Introduction to Business

Introduction to Business
Second Edition

Joseph T. Straub
Valencia Community College

Raymond F. Attner
Brookhaven Community College

Kent Publishing Company
Boston, Massachusetts
A Division of Wadsworth, Inc.

To Pat and Stacey (J.S.)
and
Donnelle — my support, my partner, my faith (R.A.)

Senior Editor: **Richard C. Crews**
Production Editor: **Marianne L'Abbate**
Interior Designer: **Trisha Hanlon**
Interior Illustration Artist: **George Nichols**
Cover Designer: **Trisha Hanlon**
Production Coordinator: **Linda Siegrist**

Cover art © David F. Hughes/Stock, Boston.

Kent Publishing Company

A Division of Wadsworth, Inc.

Printed in the United States of America

1 2 3 4 5 6 7 8 9 — 89 88 87 86 85

Library of Congress Cataloging in Publication Data

Straub, Joseph T.
  Introduction to business.

  Includes bibliographies and indexes.
  1. Industrial management. 2. Business. I. Attner, Raymond F. II. Title.
HD31.S6965 1985   658   84-20115
ISBN 0-534-04173-6

Preface

Basic Intent

This edition of *Introduction to Business* welcomes Professor Raymond F. Attner as co-author. Professor Attner's background and expertise complement and enhance the basic intent of the first edition, and that intent is reaffirmed here: we feel that *Introduction to Business* fills an obvious need for a text that is written by authors who teach the course as the mainstay of their careers. We enjoy an intimate and perceptive relationship with the course and with our students, and that relationship is reflected in the superior quality of our text.

Colleagues agree that the introductory business course is a cornerstone of many college programs. Accordingly, the text that is adopted for that course will have to meet the needs and expectations of students and professors alike. This edition of *Introduction to Business* meets the challenge surpassingly well.

By placing business in perspective and surveying the topic in a contemporary and thorough fashion, our text gives students a solid foundation in the introduction to business course and equips them for future success in advanced business courses. We realize, of course, that non-business majors may take the introductory business course as an elective. These students will benefit from our comprehensive coverage of a subject that affects every aspect of their daily lives, no matter what their present or future career interests. Our text will prepare all students to make more astute consumer decisions and to appreciate the profound role that business plays in today's society.

Organization

Our decisions on part and chapter sequencing were based on an extensive market survey of professors who teach the introduction to business course. The organization that we have selected reflects their consensus.

Part One, The Business Setting, guides students into the course by examining the role of business in our economy, and by exploring the features and characteristics of unincorporated business and of corporations. Unlike competitors, we acknowledge the complexity and popularity of corporations in today's business world by devoting an entire chapter to that form of organization.

Part Two, The Human Side of Business, discusses the importance of and need for management, the functions managers perform, the roles played, and the skills necessary to manage. It then addresses the processes and concepts involved, and alternative designs that managers utilize to create organizations. Following this, we explore the principles and processes involved in planning for, recruiting, selecting, orienting, training, appraising, and compensating their organizations' human resources. This leads to a chapter on the importance of and approaches to working with human resources by building an organizational climate, creating the opportunity for motivation, and providing leadership. Part Two ends with a chapter on labor relations, including exceptional coverage of the principles and objectives of unions, labor history and legislation, the reasons employees join unions, labor and management tactics, the collective bargaining process, the grievance procedure, and a discussion on mediation and arbitration.

Part Three, Production and Marketing Activities, examines and illustrates current production principles and techniques, and then investigates marketing principles and the elements of product, promotion, distribution, and pricing strategies. You will discover that our coverage of these important areas is thorough, logical, up-to-date, and exceptionally illustrated with examples from many well-known companies.

Part Four, Finance and Information Systems, contains chapters on money and financial institutions, finance, risk and insurance, gathering and processing data, and accounting. Our accounting chapter is purposely preceded by one on gathering and processing data so that students will better appreciate the widespread impact of computers on business operations and on the life-styles of individuals who own, or who plan to purchase, a personal computer. And we cover the subject of accounting in a fashion that introductory students can readily understand without oversimplifying or distorting this complex but essential topic.

In Part Five, Special Challenges and Issues, we investigate the topics of small business and franchising, multinational business, legal concerns, and the social and ethical environment. Our quarter-century's worth of classroom teaching experience and our market survey data convinced us to reserve small business and franchising until this point in the text. By prefacing that discussion with chapters on forms of business organization, human relations, production, marketing, finance, and information systems, our book truly prepares students to comprehend and appreciate the concerns of small-business owners or franchisees more effectively than any competitor.

Pedagogical Devices

As dedicated classroom teachers, we devoted a great deal of time and effort to create pedagogical devices that will help students maximize their learning experience with our text. The array we offer is second to none.

Chapter Outline

Each chapter opens with a topical outline of the areas that will be covered. This provides students with a general framework for upcoming discussion.

Chapter Objectives

These establish the learning benchmarks by which students' success will be measured. Organized according to discussion sequence within each chapter, they clarify what the student must do to master the material presented.

Opening Quotation

Each chapter opens with a quotation: an icebreaker related to one or more concepts that are addressed in the chapter. It's an upbeat way to begin each new area of study.

Up Front

This is a personality profile featuring an individual who has constructed a career based on concepts discussed in the chapter in which it appears. We selected our Up Front personalities based on their degree of success in a chapter-related area. They are positive role models for students of all ages. In addition, our Up Fronts personalize the chapter and give it a real-world orientation and a humanness. The persons we have chosen constitute an age, sex, and ethnic mix to which all students can relate.

Nearly all the Up Fronts in this edition are new. A few, including Nolan K. Bushnell and Lee A. Iacocca, were judged to be fully relevant to this edition and so were preserved and updated to reflect changes in the dynamic careers of the individuals involved.

Pause and Ponder

These features, which appear at strategic points twice in each chapter, pose thought-provoking questions that students may answer by referring to material just read and/or personal experience. They encourage introspection and reflection while providing a necessary study break.

The Straight Line

This element complements the chapter's Up Front with a profile of a company or group whose operations are linked with chapter concepts or principles. Like the Up Fronts, The Straight Lines give the text real-world orientation and credibility — students can see how the material they study is actually applied or how it affects the operations of an identified business firm. And nearly all The Straight Line features are new to this edition.

Summary

Each chapter closes with a narrative summary of salient topics. Students may use the summary for a general review and for placing the material in perspective after studying the chapter in depth.

Key Terms

These are listed after each summary so students may review the entire chapter's terms in one spot. Terms are alphabetized in each list.

For Review and Discussion

We provide an exceptionally generous amount of review and discussion activities that require students to apply chapter principles, and to study and comprehend the vocabulary and concepts that the chapter presents. Our review and discussion activities are coordinated, of course, with the objectives at the beginning of the chapter. Mastery of the review and discussion items ensures that students will accomplish the chapter objectives.

Applications (Cases)

This edition features two new cases in each chapter. Our cases and the accompanying discussion questions also encourage students to explore, reflect on, and apply their learning to business situations. Many cases are based on the experience of identified business firms. References are provided where appropriate. Our cases, like the Up Fronts and The Straight Lines, blend theory with practice. They are excellent devices for generating classroom discussion and independent thought.

Careers

Students are eager to learn how companies prepare them for careers in certain business areas. To meet that expectation, we provide Career Capsules at the ends of Parts Two, Three, and Four. These describe the qualifications, training, advancement opportunities, and career paths that large employers such as Levi Strauss, Caterpillar Tractor, Atlantic Richfield, and General Foods offer qualified individuals. The Career Capsules expand our text's real-world orientation by giving students a glimpse into career opportunities and challenges offered by companies whose names are household words.

Our exploration of careers would not be complete, of course, without a formal discussion of career planning and job searches. We address those subjects specifically in Appendix A, The Business of Getting a Job. There we examine in detail how to choose a career (including selection of a major in college), prepare a résumé, locate job openings, and deal with company recruiting activities (including successful interviewing and job offer evaluation). This outstanding feature of our text may be incorporated into your classroom discussion or reading assignments whenever you feel it is appropriate.

Terminology

Command of business vocabulary is an integral goal of any introduction to business course, and our text ensures that this will be achieved through several techniques. Each term is printed in boldface and defined in italics where it first appears. It is also printed in color in the margin to draw students' attention to it during chapter review. As mentioned previously, key chapter terms are conveniently grouped at the end of each chapter. Finally, every key term in the text is repeated, along with its text definition, in a comprehensive glossary at the end of the book. Our reviewers confirm that no other introduction to business text goes to such lengths to help students gain a firm command of the language of business.

Treatment of Small Business and Franchising

We mentioned earlier, and we believe it's worth repeating, that we lead students into small business and franchising more logically and effectively than competing texts do. The first four parts of our text examine areas that are prerequisites to understanding such a topic: legal forms of organization, personnel, management, motivation, labor relations, production, marketing, finance, risk management, data processing, and accounting. *After* students have studied those areas, we introduce them to small business and franchising. We are convinced (and our reviewers have confirmed) that this is the most academically sound way to organize an introductory text. To place the small business and franchising chapter before a discussion of essential business topics does students a grave injustice. We successfully avoid that oversight and your students will benefit accordingly.

Graphics

Our array of graphics — more effective and impressive than any competing text's — was designed for maximum educational benefit. Significant chapter information and relationships are captured visually through the dramatic use of a second accent color combined with highly informative tables and figures throughout each chapter. These give our book exceptional visual appeal and enhance the impact of the multitude of pedagogical devices mentioned earlier.

A Commitment to Credibility

We further distinguish ourselves from competitors through our commitment to credibility. That simply means that this book was researched and written *entirely* by us. No chapters or pedagogical items were ghostwritten by colleagues, student assistants, or others whose labor we claim as our own. Our "total immersion" approach, although demanding intense labor and time, has resulted in a text with integrity. By being fully responsible for and intimately knowledgeable about our book's contents, we were able to refer students ahead to upcoming discussion (or back to previous material) at strategic points. We thus unite the book's contents so students understand how various subjects relate to one another in the operation of a functioning business.

Supplemental Items

We realize that many professors place great value on the supplemental items that accompany a text. Our commitment to excellence is obvious here, too. With the help of our publisher, who conducted a market study to determine what the essential components of the supplemental package should be, we provide the following items.

Student Study Guide

Co-authored by Nancy Carr of the Community College of Philadelphia and James McHugh of St. Louis Community College at Forest Park, this self-paced learning aid contains questions in several formats that promote thorough vocabulary mastery and command of chapter concepts.

Instructor's Manual

As career instructors of the introduction to business course, we have prepared a most valuable, efficient, and practical instructor's manual. It contains:

- Detailed lecture outlines for each chapter, including enrichment vignettes
- Suggested course outlines for 7- and 14-week courses
- Several hundred 16mm films available from 33 sources and coordinated with text chapters
- Suggested business periodicals for library reference
- Sources of guest speakers and tips on how to select a subject and a speaker, prepare for the visit, and follow up after the speaker's appearance. We also include a section on teleconferencing, a way in which key business executives may interact with your students through conference calls.
- Course building activities that will help you gather material to supplement and enhance classroom discussion. This section also contains a mailing list to request material from *Fortune*'s top 200 companies, ranked according to 1983 sales and 26 of the nation's leading franchise firms.

— Answers to all the questions and case problems contained in the Study Guide.

One Hundred Acetate Transparencies

These are keyed to the text chapters, but they contain new information not provided in the book. They may be used in conjunction with our detailed lecture outlines to illustrate various chapter concepts, promote class discussion, and supplement your personal file of transparencies.

Test Bank

A comprehensive test bank containing over 2000 questions is provided to adopters of *Introduction to Business*, Second Edition. The test bank, which follows a chapter-by-chapter format, is structured according to chapter objectives. There is a balance between true/false and multiple choice questions.

New in This Edition

We are indebted to Kent's Review Board reviewers, who are acknowledged on page xi, for input that resulted in numerous changes and additions. We want potential adopters to know that this edition of *Introduction to Business* is the product of a thorough and meticulous revision and that it required many hours of research and writing. Statistics and references have been updated in chapter body discussion, charts, and tables — from cover to cover. On a chapter-by-chapter basis, some of the most outstanding changes are:

Chapter 1 The Role of Business in Our Economic Setting
- A new section on the characteristics of private enterprise
- A new section on the history of American business

Chapter 2 The Unincorporated Business
- A new section on the rights and obligations of partners under the Uniform Partnership Act
- An expanded discussion on partnerships

Chapter 3 The Modern Corporation
- An updated discussion of S corporations (formerly titled Subchapter S corporations) that includes the effects of the Subchapter S Revision Act
- The breakup of AT&T (summarized in The Straight Line)

Chapter 4 Managing Business Organizations
- A new section providing a thorough explanation of each level of management's responsibility for the performance of the management functions — the universality of management
- A new section explaining the importance of management roles and providing examples of managerial roles

Chapter 5 Creating an Organization
- A new section discussing the step-by-step process for organizing
- An expanded discussion on delegation, including the relationship of delegation, authority, responsibility, and accountability

Chapter 6 Personnel: Acquiring and Developing Human Resources
- A new section on the legal environment of human resources management
- An expanded discussion on the selection process including specific dos and don'ts

Chapter 7 Managing People: Motivation and Leadership
- A new section discussing the importance of developing a positive work environment to increase motivation
- A new section establishing Theory X and Theory Y as the basis for a manager's motivation and leadership approaches

Chapter 8 Labor Relations
- A new section discussing the principles and objectives of unionism
- A new section discussing the goals and directions of unions

Chapter 9 Producing the Product
- A new section discussing the use of robots on production lines

— Discussion of the Japanese inventory management technique, *kanban*, in a chapter-end case

Chapter 10 Marketing and Product Strategy

— A new section on the process of marketing
— A new section discussing the components of product strategy

Chapter 11 Marketing Promotional Strategy

— A new section discussing the roles and importance of promotional strategy
— A new section providing an explanation of the communication process utilized by promotion

Chapter 12 Distribution and Pricing Strategy

— A new section discussing the importance of distribution strategy
— A new section discussing the importance of pricing strategy and pricing objectives

Chapter 13 Money and Financial Institutions

— An expanded discussion of the Consumer Price Index, including the CPI-U and the CPI-W
— A new section discussing the trend toward interstate banking

Chapter 14 Financing for Profits

— Discussion of the impact of the 1982 Tax Equity and Fiscal Responsibility Act on bond formats
— New information on adjustable rate or "floating rate" preferred stock and "zero coupon" bonds

Chapter 15 Risk and Insurance

— Additional information on how companies may avoid risks and an expanded discussion on the practice of self-insurance
— New section on criteria required for an insurable risk
— New material on no-fault auto insurance, universal life insurance, and hazardous waste insurance required by the Environmental Protection Agency

Chapter 16 Gathering and Processing Data

— Expanded discussion of a management information system
— New section on the popularity and uses of personal computers

Chapter 17 Accounting for Profits

— New section discussing the various groups that use accounting data
— New discussion of the CPA's responsibility to maintain "professional skepticism" regarding possible fraud

Chapter 18 The Small Business and Franchising

— Expanded discussion of venture capital firms
— Expanded discussion of franchising

Chapter 19 Multinational Business

— A new section discussing why businesses go international
— A new section discussing barriers to international trade

Chapter 20 Business Law and the Legal Environment of Business

— New discussion of secrecy as an alternative to patenting
— New material on governmental response to regulation, including discussion of the work of the Private Sector Survey on Cost Control

Chapter 21 The Social and Ethical Environment of Business

— A new section on the evolution of social responsibility
— A new section discussing the need to implement social responsibility and the social audit

Appendix A The Business of Getting a Job

— New section on networking as a method of obtaining job interviews

Appendix B The Stock Market and Personal Investing

— Added remarks about the insurance brokerage firms must carry against loss or theft of stocks carried in street name

— Added material on *scripophilists* (persons who collect unusual securities certificates)

. . . And Gratitude to Our Publisher's Editorial Staff

Reviewers provided valuable advice on our textbook's content, but it was our publisher's editorial staff that converted the finished manuscript into reality — the bound book that you're holding now. We are profoundly grateful to our editorial partners in this effort.

Dick Crews, our acquisitions editor, contributed market knowledge, hearty encouragement, diplomacy, patience, foresight, and enthusiasm for new ideas that buoyed our spirits throughout the project. He helped make a very long task a very pleasant one.

We also wish to thank the public-spirited, education-oriented businesses and other organizations that contributed to this book so generously. The illustrative materials they allowed us to use bring many chapter concepts to life— yet another factor that makes this book exceptional.

Finally, we wish to express our appreciation and love to our families for their consistent encouragement and vital support.

Joseph T. Straub
Raymond F. Attner

A Salute to the Kent Review Board

Although this text is a product of our authors' own research and writing, the work was reviewed extensively by a select number of highly qualified professors teaching introduction to business courses. Our Review Board made suggestions on chapter content, topical sequence, pedagogy, and graphics, which helped the new edition to be the most effective teaching and learning

package possible. I acknowledge with gratitude the help, advice, and support of the following professionals, whose involvement with this new edition has greatly enhanced the final product.

Richard C. Crews
Executive Editor
Kent Publishing Company

Introduction to Business Editorial Review Board

Raymond Boglioli
State University of New York at Farmingdale

Frank M. Falcetta
Middlesex Community College

Robert M. Fishco
Middlesex Community College

Glenn J. Gelderloos
Grand Rapids Junior College

Donald J. Gordon
Illinois Central College

James M. McHugh
St. Louis Community College at Forest Park

Dennis Pappas
Columbus Technical Institute

W. Arthur Parrish
Belleville Area College

J. J. Quinn
Camden County College

Paul L. Schmitt
St. Clair Community College

Margaret E. Sprencz
Dyke College

Frank G. Titlow
St. Petersburg Junior College

Brief Contents

Contents

Part 2 The Human Side of Business   79

Chapter 4 Managing Business Organizations   80

Chapter 5 Creating an Organization   106

Chapter 6 Personnel: Acquiring and Developing Human Resources   134

Chapter 7 Managing People: Motivation and Leadership   170

Chapter 8 Labor Relations   204

Part 3 Production and Marketing Activities

Chapter 9 Producing the Product

Chapter 10 Marketing and Product Strategy

Chapter 11 Marketing Promotional Strategy   298

Chapter 12 Distribution and Pricing Strategy   328

Part 4 Finance and Information Systems   357

Chapter 13 Money and Financial Institutions   358

Chapter 14 Financing for Profits   388

Chapter 15 Risk and Insurance   420

Chapter 16 Gathering and Processing Data 458

Chapter 17 Accounting for Profits 496

Part 5 Special Challenges and Issues 525

Chapter 18 The Small Business and Franchising 526

Chapter 19 Multinational Business   554

Chapter 20 Business Law and the Legal Environment of Business   584

Chapter 21 The Social and Ethical Environment of Business   612

Introduction to Business

Part

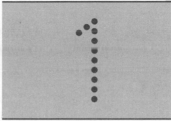

The Business Setting

The Role of Business in Our Economic Setting

Chapter Outline

Chapter Objectives

After studying this chapter, you should be able to:

1. Describe the types of business firms that compose the American business system.
2. Describe the characteristics of the private enterprise system and how it functions.
3. Identify and explain the four factors of production.
4. Distinguish between the economic systems of capitalism, socialism, and communism.
5. Explain the evolution of the American business system.
6. Identify and discuss the challenges that business will face in the future.
7. Identify four reasons for studying business.

Down in Alabama there was an old man with a rowboat. He made his living ferrying passengers across the river. He was asked, "How many times a day do you do this?" and he said, "As many times as I can, because the more I go, the more I get. And if I don't go, I don't get." That's the spirit of free enterprise I hope each one of you will have throughout your lives.
— C. M. Kittrell, executive vice-president,
Phillips Petroleum Company

Up Front   Nolan K. Bushnell

The Video King Returns from Exile

How would you like to start a new industry — video games — with only $350 in cash (and $350 from an associate) and sell out at the age of thirty-three, netting a cool $15 million for yourself? Nolan K. Bushnell, a young computer whiz, did exactly that — turned his ideas for a computer-operated video Ping-Pong game into a company that became too successful for him to continue to run.

Bushnell's rise to success was meteoric. Sales of his company, Atari, soared to $39 million in its fifth year of operation. It became the fastest-growing company in American history and Bushnell could not keep up with the demand. He began to see licensees and competitors producing and selling more units than Atari, which had insufficient cash to keep up with demand. Video games mushroomed into one of the hottest-selling consumer items.

Bushnell decided the time was right to bail out. He sold his interest to a company that had enough capital to meet the booming demand for video games — Warner Communications — and he moved on to his next venture (and adventure), Pizza Time Theatre.

Pizza Time combines electronics with self-service pizza parlors to offer customers "live" theater. The performers are not your usual entertainers but com-

Business is everywhere in America, and everyone is a part of it. The pizza you eat, the jeans you wear, the car you drive, the television you watch — all are produced, distributed, and sold by businesses. To be able to buy these things, you earn money working in a business. The bank where you keep that money is a business.

Products you buy are created by the work of many businesses. Think of a loaf of bread: first a farmer grew the wheat with the help of fertilizer supplied by a chemical company; when it was ripe, he harvested it using a machine he bought (with the help of a bank) from a manufacturer. He trucked the wheat to a mill, which ground it into flour and sold it to a bakery. That company brought the flour by train to its plant, where it was combined with other ingredients bought from other suppliers to make bread. The bakery then wrapped the bread in plastic bought from yet another company. Using the trucks it bought from a truck manufacturer, the bakery transported the bread to a retail store, where you were able to purchase it.

Figure 1.1 provides an illustration of the number and variety of the businesses involved in placing that loaf of bread on your

puter-controlled robots. The cast of characters is headed by Chuck E. Cheese, an oversized rat, who tells jokes and serves as master of ceremonies. A video game arcade is also available for customers who want to entertain themselves.

Pizza Time fell on hard times last year and the worth of Bushnell's personal stock fell from $23 million to $9 million. Part of his agreement with Warner Communications required that he not compete in the video game business for 7 years. The 7 years were up October 1, 1983, just as the time was right for Bushnell to leave Pizza Time. On January 31, 1984, he resigned the chairman's office with Pizza Time, although he remains the company's largest stockholder. Pizza Time Theatre, Inc., filed for reorganization under Chapter 11 of the bankruptcy laws on March 28, 1984.

Bushnell, meanwhile, at age forty-one is off and running in new directions. He is working on an interactive television system (ACTV), a new home robot (Androbot), and after his 7-year absence from the game business, he is back with what may be the next generation of video games — environmental games that will be "lived" through the senses of sight, sound, touch, taste, and smell.

For more about Nolan K. Bushnell, see United Press International, "Pizza Time Chain Files for Reorganization," *Dallas Morning News*, 29 March 1984, p. 2-D.

table. This example sets the stage for our discussion of the American business system: its characteristics, its operations, its history, and its future directions.

The Business of Business

When you think of "business" what picture do you have in your mind — Xerox, American Airlines, American Telephone and Telegraph? If so, you are on the right track. But business in America is more than the large corporations with which we are all familiar. Businesses come in all shapes and sizes. Business is the neighborhood service station, the beauty shop, the dry cleaners right down the street, the veterinary clinic where we board our pets, and the "mom-and-pop" store. Simply put, business means variety: pets, gasoline, food, office products.

Despite the variation in size and activity, each of these examples is a **business** because each is *an organization engaged in producing*

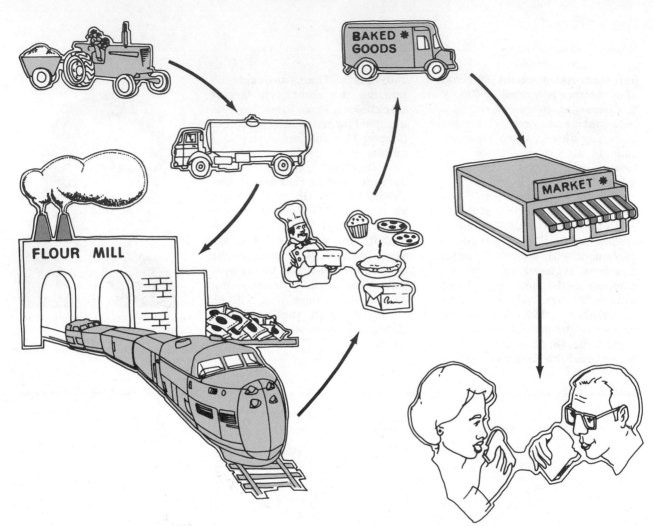

Figure 1.1 Businesses Involved in Putting Bread on Your Table

goods and services to make a profit. This definition highlights some other points about business.

Goods- and Services-Producing Firms

Businesses are either goods-producing or service-producing firms. Goods-producing firms, such as mining, construction, and manufacturing firms, produce tangible products or **goods** — *commodities that have a physical presence.* Service-producing firms provide **services** — *activities that benefit consumers or other businesses.* Transportation firms, insurance companies, beauty shops, and repair shops are all examples of service businesses.

goods

services

The Role of Profit

Regardless of whether a business produces a good or provides a service the common ingredient is profit. **Profit** is *the difference between a business's total revenues or sales receipts and the total of its production costs, operating expenses, and taxes.* In our bread bakery example the bakery has to pay for its raw materials (flour, butter or shortening, yeast, salt), equipment (mixers, ovens, wrapping machines), employees, and the energy it uses. When the bakery sells the bread to the supermarket, it charges more than the cost of making the bread. That extra part of the selling price is profit.

profit

Why do businesses want profit? Profit is the ultimate goal of business. It is the measure of success for the businessperson and the reward for taking a chance. Each person who operates a business is risking money. The baker does not know that people will buy the bread when it is produced; but money is invested in the business on the possibility that people will buy. The baker is taking a chance, a risk. Were there no profits, it would not be worthwhile for the baker to risk the money.

Private Enterprise: The American Business System

The baker in our previous example was able to invest money and receive a profit because of the type of economic environment found in America. This environment is known as the private enterprise system. Let's examine it.

Characteristics of Private Enterprise

The **private enterprise system** is *an economic system where both the resources necessary for production and the businesses are owned by private individuals, not by public institutions like the government.* Private enterprise is based on four principles or rights: the right to private property, freedom of choice, profits, and competition.

private enterprise system

The Right to Private Property. In the private enterprise system individuals have the *right* to buy, own, use, and sell property as they see fit. This right of ownership includes land, buildings, equipment, and intangible property such as inventions.

The Right of Freedom of Choice. The private enterprise system also provides the right of freedom of choice. This freedom of choice applies to the individual's right to decide what type of work to do, where to work, and how and where money is to be spent. This means that people can work for others or work for themselves if they so choose. It also means that a person is free to change jobs and work to improve his or her economic position in life.

The Right to Profit. In the private enterprise system, the person who takes the chance in starting the business by investing is guaranteed the right to all profits. This right is what attracts people to begin businesses, and it is the ultimate goal of business. Inherent in starting a business is the freedom to fail. Not all entrepreneurs are successful, but the opportunity is there to start a business and reap the rewards.

The Right to Compete. Under the private enterprise system people have the freedom to compete with others. Competition, along with profit, is the cornerstone of the private enterprise system. Competition pits one company against another in the struggle to attract and retain the consumer. Companies compete by developing better products, altering prices, developing unique advertising programs, and having the product or service where and when the consumer wants it. The benefit to the consumer: competition makes for better products and more responsiveness to consumer needs.

The Factors of Production

The private enterprise system, as do all economic systems, requires resources for its business to produce goods and services. *The resources used to provide goods and services* are the **factors of production:** *land, labor, capital, and entrepreneurship.* These four factors are blended together by a business to produce goods and services as shown in Figure 1.2. Let's examine each.

factors of production

land

labor

Land is *the natural resources that can be used to produce goods and services.* Natural resources are all resources growing on and under the earth's surface, such as trees, minerals, oil, and gas.

Labor is *the total human resources required to turn raw materials into goods and services.* It would include all employees of the business from top management through the entire organization structure.

Pause and Ponder

As a businessperson which one of the four rights of the private enterprise system is the most important to you? Why? If one or two of these rights are removed can the private enterprise system continue to function? Why?

Gallery 1
American Business: A Preview of Its Many Forms

The cornerstone of American business continues to be the small business operation. An example is Ben's Barber Shop, almost as easily recognized by the red-white-and-blue ornament on its storefront as by its name.

Small businesses clustered in one locale, like this pizzeria and flower shop on a New York City street, can provide a variety of goods and services to meet the multiple demands of consumers.

The general store — the original "department store" — is
still very much a part of the
American business scene. This
roadside general store doubles
as a gas station, which is not
uncommon in rural areas.

Urban shopping malls, like this one in Baltimore, are relatively new on the business scene. They also provide consumers with a wide variety of goods and services, and they help consumers make effective use of their time.

Franchising is an alternative for entrepreneurs who wish to go into business for themselves. Burger King restaurants are a familiar sight: they are part of a large, nationwide chain of franchises.

Coca-Cola is sold on a national and international scale. It's a sure bet you'll find it in the pizzeria in New York City, in the roadside general store, or even near the Dead Sea in Israel. Coca-Cola in Hebrew is still Coke!

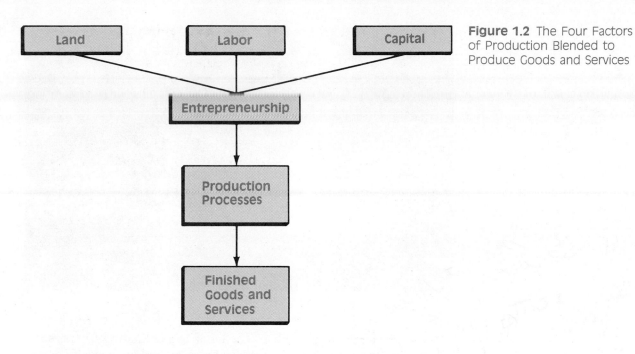

Figure 1.2 The Four Factors of Production Blended to Produce Goods and Services

Capital is *the total of tools, equipment, machinery, and buildings used to produce goods and services.* In this case capital does not refer simply to money. Money by itself is not productive; but when it purchases drills, typewriters, forklifts, and the building to place them in it becomes productive.

capital

Entrepreneurship is *the group of skills and risk taking needed to combine the other three factors of production to produce goods and services.* Entrepreneurship is the catalyst — like heat to a fire. It is supplied by an **entrepreneur,** *an individual or individuals who are willing to take risks in return for profits.*

entrepreneurship

entrepreneur

How Private Enterprise Functions

In the private enterprise system (unlike other economic systems we will discuss), the factors of production are owned by individuals in households. (In economic terms a **household** is *any person or group of people living under the same roof and functioning as an economic unit.*) Businesses must pay the members of the households in order to acquire the factors of production. The household members in turn receive various types of income to supply the factors of production. Table 1.1 reveals the type of income received for each factor of production. As a further illustration Figure 1.3 and the following step-by-step process provide an explanation of how the private enterprise system operates.

household

In this example:

1. Your business needs to hire two employees.
    — The factor of production, labor, is to be found living in the households.

Here are the factors of production in action — land, labor, capital, and entrepreneurship.

— The business purchases the labor by persuading the persons in the household to go to work for an agreed-on wage (income).

2. The business then combines the labor of the employees with natural resources, capital, and entrepreneurial skills to produce goods and services.

— The individuals in the households need or want the goods produced by the business.

— Using the income received as wages, the individuals in the households go to the marketplace and purchase the goods and services produced by the company.

3. The business then takes the money received from the sale of the goods and services and uses it to purchase more factors of production.

The result of the circular flow of resources and income: people seeking profit go into business, which creates jobs and income for households. With their incomes, households purchase goods and services, which in turn, support business and make it profitable.

Our discussion of the private enterprise system and how it functions has set the stage for a discussion of how our economic system functions in comparison with other economic systems.

Table 1.1 Income Received for the Factors of Production

Factor of Production	Income Received
Land	Rent
Labor	Wages or salaries
Capital	Interest
Entrepreneurship	Profit

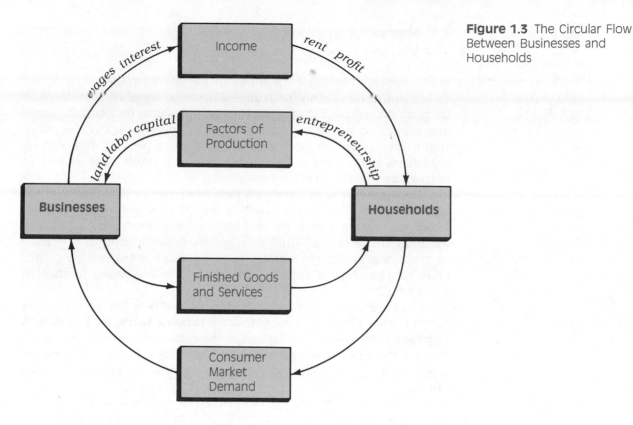

Figure 1.3 The Circular Flow Between Businesses and Households

Economic Systems

An **economic system** is *the method society uses to allocate its resources (land, labor, capital, and entrepreneurship) to satisfy its needs.* What distinguishes one economic system from another is the control of the factors of production and the interaction of business, government, and consumers. In the modern world there are three primary types of economic systems.

economic system

Capitalism

The system we have been referring to as the private enterprise system is also called capitalism. **Capitalism** is *an economic system where the factors of production are in private hands.*

capitalism

As originally described by Adam Smith in his eighteenth-century book *Wealth of Nations,* our economic system was **pure capitalism** *or* a **market economy,** one *in which economic decisions are made freely according to the market forces of supply and demand.* In this system the economic questions of

pure capitalism *or* market economy

   — What is to be produced?
   — How much will be produced?
   — Who will produce it?

Source: From *The Wall Street Journal*, permission Cartoon Features Syndicate.

— How much will it cost?
— Who will get it?

are determined by the consumers in the marketplace.

In pure capitalism consumers demand more of a product as its price decreases. This follows the commonsense notion that people are willing to purchase something if it costs less. On the other hand, producers are more willing to supply a product that can be sold for a higher price. Being motivated by profit, they expect to earn more profit when they supply more.

In pure capitalism the two factors of supply and demand will balance each other out in such a way that some middle ground called an equilibrium price will be achieved. Producers will make as many units of a product as consumers are willing to purchase at the price producers must charge to make a reasonable profit. (The relationship of supply and demand is discussed further in Chapter 12.)

laissez-faire *or* hands-off approach

In pure capitalism industry and individuals use resources as they choose. The *government* takes a **laissez-faire, *or* hands-off, approach** and *does not interfere in the economic system.* Producers and consumers pursue their own self-interests. Producers make as much as they can sell and consumers buy as much as they can afford.

In·this system each person behaves in the best interests of society, as if guided by an invisible hand. The marketplace is regulated by the interaction of the buyers and producers. If a company produces a defective product or charges too much for the product it is rejected by consumers. As a result, the producer has to improve the quality of the product or reduce the price to make any sales. The marketplace, in essence the invisible hand, regulates economic conduct. Government does not have to do any regulating.

Mixed Capitalism

mixed capitalism

Over time the United States has evolved to a system of **mixed capitalism,** which is *an economic system based on a market economy with limited government involvement.* The government has abandoned the principle of the invisible hand in favor of a more visible involvement in economic life.

In mixed capitalism the government has two economic tools: the power to tax and the power to spend. By taxing individuals and businesses it acquires funds to provide essential public programs: defense, education, transportation, and social services. In turn the money spent for these services creates more demand for the goods and services produced by businesses.

In addition, the government has become involved in the economic system through:

— Government-owned entities such as the Tennessee Valley Authority, which provides power to rural communities

— Government agencies that regulate the activities of some businesses, as when the Food and Drug Administration prevents a pharmaceutical company from selling a new medicine until tests are made

— Government involvement in employer-employee relations, for example, setting a minimum wage and initiating programs to create jobs for the unemployed

The government also has become involved in all facets of business operations. Table 1.2 provides a summary of the areas of government involvement in business activities.

Communism

Another economic system is **communism.** This is *an economic system under which the government controls the factors of production.* Land, labor, and capital are under the control of the government and entrepreneurship is supplied by the government.

As a result, all the economic decisions about production, distribution, consumption, and property ownership are made by the government. It decides what will be produced, who will produce it, how many units will be made, how much it will cost, and who will receive it. Supply and demand and competition have no influence in this system. Central government planners make all the economic decisions about production and resource allocation.

communism

Table 1.2 Government Involvement in Business Activities

Area	Government Authority
Employment practices	Equal Employment Opportunity Commission
Safety in the workplace	Occupational Safety and Health Administration
Food and drug quality	Food and Drug Administration
Compensation practices	Department of Labor
Product safety	Consumer Product Safety Commission
Management and labor relations	National Labor Relations Board
Employee retirement	Department of Labor
Business financing	Securities and Exchange Commission
Competitive practices	Federal Trade Commission
Interstate transportation	Interstate Commerce Commission
Communications	Federal Communications Commission
Waste disposal	Environmental Protection Agency

Socialism

socialism

Socialism is *an economic system in which much ownership is private, but the government controls the operation and direction of basic industries.* This control and direction are based on the belief that there are certain products and services that everyone should have. In essence this means that these need to be controlled so that all people will have them — not just those people who have enough money.

The industries normally under control of the government include mining, steel production, transportation, communication, health care, and auto manufacturing. In Sweden, for example, the government owns the transportation network, communications, the banks, and the mining, steel, and chemical industries.

Modern Economic Systems

When you examine the economic systems in the world today you will discover that no examples of pure capitalism or pure communism exist. Most economies are grouped in the center of a continuum that stretches from the complete private ownership and market economy of pure capitalism to the total public ownership of communism. This continuum, with some modern examples, is shown in Figure 1.4.

Even in the Soviet Union, some private enterprise exists. Private vendors, for example, can be seen in railroad stations and on country roads selling home-grown flowers and vegetables. Other economies that are called communist have even more traces of private ownership. Yugoslavia has developed an interesting variation of public ownership, with production decisions being made at the factory, rather than by the central government, and being regulated by supply and demand.

Comparing Economic Systems

Comparing economic systems is difficult because they are organized differently; the goals and conditions under which they operate are different.

One yardstick for measuring the performance of an economy

gross national product (GNP) is its **gross national product (GNP),** *the total market value of all*

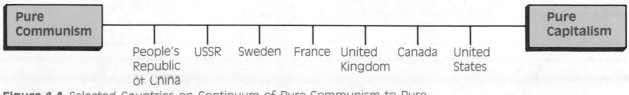

Figure 1.4 Selected Countries on Continuum of Pure Communism to Pure Capitalism

goods and services that a country produces in one year. Table 1.3 shows the comparative GNPs of selected countries. Using this measure the United States, the Soviet Union, and Japan far outdistance all other countries in output.

Another measure developed by economists is to divide total GNP by the country's population, which produces a figure called *GNP per capita* (literally, "per head"), or per person. (This figure is also known as the *standard of living.*) A look at this column shows that Switzerland, which had been last, is now first. China, which had been grouped in the center, falls to the bottom. The numbers also reveal that it is impossible to say that one economic system is superior to another. While the largely capitalist United States does better than the communist economies, it trails a socialist economy, Sweden. And although the Soviet Union does not perform as well as Sweden, it is very close in output to the United Kingdom, which has a socialist economy. East Germany, another communist country, leads the United Kingdom.

Statistics do not tell the whole story of the economy. Because they have different objectives, another basis of comparison is to examine their areas of emphases and their means of accomplishing these. Table 1.4 summarizes the characteristics of the economies of the United States and the Soviet Union, revealing the primary areas of the two economic systems.

Table 1.3 Total and per Capita GNP for Selected Countries
Source: U.S. Bureau of the Census, *Statistical Abstract of the United States: 1984*, 104th edition (Washington, D.C., 1983), p. 865.

Country	Total GNP (in Billions of U.S. Dollars)	Country	GNP per Capita (in Billions of U.S. Dollars)
United States	2,370.0	Switzerland	16,210
Soviet Union	1,290.8	Sweden	13,032
Japan	1,044.9	West Germany	12,485
West Germany	769.1	United States	10,408
China	500.5	Japan	8,946
United Kingdom	403.8	East Germany	7,924
East Germany	132.3	United Kingdom	7,210
Sweden	108.2	Soviet Union	4,861
Switzerland	103.7	China	487

Table 1.4 Comparison of the Economies of the United States and the Soviet Union

Characteristic	United States	Soviet Union
Source of economic decisions	Some by government, most by households and businesses	All by government
Land	Some owned by government, most owned by private parties	All owned by government
Capital	Some owned by government, most owned by private parties	All owned by government
Labor	Large freedom of choice in career and work place; some unemployment	Some freedom of career choice, limited ability to choose work place; very low unemployment
Entrepreneurship	Individual right to own business and retain profits	Provided by government; some incentives for superior performance
Availability of consumer goods	Plentiful	Scarce
Income distribution	Largely uncontrolled; fairly unequal	Largely controlled; fairly equal
Stability of economy	Uncontrolled, fluctuates greatly	Controlled, but fluctuates some

In the United States, the emphasis is on the freedom of the individual to make choices. Individuals own the factors of production, have freedom to choose their careers and where they want to work and live, and have the right to profits, the reward of their entrepreneurship. The cost of that freedom is greater instability: income is not distributed fairly, the individual may face unemployment, and the economy itself is unstable, fluctuating from boom to depression.

The Soviet Union's main goal is to provide greater security, guarding against both the fluctuations of the economy and the instability of unemployment. To provide that security, the government takes greater control of the economy and allows the individual less freedom of choice.

Up to this point we have taken an in-depth look at our business system and how it operates compared with other systems. But what are the "roots" of the system? Let's take a look at the historical development of American business.

A Brief History of American Business

The American business system is far different from what it was 50 or 100 years ago. Over the course of time it has undergone a number of significant changes.

The Colonial Era

The American business system in the colonial era was agriculturally based: society depended on the production of agricultural products as the basis of commerce. In addition, the economy was closely tied to England. In exchange for raw materials and precious metals, England exchanged finished goods and provided financing.

During this time the most common form of industry was provided by the cottage system. In this system workers were contracted by merchants to produce goods at home. The workers were in essence independent, highly skilled subcontractors who became specialists in producing certain goods. These goods were in turn sold by merchants in their stores.

The Industrial Revolution

The Industrial Revolution, which began in the mid 1700s, dramatically changed the American business system. The implementation of both power-driven machinery and new production methods changed the manufacturing processes. Instead of skilled craftsmen hand-producing products in cottages, factories were built and the goods were mass-produced. The skilled workers left their homes and became employees in the factories.

Other ingredients further directed the march toward industrialization. With the invention of the reaper, agriculture became more mechanized; labor flooded our shores as a result of the political and economic problems in Europe; communication was revolutionized by the telegraph; and the railroads pushed the boundaries of the country to the Pacific Ocean.

Growth of Modern Industry

During this time period America was transformed from the doorstep of industrialization into an industrial nation. A number of developments contributed to that evolution.

For the first time all the factors of production were abundantly available within our national boundaries. We were no longer dependent on European countries. The reliance on foreign capital was removed with the development of a national treasury and the establishment of a better quality banking system. Technology supplied the telephone to improve communications. Entrepreneurs such as Rockefeller and Carnegie were able to mesh the factors of production.

Toward the end of this era America survived the Great Depression. During this experience the concept of pure capitalism and the market economy was greatly modified by the role of the government. The invisible hand in the marketplace was replaced by the government through such measures as Social Security, regulation of securities, and bank insurance.

An International Industrial Power

Since the conclusion of World War II the United States has been the world's leading industrial power. Combining the immense production capabilities of its manufacturing facilities with managerial talent and financial resources has enabled America to provide the best standard of living for its citizens and to assist the economic development of other nations. The country has evolved from the ability simply to produce goods, even if demand exceeded supply, to the adoption of marketing based on identified consumer needs. These developments together with the growth in the standard of living and technology have gradually resulted in a movement of the United States to a service-oriented economy.

Business Today and Tomorrow

One conclusion that can be reached from this review of the American business system is that change and evolution are a way of life. Successful businesses and businesspersons have responded well to changes. Those that did not respond well, failed. Before we look at some trends for the future, let's take a look at three examples from our immediate past that emphasize our point.

One of the greatest changes in American life has been television. Something that was only a novelty in the 1940s became widespread in the 1950s and today almost every home has a television; many have more than one. Each set gives its owners access to information and entertainment. Each set also provides something for business: a huge audience, millions of people reachable by advertising. It is a direct communication link to a company's products and services.

The action of the Organization of Petroleum Exporting Countries (OPEC) raised the oil prices during the 1970s. As a result American consumers began turning away from the larger American cars in favor of fuel-efficient foreign cars. Today more than a third of the cars bought in the United States are of foreign manufacture — a fact that threatens the future of the American automobile industry and the industries that support it.

Though mechanical data processing first began late in the nineteenth century, it was not until the 1960s and 1970s that computers were available for widespread use. Today computers are revolutionizing business by helping small-business owners figure out their accounts, giant insurance companies handle their massive record-keeping chores, and manufacturers design new products.

These three illustrations have affected our communications capability (television), our desire for and ability to be self-sufficient (OPEC), and our capacity to transfer and process information (computers). Many more examples could be cited, but these serve the purpose of emphasizing the importance of working with change and of being adaptable.

What trends and challenges does business need to be aware of for tomorrow?

- **The Growing Scarcity of Resources** As energy sources continue to diminish, business will have to devise new ways to provide goods and services that use less energy or else find alternative sources of energy.
- **The Importance of International Business** The scope of international business involvement continues to expand. Both the number of businesses involved and the percentage of business transacted on an international scale continues to increase.
- **The Challenge of Technology** Industries are in the midst of a technologic revolution. Computer technology is evolving at breakneck speed; robotics and laser technology also are making their presence felt in the workplace. Heavy industries like steel and automaking will have to update their facilities with new technology to compete.
- **The Need for Improved Productivity** Managerial talent will have to be focused on the productivity dilemma: our output per worker is not keeping stride in relationship to the rest of the world. Answers are needed to maintain our production capabilities.
- **The Increased Importance of Business's Social Responsibility** More demands will be placed on the business sector to accomplish the dual objectives of profitability and social responsiveness.

Some businesses will meet these challenges, as in the past. Those will be the businesses that survive; the firms that cannot adapt will fail. The excitement of business is that it allows people to observe their environment and respond creatively to it. People receive much satisfaction and can find great rewards in creating solutions to

The challenge of technology — the computerized work station is here.

problems, and business provides them with the opportunities to do so.

Why Study Business?

After reading and studying the first chapter it is appropriate to discuss why people study business and how the upcoming chapters can help meet these goals. People study business for many reasons. Some people are preparing to pursue careers in one of the major fields of business. Others want to become better-informed consumers, understand their rights, and avoid purchasing problems. The following are some of the reasons that people study business.

— **The Impact of Business** Business is a major force in American life. It affects us in our daily activities. It is always present — in newspaper stories or on television and radio broadcasts. Business provides most of the jobs that enable people to earn money, and it offers the goods and services that people spend that money on. As a result of the dominant role business plays in our lives people have a natural curiosity to learn more about it. People take up the pursuit of business to be able to understand the "hows and whys" more thoroughly.

— **Career Choice** Studying business can help in the selection of a career. Too often job selection is by accident and not well designed. By becoming knowledgeable about the areas involved

Business makes an impact on our daily lives. It provides us jobs so we can buy goods and services.

in business and business practices a better quality decision can be made. An aid in making a career choice can be found in the appendix titled "The Business of Getting a Job." This material outlines the steps to follow in choosing a career and in getting a job in a chosen field.

— **Business Ownership** Owning a business is the goal for many individuals. If a person wants to increase the chances for success, one approach is to study business operations. A knowledge of accounting, management, marketing, risk management, and finance is a necessity for a small business as well as for a large one. The difference is that as a small-business owner a person must be knowledgeable in all areas.

— **More Knowledgeable Consumer** One role everyone plays in relationship to business is that of consumer. When a company advertises a product, has just sold the last one when the consumer arrives but conveniently has a more expensive model available, what should the consumer do? When a contractor does not meet specifications on remodeling a room, what options are available? Each person has a need to improve his or her consumer skills. Studying business can provide some of the information to be a better-informed consumer.

The Organization of This Book

The material contained in the upcoming chapters will help in meeting these goals for studying business:

— Chapters 2 and 3 will examine the legal forms business can take: sole proprietorship, partnership, and corporation.

— Chapters 4, 5, 6, 7, and 8 will introduce the "people" side of business: how to manage, how to hire and train employees, how to organize a business, how to provide for motivated employees, and how to achieve good labor relations.

— Chapters 9, 10, 11, and 12 will discuss the major activities of a business in making and marketing its goods or services: production, marketing, promotion, distribution, and pricing.

— Chapters 13, 14, 15, 16, and 17 will examine the support systems that businesses need to conduct business profitably: the banking system, financing, insurance, gathering and processing data, and accounting.

— Chapter 18 provides the opportunity to apply the business practices to the operation of an independent small business or a franchise.

— Chapters 19, 20, and 21 discuss issues that confront American business: competition in an international economy, the legal setting of business, social and ethical concerns of business.

The Straight Line

America
Land of Limitless Ideas and Opportunities

I do not choose to be a common man. It is my right to be uncommon — if I can. I seek opportunity — not security. I do not wish to be a kept citizen, humbled and dulled by having the state look after me.

I want to take the calculated risk, to dream and to build, to fail and to succeed.

I refuse to barter incentive for a dole; I prefer the challenges of life to the guaranteed existence; the thrill of fulfillment to the stale claim of Utopia.

I will not trade my freedom for beneficence nor my dignity for a handout. I will never cower before any master nor bend to any threat.

It is my heritage to stand erect, proud and unafraid; to think and act for myself, to enjoy the benefit of my creations and to face the world boldly and say: This, with God's help, I have done. All this is what it means to be an Entrepreneur.

— Official Credo
of American
Entrepreneurs
Association

Here are a few examples of Americans who turned their ideas, their dreams, into realities and profits:

Telepraisal. A recent innovation in art appraisal is a phone-in service started by Carol Prisant and her son, Barden, in October 1982. Located in Roslyn, New York, and using a toll-free number and a computerized catalog with more than 50,000 artists and 5 years of sales records, the Prisants have appraised 4,000 paintings. The company also helps match potential buyers and sellers.

Class Reunions. Organizing class reunions isn't as much fun as attending them Judy and Shell Norris discovered in talking with friends at their high school and college reunions. So in 1982 the Norrises started a new business booking class reunions. Their services include planning and booking the events, running the show, and even locating missing class members. Their efforts were rewarded with $60,000 in income for 1983. Shell has now quit his regular job and he and Judy are interested in franchising nationally.

Summary

A business is an organization engaged in producing goods and services to make a profit. Businesses come in all sizes, shapes, and varieties but may be divided into goods-producing and service-producing firms. Regardless of what they produce, the common ingredient is profit.

The American business system is known as private enterprise because the factors of production and the businesses are owned by private individuals and not by public entities like the government. This system is based on the right to private property, the right to freedom of choice, the right to profit, and the right to compete.

Meter Messages of Los Angeles. This idea has turned parking meters into miniature billboards. The company currently buys the space from the city government in eleven cities nationwide and sells it to advertisers. Meter Messages will also make and install stick-on ads for an additional fee. The business in St. Louis has the possibility of turning a $1 million profit this year.

The Timeshare Kitchenware Packages. This service provides a kit with everything you need to stock a bare vacation kitchen. Beverly Margolis started her business 3 years ago after her own vacation misadventure. She had sales of $300,000 the first year, topped $4 million the second year, and expects $6 million for 1983. Her prepared packages range from $325 to $2,200 (the gourmet kit). Margolis tapped into her market through the timeshare developers' national association.

Business is on the move — on wheels, that is. Enterprising individuals are taking a variety of goods and services *to* the consumer in specially equipped vans:

— *Decorating Den Systems* of Indianapolis now has 140 franchises taking decorating samples to the homeowner for on-the-spot tests with color schemes under existing lighting conditions.
— *Petvacx* in Wheaton, Maryland, has a van equipped with $24,000 worth of veterinary supplies to provide for most pet needs on house calls.
— *Wheels of Vision* in New York City is a traveling optician/optometrist team that mainly provides service to the elderly.
— *Now or Never* is a mobile fitness franchise in Los Angeles that uses vans fitted with $10,000 worth of physical fitness equipment. A trained coach (who also serves as driver) makes house calls for $50 an hour.
— *Brown Bag* is a meal wagon that delivers several hundred made-to-order sandwiches each day to workers in the Glenview, Illinois, area at lunchtime.

For more about entrepreneurial ventures, see "Entrepreneur's Credo," *Entrepreneur,* April 1984, p. 5; Joan Wester Anderson, "Bagging It," *Entrepreneur,* April 1984, p. 62; Carol Dilks, "Business on the Move," *Nation's Business,* March 1984, pp. 66, 68; "Timeshare Kitchenware Packages," *Entrepreneur,* March 1984, p. 11; "Organizing Class Reunions," *Entrepreneur,* March 1984, p. 13; "Meter Messages Inc., of LA," *Inc.,* January 1984, p. 20; and "Telepraisal," *Inc.,* November 1983, p. 25.

To produce goods and services in the private enterprise system the four factors of production (land, labor, capital, and entrepreneurship) are obtained from the individuals that own them in exchange for income. Once the factors of production are combined, they are sold to individual consumers. The consumers purchase these goods with the money obtained by selling the factors of production.

The three basic economic systems are capitalism, communism, and socialism. An economic system is the method society uses to allocate its resources to satisfy its needs. In the United States the private enterprise system is an economic system called capitalism. In capitalism the factors of production are in private hands. Our original economic system, pure capitalism (no government interference), has evolved to mixed capitalism in which the government plays an active role.

Communism is an economic system under which the government controls the factors of production. Supply, demand, and competition have no influence. Central government planners make all the economic decisions about production and resource allocation.

Socialism is an economic system in which much ownership is private, but the government controls the operation and direction of basic industries. The control is to ensure the enforcement of a belief that there are certain products and services everyone should have and that these should not be dependent on whether or not a person has money.

The American business system today is far different than it was 50 or 100 years ago. It has undergone significant changes as it has evolved from the colonies through the Industrial Revolution to become a national and international industrial power. More recently the country, because of the increased standard of living and growth in technology, has evolved to a service-oriented economy.

One of the lessons that the evolution of business in America has taught us is that change is constant and that survival depends on being able to adapt. Those companies that adapt are still in business. Those that did not are not. Business faces the future challenges of productivity, diminishing resources, international business, technology, and social responsibility.

People undertake the study of business for different reasons. The most common are to understand the overall impact of business, to assist in selecting a career, to prepare for business ownership, and to become a more knowledgeable consumer.

Key Terms

business	factors of production	mixed capitalism
capital	goods	private enterprise system
capitalism	gross national product (GNP)	profit
communism	household	pure capitalism *or* market economy
economic system	labor	
entrepreneur	laissez-faire *or* hands-off approach	services
entrepreneurship	land	socialism

For Review and Discussion

1. Distinguish between a goods-producing and a services-producing business.

2. Describe the importance of profits to a businessperson. How is profit determined?

3. List and describe the four rights, or principles, of the private enterprise system.

4. What are the four factors of production? Give an example of each.

5. Explain the interactions of businesses and households (individuals) in the private enterprise system.

6. What is the concept of the "invisible hand"?

7. Distinguish between pure capitalism and mixed capitalism.

8. Who controls the factors of production in communism? How are the economic decisions made?

9. Describe the basic belief underlying socialism.

10. Distinguish between socialism and communism.

11. What effect did the Industrial Revolution have on the production processes of America?

12. What challenges face business in the future?

13. List and explain the reasons people study business.

Applications

Case 1.1 The New Capitalism

In the historical development of the United States, its economic system has evolved from pure capitalism to mixed capitalism. During the colonial period pure capitalism functioned through the cottage industry. As an independent businessperson each cottage controlled the factors of production and took the risk of producing the products for sale at the marketplace. Whatever resources were used in the production of products came from the land. Labor was supplied by the family. Tools and equipment were also part of the capital resources of the cottage environment.

With the advent of the Industrial Revolution, pure capitalism began to change, eventually to disappear. Now there is evidence of a rebirth in Hong Kong and the United States. In the face of the rapidly changing world a form of almost pure capitalism has emerged. The British Colony of Hong Kong is a thriving cottage industry. Each household unit is an independent entrepreneur blending the factors of production into finished goods for sale in the international marketplace. Clothing, toys, and cloth goods are the specialty items of this near relative of pure capitalism.

A second potential rebirth of the cottage industry has been discussed for America. With the development of personal computers many futurists predict a thriving cottage industry here. In this scenario a person would no longer commute to work but would stay at home and transact business — the new capitalism.

Questions

1. Why do you think the cottage industry in Hong Kong has emerged in the face of industrialization in the world?

2. What do you think the possibility of a cottage industry is in the United States?

3. Which industries would most likely be adaptable to the cottage approach?

4. What factors would have to change to see this become a reality?

Case 1.2 Concealed Capitalism

An economic phenomena is taking place in the Soviet Union. In recent years it has become known that two distinct economic systems are operating side-by-side within its national borders.

The official system, communism, places the factors of production under the control of the state. State factories and stores manufacture and market goods as directed by the national planners. The resources for these goods are carefully allocated and monitored by the central agency. Norms, established by government laboratories and institutes, detail the amount of raw materials needed and the acceptable wastage for the production of goods. Once the goods are produced they are distributed through a government-controlled network of wholesalers and retailers. Prices are established by the government for the goods intended for the final consumer.

Within this state-controlled monopoly, however, the private enterprise system is producing shoes, clothing, handbags, sunglasses, and other consumer goods. It competes side by side with the state system. Its advantage: efficiency and the ability to follow the fashion trends as quickly as they emerge in the Western nations. The government takes months to approve production of an item in state-run factories; the entrepreneur avoids this obstacle.

How is this possible? The goods are produced on the same equipment, which is operated and managed by the same personnel who produce the state-controlled goods. Capital and supplies are provided by private entrepreneurs who own the goods and eventually sell them for profit.

This system within a system functions under the eyes of the state agencies through an elaborate system of reallocation of resources and bribery. "Inducements" are given to planners to inflate the estimates for the amount of material needed for the production of goods and the goods themselves are not always produced to exact specifications. Once the goods are manufactured they are distributed through the state-controlled network of wholesalers and retailers who also support the "second" system. The employees of the store are willing to sell the goods for one-third of the profit.

The individuals who operate within the underground economic system do so at personal risk. When an entrepreneur is successfully identified and brought to trial for economic crimes against the state, the punishment normally prescribed is a lengthy period of confinement at a labor camp.

Questions

1. Why would underground entrepreneurs risk imprisonment to create these business ventures?

2. What conclusions can you draw about communism and capitalism as economic systems from this case?

3. "It's not the money, it's the fact that it's my business." Relate this statement to this case situation.

The Unincorporated Business

Chapter Outline

Chapter Objectives

After studying this chapter, you should be able to:

1. Describe the characteristics of a sole proprietorship as a form of business.
2. List and describe the major advantages and disadvantages of a sole proprietorship as a form of business ownership.
3. Explain the nature of and process involved in creating a partnership.
4. List and describe the major advantages and disadvantages of a partnership as a form of business ownership.
5. Describe the purposes and characteristics of a joint venture.
6. Explain the nature of silent, secret, dormant, and nominal partners.

To be a success in business, be daring, be first, be different.
— Marchant

Eugene Kohn

From Kohn to Kohn Pedersen Fox Associates

In 1976 Gene Kohn started his own architectural firm. He began the transition from working for someone else to working for himself by interviewing large investors and corporate clients about their architectural needs from their perspectives. From the information gained Kohn established the operating philosophy for his firm: (1) His firm would be service oriented. Individual attention would be *the* primary rule. (2) His firm would design structures based on their function and the proposed structures' surroundings. Architectural designs would *fit* their context.

Two concerns of any business wanting to stay in business and do well should be product quality, service quality, and fiscal responsibility. Kohn *expected* quality from himself and his associates and he assumed his clients would expect it too. Therefore, to him, quality was a given. Fiscal responsibility, including treating the client's budget as though it were your own, became an organization rule.

With this broad philosophy, one "given" and one "rule," Kohn formed the successful New York City firm Kohn Pedersen Fox Associates (KPF). By 1982 there were 7 partners and 150 employees working all over the world. There are three managing partners who have primary responsibility for

One of the major decisions an entrepreneur must make is to determine which legal form of business ownership to use in creating a business venture. There are three basic forms of business ownership:

1. Sole proprietorship
2. Partnership
3. Corporation

Which of these legal forms of business ownership is best? There is no simple answer to that question. The type and scope of operations, the nature of the product, and the goals of the entrepreneur can influence the decision on the best form. Figure 2.1 shows approximately how many of each type were in operation in the United States recently.[1]

In this chapter we will examine sole proprietorship and partnership — how they are created, their advantages, and disadvantages. Chapter 3 will discuss corporations.

management of projects and staff responsibility in three separate areas: new business development is headed by Kohn; business and financial affairs is the main concern of Sheldon Fox, an original partner; and staffing and employment is handled by Robert Cioppa. The three primary design partners are William Pedersen, who is also an original partner, Arthur May, and Bill Louie.

To remain true to Kohn's philosophy, each project is headed by a team composed of at least one managing partner and one design partner. As the firm has grown, additional partners have been added to keep personalized client attention a top priority. In addition, KPF has established a wholly owned subsidiary, headed by Patricia Casey, which is responsible for early involvement in projects in the areas of planning and interior design. Kohn's firm provides the total package — a fully integrated environment.

Customers are pleased with the personal attention and with the attention to detail. Clients like KPF's professionalism, experienced staff, and personal commitment. Add distinctive architectural design to the package and you have KPF, an internationally respected and phenomenally successful young firm.

For more about Eugene Kohn and his firm, see the four-story profile published in *Progressive Architecture* (October 1983, pp. 69–91).

The Sole Proprietorship

The **sole proprietorship,** as the name implies, is *a business owned by one individual.* It is the oldest and most common type of business. As shown in Figure 2.2, in a recent year sole proprietorships accounted for almost 80 percent of all businesses in the United States. That means sole proprietorships account for more than three out of four businesses; however, they have less than 10 percent of total sales and only 18 percent of the profits when compared with partnerships and corporations. Sole proprietorships are typically small-business operations such as drugstores, variety shops, and delicatessens or service businesses such as barbershops and repair shops.

In the eyes of the law, the owner and the company in a sole proprietorship are inseparable. From a business standpoint the sole proprietor not only owns the business but also is responsible for the operation of the business. In the eyes of the public and business suppliers, the sole proprietor is considered to be the business. But

sole proprietorship

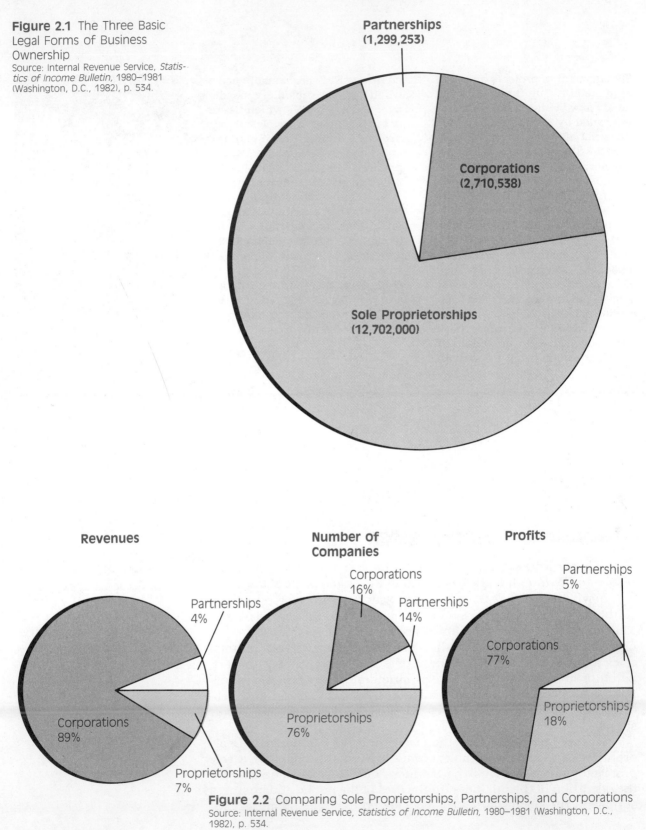

Figure 2.1 The Three Basic Legal Forms of Business Ownership
Source: Internal Revenue Service, *Statistics of Income Bulletin*, 1980–1981 (Washington, D.C., 1982), p. 534.

Partnerships
(1,299,253)

Corporations
(2,710,538)

Sole Proprietorships
(12,702,000)

Revenues

Partnerships
4%

Corporations
89%

Proprietorships
7%

Number of Companies

Corporations
16%

Partnerships
14%

Proprietorships
76%

Profits

Partnerships
5%

Corporations
77%

Proprietorships
18%

Figure 2.2 Comparing Sole Proprietorships, Partnerships, and Corporations
Source: Internal Revenue Service, *Statistics of Income Bulletin*, 1980–1981 (Washington, D.C., 1982), p. 534.

The sole proprietor is the business in the eyes of the law, the public, and suppliers.

being a sole proprietor does not mean working alone; a sole proprietorship has as many managers and employees as the scope of operations requires.

The advantages of a sole proprietorship are related to its freedom of operation and its simplicity. It also has its drawbacks.

Advantages of Sole Proprietorships

Ease of Formation. The sole proprietorship is the easiest and least expensive form of business to create. Normally once a sole proprietor has decided on a product or service to sell, he or she is in business. Legal requirements are minimal. With the exception of licenses for health and food services, permits for construction firms, beauty salons, and barbershops, and having to conform to zoning requirements, no permission is needed to enter business.

Retains All Profits. As the sole owner, a proprietor is entitled to retain all profits. The profits of the business flow directly to the owner.

Freedom in Decision Making. As the owner and the boss, the sole proprietor enjoys freedom and flexibility in decision making. The decisions can be made promptly, without consulting others.

Personal Satisfaction. Sole proprietors can enjoy the satisfaction that comes from personal achievement. Entrepreneurs who form sole proprietorships are highly motivated to achieve, desire independence, and place success or failure solely within their abilities. As a result of their actions they personally can enjoy the rewards.

Ease of Dissolution. A sole proprietorship can be ended as easily as it was begun. All the owner must do is pay the bills, close the doors, and cease operation.

Tax Advantage. Sole proprietorships are not taxed as a business. The income of the business becomes the income of the owner and is taxed as personal income.

Disadvantages of Sole Proprietorships

unlimited liability

Unlimited Liability. Legally, a sole proprietor has **unlimited liability.** This refers to *the owner's personal responsibility for any debts or damages incurred by the operation of a business.* If the business does not have enough money to pay its bills, the proprietor has to pay them with his or her own money. If the proprietor does not

creditors

have enough money, the business's **creditors,** *those to whom the company owes money,* may legally claim the owner's personal assets.

assets

(**Assets** are *things of value that businesses, government, or individuals own,* objects such as a car or a building.) In one case the sole proprietor of an Italian restaurant had obtained the necessary kitchen equipment, furniture, and fixtures by paying $8,000 from his personal savings and borrowing the rest from his bank. When several nationally known fast-food restaurants opened nearby, competition for customers became fierce. Business soon declined to a point where he could no longer make payments to the bank. The bank repossessed his equipment and sold it to satisfy the unpaid balance on the loan. Unfortunately the proceeds did not cover the amount he owed, so the bank also attached (obtained the legal right to seize) and sold his new Datsun 280ZX and a piece of land that he had inherited from his parents.

Limited Funds for Expansion. A sole proprietorship's financing consists of what the owner can contribute and borrow. Borrowing ability depends on the value of the proprietor's business and personal assets. In addition, lenders may be somewhat reluctant to risk their funds on an unproved operation whose success depends on one person.

Lack of Business and Management Skills. By its nature a sole proprietorship places the demands for business and management skills on one person — the owner. One person can hardly be an expert in such broad and diverse fields as finance, accounting, marketing, production, and law. As a result managing a sole proprietorship is often difficult, and success may be impeded by the owner's limitations.

Pause and Ponder

One of the disadvantages of a sole proprietorship is the inability to attract and retain qualified individuals. What specific ideas can you suggest to attract qualified employees? What techniques are available to retain qualified employees?

Joe might be one of the best body-and-fender repairers in town, but that does not mean he has the business expertise to run his own repair shop profitably. A sole proprietor must be a jack-of-all-trades, which is no easy task — as many have discovered.

Difficulty in Attracting Employees. An additional shortcoming of sole proprietorships is the lack of opportunity for employees. Because chances for advancement often are quite limited in a small firm, owners have difficulty hiring and keeping highly talented, ambitious employees.

Limited Life. A sole proprietorship has a limited life as a business; it lacks continuity. If the owner dies or is permanently unable to continue operations because of a disability, then the firm is legally dissolved. It cannot be handed down to the owner's heirs, only its assets can.

In spite of all these disadvantages, sole proprietorships are a significant factor in the world of business. For people who want to get into business and be independent, the sole proprietorship is an attractive alternative. Table 2.1 sums up the advantages and disadvantages of sole proprietorship.

"4:15. Right about now I would be at the bank making a deposit."
Source: From The Wall Street Journal. Courtesy Herb Brammeier Jr.

Failure for most sole proprietorships is the result of limited business and management skills.

Table 2.1 Advantages and Disadvantages of Sole Proprietorship

Advantages	Disadvantages
Ease of formation	Unlimited liability
Owner receives all profits	Limited funds for expansion
Freedom and flexibility in decision making	Lack of business and management skills
Personal satisfaction	Difficulty in attracting employees
Easy to dissolve	Limited life; business lacks continuity
Tax advantages	

Partnerships

partnership

A **partnership** is *an association of two or more people who are co-owners of a business for profit.* Partnerships are created to pool talents, provide more financial resources than are possible with a sole proprietorship, and at times to provide a base of support for each of the individuals who wish to enter a business but do not want to "go it alone."

Forming a Partnership

A partnership may be entered into by simply discussing a business proposition with a prospective partner or partners and reaching an agreement. This approach has limitations: people may forget what they agreed to, difficult times may force the business to dissolve which can result in decisions being made emotionally, and differences of opinion may create misunderstandings.

articles of partnership

A better solution is to have an experienced lawyer draw up written **articles of partnership.** These make up *a contractual agreement that establishes the legal relationship between partners.* Figure 2.3 presents a typical articles of partnership agreement.

Advantages of a Partnership

Ease of Formation. Like proprietorships, partnerships are easy to form. No state approval is required to form a partnership, nor does it have to be in writing to be legal (though it is advisable, as previously stated). Once basic agreements on profits, responsibilities, finances, and termination procedures are resolved, a partnership can begin.

Pooling of Knowledge and Skills. In a partnership two or more persons can pool their knowledge and skills and operate more effectively than one person might. For example, one partner can provide management expertise while another provides marketing skills.

More Funds Available. By pooling their financial resources, partners have more money available for meeting the financial needs of their business. These combined assets often give a general partnership a better credit rating than that of a sole proprietorship. In addition, because of the ability to offer a partnership to another person, the partnership has a method of attracting more funds for operations and expansion.

Ability to Attract and Retain Employees. As you remember, sole proprietorships often have trouble attracting and retaining superior employees because there are few opportunities for advancement. A partnership can overcome this, however, because valuable employees can be made partners in the firm. This is common practice in law and accounting firms.

<figure>

Partnership Agreement

This partnership contract and agreement entered into this the   day of
19   , by and between

WITNESSETH: The parties hereto agree that they will become and be partners in a business for the purpose and on the terms and conditions hereinafter stated.

1. The name of the partnership shall be:

2. All of the partnership business shall be carried on in the partnership name.

3. The business or businesses of this partnership are as follows:

4. The principal place of business for the partnership is:

5. The period of duration of the partnership shall be from the date of the execution of this instrument until the   day of   , 19   .

6. The assets of the partnership are and were contributed as follows:

7. Each of the partners shall share in the profits and losses of the business equally.

8. Each of the partners hereby agrees to give his undivided time and attention to the business of the partnership, and to use his best efforts to promote the interests of the partnership.

9. It is understood and agreed that books of account of the transactions of the partnership shall be kept at the principal place of business of the firm, and shall be at all reasonable times open to the inspection of any partner.

10. Any or all of the partners shall be permitted to draw from the funds of the partnership as follows:
Such sums shall be charged to him and at the annual accounting shall be charged against his share of the partnership profits. In the event that his share of the profits shall not be equal to the sum so drawn, the deficiency shall be deducted from the sum to be drawn at the next pay period.

11. Checks on the bank account of the partnership may be signed by any partner, but only for partnership obligations, and no party shall sign checks to withdraw money for any purpose except to pay partnership debts or obligations.

</figure>

Figure 2.3 A Typical Articles of Partnership Agreement

Figure 2.3, continued

12. Any or all partners shall, on every reasonable request, give to the other partner or partners a true account of all transactions relating to the business of the partnership, and full information of all letters, writing, and other things which shall come into his hands concerning the business of the partnership.

13. No partner shall, without the written consent of the other or others, become bail or surety for any other person, nor lend, spend, give, or make away with any part of the partnership property or draw or accept any bill, note, or other security in the name of said partnership.

14. Any partner may retire from the partnership at the expiration of any fiscal year on giving to the other partner or partners one month's written notice of his intention to do so.

15. When, in case of dissolution of the partnership by death, the survivors desire to continue the business, the value of the good will of said business shall be determined by appraisal. Said surviving partner or partners shall appoint one appraiser, the representative of the deceased shall appoint a second appraiser, and the two appraisers shall appoint a third. The decision of the three appraisers as to the value of the good will and other assets of the partnership shall be binding on the surviving partner or partners and the representatives of the deceased partner. The continuing partner or partners shall assume all of the existing firm obligations and hold the estate of the deceased partner harmless from all liability thereon.

16. In the event that the partnership shall terminate other than by death of one of the partners, the partnership business shall be wound up, the debts paid, and the surplus divided between the partners in accordance with their interest therein.

IN WITNESS WHEREOF we have hereunto set our hands this   day of
            , 19   .

ACKNOWLEDGMENT

STATE OF TEXAS

COUNTY OF

BEFORE ME, the undersigned, a Notary Public in and for said County and State, on this day personally appeared

known to me to be the person   whose name   subscribed to the foregoing instrument, and acknowledged

to me that   he   executed the same for the purposes and consideration therein expressed.

GIVEN UNDER MY HAND AND SEAL OF OFFICE, this the   day of   A.D. 19

Notary Public in and for   County, Texas

Tax Advantage. As with a sole proprietorship, the profit from a partnership venture is not taxed as a business. Any profits become personal income of the partners and are taxed as personal income.

Disadvantages of a Partnership

Those who think that the divorce rate is high should look at the statistics for partnerships. Business marriages, like personal ones, can fall apart quickly and with little warning. Anyone who enters into a partnership should recognize the potential pitfalls of the relationship in advance.

Unlimited Liability. As with sole proprietorships, each partner is personally liable for the financial obligations of the firm. If one partner incurs liabilities in the name of the partnership that exceed the wealth of the business and his or her personal wealth, the other partners' assets might be used to pay off the debts.

Limited Life. Partnerships lack permanence or continuity. When a change in partners occurs, the business must be formally ended under the old partnership and recreated under a new one. If one partner dies or becomes physically or mentally disabled, the partnership is legally dissolved. The same would be true if one partner decided to withdraw from the firm or a new partner were admitted. Problems of this nature sometimes can be minimized if the articles of partnership clearly define the action to take when a partner enters, leaves, or becomes incapacitated.

Potential Conflict Between Partners. Partners sometimes have scant knowledge of each other's characteristics before they begin business. Is it any surprise that conflicts of personalities, ideas, and interests among partners can often be the downfall of a business? Disharmony can be a significant disadvantage to the partnership as a form of business organization. People as well as assets must be combined successfully. Eugene Jennings, a professor of business administration, points out that partnership is the most personal and intimate type of business arrangement because two people who have equal amounts of authority must work together. The only way partnerships can survive is to respect this equal authority and to have equal division of responsibilities.[2]

Difficulty in Dissolving the Business. Once the partnership is formed, a partner cannot withdraw from the business by selling his or her partnership investment without the other partners' consent. If a partner decides that forming the partnership was a mistake, that partnership interest would have to be sold to someone who was acceptable to all partners. Table 2.2 sums up the advantages and disadvantages of partnerships.

Types of Partnerships

General Partnership. There are two types of partnerships. A **general partnership** is *an association of two or more people, each with unlimited liability, who are actively involved in the business.* In

general partnership

Advantages	Disadvantages
Ease of formation	Unlimited liability
Pooling of knowledge and skills	Limited life
More funds available	Potential conflict between partners
Ability to attract and retain employees	Difficulty in dissolving the business
Tax advantages	

Table 2.2 Advantages and Disadvantages of Partnerships

general partner

a general partnership *each* partner is a **general partner,** *having specific authority, specific operational responsibilities, and unlimited liability.* There are approximately one million general partnerships in the United States, representing approximately 8 percent of all businesses. Most of these are service companies, such as real estate and securities brokerage firms, insurance companies, law and accounting firms, engineering firms, and medical and dental clinics.

General partnerships, like sole proprietorships, are relatively simple to establish, but their operation is somewhat more complicated. Partners must work very closely with each other, and the acts of one can legally commit or bind the rest. In a general partnership all partners can be held personally responsible for any business-related debts incurred by one partner.

In an attempt to clarify the rights and responsibilities of general partners, the Uniform Partnership Act was created. Adopted by all states except Louisiana and Georgia, it brings uniformity to several aspects of general partnership operations. It also sets forth steps to be followed in dissolving a partnership. Any general partnership agreement must be constructed within the limits of this law in states that have adopted it.

Under this act each partner has the *right to:*

— Share in the management of the business
— Share in the profits
— Receive repayment for investments
— Receive repayment for payments made on behalf of the partnership
— Receive interest on any advances made to the business
— Have access to the financial records of the business
— Have a formal accounting of the financial affairs of the business

In addition, each partner has the *obligation to:*

— Contribute toward any losses incurred by the partnership
— Work for the partnership for a share in the profits rather than pay
— Agree to a majority vote or third party arbitration when differences of opinion occur
— Provide other partners with information known personally about the partnership
— Provide an accounting to the partnership of all profits made from the partnership arrangement

limited partnership

Limited Partnership. The second type of partnership is known as a **limited partnership.** It is *a partnership arrangement in which the liability of one or more partners is limited to the amount of assets they have invested in the firm.* A limited partnership cannot be formed unless a state allows it. All states except Louisiana have adopted the Uniform Limited Partnership Act to govern limited partnership operations consistently.

A limited partnership must have at least one general partner to assume unlimited liability for the debts of the firm. It may then take in any number of **limited partners,** *partners who are legally barred from participating in the partnership's management but enjoy limited liability for debts incurred by the firm.* Limited partners stand to lose only the assets that they have contributed to the company if the creditors sue to recover unpaid debts.

limited partners

Because they enjoy limited liability, limited partners' rights are restricted in several ways:

1. Their names may not appear in the name of the business.
2. They are not allowed to participate in management.
3. They must not provide any services to the firm.

If a limited partner plays an active role in management, he or she may be stripped of limited liability and declared a general partner. For example, an attorney representing the creditors of a limited partnership obtained a document signed by a limited partner with the title *manager* after that partner's name. The court held that this was evidence of active management, and the limited partner was declared personally liable for $5,000 of the company's unpaid debts.

Why form a limited partnership? A limited partnership has some attractive features including:

— The ability to obtain additional funds for the business without general partners having to share management decisions
— The ability to change (through death, withdrawal, or other circumstances) the combination of limited partners without causing the business to be legally dissolved
— The ability as a limited partner to share in the profits without risking more than the amount of the investment

Because of these advantages limited partnerships have become an investment alternative in raising funds for motion pictures and in

Pause and Ponder

The two types of partnership options to choose from are general and limited partnerships. What factors would you consider important in selecting one form over the other? Given the option, which form would you select? Why? If you selected a limited partnership would you become a limited or a general partner? Why?

Sports teams use limited partnerships to attract investors.

syndicating thoroughbred horses. Silver Screen Partners and Delphi
II offered investors the opportunity to become limited partners in
movie productions for a $5,000 investment.[3]

With the expense of horse racing rising so fast, the need to
acquire additional capital initiated the development of limited partnerships. For $40,000 to $75,000 an individual investor can become
a limited partner in either a racehorse or breeding stock.[4]

Naturally limited partnerships have disadvantages. First, the
general partner or partners must assume the burden of full financial
liability. Second, if a general partner withdraws from the business,
the partnership arrangement is terminated.

Table 2.3 provides a comparison of sole proprietorship, general
partnership, and limited partnership. Each has its advantages and
disadvantages.

Joint Venture

joint venture

Although general and limited partnerships are the two major types
of partnership arrangements, a third type exists that is designed
for short-term projects. A **joint venture** is *a partnership established
by two or more persons to carry out a specific "adventure" or
undertaking. It usually is dissolved after the objective has been
achieved. For the duration of the agreement, each partner has
unlimited liability.* Joint ventures are fairly common in real estate:
several persons pool their financial resources, purchase a large parcel
of land — perhaps develop it — divide it, and resell it.

Joint ventures also are used by firms that want to do business

Table 2.3 Comparison of Sole Proprietorship, General Partnership, and Limited Partnership

Factors	Sole Proprietorship	General Partnership	Limited Partnership
Liability	Unlimited	Unlimited	Limited for limited partner only
Formation	Minimum effort; low start-up costs	Minimum effort; hard to find suitable partners; low start-up costs	Documentation of type of partners; low start-up costs
Dissolution	Minimum	Agreement needed between partners	Agreement needed between partners
Duration	Life of the owner	Legally terminated at death or withdrawal of a partner	Legally terminated at death or withdrawal of general partner
Decision making	All decisions by owner	Cooperation required in decision making	Cooperation required in decision making if more than one general partner
Ability to acquire funds	May be difficult to raise additional capital	Easier to raise additional capital than sole proprietorship	Unlimited ability to raise additional capital
Ability to acquire and retain employees	Little to offer potential or present employees	Can offer partnership	Can offer partnership
Business and management skills	Limited ability to possess all necessary business and management skills	Greater opportunity to have necessary business and management skills	Greater opportunity to have business and management skills
Tax	Taxed as personal income	Taxed as personal income	Taxed as personal income

in a foreign country. One firm enters into a joint venture with another firm that is already established in the other country. Several years ago A. H. Robins, a pharmaceutical company, agreed to join with the German pharmaceutical firm of Boehringer Sohn, Ingelheim to build a chemical plant in Petersburg, Virginia. Each firm had a 50 percent interest, and neither had to bear the full cost and risk of the project.

A joint venture proposal from Sears, IBM, and CBS would unite three firms dominant in their respective industries in the videotape business. All three view this business as an important tool for buying services and merchandise at home; each in turn brings its area of expertise to the joint venture.[5] (The automobile world has been dazzled by the joint venture created by General Motors and Toyota.

In addition to partners being identified by the types of partnerships, partners often are referred to by other names: silent,

The Straight Line

The Dallas Cowboys

Bright Group Buys the Team

On March 19, 1984, the National Football League (NFL) approved the sale of the Dallas Cowboys for a record $60 million, officially ending the Clint Murchison era, which spanned 24 years. The new owners are the eleven members of a limited partnership headed by general partner H. R. (Bum) Bright, who is the largest shareholder in the Dallas Cowboys Football Club, Ltd. with 17 percent. For $20 million, Bright also purchased the Texas Stadium Corporation from Murchison, which gives him total control to operate the facility.

The group of Texas businessmen who formed the partnership vary in age from the youngest, who is 33, to the oldest, who is 65, and their percentage of ownership ranges from 3 to 17 percent. Five of the eleven are native Texans. The business interests of the eleven men are diversified. Among them are board chairmen of banks, the board chairman of an investment firm, the president of a barge line, and owners of real estate firms, real estate management firms, real estate development firms, auto dealerships, and a savings and loan firm. Many of the men sit on various boards, including banks, service companies, universities, a medical center, the Salvation Army, and Time, Inc. They are all men of stature whose common interest in the Dallas Cowboys

secret, dormant, or nominal. What do these terms mean and what effect do they have on partnerships?

Special Partner Classifications

Partners may have specific classifications or restrictions that affect their involvement with management or their visibility to the public.

silent partner

A **silent partner** is *a partner who assumes no active role in managing the firm, but who may be known to the general public as a partner.* Such a person provides a business with funds solely to get a piece of the action, that is, to earn income. Often the silent partner is a person with money available for investment but with no time or skills to contribute to management. The law requires limited partners to be silent partners.

secret partner

A **secret partner** is *a partner who may be an active manager but does not want his or her identity revealed to the general public.* Secret partners may have several reasons for wanting their identity kept from view. One example is a parent who gives financial support to a son's or daughter's business but prefers that the public be

brought them together to form a partnership

Tex Schramm, with a 3 percent share, was named managing partner of the new firm and was given the voting trust, which gives him the power to represent the Cowboys in NFL matters and eliminates the need for a majority owner. But as Bright pointed out — as in the case of any large company — the firm's partnership can exercise its rights to replace Schramm should it ever become necessary. A letter to this effect was sent to NFL commissioner Pete Rozelle. This letter explains replacement proceedings.

In outlining Schramm's responsibilities, Bum Bright stated that Tex will have absolute authority to run the ball club. He will have the authority to hire, fire, release, or trade players and to hire and fire coaches, administrative personnel, and secretaries. He will make all decisions pertaining to the club's operations. In short, as the Cowboys' official representative, Tex Schramm has exclusive and continuing authority to act for and on behalf of the Cowboys in all matters, including any NFL related business. He answers only to Bum Bright, and the other nine partners deal with him only through Bright.

For more about the Cowboys purchase, see Gary Myers, "NFL Approves Cowboys Sale to Bright Group," *Dallas Morning News*, March 20, 1984, p. 1; and Gary Myers, "New Owners Can Replace Schramm," *Dallas Morning News*, March 21, 1984, pp. 1B–2B.

unaware of this involvement. Another is a physician who is a partner in a funeral home.

A **dormant *or* sleeping partner** is *a partner who is both secret and silent. This person is only interested in investing funds in the company for financial profit.*

dormant *or* sleeping partner

A **nominal partner** is *an individual who is neither a part-owner of the partnership nor an active participant in the firm's affairs. Often this is a well-known person who lends a famous name to the company.* Nominal partners' responsibilities should be defined clearly. If a nominal partner misleads or deceives outsiders into thinking that he or she is a genuine partner, the true owners (and possibly the nominal partner) could be liable for debts and other commitments that the nominal partner makes.

nominal partner

Summary

This chapter examines two categories of unincorporated businesses: sole proprietorships and partnerships. A sole proprietorship is a business owned by one individual. Legally the owner and the company are inseparable. Sole proprietorships have a number of advantages including:

— Ease of formation
— Retains all profits
— Freedom in decision making
— Personal satisfaction
— Ease of dissolution
— Tax advantages

A sole proprietorship also has certain disadvantages.

— Unlimited liability
— Limited funds for expansion
— Lack of business and management skills
— Difficulty in attracting employees
— Limited life

A partnership is an association of two or more people who are co-owners of a business for profit. A partnership can be created orally or in writing. It is recommended that it be developed in writing through an articles of partnership agreement. A partnership has a number of advantages including:

— Ease of formation
— Pooling of knowledge and skills
— More funds available
— Ability to attract and retain employees

Roger B. Smith, chairman of General Motors, and Eiji Toyoda, chairman of Toyota Motor Company of Japan, inaugurate their joint venture in Fremont, California.

- Ownership commitment and support
- Tax advantages

As with sole proprietorships, it does have disadvantages:

- Unlimited liability
- Limited life
- Potential conflict between partners
- Difficulty in dissolving the business

There are two types of partnership: general partnership and limited partnership. A general partnership is an association of two or more people, each with unlimited liability, who are actively involved in the business. A limited partnership, on the other hand, is one in which the liability of one or more partners is limited to the amount of assets they have invested in the firm. A limited partnership must have at least one general partner who assumes unlimited liability. In a limited partnership the limited partner legally is barred from participating in managing the firm.

A joint venture is a partnership form developed for short-term projects. It is a partnership established by two or more persons to carry out a specific adventure or undertaking. It usually is dissolved after the objective has been achieved. For the duration of the agreement, each partner has unlimited liability.

Partners are often referred to by different terms depending on the restrictions imposed by the type of partnership and the visibility to the public. They are classified as silent, secret, dormant (sleeping), or nominal.

Key Terms

articles of partnership
assets
creditors
dormant *or* sleeping partner
general partner

general partnership
joint venture
limited partner
limited partnership
nominal partner

partnership
secret partner
silent partner
sole proprietorship
unlimited liability

For Review and Discussion

1. It has been said that in the eyes of the law, suppliers, and the public, a sole proprietor is the company. Explain.

2. "Forming a sole proprietorship is as easy as simply hanging out your shingle and beginning business." Explain.

3. Describe the major disadvantages of a sole proprietorship.

4. "A partnership does not have to be in writing to be legal, but it is a good idea to create an articles of partnership." Discuss this statement.

5. Describe the advantages and disadvantages of a partnership as a form of business ownership.

6. Given a choice of becoming a general partner or a limited partner in a limited partnership arrangement explain why a person would decide to choose each alternative.

7. Describe the burden placed on a general partner in a limited partnership arrangement.

8. Explain the rights and obligations of a partner under the Uniform Partnership Act.

9. What is the purpose of creating a joint venture?

10. Describe the characteristics of the following kinds of partners: a. silent, b. secret, c. dormant, and d. nominal.

Applications

Case 2.1 Making the Right Choice

Annie Marangi reviewed the options available to her once again:

- Continue to go it alone as a sole proprietorship
- Create a general partnership with Chris and Ed
- Establish a limited partnership with two investors who would "bankroll" her for a healthy share of the profits

Though each of the options was appealing, each had its disadvantages. Continuing her veterinary practice by herself would put a strain on cash availability. To have the kind of physical facilities she wanted (dog runs, modern surgical equipment, and some additional help), Annie *really* needed the money supplied by a partnership of some sort. In addition, there was absolutely no one else to rely on for technical information, and she could *never* get sick.

Creating a general partnership brought a cloud of uncertainty. Being as independent as she was, how would decisions be made on finances, marketing, and personnel? Although Chris and Ed had been friends since medical school, she had never worked with either of them on a regular basis.

There was another problem. Each of the potential partners was not going to invest the same amount of money: Chris was to invest $50,000, Ed $35,000, and Annie $20,000 plus facilities. Ed and Chris did not appear to have any concerns about this, but it did bother Annie. Partners were supposed to be equal on everything — investments, work, and profits.

Forming a limited partnership presented a different type of dilemma. If agreed to, under the terms of the partnership the two potential limited partners and she would divide the profits 60-40. Giving someone 40 percent of the profits simply for the use of money did not seem equitable. This concern was explained away by one of the investors with the comment, "Well, Annie, you have all the freedom in the world to make decisions with our money. It's yours to make or break — like a game of Monopoly."

After looking at the options Annie was still undecided. "I'll just sleep on it overnight. In the morning I'll wrestle with it some more."

Questions

1. What are the advantages of each proposal?
2. Which proposal should Annie adopt? Why?
3. How would you solve each of Annie's concerns about the three proposals?

Case 2.2 An "Informal" Partnership

"But we've had a partnership all these years. We built the business from nothing. It was a labor of love. Al would produce, sell, and pack the shipping cartons. I handled the rest — typed invoices, answered the phone, did odds and ends — just everything.

"*We* grew the business over the years. Eventually we hired some employees, built a small combination office-warehouse, and made it our full-time business. Our kids worked in the summer to help us out. It was a real family business.

"After all those years and hard work the company did well. We had one hundred employees and a regional reputation. Now you are telling me that John Briggs and Company no longer exists? That:

- The death of my husband has ended the business.
- The business was legally a sole proprietorship and not a partnership.
- My husband did not designate in his will that the assets of the business were to be left to me.
- I'm not identified anywhere — bank statements or company documents.
- Even though John never made a decision without consulting me, I was never a partner because everything was in his name.

"I just can't believe we did this to ourselves."

Questions

1. What does this case tell you about "partnerships"?
2. What specific point is made about a sole proprietorship as a form of business?
3. What two alternatives are available to prevent this type of situation from recurring?

The Modern Corporation

Chapter Outline

Chapter Objectives

After studying this chapter, you should be able to:

1. Summarize the nature and significance of the corporation as a form of business organization.
2. Describe the steps involved in forming a corporation.
3. Identify and explain the different categories of corporations based on place of chartering, restrictions on stock ownership, and reasons for existence.
4. Describe the internal organization of a corporation.
5. State in your own words the principal advantages and disadvantages of the corporate form of business organization.
6. Discuss the general conditions and benefits of organizing an S corporation.
7. Present the differences between an acquisition, a merger, and an amalgamation or consolidation.
8. Describe the various types of mergers that can occur among corporations.
9. List and describe the features of corporations formed for profit and those formed for nonprofit purposes.

A corporation is an artificial being, invisible, intangible, and existing only in contemplation of law. Being the mere creature of law, it possesses only those properties which the charter of its creation confers upon it, either expressly, or as incidental to its very existence.

— *John Marshall, former chief justice of the United States Supreme Court*

Up Front   Lee Iacocca

The Challenge Continues

Iacocca, the son of Italian immigrants, joined Ford Motor Company as a trainee in 1946 after earning a master's degree in engineering from Princeton. During the next 32 years, Iacocca charmed or clawed his way — it depends on whom you ask — to the presidency of Ford and a yearly salary of $978,000. En route he conceived and introduced the Ford Mustang, one of Ford's best-known products (first-year sales in 1964 were 418,000 cars, a record that stands to this day).

Things changed abruptly when the bright, hard-nosed Iacocca was fired by chairman Henry Ford II on July 13, 1978. A millionaire by then, Iacocca could have slipped into obscurity and a comfortable retirement — not a likely fate for a person with his drive, ambition, and talent.

On November 2, 1978, the financially desperate Chrysler Corporation, which had reported a record loss of $158.5 million in the previous 3 months, announced the hiring of Lee Iacocca as president, a position that required saving the company from impending collapse. Iacocca has met the challenge with characteristic bravado.

In the fall of 1979, with Chrysler's bankruptcy imminent, Iacocca summoned all his skills of persuasion to have Congress pass a bill guaranteeing $1.5 billion worth of loans from private sources to rescue the troubled company. Other badly needed aid also was secured. The United Auto Workers agreed to defer wage increases for 3 years to help give the company a chance to get back on its feet. Under pressure from Iacocca, Chrysler suppliers and lenders agreed to relax payment terms. These respective concessions enabled Chrysler to obtain more badly needed cash. (The company reportedly spends $5 million each working hour just for daily operating expenses.) With the company's financial burden temporarily lightened, Iacocca channeled his energy toward improving Chrysler's long-term operating efficiency and cutting costs to the bone. Losses persisted between 1979 and 1981, however, fueled by the combined effects of Japanese competition, national economic woes, and the lingering effects of the company's previous operating practices. During that 3-year period Chrysler lost $3.3 billion.

By mid-1983, Iacocca had closed 16 of Chrysler's 52 American plants and sold its foreign plants and nonautomobile businesses. The work force was pared from 157,000 employees in 1978 to 82,000 in 1983, which saved the company more than half a billion dollars annually in payroll expense. By eliminating excessive buyer options on things such as window tinting and body trim, Iacocca reduced the number of parts used to build Chrysler cars by 43 percent, which saves the company approximately $300 million per year. He also terminated Chrysler's unique and costly practice of manufacturing cars in advance of dealer orders and parking them outside to become weather-beaten, then sold at reduced prices. The company now gears its production plans to dealer orders actually in hand.

Chrysler Corporation advertisements began featuring a new star — Lee A. Iacocca — who convincingly personified the spirit of "The New Chrysler Corporation" by telling potential car buyers, "You can go with Chrysler, or you can go with someone else — and take your chances." By then Iacocca, a veteran at taking chances, *was* Chrysler Corporation in the minds of his employees and much of the American public. The earthy president-turned-pitchman seemed to be dragging the company back from the grave.

The future looked promising for Chrysler by 1983. Drastic survival measures implemented by Iacocca and his hand-picked top managers, coupled with an improving national economy and an industry-wide emphasis on quality, began to bear fruit. The leaner, more competitive company only needed to sell 1.2 million cars each year to earn a profit (compared with 2.3 million in 1980), and it had $900 million in cash available to pay day-to-day business expenses. Dealers had ordered every car the company could make before its plants shut down to convert to 1984 models, and Chrysler's share of the automotive market rose to 12 percent. Iacocca was voted the most admired business manager in the United States in a Gallup poll.

Perhaps the most triumphant moment of 1983, though, was the day Lee Iacocca announced to the National Press Club in Washington, D.C., that Chrysler would pay off the last $800 million of its guaranteed loans that September: 7 years before the due date.

Is Iacocca's work finished at Chrysler Corporation? Not by a long shot. Under his stewardship Chrysler Corporation now produces only small and midsized automobiles, which means that it cannot compete on a model-for-

model basis with much larger competitors such as General Motors. There are also indications that the American public once again may want larger, less fuel-efficient cars, especially if gasoline prices remain stable or decrease. Furthermore, an increase in interest rates would depress the new car sales that Chrysler desperately needs to sustain its newly regained sales momentum and avoid a possibly fatal financial relapse.

While acknowledging that the battle is far from over, the forthright, confident, and flamboyant fifty-nine-year-old Iacocca pursues new directions for Chrysler. For example, the company has invested $700 million in the production of a 40-mile-per-gallon van/station wagon (the Plymouth Voyager or Dodge Caravan — they are basically the same), which was introduced in early 1984. This unique new vehicle can haul seven passengers comfortably while fitting into a standard garage. Iacocca also is working toward what has been called *Global Motors*, a concept that may unite Chrysler Corporation in joint ventures (see Chapter 2) with various automakers and parts producers around the world. Such an arrangement could enable Chrysler to compete in all markets with General Motors and Ford.

Applauded by employees, peers, and the public at large, Iacocca seems to have proved beyond doubt that he is the ideal person to engineer Chrysler's recovery. Remarked one New York banker, "Lee is a man who can instill leadership in a crisis. He knows his business from front bumpers to back ends. He is the right man at the right time."

For more about Lee A. Iacocca, see "$1 Billion for the UAW," *Fortune*, October 3, 1983, p. 6; Tom Nicholson with James C. Jones, Marilyn Achiron, and Rich Thomas, "Back to Cruising Speed," *Newsweek*, July 25, 1983, p. 63; John Koten, "Iacocca Says He Will Stay at Chrysler," *The Wall Street Journal*, July 11, 1983, p. 21; Alexander L. Taylor III, "Iacocca's Tightrope Act," *Time*, March 21, 1983, p. 50; Tom Nicholson with James C. Jones, "Iacocca Shifts into High," *Newsweek*, February 14, 1983, p. 64; and Carey W. English, "Chrysler: Classic Turnaround in U.S. Industry," *U.S. News & World Report*, February 14, 1983, p. 68.

In Chapter 2, we examined two important legal forms of business ownership — the sole proprietorship and the partnership. In this chapter we explore a third legal form of business ownership: the corporation. Although there are approximately five times as many sole proprietorships in the United States as corporations, corporations are responsible for between 85 and 90 percent of all sales. Corporation ownership is widespread, and corporations employ millions of workers. Their influence on society at all levels — local, national, and international — is substantial.

What Is a Corporation?

You learned earlier that forming a sole proprietorship or a partnership is relatively simple. You also learned that the owners of such unincorporated businesses ordinarily cannot be separated from their firms: they are the firms. A **corporation,** however, is *a legal form of business organization created by a government and considered an entity separate and apart from its owners.* In effect it is an artificial person that has been created by law. Its birth certificate is the **corporate charter,** *a document issued by a government that contains all information stated in the original application for a charter plus the powers, rights, and privileges of the corporation as prescribed by law.*

    A corporation can sue or be sued, make contracts, own property, and even be a partner in a partnership. In contrast to other legal forms of organization, the corporation does not cease to exist when its owners die. It is distinct and apart from its **shareholders or stockholders,** who are *a corporation's owners but frequently not the individuals who control and manage the firm day by day.* **Stock certificates,** *documents that provide legal evidence of ownership of shares in a corporation,* are issued to the shareholders. (Figure 3.1 shows you an example of a stock certificate.) Most shareholders have little or nothing to do with management, as you will see later in the chapter.

corporation

corporate charter

shareholders *or* stockholders

stock certificates

How to Incorporate

In the previous chapters we discussed what might happen when two people go into a business venture together. Let's assume that the two of you have considered both the sole proprietorship and partnership forms of organization, but have decided to incorporate the business. How would you go about forming a corporation?

    First, you would apply to the appropriate state official, frequently the secretary of state, for permission to incorporate. A lawyer can help you with this. A **certificate (articles) of incorporation** is *the application to incorporate that must be filed with the secretary of state, which becomes the corporation's charter after it is approved.*

certificate (articles) of incorporation

Figure 3.1 Sample Stock Certificate
Source: Courtesy Bethlehem Steel Corporation. Reproduced with permission.

Some states permit one person to form a corporation; others require a minimum of three. The people who form a corporation are called *incorporators* and usually serve as the corporation's directors until the first stockholders' meeting, when a board can be elected. If you wish to be the sole director of a corporation but the state requires three incorporators, you may ask relatives or your lawyer and accountant to serve. These two individuals may then bow out at the first meeting.

The charter describes the corporation's purpose and its intended business. Because the corporation cannot engage in any business not included in the charter, the articles of incorporation may list a wide variety of business activities. Doing so makes it unnecessary to apply for a charter amendment should the corporation enter a business different from its original one. A charter generally includes the following information:

1. Company name; names and addresses of incorporators; location of main office
2. Purpose for which the corporation is being formed
3. Length of life (may be perpetual)

4. Amount and kind of stock the corporation wants authorization to issue
5. Names, addresses, and powers of the original board of directors
6. Dates and times of shareholders' and directors' meetings
7. Names of initial subscribers to stock shares
8. Procedure to amend, alter, or repeal any provision contained in the original articles of incorporation (if the law permits)

Types of Corporations

domestic corporation

foreign corporation

alien corporation

open corporation

Corporations fit into one of three categories, depending on where they are chartered. To illustrate, assume that a corporation is chartered in New Jersey. In that state, it would be a **domestic corporation,** *the term applied to a corporation in the state where it is incorporated.* In the other forty-nine states, it is considered a **foreign corporation,** *the term applied to a United States corporation in states other than the one in which it is incorporated.* If the same company did business in other countries, they would consider it an **alien corporation,** which is *a firm incorporated in a country other than the one in which it operates.* For example, Porsche, the German automobile manufacturer, is considered an alien corporation by the United States. Figure 3.2 presents these relationships visually.

Corporations also may be classified as open or close. Those like General Foods or International Business Machines are considered **open corporations;** each is *a corporation whose stock can be*

Figure 3.2 Three Classifications of Corporations: Domestic, Foreign, and Alien

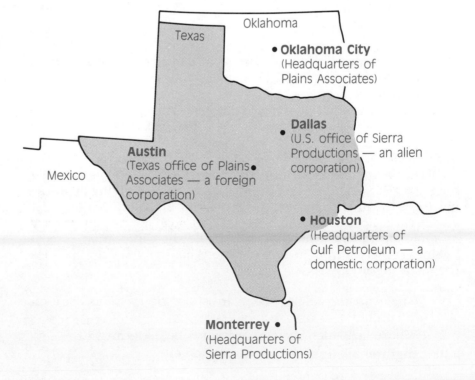

Oklahoma

Texas

• **Oklahoma City**
(Headquarters of
Plains Associates)

• **Dallas**
(U.S. office of Sierra
Productions — an alien
corporation)

Austin
(Texas office of Plains•
Associates — a foreign
corporation)

Mexico

• **Houston**
(Headquarters of
Gulf Petroleum — a
domestic corporation)

Monterrey •
(Headquarters of
Sierra Productions)

purchased by anyone who can afford the price. A **close corporation,** close corporation
or one that is closely held, is *a corporation whose stock cannot be purchased by the general public; it is usually owned by a few individuals.* Often these are family members who agree not to sell stock to outsiders because they fear losing control of the firm. Corporations such as Ford Motor Company, Levi Strauss & Company, and Adolph Coors Company began as closely held companies and later went public (sold stock to the general public). Usually a corporation does this to raise additional capital for expansion. (The subject of financing with stock and the kinds of stock that may be sold will be explored in detail in Chapter 14.) Many large corporations, however, remain closely held to this day, including United Parcel Service and Hallmark Cards.

How Corporations Are Organized

For the moment, assume that you and your friend have received a corporate charter and issued stock to twenty other persons. You would then call a meeting of the stockholders for the purpose of approving your **bylaws,** which are *internal rules that govern the*   bylaws
general operation of a corporation. The bylaws may repeat some of the charter's provisions and include the following points as well:

— Quorum required for holding stockholders' meetings
— Voting privileges of stockholders
— Number of directors; method of electing them; method of creating or filling vacancies on the board of directors
— Time and place of directors' meetings; requirements for a quorum
— Method of selecting officers; titles; duties; terms of office; salaries
— Transfer restrictions on stock certificates; procedure for recording new owners on company books
— Procedure for declaring dividends on stock
— Authority to sign checks
— Procedure for amending bylaws

Table 3.1 compares the ownership and management of a corporation to that in a sole proprietorship and a partnership. The owners of a corporation are the stockholders, but they do not run the business. They give the authority to develop the company's policies to the board of directors, who have been elected to represent them. The board members select the company's officers: president, treasurer, and secretary. A corporation's officers, rather than its board of directors, are responsible for carrying out its day-to-day activities. If the firm is large enough, it will employ and supervise specialized managers in fields such as marketing, production, finance, and personnel management.

Although sole proprietorships and partnerships can be managed by people who are not the owners, as Table 3.1 shows, such a

Table 3.1 Comparing Ownership and Management in the Three Forms of Business

	Sole Proprietorship	Partnership	Corporation
Ownership	Proprietor	Partners	Stockholders
Management	Proprietor or person chosen by proprietor	Partners or person chosen by partners	Corporate officers who are chosen by board of directors, who are elected by stockholders

practice is unusual. It is much more typical for the owners to manage these two forms of business.

Few stockholders in corporations, however, expect to exert control over corporate activities. In its more than 100 years of existence, American Telephone and Telegraph Company (AT&T) accumulated assets of more than $113 billion, more than any other corporation in the world. Before embarking on a recent reorganization (see The Straight Line, pp. 72–73) it had over 1 million employees, 24,000 buildings, 177,000 motor vehicles, and 3 million shareholders.[1] If you own ten shares of General Motors (GM) common stock, you are a part-owner of a giant corporation. But you exercise little if any control over the firm because there are 1,035,000 other shareholders.

Stockholders tend to know or care little about the operation of the firm. They are more interested in the earnings or growth potential of their investment. Also, in many large corporations, no individual holds more than 1 percent of the outstanding stock, hardly enough to exercise control over corporate activities. In widely held corporations where stockholders are scattered and unable to contact each other conveniently, however, one stockholder could exert considerable influence with less than 51 percent of the stock. In fact, a person with 20 percent of the stock could get effective control of the corporation.

Generally, however, the corporate management — the officers — control the internal affairs of most large corporations. And that management is largely self-perpetuating. Stockholders' influence can be felt only if they organize themselves into a group with a collective interest and vote their shares together to change the management or reject management policy. As long as the stockholders feel that management is running the corporation well and their own investment is secure and profitable, though, the management will be left alone.

Management has to report to the stockholders, however, in two ways: in the annual report, which describes the corporation's operations and financial status, and in the stockholders' meeting. The bylaws of each corporation specify when the meeting must be held. At the meeting, the stockholders have the opportunity to chal-

Pause and Ponder

In recent years, immensely wealthy foreign companies and individuals (notably those from the oil producing Middle Eastern nations) have purchased huge amounts of United States real estate and large blocks of stock in United States corporations. Do you believe there should be legal restrictions on the amount of American property and stock that noncitizens and alien corporations may own? Why or why not?

lenge management's decisions. Few stockholders attend these meetings, again because of the relatively small size of their holdings and their lack of interest in operational details. In a remarkable case of stockholder apathy, the annual meeting of Tensor Corporation, a manufacturer of lamps, was attended by exactly one stockholder who was not a director or an officer. Tensor's president claimed that the fellow, who lived nearby the meeting place, came mostly to enjoy the refreshments.[2]

Corporate management must obtain the stockholders' approval on certain issues. The bylaws always specify which matters this is true for, often including such things as the acquisition of another company or the issuing of new stock. Even so, all stockholders will not attend the meeting. A stockholder may mail the company a **proxy,** which is *a document that expresses a stockholder's voting intentions on corporate matters when he or she cannot attend the annual meeting.* Proxies are like absentee ballots in political elections, although the forms used to solicit them often state that if the proxy is not returned by a certain date, the stockholder's votes will be cast in a manner specified by management.

proxy

At a corporation's annual meeting, stockholders may express their concerns and recommendations to management face to face.

Advantages of Corporate Organization

limited liability

Corporations, too, have their advantages and disadvantages. One of the key drawbacks of sole proprietorships and partnerships — unlimited liability — is avoided under the corporate form of organization. Owners of a corporation enjoy **limited liability,** which is *a feature inherent in corporations;* it means that *stockholders' responsibility for debts is restricted to the amount of their investment in the corporation.* One practical point should be mentioned here. A corporation that decides to borrow money may have trouble doing so if its assets are inadequate security for the loan. A lender may then require one or more stockholders with substantial personal assets to cosign the loan agreement with the corporation. The stockholders who agree to such an arrangement voluntarily relinquish their limited liability for their company to borrow funds.

A second advantage is ease of expansion. Corporations can raise funds by selling stock, a financing device that does not exist for sole proprietorships or partnerships. Corporations also can borrow against the value of their assets by selling bonds. Both of these corporate securities will be explored in detail in Chapter 14.

A third advantage of corporations is the ease of transferring ownership. Stockholders can transfer their shares to someone else merely by endorsing the stock certificate in the space provided on the back.

Relatively long life is a fourth advantage. Corporations, unlike sole proprietorships and partnerships, can be chartered for perpetual existence. They do not terminate with the death or incapacitation of the stockholders-owners. In fact, approximately twenty American corporations can trace their roots to before the Revolutionary War.[3]

A fifth advantage of incorporation is the greater ability to hire specialized management. As we said earlier, most sole proprietorships and partnerships are managed by the owners. One reason is that these people are often entrepreneurs who want to run their own business. Another reason is that these businesses are usually smaller and cannot afford to bring in sought-after managers. Corporations, on the other hand, have the facilities and money necessary to attract top talent to management jobs in critical business areas such as labor-management relations, finance, marketing, manufacturing, and personnel. Unlike sole proprietorships and partnerships,

Pause and Ponder

Why might a corporation be a desirable general partner in a limited partnership? What problems might arise from having such a partner? Would a corporation exercise more power than an individual person acting as a partner? Why or why not?

corporations can replace top managers if their performance is unsatisfactory.

Disadvantages of Corporate Organization

Corporations also have their disadvantages. One drawback is that they are normally more expensive and complicated to organize than the other forms of business. It is usually necessary to hire a lawyer to draft the articles of incorporation, and states require the payment of a charter tax, filing fees, and various other costs.

Taxation can be a further disadvantage. The Internal Revenue Service taxes the earnings of sole proprietorships and partnerships at the graduated personal income tax rate, which is often less than the 46 percent maximum tax rate applied to the earnings of corporations. Taxes are not a consistent problem, however. We mentioned earlier that expert managers could be hired, and often these experts can help a large corporation legally avoid the full 46 percent tax rate. In one recent year, such large corporations as Ford Motor Company, Lockheed Corporation, and Western Electric paid considerably less than the maximum tax rate.

Exercising every citizen's right to take full advantage of federal tax laws, corporations, like individuals, can minimize their tax burden through such actions as:

1. Allocating certain kinds of revenue over several years' operations, which may reduce the total amount of tax paid on that revenue
2. Spreading certain kinds of operating losses over several years, which will reduce the firm's taxable income for each of those years
3. Selling unprofitable investments or subsidiary companies and using the loss to decrease taxable earnings over several years
4. Depreciating assets using the highest annual rate allowed under current tax laws, thus reducing the amount of revenue subject to income tax
5. Purchasing certain costly equipment or making major improvements whose value may be deducted from income taxes owed under current tax laws

In addition to federal income tax, corporations must pay taxes in each state where they do business, if the state levies a corporate income tax. Then the stockholders must pay personal income taxes on the corporate profits paid to them as dividends on their stock. The fairness of this double taxation has been questioned for many years by corporations, stockholders, and legislators alike.

Government restrictions and reporting requirements are generally more extensive for corporations than for other businesses. As a result, corporate activities lack the freedom and privacy enjoyed

Large groups of employees work to prepare the many government reports required of a large corporation.

by the other forms of business ownership. In addition to federal reporting requirements and restrictions, corporations also must comply with the demands of each state in which they operate. Depending on a company's operations and products, legally mandated paperwork can be mind-boggling. Most large corporations must report sources of revenue, debts, expenses, and a host of other financial information. This information, which often becomes a matter of public record, can be examined by competitors and other interested parties. Such loss of secrecy about operations can hurt a corporation's competitive position in the marketplace.

Finally, employees in large corporations may lack the personal identification with and commitment to corporate goals that those of smaller organizations often enjoy. This may be more the fault of management's attitude than of the company's form of organization. After all, the employee-owners of small family corporations display considerable identification with and interest in operations.

Table 3.2 summarizes the advantages and disadvantages of the corporate form of organization, along with those of the sole proprietorship and general partnership you learned about in Chapter 2.

The S Corporation

One way of avoiding the tax disadvantages of corporations while enjoying the advantages of incorporating is available to business that qualifies as an **S corporation.** This is *one that may elect, under Subchapter S of the Internal Revenue Code, to be taxed as a sole proprietorship, if owned by one stockholder, or as a partnership, if owned by several stockholders.* If the owners choose

S corporation

Table 3.2 Comparing Advantages and Disadvantages of the Three Forms of Business Ownership

Form of Ownership	Advantages	Disadvantages
Sole proprietorship	Easy to establish. Owner retains all profits. Owner enjoys relative freedom and flexibility in decision making. Owner gets satisfaction and independence. Easy to dissolve.	Owner has unlimited liability. Funds for expansion may be difficult to obtain. Owner's lack of business skills may impede success. Employees lack opportunities. Business lacks continuity; it dies when owner dies.
General partnership	Individuals with diverse talents can pool knowledge and skills. More funds may be more easily available than for sole proprietorship. There is the potential for a better credit rating than sole proprietorship can obtain. Valuable employees can be retained by allowing them to become partners.	Partners may have conflicting personalities, ideas, and interests. Business lacks permanence. General partners have unlimited liability. Investments are frozen. Value of partners' claims may be disputed.
Corporations	Owners have limited liability. Easy to expand. Easy to transfer ownership. Business can have relatively long life. First-rate, specialized managers can be hired and kept more easily.	More expensive and complicated to organize. Taxes are frequently higher. Government restrictions and reporting requirements can be costly and time consuming. Employees may lack identification with and commitment to corporate goals.

this tax treatment, the corporation pays no corporate federal income tax. Instead, the shareholders declare their share of the firm's taxable income as personal income (regardless of whether the amount was actually paid to them), and it is taxed at their personal income tax rate, which is often less than the maximum corporate rate of 46 percent.

The Subchapter S Revision Act of 1982 made several significant changes in the conditions and qualifications that apply to S (formerly called Subchapter S) corporations. Major conditions are:

1. The firm must be chartered in the United States.
2. Only one class of stock may exist.
3. A maximum of thirty-five stockholders is allowed.
4. Shareholders must be individuals or estates.
5. Nonresident aliens and other corporations are not permitted to be shareholders.

To Potential Small-Business Owners

Small business is an essential part of the United States economic system. The National Small Business Association reported to a House of Representatives subcommittee that small businesses make up 98 percent of all companies, sell 72 percent of all merchandise bought by final consumers, sell 82 percent of all services, and provide jobs for 59 percent of the nation's private, nonagricultural work force. Some readers of this book expect to start small businesses in the future. If that is your goal, you will want to read Chapter 18, "The Small Business and Franchising." We believe, however, that you will gain the most value from that chapter if you study our material on management, human relations, production, marketing, and finance *first*. Consequently, we explore those topics in Chapters 4 through 17 as groundwork for our discussion of small business and franchising.

---

6. All shareholders must agree to have their corporation taxed as an S corporation.
7. S corporation status may be terminated by a majority vote of the shareholders. (Under previous regulations, one minority shareholder could prevent the termination of S corporation status.)
8. The Internal Revenue Service may terminate S corporation status for a company whose passive income (from royalties, rents, dividends, and interest) exceeds 25 percent of annual gross sales for 3 consecutive years. Federal income tax must be paid on the excess amount in any given year.

If S corporation tax treatment sounds good to you, and you are able to meet the above conditions, you still should ask an experienced lawyer and accountant for their advice. It is possible, for example, that tax laws in your state do not recognize S corporations. That would mean that while avoiding federal corporate income taxes, your S corporation would still have to pay state corporate income taxes. Federal and state tax laws are quite complex, and they change from year to year.

Business Combinations

Businesses combine to achieve greater profitability, efficiency, and competitiveness. After forming a corporation — let's call it Yankee Pedaler Bicycle Corporation — your original company can be combined with others in one of several ways.

Acquisition

Acquisition *results when one firm buys a majority interest in another, but both retain their identities.* Corporations that want a reliable supply of parts and materials or guaranteed markets for their products often use this tactic. They simply purchase enough of the outstanding shares of a supplier or a customer to exercise a controlling interest in that firm.

acquisition

To prevent periodic shortages of tires, tubes, and bicycle chains and to increase retail sales, you could buy controlling interest in Big Wheel Tire Company, Continuous Chain Corporation, and House of Spokes Bike Shops. Figure 3.3 shows the organization that would result. That should solve your supply and marketing problems.

Merger

A **merger** *occurs when two or more companies become a single enterprise; the controlling corporation retains its identity and absorbs the others.* Powerful entrepreneurs once eliminated competitors this way. United States Steel Corporation, American Tobacco Company (now American Brands), du Pont, and Standard Oil Company were born during the first wave of mergers between 1881 and 1911. In 1899 alone, 1,028 companies completely disappeared as a result of merging with other firms.

merger

Mergers are still popular today. In 1982, for example, 2,346 companies joined forces by merger and 2,533 had merged by the end of 1983, a 9-year record. Phillips Petroleum Company played the lead role in these 1983 mergers by purchasing General American Oil Company for $1.1 billion in cash and stock. American General Corporation purchased Gulf United Corporation for $1 billion in stock, and Goodyear Tire and Rubber Company bought Celeron Corporation for $809.7 million in stock.[4]

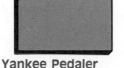 Owned by Yankee Pedaler

**Yankee Pedaler
Bicycle Corporation**

Figure 3.3 Yankee Pedaler Grows by Acquisition

Big Wheel Tire
Company

Continuous Chain
Corporation

House of Spokes
Bike Shops

Final preparations for the largest merger in United States history began in mid-1984 when Standard Oil Company of California (SOCAL) purchased Gulf Corporation for $13.4 billion. Other leading mega-mergers ranked according to cost are Texaco Inc. and Getty Oil Company ($10.1 billion), du Pont Company and Conoco ($7.4 billion), and Marathon Oil and U.S. Steel ($6.5 billion).[5]

horizontal merger

There are three different kinds of mergers. A **horizontal merger** *occurs when one firm purchases other firms that produce similar or competing products.* This results in greater production economies and reduced competition, but as you will see later, the Federal Trade Commission and Department of Justice regulate such mergers closely. Flowers Industries of Thomasville, Georgia, has grown impressively by horizontal merger during the last two decades. Begun in 1919 by William Flowers as a bakery and ice cream shop, the company started to grow by horizontal merger in 1964 after his son, William Flowers, Jr., assumed control. After 20 years of horizontal mergers the firm now owns 27 bakeries in 13 states, which makes it the largest independent bakery in the United States. Despite this dramatic expansion, Flowers family members still own 30 percent of the stock.[6] If you staged this kind of merger, you would buy bicycle companies, perhaps in other parts of the country, in exchange for stock in Yankee Pedaler, as shown in Figure 3.4

vertical merger

Vertical mergers were common from 1921 to 1929. A **vertical merger** *occurs when one firm unites with others that contribute to its product's manufacture or distribution.* It usually is intended to guarantee sources of parts or sales outlets, so it can be used as an alternative to acquisition in attaining these goals.

A company that merges vertically with others controls the raw materials, production, distribution, and marketing of a product. In their infancy automakers bought glass, adhesives, shock absorbers, batteries, and ignition parts from independent companies. Over the

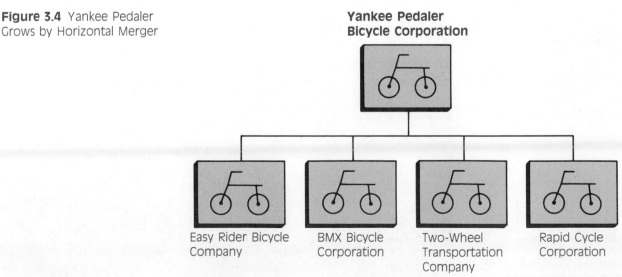

Figure 3.4 Yankee Pedaler Grows by Horizontal Merger

years suppliers of these items were acquired in vertical mergers, and most are now the exclusive suppliers of a parent firm. Vertical mergers have resulted in such entities as fully integrated oil companies like ARCO (Atlantic Richfield Company), which owns everything from offshore drilling rigs in the Gulf of Mexico to gasoline pumps at the corner service station. Vertical mergers are less likely than horizontal mergers to encounter antitrust difficulties.

If Yankee Pedaler Bicycle Corporation underwent a vertical merger, it would absorb companies that produced the chains, tires, wheels and fenders, handlebars and grips, seats, lights, and horns for its bicycles. Adding a chain of bicycle stores would complete the production and marketing system, as illustrated in Figure 3.5. After this kind of merging, the company would be virtually self-sufficient.

A **conglomerate merger,** which *occurs when one firm buys other firms that make unrelated products,* has become a natural response to government regulation of monopolies. The wave of mergers that occurred during the 1960s and early 1970s saw many of these.

conglomerate merger

To expand profitably is the main goal of a conglomerate merger. Another purpose of combining unlike firms is to diversify operations and thus vary sources of income for the parent company. Conglomerates avoid putting all their corporate eggs in one industrial basket.

Yankee Pedaler Bicycle Corporation

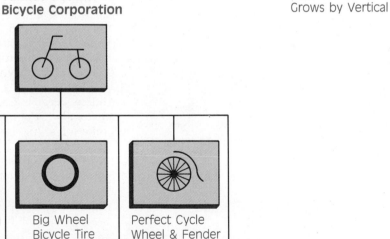

Figure 3.5 Yankee Pedaler Grows by Vertical Merger

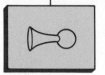

"It doesn't matter where you get it, Mister — we're owned by the same conglomerate."
Source: From *The Wall Street Journal*, permission Cartoon Features Syndicate.

Hard times tend not to fall on all industries at once or with equal severity.

R. J. Reynolds Industries is well known as the largest cigarette company in the United States; however, this firm also owns the first and largest containerized shipping company in the world (Sea-Land Industries Investments), the nation's largest fruit and vegetable processor (Del Monte Corporation), the nation's second largest wine and distilled spirits producer (Heublein), and the nation's second largest fast-food chain (Kentucky Fried Chicken Corporation). J. Paul Sticht, the company's chief executive officer, reported in a speech to the National Food Processors Association that his firm processes more agricultural products than any other company in the Western world.

Table 3.3 presents selected subsidiary firms owned by two large conglomerates. Note the variety of businesses these corporations are involved in. If the Yankee Pedaler Bicycle Corporation decided to undertake a conglomerate merger, it would purchase several well-managed firms that make a variety of products with promising consumer demand.

Table 3.3 Two Conglomerates and Selected Subsidiaries

Parent Company	Selected Divisions and Subsidiaries[a]
American Brands, Inc.	Acme Visible Records, Inc. (business forms)
	Acushnet Co. (golf equipment)
	American Cigar
	American Tobacco Co. (cigarettes)
	James B. Beam Distilling Co. (distilled spirits)
	Franklin Life Insurance Co.
	Gold Belt Manufacturing Co. (printing and laminating)
	Andrew Jergens Co. (toiletries)
	Master Lock Co. (combination and key locks)
	Pinkerton's, Inc. (security and investigative services)
	Sunshine Biscuits, Inc.
	Swingline, Inc. (staplers and fasteners)
	Wilson Jones Co. (business forms)
Tenneco, Inc.	J. I. Case Co. (construction and farm equipment)
	Monroe Auto Equipment Co.
	Newport News Shipbuilding & Dry Dock Co.
	Packaging Corporation of America
	Philadelphia Life Insurance Co.
	Speedy Muffler King, Inc.
	Tenneco Oil Co.
	Tenneco Uranium, Inc.
	Tennessee Gas Transmission Co.

[a]The selected subsidiaries may in turn own all or part of other corporations.

Amalgamation or Consolidation

An **amalgamation *or* consolidation** *occurs when one firm combines with others to form an entirely new company; former identities are relinquished.* Expressed as a formula,

Company A + Company B + Company C = Company D

This is an alternative to the types of merger discussed previously. The companies sacrifice their former identities for the sake of a new combination and a fresh public image. Amalgamation is what happened in 1917 when the individual corporations that manufactured Oldsmobiles, Buicks, Pontiacs, and Cadillacs combined to form General Motors Corporation. (Two years later, this new firm absorbed Chevrolet in a merger.) More recently, Standard Brands and Nabisco consolidated to form Nabisco Brands.

Applying this concept to your fictitious corporation, you could consolidate with other companies and adopt the new name and image of Amalgamated Manufacturing Corporation.

amalgamation or consolidation

Regulating Combinations

While mergers, acquisitions, and amalgamations are common in business, corporations are not free to engage in any combination they want. The government is concerned that colossal companies will control too much business and endanger competition. To monitor business combinations, the federal government uses the Federal Trade Commission and the Justice Department.

A government agency established by the Federal Trade Commission Act of 1914, the **Federal Trade Commission (FTC)** *is a quasi-judicial body empowered to issue cease-and-desist orders against companies whose combinations would significantly lessen competition.* A firm that disregards one of these orders may be fined up to $10,000.[7] The FTC also investigates false or misleading advertising claims, regulates product labeling and packaging, and ensures that borrowers are told the true cost of consumer loans and charge accounts.

Federal Trade Commission (FTC)

The **Department of Justice,** *an arm of the federal government, works closely with the FTC to preserve competitive markets through investigations by its Antitrust Division.* This division investigates company activities that lead to one or a few firms so dominating an industry that they control the supply or cost of a product, enabling them to squeeze out competitors and charge extremely high prices.

Department of Justice

Both of these regulators may dispute a proposed business combination. They also may bring legal action to break up large firms that have excessive control over products and prices within their industries. A Department of Justice case filed in 1970 sought to dissolve massive International Business Machines Corporation (IBM), while neglecting to clarify precisely what illegal acts the firm was accused of. This case, nicknamed the Methuselah case, involved more than 300 lawyers and generated 66 *million* pages of depositions and other legal paperwork. As proceedings dragged on, IBM's share of the market decreased from 70 percent to an estimated 62 percent in 1981 owing to more aggressive foreign and domestic competitors and new technological advances. The Department of Justice finally dropped the suit 13 years later.[8]

In recent years the Department of Justice has displayed more tolerance for business combinations. Discarding a 1968 guideline that marked a combination for investigation if fewer than five companies controlled 60 percent of the market, the department now applies a more precise and logical mathematical formula to proposed combinations. This yardstick considers both the number of firms in the market and the relative power of each.

Other Types of Corporations

So far we have discussed only private, profit-seeking businesses. Now we will look at some alternatives to private ownership: government corporations and nonprofit corporations, including cooperatives.

Government Ownership

government *or* public corporation

A **government *or* public corporation** is *a corporation organized by a city, county, state, or federal government to serve a specific segment of the population.* First created during World War I to provide the financial and operating flexibility required by emergency programs, government corporations soon became common in most countries and at all levels of government.

The Tennessee Valley Authority (TVA) and the Federal Deposit Insurance Corporation (FDIC) are well-known examples of government corporations. In 1933, when President Franklin D. Roosevelt recommended that the TVA be established, he stated that "the government's purpose is to provide an agency clothed with the power of government but possessed of the flexibility and initiative of private enterprise." A more recent example of a public corporation is the government's Synthetic Fuels Corporation. Set up in the late 1970s, it controlled $15 billion available to private companies for developing processes to convert coal into oil and natural gas. It is reportedly scheduled to be phased out by 1985, but by then this government corporation will have distributed approximately $10 billion of its funds to private industry to subsidize construction of several synthetic fuel plants.[9]

Government corporations at all levels have been created for many purposes. Some cities and townships, for example, carry out their governmental responsibilities under a corporate charter issued by the state. (They issue no stock.) Atlanta and San Francisco are examples of municipal government corporations. Pennsylvania, West Virginia, and sixteen other states have created public corporations to control the sale of liquor. In these states, liquor can only be bought from one source — the state store.

Some government corporations are responsible for providing a public service regardless of profit or loss. Others must be self-supporting. Federal Prison Industries is an example of a self-supporting government corporation. This corporation is chartered by the federal government to sell goods and services to federal agencies through seventy-four industrial operations in thirty-five federal penal institutions.

When we discussed socialist economies in Chapter 1, we mentioned that in such an economic system the government owns the major industries. *The change from private ownership of an industry to government ownership* is a process known as **nationalization.** The banks of France recently were nationalized by President François Mitterrand. Many of the countries of Europe are socialist and have nationalized industries.

nationalization

Nationalization also occurs in the countries of the Third World — Asia, Africa, and South America. The economically disadvantaged countries in these regions sometimes take control of important industries previously run by foreign companies.

Some government corporations compete directly with private corporations for world markets. For example, Scandinavian Airlines System (SAS) and Air France (both government-controlled airlines) compete with TWA (Trans World Airlines), a privately owned American corporation. Renault, a French government-owned automaker, competes with General Motors and Ford, private American corporations.

Nonprofit Corporations

Some corporations are considered **nonprofit corporations.** These are *organizations formed to further the interests and objectives of educational, religious, social, charitable, and cultural groups.* No

nonprofit corporations

Many groups, including The American National Red Cross, are organized as nonprofit corporations.

The Straight Line

The Breakup of AT&T

For Whom the Bells Toll

What would happen if the Department of Justice fragmented the nation's largest corporation? Well, it did so on January 1, 1984. The ultimate effects, while uncertain at this time, should make life interesting if not confusing for 57 million residential and 7 million business customers.

In 1974 the Department of Justice filed charges against American Telephone and Telegraph Company (AT&T) for having excessive control over the communications industry. The ensuing 8-year battle about its dismantling cost both sides approximately $375 million. In 1982 the Justice Department agreed to drop the case if AT&T would sever all ties with its 22 local operating companies throughout the country. A resolution finally was reached after considerable negotiation.

As part of the settlement, AT&T created seven independent corporations that began providing local phone service in their respective regions on January 1, 1984. Another ingredient of the settlement allowed AT&T to retain ownership of Western Electric, which manufactures telephones and other telecommunications equipment (more than 390,000 products in all) and is a leading producer of computer memory chips. The new regional telephone companies will be free to buy equipment from any company, so AT&T no longer will have a captive market for Western Electric's products.

Resolving the issue of share distribution in the new regional companies will be complex indeed. The 3.2 million AT&T shareholders will receive one share in each of these seven companies for every ten shares formerly held in AT&T. This aspect of the breakup reportedly will require a staggering 100 *billion* stockholder transactions, but problems hardly end there.

Down through the years, parent AT&T distributed some of the money it charged for long distance calls to its 22 subsidiary companies. This meant that for generations customers weren't charged the full cost for local service. Today, however, each of the seven regional companies must charge the full rate for local service and bills have been predicted to rise between 10 and 20 percent as a result.

The new company that owns

stock is issued, but the members of the organization enjoy the advantage of limited liability. The American Automobile Association, most private colleges and universities, and the American Cancer Society are examples of nonprofit corporations.

As indicated by their name, nonprofit corporations do not exist to make a profit. They can, however, have a surplus of collections (dues, for instance) over expenses. This surplus can then be used by the nonprofit corporation to expand facilities or services or to give raises to employees. But that surplus is not a profit because it is not distributed as earnings to shareholders.

AT&T's long-distance facilities, AT&T Communications, proposed charging individual consumers $2 per month and business users $2.90 per month for access to its long-distance lines. The fees, which were planned to escalate to $4 and $6 per month respectively by 1986, were denied by the Federal Communications Commission until mid-1985 at the earliest. Although AT&T Communications planned to reduce its long-distance charges (as it no longer will have to subsidize local service with long-distance rates), any savings realized by individual users would have been offset by the access fee.

Telephone customers may now receive three separate bills in the same envelope: one for monthly service and regional long-distance calls from the regional telephone company; one for rental of the telephone itself, unless they chose to buy it outright; and one for long-distance calls, if they use AT&T Communications for long-distance service. Several other companies such as MCI Communications, Southern Pacific Communications, and General Telephone's Sprint offer competing long-distance service.

Although these competing companies may charge lower rates per minute for long-distance calls, the difference is offset in most cases by their monthly rental fee. Furthermore, callers may have to punch more than 22 digits (touch-tone service is required) to tap into the long-distance service provided by these firms. AT&T must eliminate this access problem by the end of 1986.

Another complication is that many subscribers may decide to have their telephones removed rather than pay AT&T's proposed $2 monthly access fee and increased local rates. This decline in customers would then force the regional companies to increase local rates to remaining customers.

Many groups, including the Defense Department, saw an advantage in having a centrally coordinated, unified, highly efficient national telephone system despite the fact that AT&T held undisputed control of the industry. For some this feeling still prevails even though the cost of service may indeed decline as significant competition enters the telecommunications market for the first time in history.

For more about the breakup of AT&T, see James A. White, "Telephone Equipment: How AT&T's Split Will Affect Ownership, Repairs and Billing," *The Wall Street Journal*, December 20, 1983, p. 33; James A. White, "Telephone Service: How AT&T's Breakup Changes Bills, Rates, Long-Distance Calls," *The Wall Street Journal*, December 21, 1983, p. 27; James A. White, "AT&T Dissolves Western Electric as Separate Unit," *The Wall Street Journal*, December 15, 1983, p. 10; David Pauly et al., "Chaos in the Phone Business," *Newsweek*, November 28, 1983, p. 92; Jane Bryant Quinn, "What You Need to Know," *Newsweek*, November 28, 1983, p. 98; Kenneth Michael, "In Broker Lingo, AT&T Breakup Is 'A Real Mess'," *The Orlando* (Florida) *Sentinel*, November 20, 1983, p. G-1; "An Interview With Charlie Brown," *The Wall Street Journal*, November 17, 1983, p. 22; David Pauly et al., "Cutting Ma Bell Along the Dotted Line," *Newsweek*, December 27, 1982, p. 55; Ronald A. Taylor, "Final Shape of Big AT&T Settlement," *U.S. News & World Report*, August 30, 1982, p. 36; Christopher Ma, "Ma Bell's Mixed Blessing," *Newsweek*, August 23, 1982, p. 52; and Associated Press International, "FCC Confirms Putting Off Phone Access Fees Till '85," *The Orlando* (Florida) *Sentinel*, January 26, 1984, p. A-5.

Cooperatives

Another type of enterprise can be included in our nonprofit classification — the **cooperative** or co-op. This is *an enterprise created and owned jointly by its members and operated for their mutual benefit.* It may be a group of consumers with a common interest or small producers whose objective is to gain greater economic power. By banding together the members enjoy the benefits of large-scale operations, for goods and services can often be bought cheaper and sold more profitably in large quantities.

cooperative

73

Some cooperatives are groups of consumers who combine their buying activities to receive quantity discounts and thus reduce their costs. Members also benefit from owning or controlling the facilities that make or sell the goods and services they desire. Many farming communities have cooperative stores that sell feed, seed, fertilizer, and equipment to members. There are also cooperatively owned houses and apartment buildings, group health plans, insurance companies, and funeral homes. Some groups have created cooperatives that buy food in large quantities and sell it to members at low prices.

Cooperatives also exist for producers. Business owners have formed producer cooperatives to buy supplies more cheaply and sell products more profitably. Such cooperatives are most common in agriculture and also appear, though less frequently, in the fishing and petroleum industries. Gold Kist, a chicken farmers' cooperative, processes some 230 million chickens a year at a highly mechanized plant capable of handling up to 35,000 chickens a day.[10] Gold Kist, like other large poultry packers, is engaged in every aspect of poultry production — grinding and blending feed, preparing, packaging, and shipping oven-ready birds to supermarkets, and converting the scraps to hot dogs or other processed meats.[11]

According to the U.S. Department of Agriculture, more than 500 cooperatives sell dairy products; 2,500 sell grain; 436 sell fruit and vegetables; 500 sell cotton; 600 sell livestock; and 150 sell eggs. Co-ops are credited with selling approximately 25 percent of all produce grown in the United States and selling 20 percent of all feed, seed, and other supplies needed to grow crops.[12]

Summary

In this chapter we examined the third basic form of business organization — the corporation, the form that accounts for more than 80 percent of all sales in the United States. A corporation is a legal entity separate from its owners. It can sue and be sued, enter into contracts, and buy, hold, and sell property in its own name. A corporation is created by the state, and its birth certificate is called a charter. Its owners are termed shareholders and hold stock certificates as evidence of their ownership.

Corporations are classified as either domestic (within their home states), foreign (from another state), or alien (from another country), depending on where they were chartered and where they conduct their business affairs. Corporations also are classified as either open or close, depending on whether their stock can be bought by the general public. Corporations raise long-term funds or equity capital by issuing stock. They may also borrow by selling bonds. These subjects will be explored in depth in Chapter 14.

Stockholders with voting rights elect a board of directors, which is responsible for developing company policy and selecting top officers. There is a gap between ownership and true control in many large American corporations. The average stockholder in a giant corporation has little involvement or interest in its affairs, caring only that the stock increases in value or the company pays regular dividends.

As is the case with sole proprietorships and partnerships, corporations have several advantages (in this case, ease of expansion, limited liability, and long life), and several disadvantages (expense of organizing, generally higher taxes, and government restrictions).

Business organizations are anything but static. New ones arrive on the economic scene daily, and older ones drop out. Some firms merge with others and lose their original identity. Some combine with others but retain their identity. Others voluntarily discard divisions or companies previously acquired. A few are required by the courts or regulatory agencies to divest themselves of previous acquisitions.

In addition to private corporations formed for profit, there are several types of corporations established for reasons other than profit making. These include government (public) corporations, nonprofit corporations, and cooperatives.

Key Terms

acquisition
alien corporation
amalgamation *or* consolidation
bylaws
certificate (articles) of
   incorporation
close corporation
conglomerate merger
cooperative

corporate charter
corporation
Department of Justice
domestic corporation
Federal Trade Commission (FTC)
foreign corporation
government *or* public
   corporation
horizontal merger
limited liability

merger
nationalization
nonprofit corporations
open corporation
proxy
S corporation
shareholders *or* stockholders
stock certificates
vertical merger

For Review and Discussion

1. What is the purpose of a corporate charter? Why should its provisions regarding future activities be expressed in general terms?

2. Assume that the Kilobyte Personal Computer Company was incorporated in the state of Arizona. The company also has operations in Nevada, Texas, and Canada. How would the state of Arizona classify the firm? Nevada? Canada?

3. What is the difference between an open and a close corporation? Why might a close corporation decide to go public?

4. What is the purpose of a board of directors?

5. Why is limited liability considered an advantage to the owners of a corporation?

6. What federal income tax option is open to the

stockholders of an S corporation? What general conditions must be met before the company can elect this kind of tax treatment?

7. What are the main reasons some firms merge with or acquire other firms? State at least one potential disadvantage of business combinations to the controlling firm, the controlled or absorbed firms, and the general public.

8. Under what circumstances might it be better to combine several companies through amalgamation than to merge?

9. What is your attitude toward government ownership of such enterprises as the Tennessee Valley Authority (TVA) and the Federal Deposit Insurance Corporation (FDIC)? Discuss some of the alternatives.

Applications

Case 3.1 Placing Directors in Perspective

The board of directors plays a major role in a corporation's success. Elected by and answerable to the stockholders, directors provide advice and counsel to top management and work closely with the corporation's chief executive officer, who is the top decison maker in the company.

Perhaps the primary qualifications of a director are experience and seasoned judgment. Most directors are chosen for their potential to contribute wisdom and objectivity to the profound decisions reached in corporate boardrooms.

Responsibilities and concerns of the board include:

- Evaluating the performance of top management and monitoring the corporation's welfare with the best interests of stockholders in mind

- Advising top managers on proposed long-term company goals and the means by which they intend to reach those goals

- Bringing objectivity and multiple viewpoints into the boardroom for the ultimate advantage of stockholders, customers, employees, top managers, and everyone else whose lives will be affected by the future prosperity of the company

- Assessing prevailing stockholder sentiment about the direction the company should take

- Evaluating proposals submitted for approval by top management before directors' meetings and preparing to challenge, advise, or otherwise provide input to management about pending actions that will have a long-term impact on the direction and health of the company

- Being prepared to oppose top management's recommendations when justified and offer constructive criticism and input to top management whenever requested or justified

Many persons who sit on corporate boards are presidents of other corporations. Some are university presidents, business school professors, or management consultants. A few so-called professional directors are retired top managers with considerable management experience who may serve on the boards of several corporations. Companies usually compensate outside directors for their services. According to a study by The Conference Board, a business research organization, the typical manufacturing company pays outside directors who also serve on committees an average of $17,000 per year.

Students of the role of corporate directors have commented that outside directors can bring necessary objectivity and varied experience to a company's board. Experiences and decisions from their own eminent careers can add valuable perspective to proposed actions. They also may think more independently and defend the interests of stockholders more vigorously than those inside directors who also work as top managers.

But inside directors can bring their own particular expertise to corporate governance. Being immersed in day-to-day operations, they are likely to be better informed on the nuts and bolts of the company than outside board members. Furthermore, inside directors may be more committed to the success of a corporation because their careers may depend on it. Outside directors, on the other hand, may choose to avoid conflict with other board members by resigning from the board rather than dealing with controversial issues or staying to resolve conflicting views over a company's future.

Questions

1. Discuss the importance of diplomacy in the work of a corporate director.

2. Members of the board of directors usually work closely with a corporation's chief executive officer. What suggestions would you have for a company's chief executive officer in responding to suggestions made by outside directors? Inside directors?

3. Provide at least one reason why an inside director may have difficulty remaining objective.

4. How may outside directors gather information about the corporation's products, markets, and stockholder image? How may such information be used advantageously?

Case 3.1 For more about the role of a corporation's directors, see Arthur M. Louis, "How a Professional Director Earns His Keep," *Fortune*, October 31, 1983, p. 140; Thomas L. Whisler, "Some Do's and Don'ts for Directors," *The Wall Street Journal*, March 21, 1983, p. 20; and Associated Press International, "Pay Raises for Corporate Directors Slow," *The Orlando* (Florida) *Sentinel*, January 23, 1984, p. E-8.

Case 3.2 Harley-Davidson: An American Tradition Fights for Survival

Some call it a cult bike, others a dinosaur; for some it's an American tradition. In any view the Harley-Davidson is unique because it is the only American manufactured motorcycle on the road.

Started in 1903, the company remained privately held by the families of founders Harley and Davidson until 1965, when it became an open corporation. In 1969 it was acquired by AMF Incorporated and operated as a wholly owned subsidiary. In 1981 it was bought by a group of Harley-Davidson executives headed by Vaughn Beals, Jr., former vice-president of AMF's motorcycle products. Beals is now chairman and chief executive officer. Willie Davidson, grandson of the co-founder and another member of the purchasing group, is vice-president for design. Today the company is a private corporation once again.

For many years the company did not have to deal with severe Japanese competition because the Japanese were building bikes with smaller engines and lighter frames than those of Harley's powerful macho road machines. All this changed in 1981, however, when Honda and other Japanese makers introduced larger-engine cruising bikes with a variety of innovations and refinements including digital instrumentation, shaft drive, and improved suspension. Their quality was reportedly better and their average price was $1,500 below Harley's competing model, the Sportster. Between 1980 and 1982 Japanese cruising motorcycles claimed approximately 19 percent of the American cruising bike market as Harley-Davidson's share declined by almost one-third to 14.3 percent.

Much of this problem could be traced to production efficiency. Harley-Davidson still machined and finished its engines manually, as it had for years, while Japanese firms used more sophisticated machinery that finished their engines faster and cheaper, if not better. Today Harley is playing catch-up in a viciously competitive market and the fate of the company may be on the line.

Money is a problem. The company has a new engine (designed by Porsche of Germany) that will be fully competitive with Japanese models — if it can be put into production. Unfortunately, the cost of tooling up to manufacture this engine and the new model bike for which it was designed (called the NOVA) will range between $15 million and $18 million. Beals and Davidson lack the money to fund this new product themselves; however, even if the funds were available, it would take approximately two years to gear up for production and get the bike on the market.

Then there's the engine noise issue. For generations the company has remained faithful to its big cylinder V-block, large-displacement engine designs. Harleys have an unmistakable throaty roar unlike any other bike on the highway, and the sound of the engine itself is a selling point. While competing Japanese bikes sound like sewing machines, Harleys sound like thunder — some riders wouldn't have them any other way. Any change in the basic sound of a Harley-Davidson would diminish its mystique in the minds (and ears) of many potential buyers.

Questions

1. Discuss the strength of sentiment that may have influenced the managers' decision to acquire their company from AMF and to keep it closely held. Under the circumstances, does it appear to be a sound decision? Why or why not?

2. Some American manufacturers have companies in Japan or elsewhere produce certain components, which are shipped to the United States for final assembly. Would you suggest this practice to Harley-Davidson? Why or why not?

3. What methods might Harley-Davidson's owner-managers use to obtain the money to finance production of the new engine and bike without losing control of their company?

Case 3.2 For more about Harley-Davidson's situation, see Steve Kichen, "Thunder Road," *Forbes,* July 18, 1983, p. 92; and Barbara Rudolph, "The Hog Lives," *Forbes,* March 30, 1981, p. 127.

Part

The Human Side of Business

Managing Business Organizations

Chapter Outline

Why Managers Are Needed

What Is Management?

Levels of Management: The Management Hierarchy

Management Functions

Planning
Organizing
Staffing
Directing
Controlling
The Universality of Management Functions

Management Roles

Management Skills

The Decision-Making Process

Summary

Chapter Objectives

After studying this chapter, you should be able to:

1. Explain why managers are necessary in organizations.
2. Explain the concept of management.
3. Identify and explain the three levels of management in a firm.
4. Identify and explain the five management functions.
5. Explain the universality of management as it relates to the levels of management.
6. Describe the roles managers are required to perform.
7. Describe the three skills — technical, human, and conceptual — required of a manager.
8. Explain the nature of and steps involved in managerial decision making.

The secret of Japanese success is not technology, but a special way of managing people — a style that focuses a strong company philosophy, a distinct corporate culture, long-range staff development, and consensus decision making.

— William Ouchi

Peter W. Schutz

An American Drives Porsche

He had never driven a Porsche and admittedly knew little about the auto industry, yet Peter W. Schutz, a German born American who had come to the United States when he was eight years old, became president of the Porsche sports car firm in Stuttgart, Germany, in December, 1980. Dr. Ferry Porsche, chairman of the board of directors, was attracted to Schutz because of his marketing background and his method of dealing with problems.

Schutz's impressive work record as an engineer at Caterpillar and at Cummins Engine in Columbus, Indiana, his experience as vice-president of marketing at Cummins, and his position as an engineer with sales expertise in charge of the engine business at Klockner-Humbolt-Deutz in Cologne, West Germany, influenced Dr. Porsche and his family to hire the American even though there were several German candidates.

Porsche had problems. Management needed to be reviewed and restructured. There were morale problems, heightened by lack of communication. There was a lack of enthusiasm among the workers, which became more evident as the time approached for the Le Mans race where Porsche had been overall winner five times. Engineers explained to Schutz, who had been with Porsche only 95 days at the time, that there was no chance for a victory with the cars they were entering. Their only goal was marketing. They wanted to race production models of the 924 and the new 944 to build up the cars' images. When Schutz questioned this decision, he was told there was no racing car ready.

Schutz would not accept defeat. He went into action; with only 62 days left before the race, he had two 936 Porsches removed from the Porsche museum — winners in 1976 and 1977. The rest is the history of determination, perseverance, and hard work. One car came in first. The other one had to have its entire engine removed and repaired but still came in thirteenth. In all Porsche won nine of the top ten places. The Le Mans victory was a testimony to Schutz's optimistic faith in the ability of the engineers and drivers to prove the worth of the Porsche.

This triumph was the impetus needed to start breaking down barriers, opening up com-

---

The world is full of organizations: the Dallas Cowboys, the corner drugstore, your neighborhood bank, the Teamsters Union. Organizations can vary in size, structure, resources, personnel, and purposes, but they do have some things in common.

Why Managers Are Needed

organization

Basically an **organization** is *a group of two or more persons that exists and operates to achieve clearly stated, commonly held objectives.* The objectives of an organization have to do with providing

munications, and giving Schutz the authority to reorganize management. He established a policy of circulating information freely through group discussions and group thinking and decision making, which resulted in increased productivity.

Schutz announced record 1983 earnings of $28.1 million on sales of $841 million. His biggest success was in America: in 1983 Porsche sold 21,800 cars in the United States as opposed to 11,200 in 1981. Since America is Porsche's largest market (with half of Porsche's worldwide sales), Schutz decided the company needed to put additional emphasis here — the company needed to be more directly involved with the customer. Schutz devised a new plan for U.S. operations that modified the distribution system and dealer arrangements. The initial plan met with dealer opposition, so Porsche revised it. Under the revised plan, all 330 dealers would qualify for franchise agreements if they met Porsche's dealer operating standards. To facilitate this, time limits were extended to enable dealers meet the standards if they wanted a franchise. The re-

sult: 97% of the dealers had signed franchise agreements by the September 1, 1984, inauguration of Porsche Cars North America.

According to John Cook, president of Porsche Cars North America, the organization's new emphasis involves a degree of excellence demanded by Porsche customers, and a degree of excellence demanded of an automobile that is not mass manufactured or mass merchandised. The new strategy focuses its energy on pleasing the person who buys a Porsche — an achiever who demands excellence. Porsche wants to have above average service to match customer needs. To do this, two distribution centers located at airports in Reno, Nevada, and Charleston, South Carolina, will receive parts and cars from Germany for fast delivery and parts warehousing. A tentative plan calls for five 747 cargo planes to deliver approximately 250 cars per week. Dealer aids include a direct computer link to corporate headquarters in Reno, technical personnel, dealer training, and a corporate marketing strategy.

For more about Peter Schutz, see David B. Tinnan, "Porsche's Civil War With Its Dealers," *Fortune*, April 16, 1984, pp. 63–68; Eleanor Johnson Tracy, "Porsche Is Doing Great — So Changes Course," *Fortune*, March 5, 1984, p. 59; and David B. Tinnan, "The American at the Wheel of Porsche," *Fortune*, April 5, 1982, pp. 78–87.

goods and services to its members or providing them to others outside the organization. To meet these objectives it is necessary for the members of an organization to work together — to become a cohesive unit. This might not happen. It is quite possible that each member might do parts of jobs that each thought important to meet the objectives, while in actuality the members might be working in opposite directions.

To ensure the success of an organization a manager is needed. A manager can be the owner, operator, or founder (or all three) of an organization as well as someone hired by an organization to give it a direction — to make decisions and commit its resources (personnel, capital, equipment) to achieve the organization's objectives. The manager is often a connecting link, a catalyst, and a driving force for change, coordination, and control in an organization.

Just what do managers do? Are all management jobs the same? If there are differences, what are they? What demands are placed on managers? Are there certain skills managers need? As you study this chapter you will examine the answers to these questions and get a better view of the management job.

What Is Management?

management

Management is defined as *the process of setting and achieving goals through the execution of five basic management functions that utilize human, financial, and material resources.* There are a number of points to remember in this definition. First, management and managers make conscious decisions to set and achieve goals; decision making is a critical part of all management activities. Second, management is getting things done through people. Once management acquires the financial and material resources for the organization, it works through the organizational members to reach the stated objectives. Third, to achieve the goals they set, managers

management functions

must execute the five basic functions. These **management functions** are *the five broad activities that managers perform to achieve organizational goals: planning, organizing, staffing, directing, and controlling.* Each of these functions will be taken up later in detail.

Managers are the catalysts that ensure the success of an organization.

Levels of Management:
The Management Hierarchy

We have been using *management* in a broad sense to describe all managers. Is management the same throughout the organization? The answer is both yes and no. Managers all perform the same management functions but with different emphases because of their positions in the company. In most organizations the management group consists of a **management hierarchy,** which is *the pyramid arrangement of the several levels of managers,* such as those shown in Figure 4.1. The specific titles managers have depend on the organizations in which they work and the actual jobs they perform. In government organizations titles such as administrator, section chief, and director are quite common. In business, titles such as supervisor, manager, vice-president, and foreperson are often used. Titles by themselves have little meaning outside the environment in which they are granted. A district manager of one company could be the equivalent of a regional manager in a rival firm.

     For our purposes we can divide managers into three basic categories: top management, middle management, and first-line management. Top management usually consists of the organization's most important manager — the chief executive officer or president — and his or her immediate subordinates, usually called vice-presidents. **Top management** are *managers who are responsible for the overall management of the organization, for establishing organizational or company-wide objectives or goals and operating policies, and directing the company in relationships with its external environment.* **Middle management** are all *managers below the*

management hierarchy

top management

middle management

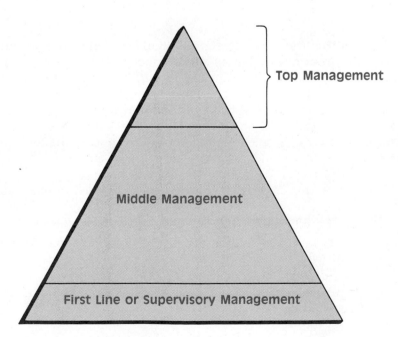

Figure 4.1 The Management Hierarchy
Source: From Warren R. Plunkett and Raymond F. Attner, *Introduction to Management* (Boston: Kent Publishing Company, 1983), p. 6. © 1983 by Wadsworth, Inc. Reprinted by permission of Kent Publishing Company, a division of Wadsworth, Inc.

first-line management

rank of vice-president but above the supervisory level. These middle managers may be titled *superintendents* or *plant managers* in their organizations. Regardless of the title, the major point is that *their subordinates are other managers. They are responsible for implementing top management policies.* **First-line management,** those at the operating level, are *the lowest level of management. Their subordinates are nonmanagement workers* — the group on which management depends for the execution of their plans.

Management Functions

You will recall that management has been defined as the process of setting and achieving goals through the execution of five basic management functions that utilize human, financial, and material resources. These five functions are planning, organizing, staffing, directing, and controlling. Although these functions are discussed separately it is important to remember that the functions are interdependent. In reality the functions are inseparable. It is not a matter of saying, "I'm going to plan in the morning, direct before lunch, organize between 1:00 and 2:30 P.M., and control from 2:30 P.M. until the end of the day." A manager must coordinate these functions. Plans cannot be carried out without acquiring human resources and organizing work groups. Controls are required to assess a plan's progress while directing subordinates on how to complete the plan. The management functions and the performance of the functions by managers are dynamic, complementary, and mutually supportive.

Planning

planning

Planning is the first function that all managers engage in because it lays the groundwork for all other functions. **Planning** is *the management function that establishes organizational goals or objectives and creates the means for accomplishing them.* It maps out courses of action that will commit individuals, departments, and the entire organization for days, months, and years to come. Planning achieves these ends after setting in motion the following processes:

1. Determination of what resources will be needed (organizing)
2. Identification of the number and types of personnel the organization will need (staffing)
3. Development of the foundation for the organizational environment in which work is to be accomplished (directing)
4. Determination of a standard against which the progress toward the objectives can be measured so that corrections can be made if necessary (controlling)

Length and Scope of Planning. The length of time and the scope of planning will vary according to the level in the company. Top-level management planning may cover a period of five or ten years and can be considered long-range planning. The plans at this level may cover expansion of the business and how it will be financed. At lower levels of management, the concern may be a plan for today's activities or planning tomorrow's work schedule.

Continuity and Flexibility. Planning is not a one-time practice. It is a continuous function that must be performed as long as the organization exists. Plans are not always achieved as originally intended. Managers — as planners — must stay flexible, because unexpected events and circumstances change original plans. An example of an organization's modifying its plans is provided by Texas Instruments. The company originally envisioned itself as a major competitor in the personal computer field. It vigorously pursued this goal until competition and supply problems indicated a change in plans was necessary. The response: eliminating the low end of the home computer line and redeveloping objectives to concentrate on computers where the company had a competitive foothold.

Sometimes organizations don't modify plans or wait until it is too late to try. A number of banks developed long-range plans based on loans to the oil industry. As the exploration for new fields of oil screeched to a halt and oil prices decreased or leveled off, banks holding those outstanding loans could not adjust their plans to balance out their loan portfolios. The result — default.

"Now, gentlemen, here's my plan."

Source: Reprinted by permission from Sales & Marketing Management magazine. Copyright 1976.

Types of Plans. Planning results in the creation of an organizational blueprint of what the organization is going to do and how it will get this accomplished. The blueprint in essence is a series of plans all focusing on the end results of the organization. **Objectives,** like destinations on a road map, are *the results that plans are made to achieve.* The objectives (also referred to as goals, targets, or purposes) give the enterprise a sense of purpose and provide standards that management can use to measure progress and decide on required changes.

objectives

To meet objectives managers often must develop another type of plan, a **policy,** which is *a plan that describes how a question or subject should be addressed; it helps guide management decisions.* Because they explicitly state what is to be done, thus ensuring consistent treatment, policies help managers make decisions on recurring topics such as:

policy

— Promotions
— Customer complaints
— Customer credit
— Disposal of records

Pause and Ponder

What policies and procedures are you familiar with through your job? Does your organization have a policy manual? What policies are included? What are the policies for sick leave, vacation, and overtime? What procedures are used to implement the policies?

— Employee eligibility for profit-sharing and stock option plans
— Use of facilities by outside organizations
— Work schedules and break periods
— Sale of surplus property
— Employee discounts on merchandise
— Vacations and sick leave

procedure

Many times the development of policies requires management to create a **procedure,** which is *a set of step-by-step, chronological instructions for carrying out a given policy.* In other words, a procedure describes *how* a policy is to be implemented. The following is an example of a policy and its accompanying procedure.

Policy
The company will fill vacant jobs with present employees whenever possible.

Procedure
1. The personnel manager will advertise the vacancy to existing employees by posting a notice and the job specification on official bulletin boards in each department.
2. Qualified employees will complete Form 1132, listing their qualifications, and forward it to the personnel manager.
3. The personnel manager will interview qualified employees who express interest and send the most highly qualified candidates to the position's supervisor for final interviews and selection.
4. If no qualified employees wish to be considered for the vacancy, it will be filled by someone from outside the company.

Organizing

organizing

Organizing is *the management function concerned with (1) assembling the resources necessary to achieve the organization's objectives and (2) establishing activity-authority relationships of the organization.* Planning has established the goals of the company and how they are to be achieved; organizing develops the structure to reach these goals.

The activities necessary to achieve the objectives are grouped into working divisions, departments, or other identifiable units primarily by clustering similar and related duties. The result, a network of interdependent units or departments known as an *organization structure*, is shown in Figure 4.2. Each unit (and each person in the unit) should have clearly defined authority, or a clearly defined list of duties, and one person to whom to report.

This organization structure of managerial relationships needs to be examined periodically and adjusted as the objectives of the company change. One thing is certain: changes that occur both within and outside the organization will require new approaches, plans, and organizational units. Chapter 5 examines the organizing function in detail.

Staffing

Staffing is *the management function that attempts to attract good people to an organization and to hold onto them.* Staffing is concerned with locating prospective employees to fill the jobs created by the organizing process. Staffing involves the process of reviewing the credentials of the candidates for the jobs and trying to match job demands with the applicants' abilities. After the employment decision has been made (the position has been offered and accepted), staffing involves orienting the new employee to the company environment, training the new person for his or her particular job, and keeping each employee qualified. Staffing also involves the development and implementation of a system for appraising performance and providing feedback for performance improvement, as well as determining the proper pay and benefits for each job. Many aspects of the staffing function are the responsibility of the personnel department — a staff department most likely to exist in an organization large enough to support such a specialized group. Chapter 6 examines the staffing function in detail.

staffing

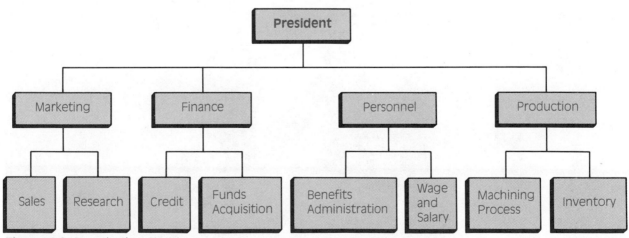

Figure 4.2 Organization Structure
Source: From Warren R. Plunkett and Raymond F. Attner, *Introduction to Management* (Boston: Kent Publishing Company, 1983), p. 185. © 1983 by Wadsworth, Inc. Reprinted by permission of Kent Publishing Company, a division of Wadsworth, Inc.

Directing

Directing is aimed at getting the members of the organization to move in the direction that will achieve its objectives. **Directing** is *the management function that builds a climate, provides leadership, and arranges the opportunity for motivation.* Each manager must plan and oversee the work of each of his or her subordinates.

In performing the directing function, the manager is faced with the challenge of providing leadership to the work group, building a climate in which individuals are motivated to perform their jobs effectively and efficiently, and communicating both operating expectations for performance as well as providing feedback on results. These individual elements of directing place a premium on the manager's ability to work with people. There are no hard and fast rules: the manager needs to be sensitive to the individuals involved and to provide ongoing guidance, coaching, and necessary information to subordinates.

In practicing leadership, the manager is not simply giving orders. Rather, the manager is making conscious decisions on how best to achieve goals through people. The dilemma for a manager becomes, "How do I best provide guidance, involve people in decisions, and build a work team when all people are different?" Part of the answer to this problem can be solved by creating a work environment in which employees are motivated to work toward their goals and the goals of the organization. This requires a manager to appreciate the uniqueness of each person in a work group and to attempt to provide an environment in which each individual has his or her personal needs fulfilled.

To practice leadership and build a climate, a manager must keep communication channels open and ongoing. A manager must communicate performance expectations, respond to employee concerns, and provide feedback on individual performance. It must

Providing leadership to subordinates is the core of the directing function.

also be a genuine exchange between the manager and the employee of ideas, concerns and actions.

Controlling

Controlling is *the management function of establishing standards, measuring actual performance to see if standards have been met, and taking corrective action if required.* The controlling function is essential. Planning chooses goals and maps out the necessary strategy and tactics. Controlling attempts to prevent failure (and to promote success) by providing the means to monitor the performances of individuals, departments, divisions, and the entire organization. It attempts to prevent problems, to determine when problems do exist, and to solve the problems that occur as quickly and effectively as possible.

controlling

The control process consists of three basic steps applicable to any persons, items, or processes being controlled:

1. Establish standards to be used in measuring progress, or lack of progress, toward goals.
2. Measure performance against standards, noting deviations from standards.
3. Take actions necessary to correct deviations from standards.

These three steps happen continuously, as shown in Figure 4.3. You can see that controlling gives management feedback on the status and progress of plans, just as a car speedometer lets the driver know if the speed limit is being observed. Also note that a control system provides management with a warning that the control device may not be realistic. It could mean that the standard is too easily met and that resources — personnel, equipment, and capital — are not being used correctly. As an example, consider a salesperson who repeatedly performs 200 percent above sales quota for a given territory. It could mean superior talent. It could also mean an inaccurate quota: the salesperson could be accomplishing the work in half the time allowed.

Managers apply many different kinds of control devices. Some are simple, others are complex and technical, but all of them are intended to inform management of progress toward objectives. Several examples of control devices are listed for your investigation.

— Employee performance evaluation
— Reports on sales, expenses, inventories, customer complaints, and accidents
— Automatic control devices to shut down malfunctioning machinery
— Budgets
— Quality assurance standards and inspections to confirm that products are meeting those standards
— Conferences

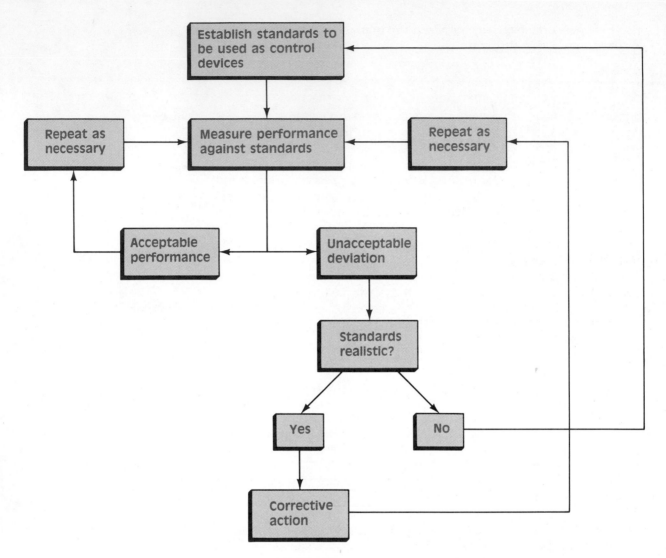

Figure 4.3 The Controlling Process

Source: From Joseph T. Straub, *Managing: An Introduction* (Boston: Kent Publishing Company, 1984), p. 453. © 1984 by Wadsworth, Inc. Reprinted by permission of Kent Publishing Company, a division of Wadsworth, Inc.

The Universality of Management Functions

universality of management

All managers do the same job regardless of title, position, or management level. They all execute the five management functions and work through and with others to achieve organizational goals. This concept, known as the **universality of management,** is shown in Figure 4.4. As you examine this figure it is important to note that although all managers perform the same functions, the various management levels require different amounts of time for each function, and the points of emphasis in each function will differ.

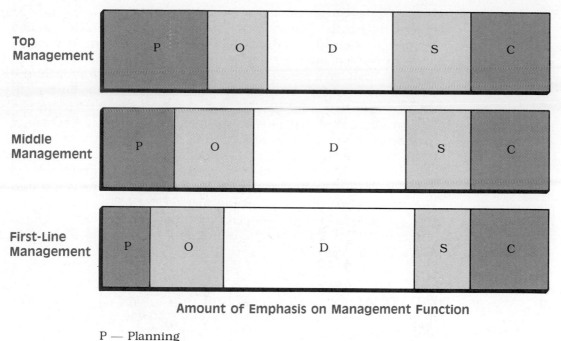

Amount of Emphasis on Management Function

P — Planning
O — Organizing
D — Directing
S — Staffing
C — Controlling

Figure 4.4 Universality of Management
Source: From Warren R. Plunkett and Raymond F. Attner, *Introduction to Management* (Boston: Kent Publishing Company, 1983), p. 10. © 1983 by Wadsworth, Inc. Reprinted by permission of Kent Publishing Company, a division of Wadsworth, Inc.

Top Management. Top-level management's job is concerned with the big picture, not the nitty gritty. The planning function for top-level management consists of developing the major purpose of the organization, the global objectives for organizational accomplishment, and the major policy statements for implementation by middle and first-line managers. Organizing at this level is viewed as developing the overall structure of the organization to support the accomplishment of the plans and then acquiring the resources for the company. The staffing function at the top level of management is concerned with policy development in the areas of equal opportunity in employment and with employee development. In addition, top management is concerned with acquiring talent to fill upper-management positions. The emphasis in directing is on company-wide management philosophy and on cultivating an organizational climate for optimum employee performance. The controlling function at this level emphasizes overall company performance relative to company objectives.

Middle Management. Middle-level management's primary job is to develop implementation strategies for the broad concepts determined by top management. For example, if the top level managers decide on a 10 percent profit objective, the job of middle managers is to translate that goal into concrete goals of their own so that the desired profit can be attained. Middle managers decide on how to do it — with new products, or new customers, or new territories. Organizing at the middle level is the making of specific adjustments in the organization structure and the allocation of the resources acquired by top management. Staffing focuses on the policy development in the areas of equal employment opportunity and employee development programs. Directing is viewed as providing leadership and support for lower-level management. Controlling is concerned with monitoring the results of plans for the specific products, regions, and subunits and making the indicated adjustment to achieve organizational objectives.

First-Line or Supervisory Management. Where top-level management is concerned with the big picture and middle-level management with its company-wide implementation, first-line management is concerned only with its immediate responsibilities. For the first-line manager, planning involves scheduling employees, deciding what work will be done first, and developing procedures to achieve the goals. Organizing may consist of delegating authority or deciding that work done by one group of people should be done by another work group. Staffing at this level consists of requesting a new employee, hiring that employee, and then training the person to perform the job. Directing includes communicating and providing leadership both to the work group and to all employees individually. Controlling at this level focuses on having the manager's work group meet its production, sales, or quality objectives.

Management Roles

Our working definition describes the manager as a person who plans, organizes, staffs, directs, and controls. Implicit in this description is the assertion that all managers, regardless of level in the organization or job title — vice-president of marketing, director of accounting services, or supervisor of clerical support — perform these functions to some degree. Now we need to know: What does the manager do to carry out these functions? The answer is that she or he must fill various roles.

role

What are these roles? And what influences which role a manager must assume? A **role** is *any one of several behaviors a manager displays as he or she functions in the organization.* As a manager attempts to perform the management job, he or she must "wear different hats" in interactions with various members of the organization. These role requirements are influenced by a manager's formal job description and also arise from the values and expectations of the manager's superiors, subordinates, and peers. Let's look at some of the roles required of a manager.[1]

- **Figurehead Role** A manager is the head of his or her work unit, be it division, department, or section. Because of this lead-person position, the manager routinely must perform certain ceremonial duties. For example, the manager may be required to entertain visitors to the organization, attend a subordinate's wedding, or participate in a group luncheon.

- **Leadership Role** The manager is the environment creator. He or she plays this role by working to improve employees' performance, reducing conflict, providing feedback on performance, and encouraging growth.

- **Liaison Role** Managers interact with others besides superiors and subordinates: they work with peer-level managers in other departments, staff specialists, other departments' employees, and outside contacts (suppliers, clients). In this role the manager is building contacts through which to gather information.

- **Monitor Role** The manager is constantly monitoring the environment to determine what is going on. This information is collected both directly, by asking questions, and indirectly, through unsolicited information.

- **Disseminator Role** What does the manager do with the information collected? As disseminator, the manager passes on to subordinates some of the information that ordinarily would not be accessible to them.

- **Spokesperson or Representative Role** The manager is the person who speaks for his or her work unit to people outside the work unit. One part of this role is to keep superiors well informed and a second aspect is to communicate outside the organization.

- **Entrepreneur Role** As the manager is exposed to new ideas or methods that may improve the work unit's operations, he or she assumes the entrepreneur role. In this role the manager initiates activities that will allow and encourage the work unit to use the ideas or methods most advantageously.

- **Disturbance Handler Role** What happens when parts of the work environment — schedules, equipment, strikes, reneged

Pause and Ponder

What roles do you expect your manager to perform? Which roles have been played successfully? Unsuccessfully? How did the results make you and your fellow workers feel?

Disturbance handler is one of the many roles managers perform.

contracts — get out of control? The manager must handle these crises as they develop.

— **Resource Allocator Role** The manager is responsible for determining who in the work unit gets the resources, and how much each person gets. These resources include money, facilities, equipment, and access to the manager's time.

— **Negotiator Role** Managers are required to spend a good portion of their time in the negotiator role. Negotiating may be required on contracts with suppliers or simply on trading off resources inside the organization. The manager must play this role because he or she is the only one in the work unit with both the information and authority negotiators need to have.

These roles are what managers actually do to carry out the functions of their jobs. Any manager who has a problem wearing any of the many hats of the job is going to have a work unit that is adversely affected to some extent.

Management Skills

In addition to being able to perform specific role demands, competent managers must draw on certain managerial skills to assemble and manage human and other resources for the achievement of organizational goals. As a manager plans, organizes, staffs, directs, and controls, he or she must have mastery of three basic skills. These skills — needed by all managers — are technical, human, and conceptual.[2]

technical skill

Technical skill is *the knowledge of and ability to use the processes, practices, techniques, or tools of a specialty responsibility area.* Examples of the technically skilled are accountants, engineers, salespersons, and quality control specialists. The manager needs enough technical skill to accomplish the job for which he or she is responsible.

Human skill is *the ability to interact with other persons successfully.* A manager must be able to understand, work with, and relate to both individuals and groups to build a teamwork environment. The proper execution of one's human skills is often called human relations.

human skill

Conceptual skill deals with ideas and abstract relationships. It is *the mental ability to view the organization as a whole and to see how the parts of the organization relate to and depend on one another.* In addition, conceptual skill is *the ability to imagine the integration and coordination of the parts of an organization — all its processes and systems.* A manager needs conceptual skills to see how factors are interrelated, to understand the impact of any action on the other aspects of the organization, and to plan long range.

conceptual skill

The importance of having these three skills depends on a manager's level of management in the organization. Technical skill is most important for a manager at the first-line management level and becomes less important as the manager moves up in the organization structure. For example, the supervisor of a word-processing department will have to know more technical information about the systems, equipment, and methods of training than the company president, who does not deal in the "how to's" of the department. Technical skill is acquired through company training programs and on-the-job experience. Figure 4.5 illustrates the relative

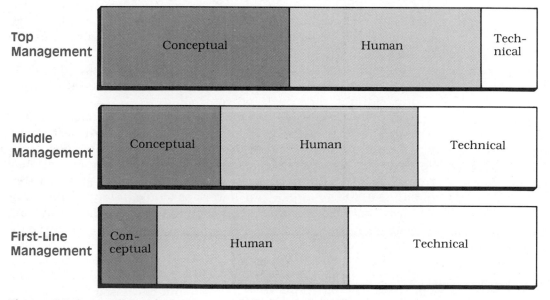

Figure 4.5 Proportions of Management Skills Needed at Different Levels of Management

Source: James A. F. Stoner, *Management,* 2nd edition (Englewood Cliffs, N.J.: Prentice-Hall, 1982), p. 19. Reprinted by permission.

amounts of each kind of skill needed by the three levels of management.

Human skill is equally important at every level in the organization. The need to be able to understand and work with people is important to all managers, but the first-line manager's position places a premium on human skill requirements because of the great number of employee interactions required. Many organizations have recognized the importance of this skill need and have developed specialized training programs emphasizing its development. As an example, Burger King supported the need for human skills when it built the $1.6 million Burger King University. One of the goals of this training program is "formalizing people skills." Instructors teach relatively inexperienced Burger King managers how to deal successfully with forty or more restaurant employees.

Conceptual skill becomes increasingly important as a manager moves up the levels of management. The first-level manager focuses basically on her or his work group; therefore, the need for conceptual skills is at a minimum. Top-level management is concerned with broad-based, long-range decisions that affect the entire organization; therefore, conceptual skill is most important at that level. Top-level management must be able to integrate the various organizational environments of law, manufacturing, marketing, labor relations, public relations, finance, and customer relations in problem solving and decision making. Conceptual skills are developed through broad-based experience and exposure to theory in university settings or company-sponsored seminars.

The Decision-Making Process

Now that we have examined the manager's job (functions), the behaviors necessary to perform the job (roles), and the skills necessary to manage, it is appropriate to look at decision making. Decision making is a part of all managers' jobs. A manager makes decisions constantly as he or she performs the functions of planning, organizing, staffing, directing, and controlling.

decision making

Decision making, *the process of making rational choices among alternatives,* is not a function of management, but rather it is a common thread within the five management functions. Managers make big and small decisions daily. Whether or not they realize it, they go through a process to make those decisions. Whether planning a budget, organizing a work schedule, interviewing a prospective employee, watching a worker on the assembly line, or making adjustments to a project, the manager is performing a decision-making process.

The decision-making process has seven steps. They are logical and simple in themselves, but they are all essential to the process. The steps are illustrated in Figure 4.6 and discussed briefly in the following pages.

— **Define the Problem** What is the particular problem you have to resolve? Defining the problem is the critical step. The accurate

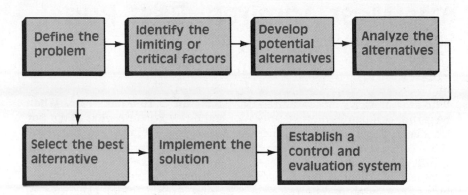

Figure 4.6 The Decision-Making Process
Source: From Joseph T. Straub, *Managing: An Introduction* (Boston: Kent Publishing Company, 1984), p. 481. © 1984 by Wadsworth, Inc. Reprinted by permission of Kent Publishing Company, a division of Wadsworth, Inc.

definition of a problem affects all the steps that follow. If a problem is defined inaccurately, every other step in the decision-making process will be based on that incorrect point. A motorist tells a mechanic that her car is running rough. This is a symptom of a problem or problems. The mechanic begins by diagnosing the possible causes of a rough-running engine, checking each possible cause based on the mechanic's experience. The mechanic may find one problem — a faulty spark plug. If this is the problem, changing the plug will result in a smooth-running engine. If not, then a problem still exists. Only a road test will tell for sure. Finding a solution to the problem will be greatly aided by its proper identification. The consequences of not properly defining the problem are wasted time and energy. There is also the possibility of hearing "What, that again! We just solved that problem last month, or at least we thought we did."

— **Identifying the Limiting or Critical Factors** Once the problem is defined, the manager needs to develop the limiting or critical factors of the problem. *Limiting factors* are those constraints that rule out certain alternative solutions. One common limitation is time. If a new product has to be on the dealers' shelves in one month, any alternative that takes more than one month will be eliminated. Resources, personnel, money, facilities, and equipment are the other common limiting or critical factors that narrow down the range of possible alternatives.

— **Develop Potential Alternatives** At this point it is necessary to look for, develop, and list as many possible alternatives — solutions to the problem — as you can. These alternatives should eliminate, correct, or neutralize the problem. Alternative solutions for a manager faced with the problem of trying to maintain scheduled production may be to start an extra work shift, to schedule overtime on a regular basis, to increase the size of the present work force by hiring employees, or to do nothing. Doing nothing about a problem sometimes is the proper alternative, at least until the situation has been analyzed thoroughly. Occasionally just the passing of time provides a cure.

The Straight Line

The Most Admired, Best-Run Companies

Profits Plus

Who are America's most admired, best-run companies? Most analysts agree they are the companies that consistently earn money. Profit, after all, is what American business is all about. But to earn money consistently requires certain attributes or characteristics that our most admired, best-run companies have in common.

Fortune's second annual survey of corporate reputations polled more than 7,000 executives, corporate directors, and financial analysts. The results published in the magazine's January 9, 1984, issue tabulated ratings on the following eight key attributes:

1. Quality of management
2. Quality of products and services
3. Financial soundness
4. Ability to attract, develop, and keep talented people
5. Innovativeness
6. Long-term investment value
7. Community and environmental responsibility
8. Use of corporate assets

The most admired corporation was International Business Machines (IBM) with a score of 8.53 on a 10-point scale. When asked by *Fortune* what IBM's key strengths are, chief executive officer John Opel replied, "A commitment to excellence and a commitment to customer service." John Young, chief executive of Hewlett-Packard (ranked third) said, "The corporate objectives provide the basic framework for the management-by-objectives system, which gives individual managers a lot of freedom to be entrepreneurial and innovative." Both CEOs commented on the values and human qualities that make their companies successful.

The management practices or characteristics shared by the best-run or most admired companies were analyzed by Thomas J. Peters and Robert H. Waterman in their best-selling book *In Search of Excellence* (New York: Harper & Row, 1982). According to Peters and Waterman, America's excellent companies share these characteristics:

1. Bias for action — don't talk about it, do it! This requires organization, communication and teaming.

— **Analyze the Alternatives** The purpose of this step is to decide the relative merits of each of the alternatives. What are the positives and negatives of each alternative? Do any alternatives conflict with the critical (limiting) factors that you identified earlier? If so, they must be automatically discarded.

— **Select the Best Alternative** By this point, the alternatives have been listed along with their corresponding advantages and disadvantages. Which should be selected? Sometimes the best solution is a combination of several of the alternatives. In trying to select an alternative or combination of alternatives,

2. Close to the customer — provide service, listen to complaints and suggestions, solve problems.
3. Autonomy and entrepreneurship — it's that old saying, "People support what they help create."
4. Productivity through people — all workers are capable of contributing to company goals from setting the goals through implementing and evaluating them.
5. Hands-on, value-driven — company values are known, shared and incorporated into daily activities.
6. Stick to the knitting — the excellent company stays within the area of its expertise. (It knows what business it does best and so that is the business it does.)
7. Simple form, lean staff — simple structure and few management layers foster communication and productivity.
8. Simultaneous loose-tight properties — *everything* in the company is interrelated. Discipline and control provide a framework for developing expectations, instilling confidence, and encouraging individual action.

In an interview update for *Management Review*, Peters discussed additional observations. According to Peters the catalyst for these eight characteristics is management by wandering (or walking) around, or MBWA. He found that managers (including top management) of the excellent companies spend a high percentage of their time talking face-to-face with employees and customers at their work stations or in their offices. He also found that the chief executives of the excellent companies tended to rise from the ranks of the manufacturing and sales functions, which tended to give these executives a better overall understanding of the organization.

In summary, successful companies focus on the fundamentals. They adapt to changing environments; they manage and integrate the management functions; they continually strive for improvement. And they have staying power — they are committed.

For more about America's top-rated companies, see Nancy J. Perry, "America's Most Admired Corporations," *Fortune*, January 9, 1984, pp. 50–62; William T. Liston, "Exploring *In Search of Excellence*," *Management World*, January 1984, pp. 28–30; "In Further Search of Excellence," *Management Review*, January 1984, p. 4; and Richard E. Cavanagh and Donald K. Clifford, Jr., "The High-Growth Potential of Mid-sized Companies," *Management Review*, March 1984, pp. 23–28, 37–41.

a solution must be found that appears to offer the fewest serious disadvantages and the most advantages. Care should be taken not to solve one problem and create another.

— **Implement the Solution** Managers are paid to make decisions, but they are also paid to get results from these decisions. A decision that just sits there hoping someone will put it into effect may as well never have been made. Everyone involved with it must know what he or she must do, how to do it, why, and when. In addition, a good alternative applied by uncommitted persons in a half-hearted way often will create problems,

not solve them. Like plans, solutions need effective implementation to yield the desired results. People must be sold on their
roles and know exactly what they must do and why. Programs,
procedures, rules, or policies must be put into effect thoughtfully.

– **Establish a Control and Evaluation System** The final step
in the decision-making process is to create a control and evaluation system. Ongoing actions need to be monitored. This
system should provide feedback on how well the decision was
implemented, what the results are — positive or negative —
and what adjustments are necessary to get the expected results.

For a manager who uses this decision-making process, the
probability of successful decisions should be improved. Why? Because
it provides a step-by-step roadmap for the manager to move logically
through decision making.

Summary

The world is full of organizations. All organizations operate to achieve
clearly stated, commonly held objectives. To achieve these objectives
it is necessary for members of the organization to work together.
To ensure the success of an organization a manager is needed.
Managers supply management — the process of setting and achieving
goals through the execution of five basic management functions
that utilize human, financial, and material resources.

The management group in an organization consists of three
basic categories: top management, middle management, and first-
line management. Regardless of the management title, position, or
level, all managers execute the five management functions and work
through and with others to achieve organizational goals. This concept
is known as the universality of management.

The five management functions — the broad activities that
managers perform to achieve organizational goals — are planning,
organizing, staffing, directing, and controlling. Planning is the
management function that establishes organizational goals or objectives and creates the means for accomplishing them. Organizing
is the management function concerned with (1) assembling resources
necessary to achieve the organization's objectives and (2) establishing
activity-authority relationships of the organization. Staffing attempts
to attract good people to an organization and to hold onto them.
Directing builds a climate, provides leadership, and arranges the
opportunity for motivation. Controlling is concerned with establishing
standards, measuring actual performance to see if standards have
been met, and taking corrective action if required.

To accomplish the management functions managers must assume various roles. A role is any one of several behaviors a manager
displays as he or she functions in the organization. Potential roles
required of a manager include those of figurehead, leader, liaison,
monitor, disseminator, spokesperson or representative, entrepreneur,
disturbance handler, resource allocator, and negotiator.

Competent managers must draw on certain managerial skills to assemble and manage human and other resources for the achievement of organizational goals. The three required skills are technical, human, and conceptual. A manager must possess these skills, and the importance of the skills depends on a manager's level in the organization. Human skill is equally important at all three levels. Technical skill is most important at the first-line level and becomes less important as the manager moves up in the organization. Conceptual skill also becomes increasingly important as a manager moves up the levels of management.

A part of all managers' jobs is decision making. A manager makes decisions constantly as he or she performs the functions of planning, organizing, staffing, directing, and controlling. The manager uses a seven-step decision-making process that includes: defining the problem, identifying the limiting or critical factors, developing potential alternatives, analyzing the alternatives, selecting the best alternative, implementing the solution, and establishing a control and evaluation system.

Key Terms

conceptual skill
controlling
decision making
directing
first-line management
human skill
management

management functions
management hierarchy
middle management
objectives
organization
organizing
planning

policy
procedure
role
staffing
technical skill
top management
universality of management

For Review and Discussion

1. Explain why managers are necessary in organizations. What specific contributions do they make?
2. What are the three levels of management in an organization? Who does each level manage? What responsibility areas does each level have?
3. Which management function is the most basic? Can the management functions be undertaken separately? Why or why not?
4. What occurs when managers perform the planning function? What is the importance of planning? Distinguish between objectives, policies, and procedures.
5. The organizing function includes what two parts? What is the result of the organizing process?
6. What is the purpose of the staffing function? What activities does the staffing function include?
7. What is the purpose of the directing function?
8. What is the purpose of the controlling function? What are the three steps in the control process?
9. What is meant by the term *universality of management*? How does this apply to present-day organizations?
10. What is meant by the term *role*? List and describe four roles managers are required to perform.
11. What three skills are needed by managers? Discuss how the need for two of these skills changes as a manager rises in the organizational hierarchy.
12. Discuss the seven steps in the decision-making process. Why does decision making overlap all of the management functions?

Applications

Case 4.1 The Life of a Manager

"Just another typical day in the life of a manager," thought Tina Welles, manager of advertising and public relations for the Schroeder Corporation, as she packed her briefcase with paperwork to be done that night. "Another day, another dollar," she said aloud as she recalled the events of the day.

1. Worked with the "top bananas" upstairs in forecasting new product sales for the upcoming year.

2. Had a short discussion with Larry on his constant tardiness. Seems he just can't leave early enough to beat the freeway rush.

3. Met with Earlene and Henri to work out the details for the upcoming Homeowners Handyman Convention. At least we know we have to create a special unit to carry this one off. And Earlene will pick the right people to work with her temporarily.

4. Completed the budget adjustment forms and sent them on for approval. I'm glad I had the opportunity to review our printouts of budget spent versus budget planned. I surely wouldn't want to run short of money 3 months ahead of time.

5. Interviewed three prospective applicants for the specialist's opening. The second applicant — Bernice Slovak — was really impressive. I hope her work references are good.

6. Took Mr. Peterson's wife on a tour of our new computer graphics area. Nothing like keeping the boss happy.

7. Completed Henri's probationary review. Seems that he needs a little more time before we can take him off probation.

8. Tried to work through Anna's problems. It certainly is difficult for her to work with both her parents being so ill. Maybe the time off we agreed on will help.

9. Attended the chamber of commerce luncheon. Made some good contacts for potential business — even the rubber chicken was good.

   "I wonder what tomorrow holds."

Questions

Using the events of Tina's day, cite specific examples to answer the following questions:

1. What management functions did Tina Welles undertake during her work day?

2. What management roles were required to complete these functions?

3. What management skills were involved in each of the day's events?

Case 4.2 Decisions, Decisions, Decisions!

Tony Salvo, manager of the Paper Products Division for Bow Industries, has been gone from work all morning to attend meetings. When he entered his office he was greeted by the following situations:

1. A preliminary report of test results on the new product has just been delivered. The lab cannot proceed with further tests until Tony responds to this report. The anticipated time: 30 minutes.

2. A telegram from Tony's salesperson in Chicago requests approval for priority processing of a large order. Anticipated time: 15 minutes.

3. A note from the boss says he wants to see Tony as soon as he arrives. Tony knows the boss always takes 30 to 60 minutes regardless of the topic.

4. The telephone is ringing: it may be Chicago.

5. Tony's production foreman wants to talk to him immediately. She heard about plans for a work slowdown to begin tonight on the third shift. Estimated time: at least one hour.

6. A note from a peer manager requests 15 minutes of Tony's time as soon as possible to discuss something of vital concern to both of them. His note does not specify the topic.

7. Tony's secretary became ill at lunch and is now resting in the company infirmary. It will take 10 minutes to check on her.

8. Three persons are seated in the outer office. Two appear to be salespersons and one a job applicant. It will take 10 minutes just to find out who they are.

9. Tony just remembered a purchase order that has to be processed today to keep the production schedule on target. Estimated time: 15 minutes.

Questions

1. In what order would you deal with these situations?

2. Explain why you made the decision to establish the priorities the way you did.

Creating an Organization

Chapter Outline

Chapter Objectives

After studying this chapter, you should be able to:

1. Explain what an organization is and why it is necessary.
2. List and describe the steps in the organizing process.
3. Identify the four forms of departmentalization and the situations in which each would be appropriate.
4. Define authority, and explain the differences among line, staff, and functional authority.
5. Relate the concept of delegation to authority, responsibility, and accountability.
6. Explain the organizational concepts of span of control and centralization and decentralization.
7. Differentiate among line, line-and-staff, functional, and matrix organization structures.
8. Explain the nature of the informal organization.

Our research told us that any intelligent approach to organizing had to encompass, and treat as interdependent, at least seven variables: structure, strategy, people, management style, systems and procedures, guiding concepts and shared values (i.e., culture), and the present and hoped-for corporate strengths or skills.
— *Thomas J. Peters and Robert H. Waterman, Jr.,*
In Search of Excellence

Up Front   Roger B. Smith

New Ideas Fuel General Motors

In January of 1984 Roger B. Smith, chairman of General Motors (GM), announced a revolutionary change in the company's structure, the first major change since the 1920s when Alfred P. Sloan divided the company into five separate car divisions. Smith plans to set up two auto groups — Chevrolet, Pontiac, and GM of Canada in one group, and Buick, Oldsmobile, and Cadillac in the other. Although Smith admits his project could be risky, if it works, the company will be set for many years.

Roger Smith has a philosophy about management that he calls the 3Rs — risk, responsibility, and reward. Like his predecessor, Smith believes that the best decisions are made by those closest to the problem; therefore,

he has increased the authority of his individual managers and supervisors. Managers are enthusiastic about Smith's reorganization. Increasing their share of the 3Rs has made them feel that they are an integral part of the company.

General Motors made a profit of $3.7 billion in 1983; production schedules are at their peak; and the company built more cars in 1984 than it built in 1983. But Roger Smith already is looking toward the future and diversification into electronics and other high-technology industries. One of GM's diversification projects is a lightweight, artificial magnet that Smith hopes to be able to sell to other industries. The company also is working on a small car,

In the last chapter you learned the importance of planning in an organization. But planning alone cannot ensure an organization's success. A company that has taken the time, energy, and money to develop quality plans needs to organize its employees to attain these goals. It must provide a structure for all jobs that makes clear who has responsibility for all tasks and who reports to whom. An organization without structure (as seen in the quotes below) can result in confusion, frustration, loss of efficiency, and limited effectiveness.

"You can't tell me what to do, only Larry can. He's my boss!"

"When did the advertising department start reporting to Frank? I thought it was part of John's department."

"Can I please have a decision on this requisition? Who do I need to go see? Who's in charge here anyway?"

In this chapter we will discuss what an organization is and why it is necessary, the organizing process, key concepts in managing

Saturn, whose method of assembly, the modular concept, is a new concept for General Motors. Rather than one long assembly line, perpendicular lines feed into a short final line where the module is built up. Each module can be tested before it is assembled into the car. This system should cut costs, raise productivity, and increase profits. The Saturn should be introduced by 1990.

From his long tenure at GM (he first started to work for GM in 1949), Smith has obtained an enviable knowledge of the company's operations and statistics: his facts and figures seldom have to be verified. Through the years he has accomplished many difficult assignments successfully and has proved his ability and willingness to make tough decisions. One of the hardest decisions he ever had to make was in the 1970s when competition forced him to recommend that the firm cut its losses and sell Frigidaire and Terex, the divisions that made appliances and earthmoving equipment. At first the other executives thought the idea was absurd, but eventually they agreed. Smith's decision proved to be wise, and he has continued to make profitable and controversial judgments for GM.

Roger B. Smith, an unassuming, outwardly complacent man, has a sense of timing and an incredible ability to know when to fight and when to fold.

For more about Roger B. Smith, see Anne B. Fisher, "GM's Unlikely Revolutionist," *Fortune*, March 19, 1984, pp. 106–112; Joe Simnacher, "GM Chief Heads Firm Down High-Tech Path," *Dallas Morning News*, February 19, 1984, p. 1-H; and "GM Redesigns Itself," *Fortune*, February 6, 1984, p. 14.

the organization, types of organization structures, and the informal organization.

What Is an Organization?

All around you are examples of organizations that you come into contact with every day — churches, social clubs, athletic teams, local governments, and nonprofit groups. What do we mean by organizations and why do they exist? An **organization** is *a group of two or more people that exists and operates to achieve clearly stated, commonly held objectives.*

organization

A business is an organization. It is created by owners and managers to achieve a specific goal: to provide a product or service to a customer at a profit. When managers create an organization they actually are developing a framework in which to (1) operate effectively, (2) reach the organization's objectives, and (3) provide

formal organization

a profit. This framework establishes the operating relationships of people: who supervises whom, who reports to whom, what departments are formed, and what kind of work is performed in each department. This framework is known as a **formal organization** — *the official organization that top management conceives and builds.* A formal organization does not just happen; it is developed by managers through the organizing function of management that was introduced in Chapter 4.

Building an Organization: The Organizing Process

Managers build (and modify) organizations by using the organizing process. The series of illustrations in Figure 5.1 show how the organizing process is applied. As you read and study the following description of the five-step process, refer to this figure to see how an organization is created.

Step 1: Consider Objectives and Plans

In Chapter 4 we mentioned that objectives and plans affect organizing and its result, the organization. Objectives dictate the purposes and activities that organizations have or will have. Managers begin the organizing process by examining the objectives of the organization. As plans change and new objectives are developed, new departments may be created, old ones may be given new responsibilities, some may cease to exist. Objectives and plans are the starting point.

Step 2: Determine the Necessary Work Activities

What work activities are necessary to accomplish the identified organizational objectives? Creating a list of tasks to be accomplished begins with those that will be ongoing tasks and ends with the unique, or one-time-only, tasks. Hiring, training, and recordkeeping are part of the regular routine of running any business; but what, in addition, are the unique needs of this organization? Does it include assembling, machining, shipping, sorting, inspecting, selling, advertising? Identify all activities necessary. Once managers know what tasks must be done, they are ready to classify and group these activities into manageable work units.

Step 3: Classify and Group Activities

Step 3 asks managers to perform three processes:

1. Examine each activity identified to determine its general nature (marketing, production, finance, personnel)
2. Group the activities into these related areas

Figure 5.1 The Organizing Process Exemplified

Excelsior Widgets Corporation

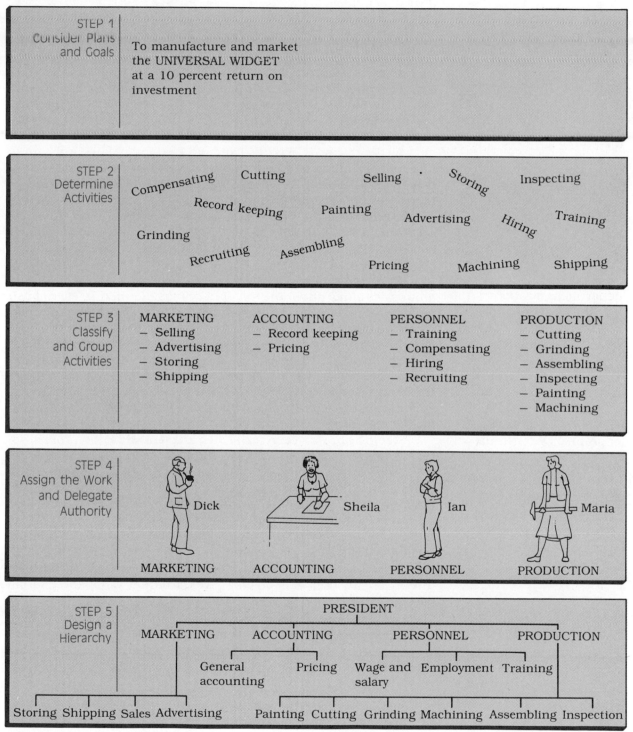

STEP 1
Consider Plans and Goals

To manufacture and market the UNIVERSAL WIDGET at a 10 percent return on investment

STEP 2
Determine Activities

Compensating Cutting Selling Storing Inspecting Record keeping Painting Advertising Hiring Training Grinding Recruiting Assembling Pricing Machining Shipping

STEP 3
Classify and Group Activities

MARKETING
– Selling
– Advertising
– Storing
– Shipping

ACCOUNTING
– Record keeping
– Pricing

PERSONNEL
– Training
– Compensating
– Hiring
– Recruiting

PRODUCTION
– Cutting
– Grinding
– Assembling
– Inspecting
– Painting
– Machining

STEP 4
Assign the Work and Delegate Authority

Dick — MARKETING   Sheila — ACCOUNTING   Ian — PERSONNEL   Maria — PRODUCTION

STEP 5
Design a Hierarchy

PRESIDENT

MARKETING   ACCOUNTING   PERSONNEL   PRODUCTION

General accounting   Pricing   Wage and salary   Employment   Training

Storing Shipping Sales Advertising   Painting Cutting Grinding Machining Assembling Inspection

3. Establish the basic department design for the organization structure

In practice, the first two processes occur simultaneously. Selling, advertising, shipping, and storing can be considered marketing-related activities. Thus they are grouped under the *marketing* heading. Assembling, cutting, machining, welding, painting, and inspecting are manufacturing processes; they can be grouped as *production. Personnel*-related activities include hiring, training, developing, recruiting, and compensating. Work that is similar in nature, tasks, processes, or skills required is placed together to achieve organizational objectives.

departmentalization

As the tasks are classified and grouped into related work units (production, marketing, finance, and personnel) the third process, departmentalization, is being finalized. **Departmentalization** is *the process of creating the basic format or departmental structure for the organization; forming groups, departments, and divisions on the basis of the objectives of the organization.* Management chooses a departmental type from function, geographic or territorial, customer, or product line.

functional departmentalization

Functional departmentalization, the most common approach, *groups activities under the major headings that nearly every business has in common* — finance, production, marketing, and personnel. These are the functions of the business, and the entire organization is divided into these major areas as shown in Figure 5.2. The functional approach is a logical way for most businesses to departmentalize. What each person or unit does or will do becomes the basis of organizing. This method helps to avoid overlap in the execution of basic business activities. Lines are clearly drawn between functional areas.

geographic *or* territorial departmentalization

Geographic *or* territorial departmentalization *groups activities and responsibilities according to geography.* Expanding companies often locate plants and sales or repair facilities in various parts of the country because of favorable labor and materials costs, tax incentives, easy access to transportation, or the need to be near customers to serve them quickly and efficiently. Referring to Figure 5.2 you can see the divisions — the Eastern Region and the Western Region — that illustrate this method. Department stores like J. C. Penney and Sears have located stores throughout the United States to be close to their customers. The Carnation Company has departmentalized regionally to sell its grocery products.

Pause and Ponder

Consider the organization where you work or have worked. What approach did management take for departmentalization? Why was this choice made? What other departmentalization choices might you suggest to management? Why would you recommend these methods of departmentalization?

Figure 5.2 Methods of Departmentalization

```
                    |
     ┌──────────┬────┴─────┬──────────┐
  ┌──────┐  ┌────────┐ ┌─────────┐ ┌──────────┐
  │Finance│  │Production│ │Marketing│ │Personnel│   Functional
  └──────┘  └────────┘ └─────────┘ └──────────┘
                            │
                    ┌───────┴───────┐
            ┌──────────────┐ ┌──────────────┐
            │Eastern Region│ │Western Region│    Geographic
            │Division      │ │Division      │
            └──────────────┘ └──────────────┘
                   │
            ┌──────┴──────┐
       ┌──────────┐  ┌──────────┐
       │Typewriters│  │Calculators│            Product
       └──────────┘  └──────────┘
                         │
               ┌─────────┼─────────┐
        ┌──────────┐ ┌──────┐ ┌─────────┐
        │Government │ │Retail│ │Hospitals│      Customer
        └──────────┘ └──────┘ └─────────┘
```

Product departmentalization *assembles the activities of creating, producing, and marketing each product into one department*, such as the typewriter and calculator departments in Figure 5.2. This form should be considered if each product requires a unique marketing strategy, production process, distribution system, or capital resources. Product departmentalization results in attention, energy, and effort being focused on a particular product. A well-known historical example of this approach is General Motors, which for years had separate divisions for each make of car, as well as a truck division, until it was modified to a large car–small car product departmentalization design.

product departmentalization

Customer departmentalization, which *groups activities and resources in response to the needs of specific customer groups*, is illustrated by the last row in Figure 5.2. A company that markets products to government agencies, to retail customers such as Sears and Montgomery Ward, and to medical institutions such as hospitals, faces an extremely difficult task. Each of these customer groups has a different set of demands, needs, and preferences. In turn each requires a different set of approaches, customs, and operations.

customer departmentalization

Step 4: Assign Work and Delegate Appropriate Authority

Management has identified the activities necessary to achieve objectives, has classified and grouped these activities into major operational areas, and has selected a departmental structure. The

Source: Drawing by Lorenz; © 1977
The New Yorker Magazine, Inc.

activities now must be assigned to individuals who are simultaneously given the appropriate authority to accomplish the task.

Step 5: Design a Hierarchy of Relationships

Step 5 requires the determination of both the vertical and horizontal operating relationships of the organization as a whole. In effect this step puts together all the parts of the puzzle.

The vertical structuring of the organization results in a decision-making hierarchy that shows who is in charge of each task, of each specialty area, and of the organization as a whole. Levels of management are established from bottom to top in the organization. These levels create the **chain of command,** or *hierarchy of decision-making levels in the company.*

chain of command

The horizontal structuring has two important effects: (1) it defines the working relationships between operating departments, (2) it makes the final decision on the **span of control** — *the number of subordinates under the direction of each manager.*

span of control

The result of this step is a complete organization structure. This structure is shown by an **organization chart** — *the visual representation of the way an entire organization and each of its parts fit together.* The organization chart has its value to managers in depicting the basic framework of the organization. Figure 5.3 illustrates that a chart can tell us:

organization chart

1. Who reports to whom — the chain of command
2. How many subordinates work for each manager — the span of control

Figure 5.3 Organization Chart: The Right Way Corporation, 19——

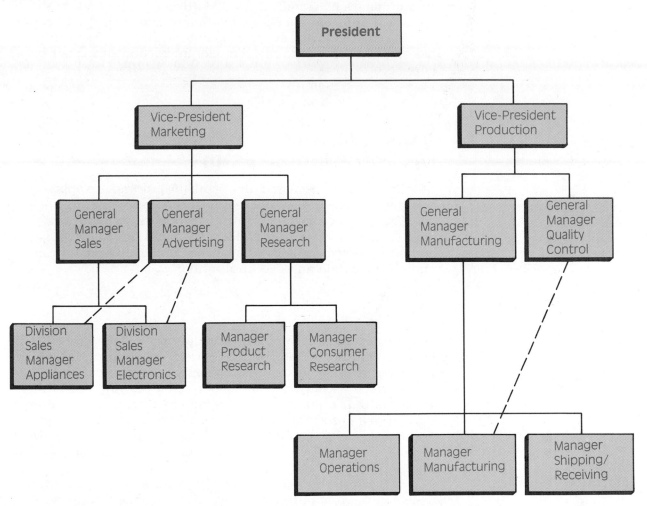

3. Channels of official communication (the solid lines that connect each job)
4. How the company is structured — by function, customer, or product, for example
5. The work being done in each job (the labels on the boxes)
6. The hierarchy of decision making (where a decision maker for a problem is located)
7. How current the present organization structure is (if a date is on the chart)
8. Types of authority relationships (solid connections between boxes illustrate line authority and dotted lines show staff and functional authority, which we will examine later)

By developing a formal organization structure and chart, management also has attempted to clarify and coordinate the work environment. Everyone should now know what to do: the tasks and responsibilities of all individuals, departments, and divisions should be clear. Confusion should be minimized and obstacles to performance removed. The interrelationship of the various work units has been developed, and guidelines for interaction among personnel have been defined.

Managing the Organization Structure

Now that we have discussed the organizing process, it is appropriate to examine some of the organizational concepts managers apply in successfully guiding the organization to reach its objectives. Specifically managers need to understand and utilize the concepts of authority, delegation, responsibility, accountability, span of control, and centralization and decentralization.

Authority

All managers in an organization have authority. They have different degrees of authority based on the level of management they occupy in the organization structure. **Authority** is a manager's tool; it can be described as *the right to commit resources (that is, to make decisions that commit the organization's resources) or the legal right to give orders (to tell someone to do or not to do something).* Authority is the "glue" that holds the organization together: it provides the means of command. Let's examine how a manager acquires authority.

It has been said that "authority comes with the territory," which means that authority is vested in a manager because of the position he or she occupies in the organization. Thus authority is defined in each manager's job description or job charter. The person who occupies the position has its formal authority as long as he or she remains in that position. In an organization different types of authority are created by the relationships between individuals and between departments. There are three types of authority: (1) line, (2) staff, and (3) functional.

Line authority defines the relationship between superior and subordinate. It is *direct supervisory authority from superior to subordinate.* Managers who supervise operating employees or other managers have line authority. Line authority flows downward in an organization directly from superior to subordinate, as Figure 5.4 illustrates.

Staff authority is *the authority to serve in an advisory capacity (the authority to advise).* Managers whose role it is to provide advice or technical assistance are granted advisory authority. Advisory authority does not provide any basis for direct control over the

authority

line authority

staff authority

Authority is not just giving orders. It is also the right to make decisions that allocate resources.

subordinates or activities of other departments with whom they consult (see Figure 5.4); however, within the staff manager's own department, he or she exercises line authority over the department's subordinates.

Functional authority is *the authority to make decisions on specific activities that are undertaken by personnel in other departments.* This concept is illustrated in Figure 5.5. The personnel manager must monitor and review compliance in operating de-

functional authority

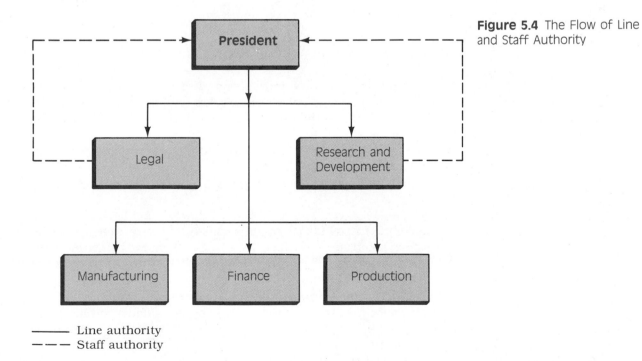

Line authority
Staff authority

Figure 5.4 The Flow of Line and Staff Authority

Figure 5.5 Functional
Authority

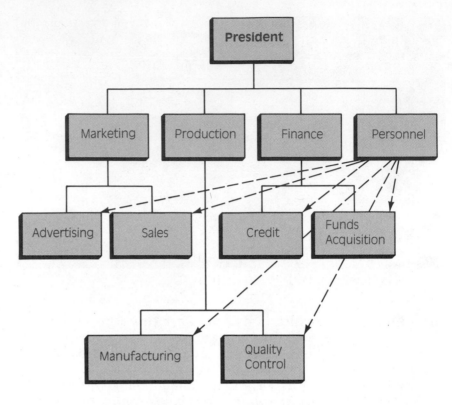

————— Functional authority

partments for recruitment, selection, and performance appraisal
systems.

Delegation

delegation

As the company grows and more demands are placed on a manager,
or because a manager wishes to develop subordinates, delegation
takes place. **Delegation** is a concept describing *the downward
transfer of formal authority from one person to another.* Superiors
delegate, or pass, authority to subordinates to facilitate work's being
accomplished.

When managers choose to delegate, a sequence of events is
created.

1. Assignment of tasks: specific tasks or duties that are to be
   undertaken are identified by the manager for assignment to
   the subordinate. The subordinate is then approached with the
   assignment (tasks).

2. Delegation of authority: for the subordinate to complete the
   duties or tasks, the authority necessary to do them should be
   delegated by the manager to the subordinate. A guideline for
   authority is that it be adequate to complete the task — no
   more and no less.

3. Acceptance of responsibility: **responsibility** is *the obligation to carry out one's assigned duties to the best of one's ability.* Responsibility is not delegated by a manager to an employee, but the employee becomes obligated when the assignment is accepted. The employee is the receiver of the assigned duties and the delegated authority, these confer responsibility as well.

responsibility

4. Creation of accountability: **accountability** is *having to answer to someone for your actions.* It means taking the consequences — either credit or blame. When the subordinate accepts the assignment and the authority, he or she will be held accountable, or answerable, for actions taken. A manager is accountable for the use of her or his authority and performance. In addition, the manager is also accountable for the performance of and actions of subordinates.

accountability

This four-step process should ensure that the process of delegation is clearly understood by the manager and the subordinate. The manager should take the time to think through what is being assigned and to confer the authority necessary to achieve results. The subordinate, in accepting the assignment, becomes obligated (responsible) to perform, knowing that he or she is accountable (answerable) for the results.

By delegating authority down through the management hierarchy, top managers and successive levels of subordinate managers parcel out decision-making authority and specific tasks to appropriate individuals on the organization chart. To be effective, authority should be delegated to the management level best suited to make the decision in question. A company president should not be the one to decide when the engine in a forklift should be overhauled.

A manager is accountable for the performance and actions of subordinates when they are assigned tasks and delegated authority.

Authority for that decision should be delegated to the lowest possible level, in this case the plant maintenance manager.

Span of Control

As managers are designing the organization structure they are concerned with the span of control. As we learned earlier, the *span of control* refers to the number of subordinates a manager supervises. There is no correct number to be assigned to each manager at the top, middle, or bottom level of the organization. The exact number for each manager is determined by:

— The complexity and variety of the subordinates' work
— The ability of the manager
— The ability and training of the subordinates themselves
— The supervisor's willingness to delegate authority

As a general rule, the more complex the subordinates' jobs, the fewer that manager's number of subordinates should be. Another predictable guide is the more routine the work of subordinates, the greater the number of subordinates that can be effectively directed and controlled. Because of these general rules, organizations always seem to have narrow spans at their tops and wider spans at lower levels.

As Figure 5.6 illustrates, it is not uncommon to find a factory production supervisor with fifteen or more subordinates. Why? Because persons who can be well trained to follow directions and routines will, once they master their tasks, require less of their supervisor's time and energies. They will know what they must do and exactly how to do it to meet their performance standards.

Conversely it is uncommon to find a corporate vice-president with more than three or four subordinates (see Fig. 5.6). Why? Because middle and upper management employees perform little that is routine. Their tasks usually require ingenuity and creativity, and their tasks are nonrepetitive.

Two managers who hold jobs at the same level in the organization should not automatically be assigned identical spans of control. While one manager may be able to supervise six people effectively, another manager in the same job may not be able to do so. Why? Because no two managers are equal in their abilities and because their subordinates have differing capabilities and levels of experience as well. The qualifications of the managers and their subordinates must be considered when creating spans of control. The more capable and experienced the subordinates, the more that can be supervised effectively by one competent manager. The less time needed to train, the more time can be devoted to producing products. In general spans can be widened with growth in experience and competency of personnel.

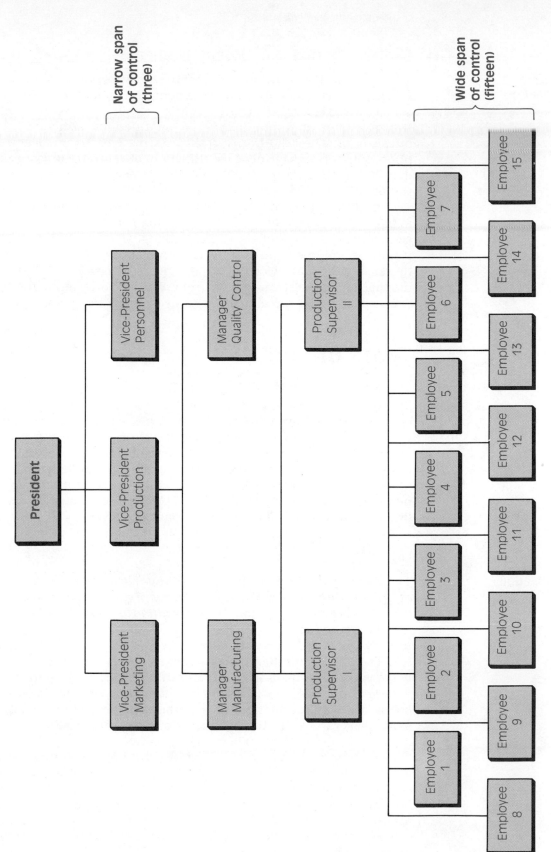

Figure 5.6 Narrow and Wide Spans of Control

Centralization Versus Decentralization

centralization
decentralization

The terms **centralization** and **decentralization** refer to *a philosophy of organization and management that focuses on either the selective concentration* (centralization) *or the dispersal* (decentralization) *of authority within an organization structure.*[1] The question of where authority resides is resolved in an operating philosophy of management — either to concentrate authority for decision making in the hands of one or a few or to force it down the organization structure into the hands of many.

Centralization and decentralization are relative concepts when applied to organizations. The top-level management may decide to centralize all decision making: purchasing, staffing, operations. Or it may decide to set limits on what can be purchased at each level by dollar amounts; decentralize the hiring decisions to first-level management for clerical workers (retaining authority for managerial decisions); and let operational decisions be made where appropriate.

Types of Formal Organization Structure

Formal organization structures are developed by companies to help achieve their specific objectives. Because the objectives of companies will differ because of resources, stage of organizational development, and philosophies of management the type of organization structure to meet these objectives necessarily will differ. In addition, as companies and their objectives change it is often necessary to adopt a new format. Management has four options from which to select: line, line and staff, functional and matrix.

Line Organization

line organization

The **line organization** structure is the simplest and the oldest form of organization. It originated in military organizations and can be best visualized by *a straight line of authority originating from the top manager that connects each successive management level until it reaches the operating employee level,* as shown in Figure 5.7. The line organization is based on direct authority. Each manager is responsible for making his or her own decisions. In making these decisions the manager is responsible for collecting and processing his or her own information without the assistance of specialists or staff advisers. This in turn provides for speed in decision making.

The line organization is most applicable to small organizations whose scope and volume of operations are limited. Managers are capable of handling all the responsibilities in this limited environment and performing the decision-making role. As the organization grows in number of employees, complexity, and scope of operations, managers find it difficult to complete all their tasks with the same degree of effectiveness. They do not have the time or special skills to perform as effectively.

Figure 5.7 Line Organization

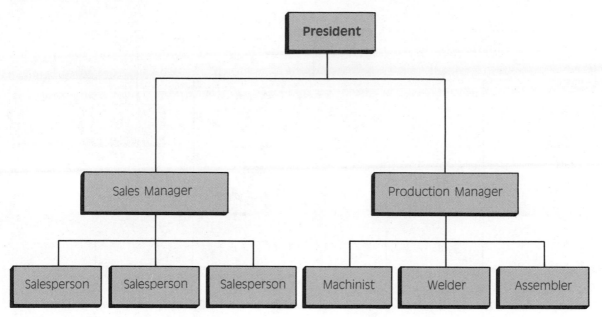

Line-and-Staff Organization

Large firms find it virtually impossible to operate effectively with a line organization. Widespread facilities, complex products, and sophisticated operations demand expert advice on such subjects as law, engineering, and human resources management. Consequently growth forces a company to employ specialists in these areas and to convert to the second type of internal organization: line and staff.

The **line-and-staff organization** structure *blends into the line organization staff personnel that advise and serve the line managers.* The line managers make decisions and take actions that directly affect the firm's performance. The staff departments and their employees advise the line personnel and thus improve their decision-making effectiveness. Staff departments possess specialized or technical knowledge enabling them to provide assistance and expertise to line managers. Figure 5.8 presents an organization developed using the line-and-staff concept. In this organization the

line-and-staff organization

Pause and Ponder

Reflect on the company where you work or have worked. What type of organization structure was present? How effective was it in assisting decision making and communication? If a change were to be made in the type of organization structure, which one would you recommend? Why?

Figure 5.8 Line-and-Staff Organization

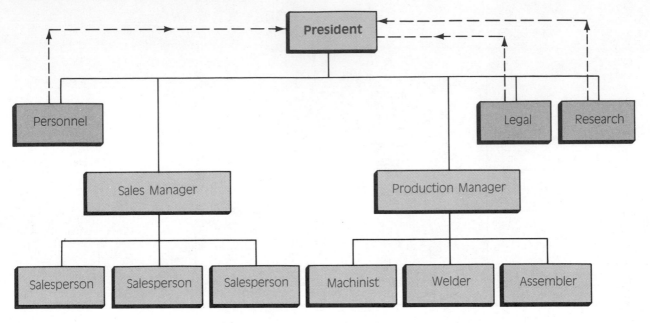

line manager is aided in decision making by personnel, legal, and research staff departments.

In a line-and-staff structure the three types of authority previously introduced are present. Line managers possess line authority — direct supervisory authority over their departments and operations. They have the authority to make decisions and to compel action. Staff managers possess staff authority. They are intended to advise line managers. They do not have the authority to give orders or force line managers to make certain decisions. Finally, some staff managers are given functional authority. They have the authority to make decisions on specific activities undertaken by personnel in other departments (see Fig. 5.8).

Functional Organization

functional organization

The **functional organization** structure is *an attempt by management to provide expert technical supervision to operating employees by providing separate supervisors for each task.* It is based on the belief that one person will not be able to provide as much expert supervision on the six tasks of an employee as would six separate supervisors. This idea, shown in Figure 5.9, originally was introduced by Frederick Taylor, the father of scientific management. Notice that the six elements of an employee's job are supervised by six technically skilled supervisors. Workers receive technical advice in cutting, trimming, polishing, assembling, painting, and packaging from six separate managers. In a line organization one manager would be responsible for all the elements.

Although the functional organization structure provides technical expertise it does create a major difficulty. As you can see, each worker has six supervisors. Even though the areas of supervision

Figure 5.9 Functional Organization

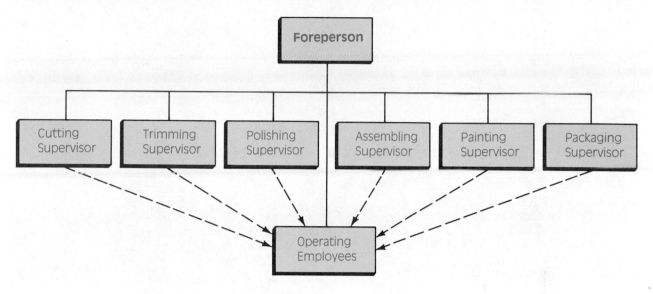

are closely defined, at times conflict and confusion can occur with supervisors attempting to control subordinates. It also violates the principle of **unity of command:** *each person in an organization should take orders from and report to only one person.* Because of these difficulties the functional structure is not widely implemented.

unity of command

Matrix Organization

The matrix organization is a relatively new approach to internal organization, which has received increasing attention in recent years. Sometimes referred to as a *project organization* structure, the **matrix organization** *temporarily groups together specialists from different departments or divisions to work on special projects.* When the project is completed, the specialists either return to their central area or are reassigned to another project.

matrix organization

The matrix approach is commonplace in aerospace companies where several simultaneous projects require the interaction of engineers, research and development scientists, and other specialized people. Figure 5.10 presents a matrix organization structure for an aerospace project. The departments — production, materials, personnel, engineering, and accounting — are permanent parts of the organization. The various project teams — Venus, Mars, and Saturn — are created as the need arises and are disbanded when the project is completed.

Members of the Venus project team are selected from the departments and are supervised for the duration of the project by the Venus project manager. During the course of the project, the technical team specialists have access to and can use the resources of their functional departments. The matrix approach utilizes the technical resources of an organization by efficiently allocating the expertise where and when it is needed.

The matrix organization builds a project team composed of members from major departments in the company.

Which Organization Structure Is Best?

Remember, organization structures are created to achieve the objectives of the organization. There is no one best organization structure. A small business can best achieve its objectives through a line structure; a medium or large business would need the expert advice provided by the line and staff organization. A company specializing in custom production — car or van customizing — may select the functional structure, while a company with an environment characterized by numerous projects may choose the matrix form. Each has its advantages and disadvantages. Table 5.1 examines the advantages and disadvantages of the four forms of organization.

The Informal Organization

Management has taken the time to develop the formal organization — departmental structures, decision-making guidelines, authority relationships, and designated managers — but functioning within the formal organization is something management did not design: the informal organization.

informal organization

The **informal organization** is *a network of personal and social relationships that arises spontaneously as people associate with each other in the work environment.*[2] It can be illustrated by the lunch bunch, the coffee-break group, the company bowling team, or just two people who meet to talk after work. It is a self grouping of people because of shared interests, social and educational backgrounds, personalities, and shared needs.

The informal organization cuts across the formal organization structure. It is not shown on the organization chart. People from

Figure 5.10 Matrix Organization Structure

Source: John F. Mee, "Matrix Organizations," *Business Horizons*, vol. 7, no. 2 (Summer 1964), p. 71. Copyright, 1964, by the Foundation for the School of Business at Indiana University. Used with permission.

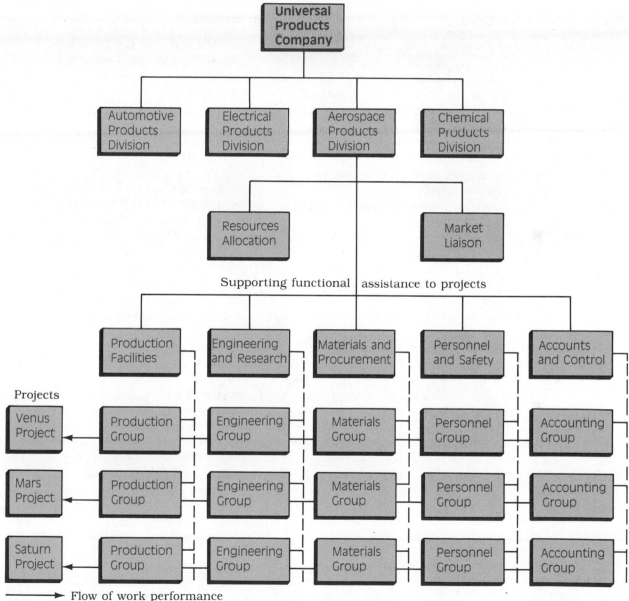

different departments and different levels in the organization interact, find commonalities, support and assist each other, satisfy needs, and provide information. Membership in an informal group and in the informal organization is voluntary and is determined by the members of the group.

Managers need to understand and work with and through the informal organization. Why? It will be present in all formal organizations. Managers cannot prevent the informal organization from forming. People naturally interact and develop relationships. It is

Table 5.1 Advantages and Disadvantages of the Four Major Types of Formal Organization

Type of Organization	Advantages	Disadvantages
Line	Decisions can be made faster. Authority, responsibility, and accountability are clearly placed. It is simple and sometimes less expensive to create and manage because no staff people are needed.	It omits the use of skilled specialists. All decisons tend to be made at upper levels, thus burdening top managers with minor details.
Line-and-staff	Staff employees provide specialized and technical information to line managers. Line managers need not be experts on highly technical subjects. Line managers' decisions may be better because of staff input.	Decisions can be delayed while staff people research problems and develop recommendations. Conflicts arise when some line managers resent staff's influence and expert status. Confusion results if staff-and-line authority and responsibility are not clear. Friction develops if staff members attempt to direct the activities of line personnel.
Functional	It provides expert technical advice to each worker. It limits the technical expertise demand on one manager.	Violates unity of command. Conflict may occur between technical experts over supervisory relationships.
Matrix	Specialists in several functions can be assigned to various projects that require their expertise. Each project has a manager who devotes full time and effort to coordinating its success. Specialists benefit from working on a broad variety of challenging assignments.	Authority relationships between functional managers and project managers may be unclear. Employees may have difficulty serving two supervisors, the functional manager and the project manager. Project and functional managers may compete for recognition, status, and money. Specialists with long-term project assignments may identify more with the project than their functional area, thus distorting their perspective.

management's job to recognize and cultivate the informal organization. If approached correctly it can aid in accomplishing the organization's objectives, provide stability, support the manager, and assist in providing information to members of the organization.

Figure 5.11 provides an illustration of the informal organization's communication system: the grapevine. Notice that the majority of the information is transmitted outside the formal channels from information known only to Manager 110. This system relies on word-of-mouth communication rather than memos. It can and does move information across as well as up and down the organization. Managers should identify and use the grapevine. By using

The informal organization is here at work.

Figure 5.11 The Informal Organization's Communication System: The Grapevine

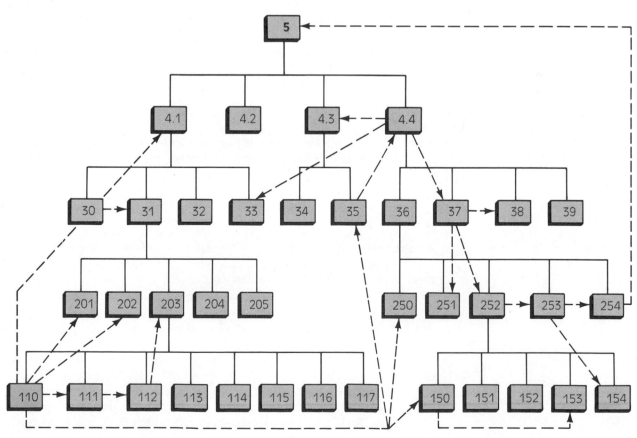

The Straight Line

Sotheby Art Auction House

Back in the Black After Reorganization

In 1982 Sotheby, the world's largest art auction house, reported its first loss since World War II — $4.5 million. One year later it was back in the black with projected fiscal year profits of $6 million.

Although the economy was partially responsible for Sotheby's losses, what the failing economy actually did was reveal weaknesses in Sotheby's management that were unable to survive an economic downturn. For 21 years the company had been virtually a one-man show. When Peter Wilson retired as chairman in 1979, the lack of organization and the management void became painfully apparent. Wilson was a chaotic, though charming, autocrat who managed according to the needs (or whims) of the moment. Without his charismatic personality forging ahead, his expert analysis of the current art situation, and his vitality to tie the various parts of the organization together, the internal collapse began (or became apparent).

Because Wilson feared over-organizing, there were no clear lines of authority, no established areas of responsibility, and no controls for holding individuals accountable. In addition, a tremendous growth spurt between 1977 and 1979 had increased personnel by 50 percent. Lacking supervision and operating procedures, employees made their own decisions and their own deals with customers. The ultimate result was increased financial drain and strain on the organization.

Wilson's departure from Sotheby's was as chaotic as his tenure there. He left hastily and without naming a successor. The

this network managers can supply accurate information to remove rumors and to provide additional information to their employees.

Summary

An organization is a group of two or more people that exists and operates to achieve clearly stated, commonly held objectives. A business is an organization created to provide a product or service to a customer at a profit. To reach these objectives it is necessary to establish a framework of operating relationships of people and activities. This operating framework is known as the formal organization.

The formal organization is developed through a series of organizing steps: (1) consider objectives and plans, (2) determine activities necessary to achieve objectives, (3) classify and group activities (functional, geographic or territorial, product, customer), (4) assign work and delegate authority, and (5) design a hierarchy

Earl of Westmoreland spent 2 years as interim chairman. He lacked not only the necessary management skills to get the company organized, but also the art background that had enabled Wilson to keep Sotheby going.

In 1982 Gordon Brunton, chief executive of International Thomason Organisation, Ltd., the newspaper and book publishing conglomerate, took the reins from Westmoreland. Previously Westmoreland had asked Brunton, a member of Sotheby's board, to develop a reorganization plan. Years of undirected expansion and increasing debt finally were brought under control by the new management's emphasis on long-range planning and cost cutting. Areas of responsibility were assigned to specific officers and managers. A new structure was established.

Some consolidation of expansion occurred. Cost-cutting methods such as "no-frills" auctions for selling low-priced goods were implemented. (A rising economy also helped.)

Sotheby now is back on its feet: ready to enter the second half of the decade with a new owner, A. Alfred Taubman, a multimillionaire real estate developer and art collector from Detroit. Taubman put the winning bid together with long-time friends Henry Ford II and Max Fisher (former head of United Brands). Although many of Sotheby's employees and their British countrymen are concerned about the new American ownership, Taubman believes his marketing skills will turn the tide for Sotheby's once again.

For more about the Sotheby art auction house, see James Fleming, "A Winning Bid for Sotheby's," *Maclean's*, October 10, 1983, p. 44; "Sotheby in the Black," *Fortune*, October 3, 1983, p. 229; Gigi Mahon, "And to All a Good Knight," *Barrons*, October 3, 1983, p. 13; "Sotheby Profit Seen," *The New York Times*, July 13, 1983, p. D17; and Gwen Kinkead, "Sotheby's Lost Art: Management," *Fortune*, May 31, 1982, pp. 123–129.

of relationships. The result of this process is a formal organization structure. This structure is shown visually by an organization chart.

Once the organization is developed, there are organizational concepts to be applied by managers to assist the organization in achieving its objectives. These concepts include:

- **Authority** Right to commit resources or the right to give orders. There are three types of authority — line, staff, and functional.
- **Delegation** The passing of formal authority to another person. It involves assigning tasks, delegating authority, exacting responsibility, and holding a person accountable.
- **Span of Control** The number of subordinates a manager supervises. There is no correct number to be assigned for each manager.
- **Centralization or Decentralization** A philosophy of organization that focuses on the selective concentration (centralization) or the dispersal (decentralization) of authority within an organization structure. The application of this philosophy

determines if decision making is in the hands of a few or is forced down the organization structure.

There are four types of formal organization structures developed by managers: line, line-and-staff, functional, and matrix. Each has its advantages and disadvantages. The organization structure selected by an organization will depend on its objectives, stage of development, and philosophies of management.

Within the formal organization is the informal organization. The informal organization is a network of personal and social relationships that arises spontaneously as people associate with each other in the work environment. Managers need to recognize and work with the informal organization as it assists the managers in meeting organization objectives.

Key Terms

accountability

authority

centralization

chain of command

customer departmentalization

decentralization

delegation

departmentalization

formal organization

functional authority

functional departmentalization

functional organization

geographic *or* territorial departmentalization

informal organization

line authority

line organization

line-and-staff organization

matrix organization

organization

organization chart

product departmentalization

responsibility

span of control

staff authority

unity of command

For Review and Discussion

1. What is an organization? Why is it necessary? What is a formal organization?

2. List and explain each step of the organizing process.

3. What are the four forms of departmentalization? Under what situations would each be appropriate?

4. What information can be obtained from looking at an organization chart?

5. What is meant by the term *authority*? Where does a manager get his or her authority?

6. What does the term *delegation* mean? How are delegation, authority, responsibility, and accountability related?

7. Is there a correct span of control? If your answer is no, what factors affect the span of control?

8. Distinguish between centralization and decen-

tralization. What is the result of each on decision making in an organization?

9. What are the advantages of a line organization? What size business should use a line organization?

10. What is the major difference between a line organization and a line-and-staff organization?

11. Describe how a functional organization would provide supervision for an employee who was responsible for assembling a product, packing the product in a carton, and completing paperwork for shipping instructions. What problems could occur?

12. When would a matrix organization be applicable?

13. How does the informal organization come into existence? Who can be a member? What is the grapevine?

Applications

Case 5.1 A Matter of Time

Jerry Stimpson had just returned to his office after spending a week with one of his new supervisors, Barbara Anson. Jerry had become concerned about the quality of work Barbara had been doing since becoming the manager of the personnel department 3 months ago.

In that time reports from Barbara to Jerry had been received after established deadlines, budget projections had obvious errors, and informal conversations with line managers revealed that Barbara did not seem to have time to discuss their personnel concerns. In addition, there were rumors on the grapevine that the once happy personnel department, staffed by sixteen veteran employees, had become disenchanted. When questioned on the telephone about these events Barbara had responded, "I'm just busy, Jerry, but things will calm down in a little while. Trust me."

But things had not improved, which prompted Jerry to make a personal visit. During this week Jerry had observed Barbara:

- Writing all job vacancy notices
- Tallying all employee time sheets
- Returning all phone calls received (her secretary simply took the person's name and telephone number)
- Conducting all employee orientations, including tours of the facilities
- Scheduling employee training sessions for all departments so that she might observe each session

In addition, Jerry had observed that Barbara's employees did not seem to have enough to do during the day. They took many breaks, gathered constantly around the coffeepot, took long lunches, and generally appeared disinterested. When questioning one employee about her job, Jerry was told, "What job? I'm not allowed to do my job."

Questions

1. What is Barbara's problem?
2. What specific actions must Barbara take to solve her problem?
3. How can Jerry hold Barbara accountable for implementing these actions?

Case 5.2 Developing an Organization Chart

Using the following information develop an organization chart for the I. M. Boss Company, manufacturer and marketer of the world's best widgets.

1. The activities being performed in the company are:
   - Machining
   - Selling
   - Hiring
   - Recordkeeping
   - Shipping
   - Training
   - Assembling
   - Advertising
   - Auditing
   - Pricing
   - Compensating
   - Painting
2. The company's president, I. M. Boss, has stated that:
   - Departments should be developed based on a functional approach.
   - There should be only *four* major functional departments.
   - The span of control should be not more than three for each department head.
   - All hiring practices should be uniform, even though all managers may hire their own employees.
3. I. M. Boss started the organization chart but was called out of town.

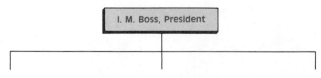

I. M. Boss, President

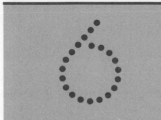

Personnel: Acquiring and Developing Human Resources

Chapter Outline

Chapter Objectives

After studying this chapter, you should be able to:

1. Summarize the nature and importance of human resources management.
2. Explain the impact of equal employment opportunity and affirmative action on human resources management.
3. Describe the process involved in human resources planning.
4. Describe internal and external sources for human resources recruitment.
5. Outline the selection process and describe each step.
6. Describe the purposes of an employee orientation program.
7. Describe the methods of employee training.
8. Identify and explain the purposes of and types of performance appraisal.
9. Distinguish between employee promotions, transfers, demotions, retirements, resignations, layoffs, and terminations.
10. List and explain the methods of employee compensation.
11. Discuss the effect of the Occupational Safety and Health Act on employee safety and health.

You can dream, create, design, and build the most wonderful place in the world . . . but it takes people to make the dream a reality.

— Walt Disney, founder of Walt Disney Studios

Up Front

Len Peach

IBM's Mr. Personnel in the UK

According to *Personnel Management*'s "Man of the Moment" series, Len Peach is "the personnel supremo of the most successful business" in the information processing industry. Born and educated in the United Kingdom, including a state scholarship to Oxford, Peach stumbled into personnel management after a stint as literary assistant to Randolph Churchill. A sponsorship to the London School of Economics in 1957 proved to be the catalyst for his move into the business world. In 1962 he joined IBM and began a 10-week training program that was cut short when his boss resigned. As a result Peach found himself promoted to management development coordinator.

His philosophy and values meshed with IBM's, which enabled him to be extremely effective in Britain and Europe. In 1971 he was made UK director of personnel and reported to the chief executive. In 1972 Peach was named group director of personnel for IBM Europe with responsibility for 93,000 people. After 3 years based in Paris but spending most of his time traveling the world, Peach returned to the United Kingdom as personnel chief and director of corporate affairs.

Peach believes that the purpose of the personnel department should be that of creating an environment in which line managers "can recruit, retain, and motivate employees to meet the present and future needs of businesses." This goal takes commitment, however, to long-term objectives, planning systems, and the other manage-

"You are only as good as your people" is an often-heard saying in management. You can have outstanding plans, but if you do not have the quality employees to carry those plans out, you are back to square one. The purpose of this chapter is to discuss the human resources function — its importance and its activities.

The Importance of Human Resources Management

For an organization to survive and prosper it must be able to identify, select, develop, and retain qualified personnel. People are the most important resource of an organization. They supply the talent, skills, knowledge, and experience to achieve the organization's objectives.

Through the planning function, management determined the objectives for the organization. In turn these objectives were analyzed through the organizing function to identify activities necessary to

ment functions, something that has been required of line managers but from which personnel managers have felt exempt. Personnel managers or departments are seen by many line managers as "a place to turn to in time of trouble." Peach thinks the personnel job is a daily job to be fully integrated into the company; and it is up to personnel managers to be effective on a day-to-day basis in the organization. He feels that it is also up to the personnel group to provide the necessary support systems to make the organization's philosophy work.

The answer to what has made Len Peach a personnel manager "supremo" is that he has worked to make the elements of IBM's personnel philosophy work:

- Respect for the individual.
- Merit pay system.
- Full employment. No IBM employee has lost as much as an hour's pay because of layoffs.
- Internal appeals procedure. It works because everyone accepts it as a process and not as a personal attack.
- Management and employee education programs.
- Outstanding internal communications. Everyone can be heard through formal and informal channels.

In recognition of his abilities and achievements, Len Peach was elected IPM (Institute of Personnel Management) president in 1983.

For more about Len Peach, see Susanne Lawrence, "Man of the Moment: Len Peach," *Personnel Management*, October, 1983, pp. 29–34.

---

achieve the objectives. Ultimately the activities form the basis for either creating or modifying job positions in the organization. The challenge at this point is for management to match personnel with the jobs identified and to provide for their long-range growth and welfare as members of the organization.

What Is Human Resources Management?

Human resources management is *the staffing function of the organization.* Sometimes identified as personnel management, *it includes the activities of human resources planning, recruitment, selection, orientation, training, performance appraisal, compensation, and safety.* Human resources management is a part of every manager's job. Each individual manager performs each of these basic human resource management activities. In small- to medium-

human resources management

sized organizations the individual manager has the majority of the responsibility for the staffing function. As companies expand operations and need more people, a decision normally is made to employ a specialist called a *human resources manager* (or a personnel manager) to assist with the more technical human resources matters. The activities involved in human resources management are then grouped in a human resources or personnel department as illustrated in Figure 6.1. The Director of Education and Training, along with the other specialists in the Human Resources Department, is responsible for assisting line managers in the operations of their departments.

One of the areas where technical assistance is needed is in the legal aspects of the human resources process. Before we examine each of the human resource activities in detail, we will discuss the legal environment of human resources management.

The Legal Environment of Human Resources Management

The legal environment influences all aspects of the human resources management process. Legislation has been enacted that focuses on discriminatory practices in employment, wages, and retirement.

Figure 6.1 An Example of the Responsibilities and Organization of Human Resources Management

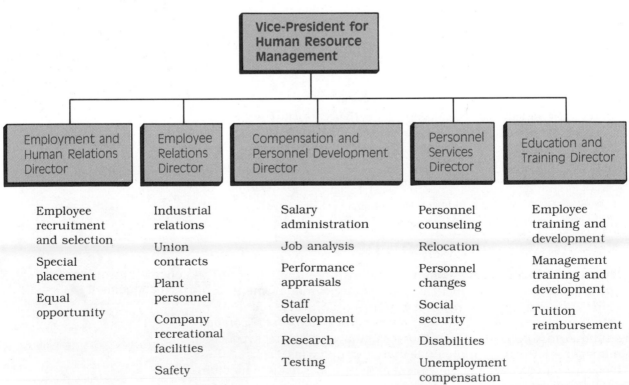

Table 6.1 provides a summary of the federal laws that affect human resources management. Two major influences in the human resources area are legislation on equal employment opportunity and affirmative action.

Equal Employment Opportunity *legislation is designed to provide an employment environment in which both job applicants and present employees are free from discrimination in their pursuit of employment opportunities.* Equal employment legislation prohibits choices made on the basis of race, color, religion, sex, age, or national origin. It is unlawful for an employer to do either of the following:

Equal Employment Opportunity

— To fail or refuse to hire or to discharge an individual because of race, color, religion, sex, age, or national origin.
— To limit, segregate, or classify employees for employment in any way that would deprive the individual of employment op-

Table 6.1 Human Resource Management Legislation

Federal Legislation	Description of Provisions
Title VI 1964 Civil Rights Act	Prohibits discrimination based on race, color, or national origin. Applies to employers receiving federal financial assistance.
Title VII 1964 Civil Rights Act	Prohibits discrimination based on race, color, religion, sex, or national origin. Applies to private employers of fifteen or more employees; federal, state and local governments; unions; and employment agencies.
Executive Orders 11246 and 11375 (1965)	Prohibits discrimination based on race, color, religion, sex, or national origin. Established requirements for affirmative action plans. Applies to federal contractors and subcontractors.
Title 1 1968 Civil Rights Act	Prohibits interference with a person's exercise of rights with respect to race, color, religion, sex, or national origin.
Equal Pay Act of 1963	Prohibits sex difference in pay for equal work. Applies to private employers.
Age Discrimination in Employment Act of 1967 and amended 1975	Prohibits age discrimination against people between the ages of 40 and 70. Applies to all employers.
Rehabilitation Act of 1973	Prohibits discrimination on the basis of certain physical and mental handicaps by employers doing business with or for the federal government.
Vietnam Era Veterans Readjustment Act 1974	Prohibits discrimination against disabled veterans and Vietnam era veterans.
Revised Guidelines on Employee Selection 1976, 1978, and 1979	Established specific rules on employment selection procedures.
Mandatory Retirement Act	Determined that an employee could not be forced to retire before age 70.
Privacy Act of 1974	Established the right of employees to examine letters of reference concerning them unless the right is waived.
Equal Employment Opportunity Guidelines of 1981	Prohibits sexual harassment when such conduct is an explicit or implicit condition of employment, if the employee's response becomes a basis for employment or promotion decisions or if it interferes with an employee's performance. The guidelines protect men and women.

portunities because of race, color, religion, sex, age, or national origin.[1]

The impact of most equal opportunity legislation is on the recruitment and selection of new employees and on promotion, compensation, training, and discharge of present employees. Recruitment advertisements can no longer specify male or female, nor can a company rely on word-of-mouth advertising to attract minorities. In the selection process questions not related to job performance are prohibited. Questions on age, sex, marital status, race, religion, national origin, color of hair, eyes, height, and weight must be eliminated on the application blank and in interviews.[2]

Affirmative Action

Affirmative Action goes beyond equal employment opportunity: it requires an employer to make an effort to hire and promote people in a protected minority. The purpose of affirmative action *programs* is *to eliminate the present effects of past discrimination on women and minorities.* When an organization takes an aggressive or affirmative role in recruiting, hiring, training, and compensating, the purposes of affirmative action should be achieved. The measurable result of affirmative action is that the organization's percentage of females, males, and minorities performing in job categories is equal to the percentage of females, males, and minorities in the relevant job market.[3]

For most organizations affirmative action is voluntary; for others it is a requirement for receiving a federal contract. A plan is developed for reaching out in recruiting to attract minorities and women, which provides the means to aggressively hire, train, and promote protected classes. In the process the organization attempts to identify and eliminate obstacles to the hiring and promotion of women and minorities.

The Human Resources Process

The activities involved in human resources management should be viewed as a series of interrelated steps that managers and specialists perform to acquire and maintain the right people in the right positions. Figure 6.2 illustrates the human resources process. Let's examine each step in detail.

Human Resources Planning

human resources planning

Well-managed firms must forecast future personnel needs carefully. They are far too important to be left to guesswork. The overall **human resources planning** process for an organization, which *includes forecasting the demand for and supply of personnel,* has three parts: (1) forecasting the personnel requirements, (2) comparing the requirements with the talents of present employees, and (3) developing specific plans for how many people to recruit (from outside the company) or whom to train (from inside). Figure 6.3 illustrates the human resources planning process.

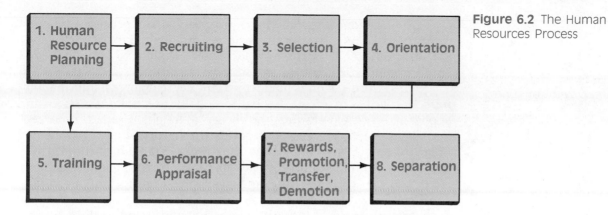

Figure 6.2 The Human
Resources Process

Human resources forecasting *attempts to predict the or-* | human resources forecasting
ganization's future demands for people and for jobs. Major factors
to be examined are the company's objective (growth, contraction,
status quo) and the employment history of the company (retirements,
resignations, terminations, promotions, and deaths). The combination of these two sources results in an initial forecast of personnel
needs.

Human resources inventory *provides information about the* | human resources inventory
organization's present personnel. What are the skills, abilities, interests, and qualifications of the present employees? The personnel
inventory allows the managers to match the organization's present
personnel strengths and weaknesses against the future requirements.

Figure 6.3 Human Resources Planning Process

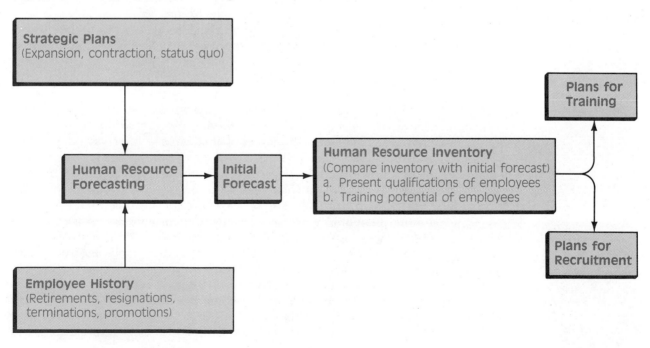

Comparison of forecast and inventory is the process of determining if anyone in the organization is qualified to fill the projected job openings. At this time the decision is made to train present employees or to recruit outside the organization.

When the decision is made to recruit new employees, information must be gathered on each position. Jobs are not tailored to fit applicants — employees must be chosen to fit jobs. Human resources managers must analyze and describe the nature of each job in the organization. At the same time they must establish minimum requirements so that suitable applicants can be hired. This information is developed through job analysis, job description, and job specifications.

job analysis

Job analysis is *the gathering and analyzing of data about a specific job so that a job description and job specification can be written.* It clarifies the nature of the work and the conditions under which it is done.

job description

Job description is *a written summary of the scope, function, duties, responsibilities, and relationships involved in a job.* The job analysis provides the data necessary to write this document. Job descriptions help management to select, orient, and compensate employees effectively. The job description, as illustrated in Figure 6.4, provides management with the job demands. Notice the function, scope, and responsibilities of the customer service representative.

job specification

Job specification is *a document that describes the characteristics and qualifications needed in someone who could successfully perform a given job.* As seen in Figure 6.5, a job specification helps managers determine an applicant's fitness for a certain position by defining qualifications for education, training, experience, and behavioral qualities the person must have to perform the job. A firm is much more likely to recruit and eventually select better employees if it has clear job specifications.

Armed with the job description and job specification, the human resources manager can now contact potential sources of applicants.

Recruitment

recruitment

By **recruitment** *the organization attempts to identify and attract candidates to meet the requirements of anticipated or actual job openings.* There are two sources of applicants — internal and external. Internal sources are the employees of the organization. A number of organizations have policies of promoting from within. This has a positive impact on the organizational members and the internal working environment. The opportunity for advancement has three distinct benefits: it can reduce turnover, provide incentive to learn jobs quickly, and assist in making the individual a functioning member of the organization faster because the person already knows the policies and expectations of the company.

There are also negatives from internal recruiting. Employees who do not get the jobs may become discontented. There is always the possibility that this policy, if taken to the extreme, can result in minimal "new blood" being brought into the organization; and

Figure 6.4 Job Description

I. **Job Identification**
POSITION TITLE: Customer Service Representative
DEPARTMENT: Policyholders Service
EFFECTIVE DATE: March 1, 1984

II. **Function**
To resolve policyholders' questions and make corresponding adjustments to policies if necessary after the policy is issued.

III. **Scope**
a. Internal
Interacts with other members of the Department in researching answers to problems.
b. External (within Company)
Interacts with Policy Issue for policy cancellations; with Premium Accounting on accounting procedures; with Accounting Department for processing checks.
c. External (outside Company)
Interacts with policyholders to answer policy-related questions; with client company payroll departments to resolve billing questions; with the Carrier to modify policies.

IV. **Responsibilities**
He/She will be responsible for:
a. Resolving policyholder inquiries on policies and coverage.
b. Initiating changes in policies with Carriers at the request of the Insured.
c. Adjusting in-house records as a result of approved changes.
d. Corresponding with policyholders regarding changes as requested.
e. Reporting to the Department Manager any problems he or she is unable to resolve.

V. **Authority Relationships**
a. Reporting relationships: reports to the manager of Policyholders Service.
b. Supervisory relationship: none.

VI. **Equipment, Materials, and Machines**
Typewriter, adding machine, and CRT.

VII. **Physical Conditions or Hazards**
95 percent of the duties are performed either sitting at the desk or CRT.

VIII. **Other**
Other duties as assigned.

---

that which is new is at a low position on the hierarchy. This may result in limited new ideas and stagnation.

One internal source is referrals of outside persons made by friends and relatives within the organization. Another method is to attract candidates by announcing job openings in company newsletters and by posting position vacancies on bulletin boards. This strategy provides all employees the equal opportunity to apply (if they see the notices). A third strategy is to conduct a search of the performance records of present employees with the intent of identifying qualified candidates and then to encourage them to apply

Figure 6.5 Job Specification

I. Job Identification
POSITION TITLE: File/Mail Clerk
DEPARTMENT: Policyholders Service
EFFECTIVE DATE: March 1, 1984

II. Education
Must have minimum of high school diploma or equivalent.

III. Experience
Must have minimum of 6 months of filing experience involving developing, monitoring, and maintaining file system.

IV. Skills
Typing skills: must be able to set up own work and operate typewriter. No minimum WPM.

V. Special Requirements
a. Must be flexible to the demands of the organization for overtime and change in work load.
b. Must be able to comply with previously established procedures.
c. Must be able to do detail work as illustrated by monitoring the location of the files and filing of files.
d. Must be able to apply systems knowledge as illustrated by anticipation of systems changes and creation of new procedures.

VI. Behavioral Characteristics
a. Must have high level of initiative demonstrated by recognizing a problem, resolving it, and reporting it to the Supervisor.
b. Must have interpersonal skills as demonstrated by being able to work as a team member and being cooperative with other departments.

for positions. This practice is not as popular as it once was because it may result in the organization's being accused of preselection for a job, that is, of not allowing all candidates for a position equal opportunity to be considered for the position.

A second potential source for candidates is outside the organization. Organizations can develop programs using on-site visits to colleges, trade schools, professional conferences, trade fairs, and high schools. This device allows the company to create impressions, answer questions, and screen applicants quickly.

Another tactic is either to place advertisements in newspapers and trade journals or to place job requisitions with unions, school placement bureaus, and private or public employment agencies. The success in using these sources will depend on how well the organization has described its performance requirements and specifications. In June of 1981 a manufacturer in St. Louis advertised for eight production workers. Three thousand people applied!

Selection

selection

Selection is *the process of deciding which candidate, out of the pool of applicants developed in recruiting, has the abilities, skills, and characteristics that most closely match job demands.* The decision comes after the candidates go through a series of steps that compose the selection process. Figure 6.6 illustrates the steps in the selection process. Let's review each step in detail.

Step 1: The Application Blank. Prospective employees are requested to complete an application blank (such as the example shown in Fig. 6.7), which provides the manager with information on the education and experience of an applicant. It also provides information about the applicant's previous growth and progress[4] on the job as well as employment stability. A final point: it can also show, simply by its requirements, a person's ability to follow instructions and his or her command of the language.

Step 2: Preliminary Interview. This step attempts to screen out the obviously unqualified from the pool of applicants. This interview may be conducted by the manager or a personnel specialist, with the information supplied on the application blank.

Step 3: Testing. The purpose of employment testing is to determine the candidate's ability to perform the job. The kinds of tests used by employers vary and are subject to certain limitations. Aptitude

A college campus is a source of external applicants for an organization.

Figure 6.6 The Selection Process

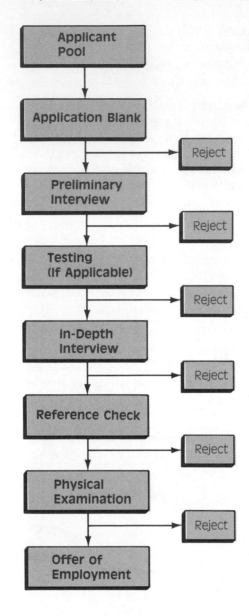

tests attempt to measure a person's ability to learn concepts and to master physical skills. Performance or achievement tests prove what a person can do at the time of testing. Personality tests measure individual characteristics and traits as well as particular motivations. They attempt to pinpoint particular strengths and weaknesses to match them to the prerequisites considered to be important in the jobholder for successful performance. Most tests need the expert administration and interpretation available only in testing agencies or through professionals, such as psychometrists and psychologists. For this reason, testing is expensive and should be used only when it is absolutely indispensable.

To avoid discrimination or charges of it, most companies use tests that have been approved or recognized as nondiscriminatory.

Figure 6.7 Sample Job Application Blank
Source: Courtesy Westinghouse Electric Corporation.

Westinghouse Electric Corporation
An Equal Opportunity Employer

Professional Employment Application

Westinghouse Building
Gateway Center
Pittsburgh Pennsylvania 15222

LAST NAME	FIRST	MIDDLE	SOCIAL SECURITY NO.

PRESENT ADDRESS (STREET/P.O. BOX)	CITY	STATE	ZIP CODE	PHONE (INCL. AREA CODE)

IN CASE OF EMERGENCY, NOTIFY (NAME, ADDRESS, PHONE (INCL. AREA CODE)   (SEE FOOTNOTE NO. 1)

IS YOUR AGE: (CHECK ONE)
UNDER 18 ☐   18-70 ☐   OVER 70 ☐

FORMER WESTINGHOUSE EMPLOYE?   YES ☐   NO ☐
SEPARATION ALLOWANCE PAID?   YES ☐   NO ☐   LOCATION

ARE YOU A CITIZEN OF THE U.S.
YES ☐   NO ☐

RELATIVES OR FRIENDS WORKING FOR WESTINGHOUSE?   NAMES AND RELATIONSHIP   (SEE FOOTNOTE NO. 1)

U.S. MILITARY HISTORY

BRANCH	DATE ENTERED	DATE DISCHARGED	TYPE OF DISCHARGE (SEE FOOTNOTE NO. 2)	HIGHEST RANK ATTAINED AND UNIT

ARMED FORCES RESERVE BRANCH OR NATIONAL GUARD   ACTIVE ☐   INACTIVE ☐   INDICATE SPECIFIC SKILLS ACQUIRED IN THE U.S. ARMED FORCES

EDUCATIONAL BACKGROUND

CIRCLE HIGHEST GRADE COMPLETED IN EACH SCHOOL CATEGORY

GRADE SCHOOL	SECONDARY SCHOOL	TRADE, TECH., BUS. SCHOOL	COLLEGE	GRADUATE SCHOOL
1 2 3 4 5 6 7 8	9 10 11 12	1 2 3	1 2 3 4	1 2 3 4

SECONDARY SCHOOL; CITY & STATE   YEAR GRADUATED   MAJOR COURSE

COLLEGES/UNIVERSITIES ATTENDED	DATES ATTENDED	DATE GRADUATED OR DATE TO BE GRADUATED	DEGREE	MAJOR SUBJECT	GRADE AVERAGE	CLASS STANDING (TOP 1/2, 1/4, ETC.)
	FROM: TO:					
	FROM: TO:					
	FROM: TO:					
	FROM: TO:					
TRADE, TECHNICAL, BUSINESS SCHOOL	FROM: TO:					

HONORS & ACTIVITIES

OUTLINE ANY EDUCATIONAL ENDEAVOR IN WHICH YOU ARE NOW ENGAGED

LIST MEMBERSHIP IN TECHNICAL OR PROFESSIONAL SOCIETIES

WORK EXPERIENCE

IF OFFERED A POSITION, BY WHAT DATE SHOULD YOU RECEIVE THE OFFER?	DATE AVAILABLE	SALARY REQUIREMENTS

IF YOU HAVE PREVIOUSLY WORKED FOR WESTINGHOUSE ELECTRIC CORPORATION, WHERE AND DATES

DESCRIBE THE TYPE OF WORK IN WHICH YOU ARE INTERESTED BY VIRTUE OF APTITUDES, EDUCATION, AND EXPERIENCE

APPLICATION WILL BE RETAINED FOR 1 YEAR IF APPLICANT IS NOT HIRED.

PROFESSIONAL EMPLOYMENT APPLICATION
FORM 36487M

ALSO COMPLETE EMPLOYMENT APPLICATION SUPPLEMENT, FORM 46646.

FOOTNOTE NO. 1 – DO NOT COMPLETE IN THE STATE OF NEW YORK

FOOTNOTE NO. 2 – DO NOT COMPLETE IN THE STATES OF MASSACHUSETTS NEW JERSEY WASHINGTON

Figure 6.7, continued

EMPLOYMENT HISTORY (PLEASE COVER EMPLOYMENT FOR PAST TEN YEARS, INCLUDING U.S. MILITARY, IF APPLICABLE)

NAME AND ADDRESS OF PRESENT EMPLOYER   PHONE: (INCL. AREA CODE)

1.
EMPLOYED FROM   TO   POSITION

NAME AND TITLE OF IMMEDIATE SUPERVISOR   CURRENT SALARY

DESCRIBE DUTIES

WHY DO YOU PREFER A CHANGE?

NAME AND ADDRESS OF PREVIOUS EMPLOYER   PHONE: (INCL. AREA CODE)

2.
EMPLOYED FROM   TO   POSITION   REASON FOR LEAVING

NAME AND POSITION OF SUPERVISOR   FINAL SALARY

DESCRIBE DUTIES

NAME AND ADDRESS OF PREVIOUS EMPLOYER   PHONE: (INCL. AREA CODE)

3.
EMPLOYED FROM   TO   POSITION   REASON FOR LEAVING

NAME AND POSITION OF SUPERVISOR   FINAL SALARY

DESCRIBE DUTIES

OTHER EMPLOYERS

EMPLOYER   DATES EMPLOYED

4.
EMPLOYER   DATES EMPLOYED

5.
PLEASE LIST TWO (2) PROFESSIONAL REFERENCES

NAME   POSITION   COMPANY   ADDRESS   PHONE: (INCL. AREA CODE)

1.

2.
LIST PATENTS, PATENT APPLICATIONS & DISCLOSURES

LIST BOOKS, ARTICLES AND THESES WHICH YOU HAVE AUTHORED

HAVE YOU EVER APPLIED FOR A SECURITY CLEARANCE?   HAVE YOU EVER BEEN GRANTED A SECURITY CLEARANCE?

YES ☐   NO ☐   DATE: YES ☐   NO ☐   TYPE OF CLEARANCE GRANTED:

IT IS THE POLICY OF WESTINGHOUSE ELECTRIC CORPORATION AND SUBSIDIARY COMPANIES, CONSISTENT WITH THE LAW OF SOME STATES,* NOT TO REQUIRE AN APPLICANT TO SUBMIT TO TAKING A POLYGRAPH, LIE DETECTOR OR SIMILAR TEST OR EXAMINATION AS A CONDITION OF EMPLOYMENT OR CONTINUED EMPLOYMENT.

*IN THE STATE OF MARYLAND YOUR SIGNATURE IS REQUIRED TO ACKNOWLEDGE THAT YOU HAVE READ AND UNDERSTOOD THIS STATEMENT. _____
                                                                                      SIGNATURE

I CONSENT TO THE WESTINGHOUSE ELECTRIC CORPORATION (OR SUBSIDIARY COMPANY) SEEKING AND OBTAINING JOB-RELATED INFORMATION CONCERNING MY PREVIOUS EMPLOY-MENT, AND I GIVE CONSENT TO MY PREVIOUS EMPLOYERS TO PROVIDE JOB-RELATED INFORMATION CONCERNING MY EMPLOYMENT TO WESTINGHOUSE ELECTRIC CORPORATION (OR SUBSIDIARY COMPANY).

MY SIGNATURE BELOW INDICATES THAT I HAVE READ, UNDERSTOOD AND CONSENTED TO THE ABOVE STATEMENT AND THAT I HAVE MADE TRUE, CORRECT AND COMPLETE ANSWERS AND STATEMENTS ON THIS APPLICATION AND ANY SUPPLEMENTS TO IT IN THE KNOWLEDGE THAT THEY WILL BE RELIED UPON IN CONSIDERING MY APPLICATION FOR EMPLOYMENT, AND I UNDERSTAND THAT ANY OMISSION FALSE ANSWER OR STATEMENT MADE BY ME ON THIS APPLICATION, OR ANY SUPPLEMENT/S TO IT, WILL BE SUFFICIENT GROUND FOR MY DISCHARGE.

SIGNED _____
              APPLICANT   DATE

PLEASE SUPPLEMENT THIS RECORD WITH A RESUME OR ADDITIONAL INFORMATION WHICH YOU FEEL WILL AID IN OUR EVALUATION OF YOUR PROFESSIONAL QUALIFICATIONS.

FORM 36487M

Pause and Ponder

Based on a job you now hold or have held, what type of tests —
if any — were given prior to employment? What type of tests would
you recommend? Why did you choose these particular types of
tests?

Managers should be concerned with four points in testing: (1) court
decisions and federal agency rulings demand that test users must
be able to show that their tests actually predict success on a job if
those tests are used to make the decision to hire; (2) the test must
be valid, that is, test what it is supposed to test and not some other
area of performance; (3) the test should be reliable; it should provide
approximately the same score each time it is administered to an
individual; and (4) the test must not exclude a significantly greater
number of minority members than it does of nonminority persons.

Step 4: In-Depth Interviews. The in-depth interview provides the applicant's prospective manager or managers (the candidate may be
interviewed by more than one person) the opportunity to verify
information on hand and to find out more about the applicant's
interests, aspirations, and expectations. It also provides the opportunity to share information about the company, the job, and its
environmental conditions. The aim is to have a two-way communication that is mutually beneficial.

In-depth interviews may be structured or unstructured. In a
structured interview, little flexibility is allowed to the manager. All
candidates are asked the same questions in the same order, with
limited time to chat. An unstructured interview allows a free-flowing
conversation; only overall topics are prepared for discussion by the
interviewer.

Regardless of the type of interview format adopted, the effectiveness of the interview is directly related to the ability of the
interviewer. The good interviewer does not spend more time talking
than listening. In addition, the interviewer must be guided by what
are acceptable inquiries. He or she must never forget that inquiries
about age, marital status, ethnic background, and religion are illegal.
Table 6.2 shows us the questions that may not be asked during
the interview or on application blanks.

Step 5: Reference Checks. Applicants normally are asked to supply
personal or work references on the application blank. Personal references — ministers, doctors, friends — are of little value to an
employer because applicants normally do not list people who will
provide negative information. Work references, on the other hand,
have value, provided the reference feels free to communicate. A
telephone conversation between former manager and prospective

Table 6.2 What Employers Are Allowed to Ask on Employment Applications and in Interviews

Source: "Checklist to Avoid Bias Pitfalls" by James Strong. Reprinted by courtesy of the *Chicago Tribune*. Copyright 1978, *The Chicago Tribune*. All rights reserved.

	Acceptable Inquiry	Discriminatory Inquiry
Name	Additional information relative to change of name, use of an assumed name or nickname necessary to enable a check on applicant's work records.	The fact of a change of name or the original name of an applicant whose name has been legally changed.
Birthplace and Residence	Applicant's place of residence. Length of applicant's residence in state and/or city where the employee is located.	Birthplace of applicant. Birthplace of applicant's parents. Requirement that applicant submit birth certificate, naturalization, or baptismal record.
Creed and Religion	None.	Applicant's religious affiliation. Church, parish, or religious holidays observed by applicant.
Race or Color	General distinguishing physical characteristics such as scars, etc.	Applicant's race. Color of applicant's skin, eyes, hair, etc.
Photographs	None.	Photographs with application. Photographs after interview, but before hiring.
Age	If hired, can you furnish proof of age?	Date of birth or age of an applicant except when such information is needed for or to: 1. Maintain apprenticeship requirements based on a reasonable minimum age. 2. Satisfy the provisions of either state or federal minimum age statutes. 3. Avoid interference with the operation of the terms and conditions and administration of any bona fide retirement, pension, employee benefit program. 4. Verify that applicant is above the minimum legal age (21), but without asking for a birth certificate. Age specifications or limitations in newspaper advertisements which may bar workers under or over a certain age.

Table 6.2, continued

	Acceptable Inquiry	Discriminatory Inquiry
Education	Academic, vocational, or professional education, and the public and private schools attended.	
Citizenship	Are you in the country on a visa which would not permit you to work here?	Any and all inquiries into whether applicant is now or intends to become a citizen of the U.S., or any other inquiry related to the aspect of citizenship.
National Origin and Ancestry	None.	Applicant's lineage, ancestry, national origin, or nationality. Nationality of applicant's parents or spouse.
Language	Language applicant speaks and/or writes fluently.	Applicant's mother tongue. Language commonly used by applicant at applicant's home. How the applicant acquired ability to read, write, or speak a foreign language.
Relatives	Names of relatives already employed by the company. Name and address of person to be notified in case of accident or emergency. Name and/or address of any relative of applicant.	
Military Experience	Military experience of applicant in the Armed Forces of the United States. Whether applicant has received any notice to report for duty in the Armed Forces.	Applicant's military experience in other than U.S. Armed Forces. National Guard or Reserve Units of applicant. Draft classification or other eligibility for military service. Dates and conditions of discharge.
Organizations	Applicant's membership in any union or professional or trade organization. Names of any service organizations of which applicant is a member.	All clubs, social fraternities, societies, lodges, or organizations to which the applicant belongs other than professional, trade, or service organizations.

Table 6.2, continued

	Acceptable Inquiry	Discriminatory Inquiry
References	Names of persons willing to provide professional and/or character references for applicant. Names of persons who suggested applicant apply for a position with the employer.	The name of applicant's pastor or religious leader.
Sex and Marital Status	Maiden name of applicant.	Sex of applicant. Marital status of applicant. Dependents of applicant.
Arrest Record	Number and kinds of convictions for felonies.	The number and kinds of arrests of an applicant.
Height	None.	Any inquiry into height of applicant, except where it is a bona fide occupational requirement.

manager is usually more useful for collecting information than a written inquiry because the applicant's former bosses can answer simply and directly with no tangible evidence that could be used against them later. An employee who received a negative written reference could decide to use it as evidence in a defamation-of-character lawsuit against the author of that reference. Credit checks are considered to be discriminatory and are a questionable practice.

Step 6: Physical Examination. Prior to tendering a job offer, some organizations require potential employees to take a physical examination. The purposes of the examination are to: (1) prevent insurance claims for illnesses or injuries that occurred prior to employment by the company, (2) detect any communicable diseases, (3) certify that the person can physically perform the work. If there are physical requirements in the job description and job specifications, they must be valid. If they are not, the company may be accused of discrimination toward handicapped workers.

Step 7: Offer of Employment. At this point, the top-ranking applicant is offered a job by management. This may involve a series of negotiations on initial salary depending on the organization's compensation philosophy.

Orientation

Once an employee is hired, it is important to bring the person into the mainstream of the organization as quickly as possible. Firms accomplish this by developing an **orientation program** — *a series*

orientation program

of activities that gives the new employees information to help them adapt to the organization and their new jobs. Its purpose is to turn "them" (new employees) and "us" (the company) into "we."

The orientation program familiarizes the employee with the duties and benefits of employment. The employee receives an overview of the company — its history, products and services, organization structure and important rules, policies, and procedures. The employee also completes appropriate paperwork, receives needed passes, has benefits explained, and reviews the job description. Finally, a sound orientation program provides the opportunity for the employee to meet co-workers, spend time with the immediate supervisor, and become familiar with the new work environment. The result: the new employee feels more secure and settled.

Training

Training *supplies the skills, knowledge, and attitudes needed by subordinates to improve their abilities to perform their jobs.* The amount and type of training depend on the type of job, the present skills of the employee, and the resources of the organization. Several training methods can be used.

— **Classroom training** is *training conducted away from the pressures of the work environment.* The employee learns the basic skills of the job and then is sent to the work force.

— **On-the-job training (OJT)** is *a technique of teaching job skills while the person performs the job.* Training normally is provided by the supervisor and co-workers.

— **Vestibule training** is *training conducted in a simulated work environment complete with sample equipment.* The trainee is placed in this environment without the pressure of meeting production figures. The United Park Telephone Company in Winter Park, Florida, uses this method for training telephone operators. They learn on model switchboards, handling simulated calls on tape, and then advance to a real board after their training is complete.

Organizations can provide training through their own facilities or locate outside sources. Some companies have developed in-house, or company, schools that hold courses of varying length at company

Margin terms: training

classroom training

on-the-job training (OJT)

vestibule training

Pause and Ponder

What type of training have you received on various jobs you performed? Was the type received appropriate for each job? What would you recommend? Why?

owned or sponsored facilities. Firms like Xerox, IBM, and General Motors all have their own training schools. Gestetner Corporation, an internationally prominent copy equipment manufacturer, trains its 350 technicians in its Yonkers, New York, training center.[5]

Another option is to develop cooperative training relationships that consist of courses offered by colleges, universities, and private organizations in response to the needs of the firm. General Motors has developed cooperative training relationships with community colleges to supplement their own in-house schools. Automotive technicians receive classroom theory, laboratory instruction, and actual on-the-job training while enrolled in the program.

Performance Appraisal

performance appraisal

Once an employee has received training and has performed in a job for a period of time it is normal for an organization to conduct a performance appraisal. A **performance appraisal** is *a formal measure or rating of an employee's job performance compared with established job standards.* Performance appraisal should be an integral part of a company's human resources management program because it:

1. Provides feedback on the success of previous training and discloses the need for additional training
2. Aids in developing plans for improvement based on agreed-on goals, strengths, and weaknesses
3. Identifies growth opportunities
4. Documents present job performance to provide managers with

Performance appraisal provides an opportunity to hear feedback and to develop plans for future growth.

information to make decisions on salary, promotion, demotion, transfer, and termination

5. Provides the opportunity for formal feedback

Each organization has its own performance appraisal system. How often a person is evaluated and how the person is appraised differ in each organization. A company may require a manager to rate an employee once or twice a year. Ideally, the more frequent the contact, the greater the opportunity to clear up misunderstandings, offer guidance, and give encouragement and support.

Companies differ on how they appraise employees. A company may use a subjective or an objective appraisal system. A **subjective performance appraisal system** is *based on the personal viewpoint of the manager.* Notice in Table 6.3 that time management, attitude, knowledge of the job, and communication are not specific. What does each mean? Also notice the rating scale — excellent, good, fair, and poor. What does each mean?

A more specific approach is shown in Table 6.4 — an **objective performance appraisal system.** In this system *the specific performance areas are identified for the employee, as are the results expected.* Figure 6.8 provides an illustration of a performance appraisal form. Is it subjective or objective?

subjective performance appraisal system

objective performance appraisal system

Personnel Changes: Moving Up and Moving On

Through the process of performance appraisal, management develops information to make employment decisions. For example, management can reward positive performance with an increase in pay based on the company's compensation program.

Other possible uses of the appraisal include decisions on promotions, transfers, demotions, and separations. In addition to management decisions for personnel changes, employees make decisions to find employment elsewhere and to retire. Human resources man-

	Excellent	Good	Fair	Poor
Time Management		✔		
Attitude		✔		
Knowledge of Job	✔			
Communication			✔	

Table 6.3 Subjective Performance Appraisal System

Table 6.4 Objective Performance Appraisal System

Goal-Setting Areas	Goals for Six Months	Actual
Production: Actual units produced	15,000 per month	
Turnover: Percentage of personnel exiting a department per month	15%	
Quality Control: Percentage of units rejected per month	3%	
Absenteeism: Number of workhours lost from job due to absentee workers	10%	
Safety: Workhours lost	50 maximum	

agers must deal with these personnel demands every day. Let's examine each.

promotion

Promotions. One employment decision is a promotion. A **promotion** is *a movement by a person into a position with higher pay and greater responsibilities.* Promotions reward competence and ambition. They act as incentives to perform above the average in one's present job and to expand one's abilities, aptitudes, and knowledge through additional training.

Promotion decisions, even though they should be rewards for performance, often are influenced by other factors. Federal and state laws affect the ways in which promotions can be made. Affirmative action programs may dictate who or what kind of person gets the promotion. Promotion of the best qualified and most eligible may be blocked by seniority rules and the union agreement. Regardless, promotions should be based as much as possible on performance.

transfer

Transfers. A second employment decision is a transfer. A **transfer** is *a lateral move from one position to another that has similar pay and responsibility levels.* Usually the differences between the jobs are minor. Management uses transfers most often to fill temporary vacancies. Sometimes positions are created as a reward to allow a person to intern with or understudy another, higher job. These "assistant to" positions help the transferee to study the higher job up close.

Transfers may be used when management is preparing to replace a person who is about to move up or out of the company. Transfers also are used to staff a new operation, department, or division with experienced workers.

demotion

Demotions. Another employment decision is a demotion. A **demotion** is *a movement from one position to another that has less pay or responsibility attached to it.* Demotion can be used for punishment,

Figure 6.8 Sample Performance Evaluation Form
Source: Courtesy Texasgulf Inc.

Texasgulf exempt employee performance review

Name (Last, First, Initial)	Product Company	Hire Date	Today's Date
	Location	Date of prior review	
Position Title	Department	Time in current position	____ yrs. ____ mos.
		Time under appraiser's supervision	____ yrs. ____ mos.

Illustrate with specific examples of job performance

Performance Levels: Distinguished, Commendable, Competent, Adequate, Marginal, Not Applicable

Job Knowledge— How effective was this employee in maintaining and developing current technical, process, procedural and other job knowledge? **Illustrate:**

Performance level: _____

Managing for Results— How effective was this employee in planning, organizing, directing and controlling job activities to achieve timely results? **Illustrate:**

Performance level: _____

Human Relations—How effective was this employee in developing and maintaining sound working relationships with others to achieve results? (This includes obtaining cooperation; resolving conflict; communicating with superiors, peers, subordinates; evaluating performance; training and developing.) **Illustrate:**

Performance level: _____

Reasoning and Judgement—How effective was this employee in applying sound thinking, problem prevention, problem solving, and decision making skills to maintain and/or improve productivity? **Illustrate:**

Performance level: _____

Accountability—How effective was this employee in utilizing the human, materials and equipment, and budget resources to maintain and/or improve cost effectiveness? **Illustrate:**

Performance level: _____

Indicate overall evaluation of this employee's performance taking into consideration the relative job-importance of each of the performance categories above. Explain:

Overall performance level: _____

Figure 6.8, continued

performance improvement plan

What specific training/development activities are planned to help this employee maintain and improve present job performance? (Ex.: job assignments, skills coaching, on-the-job training, vacation relief, general/specific educational programs, trade/professional association, internal training programs, outside seminars, community groups, etc.)

Training/Development Activity	Planned Start Date	Planned Completion Date

Employee's comments on this performance review and improvement plan:

_____
Signature   Date

Appraiser's comments on this performance review and improvement plan discussion:

_____
Signature   Title   Date

Reviewed by:

_____
Signature   Title   Date

Tg 380

but most organizations refuse it as an option, preferring instead to suspend the employee or assess a financial penalty through the forfeiture of pay. The reason for this reluctance is that a demotion staffs a position with an embarrassed and often angry worker who is not likely to be productive or any better behaved than he or she was in the former position.

Demotions have their place in staffing, however. When a demotion is made to keep an employee, as a temporary measure it can be an important staffing solution. If a person's job is being eliminated, he or she may be offered a position that represents a demotion. There is no shame or embarrassment attached to such a move, only concern for the individual. The motive is to give the person time to retrain or become qualified for a higher position.

Separations. The last category of employment decision making by management is separation. **Separation** is *the loss of an employee to an organization through layoff, termination, retirement, or resignation.*

> — A **layoff** is *a temporary separation dictated by the level of business a company is experiencing.* When and if business conditions improve employees are recalled to work. Companies have developed layoff procedures that attempt to combine affirmative action, performance, and seniority to determine the order of layoff and recall. Despite this balancing attempt, layoffs tied to affirmative action have caused bitterness among workers with seniority who have been laid off while their less experienced affirmative-action-hired counterparts have remained on the job.[6]
>
> — **Termination** is *a permanent separation from the company.* An employee is terminated, or fired, owing to unsatisfactory performance or violation of work rules.
>
> — **Retirement** is *a person's intention to stop working for the rest of his or her life.* Many companies have mandatory retirement ages, although the 1978 amendment to the 1967 Age Discrimination Act prohibits private employers with twenty or more employees from forcibly retiring workers under the age of seventy on the basis of age alone. Other companies have developed early retirement programs as an incentive for developing loyalty. These programs also provide younger employees with the opportunity for potential advancement by encouraging older workers to retire, which opens up senior positions.
>
> — **Resignation** is *a voluntary separation in which a worker leaves to accept another position.* Workers resign for varied reasons — to take more challenging or rewarding jobs, to move to other parts of the country, or to pursue new careers.

separation

layoff

termination

retirement

resignation

Organizational Responsibility. Organizations have the responsibility for the employment process. In bearing this responsibility organizations must safeguard against management practices that may be discriminatory and that can result in management malpractice suits. The number of suits is on the rise because of management dismissals — firings involving sex, race, age, national origin, physical handicaps, or violation of good faith between employer and employee.[7]

Compensation

Compensation of employees is a major responsibility area in human resources management. Human resources managers are charged with the job of designing a program to attract and retain qualified applicants. In doing this the manager must measure the worth of each job and establish compensation that is fair in relation to other jobs in the organization and in the geographic area. Companies normally offer several forms of compensation based on the job itself and the effect of outside influences.

What Influences Compensation?

Fair Labor Standards Act

Legislation, a union contract, rising prices, and competitive activities all influence management's pay system. The **Fair Labor Standards Act** is *a 1938 federal law that requires most employers to pay a minimum hourly wage and overtime pay of one-and-one-half times the base rate for any hours worked in excess of 40 per week.* Executives and professional employees are exempt from this overtime provision, and the law also applies in different ways to different types of businesses. It has been amended extensively since the original minimum wage of $0.25 an hour went into effect in 1938; the current minimum wage is $3.35 an hour.

Unionized workers and management may negotiate a contract that specifies certain pay rates and a program of pay increases. Rising prices affect a firm's pay rates by forcing them upward because management wants the company to seem fair and attractive to applicants and to hold on to current employees. Occasionally managers find that skilled workers or professionals who are in short supply (such as petroleum engineers) can demand higher than normal pay, and competitors' pay scales must be closely matched if a firm wants to attract and retain the best applicants.

How Compensation Is Set

job evaluation

Human resources managers use **job evaluation** as *a technique of placing each job within its order of importance in the organization to establish its proper compensation.* Factors such as responsibility, education, skill, training, and working conditions may be examined to help management decide where each job fits. The result is a job ladder, or hierarchy, that reaches from the company president to the lowest level of workers.

Once jobs have been evaluated and placed in their order of importance, management — taking into account such previously mentioned factors as legal requirements and supply and demand — creates **pay grades.** These are *pay categories that relate dollar values to the job ladder developed through job evaluation.* Each job may have a pay range of several thousand dollars, so jobholders do not have to be promoted to get a raise.

pay grades

Types of Compensation

Compensation for a job is based on either time put into a job or what is produced on the job. In addition, compensation can be provided through bonuses, profit sharing, stock options, and pensions. Let's examine each.

Wages is *compensation based on hours worked* while **salary** is *compensation based on weeks or months worked.* It is intended to provide pay for the hours worked and not for what is produced. An hourly wage is the means of compensation generally provided for lower-level jobs in the organization. Managerial, professional, clerical, and secretarial employees normally are paid by salary.

wages
salary

Compensation based on production, known as **piecework,** *pays employees according to the number of units they produce.* As an example, agricultural workers may be paid according to the number of boxes or bags of produce picked. In sales, employees may receive a **commission** — *a percentage paid to a salesperson of the price of each item sold.* Crown Zellerbach loggers in Washington and Oregon swapped hourly rates averaging $12 for pay based on output. The results — more productivity and satisfaction.[8]

piecework

commission

After the base method of compensation is determined, management may choose to provide a bonus, profit sharing, stock options, and pensions.

Bonus. A **bonus** is *incentive money paid to employees in addition to their regular compensation.* It may be based on superior production, effective cost control, company earnings, or other performance factors. Some salespeople, for example, may receive a bonus for exceeding sales goals.

bonus

Profit Sharing. **Profit sharing** refers to *paying a portion of company profits to employees as a performance incentive in addition to their regular compensation.* Firms such as Kaiser Aluminum & Chemical, Xerox, and IBM have long realized that sharing in a company's profits can give employees greater feelings of belonging and commitment, with a corresponding increase in motivation, morale, loyalty, and productivity.

profit sharing

Stock Option. A **stock option** is *a plan that permits employees to buy shares of stock in the employee's firm at or below the present market price.* Some firms have payroll deduction plans to encourage employee participation, and occasionally top managers receive stock

stock option

options, bonuses, and salary in a total compensation package. Companies may set aside large blocks of shares to sell directly to employees. This tactic has been employed successfully by Apple Computer, 3 Com Corp, and Seagate Technology as a means of attracting and retaining qualified people.[9]

pension plan

Pension Plan. Employers also may create a **pension plan,** which is *a program to provide a retirement income to workers by holding a percentage of their earnings in reserve.* The amount is then paid to them after their employment with the company ends. Pensions are not collected only on retirement; employees who qualify for pension benefits can receive a lump-sum payment of their benefits when they resign or are fired. Employees' contributions to the plan are matched by some companies with contributions made from company profits.

fringe benefits

Indirect Compensation: Employee Fringe Benefits. In addition to direct compensation for the job being performed, human resources managers build into the work environment **fringe benefits** — *nonfinancial rewards provided for employees.* Most of them fit into one of the following categories.

- Life, health, and dental insurance
- Paid vacations
- Sick pay
- Holidays, funeral leave, and emergency leave
- Discounts on merchandise or services
- Paid lunch and rest periods
- Tuition reimbursement
- Child care

Indirect benefits typically have averaged between 22 and 35 percent of a company's payroll.

Some firms are moving to provide a "cafeteria" plan for fringe benefits, in which employees can choose a combination of insurance and other options best suited to their individual and family circumstances. E-Systems recently applied such a plan to a group of employees.[10] Another emerging trend is the number of businesses getting involved in child care benefits. Walt Disney World and Intermedics are but two of many firms providing this option.[11]

OSHA: Regulating Safety in the Work Place

Human resources management also involves providing for the health and safety of the employees in the work environment. In focusing on this activity a major influence is the **Occupational Safety and Health Act.** Enacted in 1971 this is *a federal law that requires most employers to create and maintain safe, healthful working conditions.* Although the self employed, farms that employ only immediate family members, and work places covered by other federal

Occupational Safety and Health Act

agencies or laws are exempt, more than 5 million work places are covered under the act.

The Scope of OSHA Activities

The 1971 act also created the Occupational Safety and Health Administration (OSHA) and empowered it to develop, implement, and enforce job safety and health standards in four categories: general industry, maritime, construction, and agriculture. In addition to complying with these standards and filing reports about this compliance, employers must display certain OSHA posters, notices, report summaries, and other material in work areas.

To check on employers, OSHA has more than 1,000 compliance officers or inspectors who visit work places. These compliance visits may occur routinely or they may be in response to employee complaints about safety or health conditions where they work. If employers do not comply at all or if they comply after OSHA's deadline date, they may be fined or penalized.

OSHA and Business

Since its creation OSHA has been tremendously controversial. Why? First, businesses complained about OSHA's scope: it had the ability to affect most companies in most industries. Second, the initial work-place rules were extremely detailed (one regulation set the distance between fire extinguishers and the floor). Finally, OSHA inspectors had the power to search work places without notice.

Cowboy _after_ O.S.H.A.

Source: Mr. James N. Devin, Independence, Missouri. © 1972. Reproduced with permission.

The Straight Line

Management Malpractice

Employees Sue Employers

Through the years life has become more complicated for employers who, for various reasons, want to dismiss an employee. This act has now literally become a federal case and lays an employer wide open to a lawsuit if an employee wants to bring charges. The charges include everything from age discrimination to operating in bad faith.

No longer can employers post dismissal notices when they merely want to cut back by laying off one or more employees. Owing to the recent changes in our laws, employees can bring what are termed *management malpractice suits* against employers. Disgruntled employees not only have access to unions and federal and state agencies to air their grievances, they also can go before the courts, asking juries to right wrongs and award compensation and punitive damages.

There is an increased aware-ness of legal remedies. Court decisions have given employees more rights and access to damages, including punitive damages. When employees are fired, they bring suits against employers based on discrimination because of sex, race, age, national origin, physical handicap, or union activities. More and more frequently the suits allege unjust dismissal, which accuses the employer of violating a contract, a covenant of good faith and fair dealing, or of inflicting emotional distress. The contention that a job is a person's right to enjoy for as long as the person does the work satisfactorily is being established by litigation. At least seven states recognize unjust dismissal as cause for action; in some instances, it is subject to punitive as well as compensatory damages. The next cause for legal action likely will be for unjust demotion.

What recourse does a com-

Although OSHA is still controversial, some changes have occurred. Approximately 1,000 of the original OSHA standards have been simplified or eliminated because they applied to obsolete manufacturing equipment, because they did not apply directly to safety, or because they were too detailed. In addition, beginning in the late 1970s OSHA began to direct its efforts more toward ensuring healthful working conditions and less toward safety. Finally, the powers of OSHA inspectors were limited by a 1978 United States Supreme Court ruling that allowed business owners to deny the inspectors entrance to companies unless they were armed with search warrants.

Summary

Once the organization is developed, the challenge to management is to match personnel with the jobs identified and to provide for their long-range growth and welfare as members of the organization.

pany have, and how can the work force be reduced without threat of a suit? It has been suggested that laying off the most recently hired employee is not an effective deterrent to a lawsuit. Instead workers and supervisors should evaluate each employee according to his or her skills and reliability. Employees then should be laid off by a strict point system, department by department.

Among the ways to avoid litigation, management needs to:

1. Rewrite the employees' handbook to remove questionable promises
2. Educate personnel directors in the legal aspects of their work
3. Include language on employee applications that clearly spells out the limitations of employment
4. Require each new employee to read and sign a copy of the work rules so there is no doubt that he or she understands work requirements and the legitimate grounds for dismissal
5. Institute formal grievance and arbitration procedures
6. Schedule more frequent and demanding evaluations of employee performance
7. Treat employees with courtesy and respect
8. Avoid hiring overqualified employees unless there is an imminent opportunity for advancement
9. Avoid blocking a terminated employee's future employment
10. Seek legal counsel when in doubt

The eventual outcome of management malpractice may be lawsuits initiated by employers who sue employees who quit without good cause.

For more about management malpractice, see Brian Heshizer and Harry Graham, "Justice Without Juries," *Management World*, March 1984, pp. 10, 11; George Stevens, "Firing Without Fear," *Management World*, March 1984, p. 11; Robert W. Goddard, "How to Avoid Employee Complaints That Could Lead to Litigation," *Management Review*, February 1984, pp. 58–61; Craig R. Waters, "The New Malpractice," *Inc.*, June 1983, pp. 136–140; and Richard Greene, "Fear of Firing," *Forbes*, April 25, 1983, p. 83.

Human resources management has this responsibility. As the staffing function of the organization its activities include human resources planning, recruitment, selection, orientation, training, performance appraisal, and compensation.

The human resources area is influenced by the legal environment. Specific employment decisions are made within the guidelines of equal employment opportunity and affirmative action.

The activities involved in human resources management should be viewed as a series of interrelated steps that managers and specialists perform to acquire and maintain the right people in the right jobs. These activities include:

— *Human resources planning*, which involves human resources forecasting, human resources inventory, and a comparison of these two to determine the need for recruiting. It also involves the development of job descriptions and job specifications as an aid to recruiting.
— *Recruitment*, which attempts to identify and attract candidates

to meet the requirements of anticipated or actual job openings. Two sources for recruitment are inside and outside the company.

— *Selection*, an activity that decides which candidates out of the pool of applicants developed in recruiting have the abilities, skills, and characteristics most closely matching job demands. The candidates go through a selection process that includes completing an application blank, a preliminary interview, testing, an in-depth interview, a reference check, and a physical examination.

— *Orientation*, which includes a series of activities that gives new employees information to help them adjust to the organization and their new jobs.

— *Training*, which attempts to supply the skills, knowledge, and attitudes needed by individuals to improve their abilities to perform their jobs. Types of training are classroom, on the job, and vestibule.

— *Performance appraisal*, which measures an employee's job performance compared with established job standards. There are two types of appraisal — subjective and objective.

The results of the appraisal process and the actions of employees cause a number of employee-personnel actions. Employees may choose to resign or retire; management may choose to promote, transfer, demote, lay off, or terminate an employee.

Human resources managers are responsible for employee compensation. They must design a program to attract and retain qualified applicants. In doing this they rate the worth of each job and establish pay grades. Compensation is based on time or on output. Additional compensation in the form of bonuses, profit sharing, stock options, and pensions also are developed. Indirect compensation — insurance, paid vacations — completes the compensation program.

Human resources management also includes providing for the health and safety of employees in the work environment. A major influence on this is the Occupational Safety and Health Act.

Key Terms

Affirmative Action
bonus
classroom training
commission
demotion
Equal Employment Opportunity
Fair Labor Standards Act
fringe benefits
human resources forecasting
human resources inventory
human resources management

human resources planning
job analysis
job description
job evaluation
job specification
layoff
objective performance appraisal system
Occupational Safety and Health Act
on-the-job training (OJT)

orientation program
pay grades
pension plan
performance appraisal
piecework
profit sharing
promotion
recruitment
resignation
retirement
selection

separation	termination	vestibule training
stock option	training	wages
subjective performance appraisal system	transfer	

For Review and Discussion

1. What is the importance of human resources management on the long-range development of a company?

2. What activities are included in human resources management?

3. What is the objective of equal employment opportunity legislation? How does this differ from affirmative action?

4. What steps are involved in human resources planning? What factors are considered in deciding to train or recruit?

5. What is the purpose of a job analysis? A job description? A job specification?

6. What are the benefits to a company of internal recruiting? Why would a company choose to recruit from external sources?

7. What is the purpose of an employment application blank?

8. What is the objective of a preliminary interview?

9. What limitations are placed on the use of testing for employment? What is validity?

10. Who should conduct the in-depth interview? Why?

11. What is the value of reference checking? How can it be improved?

12. What is the purpose of a preemployment physical examination?

13. What elements are included in an orientation program? What is the purpose of orientation?

14. Contrast on-the-job training with vestibule training. When might you use each?

15. What is the purpose of performance appraisal? Distinguish between subjective and objective appraisal.

16. Distinguish between transfers, promotions, and demotions; between layoffs and termination; between resignations and retirements.

17. What factors does a human resources manager analyze in developing a compensation program?

18. What are the two basic types of compensation? How do they differ?

19. Explain the different characteristics of stock options, profit sharing, and bonuses.

20. Discuss how the Occupational Safety and Health Act affects employee working conditions.

Applications

Case 6.1 A Quality Decision?

Judy Bartholomew, Director of Employee Relations for King's Quality Stores, was involved in a heated discussion with her boss, Jessie Hernandez, Vice-President of Human Resources.

Judy But, Jessie, I think we have more to lose than gain if we adopt your idea. I'm really concerned about using lie detectors as part of our selection process! What is the emotional cost to a person if we make a mistake?

Jessie It will improve the chances of selecting a better qualified candidate. I'm convinced that if we couple the polygraph with personality tests that the Willis Company uses, we'll significantly improve the quality of the people we hire.

Judy Jessie, we don't have any hard evidence that polygraphs do what they say they can do. Besides, I really don't feel good about hooking everyone up to a lie detector.

On point number two, why personality tests? Right now our selection process calls for the prospective employee to complete an application blank and to receive a preliminary interview, an in-depth interview, a reference check, and a physical. That's pretty thorough.

Jessie Judy, I want people with integrity working here. I also believe that we have to have the right personality in the right job. Don't you agree?

Judy was unable to reply. She was concerned about sound personnel practices as well as maintaining her objective viewpoint in personnel practices. Her reply needed to contain both elements.

Questions

1. Does the use of a lie detector test invade a person's right to privacy?

2. What did Judy mean by "I think we have more to lose than gain if we adopt your idea"?

3. Is Judy correct — do the benefits override the costs?

4. What are the purposes of employment tests? What should the personality tests indicate? Do they?

5. Help Judy develop an answer. Write a response to Jessie Hernandez concerning the use of lie detectors and the personality tests.

Case 6.2 What's Fair and What's Right?

Synco Supplies is a rapidly expanding industrial supply house located in Baton Rouge, Louisiana. Over the past 3 years it has grown from twenty-five employees to eighty. With more expansion in sight, Synco decided to employ a full-time human resources manager. The person chosen for the job was Kevin McCord, a recent college graduate with 1 year of experience in personnel.

As part of Kevin's orientation to Synco Supplies, he had arranged a series of interviews with department heads. These sessions were designed to acquaint both parties and to provide Kevin with some information on the company's past history.

Kevin was involved in a session with Harold Armes, Director of Customer Services. The "Silver Fox," as Harold was known, was considered a wily manager, always looking for an angle. Everything was progressing as planned until Harold began to relate a story about one of his subordinate managers.

"Before we promoted Roseanne to her supervisory position she was only making $10,000 a year. The job she was promoted into calls for a minimum base of $20,000 per year. Well, I just couldn't see raising Roseanne all the way to that salary at once because we were buying an unknown quantity.

"I told her I had two choices. One, to promote her or, two, to go outside the organization and hire an experienced person. I made an agreement with her that within 18 months she would be making the base salary called for.

"I have been putting through raises for her, but it seems she is unhappy with the situation and has been pushing me to get her to the base level. I can't understand it, after only 10 months she is earning $16,000. You're the management expert, what do you think about it?"

Questions

1. Is what Harold has done within the guidelines of equal employment and affirmative action?

2. How does Harold's action relate to good compensation practice (pay the person or pay for the job)?

3. If you were Kevin, how would you respond from both the law and compensation practices?

4. What recommendation would you make?

7

Managing People: Motivation and Leadership

Chapter Outline

Chapter Objectives

After studying this chapter, you should be able to:

1. Explain the importance of, and the manager's role in, developing a positive work environment.
2. Explain the influence of Theory X and Theory Y on leadership, motivation, and the work environment.
3. Explain the importance of managers' recognizing individual differences and needs and their influence on motivation.
4. Summarize the motivational theories of Maslow and Herzberg and explain the implications of each on employee motivation.
5. Describe the effect of leadership on employee performance.
6. Identify and explain the three factors that influence the choice of leadership style.
7. Describe the three major styles of leadership.
8. Discuss the concept of morale and its effect on quality and quantity of work.
9. Describe techniques that managers and organizations can use to improve the work environment, increase motivation, and improve morale.

Treat people as if they were what they ought to be and you help them to become what they are capable of being.
— Johann W. von Goethe, German poet

The Truth According to Treybig

James G. Treybig (pronounced try-big), a Texas native in his mid-forties, is founder and president of Tandem Computers in Cupertino, California. Jimmy T., as the Tandem people call him, received his B.S. and M.B.A. degrees from Stanford. Before starting Tandem, he worked for several years in sales and marketing at Texas Instruments and Hewlett-Packard and in venture capital in San Francisco.

Since its founding in the midseventies, Tandem Computers has been remarkably successful. Projected sales for 1984 are over $1 billion. Credit for the firm's tremendous success goes to Treybig, who also is responsible for its elaborate management scheme.

Treybig's style is typified by his philosophy that most people need less management. He relies on ideology and incentives to keep employees satisfied in their work and to increase production figures, and he has successfully combined capitalism and humanism to

achieve his goals. There are no time clocks at Tandem. The employees are paid for the amount of work they produce — not for the amount of time they work. Managers may not always know how many hours the employees work, but they do know the results in terms of productivity.

Treybig's management philosophy covers the spectrum of incentives, including monetary and recreational. He offers generous stock options, worth $100,000 to the employees who have been with Tandem since it was founded. The recreation includes jogging trails, space for exercise and yoga classes, company-supplied barbecues for employees working overtime, a swimming pool, and a weekly beer bust.

The indoctrination program is extensive as Tandem recognizes that the key to success is a good staff. It encourages loyalty, hard work, self-esteem, and respect for co-workers, and it gives each employee an overall understanding of the company's business and of

In the previous chapter you were introduced to the concepts involved in staffing the organization. The manager now needs to direct energy and attention to the people selected to fill the positions. Organizations flourish through the efforts of individuals. Because people are the most important resource a manager has, managers must learn to work effectively with them and through them.

This chapter focuses on human relationships in the work environment. Managers who understand why people act in certain ways will be more successful in moving an organization toward its goals than those who see management as a mechanical, impersonal series of activities.

the 5-year plan. Employees feel that they are a part of the team and have a sense of pride in being trusted with corporate information.

But all cannot and does not go smoothly all the time. As Treybig knows, initiating and maintaining are separate functions — and maintaining is the more difficult. Too much emphasis on growth and not enough on maintaining the "small-company" culture contributed to Tandem's management and revenue problems in 1982. The company realized that additional internal controls were needed to manage its rapid growth in order to maintain its desired growth rate and percent of profits.

Treybig began working on ways to remain true to his management philosophy — regardless of company size — while continuing to increase profits. His concern for open communication with all employees led him to invest heavily in a Tandem television network designed to keep employees in all locations in touch with corporate headquarters. After some trial and error and listening to employees' input, Tandem television is getting its job done through training programs, marketing presentations, divisional meetings, and "Tandem Talk," a monthly discussion between Treybig and company officers. Tandem is once again maintaining its small-company culture based on Treybig's management philosophy as summed up in "The Truth According to Treybig":

1. All people are good.
2. People, workers, management, and company are all the same thing.
3. Every single person in a company must understand the essence of the business.
4. Every employee must benefit from the company's success.
5. You must create an environment where all of the above can happen.

For more about Jim Treybig, see "Prime Time at Tandem," *Inc.*, June 1983, pp. 37, 38; "An Acid Test for Tandem's Growth," *Business Week*, February 28, 1983, pp. 64, 66; and Myron Magnet, "Managing by Mystique at Tandem Computers," *Fortune*, June 28, 1982, pp. 84–91.

Developing a Positive Work Environment

Once an organization has acquired the best possible human resources to perform a job, each manager is faced with the challenge of creating a positive work environment where the employees can grow. The work environment is the key to developing and maintaining motivated workers who will achieve organizational objectives. What elements should a manager focus on in creating this climate? Managers create a positive climate by:

— Recognizing people as individuals
— Acquiring resources for goal accomplishment
— Providing rewards based on performance
— Developing, communicating, and reinforcing expectations for performance, group citizenship, initiative, and creativity
— Encouraging risk taking
— Providing for participation in goal setting

What is the result of this effort? The manager creates a stable work environment where expectations are known, the individual is appreciated, individual goals can be met, all people receive equitable treatment, trust exists, and motivation is supported. The challenge for management is to provide the leadership that can create this climate.

Philosophy of Management: Theory X and Theory Y

philosophy of management

A factor that sets the foundation for creating the work environment is *a manager's* **philosophy of management** *or attitude about work and the people who perform that work.* The manager's philosophy is important because it influences both the leadership and motivation approaches a manager will select. A manager who sees subordinates as ambitious, eager, wishing to do work well, wanting to be independent, and enjoying work will take far different actions than a manager who sees subordinates in an opposite vein.

Douglas McGregor, a professor of industrial management, has provided two sets of assumptions about workers. These sets of assumptions — Theory X and Theory Y — serve as a philosophic base for a manager's approach to working with subordinates.

Theory X

Theory X *is a philosophy of management with a negative perception of subordinates' potential for work and general attitudes toward work. It assumes that subordinates dislike work, are poorly motivated, and require close supervision.* A manager who has these beliefs would probably control the group, use negative motivation, and refuse to allow individual employee decision making. Table 7.1 provides a full view of Theory X.

Theory Y

Theory Y, on the other hand, is *a philosophy of management with a positive perception of subordinates' potential for and general*

Pause and Ponder

How would you describe your work environment? Do you feel you receive support and appreciation? Are you treated as an individual? Is there trust in the environment? Why or why not?

Theory X	Theory Y
People basically dislike work and avoid it whenever possible.	Most people find work as natural as play or rest and develop an attitude toward work based on their experience with it.
Because most people dislike work, they have to be closely supervised and threatened with punishment to reach objectives.	People do not need to be threatened with punishment; they will work voluntarily toward organizational objectives to which they are committed.
Most people prefer to be told what to do, have little ambition, want to avoid responsibility, and want security above all else.	The average person working in a good human relations environment will accept and seek responsibility.
	Most people have a high degree of imagination, ingenuity, and creativity with which to solve organizational problems.
	Although people have intellectual potential, managers only partially utilize it in modern industrial life.

Table 7.1 Theory X and Theory Y Assumptions About Workers

attitudes toward work. It assumes, as shown in Table 7.1, *that subordinates can be self-directing, will seek responsibility, and find work as natural as play or rest.* The natural outcome of this belief is a manager who encourages people to seek responsibility, involves people in decision making, and works with people to achieve their goals.

The important point about Theory X and Theory Y is that the philosophy a manager has about people influences the type of work climate a manager tries to create and ultimately how people are treated. Remember, managers — like all people — often reap the attitudes they sow. If you expect someone to not perform, eventually that may happen. A direct outcome of a manager's philosophy of management is the ability to recognize and work with people as individuals.

People Are Individuals

All of us are individuals. We have different personalities. We think differently. We all have different needs, wants, values, expectations, and goals in life. We are not made from the same mold. We all want to be treated as a special person because we are unique. We all are at different places in our lives. We perceive things differently depending on where we are at various times. Being liked may be important to us today; a year from now it may be more important to us to be recognized for what we have accomplished.

Managers need to recognize people as individuals and to work with their individual differences. This recognition goes one step further. Because each of us is an individual, we all are motivated differently. The more managers know about motivation, the more successful they will be in working with people. Let's examine motivation.

Motivation

motivation

An employee's ultimate productivity and success in the organization hinge on **motivation,** *feelings that drive someone toward a particular objective.* By understanding and applying basic motivational concepts, managers can create an environment that supports a worker's desire to work, thereby getting the extra effort. One factor to look at is an employee's needs.

Needs and Motivation

needs

Each of us has **needs,** *deficiencies a person is feeling at a particular time or things that are missing from a person's life.* These needs create tension that results in wants. This in turn leads us to perform some act that relieves that tension. We then remain satisfied (tension satisfied, needs and wants fulfilled) until the next need occurs and the cycle starts again. Figure 7.1 illustrates how needs motivate people.

Needs can be strong motivators in the work environment when there is a way provided by management to satisfy these needs. For example, employees who want to join a country club, move to a more desirable neighborhood, or send their children to expensive private colleges may do superior work to earn a promotion if that promotion brings a pay increase to make those things affordable. Salespeople who are paid on commission also may work hard because their efforts translate directly into dollars, which they need to maintain or improve their present standard of living. Managers are responsible for providing the work environment where people can meet their needs. As a result, the needs of the organization will be met, employees will be motivated, and productivity will be increased.

Managers also need to recognize that a satisfied need does not motivate people. If you have the home you always wanted and know you can afford the food you want whenever you are hungry, then these things no longer motivate you. But something else does: more complex needs, such as more prestige, may become a priority for you. The challenge for management is to provide the ability to satisfy these more complex needs in the work environment.

"Now then, what makes you feel that we're dehumanizing you, 624078?"
Source: *The Wall Street Journal.* Reproduced with permission of Eli Stein.

Maslow's Hierarchy of Needs

A tool managers can apply to understand human needs was developed by Abraham H. Maslow in his book *Motivation and Personality.*[1] Maslow developed a five-level sequence, or hierarchy, of human needs,

Figure 7.1 Basic Motivation Models

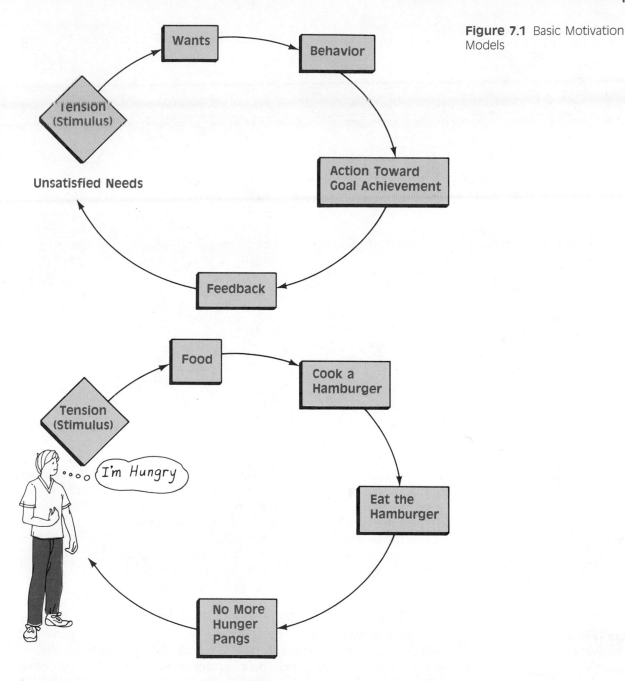

which is shown in Figure 7.2. A major point of this hierarchy is that each need level must be generally satisfied before the person attempts to fill those needs on the next level. The first two needs are considered primary, or lower-order, needs; the remaining three are secondary, or higher-order, needs. Let's discuss each of these levels.

Physiological need is *the fundamental need for food, clothing, and shelter.* People must be able to satisfy this need before they acknowledge any of the higher ones. Someone who faces death by

physiological need

Figure 7.2 Abraham Maslow's
Hierarchy of Human Needs
Source: Abraham H. Maslow, "A Theory
of Human Motivation," *Psychological
Review* 50 (1943): 370–396.

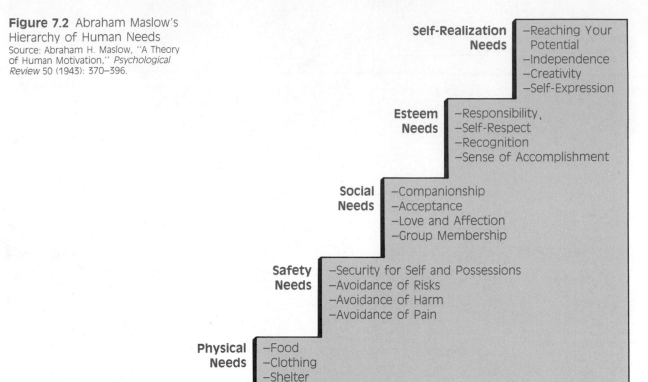

starvation or exposure may resort to murder or cannibalism to meet
fundamental, life-sustaining needs, despite what society might think.
Work satisfies these needs if an employer pays wages or salaries
that allow employees to buy the simple necessities.

safety and security need

The **safety and security need** is *the need to avoid bodily
harm and uncertainty about one's well-being.* People become conscious of this need after they fulfill the first one. This kind of need
satisfaction would come from tenure for a college professor, a union
contract defining policies and procedures for layoff for a steelworker,
or insurance and retirement programs for employees.

social need

Social need is *the need to be accepted by people whose
opinions and companionship you value.* On the job pleasant relations with co-workers help people meet these needs. The traditional
office conversation at the water cooler reflects employees' needs to
interact socially as well as in their official business roles. The groups
employees form at lunchtime are also a result of their need to be
social. In other areas of life, involvement in religious, civic, and
professional organizations and activities with family and friends
satisfy them.

esteem need

Esteem need is *the need to feel important, admired, and
worthwhile.* Like the previous level of need, this one is fulfilled by
a combination of activities on and off the job. Although work can
fulfill this need by giving out prestigious promotions, a high salary,

and organizational status symbols, some employees disregard job-related fulfillment, choosing instead to pursue an outside activity that brings them praise and respect from others. Perhaps you have worked with someone who, although not a spectacular employee, was a recognized expert on rare coins, an authority on boating safety, or the local baseball commissioner.

Self-actualization *or* self-realization need is *the need to get the maximum reward from one's life experience; to maximize one's skills, abilities, and potential.* The capstone in Maslow's hierarchy, it is reaching your potential. A characteristic of people who are self-fulfilled through their work is rising to the top of an organization, a trait shown by many top executives of large corporations.

self-actualization *or* self-realization need

Companies can offer incentive programs that are targeted to satisfy employees' esteem needs.

The possibility of attaining self-fulfillment in work attracts many entrepreneurs to start their own businesses. Self-actualization also can be achieved by pursuing a variety of activities: a multimillionaire business owner who takes flying lessons and teaches lifesaving techniques at the local Red Cross or a registered nurse who lobbies for environmental issues and restores furniture both combine work and hobbies to achieve self-fulfillment. Table 7.2 presents twenty-three jobs rated according to boredom — those at the top of the list contribute least to this need's fulfillment.

Maslow's view of motivation challenges and assists managers to identify the needs of each worker — an often difficult task. By analyzing comments, attitudes, quality and quantity of work, and personal circumstances, the manager can identify the particular level of need that each one is trying to satisfy. Then the manager can try to build into each job the opportunity to satisfy those needs.

Table 7.2 Twenty-Three Typical Jobs Rated According to Boredom
Source: "Twenty-Three Typical Jobs According to Boredom" from *The Book of Lists* by David Wallechinsky, Irving Wallace, and Amy Wallace. Copyright © 1977 by David Wallechinsky, Irving Wallace, and Amy Wallace. By permission of William Morrow & Co.

Job	Boredom Rating[a]
1. Assembler (work paced by machine)	207
2. Relief worker on assembly line	175
3. Forklift-truck driver	170
4. Machine tender	169
5. Assembler (working at own pace)	160
6. Monitor of continuous flow goods	122
7. Accountant	107
8. Engineer	100
9. Tool-and-die maker	96
10. Computer programmer	96
11. Electronic technician	87
12. Delivery service courier	86
13. Blue-collar supervisor	85
14. White-collar supervisor	72
15. Scientist	66
16. Administrator	66
17. Train dispatcher	64
18. Policeman	63
19. Air traffic controller (large airport)	59
20. Air traffic controller (small airport)	52
21. Professor with administrative duties	51
22. Professor	49
23. Physician	48

[a]Based on interviews with 2,010 workers performing twenty-three different jobs, the Institute for Social Research at the University of Michigan drew up "boredom factors" for each occupation. The average was considered to be 100, and the higher the rating the more boring the job.

Workers' Circumstances	Levels of Need Demanding Satisfaction	Need Satisfying Actions
Two children entering college next year	Physiological/safety	Increase pay or train and promote to higher-paying job if justified; confirm job security.
Complains of not being appreciated	Ego/self-esteem	Examine job performance; find reasons for praise. Accept suggestions where applicable; build closer rapport.
Expresses concern over present firm being bought by a competitor	Safety	If possible, reassure that jobs will not be eliminated; otherwise frankly admit that certain jobs will be abolished; encourage and assist those affected to seek employment elsewhere.
New addition to closely knit work group feels uncomfortable; has difficulty becoming one of the gang	Social	Hold an open house at your home for subordinates, creating an opportunity for the newcomer to meet peers in an informal setting; encourage participation in company recreational activities; sponsor for membership in professional organizations.

Table 7.3 Workers' Needs and Appropriate Managerial Responses

Every supervisor is a catalyst to motivation. If the work experience is improved, thus satisfying certain needs more fully, employees will be motivated and the manager will harvest the benefits along with them. Table 7.3 presents examples of workers' circumstances, levels of need that they indicate, and supervisors' actions that satisfy those needs.

In addition to Maslow's model, a second theory has been developed to assist managers with motivation — the motivation-maintenance theory.

Herzberg's Motivation-Maintenance Model

Frederick Herzberg, another well-known observer of management, developed a theory of motivation in his motivation-maintenance model.[2] Herzberg's research indicates that two sets of factors, or conditions, affect how people behave in organizations. These two sets of factors are maintenance and motivation factors.

maintenance *or* hygiene factors

Maintenance Factors. The first set, **maintenance *or* hygiene factors,** are *those job factors that prevent dissatisfaction but do not generate satisfaction or motivate workers to greater effort.* They include the following:

1. Salary: adequate wages, salaries, and fringe benefits
2. Job security: company grievance procedures and seniority privileges
3. Working conditions: adequate heat, light, ventilation, and hours of work
4. Status: privileges, job titles, and other symbols of rank and position
5. Company policies: the policies of the organization and the fairness in administering those policies
6. Quality of technical supervision: whether or not the employee is able to receive answers to job-related questions
7. Quality of interpersonal relations among peers, supervisors, and subordinates: social opportunities as well as the development of comfortable operating relationships

Herzberg found that these factors are taken for granted. Workers feel that management is morally obliged to provide them, so when they do exist the response is neutral. A package of such fringe benefits as sick leave, paid vacations, health and life insurance, and a pension plan will not make workers do more than they must. Take them away, though — cancel company-paid medical insurance — and employees quickly become dissatisfied.

motivation factors

Motivation Factors. The second set, **motivation factors,** are *those job factors that provide satisfaction and therefore motivation, but whose absence causes no satisfaction to be achieved.* Herzberg's motivation factors are:

1. Achievement: opportunity for accomplishment and for contributing something of value when presented with a challenge
2. Recognition: acknowledgment that contributions have been worth the effort and that the effort has been noted and appreciated
3. Responsibility: acquisition of new duties and responsibilities, either through the expansion of a job or by delegation
4. Advancement: opportunity to improve one's organizational position as a result of job performance
5. The work itself: opportunity for self-expression, personal satisfaction, and challenge

Imagine a worker in a manufacturing plant who has a chance to advance to foreman. This opportunity may make that worker more satisfied with the job and motivated to do it more efficiently and productively. If the job contained only those fundamental maintenance factors mentioned earlier, however, the person would not necessarily become dissatisfied with it, and he or she could perform satisfactorily nonetheless.

Figure 7.3 illustrates the maintenance or hygiene and motivation factors. The hygiene factors operate in a range between no dissatisfaction if they are present in the work environment to high job dissatisfaction if they are not present. The motivators, if present in the work environment, can provide high satisfaction; if not present no satisfaction can result.

After studying Herzberg's factors, you can understand why employers who try to motivate employees with pay raises and other basic factors of job satisfaction are bound to be disappointed. If management includes automatic cost-of-living allowances in the company's compensation program to help workers keep pace with rising prices, for example, these pay increases simply maintain the status quo; they have no motivational power. Employees perceive them as maintenance factors — things that management should give them because it's only right.

Herzberg's Challenge to Managers. Herzberg's view of motivation differs from, but does not conflict with, Maslow's view. The supervisory challenge from Herzberg's standpoint is to give workers the basics, the maintenance or hygiene factors, and enhance the job with ingredients that employees do not take for granted. Review the list of motivational factors and you will see that practically all supervisors have the power to make subordinates' jobs more rewarding by granting them more responsibility, praising their accomplishments, and making them feel that they are succeeding. Top management, by designing and guiding the overall organization, can create an en-

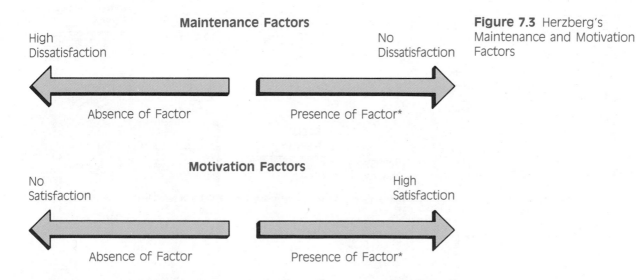

Maintenance Factors

High
Dissatisfaction

No
Dissatisfaction

Absence of Factor

Presence of Factor*

Motivation Factors

No
Satisfaction

High
Satisfaction

Absence of Factor

Presence of Factor*

Figure 7.3 Herzberg's Maintenance and Motivation Factors

*The quality of each factor present also influences each employee's level of satisfaction or dissatisfaction.

vironment that fosters personal growth and advancement throughout the hierarchy.

Figure 7.4 provides a comparison of Maslow's and Herzberg's views. The maintenance factors are similar to Maslow's physical, safety, and social needs levels. The motivation factors are similar to his esteem and self-realization needs.

Managers build a comfortable work environment that encourages motivated employees by providing leadership to the employees. In the next section we will discuss leadership.

Leadership

leadership

Whenever one person influences an individual or group toward accomplishing an objective, leadership occurs. **Leadership** is thus defined as *the process of influencing a group or individual to set or achieve a goal.*

There is no one correct way to lead an individual or group. In different situations a manager is required to be an educator, counselor, judge, spokesperson, initiator of action, or order giver. How managers choose to lead — their styles — will depend on the interactions among the manager (leader), the subordinates (the led), and the organizational environment (work and the work situation).

Leadership can be viewed as a special relationship between each manager and each individual or group. This relationship is in turn influenced by the work environment. Figure 7.5 illustrates the relationships within the leadership setting. Employees with no

Figure 7.4 Comparison of Maslow's Needs Hierarchy and Herzberg's Maintenance and Motivation Theories

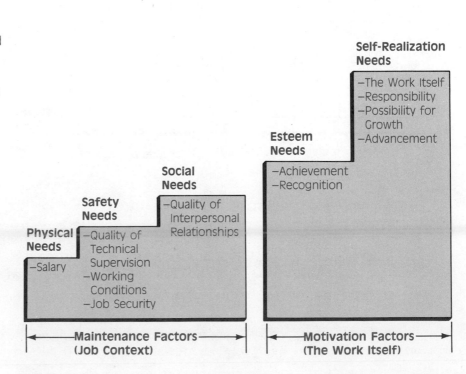

training or experience need to be told what to do and how to do it, while experienced employees do not need as much direction. A job environment that calls for creativity (research laboratory) may require a manager to provide assistance, not to direct activities. Leadership can be viewed as situational: style needs to be adjusted to the situation.

In practicing leadership managers use different leadership styles. What are they and why are they used?

Styles of Leadership

Leadership style is *the approach a manager uses to influence subordinates.* This influence may take the form of making a decision for a subordinate, guiding the subordinate in decision making, or simply providing a topic for a subordinate to decide on. Thus a manager has a number of options for a decision-making style. Robert Tannenbaum and Warren Schmidt[3] have presented this range of styles in the continuum of leadership behavior shown in Figure 7.6. A manager can choose any of these styles depending on the situation.

leadership style

The range of styles shown on the continuum can be grouped under three headings: autocratic, participative, and free-rein. Let's discuss each in relationship to the continuum.

The **autocratic leadership style** is *characterized by decision making solely by the manager; subordinates are excluded from the process.* Variations of this approach find the manager making the decision and then "selling" it to employees or making the decision and allowing the group to ask questions. This type of leadership style is appropriate in dealing with crises, short deadlines, new trainees, or less motivated subordinates who need firm supervision. Managers who use the autocratic leadership style inappropriately, however, deny themselves the value of subordinates' suggestions and talents. In addition, limited involvement in problem solving can hinder a subordinate's ability to handle additional responsibility and will limit the opportunity for promotion.

autocratic leadership style

The **participative leadership style** is *characterized by the manager involving the subordinates in the decision.* The involvement in decision making is a matter of degree. It can range from the first to the last of the following four options of participation.

participative leadership style

Figure 7.5 The Leadership Situation

— The manager presents a tentative solution subject to change based on employee input.
— The manager presents a problem to the employees, asks for their input, and makes a decision.
— The manager defines a problem and the employees make a decision.
— The managers and employees jointly make a decision. (The manager and employees are equal.)

The use of the participative style should aid in building individual employee support and assist in developing the employees' talents.

Figure 7.6 Continuum of Leadership Behavior (Tannenbaum and Schmidt)

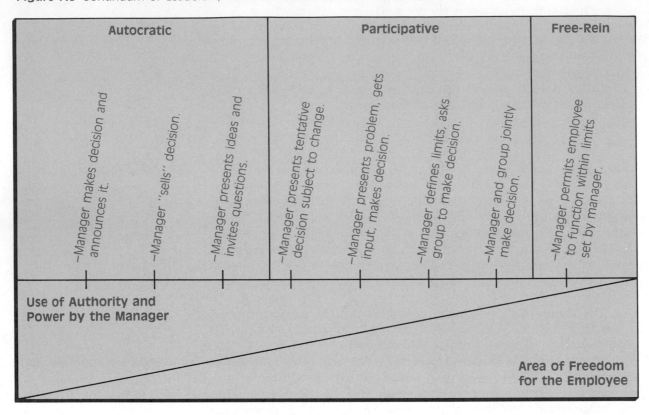

Autocratic	Participative	Free-Rein

—Manager makes decision and announces it.

—Manager "sells" decision.

—Manager presents ideas and invites questions.

—Manager presents tentative decision subject to change.

—Manager presents problem, gets input, makes decision.

—Manager defines limits, asks group to make decision.

—Manager and group jointly make decision.

—Manager permits employee to function within limits set by manager.

Use of Authority and Power by the Manager

Area of Freedom for the Employee

Participation is based on the theory that "two heads are better than one." Tapping the talent of employees who know and understand the job should improve the quality of decision making. In addition, taking part in the decision makes it "ours" not "yours." Finally, people who have been involved in decisions will be better able to exercise judgment and handle more responsibilities.

free-rein or laissez-faire leadership style

The **free-rein or laissez-faire leadership style** is *characterized by the leader permitting the subordinates to function independently.* The leader exercises little direct supervision over subordinates, allowing them to use considerable judgment in accomplishing tasks. In applying this style the leader either sets limits and followers work out their own problems or the individuals set their own goals. Free-rein leadership works well when employees understand and support company objectives and know the framework within which they must work.

A manager would use a free-rein style when dealing with competent, motivated people who have the knowledge and skills to accomplish tasks without direct supervision. The director of a medical clinic, for example, does not have to be involved in every decision made by a staff of doctors. The same is usually true of the director of a laser research laboratory or the senior partner in a firm of certified public accountants.

Pause and Ponder

Think about a manager you have known. Did the manager use different leadership styles? If your answer is yes, when were these used and what was your reaction? If the answer is no, should others have been used? Why?

Which Style Is Best?

The answer to the question is — it depends. Remember, the best leadership style depends on the situation: the leader, the led, and the work environment. A successful manager needs to vary the leadership style depending on the situation. By providing appropriate leadership the manager will increase the opportunity to develop motivated workers and create a positive work environment. In turn the morale of the work force should be high.

Morale in Organizations

Morale is *the attitude workers have toward the quality of their total work life.* In reality, morale is a measurement of the quality of the work environment. Morale is important because the workers' attitudes toward the total work life affects the quality and quantity of output.

     Generally speaking, high quality and quantity of output is an indicator of high morale. When attitudes toward work are poor, management often has trouble maintaining a high quality or quantity of output.

     What factors affect the quality of work life? Figure 7.7 illustrates the factors that General Motors sees affecting morale. The importance of these factors is that they individually and collectively aid in creating a work environment where workers receive satisfaction and are motivated in their jobs — leading to higher quality and quantity of output.

morale

Preventing Morale Problems

Perceptive, employee-oriented managers constantly inspect the work environment for clues that morale is on the downswing. Several of the most significant clues are:

1. Lateness
2. Absenteeism
3. High turnover
4. Employee strikes
5. Production sabotage

Figure 7.7 Factors That General Motors Sees Affecting the Quality of Work Life
Source: General Motors Corporation.

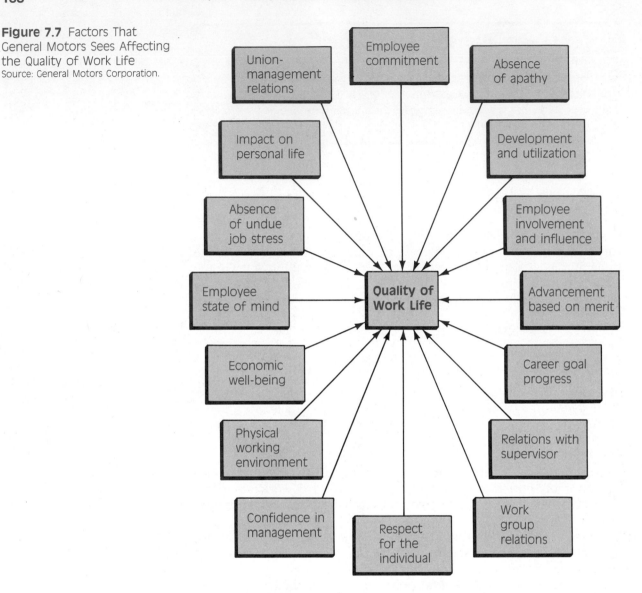

6. Increased rejection of products by quality assurance inspectors
7. Decreased productivity
8. Disregard for safety rules; carelessness that results in injuries
9. Extreme criticism of policies, procedures, and rules
10. Excessively critical comments made during exit interviews

These clues lead a manager to search for the causes. They may result from inadequate training, low pay, faulty material or machinery, or an employee's personal problems. Regardless of the source, a manager must recognize and deal with the problems to maintain a positive work environment.

Managers can do several things to uncover clues to poor morale. One approach is to check company records on tardiness, absences,

In an attempt to improve the total quality of work life, many companies (like Shaklee Company) provide physical exercise facilities.

quality rejects, and comments received during exit interviews. Another approach is to observe and listen: employees' comments to each other, direct remarks to their supervisors, and informal communications through body language are all clues to work attitudes. As an example, one ride attendant at a sprawling amusement park confided: "Whenever we think the higher-ups aren't listening to us or giving us the attention we deserve, we just screw up the roller coaster. The big boys come running to find out what went wrong, which gives us an hour or so to talk to them and get things off our chests. After the problem is fixed and they leave we feel better, like they know we're alive, and things run fine until we start feeling ignored again. Then another breakdown happens." The investigating managers did not read the situation for what it was, a morale problem masquerading as a mechanical one.

A more formal way to check on morale is by conducting an employee attitude or opinion survey. This is a questionnaire that lets workers express their feelings about their jobs anonymously. It is thorough. All workers can be given the questionnaire if management wishes. It is a way to gather honest responses about employee morale. One part of an employee attitude survey appears in Figure 7.8.

Resolving Morale Problems

The problem areas identified through a search of company records, observation, or an attitude survey must be resolved. If not, the situation will worsen, not go away. As an example, after Walt Disney World's management tabulated and analyzed responses to an employee opinion survey, they made some changes.

Figure 7.8 Partial Employee Attitude Survey[a]
Source: Edgar F. Borgatta. Reproduced with permission.

Please answer each question to show how you feel. The only correct answer is your frank opinion. Please do not sign your name on this questionnaire. (Answer each question in one of the following ways: definitely no, probably no, probably yes, or definitely yes.)

1. Do you get feedback (information about your performance) in a way you feel treats you like a mature and responsible person?

2. In the last couple of months have you thought that you would like to quit or change jobs because you do not like the work itself?

3. Is it possible for you to know whether you are doing well or poorly on your job the way it is run now?

4. Do you feel that your job is set up so that it is too closely supervised?

5. Does your job, as presently structured, give you reasonable opportunities for individual recognition?

6. Do you feel that parts of your job could be eliminated without really affecting the work of your organization?

7. Do you feel your job is monotonous, that the work itself provides no basic interest?

8. Do you have a reasonable say in deciding how your job is to be carried out?

9. Do you get enough information to allow you to control your own work process?

10. Do you feel you have to have things checked unnecessarily by supervisors?

11. Do you feel your present assignment is a job where you can continue to learn?

12. Do you feel that you waste a good deal of time because of the way you have to do your job?

13. Do you like the work itself that you are actually doing?

14. Do you feel that you decide exactly how you do your own work?

15. Do you feel your work is set up in such a way that your supervisors can let you know when you are doing well?

16. Do you feel your work is checked too much?

17. Do you feel your present assignment is a good one for a person who wants to be advanced in this business?

18. In carrying out your job, do you feel much of your time is wasted because the work is not well organized by the company?

19. When you are away from work, do you think of your job as something you look forward to?

20. Do you get enough information about how you are doing in your work to allow you to correct errors and improve your performance?

21. Do you feel your job could operate well with less supervision?

22. Do you feel your job is a "dead end" as far as a work career is concerned?

23. Do you feel your job is organized so that it is as easy as possible to carry out effectively?

24. Do you find your work interesting enough to talk about it with people outside of your work situation?

25. Do you feel you get enough feedback about your work?

26. Do you feel that your job is a place where you can continually learn something worthwhile?

27. Do you find your job less interesting than, say, six months ago?

28. Do you get enough opportunity to correct your own errors in how you do things?

29. Do you find that the longer you hold your job, the more boring it becomes?

30. Do you feel satisfied with the way in which you get feedback about your work?

[a]For reasons of space, only the first part of the survey is reproduced here.

1. Increased hourly pay for more than 70 percent of the employees in certain job categories
2. Reduced by 1 year the length of service required to qualify for 3 weeks of vacation
3. Added another paid holiday (a day to commemorate the opening of the park)
4. Agreed to investigate the need for a day care center for employees' children
5. Built an employees' gas station to sell fuel to workers on a nonprofit basis
6. Gave employees a 20 percent discount on parts and labor for repairs at the car care center
7. Simplified transfer procedures among jobs and posted regular bulletins announcing job openings

Working to identify areas that can negatively affect the work environment is important. Still more important are the techniques a manager can utilize to improve the work environment, increase motivation, and improve morale.

Improving the Work Environment, Motivation, and Morale

What can managers do to improve the work environment and ultimately increase motivation and improve morale? The answer depends on the skills and interests of the individual manager as well as on the support provided by the manager's organization. Generally approaches to be taken can be placed in three categories: management techniques and practices, techniques focused on job redesign, and techniques that provide work flexibility. Figure 7.9 summarizes these techniques.

Management Techniques and Practices

The individual manager has a number of tools available to improve the environment for employees. These tools are within the control of the manager and generally depend on his or her managerial philosophy and leadership style. These include praise and recognition for work well done, delegation, participative management, management by objectives, quality circles, and applying people principles.

Praise and Recognition for Work Well Done. We all like to be praised for something we have done. Giving deserved praise may seem like an obvious way to improve the work environment, but how many managers consistently do it? Supervisors who know subordinates as feeling individuals know that they value praise. They may redouble

Figure 7.9 Techniques for Improving the Work Environment

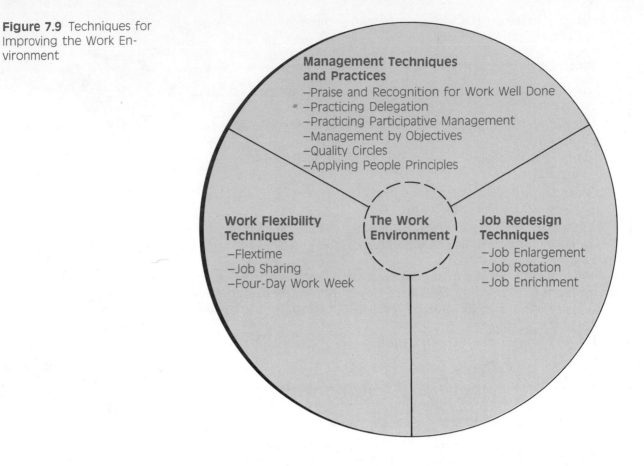

their efforts after well-deserved congratulations or recognition for a job well done. To most workers, honest praise and recognition are powerful motivators. The result may be higher productivity and morale. Hillenbrand Industries, a producer of caskets and hospital beds, went public with its praise: it once printed the names of all 3,396 employees on the cover of its annual report to stockholders.[4]

Managers need to be sensitive to the needs of employees for praise and recognition. If an employee does a good job and receives no praise a negative reaction can develop. Wouldn't it be logical to think that no one cares if good work goes unnoticed? The response — "If they don't care, why should I?"

Practicing Delegation. Providing the opportunity for employees to make important decisions, even those with a relatively high degree of risk, also improves the work environment. When a manager delegates, he or she gives employees the freedom to succeed or fail. This in turn encourages creative thinking and decision making.

Any manager can delegate. It is a personal philosophy that a manager can use without a formal order from top management. Those managers who delegate authority must realize that not all employees are comfortable making important decisions. It is up to the manager to encourage these employees to take risks.

Practicing Participative Management. Like delegation, participative management can be used by all managers. How? The supervisor simply provides the opportunity for subordinates to have a greater voice in decisions that affect them. Participative managers are comfortable with this approach. When workers are involved in decisions and changes that directly affect their jobs, the experience helps them fulfill their self-esteem and self-actualization needs. In addition, participation acknowledges them as thinking individuals, taps their talents, and aids in developing them.

Participative management produced especially impressive results among the 3,800 workers at General Motors' Chevrolet Citation assembly plant in Tarrytown, New York. The plant was once burdened with 7 percent absenteeism, a backlog of up to 2,000 unsettled grievances, and poor product quality. Then, during one retooling period, management took the dramatic step of inviting workers to recommend assembly-line changes.

The cost-saving suggestions that came out of this informal discussion led to regular meetings in which production workers and supervisors talked about ways to increase efficiency and resolve grievances. Before long, workers disclosed superior assembly techniques they had once kept to themselves (such as how to seal windshields better), to the surprise of co-workers, supervisors, and engineers. When body-shop workers joined forces to improve welding quality, faulty welds declined from 35 percent to 1.5 percent. As participative management gained momentum at Tarrytown, the list of unsettled grievances dropped to fewer than forty and absenteeism fell to 2.5 percent.[5]

Management by Objectives. An excellent technique to guarantee participation is management by objectives. **Management by objectives (MBO)** is *a technique designed to improve motivation and commitment by having the manager and employee jointly set objectives, assess progress on the objectives, and evaluate the end results.* Management by objectives allows employees to understand goals fully. Because employees are involved in a joint goal-setting process, there is a greater commitment to meeting these goals. Finally, the employee knows specifically how she or he will be evaluated.

management by objectives (MBO)

The following steps, illustrated in Figure 7.10, are used in implementing MBO.

1. The employee and manager meet to review the employee's job description.
2. The employee and manager jointly develop the subordinate's goals for the agreed-on time period.
3. The employee and manager meet periodically, at agreed-on times, to review the employee's progress toward the goals.
4. At the end of the specified period, the employee and manager jointly evaluate the employee's performance on the goals.

Management by objectives results in a mutually agreed-on series of goals for the employee. It also opens up communication from

Figure 7.10 The Management by Objectives Process

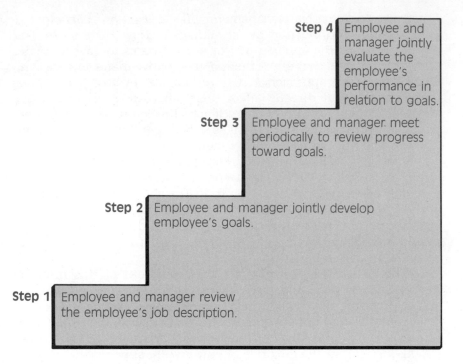

Step 4 — Employee and manager jointly evaluate the employee's performance in relation to goals.

Step 3 — Employee and manager meet periodically to review progress toward goals.

Step 2 — Employee and manager jointly develop employee's goals.

Step 1 — Employee and manager review the employee's job description.

manager to employee. Finally, it gives the subordinate specific indicators of how he or she will be evaluated.

If management by objectives is used in the entire company, it becomes both a planning system and a performance appraisal system. It will link all the levels of management together. Each manager will negotiate with the next lowest level of management on specific goals, which will help the people and the organization achieve their objectives.

quality circle

Quality Circles. Another worker participation opportunity is provided by a quality circle. A **quality circle** is *a cooperative effort by workers and supervisor to find ways to improve operations and quality.* Quality circles focus their attention on gaining workers' input and cooperation in programs of cost reduction and improvement.

More than 750 United States corporations use quality circles and the number is growing rapidly. The fifty-five or so blue-and-white-collar circles operating at Northrop Corporation's California Aircraft Division have contributed significantly to reducing by 50 percent the costs of the Boeing 747 parts they make. Hewlett-Packard, an electronics manufacturer, started quality circles in 1979 and currently has over 500; it too has benefited significantly from cost reduction and methods improvements.[6]

Quality circles rely on the commitment of all company personnel. They operate at the supervisory levels of most firms. They involve workers voluntarily participating. Quality-circle sessions are held regularly — most daily — to focus on only one problem that the supervisor or participants wish to consider. Suggestions are brainstormed, refined, and forwarded to management for consideration.

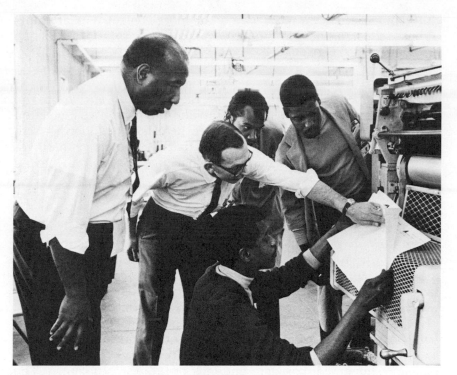

Quality circles focus on employee involvement to improve products and techniques.

Feedback is designed to be immediate so that progress can be seen and contributions noted.

Applying People Principles. In addition to the ideas previously mentioned, managers can aid in developing a quality work environment by applying some "people principles." Managers should be sensitive to (1) letting employees make decisions on areas where they have the authority and competence and (2) ensuring that employees are accountable to only one supervisor.

People principle number one is known as the **exception principle** — *routine actions and decisions should be handled by subordinates; only exceptional decisions should be referred to a higher level.* The result of this principle is that decisions are made where they are supposed to be made and trust is developed in the environment.

exception principle

People principle number two is known as the unity of command principle — each person in an organization should take orders from and report to only one person. This minimizes confusion and keeps the employee out of the middle. Who should an employee listen to if two managers are giving different directions? As mentioned in Chapter 5 this problem sometimes occurs with functional authority.

Techniques Focused on Job Redesign

To improve the work environment management has attempted to redesign jobs to put challenge and other psychological rewards into the work. Through job redesign employees can be provided with different experiences, more variety, or more control. The attempts at job redesign include job enlargement, job rotation, and job enrichment.

job enlargement

Job Enlargement. Job enlargement *increases the variety or the number of tasks a job includes.* It can add to a person's satisfaction with and commitment to the job when he or she is suffering from underload and boredom. A person's sense of competence improves as the volume of output does. The challenge comes from having more and different tasks.

job rotation

Job Rotation. Job rotation *assigns people to different jobs or different tasks to people on a temporary basis.* The idea is to expose people to various jobs and how the jobs relate. Assembly-line workers may be assigned one set of tasks one month and another set of tasks the month after that. Job rotation can be used to cross train, which in turn makes employees better resources.

Job rotation can help stimulate people to higher levels of contributions and renew people's interests and enthusiasm. But managers should realize that once the novelty wears off and the new tasks are mastered, boredom and lack of interest can return. The time value will depend on the employee's personal feelings toward the experience.

job enrichment

Job Enrichment. Job enrichment is *directed at giving the worker more authority over the work, providing a variety of tasks, and increasing responsibility.* Job enrichment applies Herzberg's motivation factors to a job, thus allowing employees to satisfy some of their psychological needs.

Specifically job enrichment is aimed at introducing new and more difficult tasks, giving the person the opportunity to control a total unit of work from start to finish, providing additional authority for decision making, and permitting workers to act as their own quality control.

When Maytag Company introduced this technique more than 15 years ago, it found that product quality increased markedly. Training costs, employee turnover, and labor expenses all declined. Management had more flexibility in making job assignments, because workers performed several tasks where they formerly did just a few. Employees were also pleased that they could set their own work pace instead of working at the speed of an assembly line.

What does job enrichment require? Although job enrichment offers impressive benefits, it means sweeping organizational changes. Management must rewrite job descriptions, provide extensive retraining, and, in manufacturing, rearrange the flow of materials and layout of machines to accommodate several assembly operations that are now condensed into one job. It is especially important that employees understand and accept the action, because workers, especially those who are unionized, may accuse management of trying to increase their work load.

In addition, job enrichment should not be a short-term experiment. Whatever changes are made should match a job's level of challenge to the jobholder's skills. Once a job is enriched, it may need to be enriched again. Once people experience the benefits of job enrichment, they will be reluctant to give them up. For the first time at work, people may experience a sense of competence, independence, and recognition — and a sense of responsibility.

Techniques That Provide Work Flexibility

Another set of techniques available to management to improve the work environment focuses on providing flexibility with the time frame that the job is done and who does the job. These techniques include flextime, job sharing or twinning, and the 4-day workweek.

Flextime. **Flextime, *or* flexible working hours,** *allows employees to decide, within a certain range, when to begin and end each workday.* It thus allows them to take care of personal business before or after work, vary their daily schedules, and enjoy more control over their lives. Companies that have adopted this approach have reported decreases in absenteeism, lower turnover, less tardiness, and higher morale.

Flextime workers must work a fixed number of hours every day, but within limits they may vary their starting and quitting times. Employees may be permitted to start as late as 10:00 A.M. or leave as early as 3:00 P.M., for example, as long as they work 8 hours before leaving.

flextime *or* flexible working hours

Job Sharing. **Job sharing, *or* twinning,** *permits two part-time workers to divide one full-time job.* This is practical in such fields as laboratory work, clerical jobs, and retail sales. Insurance companies, banks, fast-food chains, and hospitals have all tried it.

Such an occupational buddy system is ideal for parents who are raising school-aged children, retirees, students, and those who prefer part-time to full-time work. Job sharers enjoy a less demanding workday and more personal freedom. Atlantic Richfield's experience with this experiment at their Los Angeles office was so satisfying that management is reviewing the potential of developing a company policy on it.[7]

Most job sharers receive prorated fringe benefits, which may include life and health insurance, sick leave, and paid vacations. Control Data Corporation, Equitable Life Assurance Society, Honeywell, and Sears have successfully used this technique.

Employers value the often complementary skills and innovative approaches that job sharing can bring to one task. Also valued is the greater enthusiasm and energy that is available because neither

job-sharing *or* twinning

The Straight Line

Intrapreneurship
Working Within the System

A decidedly different approach to employee motivation in the 1980s is encouraging entrepreneurship within the corporate structure. The idea of intrapreneurship, a word coined and trademarked by consultant Gifford Pinchot, III, is being implemented successfully in companies such as Levi Strauss, Control Data, Allstate Insurance, and Gould.

Intrapreneurship is being credited with motivating bright employees, making them and their companies more productive, and with enabling companies to hold on to their best employees. Allowing employees the necessary freedom to innovate and to take risks is not the norm.

Two schools that have developed programs designed to help organizations create an environment for intrapreneurship are the School for Entrepreneurs at Tarrytown Conference Center in Tarrytown, New York, and the ForeSight Institute, a joint venture of the Naisbett Group, Washington, and the ForeSight Group, Stockholm. The ForeSight Program teaches employee-students how to develop business plans and how to use company resources to turn their ideas into realities. The program also helps companies create supportive environments for intrapreneurship.

Harvard, Yale, Stanford, and Northwestern are among the many

---

person must do a full day's work. Sometimes a position can be split into two distinct parts — data gathering and report writing, or assembly and testing — and each employee can perform the function that he or she does best.

Work sharing has other benefits for the work force. During the recent recession work sharing saved 1,000 jobs for Motorola Corporation. Rather than laying people off, the jobs were shared. When conditions improved, management had experienced employees and did not have to hire employees for new positions.[8]

Four-Day Workweek. The 4-day workweek has received mixed reviews from both employers and employees. Reactions vary from delighted to disgruntled. Du Pont has experimented with a complex modification of this technique since 1974 at six plants operating around the clock, 7 days a week. Employees work 12-hour shifts for 3 or 4 days; each receives 2 weekends off every 4 weeks; no one works more than 7 nights during a 4-week period.[10] After the program began, commuting time to work decreased 30 percent. Workers had more time for family activities, outdoor sports, and socializing. They expressed more job satisfaction, and there were no problems with safety, turnover, or absenteeism, despite the long working hours of each shift. The 12-hour-shift rotation schedule for the plant in Florence, South Carolina, appears in Table 7.4 on page 200.

business schools that have changed the emphasis of their entrepreneurship programs from business startup to entrepreneurship within big business. Courses in adapting to change, risk taking, and new product innovation have proliferated in the 150 plus schools that now offer corporate entrepreneurship programs.

Internal entrepreneurship has been encouraged at Levi Strauss since 1982 when the company budgeted $3 million for new idea development. One of the ideas funded, Two-Horse Brand Jeans, became the most profitable product in its division. As a result of 1982's success, Levi earmarked $4 million in 1983 and again in 1984 for funding intrapreneurship.

Companies that consider intrapreneurship as a tool for increasing motivation and productivity and for decreasing turnover should be prepared to deal with issues of risk, allowing employees to fail without fear of retribution or firing; of financial backing, not just "pat on the backing"; of time to experiment, not added on to the end of a full workday; and of credit or recognition due to the individual, in the form of promotions, additional project funding, or a stake in his or her own company.

For more about intrapreneurship, see Gifford Pinchot, *Intrapreneuring: Why You Don't Have to Leave the Corporation to Become an Entrepreneur*, Harper & Row (New York), 1984; Sharon Nelton, "Finding Room for the Intrapreneur," *Nation's Business*, February 1984, pp. 50–52; "B-Schools Try to Churn Out Entrepreneurs," *Business Week*, March 1984, p. 102; and "Every Employee an Entrepreneur — Inc. Interview with Allan Kennedy," *Inc.*, April, 1984, pp. 106–117.

Summary

Once an organization has acquired the best possible human resources to perform a job, managers are faced with the challenge of creating a positive work environment where employees can grow. The work environment is the key to developing and maintaining motivated workers who will achieve organizational objectives.

An influence on the work environment created by a manager is the development of a management philosophy. Theory Y is a positive philosophy about people at work; Theory X is a negative philosophy of management. A direct outcome of a manager's philosophy of management is the ability to recognize and work with people as individuals.

As individuals we all are motivated differently. Maslow's hierarchy of needs theory and Herzberg's motivation-maintenance theory provide managers with tools to help provide for motivation in the work environment. Though approached differently, Herzberg's motivational and maintenance factors provide for the same needs identified in Maslow's hierarchy.

Managers aid in building a supportive work environment by providing leadership. Managers alter their leadership styles depending on the interaction of the manager, the employee, and the particular work environment. Managers can select the appropriate style from three options: autocratic, participative, or free-rein.

Table 7.4 Du Pont Florence Plant, 12-Hour Shift Rotation[a]

Source: Reprinted with permission from *World of Work Report*, February 1978, p. 19. © Work in America Institute, Inc., Scarsdale, New York.

Week[b]	Monday	Tuesday	Wednesday	Thursday	Friday	Saturday	Sunday
1	6 A.M.–6 P.M.	6 A.M.–6 P.M.	6 A.M.–6 P.M.	6 A.M.–6 P.M.	Off	Off	Off
2	Off	Off	Off	Off	6 P.M.–6 A.M.	6 P.M.–6 A.M.	6 P.M.–6 A.M.
3	6 P.M.–6 A.M.	Off	Off	Off	6 A.M.–6 P.M.	6 A.M.–6 P.M.	6 A.M.–6 P.M.
4	Off	6 P.M.–6 A.M.	6 P.M.–6 A.M.	6 P.M.–6 A.M.	Off	Off	Off

[a]Workers must rotate among all three shifts to get an even spread of experienced people on each shift.
[b]Weeks 1 and 3 are 48 hours; weeks 2 and 4 are 36 hours.

How well managers have done in providing leadership to build a motivated work environment can be judged from the general morale of the work force. Morale is important because it affects the quality and quantity of output produced. It is important for managers to monitor the morale of employees and make adjustments to the work environment to maintain positive morale.

Managers and organizations have techniques to maintain and improve the work environment, increase motivation, and improve morale. Generally the techniques can be placed in three categories:

1. Management techniques and practices
   Praise and recognition
   Delegation
   Participation
   Management by objectives
   Quality circles
   People principles
2. Techniques focused on job redesign
   Job enlargement
   Job rotation
   Job enrichment
3. Techniques that provide work flexibility
   Flextime
   Job sharing
   4-day workweek

Key Terms

autocratic leadership style
esteem need
exception principle
flextime *or* flexible working hours

free-rein *or* laissez-faire leadership style
job enlargement
job enrichment
job rotation

job sharing *or* twinning
leadership
leadership style
maintenance *or* hygiene factors

management by objectives (MBO)	participative leadership style	self-actualization *or* self-realization need
morale	philosophy of management	social need
motivation	physiological need	Theory X
motivation factors	quality circle	Theory Y
needs	safety and security need	

For Review and Discussion

1. Why is it important for a manager to develop a positive work environment?

2. When a manager says, "We have a positive work environment here," what factors could be cited to defend this statement?

3. Why is it important for a manager to develop a positive philosophy of management?

4. Distinguish between Theory X and Theory Y as philosophies of management. How would the adoption of each by a manager influence the work environment?

5. In what ways are people different? Why is this important for a manager to recognize?

6. As a manager, how would you react to this statement: "It is up to the employee to satisfy his or her own needs, I don't have the time"?

7. Explain each of Maslow's five levels of need. Why is Maslow's model known as a hierarchy of needs?

8. Differentiate between Herzberg's motivational factors and maintenance factors. What does the presence or absence of each mean to the work environment?

9. Why is it important for a manager to monitor the morale of employees? What methods can a manager use to do this?

10. For each of the following management techniques, explain how the application of these by a manager will improve the work environment.

    a. Praise and recognition
    b. Delegation
    c. Participation
    d. Management by objectives
    e. Quality circles
    f. People principles

11. Distinguish between job enlargement, job rotation, and job enrichment. Which offers the most potential in an organization?

12. Why should an employer consider the use of flex-time? What are the benefits to an employee?

13. Why would an employer not want to encourage job sharing? What are the benefits to both the employee and the organization?

14. Develop a proposal to present to management supporting the conversion of your job (or one you have held) to a 4-day, 40-hour workweek. Include the advantages and disadvantages you can identify.

Applications

Case 7.1 Modern Is Best

John McNulty, accounting department manager, sat back in his chair and remembered his thoughts of 3 months back. He had just said goodbye to the work crew after they had installed the new modular office system. "Very appealing to the senses, leads to more productivity for the employees, and is right on the leading edge of technology," were the words he had used to describe the system to his boss Terri Tyler, the director of finance who approved its installation.

The redesign of the office had been an idea de-veloped by John after attending a seminar in Washington, D.C., titled "Bringing Technology to the Office Environment." John had been excited by what he had seen and heard.

The new concept of creating a separate office space for each employee by using 8-foot-high partitions was ideal. This would give his office staff of ten women and five men maximum privacy and ultimate productivity. It would be far better than having all the desks in a big open room where everyone could see everyone else, where they talked constantly, and even pulled their chairs together and held impromptu meetings.

John wasn't so sure about his decision now. His once highly efficient work group had not been performing well. Work was not being completed on time and what was being completed was inaccurate. Neither of these results was acceptable in an accounting department. In addition, John had observed that:

- Two or three of the members of the work group seemed distracted and daydreamed.
- A number of employees appeared moody and more sensitive.
- The lighthearted approach to working together seemed to be missing.
- People seemed reluctant to leave their work areas.

John had analyzed all the elements in the work environment to determine what had caused the change. Everything was the same, except for one thing — the modular office.

Questions

1. Which one of Maslow's five needs do you think has been influenced by the installation of the modular office? Why?
2. How would you advise John to modify the modular office to provide the opportunity for people to satisfy the need that has been limited?
3. If you were John, what would you have done differently when you made the initial decision to install the modular office?

Pg 185

Case 7.2 The New Supervisor's Dilemma

Maria Valdez was nervous as she sat outside the vice-president of personnel's office. Yesterday afternoon she had been told to be in Mr. Kline's office at nine o'clock sharp. Nothing else — just be there at 9:00 A.M. After what seemed like an eternity Maria was directed into Mr. Kline's office.

"Good morning, Maria. Have I got some good news for you," Mr. Kline began. "We have been watching your progress. You have done an excellent job on the receiving dock, and we also know you have made a strong effort to improve your background. I've seen the tuition reimbursement requests for your classes at the college . . . business, I believe. Well, Ms. Valdez, we want you to take over the receiving department at our Southside operation. It's not that big, but you'll have a chance to see if you really like management. What do you think?"

"Mr. Kline, I surely would like the opportunity to try, but I've never managed anyone. I know about receiving but I don't know the people at Southside."

For the next hour Maria and Mr. Kline discussed the Southside personnel. Now, as Maria dressed for work on her first day as a manager, she recalled the employees' names and the descriptions given by Mr. Kline.

Joel Peterson — has been with the company 10 years, and in his present position 4 years. He gets his work done, makes no mistakes in the technical part of his job, and rarely gets involved in any discussions with his fellow workers. A loner — when work is done, he takes off on his motorcycle.

Rich Rasmussen — has been with the company 6 months. He just recently came off his initial probationary period. "Eager, but lacks knowledge of the job," were Mr. Kline's exact words. He also has the reputation for trying to do something without having any idea where to start or why. Has a future with the company if he will settle down.

Idella Washington — has spent her 3 years with the company at the Southside location in her present position. She is careful, sets goals for herself, and wishes to advance. She has made numerous suggestions in the past to her previous supervisor, none of which were implemented. She has studied her job carefully and has taken night courses in distribution procedures.

Questions

1. What leadership style should Maria use with each person?
2. Why did you make the selection you did?

Labor Relations

Chapter Outline

Chapter Objectives

After studying this chapter, you should be able to:

1. Summarize the basic principles of unions and the primary objectives unions have for their members.
2. Trace the historical development of the labor movement.
3. Summarize the major legislation affecting labor-management relations and collective bargaining.
4. Identify the current trends and directions of the labor movement.
5. Discuss four reasons why people join unions.
6. Contrast the tools management and labor have to achieve their objectives.
7. Describe the roles of collective bargaining, mediation, arbitration, and a grievance procedure in labor-management interaction.

Long ago we stated the reason for labor organizations. We said that union was essential to give laborers opportunity to deal on an equality with their employer.

— United States Supreme Court

Up Front

Vicki Saporta

The Teamsters' Director of Organizing

The appointment of Vicki Saporta as director of organizing for the International Brotherhood of Teamsters was unprecedented: she is the only woman organizing director of a major union. A graduate of the School of Industrial and Labor Relations at Cornell University, Saporta comes well equipped to handle her new responsibilities.

A tireless worker she has, over a ten-year career, successfully organized in almost all of the Teamsters' diverse jurisdictions. These include campaigns among employees working in the following sectors: airlines, trucking, health care, manufacturing, clerical, public service, and warehousing, among others. Saporta's organizing efforts have taken her to all parts of the country — from the East Coast to the West Coast, and from the Midwest to the Deep South. Averaging 225 days per year on the road, her experience in the field has given Saporta a full understanding of the problems of today's organized workers.

The Teamsters, with 1.9 million members, is North America's largest labor organization, representing employees in every walk of life. They have 705 local unions throughout the United States and Canada and a full-time staff of 7,500 who organize, negotiate contracts, and service the membership in a variety of ways. In her one year as director of organizing, Saporta has structured the department to help local unions become more effective in their organizing efforts. The department provides the following services:

Mentioning the word *union* at a social gathering does not draw neutral reactions. In some quarters unions are seen as unnecessary, too powerful, a cause of problems for business, and a major contributor to low productivity in America. On the other side of the coin, unions are viewed as essential to protect workers, an aid in providing a quality work life and, in some eyes, a partner with management for long-range profitability.

Regardless of the perception, unions and management will continue to interact in the work environment. Why do some organizations have unions while others do not? What role does a union play within an organization? How do unions and management function together through collective bargaining? The answers to these questions will be provided in this chapter. But before we deal with these, a good starting point is a brief discussion of what unions are and why they exist.

1. *Training.* One-day to full-week intensive training sessions are held for organizers, agents, and stewards to sharpen their organizing skills.
2. *Advice.* Locals are able to call with a variety of problems or to discuss various campaign strategies.
3. *Information.* Local unions are able to get information on specific management consultants and their techniques, as well as complete company profiles.
4. *Materials.* The department has developed videotapes, which locals can show at their organizing meetings, and new, effective organizing leaflets. Organizing items, such as T-shirts, caps, and buttons, can also be ordered from the department.
5. *Manpower.* Expert staff is available to assist locals with their organizing efforts.
6. *Money.* Grants are available from the union to help finance organizing campaigns.
7. *Coordination.* Joint campaigns among various Teamster locals and other international unions are coordinated by the department.

Teamster local unions have enthusiastically utilized the services of the new organizing department. In the past year, the International Brotherhood of Teamsters has increased by 104,000 new members.

For more about Vicki Saporta, see Gilbert T. Sewall, "Rising Union Leaders: Sobered But Scrappy," *Fortune*, December 26, 1983, pp. 155–161; Dennis R. Whitehead, "Meet the Teamsters' New 'Miss Dynamite'," *Business Week*, October 3, 1983, pp. 107–110.

What Is a Labor Union?

A **labor union** is *a legally sanctioned, formally organized association of workers who have united to represent their collective views for wages, hours, and working conditions.* Labor unions are created by workers to provide a method to deal with management more effectively. The "collective voice" of a union in essence offsets the power of management.

labor union

Why Do Labor Unions Exist?

Management develops a work environment that either discourages or encourages unionization. An enlightened management team that is sensitive to the needs of workers, treats them fairly, develops written policies and grievance procedures, and provides for quality of work life probably will not be unionized. Companies like Texas Instruments, Otis Engineering, and Forney Engineering provide for the needs of employees and are not unionized. When employees feel that they cannot fulfill their needs, that their voices are not being heard, and that they are not treated equitably, unionism is a viable alternative.

The Principles of Unionism

Unions are based on three basic principles:

— Strength through unity
— Equal pay for the same job
— Employment practices (promotion, raises, layoffs) based on seniority

These principles are the cornerstone of the labor movement. They have in turn served as the foundation for the primary objectives that unions in general have for their members. Among these objectives are:

— Higher pay
— Shorter hours of work on a daily, weekly, or annual basis
— Improved working conditions — both physical and psychological
— Improved job security

Over the years these guiding principles and objectives have formed the basis for union actions. Before we discuss unions and management actions it is more appropriate to review briefly the history of labor and the laws that affect union and management interactions. To help you follow this history, Figure 8.1 provides a guideline of the important events in labor-management relations.

Figure 8.1 Important Events in the History of Labor-Management Relations

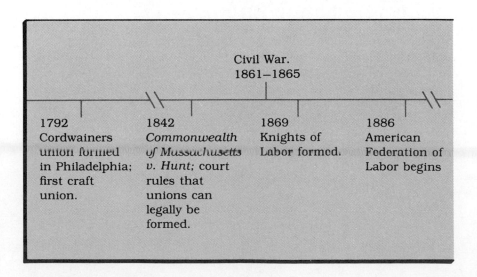

Civil War.
1861–1865

1792
Cordwainers
union formed
in Philadelphia;
first craft
union.

1842
*Commonwealth
of Massachusetts
v. Hunt;* court
rules that
unions can
legally be
formed.

1869
Knights of
Labor formed.

1886
American
Federation of
Labor begins

A Brief History of the Labor Movement

The Struggle for Legality

Unions have existed in the United States in one form or another for nearly 200 years. They began in 1792 with an alliance of cordwainers (shoemakers) in Philadelphia. By 1800 unions of carpenters and printers had sprung up in Baltimore, Boston, and New York.

These fledgling unions rarely survived for long because the courts of the day had declared them unlawful conspiracies "pregnant with public mischief and private injury."[1] Finally, in the 1842 case of *Commonwealth of Massachusetts* v. *Hunt*, Chief Justice Lemuel Shaw of the Massachusetts Appellate Court reversed precedent by declaring, "We cannot perceive that it is criminal for men to agree together to exercise their own acknowledged rights in such a manner as best to subserve their own interest." For the first time in American history, a court ruled that workers (in this case shoemakers) legally could form a union to promote better working conditions as long as they pursued "virtuous ends by virtuous means."[2]

Although the Massachusetts ruling opened the door for union formation, it was not opened too wide. Until the 1930s, workers had to struggle for whatever power they could get to influence their working conditions, wages, hours, or benefits. Despite the fact that unions were no longer illegal, unions had little or no power.

The Early Craft Unions

Most of the early unions were considered **craft, *or* trade, unions,** which are *associations of workers with a specific skill:* iron molders, locomotive engineers, carpenters, printers. The first truly national union, the Knights of Labor, which was formed in 1869 as a secret, somewhat ritualistic society of garment cutters, came out of hiding

craft *or* trade unions

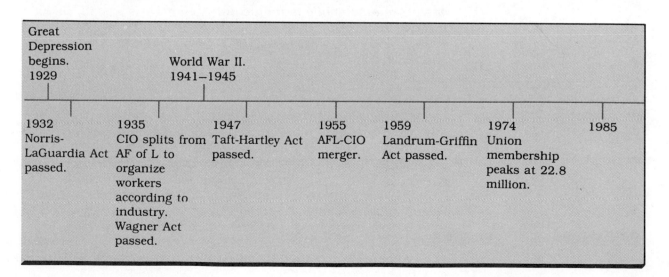

Great Depression begins. 1929		World War II. 1941–1945					
1932 Norris-LaGuardia Act passed.	1935 CIO splits from AF of L to organize workers according to industry. Wagner Act passed.	1947 Taft-Hartley Act passed.	1955 AFL-CIO merger.	1959 Landrum-Griffin Act passed.	1974 Union membership peaks at 22.8 million.	1985	

Samuel Gompers, the first president of the American Federation of Labor, set his sights on the bread-and-butter interests of workers.

in 1878 and numbered as many as 700,000 members by 1886. The Knights wanted to create one huge, centrally managed organization to represent farmers, laborers, and other groups of working people regardless of skill. They attempted to achieve their goals through political action and social reform. As a result of poorly defined goals and a series of unsuccessful strike actions, their membership began to dwindle. By 1890 membership had declined to 100,000 workers; the Knights were dissolved in 1893.

The American Federation of Labor

The dissension that caused the end of the Knights of Labor eventually resulted in the establishment of the American Federation of Labor (AFL). Several disenchanted members formed the Federation of Organized Trades and Labor Unions, which became the American Federation of Labor, a union of trade unions, in December 1886. Samuel Gompers was elected its first president. Its members consisted primarily of skilled workers. Gompers set his sights on the "bread and butter" interests of his members. The union focused its energies on raising the wages of its members and improving working conditions. The result: by 1887 unions representing more than 600,000 people were affiliated with the AFL. By 1920 almost three-fourths of all organized workers belonged to unions that had joined the coalition. The decision to permit member unions considerable independence over their affairs (unlike the Knights of Labor who had sought to centralize control) also aided the AFL's growth.

The Committee for Industrial Organization

industrial unions

Although the AFL recruited unions organized according to craft, militant coal miner John L. Lewis believed that greater emphasis should be placed on creating **industrial unions** — *associations of workers employed within a given industry, such as coal mining or steel or automobile manufacturing, regardless of skill.* In 1935 this philosophical difference caused Lewis to establish the Committee for Industrial Organization (CIO), which separated from the AFL and quickly rivaled it in size.

The AFL-CIO

After two decades of intense competition between the AFL and the CIO, in 1955 the two groups set aside their collective differences and merged into one national organization — the American Federation of Labor and Congress of Industrial Organizations (AFL-CIO), headed from its beginning until his death in 1979 by George Meany, a former plumber from the Bronx. This association gathered together unions representing 16 million workers — more than 85 percent of all union members in the United States at that time. Approximately half of the 200 individual unions in the United States now belong to the AFL-CIO.

From 1930 to 1960: Labor and the Law

The years leading up to the 1930s are sometimes called the repressive phase of the labor movement. Because many judges came from wealthy backgrounds, they tended to represent the interests of their peers. Without laws or court decisions to aid them, unions generally were ineffective when it came to recruiting and representing workers in negotiations with management. In addition, many people considered union activity unpatriotic until the Great Depression of the 1930s.

The Depression, during which unemployment approached 25 percent, shifted public sentiment away from business and toward unions. With the 1932 election of Franklin D. Roosevelt (who sympathized with working people despite his wealthy background), the pendulum swung to the unions' side, and the Norris-LaGuardia Act and the Wagner Act were passed, promoting the formation of unions. As a result, total union membership grew from fewer than 4 million in 1935 to almost 15 million by 1945. (Table 8.1 presents a detailed look at these two laws and other important legislation.)

In 1946 approximately 113 million worker-days were lost to **strikes,** *temporary work stoppages by employees to protest certain working conditions and reinforce demands for their correction.* Public sentiment shifted away from unions when such industries as coal and public utilities were temporarily paralyzed, inconveniencing millions of citizens. In this climate of growing criticism of unions, Congress voted the Taft-Hartley Act into law and overrode President Truman's veto of it. This law, which amended the Wagner Act, gave the president sweeping power to deal with work stoppages that impaired the nation's welfare, and it restricted labor's activities in the same manner that the Wagner Act restricted management's.

Moves to balance the legal power that labor received in the late 1930s persisted into the 1950s. A number of states, acting under authority granted them by the Taft-Hartley Act, passed **right-to-work laws,** which *allow workers to obtain and keep jobs without having to join or pay money to a labor organization.* Twenty states have enacted such legislation.

The year 1959 saw passage of the Landrum-Griffin Act, which attempted to protect unions from any mismanagement, financial corruption, or unethical practices on the part of their top officials.

strikes

right-to-work laws

The Unions Today

Union Membership

Although union membership has increased in total numbers over the years, the Department of Labor reports that the percentage of the total work force that belongs to unions declined from 24.5 percent in 1971 to 20.5 percent in 1980. Figure 8.2 traces union membership from 1971 through 1981.

In addition to the declining numbers, unions won 45 percent of elections held in 1984 under the National Labor Relations Board

Table 8.1 Major Federal Labor Legislation Since the 1930s

Law, Year	Provisions
Federal Anti-Injunction Act (Norris-LaGuardia Act) of 1932	*Prohibits courts from issuing injunctions against labor's nonviolent protest activities,* such as strikes and picketing. *Requires an open hearing before the issuance of an injunction.* *Outlaws "yellow dog" contracts,* in which employees agree not to join a union.
National Labor-Relations Act (Wagner Act) of 1935	Prohibits management from interfering with threats or questioning with employees' right to organize, join, or assist a union. Prohibits management from giving financial or other support to a union, to avoid having a union dominated by or dependent on the employer. Prohibits management from using employment practices to discriminate against prounion workers or reward antiunion workers: it prevents companies from firing or demoting current employees; from refusing to rehire employees who participated in a strike; and from refusing to hire qualified applicants because of union membership. Prohibits management from discharging or otherwise discriminating against an employee who files charges or testifies against the employer in labor relations cases. *Requires management to bargain in good faith* about wages, hours, and other employment conditions with the union that workers lawfully chose as their bargaining representative. (Management is not required to agree with or concede to union demands, but it must agree to meet at reasonable times and be open to discussion.) *Establishes the five-member National Labor Relations Board to supervise employee elections for union representation, and to prevent and remedy unfair labor practices by either employers or unions.*
Labor-Management Relations Act (Taft-Hartley Act) of 1947	*Permits the president of the United States to seek an 80-day injunction to delay a strike or lockout if evidence suggests that the strike would "imperil the national health and safety."* *Declares the following union activities to be unfair labor practices:* 1. *Closed shops and secondary boycotts.* 2. *Featherbedding* (forcing an employer to hire unnecessary workers). 3. *Refusal to bargain in good faith.* *Empowers states to pass "right-to-work" laws,* permitting employees to work without joining or paying dues to a union. Prohibits unions from charging excessive or discriminatory initiation fees or dues.
Labor-Management Reporting and Disclosure Act (Landrum-Griffin Act) of 1959	Requires union officers to permit members to nominate candidates for union office, vote in elections, and dispute union election results. Stipulates that all union members must be allowed to examine the contracts negotiated between the union and management. *Requires unions to file copies of their constitutions, bylaws, and various reports (including financial statements) with the secretary of labor, where they become public record.* Bars persons convicted of certain felonies from serving as union officers. *Requires that union officers be bonded (insured)* if the union has property and annual dues collections of more than $5,000.

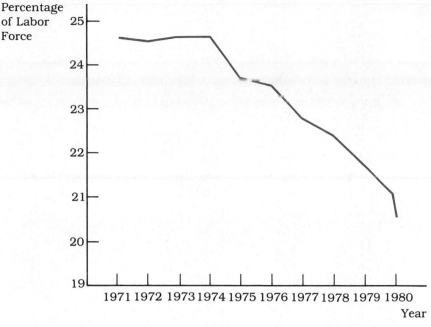

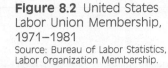

Figure 8.2 United States Labor Union Membership, 1971–1981
Source: Bureau of Labor Statistics, Labor Organization Membership.

to determine whether employees wished to organize. This figure, as illustrated in Figure 8.3, is down from the 94 percent recorded in 1937.[3] Along with this trend are the negative statistics for unions in decertification elections. The number of decertification elections, in which workers can vote out a union, has increased from less than 200 per year in the late 1940s to 1,000 in the early 1980s. Figure 8.4 shows that unions now lose three-fourths of the elections.[4]

Union membership still is highly concentrated in such basic industries as steel, aluminum, transportation, communications, and rubber; however, virtually all workers in these industries are union members. Such white-collar workers as clerical, technical, and professional employees joined unions in record numbers during the 1970s. Agricultural workers, government employees, and women in a variety of industries also account for a higher percentage of union membership today than ever in the past.

Beyond the Numbers

Unions of today are dealing with other types of concerns: gains offset by losses, rising operating costs, and a question of power. The state of the economy in the early 1980s affected overall union membership. Through plant closings and layoffs the AFL-CIO lost approximately 1.2 million American members from early 1982 through mid-1983. The American Federation of State, County, and Municipal Employees lost, and eventually recovered, 35,000 members as a result of layoffs in state and local governments. During this same period the United Steelworkers, United Auto Workers, and United Mine Workers had similar experiences.

Figure 8.3 Percent of
Elections Won by Unions

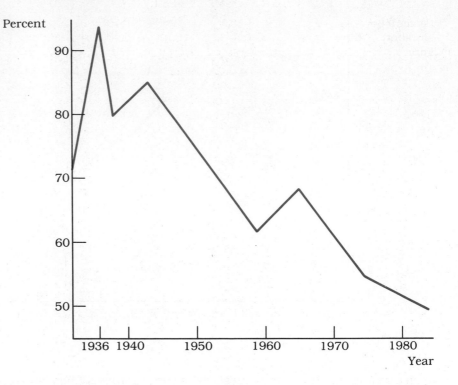

Figure 8.4 Number of
Decertification Elections

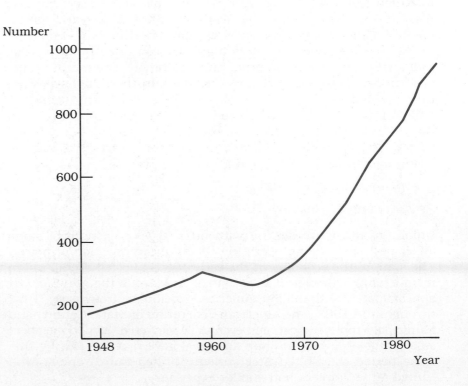

The loss of members in turn affects the unions' ability to provide staff support, hold regional conferences, and ultimately to recruit members. For the first time in history, the steelworkers union had staff layoffs; similar layoffs of staff have been experienced by the United Mine Workers. In addition to the staff cutbacks, regional conferences had to be canceled. Both of these factors affect the unions' ability to recruit members, train existing ones, and spread its "gospel."

The loss of operating funds and members also clouds the picture on labor's clout. With dwindling resources and fewer numbers there is concern among labor leaders over less power both at the bargaining table and in Congress.[5]

Growth of Employees' Associations

The image of hard-core labor unions has limited the effectiveness of union attempts to organize white-collar workers. An attractive alternative for those who do not want to be identified as union members is an **employees' association,** which is *an organization that represents an occupational group, but appeals to white-collar workers.*

employees' association

The Airline Pilots Association, the Classroom Teachers Association, and the Association of University Professors are viable organizations that represent this approach. The goals of each association are focused on its own group. The goals include not only wages, hours, and working conditions, but also special objectives; quality education, institutional autonomy, and academic freedom might be examples for college teachers. An employees' association is such an attractive alternative that the Department of Labor reports that roughly 40 percent of all organized white-collar employees belong to associations. Table 8.2 presents membership figures for the ten largest unions and employees' associations.

Organization	Members (in Thousands)
Teamsters (Ind.)[a]	1,891
National Education Association	1,684
Automobile Workers (Ind.)	1,357
Food and Commercial	1,300
Steelworkers	1,238
State, County	1,098
Electrical (IBEW)	1,041
Carpenters	784
Machinists	754
Service Employees	650

[a]All organizations not identified as (Ind.) are affiliated with the AFL-CIO.

Table 8.2 Membership of the Largest Labor Organizations
Source: U.S. Department of Labor, Bureau of Labor Statistics.

Goals and Directions

Historically unions have concentrated their efforts on blue-collar workers. With the bulk of these workers in steel, communications, and transportation unionized and with the percentage of blue-collar jobs decreasing, the union has focused its attention on other areas, specifically in:

— Unionizing federal, state, and local government employees
— Organizing white-collar employees in insurance, banking, and retail trades
— Directing energy to the new high-technology industries through organizing coalitions[6]
— Rebuilding an image of power that was damaged by wage concessions made during the early 1980s recession economy
— Focusing energies on offsetting aggressive management tactics (i.e., restructuring companies to avoid union contracts, hard-nosed bargaining, providing what the union would negotiate for)[7]
— Attempting to organize auto factories managed by Toyota and Nissan who have "imported" Japanese labor theory to create a quality environment
— Directing organizing efforts to the emerging numbers of career women in the labor force[8]
— Developing strategies to overcome the accusations that unions are a contributing factor in lower productivity
— Working to organize public schoolteachers and college educators

A goal of labor groups is organizing the emerging numbers of women in the work force.

Table 8.3 provides an illustration of the changes in union membership that support these objectives.

Now that we know where unions have been and what their future direction is, let's examine why people join unions.

Why Do Workers Join Unions?

There is no single reason why more than 20 percent of today's work force belongs to unions, but several of the more common contributing factors are:

1. To acquire more power
2. To improve working conditions
3. To get or keep a job
4. To improve economic position

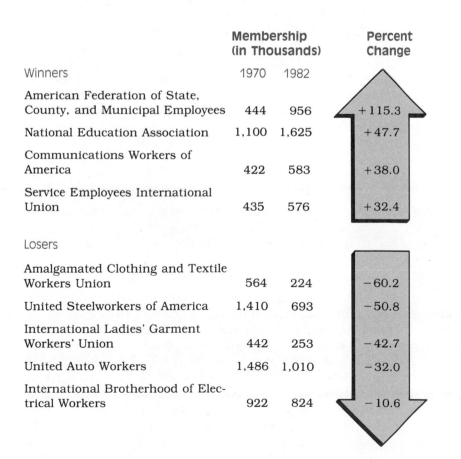

	Membership (in Thousands)		Percent Change
Winners	1970	1982	
American Federation of State, County, and Municipal Employees	444	956	+115.3
National Education Association	1,100	1,625	+47.7
Communications Workers of America	422	583	+38.0
Service Employees International Union	435	576	+32.4
Losers			
Amalgamated Clothing and Textile Workers Union	564	224	−60.2
United Steelworkers of America	1,410	693	−50.8
International Ladies' Garment Workers' Union	442	253	−42.7
United Auto Workers	1,486	1,010	−32.0
International Brotherhood of Electrical Workers	922	824	−10.6

Table 8.3 Changes in Union Membership
Source: *Newsweek*, September 5, 1983, page 49. Copyright 1983, by Newsweek, Inc. All rights reserved. Reprinted with permission.

Rising union membership in the service sector is helping to offset labor's dramatic losses in old-line industries.

To Acquire More Power

The collective voice is more powerful than that of one person. Management is management and has the power of the company and the authority contained in the job description. A single worker voicing a safety demand, questioning a work policy, or protesting against perceived arbitrary management practices faces the immediate possibility of being fired. But the power contained in a united work force with a spokesperson management *must* listen to, can offset and equalize management power. Strength in numbers acquires power.

To Improve Working Conditions

In the initial days of the union movement, improving working conditions was one of the most important reasons for the unions' development. Unions might not have reached their present strength if early managers had been more concerned about the welfare of their employees. Long hours and unsafe working conditions were commonplace. In 1900 the average work day was 10 hours, 6 days a week. Thirteen-year-old boys labored in iron foundries and coal mines for as little as 50¢ a week. Many clothing factories rightfully earned the label *sweatshop.* If workers were injured on the job — even because of the employer's negligence — the courts of the day usually applied the assumption-of-risk doctrine, ruling that the employees worked at their own risk. Workers found that the only way to overcome these oppressive conditions was to organize. Today the concern is to maintain the safe working conditions and to monitor the quality of the work environment.

To Get or Keep a Job

Joining a union may be a way to get or keep a job. Depending on what type of shop or bargaining-agent agreement is established in the contract, joining a union may be the way to get a job or a condition of employment.

closed shop

Closed Shop. Before the Taft-Hartley Act, strong unions negotiated **closed shop** *agreements stipulating that employees had to be union members at the time they were hired.* Although this is formally outlawed today, it is often practical for a person wanting a job to join a union. In states without right-to-work laws, union membership may be required for regular employment in such occupations as printing or construction. In addition, some labor-management agreements stipulate that management will first go to the union hiring hall to fill any openings. The likelihood of a nonunion applicant's being hired is remote in such a case.

union shop

Union Shop. States without right-to-work laws can have **union shop** *agreements stipulating that a company's new employees must* *join a union within a certain number of days after being hired in order to keep their jobs.* In essence this is joining a union as a condition of employment.

Agency Shop. Although union membership is not mandated in an **agency shop,** *nonunion members must pay union dues because the union acts as their agent when bargaining with management.* That reason alone is normally a reason to join the union officially.

agency shop

Simple-Recognition Shop. In some states with right-to-work laws, the **simple-recognition shop** exists. This is *an arrangement wherein all employees, whether union members or not, receive the same pay, work assignments, and benefits.* The fact that non-union employees get identical treatment may seem unfair to workers whose union dues paid for the negotiations. Consequently employees who decline union membership may find co-workers pressuring them to join unions.

simple-recognition shop

Open Shop. In an **open shop** *workers have not elected a union to represent them in dealing with management.*

open shop

Keeping a Job. In addition to the specific requirements of a contract to join a union, union membership provides job security. Union members view their union as a defense against arbitrary personnel decisions by management. Labor-management contracts specify the procedure that management must follow when assigning work to union members, taking disciplinary action (including firing), laying off workers, or recalling those who were previously laid off. Worker seniority figures prominently in the procedures followed for layoffs, recalls, and work assignments.

Union contracts negotiated in recent years have provided lifetime security for employees; the U.S. Postal Workers revolutionized job security with their contract. The United Auto Workers followed the Postal Workers' lead in their pact with Ford Motor Company: in exchange for money-saving concessions this contract ensured that 80 percent of the workers would have jobs until retirement.[9]

To Improve Economic Position

One of the basic objectives of unionism is to raise wages and benefits of employees. Many union workers believe that union membership is the best route to a higher standard of living. Once again the collective voice and the collective ability to withhold services is a strong bargaining tool. In addition to higher wages, many labor-management contracts provide automatic pay increases when prices rise, a number of paid holidays each year, paid vacations, health, life, and dental insurance, and, in some industries, a guaranteed retirement income.

Does membership in a union really improve economic position? Although some unions — United Auto Workers and Greyhound — have had to settle for reduced wage programs, on the whole the results of collective bargaining have led to above-market compensation in the unionized labor force of from 10 to 20 percent.[10] A further testimony to the effectiveness of unions is cited by Peter Drucker, who noted that the annual compensation package for nonunionized workers is $30,000 per year including fringes and benefits. On the other hand, fulltime workers in the unionized smokestack industries (e.g., steel) average $50,000 a year.[11]

Now that we know why people join unions, let's examine the techniques that management and labor employ in attempting to achieve their objectives.

Management Tools:
Illegal and Legal

Illegal Antilabor Tools

Before the Wagner Act made it illegal to do so, management regularly discharged or laid off employees who attempted to organize unions. These workers, who were branded as labor agitators, often had difficulty getting jobs elsewhere in the vicinity.

blacklist

To discourage workers from unionizing, employers within a region would create a **blacklist,** *a list of prounion workers in a given area.* These lists were circulated widely among firms, and workers whose names appeared on them often were denied employment. This approach discouraged many would-be union organizers from actively supporting the labor movement. It too was declared illegal by the Wagner Act.

"yellow dog" contract

Another antiunion tactic in the early 1900s was to require employees to sign a **"yellow dog" contract,** *an agreement by workers that they will not join a union.* Employees who later violated such a pact would be fired for breach of contract. The Norris-LaGuardia Act made these agreements illegal.

What can management legally do? There are legal options, and they are discussed next.

Lockout

One way to counteract employee demands is the **lockout,** in which *management locks the doors and prevents workers from entering the building.* Although effective in crushing workers' demands during the 1930s, this tactic rarely is used today because it produces so much negative publicity for management. In addition, management normally cannot sustain a lockout, because such a work stoppage, even if voluntary, loses sales, profits, and market share to competitors. But the threat of a lockout by paper- and pulp-mill owners in British Columbia served as the incentive to bring the International Woodworkers of America and two other unions to resume negotiations on a 3-year contract pact.[12]

Plant Closings

In some instances management has sold a plant and moved away rather than surrender to labor's demands. This was the case when the textile industry migrated from New England to the South to find cheaper, nonunion labor. Some firms have put individual plants on the market in the wake of wage demands that they said would make it impossible for them to operate at an acceptable profit. In recent months Ford threatened to shut its Edison, New Jersey, car assembly plant[13] and its River Rouge Steel Mill in Dearborn, Michigan, if the United Auto Workers did not accept contracts with cost-saving concessions.[14] Swift Independent Packing Company closed two processing plants and two sales facilities in the wake of a contract rejection by the United Food and Commercial Workers Union.[15]

In addition, a major policy decision by the National Labor Relations Board, which allows employers to move operations to a nonunionized facility to avoid the higher costs of a union contract, probably will result in more plant closings. The National Labor Relations Board stated that these moves were legal as long as companies have satisfied their obligation to bargain with the union and if the contract does not specifically restrain it.[16] Another element of this approach is the threat to close operations entirely through filing bankruptcy. Eastern Airlines and Greyhound Bus Lines both threatened bankruptcy unless labor made major concessions during contract talks. Although management viewed bankruptcy as a real possibility, labor considered it a misuse of bankruptcy laws to revoke union contracts.[17]

Injunction

A legal solution for employee protests, an **injunction** is *a court order prohibiting a party from performing an unjust, inequitable, or injurious act.* When employees stop work or otherwise protest undesirable working conditions, management can obtain an injunction ordering employees back to work. The Norris-LaGuardia Act (see Table 8.1) requires management to supply specific evidence of potentially irreparable injuries before the courts will order workers to stop their protest activities.

On three separate occasions an injunction was issued to prevent strikes by the Brotherhood of Locomotive Engineers (BLE) against Conrail, the federally subsidized northeast corridor rail freight line. The reason given for the injunction: "a strike by the BLE threatens to interrupt interstate commerce, substantially depriving a section of the country of essential transportation service. Additionally, a strike on Conrail would disrupt service to the rest of the country because other railroads would be unable to interline with Conrail."[18]

Strikebreakers

strikebreakers

Companies may attempt to operate during a strike by employing outside **strikebreakers** (called *scabs* by the strikers and their supporters). These are *workers who perform the jobs until the striking workers come to terms with management.* Labor experts believe that the use of strikebreakers will accelerate in a continuation of the trend toward hard-nosed concession bargaining that began in the country's recent economic recession. Companies that have employed this tool recently include Phelps Dodge Corporation, Magic Chef, Whirlpool Corporation, and National Metal Crafters.[19]

Management-Run Operation

As an alternative to hiring strikebreakers, some firms attempt to keep minimum production flowing by having supervisory, technical, or clerical personnel run the equipment when regular operators walk off the job. Several large oil companies have used this method to keep refineries operating in the wake of strikes by the Oil, Chemical, and Atomic Workers International Union, which represents most refinery workers. American Telephone and Telegraph has used this technique for years during its contract renegotiation phases. This practice was again successfully implemented during the summer 1983 strike by workers.[20]

Employers' Associations

employers' association

Competing firms have been known to form an **employers' association,** *a group that represents several companies in bargaining with a union that has organized their workers.* Because master contracts often cover many firms and thousands of employees within one industry, employers' associations provide management with greater bargaining strength.

Bargaining through associations is common in the coal, steel, construction, railroad, and trucking industries, where firms share the cost of highly qualified negotiators, a significant advantage for firms that cannot afford to hire their own; for example:

During the Bell System strike of 1983, supervisory personnel worked at the equipment to keep the business operating.

— Rail carriers formed the National Railway Labor Conference to bargain with twenty unions representing several groups of railroad workers.

— More than 600 trucking companies formed Trucking Management, which acts as their agent in contract negotiations with the giant International Brotherhood of Teamsters.

— Coal producers have dealt with the United Mine Workers of America through the Bituminous Coal Operators' Association, which is authorized to act for 130 coal companies in 14 states.

Lobbying

Management may resort to formal, expert **lobbying,** which is *employing persons to influence state and federal legislators to sponsor laws that further one's own interests or inhibit those of one's opponents.* Large companies, employers' associations, and trade associations of companies in various industries hire professional lobbyists to represent the interests of management to legislators.

lobbying

The Power of the Press

When a labor-management dispute arises, labor sometimes gets the lion's share of the publicity. Striking workers are interviewed by representatives of the news media, and their protest activities attract considerable public interest. Management, on the other hand, may have to spend money to air its side of the dispute, usually by purchasing full-page advertisements in newspapers and requesting equal time with labor leaders on radio and television.

Now that we have looked at management's tools, let's see what techniques labor has available.

Labor Tools

Strikes

A strike was defined earlier as a temporary work stoppage by employees to protest certain working conditions and reinforce demands for their correction. Former AFL-CIO president George Meany once asserted that "It is the right to strike that gives meaning to collective bargaining. It is the right to strike that gives a union spokesperson some measure of equality at the bargaining table." Most employers would at least agree with Meany that the strike is a powerful weapon, one that can have a lasting impact on an employer, an industry, or even an entire nation.

In the air traffic controllers' strike of 1981, almost 13,000 of the 15,000 members of the Professional Air Traffic Controllers Organization (PATCO) struck against the federal government. Because federal employees legally are prohibited from striking, President Reagan fired the 11,500 PATCO members who did not return to work within 48 hours. Military air traffic controllers, supervisors, nonstriking controllers, and trainees who applied for the fired controllers' jobs were brought into airport control towers nationwide. But the strike had an impact on business: the air traffic control system operated at 59 percent of its former stength and airlines were forced to reduce schedules and suffered many delays.[21]

Although strikes make news, they are the exception in labor-management relations rather than the rule. According to the Department of Labor, work time lost to strikes in any given year averages less than one-half of 1 percent of working time, and most strikes are settled in 2 weeks or less.

The strike is a labor tool designed to equalize power between labor and management at the bargaining table.

Picketing

"It pays to advertise," an old Advertising Council slogan, applies to workers' grievances too. In **picketing,** *workers publicly air their complaints against an employer by staging a demonstration outside the building, with protest signs and explanatory leaflets.* Although most picketing occurs during strikes, some is informational, designed to acquaint the public with the workers' side of a dispute that has not yet escalated into a strike. Figure 8.5 provides an illustration of material distributed during a picketing action. It in essence asked for a boycott.

picketing

Boycott

Another union tactic, a **boycott,** is *a refusal to do business with a given party until certain demands are met.* There are two types of boycotts. A **primary boycott** occurs when *employees or a union*

boycott

primary boycott

Please Don't Shop at Colonial Plaza Mall Stores

The working men, women, and retirees of Carpenter's Local Union 1765 urge you not to shop at Colonial Plaza Mall Shops because of the builders, Thompson Construction Company, Contract Construction, Scandia Inc., Kelley's Concrete, and their contributions to substandard wages.

Colonial Plaza Mall stores under construction are being built by Thompson Construction Company, Contract Construction, Scandia Inc., and Kelley's Concrete who pay substandard wages and fringe benefits. The use of contractors who pay substandard wages and benefits is a drain on our local economy. The payment of substandard wages diminishes the purchasing power of working persons who are also customers and neighbors in this community. Our members cannot maintain their living standards due to the substandard wages paid by Thompson Construction Company, Contract Construction, Scandia Inc., and Kelley's Concrete at Colonial Plaza Mall Construction sites. Moreover, the use of the contractors paying substandard wages undermines the business of fair labor contractors who build with skilled labor under union standards.

With so many shopping centers in the area, why not purchase your merchandise at one built by contractors using union labor, which ensures skilled labor under union standards?

We ask you to support our protests against substandard wages and working conditions by refusing to buy any merchandise at the Colonial Plaza Mall Stores until the building contractors, Thompson Construction Company, Contract Construction, Scandia Inc., and Kelley's Concrete, are willing to pay wages consistent with the area.

The picketing is informational and does not have organization, recognition, work jurisdiction, or bargaining as an objective. Employees of this and other employers are not requested to refrain from working or performing services.

Please Do Not Litter

Figure 8.5 Informational Picketing Literature
Source: Courtesy United Brotherhood of Carpenters and Joiners of America. Figure is for educational purposes only.

agree not to purchase goods from a particular firm. The AFL-CIO executive council, for example, requested a union boycott of Procter & Gamble detergents, claiming that management used delaying tactics and obstructive bargaining in negotiating with the union that workers had elected at the company's Kansas City plant.[22] The AFL-CIO went one step further in its boycott program of Procter & Gamble. Not only did it initiate a primary boycott, but it also encouraged consumers to boycott Procter & Gamble products, as shown in Figure 8.6.

Figure 8.6 Encouraging Consumer Support for Boycotting a Company's Products
Source: Courtesy of The United Steel-workers of America.

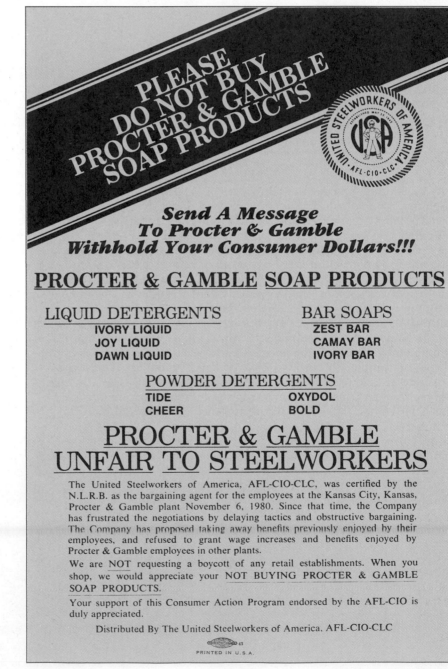

Primary boycotts are legal, but workers' participation historically has been more symbolic than actual. As a rule, even the largest primary boycott will not decrease a firm's sales impressively, so companies are rarely upset to find themselves on the AFL-CIO's boycott list, which at any given time contains the names of approximately a dozen firms.

A **secondary boycott** consists of pressure aimed at firms that buy from or sell to a firm that is engaged in a labor-management dispute. These *third-party companies are threatened with harassment and internal labor problems if they continue to do business with the target firm.* The Taft-Hartley Act outlawed secondary boycotts.

secondary boycott

Public Relations

Unions realize, as do companies, that it is important to create and project a favorable public image to consumers and potential members. Adopting this attitude with verve, the International Ladies' Garment Workers Union in the 1970s staged a landmark $2.5 million public relations campaign that included television, radio, and print advertisements centered around a song that urged consumers to "look for the union label." The National Education Association, the United Auto Workers, and many other unions also have developed costly image-building programs.[23]

Lobbying and Political Activities

Unions, like management, have a strong professional lobbying effort. They attempt to influence the direction of leglislation and enlist the support of legislators sensitive to labor's concerns.

Additionally, unions back political figures who have strong labor views. By providing financial and election worker support the unions attempt to have people elected who will promote labor's programs. Unions also have begun organizing their retirees to lobby and to work in election campaigns. The United Auto Workers, the United Mine Workers, and the Teamsters have all adopted this technique to add numbers and experience to their staffs.[24]

Pause and Ponder

Think of a labor-management situation you have read about or seen on television. What tools of labor were being utilized? What tools was management using? How effective was each side in dealing with the situation?

Collective Bargaining

collective bargaining

The Wagner Act guaranteed employees' legal right to form unions. Once a union is elected according to the law's procedures, it becomes the workers' official bargaining agent and **collective bargaining** takes place. This is *the process whereby employer and employee representatives jointly negotiate a contract that specifies wages, hours, and other conditions of employment.* Collective bargaining establishes a process and a set of governing guidelines under which management and labor work through the negotiation of contractual terms. In addition, collective bargaining includes the ongoing relationship between management and labor with administration of the contract.

Good-Faith Bargaining

In collective bargaining management and labor meet together to "hammer out" the terms of the contract. Over a period of days, weeks, or months the two parties work on the eventual agreement. Under law both parties are required to negotiate wages, hours, and terms and conditions of employment in "good faith." This means that both parties negotiate, and when one party makes an offer, the other side agrees or matches it with a counteroffer. It does not mean that either management or labor must agree to a proposal or that either party must make a concession.

What Management and Labor Bargain For

Negotiation sessions differ from industry to industry, but normally bargaining is done on wages, conditions of work, employment procedures, methods of settling disputes, safety, management's rights, and labor's rights. It is during this process that the balance of power in an organization is determined. What management "gives up" labor receives and vice versa.

A recent development in union-management bargaining has been labor's concessions to management in wages and total compensation packages. The United Auto Workers and the United Steelworkers are two of the larger unions that have made major wage and fringe-benefit concessions as a result of economic recessions.[25] Table 8.4 provides a list of topics normally included in a contract.

Ratification by Members

When the two parties have "tentatively" agreed to a contract, it is submitted to the members of the union for ratification. The ratification process may be complex or simple. In the case of a local union, the contract needs only to be voted on by that membership. For a national union (e.g., United Auto Workers, Teamsters) each local union affected by the national agreement must vote to accept or reject the contract.

Employment Practices	**Grievances**	**Table 8.4** Topics Normally Included in a Labor Contract
Hiring Procedure	Grievance Procedure	
Discharge	Arbitration (voluntary, mandatory)	
Layoff Plan	Disciplinary procedures	
Reinstatements		
Terminations	**Wages**	
Seniority		
Transfers	Bonus payments	
Job-posting practices	Piece rate	
	Shift differentials	
Work Assignments	Severance pay	
	Overtime pay	
Work loads	Job evaluation	
Work hours	Base wages	
Work breaks		
Subcontracting	**Benefits**	
	Discounts on company products	
Management and Labor Rights	Profit sharing	
	Sick leave	
Management rights clause	Group insurance	
Union security	Vacations	
	Pensions	

Mediation and Arbitration

When representatives of labor and management reach a stalemate in negotiations, they may resort to **mediation,** *a process by which an impartial person acceptable to both sides encourages them to communicate, bargain, and work toward a satisfactory compromise.* The mediator, who has no authority to decide the issue, proposes solutions to the dispute and acts as a friend to both parties. Mediation can fail, however, when labor and management are poles apart and a strong adversary relationship exists.

mediation

    In severe disputes that mediation fails to settle, or when mediation simply is bypassed, **arbitration** may take place. Here *labor and management empower an impartial third party called an* arbitrator *to act as judge and hand down a legally binding decision that both sides have agreed in advance to accept.* Arbitration is voluntary when both parties agree to submit disputed issues to a final judgment. The law may call for compulsory arbitration when deadlocks arise, for example, between city governments and such groups as firefighters, law enforcement officers, or other employees whose jobs influence the public welfare and safety.

arbitration

    Almost all labor-management contracts contain an arbitration clause. Labor and management can turn to two important agencies, one public and one private, to help them resolve disagreements peacefully. Each can provide the following services:

1. Examine labor-management disputes with greater objectivity
2. Devise creative solutions to a dispute that neither side may have considered
3. Recommend specific contract terms and language that has been acceptable to both parties in similar cases
4. Provide data that may help labor and management clarify their respective demands and smooth the way for successful negotiations
5. Inform the parties of current trends in labor-management relations in other parts of the country

The Federal Mediation and Conciliation Service

The Federal Mediation and Conciliation Service (FMCS), a federal government agency, will help settle a broad range of labor-management disputes. Functioning under a director appointed by the president of the United States, the FMCS was created by the Taft-Hartley Act to resolve disputes before they reach a crisis or to help settle existing strikes or lockouts rapidly.

Mediation through the FMCS is free and voluntary, and it can be requested by either party to help settle a conflict. In fact, the Taft-Hartley Act requires parties to a labor-management contract to file a dispute notice if they cannot agree on a new pact 30 days before their present one expires. An FMCS mediator then meets with them to see if they want assistance. (Approximately 95 percent of such cases are usually settled without mediation.)

The FMCS also maintains and makes available a roster of over 1,300 independent arbitrators who are qualified to handle disputes on subjects such as wages, hours, working conditions, fringe benefits, and job assignments. Labor and management jointly choose an arbitrator and share the arbitrator's fee equally. Arbitrators on the FMCS roster must adhere to the ethical standards and procedures contained in the code of professional responsibility for arbitrators of labor-management disputes, and their impartiality is rarely questioned. The purpose and spirit of the Federal Mediation and Conciliation Service was reflected on matchbooks commemorating the service's 30th anniversary. They read, "Call us before striking."

"Another setback — the mediators just went out on strike."
Source: © 1979 by Sidney Harris — *The Wall Street Journal.*

The American Arbitration Association

The American Arbitration Association (AAA), a private nonprofit group, also can be used to resolve disputes. This organization follows a procedure similar to the FMCS in providing a list of suggested arbitrators containing more than 1,800 names. It stands ready to handle anything from property boundary arguments and partnership friction to labor-management issues.

The AAA charges an administrative fee per case, and the arbitrator selected by the parties charges a separate fee for services rendered. The AAA helps to settle over 16,000 labor-management disputes a year.

Both mediators and arbitrators have grown in national recognition in recent years. As a result of strikes in professional sports — football, baseball, and basketball — the use of the third party to work through contracts has become well known. In addition, a National Labor Relations Board decision to refer labor disputes initially to arbitrators and to refuse in more instances to overrule arbitrators' findings may result in expanded use of arbitration.[26]

Grievance Procedures

Once a contract is negotiated and ratified, the rights of management and labor are established. But regardless of how well the contracts are worded, **grievances,** *disputes caused by contract violations or different interpretations of contract language,* can arise at any time. As a result virtually all contracts include a **grievance procedure,** *a series of steps to be followed by an employee whose complaint to a supervisor has not been resolved satisfactorily.* Grievance procedures enhance industrial relations by providing a safety valve for tensions and a remedy for disputes that arise between management and workers.

grievances

grievance procedure

The steps in a grievance procedure are not standardized in all labor-management contracts, but a typical sequence of events is as follows:

— **Step 1** If the employee and the supervisor cannot settle their dispute together, the worker informs the **union steward,** *a worker who is both an employee and a union representative.* This person meets with the supervisor to negotiate the matter.

union steward

— **Step 2** If the union steward and the supervisor cannot reach agreement, the matter may be forwarded to the chief union steward and the supervisor's boss.

— **Step 3** If the parties in Step 2 cannot reach a mutually acceptable settlement, the dispute is referred to local union officials and local company managers, who sometimes meet as a committee to resolve the grievance.

— **Step 4** If the dispute is not settled at Step 3, top company management and top union officials confer on the matter.

— **Step 5** If the parties in Step 4 cannot agree, the matter is typically referred to arbitration.

The grievance procedure is established to provide management and labor with a channel to keep communications open. In turn this aids in maintaining the work environment.

The Straight Line

The George Meany Center

Trade Unionists Also Go to School

These days of lean budgets for academic institutions do not seem to have hit one organization with the same force that others have experienced. The institution is the George Meany Center for Labor Studies, a 47-acre campus in Silver Springs, Maryland, a suburb of Washington, D.C.

Founded in 1969, the campus has facilities that include 100 guest rooms, with overnight accommodations for 130. Each room has its own private bath and study center. There is a pleasant cafeteria with good food, 7 classrooms and several smaller breakout rooms, and a 200-seat auditorium with a stage for live performances.

The center is equipped with the latest electronic teaching aids, including video- and audiotape recorders and players, overhead projectors, 35-mm motion picture projectors, and 16-mm carousel slide projectors. In a recent year the center offered forty-three institutes, workshops, and programs for trade union leaders.

Enrollment is open to any full-time officer, representative, or staff employee of any labor organization affiliated with the AFL-CIO, its departments, state federations, and local central bodies. In 1978, the first year the campus was fully operational, more than 3,200 trade unionists made use of its facilities. In addition to the center's labor study courses, AFL-CIO unions ran forty-two training programs of their own on the campus. Thirteen departments or related organizations of the AFL-

Summary

A labor union is a legally sanctioned, formally organized association of workers who have united to represent their collective views for wages, hours, and working conditions. Labor unions are created by workers to provide a method to deal with management more effectively and to equalize the balance of power. Unionism is based on three principles: strength through unity, equal pay for the same job, and employment practices based on seniority.

Labor unions, considered illegal conspiracies in this country until 1842, have come a long way since the turn of the century. Beginning with craft, or trade, unions, which organized skilled workers, they had expanded by the 1930s to recruit workers in various industries. Major union organizational accomplishments include the development of the AFL, the CIO, and the eventual union of both to create the AFL-CIO.

Union growth during the 1930s was accompanied and encouraged by the passage of the Norris-LaGuardia Act and the Wagner Act, federal laws that protect workers' rights to strike and to form unions. These rights were modified somewhat by the Taft-Hartley Act of 1947. The Landrum-Griffin Act of 1959 addressed the financial responsibility of union officials and members' rights.

CIO sponsored programs at the center.

Typical of the seminars offered are "The Union Administrator and Business Agent"; "Psychology of Union Leadership"; "Negotiating Techniques in Collective Bargaining"; "Organizing Techniques"; "Effective Union Action on Civil Rights"; and "Dimensions of Corporate Power."

The George Meany Center also offers union leaders the opportunity to study for a college degree without interrupting their union work. The center has joined forces with Antioch University to offer a flexible college degree program. And the center gives some college credits for skills learned through experiences in the labor movement.

All is not study and hard work at the center, though. It also boasts a 27-acre recreation area where students can play tennis, volleyball, and softball, or just go for a hike. Ping-Pong, pool, cards, checkers, and chess are available for rainy evenings. Through a grant from the National Endowment for the Arts, the center offers a continuing series of art exhibits displaying the painting, sculpture, and photography of American artists.

With its intensive, probing class and discussion programs, the George Meany Center for Labor Studies offers leaders of the labor movement opportunities to make their movement more effective in the years to come.

For more about the George Meany Center, see the center's latest catalog, which you can get by writing 10000 New Hampshire Avenue, Silver Springs, MD 20903.

Today's labor movement is faced with representing a lower percentage of the total labor force, an image problem, and the perceived loss of power at the bargaining tables and in Congress. The future directions of the union movement include organizing high-technology industries, service industries, education, and women in the labor force.

Workers form unions to increase bargaining power, obtain better working conditions, improve job security, and improve their economic positions. Through unionization they are able to have a collective voice to deal with management.

Both parties have their respective tactics or tools when a dispute arises. Until such tactics were outlawed, management could fire, lay off, or blacklist employees involved in union organizing activities or require them to sign "yellow dog" contracts before they were hired.

Managers can legally:

— Close plants
— Lock out employees
— Hire strikebreakers
— Use management personnel

233

   – Obtain a court injunction
   – Use the power of the press
   – Lobby
   – Form employers' associations

On the other hand, labor can:

   – Strike
   – Boycott
   – Picket
   – Utilize public relations
   – Rely on lobbying and political activities

Once employees have elected a union to represent them, the collective bargaining process between management and labor begins. Both parties are charged with bargaining in good faith. Normally contracts include conditions on wages, hours, time off, benefits, and procedures for laying off or discharging employees.

If contract negotiations stall, a third party, either a mediator or an arbitrator, may be utilized. To receive help in mediation or arbitration cases, labor and management may call on the Federal Mediation and Conciliation Service or a private organization, the American Arbitration Association.

Grievances may occur after a contract is agreed on. Grievances are caused by contract violations or by different interpretations of contract language. A grievance procedure normally is provided for as part of the collective bargaining process to resolve these situations.

Key Terms

agency shop
arbitration
blacklist
boycott
closed shop
collective bargaining
craft *or* trade unions
employees' association
employers' association
Federal Anti-Injunction Act (Norris-LaGuardia Act) of 1932
grievance procedure
grievances

industrial unions
injunction
Labor-Management Relations Act (Taft-Hartley Act) of 1947
Labor-Management Reporting and Disclosure Act (Landrum-Griffin Act) of 1959
labor union
lobbying
lockout
mediation
National Labor Relations Act (Wagner Act) of 1935

open shop
picketing
primary boycott
right-to-work laws
secondary boycott
simple-recognition shop
strikebreakers
strikes
union shop
union steward
"yellow dog" contract

For Review and Discussion

1. Why do labor unions exist?
2. What are the three guiding principles of unionism? How have those been translated into labor's basic objective?

3. Distinguish between the type of union that would affiliate with the original AFL and the original CIO.
4. Summarize the key points of each of the following:

a. Federal Anti-Injunction Act (Norris-LaGuardia Act)

b. National Labor Relations Act (Wagner Act)

c. Labor-Management Relations Act (Taft-Hartley Act)

d. Labor-Management Reporting and Disclosure Act (Landrum-Griffin Act)

5. What is the status of union membership today in terms of actual percentage of membership, certification elections, and decertification actions?

6. Comment on the following statement: "The 'clout' of unions is less."

7. Comment on the statement "The bread and butter days of unionism are over. Unions have to develop new directions."

8. Identify four new directions unions will be focusing on.

9. Does a union give employees a greater voice? Is this true in all companies? Why or why not?

10. What conclusion can you draw on the effectiveness of unions in their objective of improving their members' economic position?

11. What types of job security are provided by a union shop? By an agency shop?

12. Why do you think management has increased the use of strikebreakers?

13. What is the key legal ingredient in management's being able to close a plant or move operations as a tool in contract negotiations according to the National Labor Relations Board?

14. What is the purpose of an injunction? Under what conditions is it granted by the courts?

15. Distinguish between a primary boycott and a secondary boycott.

16. What is meant by collective bargaining? What does bargaining in "good faith" mean?

17. Comment on the statement "The collective bargaining process establishes the balance of power in an organization."

18. Distinguish between mediation and arbitration; between voluntary and compulsory arbitration.

19. What is a grievance? How can it be resolved?

Applications

Case 8.1 The Super Sub

Life had certainly changed for Ron Robisky. His whole work life had become a series of "rules, regulations, procedures, dos, and don'ts" as he was fond of saying while gulping down his supper. "My whole approach to my job, my flexibility, and even my special deals with Jim Flannigan have gone by the wayside with this union stuff."

For the past 3 years he had worked at Valve Systems, a repair shop specializing in repairing and reconditioning pipeline valves in the oil and gas industry. Ron was referred to by Jim Flannigan, the controller and warehouse manager, as my "super sub." The title was very appropriate. Ron:

– Was in charge of the physical inventory of repair parts and supplies

– Did all the shipping and receiving for the company

– Drove a delivery truck when the regular driver was unavailable or during busy times

– Worked on repairing valves (under the supervision of a lead person) when Valve Systems received a rush repair order from any one of the major oil refineries

– Put the finishing touches on the repaired valves

by operating the paint booth, attaching the repair tags, and coding the valves

Ron literally had the "run of the place." He worked in any department that needed his help. He worked irregular hours — sometimes from 5:00 A.M. until 8:00 P.M. or, on other occasions, from 1:00 to 5:00 P.M. This arrangement worked well. As a senior business administration major at the local college, it gave Ron time to study and gave the company the flexibility to have Ron work when needed.

But all this had changed. Valve Systems had become a union shop 3 months ago. The decision to unionize was supported by management: it gave the company easy access to their customers who were unionized. As Lloyd Elkins, the Field Service Vice-President, had remarked, "Being a card-carrying company is a lot more comfortable going into those refineries to repair valves, than being considered scabs by the workers. They just dislike nonunion companies."

The vote for the union shop had altered Ron's work life. Although his hourly pay had been increased, he:

– Had a specific job title that defined his duties

– No longer could move from department to department when work was needed

– Had to pay union dues that amounted to almost his entire increase in pay

– Could no longer be asked to work overtime until all the senior people had been asked

– Could no longer work the number of hours he needed to meet his expenses: his irregular pattern of hours often threw him into the overtime category for daily work (In the past his overtime was determined on a weekly basis.)

– Lost his flexibility to approach Jim and work out his own deals

– Was chastised by the shop steward for working during breaks and starting back to work before the lunch hour was over

Questions

Evaluate Ron's situation using the four reasons given in the section on why workers join unions.

1. How does Ron's personal experience compare with these guidelines?

2. What characteristics of Ron and his particular job would result in this situation?

3. What conclusions can you draw about people, unions, and the work environment from this case?

Case 8.2 Trouble on the Hill

"You're doggone right I'm unhappy! Can't you see we need to do something about this? I've told you and told you, if we had a union this just wouldn't happen. There is no way that forklift would not have been fixed when we reported the problem with the hydraulics. Now the darn thing gives way with a load of boxes on it and we almost get killed! When are we going to get smart?"

Tony Adamski, lead stockperson, was a reasonable man, but he felt that the only answer for the employees of Hillyard Industries was to vote in a union. Over the past few months a number of situations had occurred that had led him to this conclusion.

– A series of repairs to equipment had not been made, such as with the forklift.

– Employees did not have appropriate safety equip-

ment (goggles, gloves, steel-toed boots) for the work they were doing.

– Promotions were made on outright favoritism, not on performance or experience.

– Overtime was given to the lowest-paid employees rather than to the people who were qualified to do the job (and who made more money).

– Wage rates were an average of 5 percent less than the other companies in the area.

– It was rumored that people doing the same job were being paid differently.

– People who had the courage to question management were being fired. Tony himself had been labeled a troublemaker because of his constant questions of management practices.

– Performance appraisals appeared to be done with the idea of keeping people from getting raises.

– Complaints or suggestions for improvements were at the mercy of the managers. If the manager was good, the complaints were listened to and some were corrected. But if the manager was insensitive, the employees' concerns were ignored.

– It was rumored that people with union backgrounds were being "targeted" to be eventually fired for "performance" weaknesses.

When Tony talked to his fellow employees, urging them to consider a union to balance the power, develop grievance systems, and to provide for security, they had two responses:

> "We need these jobs. If we get too aggressive we'll get fired."

> "Tony, if you feel this way, why don't you report all this to OSHA, the wage and hour boys, and to the equal employment opportunity commission? They can handle this."

Questions

1. How would you evaluate the work environment of Hillyard Industries?

2. How do these situations relate to the four reasons given for why workers join unions?

3. How would having a union solve each of these situations?

4. As a member of Hillyard's management team what would you do to prevent unionization?

Personnel and Management

Personnel Management with Levi Strauss

The employees who work for some large companies could populate a medium-sized city. Consequently, the demand for personnel or human resources management managers grows with industrial expansion. In fact, the number of personnel workers is expected to grow faster than the average for all occupations through the 1980s. Those who build careers in human resources management make an important contribution to their companies and to their fellow workers by maintaining meaningful communications between management and workers at all levels. They make the firm a more efficient and more human place to work.

Levi Strauss & Company, a 134-year-old firm whose jeans are famous around the world, offers gratifying careers in personnel for qualified college graduates. The company has openings in such areas as organization development and training, industrial relations, benefits administration, executive development, and compensation within its various divisions and in its home office in San Francisco.

Although Levi Strauss has different qualifications for each entry-level job in personnel, the company places great value on advanced college degrees. It generally prefers graduates who have earned at least a master's degree (ideally, a master of business administration) or those who hold a bachelor's degree and between 1 and 3 years of personnel experience.

Employees who demonstrate exceptional leadership are invited to join the company's management development program (MDP), which accelerates their advancement. Members of this fast-track program train intensively under the guidance of a sponsoring manager for between 9 and 12 months. They also receive on-the-job training in merchandising, finance and business planning, operations, and sales, after which they receive a permanent assignment. Continued specialized training is available for those who exhibit exceptional potential. The company prefers that MDP candidates have an M.B.A. or 1 to 5 years of work experience in the area of their preference.

Levi's strong degree orientation is not unusual. Most corporate employers encourage employees to earn advanced degrees by attending classes part time at nearby accredited colleges. Levi Strauss mirrors the attitude of most companies by viewing further education as an integral part of an employee's career.

If you become part of the personnel area of this company (and perhaps move into the MDP program), you will become part of an organization that is as concerned about the quality of its employees as the quality of its products. Its commitment to providing a challenging and gratifying career to qualified applicants may best be summarized in the title of one of its recruiting brochures: "Career Opportunities You'll Never Outgrow."

Plant Operations at Caterpillar Tractor

Caterpillar Tractor Company is the world's largest manufacturer and marketer of a broad line of earthmoving equipment. It has facilities in eighteen states and twelve foreign countries. To remain a leader in a competitive industry, the company recruits college graduates with degrees in business, engineering, computer science, and various other fields. This career capsule presents the Caterpillar training program that prepares newly hired graduates to work in management at its manufacturing plants.

The company seeks creative, assertive, self-starting, and people-oriented individuals to work in plant operations. While acknowledging that engineering, industrial technology, and mechanical technology degrees are desirable, the company welcomes applicants regardless of academic background. All they must have is solid mechanical aptitude.

Newly hired applicants first complete the company's 12-month plant operations training (POT) program, which includes three phases. The first phase, 13 weeks of company orientation, begins by rotating the trainee through such areas as the product proving ground, machine tool laboratory, and welding laboratory under the direction of a training staff member. Then comes classroom training in which trainees relate their experiences during rotation to on-the-job situations. Trainees also use this time to study Caterpillar's policies and procedures.

The second phase puts trainees to work for 35 weeks in a manufacturing plant, serving either in a staff capacity or as a shop foreman. Most trainees also receive a limited amount of assembly line supervision experience in this phase.

In the final phase, only 1 week long, trainees receive a broader view of Caterpillar's activities by visiting a Caterpillar dealer and suppliers, as well as Midwestern plants. With this year-long preparation behind them, trainees are assigned to a line job in factory supervision or a staff job in manufacturing staff services.

Those in factory supervision usually start work as shop foremen and supervise workers on the second or third shift of the plants to which they are transferred. Later they may be promoted to higher managerial positions at the plant level. Eventually they may reach companywide administrative jobs.

Trainees who choose the manufacturing staff services career path assist factory managers in running the plants more effectively. Their contribution comes through work in such specialized areas as employee relations, labor relations, planning, or education and training.

Caterpillar encourages its full-time regular employees to embrace education as a lifelong process. The company's educational assistance plan pays 70 percent of the tuition and other required fees (such as registration and laboratory costs) for job-related courses that improve present or future job performance or earn them a high school equivalency diploma or an advanced college degree.

Part

Production and Marketing Activities

Producing the Product

Chapter Outline

Chapter Objectives

After studying this chapter, you should be able to:

1. Discuss the influence of production on our standard of living.
2. Differentiate between processing and manufacturing companies.
3. List the three kinds of factors to consider when choosing a plant site, and give examples of each.
4. Contrast motion study and time study and evaluate their use in production management.
5. Compare the four major production processes, giving examples of each.
6. Discuss how robots may be used for certain production jobs and how their use may benefit both labor and management.
7. List the steps involved in a typical purchasing procedure and summarize the purchasing policies that management may follow.
8. Describe the steps involved in production control.

Quality control is not just a little room adjacent to the factory floor whose occupants make a nuisance of themselves to everyone else. Quality control is — or should be — a state of mind.
— Dr. Norihiko Nakayama, president,
Fujitsu America

Up Front   McBride and McKenzie

The Key Ingredient for M & M Was Hard Work

What use would two pharmacists have for a pool cue and a 55-gallon drum? For pharmacists Cornell McBride and Therman McKenzie, they were the production equipment of what is now a successful hair-care manufacturing firm, M & M Products Company.

As pharmacy students in Atlanta, McBride and McKenzie saw a demand for a product that would moisturize black men's hair. Equipped with their background in pharmacy, the two set to work with verve to invent such a product. By the time they graduated and began working as pharmacists

for a large drugstore chain, the product — Sta-Sof-Fro — had been perfected. The first production run was mixed in McBride's cellar using that 55-gallon drum and pool cue. Their obvious determination to succeed moved suppliers to set aside enough chemicals to meet their needs even when stock was insufficient to fill orders from major manufacturers.

The two entrepreneurs soon discovered that inventing and producing their product did not guarantee success. It still had to be sold. Encountering lukewarm response from large retail stores,

In this part of the book, we will focus on the central functions of business: making, selling, promoting, and distributing products. Production is an integral part of this business activity: you cannot sell what you have not made. The age-old questions of production are at the heart of business: how can I make more products, make them cheaper, and make them better?

The Nature of Production

The United States enjoys a high standard of living because companies make goods in adequate numbers to fulfill consumer demand. In doing so, they create jobs for millions of Americans and encourage a flourishing service industry to maintain and repair the articles made. Here are a few of the support industries that provide the auto industry with required materials, parts, and supplies:

- Glass
- Metals
- Fiberglass
- Plastics
- Rubber
- Leather
- Abrasives
- Paint
- Carbon
- Cork
- Paper
- Textiles

That is not all; various other businesses rely on cars for their livelihood by servicing existing autos or auto owners:

the two began selling Sta-Sof-Fro to small retailers out of the trunks of their cars. By 1974 they decided to quit their jobs as pharmacists to devote their full energies to making M & M Products succeed. Then, in 1978, a change in black men's hairstyles occurred that ensured success for McKenzie and McBride's product — the curl. This style required that hair be moisturized, and Sta-Sof-Fro was the only product on the market that would do the job. Hair stylists regularly began recommending it to their curl customers.

Sales rocketed from $4.2 million in 1978 to $27 million in 1980, and M & M Products shot from the 99th to the 13th largest black-owned company in terms of sales. By 1982 sales hit a record $43 million and the company was the eleventh-ranked black-owned business in the nation. Employees, products, and other areas of the firm grew accordingly. By late 1983 M & M Products Company employed 400 workers, sold 65 different hair-care products, and spent $4 million just to advertise its product line throughout the United States, Europe, Africa, Canada, and the Caribbean.

For more about Cornell McBride and Therman McKenzie, see Ezra K. Davidson, "Success of Hair-Care Company Illustrates Progress of Black-Owned Businesses in U.S.," *The Wall Street Journal*, September 15, 1983, p. 33.

- Maintenance and repair businesses
- Replacement parts firms
- Aftermarket businesses selling such items as radios, paint, and tires
- Petroleum-based products dealers
- Insurance companies

The Motor Vehicle Manufacturers' Association reports that more than 16 percent of the United States nonagriculture-employed work force has jobs somehow related to the automobile industry. Production is clearly a significant factor in the world of business.

What Is Production?

Production is *a business activity that uses people and machinery to convert materials and parts into salable products.* Two types of companies engage in this activity. A **processing company,** the first type, is *a firm that converts natural resources into raw material.* Forest products, petroleum, steel, bauxite, meat-packing, citrus, and leather-tanning companies are processors. The second type of production company, a **manufacturing company,** is *a firm that converts raw materials and component parts into consumer and industrial goods.* Farm equipment, stereo, computer, and appliance makers are manufacturing companies. This is what most people

production

processing company

manufacturing company

have in mind when they think of production: long assembly lines where workers add parts to a growing object until it finally appears as the product. Our discussion will concentrate on manufacturing firms, but many of the principles discussed and introduced are important in both kinds of production.

Products are often used to make other products, so one firm's finished product may be another's component part. This kind of interdependence is common. Tens of thousands of firms rely on one another for essential parts, subassemblies, and supplies that support or become part of an end product.

Managing Production

production management

Production management is *the job of coordinating and controlling all the activities required to make a product.* It begins well before actual production. Managers who represent production, marketing, finance, and other areas must jointly decide what product to make, based on their analysis of consumer wants and needs (more on this in Chapter 10). Once a product has been chosen, management determines where and how to produce it. Materials, parts, equipment, supplies, subassemblies, and employees must appear in the right quantities, places, and times. Effective production managers co-ordinate people, dollars, machines, and materials as economically and efficiently as possible to create a marketable product.

Choosing a Plant Site

Actual production cannot begin until a plant is built, but the original plants of many prominent manufacturing companies were situated in humble and sometimes illogical places. Liquid Paper correction fluid for typing errors was first brewed up in a kitchen. Everest & Jennings International, a worldwide producer of wheelchairs and other medical equipment, began in 1933 in Harry Jennings's one-car garage. Several years later Jennings and his partner, Herbert Everest, tripled the size of their physical plant — by moving to a three-car garage. Hewlett-Packard Corporation, TeleVideo Systems, and hundreds of other well-known companies have begun in such modest surroundings.[1]

No matter how accidental or casual the origin, the management of a thriving company must eventually select a permanent plant location. This is a matter for careful thought and investigation.

Location Decisions

A plant location always leaves something to be desired. A site with an exceptionally good supply of skilled workers may be remote from prime market centers, raw materials, or both. Available transportation

Plants mean prosperity. Large manufacturing plants, such as this sprawling Nissan truck facility in Smyrna, Tennessee, employ thousands of citizens in an area.

may not be the most economical or efficient to ship parts and materials in and finished products out. State and local regulations can weave a web of red tape around an otherwise attractive location. The point is to select the best site available — the one with the greatest advantages and fewest drawbacks.

Location decisions often are made by committees of top executives who examine and weigh every factor from taxation and transportation to community services and climate. They may evaluate several potential sites in several different states, because the firm will have to live with the decision for years to come.

Although plant site requirements vary with the individual firm, product, and intended market, a location decision is based on three general concerns. The "Three Ps" of plant location are illustrated in Figure 9.1 and discussed in the sections that follow.

Proximity Factors

Proximity to customers or to raw materials is often an either-or decision. Someone in the dairy business, for example, may want to avoid the need to refrigerate and ship perishable eggs and milk over long distances, and so may locate near major markets. In Florida, Irwin and Cobia boat manufacturing companies are located in the midst of their best markets.

On the other hand, if you made television sets or stereo equipment, nearness to customers would be less important because customers are not concentrated in specific areas, the goods are not perishable, and shipping costs are relatively low in relation to the selling prices of the items.

Occasionally closeness to raw materials overrides the advantage of being close to markets, especially when these materials are expensive to ship. Timber, for example, is heavy, and shipping it great

Figure 9.1 The "Three Ps" of
Plant Location

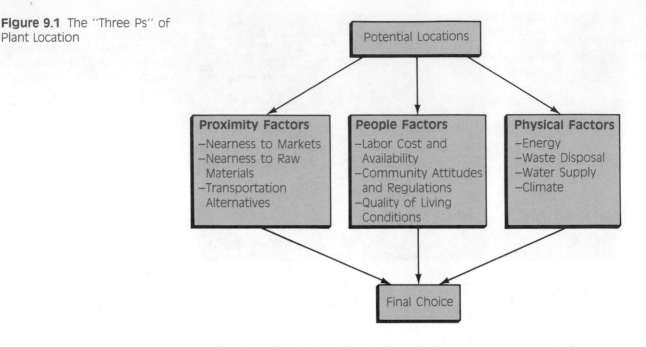

distances is costly, so the paper mills of Maine and Georgia and
the furniture plants of North Carolina are located near forests. Steel
mills in Pennsylvania and West Virginia are built near iron ore and
coal deposits, which give them access to both fuel and raw materials.
Glass container manufacturing plants are located near large bodies
of sand in Pennsylvania and West Virginia.

The third proximity factor that affects a plant site decision is
the availability of transportation. The options include rail, highway,
air, water, and pipeline. The best choice depends on the individual
case. If management is worried about perishability or rush shipments,
nearness to airports might be important. Dole pineapples, for example, are transported from Hawaii by plane instead of ship because
of their perishability. Heavy, bulky products like earth-moving
equipment are shipped cheapest by rail or water, and fluids by
pipeline. Highway transportation is popular for most products.

Along with its primary shipping method, a firm needs alternatives available in emergencies or when bad weather, strikes, or
other unforeseen events temporarily shut down the main choice.
Furniture plants, for example, may ship mainly by rail, but use
trucks for emergency shipments. Nissan officials chose Tennessee
for a truck plant because 60 percent of the parts needed to build
the trucks would have to be shipped in by rail or highway, and
Tennessee is crisscrossed by key railroads and interstate highways.

People Factors

People — their numbers, skills, and attitudes — also influence the
choice of a plant site. Although some firms actually have attracted
a skilled work force to a plant site with otherwise appealing features,

producers usually try to build where an adequate supply of skilled labor already exists. A company may, however, have to shoulder the burden of training a large supply of willing but unskilled applicants.

Aside from labor supply and skills, another people factor is the prevailing wage. If companies in a region pay higher-than-average wages, management of a firm intending to move may look for a location in an area where pay tends to be lower.

Community attitudes toward new businesses are a concern too. Area business leaders may become hostile toward a new company that pays significantly higher wages than existing businesses, because this would pressure established firms to pay more or lose workers to the newcomer. Production processes that threaten the environment may place community pressure on city, county, or state regulatory bodies to deny the company operating permits. Although Wellston, Ohio, welcomed a Jeno's frozen pizza plant for the 1,000 jobs it provided, the relationship grew strained after the plant started running. Wellston's sewage system, ill-prepared to handle the by-products of frozen pizza production, was overwhelmed by a steady stream of sludge composed of flour, pepperoni, tomato paste, and other assorted pizza ingredients. City officials arranged financing for half a million dollars' worth of equipment to dehydrate the material so it could be buried while 400,000 gallons of the stuff backed up in holding tanks.[2]

Hawaii creates imposing bureaucratic barriers to all types of businesses. Its state plan for business regulation passed in 1978 levies a 4 percent use tax on equipment shipped into the state and a 0.5 percent excise tax on manufactured products. The state's labyrinth of commissions and agencies may require up to 6 years to approve construction of a light industrial manufacturing plant.[3]

State and local regulations and restrictions should be inspected before a location decision is made. It may take several months to several years to obtain operating permits for certain kinds of processing or manufacturing plants, such as petroleum refineries.

Regulatory agencies frequently require firms to submit an **environmental impact study,** which is *a report describing how a proposed plant will alter the quality of life in an area*, covering such topics as air, water, and noise pollution; wildlife displacement; effect on natural plant life; and increased load on transportation facilities, sewage treatment plants, and water and energy supplies. This kind of preliminary work can be very expensive and time consuming, and there is no guarantee that once it is completed the necessary approvals will be granted.

environmental impact study

On the other hand, many states and cities try to sell a large company on the advantages they can offer, because new manufacturing plants mean jobs, prosperity, and increased revenues. A large plant employing several thousand people can make the difference between economic distress and prosperity in some regions, which states, counties, and local business associations acknowledge in their appeals to new corporate residents. Approximately twenty-seven states now provide staffing assistance as an incentive to attract new companies. Michigan, a leader in such efforts, reportedly spends almost $1 million per year to assist new companies in recruiting, selecting, and training a work force.[4]

Many states and communities offer reductions in taxes to encourage plant construction. The state of New York has exempted research-oriented manufacturing equipment, machinery, and inventories from state and local taxes. During negotiations for a Nissan Motor Company plant near Smyrna, Tennessee, state officials agreed to help train workers and approved concessions that will save Nissan $1.7 million in state taxes by 1990.[5] Figure 9.2 shows an advertisement placed by the city of San Antonio, Texas, appealing to high-technology companies and emphasizing the city's benefits.

Figure 9.2 Cities and States Attempt to Influence Firms in Their Location Decisions
Source: Courtesy of the San Antonio Economic Development Foundation.

Management may also want to evaluate the community's living conditions — housing, educational, recreational, and cultural facilities — because these help to attract employees and keep them contented once they are hired.

Physical Factors

Operating a manufacturing plant without heat, light, and power would be as easy as running your car without gas, oil, and water. Managers who research suitable plant sites must investigate the supply and the cost of electricity and other forms of energy. If a plant's projected energy demands would overtax existing supplies, management must either negotiate with the suppliers to expand their facilities to accommodate the plant's needs or look for a location with better service.

In addition to energy supplies, other physical factors that might be considered, depending on the nature of the product, include the waste disposal facilities, climate, and water supply.

Productivity Studies

Managers must estimate each worker's productivity during a work period to employ enough workers to produce a certain quantity of units on schedule. Productivity estimates also are used in drawing up a budget for labor costs and perhaps constructing a piece-rate wage system based on each employee's output.

Motion and time studies are needed whenever management must know how many units a worker can produce in a certain situation. These studies also allow the firm to add a portion of each worker's hourly wage to each unit's total cost. Companies that do not perform motion and time studies may hire too many or too few workers to do the jobs at hand or compute a unit price too low to recapture the product's cost, let alone earn a profit. In addition, it is important for management to design production jobs with enough motions and variety to make them challenging to workers. Repetitious, unchallenging jobs often cause high turnover; workers are virtually bored to death with their tasks.

Pause and Ponder

Consider a manufacturing plant located in your area. List the proximity, people, and physical factors that may have caused the firm to build there. Which of these factors, if any, have changed since the plant was built? Does the change make the location more or less attractive than it was originally? What does this tell you about the effect of time on a plant location decision?

Motion Study

motion study

A **motion study,** conceived and refined by management pioneer Frederick W. Taylor, is *a study that identifies the number and kind of movements required to perform a given operation.* The purpose is not to make employees work *harder,* but to help them work *smarter* — to condense the job into an economical series of steps that are more efficient and less tiring than those used before. Often employees find that they can produce more with less effort after their motions have been studied and refined.

Total simplification is not a desirable end, though. Extremely menial jobs can be terribly unmotivating and boring. So while you want to eliminate wasted motion, the work should offer enough challenge that employees are not dehumanized. Nevertheless, workers who now stand may have their work layout rearranged so they can sit down, and those who pick up and lay down several hand tools to perform a series of operations may be given a device that does the work of several of the old tools with a single squeeze.

Copying machines that collate documents after they have been copied are a good example of motion-reducing machinery. They save the motion that would be required to hand-collate the pages. McDonald's has designed a french fry scoop that fills a bag with one pass through a bin of fries.

Time Study

time study

A **time study** is *a study that determines the amount of time an average worker takes to perform a given operation.* After motion study has been used to refine movements and gain efficiency, a time study of a large cross-section of workers doing the same task allows management to determine the average time it takes to complete a particular job. This permits supervisors to estimate production volume per work shift and lets management prepare budgets accordingly. Firms that pay production workers on a piece-rate wage plan, as discussed in Chapter 6, use motion and time studies to establish average production volume per worker and to create a base pay rate from there.

Applying Productivity Studies

Many jobs lend themselves to motion and time study. Meter readers are expected to read a certain number of water or electrical meters in a typical residential area each day; telephone operators are responsible for processing a certain number of operator-assisted calls an hour. When you had your car fixed, the repair shop probably used a flat-rate manual to compute its labor charges. That book lists standard times required to perform specific maintenance and repair jobs on various makes and models of cars.

Workers tend to be wary of motion and time studies, believing that management is trying to get more work for less pay. As a result, they may try to mislead the observer by reducing their normal work pace while under study. Observers, who are usually industrial engineers, can adjust for this normal worker reaction mathematically.

Management should explain in advance what the motion and time studies are intended to do, emphasizing the budgeting and personnel planning purposes mentioned earlier in this section. Supervisors, working closely with industrial engineers, should notify workers when they will be observed and reassert the reasons for these studies.

Production Methods

All products cannot be made the same way: the nature of the product determines how it will be produced. Traditionally, these methods have been classified as analytic, synthetic, continuous, and intermittent. In the following sections, we examine each one briefly.

Analytic and Synthetic Processes

In the **analytic process,** *raw materials are broken down to form new products.* An example of this is petroleum refining: crude oil is processed and converted into a vast array of end products, as shown in Figure 9.3.

analytic process

In a sense, the **synthetic process** is the opposite of the analytic process, because *materials are combined instead of separated to form a certain product.* Glass manufacturing illustrates the synthetic process, because it combines lime, sand, potash, soda, and other elements to make a product with a unique appearance and characteristics different from any of these ingredients. Aluminum production is another example of the synthetic process because processed bauxite is combined with lime and ash. The synthetic process has two variations, the fabrication and the assembly processes.

synthetic process

The **fabrication process** is *a variation of synthetic production in which new products are created from those already manufactured by changing their form.* Calvin Klein jeans, for example, are created from cloth, buttons, zippers, trim, and thread joined together according to a pattern. Shoes and handbags, kitchen cabinets, baked goods, tires, and flashlight batteries arc also produced by fabrication.

fabrication process

The **assembly process** is *the variation of synthetic production in which materials or parts are combined without substantial changes.* Beechcraft airplanes are made almost entirely by the assembly process. The firm takes Avco Lycoming or Continental engines and ready-made instruments, landing gear, propellers, and other components from outside companies and puts the entire airplane together. Ford automobiles, which are also built by the assembly process, contain over 13,000 parts that must be joined together to form the finished product.

assembly process

Figure 9.3 Analytic Production Process: Petroleum Refining
Source: Courtesy Shell Oil Company.

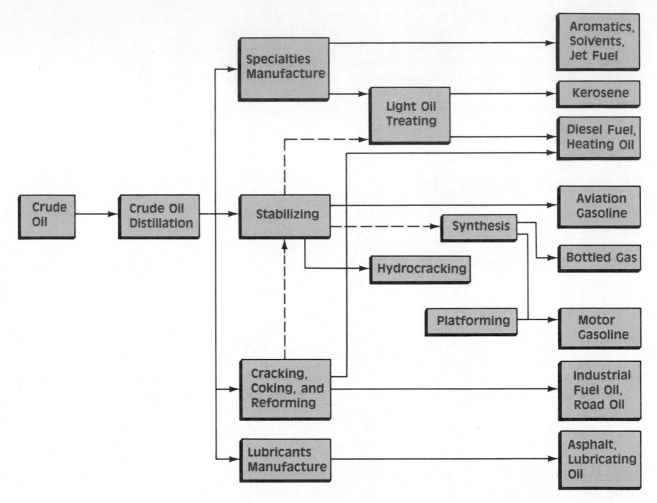

The fabrication process is used to make many products, including Cabbage Patch dolls.

Those stereo speakers that can vibrate the living room walls and deafen the neighbor's dog probably went through an assembly process similar to this one.

Continuous and Intermittent Processes

Production processes are called analytic or synthetic because of what is done to raw materials. Another way of classifying production methods is how they are performed over time. **Continuous process** is *a production method that uses the same machinery to perform the same operations repeatedly over relatively long periods of time.* Synthetic fibers, chemicals, Bic pens, and disposable razors are made by this process. Machinery runs for months at a time with few if any changes in methods or equipment. A continuous process is used for making cars. Understandably plant closings to retool for new models that will be made with a continuous process require several months: many tools and dies must be replaced and other extensive changes are necessary. Retooling at a General Motors Corvette plant in Bowling Green, Kentucky, for example, closed the plant from August to February.[6]

    A firm that uses an **intermittent process** is engaged in *a production process that shuts down equipment periodically and readjusts it to make a slightly different product; production does not run the same day in and day out.* The intermittent process is used by **job shops,** *companies that make products to customers' individual specifications.* Custom gunsmiths and guitar-makers use an intermittent process: no two units are identical. The security-vehicle (armored-car) firms that have flourished with the epidemic of international terrorism are vivid examples of intermittent process production. They do custom work by reworking a Cadillac or Lincoln Continental, in the spirit of James Bond, enabling it to conceal machine guns, spread oil slicks in the path of pursuing vehicles, release smoke bombs, start by remote control (to check for booby

continuous process

intermittent process

job shops

Wood, glue, and metal are harmonized into a custom guitar by a skilled craftsman using the intermittent production process.

traps), and withstand grenade and machine gun attacks with armor plate and bulletproof glass.

Management's choice of a continuous or intermittent process is governed by the nature of the product and the market the product is meant for. Custom-made products must be manufactured by intermittent process because manufacturing must stop with the completion of each unit. Mass production of identical units lends itself to a continuous process, but even some mass-produced items have elements of an intermittent process. Printers manufacture thousands of books in a continuous process, for instance, but must make changes when they print another book.

Robots on the Production Line

robot

The last 2 decades have brought a pronounced trend toward the use of robot assembly techniques in a number of manufacturing companies. In the context of manufacturing, a **robot** is defined by the Robot Institute of America as *a reprogrammable, multifunctional manipulator designed to move material, parts, tools, or specialized devices through variable programmed motions to accomplish a variety of tasks.* First installed on General Motors and Ford Motor Company assembly lines in 1961, robots are used today for repetitive jobs such as spray painting, spot welding, and grinding; handling plutonium or other hazardous materials; and working in environments that are otherwise hostile to humans.

Although robots may require changes in a plant's layout and

Robot assembly is now common on automobile production lines, such as this one at Chrysler Corporation.

work flow (total costs to buy and install one may exceed $100,000), ultimate savings can be impressive — $6 per hour to operate some robots compared with $19 per hour in wages and benefits paid to an auto assembly worker. Productivity naturally improves because these machines may be operated nonstop 24 hours per day if necessary. Robots also may be reprogrammed to perform different sequences of rote movements, so they are not limited to just one specialized task. Some are only "down" (in need of service or repairs) an average of 2 percent of the time, and at least one robot manufacturer — Prab Robots — will lease as well as sell them. Manufacturers have reported increases in output ranging from 30 to 300 percent after robots were installed. General Motors, presently the largest industrial robot user with more than 1,800 companywide, expects to have more than 14,000 by 1990. And while as many as 24,000 autoworkers may be displaced (job security clauses in union contracts call for retraining in other work), robots actually will create jobs for programmers, engineers, and hydraulic and electronic technicians to maintain and repair them.[7] Phillips Petroleum Company reports using more then sixty robots costing $20,000 apiece to weigh samples, measure chemicals, and perform other routine laboratory functions.[8]

Materials Management

Once you have chosen a product, built a plant, planned for workers' productivity, and determined which production method to follow, you will have to buy and control the materials needed to make the product. Materials management is a crucial concern in the production of anything from skateboards to computers. Consider that minor miracle, the car. If thousands of such seemingly insignificant parts as rubber seals, mounting brackets, and door handles had not been brought together at the required assembly points, hundreds of workers would have been idle and thousands of dollars lost as the assembly line ground to a halt. In late 1983 the shortage of several instrument panel components obtained from an outside supplier temporarily shut down two General Motors plants that manufactured Pontiac Firebirds and Chevrolet Camaros. Production difficulties at a supplier's plant delayed delivery of a carburetor plug retainer needed to correct a defect in 491,000 small General Motors cars that were recalled in early 1983.[9] Business historian and author Harold C. Livesay once saw a grim group of Chrysler Corporation employees attack a locked boxcar in a railroad yard to get the bolts they needed. With no time to unload the boxcar, the crew began cutting holes in it with an acetylene torch. Citing a cost of $40,000 per hour to stop the production line, the workers swore that the company would pay for the damaged railroad car and any fines associated with their assault.[10]

The Purchasing Function

Production thrives on machinery, raw materials, parts, and supplies, all of which may be bought. As a firm expands, it will centralize and coordinate responsibility for buying the items it needs in a purchasing, or procurement, department.

purchasing agent

A **purchasing agent** (sometimes called a PA, or procurement specialist) is *a company's in-house expert on where to buy various products. Each will buy a broad or narrow line of products, depending on the size and complexity of the company and the characteristics of its end product.* In a very small machine shop, for example, the owner may make all the buying decisions. In companies the size of McDonnell Douglas or International Business Machines (IBM), you may find one purchasing agent in charge of buying electronic components, another who buys only steel, and one who buys janitorial supplies and office equipment. The importance of careful purchasing was emphasized by the manager of corporate purchasing for Atlantic Richfield Company, who claimed that reducing purchase prices by just 1 percent companywide would save the firm $25 million per year.[11]

Although purchasing agents make many buying decisions, their authority is limited. Purchases that exceed a certain dollar amount may require the purchasing manager's approval or even that of top company management. Regardless of who does the purchasing, **purchasing procedure**

most companies establish a **purchasing procedure,** *a series of steps that a company follows when buying products.* Figure 9.4 shows a typical purchasing procedure.

Proper specifications are vital when buying something from an outside supplier or vendor. A producer may use the vendor's regular specifications — these exist for such standard items as

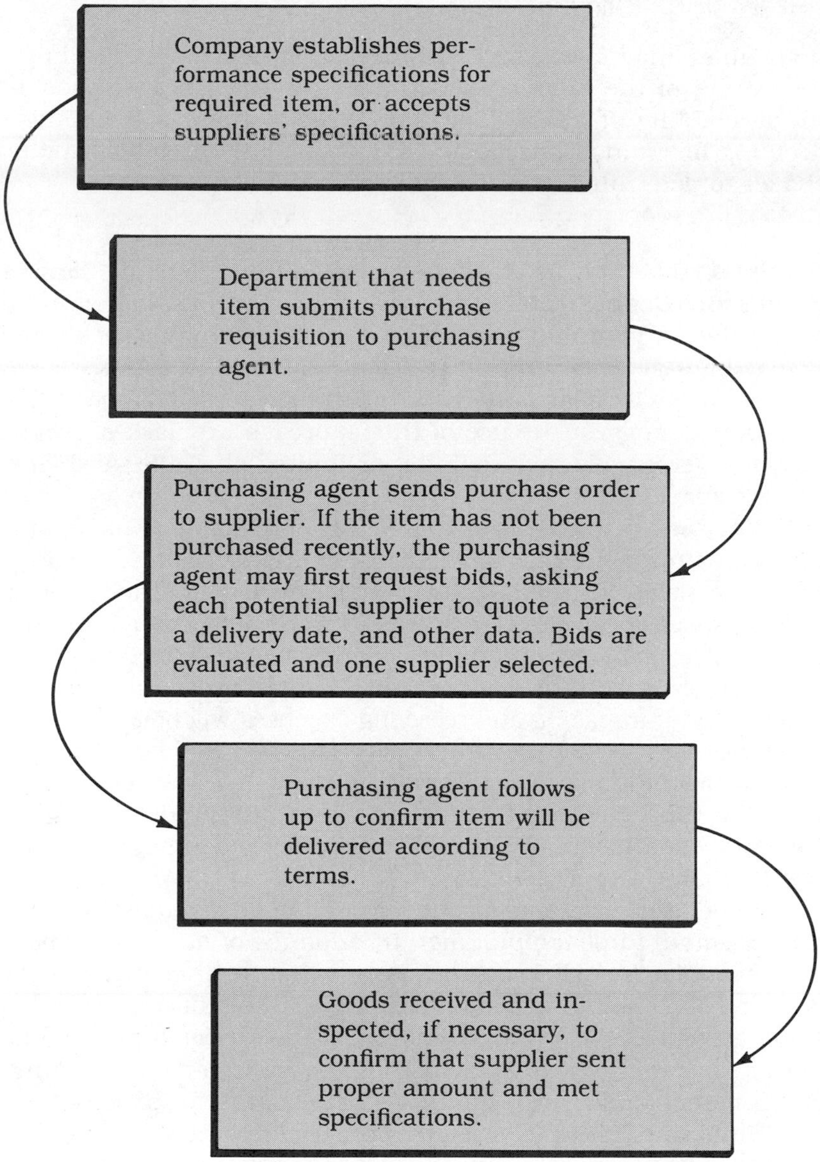

Figure 9.4 A Typical
Purchasing Procedure

Company establishes performance specifications for required item, or accepts suppliers' specifications.

Department that needs item submits purchase requisition to purchasing agent.

Purchasing agent sends purchase order to supplier. If the item has not been purchased recently, the purchasing agent may first request bids, asking each potential supplier to quote a price, a delivery date, and other data. Bids are evaluated and one supplier selected.

Purchasing agent follows up to confirm item will be delivered according to terms.

Goods received and inspected, if necessary, to confirm that supplier sent proper amount and met specifications.

fasteners, steel, and various electrical components — but some producers prefer to dictate custom specifications that the vendor must meet. Lincoln Electric Company, a producer of arc-welding equipment, purchases from steel mills coils of wire that must be made to an exact Lincoln recipe. The firm's metallurgic engineers, working closely with the steel mills, establish the specifications. Each coil is tested from beginning to end after it arrives at the Lincoln plant.[12]

Companies that buy products whose failure could cause serious harm or financial loss may even conduct **on-site inspection,** in which *the buyer's inspectors examine purchased items throughout the supplier's manufacturing operations.*

on-site inspection

Purchasing Policies

Companies may follow several purchasing policies, depending on the nature of the product, consumer demand, storage space, and the availability of funds. The first three of these policies involve deciding how much purchasing to do; the last three help the purchaser to determine who to buy from.

hand-to-mouth purchasing

Policies on Quantity. As might be expected from its name, **hand-to-mouth purchasing** involves *purchasing an item in small quantities, as needed.* If your end product has an uncertain market demand, it may be wise to buy parts on a hand-to-mouth basis so you will not be stuck with a large inventory should demand disappear. Other factors that suggest the use of this approach are: lack of funds to buy a larger supply; perishability or limited shelf life; and lack of storage space.

forward purchasing

    Forward purchasing is *a policy of purchasing relatively large quantities to fill needs over longer periods of time.* Normally the purchase price, shipping charges, and purchasing and receiving expenses will be lower as a result of forward purchasing. Producers may charge less per unit on a large order because fixed production costs will be spread over more units. Shipping in bulk also saves money, and purchasing and receiving expenses will be lower because the paperwork is cheaper to process for one large shipment than for a series of small ones. Forward purchasing assumes that you have the funds to spend, a place to store the product, long shelf life, and a market that will remain strong long enough for you to use this large supply.

anticipatory purchasing

    Under **anticipatory purchasing,** *a purchasing agent stockpiles an extremely large supply, well in advance of need, anticipating future problems* such as a shortage or a drastic price increase. This is a kind of gambling: the buyer, betting that the uncertain condition will materialize, fills up a warehouse. If the expected problem does not arise, the purchasing agent could be criticized for spending so much money and using so much storage space for so long.

    Final consumers followed this practice during a rumored toilet paper shortage several years ago. The shortage never materialized, but some householders were buying the stuff by the case. Gasoline stored in privately owned underground tanks and sugar stockpiled at low prices are examples of anticipatory purchasing by final consumers and companies alike.

Policies on Suppliers. Purchasing agents must identify suitable suppliers, but this does not necessarily mean the firms with the highest quality or lowest price. In addition to quality and price, the suitable supplier must be able to offer adequate production capacity to fill requirements, meet delivery schedules, offer a sound guarantee, and provide reliable service. The purchasing agent for a given item should keep records of suppliers who meet these conditions. To ensure supply, quality, or reliable delivery, a company may try to create a **captive supplier,** which is *a vendor firm in which the customer firm owns controlling interest or from which it obtains an exclusive supply contract.* The latter arrangement gives the buyer a legal right to all the units that the vendor produces. When shortages occur within an industry, it can be comforting to have a captive supplier and thus be assured of adequate stock.

captive supplier

Many purchasing agents are wary of **single-source purchasing,** which is *buying a product from one company only.* Rather than putting all their eggs in one basket, some firms buy standard items from several vendors. Then, if one vendor cannot fill an order, more units can be requested from one or more of the others.

single-source purchasing

Bid purchasing is *a policy of requesting bids from several vendors and selecting the most attractive one.* This does not always mean the cheapest, because the purchasing agent considers such factors as the vendor's production capacity, quality, guarantee, and others referred to earlier. The Orlando, Florida, police department displayed this kind of reasoning when it bought Kawasaki motorcycles instead of the less expensive Harley-Davidsons. Department officials said that although Kawasakis cost more, they were easier to service, more reliable, and in the officers' opinions more comfortable to ride. Firms that buy strictly from low bidders may find that in the long run they have not saved money at all: a cheap part might fail to hold up, or the vendor might provide poor service and repairs.

bid purchasing

After decades of paying nonnegotiated prices and buying from all the major steel companies, General Motors (GM) adopted a bid-purchasing policy for its steel requirements in the early 1980s. In addition to making demands for improved quality, the company also informed bidders that it would evaluate such criteria as financial condition and the range of products each firm's facilities could produce. General Motors requested price quotations on more than 5,000 items used at 53 manufacturing plants throughout the country.

This revolutionary change by one of the nation's largest steel customers had positive results. At least one steel company offered a volume discount and extended credit for 30 days, while helping GM to reduce the various standards for thickness by half. Shipments were consolidated as GM reduced the number of mills it dealt with from 341 to 272. Demands for improved quality caused the steel companies themselves to address quality as never before, which caused rejected material to drop to just a few hundred tons per year.[13]

Contract purchasing occurs when *the company negotiates with the supplier (perhaps after soliciting bids) a contract that defines prices, delivery dates, and other conditions of sale.* It is common practice with the United States government, especially the armed forces, which contract for everything from fighter planes to backpacks. Most contracts are quite complex and lawyers may be needed to represent each party in establishing and clarifying all the terms. Contract purchasing is also a good way to assure yourself of an adequate supply if a shortage develops.

contract purchasing

A **make versus buy *or* in-house versus out-of-house** policy decision answers *an either-or question: whether to create your own*

make versus buy *or* in-house versus out-of-house

supply of an essential item or rely on an outside producer to make it for you. Some suppliers already have the specialized equipment, engineering, materials, and assembly personnel to turn out a superior part. It is usually more practical to buy from them than to try to do it yourself. For example Teleflex, a prolific manufacturer of mechanical and electronic control devices, makes throttle systems for General Electric, Pratt & Whitney, and Rolls-Royce aircraft engines and various kinds of controls used on Boeing, Fairchild, Lockheed, and McDonnell Douglas aircraft and Bell, Hughes, and Sikorsky helicopters. The company's automotive division produces control devices for sun roofs, vent windows, automatic transmissions, accelerators, and floor-shift/park-lock mechanisms used in General Motors, Ford, and Chrysler vehicles. Another division manufactures mechanical and hydraulic steering systems, engine control systems, electrical instruments, hardware, and accessories for the power and sailboat market.

In the early 1980s Chrysler Corporation, which once bought half the parts that went into its vehicles, increased that portion to 70 percent after reexamining its make-versus-buy position. For example, management saved $50 million in research and development expenses by subcontracting the design of a starter motor to an outside supplier. Discovering that seat springs could be bought for 75 percent of their in-house production cost enabled the company to close a Canadian manufacturing plant.[14]

A manufacturer who decides to make a part must be able to allocate production space to it, buy material and equipment, and hire or train workers to produce it. Demand for the item must be strong enough to justify committing resources to it, and the final unit cost for in-house manufacture should be equal to or less than that of outside suppliers.

Anheuser Busch owns plants that supply barley malt for its brewing operations; cans are supplied by a wholly owned subsidiary, Metal Container Corporation. On the other hand, IBM reportedly buys rather than makes approximately 70 percent of the parts for its PC personal computer, a policy that was continued on the PC Jr. model introduced in late 1983. Disk drives for the PC Jr. are produced by a California company, keyboards by an Idaho firm, and sound chips by a Texas company. Another company hired by IBM assembles the final product at a plant in Tennessee.[15] Similarly,

Pause and Ponder

In recent years General Motors, Mead Corporation, Sears, and other companies have become more concerned about the quality of items purchased from suppliers. What incentives could companies of their size give suppliers to raise their quality standards? How might the suppliers, in turn, influence their employees to pay greater attention to quality? Name at least one way in which consumers ultimately will benefit.

Apple Computer's Macintosh model has disk drives made by Sony, video display screens by Samsung, and other components by Motorola and Hitachi.[16]

The make-or-buy question should be asked periodically about heavily used items. Changing conditions may suggest and prompt a move to the alternative.

Inventory Control

Inventory control *balances the need for adequate stock against the costs of purchasing, handling, storing, and keeping records on it.* All of this demands that management evaluate present consumption rates and anticipate future needs. Inventory control is an attempt to keep enough material on hand to satisfy production requirements and at the same time avoid tying up too much capital in inventories. Imagine the challenge Ford Motor Company faces controlling its reported 50,000 production items. Even smaller products like the one-cylinder engines that Briggs & Stratton Corporation manufactures for power mowers and snow blowers may contain up to 500 parts.[17]

Inventories represent a considerable investment, and the related costs of carrying them, listed in Table 9.1, make efficient control even more important. Inventory shortages can trigger as many difficulties as excesses can. A producer who runs out of an essential item loses sales and customer goodwill. Inventory shortages also increase costs. The unavailability of one indispensable part will stop a production line and workers will be idle until the missing piece arrives. If delays caused by inventory shortages have to be made up through overtime work, the producer may lose money on the order if the overtime wages cannot be passed on to the customer.

inventory control

Table 9.1 Costs Associated with Carrying Inventory

Storage Costs

1. Cost of building the storage facility, including interest on borrowed funds.
2. Value of the storage space assigned to the inventory.
3. Additional cost of purchasing other items in smaller quantities because of space now occupied in the warehouse.

Handling Costs

1. Equipment and materials (forklifts, conveyors, pallets, bins, racks, dollies, record cabinets, requisition forms).
2. Personnel (warehouse workers, record clerks, managers to supervise their work).

Other Costs

1. Loss caused by obsolescence, seasonal changes, shifts in customer demand, and physical wear while in storage.
2. Inventory taxes that may be levied by government agencies.
3. Interest paid on money borrowed to buy the inventory.

Finally, machines that are run faster or longer than usual to reduce the backlog will suffer greater-than-normal wear and tear.

economic order quantity (EOQ)

Inventory control managers often apply the standard of an **economic order quantity (EOQ)** to their work. To derive this figure, a purchasing agent *compares the cost of buying an item in various quantities with the cost of carrying those units in stock, and identifies the point at which the cost of the item and the cost to store it are equal.* That amount, the economic order quantity, is the best amount to buy. This computation is shown graphically in Figure 9.5.

An inventory control system also will determine consumption rates for each item and identify the point at which it is necessary to order additional stock. This should not be when all units are gone. Some units, called *safety stock*, should be on hand to meet production demands until the new order arrives. In determining reorder points, purchasing agents and inventory control employees must be aware of **lead time,** *the time a supplier requires to process and ship an order.* When lead time changes, purchasing agents have to revise their schedules to keep production flowing smoothly.

lead time

Production Control

production control

Production control, one of the most important concerns in making a product, is *coordinating the interaction of people, materials, and machinery so that products are made in the proper amounts at*

Figure 9.5 Determining Economic Order Quantity

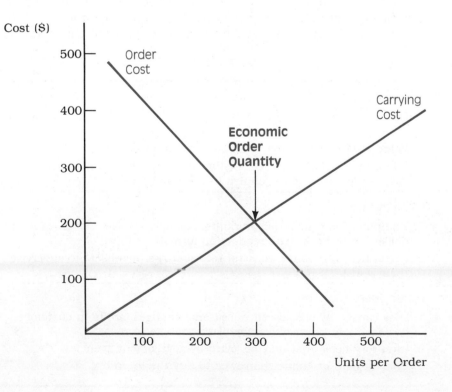

the required times to fill orders. Six steps are involved: planning, routing, scheduling, dispatching, follow-up, and quality assurance. The sequence of these steps is illustrated in Figure 9.6.

Planning

Successful production, like other successful business activities, is based on planning. Production planners know what materials, equipment, processes, and working time must be allotted to make a given item. Often they are former production workers themselves, so they can visualize the end product at various stages of completion, knowing from experience what remains to be done.

The **production plan** is *a document that contains a list of materials and equipment needed to manufacture a finished product that also specifies which operations will be performed in-house or out-of-house.* In addition, this plan reveals any operations that require special machinery or equipment to be brought out of storage or purchased and set up when the product reaches a particular stage of completion.

production plan

Production planners are like orchestra conductors. They coordinate the performances of purchasing, manufacturing, shipping, and marketing, all of which contribute to or need information about the status of an order at various stages of completion.

Routing

Routing is *the production control step in which a logical sequence is established for the operations that the product must undergo on its way to completion.* Each job's path is defined, thus determining what work will be done at what point. The person handling routing for a brewery must take into account all of the following steps: germinating the barley grain, cleaning it, milling it, weighing it,

routing

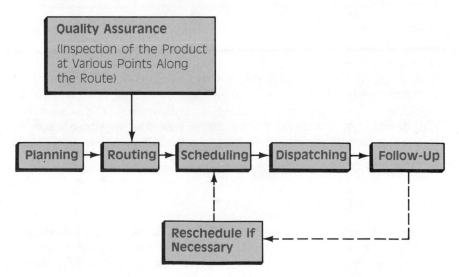

Figure 9.6 Steps in Production Control

cooking it, blending it with water, removing the grain solids to produce a clear liquid, brewing the liquid, straining out hops, cooling the liquid, fermenting it, and aging, filtering, and packaging the beer.

Scheduling

scheduling

Scheduling is *the production control step that allots time for each operation along the route.* Knowledgeable production planners are an asset here. Schedules that allow too much or too little time can lead to slack periods in various departments, causing wasted time and perhaps employee layoffs, or create bottlenecks that back up work at certain points, causing late deliveries and canceled orders. Production planners also have to take nonwork time into account. Once they are painted, auto bodies have to sit in a drying booth for some time before further work can be done. A production planner who does not know how much time to allow will leave workers idle at the next step along the route.

A product rarely follows the orginal schedule from start to finish. Production planners must reschedule work in process because of canceled orders and customer requests for earlier delivery dates or because of machinery breakdowns, design changes, strikes, and inclement weather, all of which can cause lost work time and delays in the delivery of essential materials.

Dispatching

dispatching

Dispatching occurs after jobs have been planned, routed, and scheduled. This is *the production control step in which a production planner releases a job to the first production department on its route.* Before dispatching, production control employees must gather up the materials and parts required by the production plan and issue them to the correct department.

Follow-Up

follow-up

Follow-up is *the production control step in which production planners monitor each job's progress along its route, and report and attempt to deal with any delays or difficulties that occur.* A job is usually identified by number so it can be traced from one operation or department to the next. Large manufacturing plants may be working on thousands of jobs simultaneously, many of which become subassemblies of others. Follow-up is essential in these cases to ensure that work moves according to schedule. When delays occur, production planners should be notified so they can bring the job back on schedule or reschedule it.

Quality Assurance

A firm does not always want to make the best product possible, but rather a product that suits its reputation and its customers' expectations and price requirements. Exceedingly high quality almost always is accompanied by a higher price, and not everyone wants or can afford the best. A company's quality standards are set with its market, reputation, and budget in mind. Porsche states that its Stuttgart, Germany, plant makes no more than sixty-seven cars per day. A Chevrolet plant in Lordstown, Ohio, can make more than that number in 1 hour; yet, there is a market for both brands.

The number of units inspected will vary. If product failure causes serious injury, financial loss, or both, companies might inspect each unit. This is the case with strategic missiles, communications satellites, astronauts' space suits, and complex electronic health care equipment. It is often impractical or unnecessary, however, to inspect every unit. If products pour off the machines by the thousands per hour (as with pencils, plastic trash bags, or nails), management makes random, or spot, inspections. This technique detects any major or repeated flaws caused by production routines or equipment, but it allows for and considers acceptable the occasional minor defect that escapes detection.

Problems may arise at various points along the production route, which creates a need for **quality assurance.** This is *the production control step in which the product is inspected at various stages along the route to ensure that it meets standards.* Quality assurance ought to be preventive as well as corrective. It should identify deviations from standards as quickly as possible and correct them before units must be rejected. Some rejected pieces may be sent through a rework area, where the flaw can be corrected. If the flaw is irreparable, however, or would cost more to repair than to make a new unit, the part should be recycled or scrapped. Quality rejects in automobile paint, upholstery, or trim are reworked, flawed steel castings are melted down and recast, and faulty pop-top can lids are discarded.

Manufacturers that do not inspect a critical part of the product or do not inspect it as thoroughly or as rigorously as need be, suffer

quality assurance

A quality assurance inspector confirms that printed circuit boards meet established standards.

The Lear Fan

Bill Lear's Rare Bird Requests Clearance for Takeoff

In 1954 inventor William Lear conceived the idea for an ultra-strong airplane built of light synthetic materials. In the days of cheap fuel, however, such a product deserved little investigation. Shelved for more than 2 decades, Lear's idea acquired new importance when the Arab oil embargo of 1974 threatened the future of economical executive air travel. Convinced that the idea's time had come, Lear became obsessed with perfecting a graphite-epoxy material of unsurpassed strength as well as a production process by which it could be molded into an airplane.

Lear was no stranger to revolutionary ideas. He invented the car radio, the radio directional finder and autopilot for aircraft, the 8-track stereo tape cartridge, and the Learjet executive jet aircraft. The Lear Fan aircraft promises to eclipse all of these, however. Its construction is unique in the aircraft industry. Although some aluminum is used at strategic points, the plane's fuselage, wings, and tail are molded from graphite-epoxy (also called carbonfibre) composites. Immune to corrosion and metal fatigue, this remarkable material is only half as heavy as aluminum — but almost twice as strong. The plane is built by layering the material in a mold, then pressure curing it in an autoclave. Competition is unlikely: any existing aircraft producer would have to discard existing production methods, equipment, and plant layouts to duplicate a Lear Fan.

The Lear Fan's design is as unique as its material and production processes. Its engines are recessed in the fuselage, which creates smoother, better-balanced flight and less wind drag. They connect by drive shafts to a transmission, which connects by a single shaft to a pusher propeller in the tail. If one engine stops running, it is automatically disengaged while the remaining one continues to drive the propeller. The plane's light weight and molded skin (which creates less wind drag than riveted surfaces) provide impressively better fuel economy. On a 350-mile trip a Lear Fan, although taking 13 minutes longer than a leading competitor, consumes 200 gallons less fuel. At $2 per gallon, a company traveling 250,000 miles per year would save approximately $300,000 in fuel costs.

This unique construction and design has caused some the consequences. Products may fail as customers try to use them, causing recalls. General Motors X-cars, for example, were recalled eight times between September 1979 and February 1983 for problems ranging from defective automatic transmission cooler hoses to rear-wheel brake lockups. Recalls are hardly confined to domestic products, however, as some American manufacturers quickly point out. Several hundred thousand Hondas were once recalled to rectify severe rusting of front suspension and body parts. A lesser-known but unusual recall occurred when a university recalled more than 3,000 diplomas awarded to a graduating class because the ink faded. While that

problems with Federal Aviation Administration (FAA) certification, however. The FAA's flight approval regulations require that each engine of a twin-engine plane power its own propeller. The Lear Fan's unique construction has required FAA inspectors to rewrite traditional certification standards.

Approval by the FAA is not all that has kept the Lear Fan grounded. Shortly after his death in 1978, the $6 million Lear provided to develop the plane was exhausted. His widow, Moya, managed to obtain $30 million from Oppenheimer & Company, a brokerage firm, and $50 million from the British government under an agreement to build the plane in Northern Ireland. Although the company received some $20 million in deposits for 260 planes, it also desperately needed "progress payments" from these customers 6 months and 3 months before their planes were delivered to keep the company aloft. Plans went awry as design modifications delayed production and final FAA certification. By mid-1982 the company had run out of money. The British government gave it a weekly dole to pay employees, some of whom received unpaid vacations that summer. The project looked as though it would never get off the ground (although a prototype model had flown for 17 minutes on January 1, 1981, to satisfy British officials).

Hoping to avoid an enormous loss, the British approached Bob Burch, a wealthy Denver businessman who had access to a cadre of equally wealthy investors whose money could keep Bill Lear's brainchild from suffering the same fate as the De Lorean automobile. Burch and his friends, who have been identified only as Americans, Europeans, and Saudis, infused $90 million into the project. Burch became the company's president and chief executive officer. Despite severe setbacks and some canceled orders, more than 270 orders for the plane were booked by 1984.

Although the Lear Fan is unquestionably one of the most intriguing aircrafts on the runways today, its future is still uncertain. Nevertheless, Burch and his management team are grimly determined to receive FAA certification by late 1984; it would be a fitting tribute to the plane's exceptional creator, William Lear.

For more about the Lear Fan, see Andrew C. Brown, "Northern Ireland's Other American Gamble," *Fortune*, November 29, 1982, p. 114; Alexander L. Taylor, III, "Saga in Epoxy," *Time*, November 15, 1982, p. 66; and Robert Rodwell, "Control of Lear Fan Ltd. Is Transferred to New Holding Company Based in U.S.," *The Wall Street Journal*, September 16, 1982, p. 34.

case was not really damaging to the manufacturer — or to the university — instances of defective products may expose manufacturers to extremely expensive product-liability suits from injured customers. (These will be discussed in Chapter 15.)

Summary

Perhaps the most fundamental production concern is where to build a plant. Managers examine the combined effects of certain proximity factors, people factors, and physical factors at various potential sites. The final choice is almost always a compromise.

The nature of the product and the market will dictate which production method a firm uses. The analytic process breaks down raw materials to form new products, while its opposite, the synthetic process, combines materials — by fabrication or assembly — to form new products. A production process can be termed *continuous*, if it makes identical units by following the same steps over a long period of time, or *intermittent*, if the product is made to customers' specifications and procedures and equipment are adjusted accordingly.

Robots, which were first installed on auto assembly lines, are now used by an increasing number of manufacturing companies. Although changes in plant layout and production flows are usually necessary, these reprogrammable automatons can increase productivity impressively while reducing wage and benefit costs and working in environments that are unpleasant or hostile to humans.

Production requires materials, parts, supplies, and equipment, so management creates a purchasing, or procurement, department and employs purchasing agents to buy the items it needs. These purchasing agents will use a combination of several purchasing policies, depending on the nature of the item, consumer demand, storage space, and available funds. Inventory control balances the need for adequate stock against the costs of acquiring, handling, and keeping records on it. Inventory control employees and purchasing agents work together to determine consumption rates for various products and ensure that enough stock is available to satisfy production requirements.

Management controls production through planning, routing, scheduling, dispatching, and follow-up, so that enough units are made when they are needed to fill orders. Management also inspects products so that the products meet standards of acceptability.

Key Terms

analytic process	hand-to-mouth purchasing	production control
anticipatory purchasing	intermittent process	production management
assembly process	inventory control	production plan
bid purchasing	job shops	purchasing agent
captive supplier	lead time	purchasing procedure
continuous process	make versus buy *or* in-house versus out-of-house	quality assurance
contract purchasing		robot
dispatching	manufacturing company	routing
economic order quantity (EOQ)	motion study	scheduling
environmental impact study	on-site inspection	single-source purchasing
fabrication process	processing company	synthetic process
follow-up	production	time study
forward purchasing		

For Review and Discussion

1. How does production contribute to the nation's economic health?

2. Comment on the following statement: "A plant site should be picked by a committee. One manager is not qualified to evaluate all the factors accurately and objectively."

3. List the proximity factors, people factors, and physical factors that companies examine when selecting a plant site. Why are most site decisions compromises?

4. What is the difference between motion study and time study? Offer examples from your own experience of how they affect your job or your personal life.

5. How do companies use motion and time studies? How might employees react to them? What would you recommend management do to encourage a positive reaction?

6. List some products made by the analytic and by the synthetic production processes. What is the difference between the two processes?

7. How would you describe the fabrication process? Compare it with the assembly process. Is it usual for a company to make a product using one or the other exclusively? Why or why not?

8. Under what conditions would a continuous production process be preferred to an intermittent one? Find several local firms that use each.

9. Justify the use of robot assembly techniques in enabling American producers to respond to foreign competitors. What impact should this trend have on employee training?

10. Comment on the following statement: "Purchasing agents, by the nature of their jobs, are subject to a number of ethical pressures that most other employees do not encounter." What might these pressures be? How do you think most purchasing agents react to them? Explain your answer.

11. Describe a typical purchasing procedure, including circumstances under which the purchasing agent would solicit bids from several vendors.

12. Summarize the distinguishing features of the following purchasing policies, and the conditions under which each may be used: hand-to-mouth, forward, anticipatory, bid, and contract purchasing, and make-versus-buy decisions.

13. What factors combine to fix an economic order quantity (EOQ)? How does this statistic influence a purchasing agent's decisions? What conditions might prompt a purchasing agent to buy more or less than the EOQ?

14. Explain why purchasing agents and inventory control employees should be concerned with the matters of reorder point, safety stock, supplier lead time, and economic order quantity.

15. Why are production planners essential to a successful manufacturing operation? Is hands-on production experience helpful to them in their jobs? Why or why not?

16. "When I'm right no one remembers; when I'm wrong, no one forgets." Why might this lament be particularly true in the production planner's job?

17. Discuss at least two circumstances that would require jobs in process to be rescheduled after they have been dispatched.

18. Do you believe follow-up could be eliminated from production control responsibilities if the various departments involved did their jobs efficiently? Why or why not?

19. Justify the need for quality assurance. Under what conditions would you recommend spot inspections, and when would inspection of every piece, or a "zero defects" philosophy, be preferable?

Applications

Case 9.1 *Kanban:* How Practical for American Companies?

A common practice among large Japanese manufacturers, the inventory control technique of *kanban* (also known as just-in-time production) is viewed as revolutionary — and extremely risky — by American manufacturers.

Kanban has impressive potential: a manufacturer could save millions of dollars in inventory cost, storage space, interest charges, materials-handling equipment, recordkeeping, and scrap if subassemblies and component parts were delivered to the production line exactly when needed. There would be no mountains of buffer, or safety, stock piled in warehouses and in storage areas adjacent to the production line. Production would flow continuously, as parts and subassemblies were delivered at one door and the finished product emerged from the other.

Although an impressive theory, the idea is enough to give a seasoned production manager hypertension. American companies traditionally have preferred to keep a comfortable supply of parts on hand because the lack of a single component may shut down an entire assembly line. Considering the number of parts that go into a car (Chrysler Corporation uses 40,000 for all its models), the complications resulting from running out of just one critical item could be enormous.

Japanese manufacturers like Kawasaki and Toyota, however, have implemented the just-in-time technique as a standard practice. In doing so, these and other foreign competitors have reduced the amount of work-in-process inventory (inventory issued to the production floor) to $150 per car, compared with $775 per car for American automakers.

Kanban naturally affects the way that production workers interact with each other and do their jobs. Lacking several days of safety stock to conceal mistakes, workers tend to try harder to avoid errors that will cause problems for colleagues at the next station in line. The absence of buffer stock also prompts workers to identify and resolve problems with malfunctioning production equipment as soon as possible. Workers also become more waste conscious under *kanban*, because there is no large stockpile of parts to rely on. Every unit becomes important because there aren't many extras available in case of loss or damage. Ford Motor Company, in contrast, reportedly has stocked as many as 40 days' worth of parts at its engine or transmission assembly plants. One General Motors Buick plant routinely held as many as 4,000 body parts in reserve.

The Japanese automakers' success with *kanban* can be traced in part to the number of suppliers they deal with. Toyota, for example, purchases from fewer than 250 companies, while General Motors may buy from 3,500 firms. Japanese suppliers often surround the plants they serve (which reduces distance, time, communications, and other factors associated with transportation), and suppliers work hand-in-hand to ensure an uninterrupted flow of material to the customer's production lines. Suppliers to United States automakers, however, are scattered nationwide.

Another reason that just-in-time production has succeeded in Japan is the limited number of options available on Japanese cars. The Honda Accord, for example, comes in just 32 variations. Taking into account the host of engines, transmissions, trim packages, interior light groups, and upholstery available, a buyer reportedly could create 69,000 different variations of a 1984 Ford Thunderbird and 32,000 slightly different Chevrolet Citations. Such an enormous range of choices in the showroom creates inventory handling, production planning, parts routing, and installation headaches at the plants.

A last, key reason for *kanban*'s success is the equipment set-up changes Japanese companies have made to accommodate a low-stock (in some cases almost no-stock) production line. Because large inventories of safety stock are not carried, machines that make body panels and other items must be set up more often. The Japanese have dedicated themselves to reducing set-up time drastically, and they've succeeded well. Toyota, the generally acknowledged originator of *kanban*, cut the set-up time for an 800-ton press that made body parts from 1 hour to 12 minutes. Set-up time for a similar piece of equipment in an American auto plant requires 6 hours. Japanese set-up time has further declined as large companies design and manufacture their machinery in-house and tailor it to their own special requirements and in-plant production flows.

Kanban's success abroad has spurred extensive discussion and some positive action by American automakers. Eliminating unpopular buyer options in axle ratios and interior fabrics and taking other efficiency measures has enabled Ford Motor Company to reduce inventories by $750 million and carrying costs by $250 million since 1980. General Motors has expressed a willingness to examine the make-or-buy issue more often and to consider dealing with outside firms that make some components more cheaply or more efficiently. One Buick plant reports changes in shipping methods that have reduced its buffer stock of body stampings 82 percent with no threat to production line stoppage. Despite these achievements, however, real implementation of *kanban* presents a formidable challenge.

Questions

1. Discuss the effect that a traditional or older plant layout would have on implementing a just-in-time production program.

2. In some American factories a production executive's salary depends on the plant's productivity. How might such an arrangement inhibit the acceptance of *kanban*?

3. What impact would the weather, strikes, and worker co-operation have on the success of a just-in-time program?

4. Do you believe it's feasible for American automakers to pursue the just-in-time concept to the same extent that Japanese companies have? Why or why not?

Case 9.1 For more about the *kanban* technique, see John Koten, "Giving Buyers Wide Choices May Be Hurting Auto Makers," *The Wall Street Journal,* December 15, 1983, p. 33; Alexander L. Taylor, III, "Iacocca's Tightrope Act," *Time,* March 21, 1983, p. 50; Richard J. Schonberger, "Why the Japanese Produce Just in Time," *Industry Week,* November 29, 1982, p. 56; Richard J. Schonberger, "Replace Old Buffers Just-in-Time? (letter)," *The Wall Street Journal,* September 21, 1982, p. 35; John Koten, "Auto Makers Have Trouble With 'Kanban'," *The Wall Street Journal,* April 7, 1982, p. 35; Charles G. Burck, "Can Detroit Catch Up?" *Fortune,* February 8, 1982, p. 34; and Craig R. Waters, "Why Everybody's Talking About 'Just-in-Time'," *Inc.,* March 1984, p. 77.

Case 9.2 Government Gouging

The armed forces, which are enormous customers of private industry, spend billions of dollars annually on everything from missiles to typewriters. Many of these products require spare parts after the sale.

The government usually buys spare parts from the original manufacturer (the prime contractor) because that firm usually keeps the engineering drawings, equipment, and other material required to make spare parts. Scandals surfaced in 1983, however, because of the high prices prime contractors charged government procurement officers for such items as wrenches, electronic components, brackets, bolts, and screws. The Navy reportedly paid $110 to one prime contractor for a diode available for $0.04 in electronics shops and $44 for a light bulb that retails for $0.17. Among the most widely publicized examples of outrageous prices were a plastic cap for the leg of a navigator's stool in the AWACS plane ($1,118) and a claw hammer ($430). Senator William Roth (Republican, Delaware), chairman of the Senate Governmental Affairs Committee, dramatized the extent of the problem by decorating a Christmas tree with miscellaneous items and their prices from prime contractors. The ornaments included transistors ($814), nuts ($2,043), bolts ($1,075), and an Allen wrench ($9,606). If purchased in hardware and electronic stores, the products reportedly would have cost $110. The Pentagon, however, paid more than $100,000 to the prime contractors who filled these orders.

One reason why this could happen relates to the federal government's enormous inventory itself. With a $40 billion stock of spare parts and 3.4 million items incoming annually, just checking the supply of a simple bolt (with a stock number of several digits) is a formidable job. Sometimes procurement officers allegedly have ordered a new part instead of taking the time and trouble to look for the item in existing inventory. Items also are often ordered strictly by stock number — no description — so a procurement officer may not be able to tell from the requisition if the product is a jet engine or a door handle.

Another reason for potential overcharging involves the original contract between the federal government and the supplier firm. Occasionally the government may allow the prime contractor to restrict access to a product's technical specifications. Essentially this means that engineering drawings and other production documents remain the property of the company. Even the government cannot obtain copies to use in soliciting bids from competing firms. In other cases the government may buy the product but not the specifications themselves, so essential production information again remains locked in the prime contractor's files.

How can a company defend charging $917 for a part that costs $0.35 at a nearby hardware store? The answer, some contractors contend, lies in production set-up expenses. Once a company is done making a certain part the tools, dies, templates, holding fixtures, and other equipment used in production are often disassembled, crated, and stored in a warehouse. If it is ordered some time in the future, the equipment must be located, moved back to the production floor, set up, adjusted, and tested. This time-consuming procedure must be followed regardless of the number of units ordered.

But what about standard items like nuts, bolts, and screws that may be found in common hardware stores? The federal government has a policy of dealing only with qualified suppliers (those who successfully pass muster on quality, reliability, and other criteria) so companies that have not taken the time, trouble, and expense to get their names on the Pentagon's approved supplier list would not be considered, regardless of the price they offered. It seems immaterial that the prime contractors often purchase component parts from thousands of small companies nationwide that the federal government has never heard of.

Questions

1. Discuss how the Pentagon's purchasing policies may restrict competition for federal government business to a few large prime contractors.

2. Do you believe the federal government should require all prime contractors to supply production specifications along with their products? Why might the prime contractors oppose such a requirement?

3. Critique the federal government's policy of dealing only with qualified suppliers.

Case 9.2 For more about the Pentagon purchasing scandal, see Joseph J. Petrillo, "The Lock Nuts Monster," *Inc.,* January 1984, p. 12; Associated Press, "Pentagon Spare Parts Adorn Costly Yule Tree," *The Orlando* (Florida) *Sentinel,* December 21, 1983, p. A-3; "Spare Parts Bills Jar the Pentagon," *Newsweek,* July 25, 1983, p. 69; and United Press International, "35-Cent Part Could Cost $916.55 if You Buy It from Boeing," *The Orlando* (Florida) *Sentinel,* May 12, 1983, p. D-2.

Marketing and Product Strategy

Chapter Outline

Chapter Objectives

After studying this chapter, you should be able to:

1. Describe the importance of marketing in a company's success.
2. List and explain the functions involved in marketing.
3. Describe the evolution of an organization from production orientation to marketing orientation.
4. Explain the marketing concept and its effect on the role of marketing in an organization.
5. Describe the marketing process.
6. Define what a market is and distinguish between industrial and consumer markets.
7. Discuss the importance of and processes involved in market segmentation.
8. Describe each of the four elements of the marketing mix.
9. Explain what a product is and distinguish between the two major categories of products.
10. Explain the importance of brands and packaging as components of product strategy.
11. Explain the four stages of the product life cycle.

Never be satisfied with your product, even if it is the best.
— Anonymous

Up Front

William H. Gates, III

Chairman of the Board at Twenty-Eight

Intelligent, ambitious, hard-working, and dedicated, William H. Gates, III, is a phenomenal success at the age of twenty-eight. In 1975 when he was a sophomore at Harvard, he and his friend, Paul Allen, wrote a BASIC programming language for one of the first commercially available microcomputers, the Altair. It sold so well that Gates made a decision that set the course for his future: he dropped out of college, and he and Allen founded Microsoft Corporation of Bellevue, Washington, of which he is chairman of the board and executive vice president. By 1980 the company had built a reputation impressive enough to attract callers from IBM.

Gates's business has now emerged as the most powerful company in the microcomputer software industry and dominates the market for the operating system software that runs business microcomputers. Microsoft had sales of $68 million in 1983, increasing to $100 million by the end of fiscal year 1984. His current goal is to control a larger, more promising segment of the applications software market, which is by far the largest portion of the multibillion dollar software industry.

His new Windows program provides a universal operating environment for the new generation of bit-mapped applications pro-

Most people, when asked what marketing is, would define it as selling a product or service. They would be partially correct. Selling is a part of marketing, but only a part. Marketing is much, much more. It involves a wide range of activities including market research, consumer behavior, product development, promotion, product distribution, and product pricing. Surprised? Curious? This chapter will introduce you to the dynamic nature of marketing.

Marketing Defined

marketing

Marketing is a group of interrelated activities designed to identify consumer needs and to develop, distribute, promote, and price goods and services to satisfy these needs at a profit. Whether an organization is large or small, whether it produces a product or provides a service, its long-range future is linked to successful marketing practices.

The old saying "Build a better mousetrap and the world will beat a path to your door" is not true. "They" must need the product,

grams. Microsoft Windows will allow independent software vendors to develop sophisticated, graphically-based, integrated software packages that run without modification on any sixteen-bit microcomputer. In addition, Microsoft Windows features a window management capability that allows a user to view unrelated applications programs simultaneously and to transfer data from one application program to another. At the time of its introduction, twenty-three personal computer manufacturers announced support of Microsoft Windows, which has the potential to become a highly successful industry standard.

Instinctively Gates believes that the future of his firm lies with applications software. He believes that half of the potential market for personal computers for business will be satisfied in 5 years and that the demand for applications software will increase as the sales growth of hardware and operating systems decreases. Moneywise, the sales growth will be phenomenal because applications programs sell to retailers for $50 to $200, whereas a manufacturer pays only about $10 per unit. William H. Gates, III, is fiercely competitive and is moving quickly toward his goal. "Software is a momentum business," he says, "and right now, we have momentum working for us."

For more about William H. Gates, III, see Stratford P. Sherman, "Microsoft's Drive to Dominate Software," *Fortune*, January 23, 1984, pp. 82–90; and "The Windows Battle," *Fortune*, March 19, 1984, pp. 7, 195.

know about it, be able to get it when and where they want it, and be able to afford it. Marketing provides the means to make the organization successful in the long run. What happens when marketing is not practiced well? An answer to that question is seen in the volatile home computer business. The market is universally having problems because of lack of marketing. Having the best product is not the answer. "We don't market," said Steven Ross, chairman of Warner Communications, explaining the problems the company has had with its Atari home computers. "We've got the best computer, but we don't market it right. I'm pulling my hair out." Ignorance of the role of marketing not only causes frustration and loss of profits, but also puts companies out of business.[1]

The Marketing Concept

Marketing was unheard of in the early 1900s. This period can best be described as one where far more people needed consumer goods than companies were able to manufacture. This intense demand

production orientation

on manufacturing led to organizations dominated by production management. Companies had a **production orientation:** where *the number one priority is to produce a good to keep up with demand.* All energies and talents were placed in the production function. Selling a good was incidental; determining consumer needs was unheard of.

As manufacturers increased their production capabilities, the supply of goods available increased and inventories of goods developed. An emphasis on selling occurred. This need to sell led to a sales-

sales orientation

dominated company — a **sales orientation,** whereby the *energy of the company is focused on selling the products produced.* The salesperson's job: (1) to make the desires of the consumers "fit" the products the company manufactures and (2) to convince the consumer to buy. The company's goal: to "Send the wagon out full and bring it back empty."

As more producers began competing for consumer dollars by making such high-demand products as automobiles, vacuum cleaners, and refrigerators, the supply of goods began to exceed the demand. Companies had to find a way to identify consumer demand.

marketing orientation

Organizations began to shift to a **marketing orientation,** which is *an emphasis on identifying the needs and wants of specific consumer groups, then producing, promoting, pricing, and distributing products that satisfy these needs and earn the company profits.*

marketing concept

Companies that are marketing oriented have adopted a philosophy for the firm known as the marketing concept. The **marketing concept** is *a belief that the company should adopt a companywide consumer orientation directed at long-range profitability.*[2] It includes the belief that all efforts of the organization should be directed at identifying and satisfying the needs of the consumer at a profit.

A prime example of a person who did not initially adopt the marketing concept is provided by Henry Ford and the Ford Motor Company. Through the early 1920s Ford Motor Company mass-produced more than one million Model T Fords off the assembly lines. When questioned about altering the style, color, or features of these cars Ford's response was, "They can have any color they want as long as it's black." A more appropriate answer to that was given by Alfred Sloan of General Motors (GM) who began redesigning the cars in GM's wide product lines each year to offer buyers styling, accessories, and luxuries that Ford's rugged, reliable Model T lacked. A contemporary example of a company that got carried away with its own technologic capabilities and lost sight of consumer needs

---

Pause and Ponder

Give two examples of companies you have dealt with that have adopted the marketing concept. Why do you feel that they have? Are there businesses you know that have not adopted the concept? Why? What effect has it had on your business relationship?

is Procter & Gamble with its Pringle's Potato Chips. Continuing to be the product no one really wants, Pringle's losses exceed $200 million.[3]

Marketing Functions

At the beginning of the chapter we defined marketing as a group of interrelated activities designed to identify consumer needs and develop, distribute, promote, and price goods and services to satisfy these needs at a profit. What are these activities?

Figure 10.1 presents the three broad categories of these activities: exchange functions, physical distribution functions, and facilitating functions. Let's examine each.

Exchange Functions

The **exchange functions,** *buying and selling,* are *complementary activities that relay products to their intended users.* Each consumer buys for his or her personal use, but other parties must perform

exchange functions

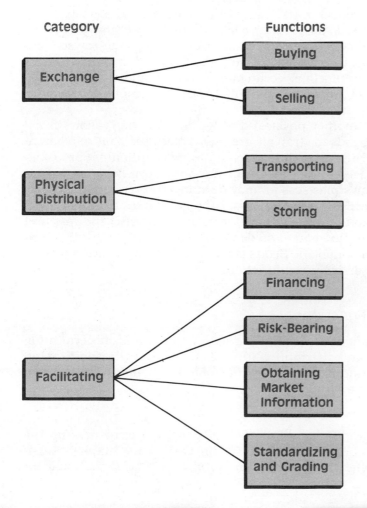

Figure 10.1 Principal Activities Involved in Marketing

**wholesalers
retailers**

buying functions that lead up to the final sale. **Wholesalers,** for example, are *firms that distribute goods to other sellers.* **Retailers** are *businesses that sell to ultimate consumers.* These retailers perform a buying function when they obtain merchandise from manufacturers or from wholesalers. (The roles of wholesalers and retailers are explored in Chapter 12.)

Selling — the other exchange function — is the critical counterpart of buying. It includes not only face-to-face meetings between sales people and potential customers, but also such sales support activities as advertising, sales promotion, service, and product repair, some of which are examined in Chapter 11.

Physical Distribution Functions

**physical distribution
functions**

Transporting and storing goods are termed **physical distribution functions.** Because members of the market segment usually are scattered throughout the country, these functions *place* products where they are wanted.

Products are shipped regularly by air, water, truck, rail, and pipeline. The method of transportation that a given producer uses depends on such factors as the perishability, durability, bulk, and weight of the product, rates charged by the carrier, and how urgently the customer needs the item. Live Maine lobsters, a highly perishable product, are flown across the country packed in wet seaweed. Oil and natural gas, because of their bulk and fluidity, can be transported conveniently by pipeline, oceangoing tankers, and rail tank cars. Forest products are shipped in bulk by rail and truck, and iron ore by rail and water.

Storage, another physical distribution function, allows firms to distribute goods to strategic areas and place them on retail store shelves when buyers need them, eliminating coordination problems caused by seasonal and uncertain demand. Toys, which sell best during the Christmas season, may be shipped several months early and stored until the season nears. Storage enables manufacturers to produce enough units to meet demand for most of the year and release them to the market as demand dictates. Products like Coppertone suntan lotion and Scotts lawn fertilizer rely heavily on storage as a physical distribution function.

Facilitating Functions

facilitating functions

Four other functions facilitate or assist companies in performing the exchange and distribution functions. These are the **facilitating functions** — *financing, risk bearing, obtaining market information, and standardizing and grading.*

Financing. The financing function aids marketing by making the exchange functions (buying and selling) easier to accomplish. Businesses may offer credit to customers, which allows them to pay for purchases over several weeks or months. Firms also may borrow funds to buy materials and parts used in the end product, which makes financing important even before the product is ready to be marketed.

Risk Bearing. Some element of risk is inherent in any business activity, especially that of marketing. Firms that are sales oriented instead of market oriented face greater likelihood of financial loss, but all companies face the risk of loss caused by competitors' marketing tactics, changes in product life cycle, and disappointing sales or profit potential.

Obtaining Market Information. Successful marketing is no accident. Managers make it happen by conducting extensive **marketing research,** which is *the facilitating function of collecting and interpreting data on customer demands and characteristics so that firms can develop new products and sell existing ones profitably.* Marketing research helps management evaluate the sales potential, demand potential, buying power, and profit potential for the firm's intended market segment. Table 10.1 lists data that marketing research must supply about a product's potential buyers.

    Accurate marketing research data are used to do the following:

— Write promotional messages that have maximum impact on the buying motives of the typical member of the market segment
— Promote product characteristics that impress most buyers

marketing research

---

1. Personal data
   a. Age   e. Marital status
   b. Sex   f. Educational level
   c. Income   g. Hobbies, favorite recreation
   d. Occupation
2. Product use
   a. Frequency
   b. Reason (personal, professional, commercial)
   c. Most popular time of year (if applicable)
3. Type of store at which product is likely to be bought (supermarket, hardware store, discount store, department store)
4. Source from which consumer is most likely to learn about product (magazine, television, radio, or newspaper advertising; friends; direct mail promotion; store displays)
5. Brands or models previously owned
6. Factors that influence a buying decision (price, warranty, design, brand name, ease of operation)
7. Housing (own or rent house or apartment; live with parents; own vacation home)
8. Credit cards that may be used to buy the product

Table 10.1 Data That Marketing Research Must Supply

- Promote the product with media that most members of the market segment will be exposed to
- Distribute a product in geographic locations where most members of the market segment live (if they are geographically concentrated)
- Identify the types of retail stores where most members of the market segment shop
- Improve existing products and conceive new products that meet consumer wants, needs, and expectations.

Standardizing and Grading. The facilitating functions of standardizing and grading permit buyers and sellers to make transactions without physically examining the product in question. If it were not for standards or grades, customers often would have difficulty comparing one product with another. Imagine, for example, the problems producers and retail stores would have with shoes or clothes if sizes were not standardized. The same holds true for light bulbs, bed sheets, flashlight batteries, tires, and the lead in the pencil you may be holding.

The Marketing Process

Having examined the activities involved in marketing, one major question needs to be answered: How does a company actually market a product or service? Figure 10.2 provides an illustration of the process involved in marketing a product or service. Briefly an organization:

1. Identifies a potential target market of consumers (age, income, location)

Gathering marketing information where consumers make purchasing decisions helps firms to develop new products and sell existing ones.

Figure 10.2 The Process of Marketing a Product

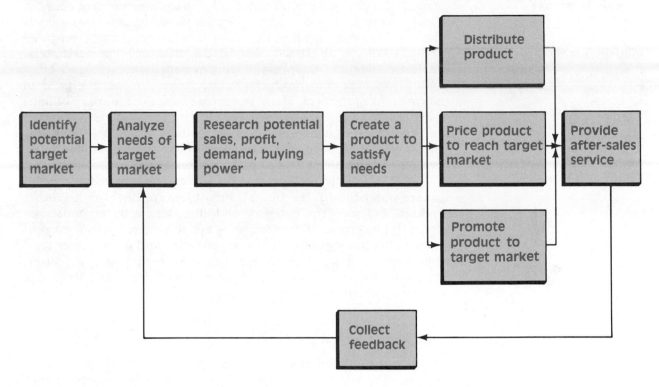

2. Analyzes the needs of the identified target market
3. Researches the potential of the target market for demand, sales, buying power, and potential profit
4. Creates a product or service intended to satisfy the needs of the target market
5. Distributes, prices, and promotes the product or service to the target market
6. Ensures satisfaction through after-sales services

The starting point is identifying a potential market.

What Is a Market?

A **market** is *a group of potential customers with the authority and the ability to purchase a particular product or service that satisfies their collective demand.* The important part of this definition is that people alone do not make a market. The people in the market, whether individual consumers or individuals buying for a business, must have the authority to make the purchase decision and have the money to be able to buy. Marketers must be careful to qualify the market. Markets are subdivided into two major markets — consumer and industrial.

market

consumer market

industrial market

Markets are categorized by who buys the products and for what purpose the purchase is intended. The **consumer market** consists of *individuals who buy products for their personal use.* The products targeted for this market are known as consumer products. (Consumer products will be discussed later in the chapter.) The **industrial market** consists of *businesses, government agencies, and other institutions that buy products to use either in operations or in making other products.* These purchases, which amount to billions of dollars' worth of goods each year, directly or indirectly support the production of consumer goods and other industrial items. Examples of industrial goods are iron ore, office supplies, drill presses, packaging machinery, and most computers.

While such products as iron ore are clearly industrial (no consumers purchase it), the buyer's intent determines whether other products fall into the category of industrial goods or consumer goods. Typing paper, for example, is an industrial good when purchased by a business for its correspondence and a consumer good when bought by a college student to write a term paper. Fertilizer, pickup trucks, and vegetables also fall into both categories, depending on how the buyer plans to use them.

Market Segmentation

Companies that market cars have recognized a simple fact: the same car cannot be sold to everyone who drives. Some people want economy, others luxury. Some people will buy Cadillac Sevilles, others Chevrolet Chevettes. It is more logical and practical to develop products for the preferences, habits, special uses, or general life-styles of a particular group of users and market them to that group. An automobile maker that appeals to particular market segments — the high fuel-economy market, the larger family market, and the youth market — may capture most of the total market by satisfying the specific needs of the smaller, more homogeneous target markets. Table 10.2 illustrates how the automobile market is segmented into smaller markets.

market segmentation

The process of dividing a total market into subgroups with similar characteristics is **market segmentation.** By splitting one big market into consumer and industrial markets we have begun market segmentation; however, these two groups are so enormous that they must be subdivided, or segmented, further to develop

Table 10.2 Automobile Market Segments

Lifestyle/Age	Income (in Dollars)		
	0–20,000	21,000–35,000	35,000–50,000
Single/22–30	Subcompact car	Compact car	Sports car
Single/31–40	Compact car	Midsized car	Foreign sports car

To market successfully, companies must identify distinct target markets within the larger mass market.

sharply defined markets for which companies can create a strategy. Two further subdivisions are necessary.

Step 1: Identify the Characteristics and Needs of the Market

By utilizing marketing research (one of the marketing activities we discussed earlier in the chapter) marketers can acquire the necessary information on consumer characteristics and needs to segment the markets, information such as:

1. Data on family income, geographic location, and race
2. Behavior patterns (e.g., amount of a specific product consumed, social status, and language spoken)
3. Physical characteristics (e.g., sex, age, and health)
4. Psychologic traits (e.g., personality characteristics and hobbies)
5. Opinions of goods on the market
6. Degree of competition

From this markets can be analyzed and subdivided in four ways.

— Demographic segmentation classifies the market into like groups based on characteristics such as age, sex, education, income, and household size.

- Geographic segmentation identifies where the consumer actually lives; for example, Portland, Maine, or Dime Box, Texas.
- Psychographic segmentation identifies like-groups based on life-styles such as peoples' activities, interests, and opinions.
- Benefit segmentation focuses on the benefits expected from a product or service. For example, diet soda may be expected to provide great taste for one group of individuals while another group may seek the soda's low-calorie benefits.

Demographic segmentation (because of the ease of reaching specific groups of consumers) and psychographics (because of the ability to consider one's psychological makeup) are the two bases for segmentation commonly used.

Step 2: Analyze the Potential of the Market

A second activity undertaken in segmenting the market after its characteristics and needs are identified is to analyze its (1) sales potential, (2) demand potential, (3) buying power, and (4) profit potential.

Sales Potential. Important market segments have sales potential, which means there is a sufficient number of prospective buyers to justify risking capital and human resources to make and market the product. This is why, to use exaggerated examples, snowmobiles are not sold in Hawaii or air conditioners in Alaska.

Forward-looking companies are especially concerned with anticipated changes in sales potential. Predictions that a segment's population will decrease, or will grow at a slow rate, may discourage entrepreneurs from appealing to that segment.

Demand Potential. Another concern in evaluating a market segment is customer demand. Customers must either demonstrate an urgent, justified need for a particular product or indicate that they can be made to want it by a company's promotional activities. The difference between the two is primarily necessity. The Frisbee, for example, is not a necessary product, but millions of customers were convinced that they wanted it. Products such as smoke alarms and antibiotic drugs, however, are sold in response to needs.

Buying Power. People are not potential customers for a product simply because they need or want it. They must also have effective demand, or buying, power — cash or credit that enables them to buy the product. Many college students may want a Porsche 924, for example, but without sufficient cash or credit they will never get beyond the tire-kicking stage. Buying power separates casual lookers from serious prospects. An important market segment needs enough of the latter to warrant producing the item.

Profit Potential. The fourth important factor in attributing importance to a market segment, and the key to all the others, is profit potential. This is the likelihood that an entrepreneur will earn sufficient profit from the units sold to justify the risk involved. Successful firms minimize the frequency and severity of bad decisions by confirming that a market segment exhibits these four features to an acceptable degree before they commit themselves to production.

Remember, a market is a group of potential customers with the authority and ability to purchase a particular product or service that satisfies their collective demand. In the process of segmenting a market, we have identified a group of consumers that have similar needs and characteristics — a target market — and we have assured ourselves that they have the authority and ability to buy. Table 10.3 shows how different market segments have specific products designed for them. Now marketers must develop plans for reaching the identified market segment or segments.

The Marketing Mix

The tools or variables a marketer works with to reach the target market segment are product strategy, promotion strategy, price strategy, and distribution strategy. *The effective meshing of product, price, promotion, and distribution strategies to achieve success* is known as the **marketing mix.** Figure 10.3 shows the relationship of the marketing mix ingredients as they blend together to focus on a target market segment.

marketing mix

Product strategy extends beyond the physical item itself to include decisions about brands, labels, trademarks, packaging, warranties, guarantees, new product development, and the product life cycle. (The remainder of this chapter is devoted to a discussion of product strategy.)

Pricing strategy is concerned with establishing prices for products that will return a profit. Pricing decisions are influenced by

Product	Market Segment
Hero dog food	Owners of large dogs
Cycle dog food	Owners of dogs at different stages of life
Gaines Burgers	Dog owners seeking convenience
CD dog food	Owners of dogs needing special diets
Good Housekeeping	Homemakers
Savvy	Female entrepreneurs and executives
Vogue	Fashion-conscious women
Flintstones vitamins	Children
Fem-iron tablets	Adult women
Geritol	Elderly people

Table 10.3 Variations of Products Designed for Market Segments

Figure 10.3 Elements in the Marketing Mix

how responsive a target market is to a high or low price, the psychological images created by prices (cheap versus quality), and the actions of competitors. William Wrigley implemented price strategy successfully by marketing a product with a low price–high volume potential: chewing gum for a nickel a pack. (We will explore pricing strategy in Chapter 12.)

Promotional strategy involves developing the correct blend of the promotional mix elements — advertising, personal selling, sales promotion, and publicity. Promotional strategy is the communication element of the marketing mix. (Promotion is the subject of Chapter 11.)

Distribution strategy involves the distribution systems and channels used to *place* the product in the customer's hands. Decisions are made concerning what shipping methods to use, how and where to store the product until it is sold, what intermediaries to use, and what sales outlets will be used in specific locations throughout the country. Produce, fresh meat, and certain health foods must be refrigerated constantly from producer to consumer or they will spoil.

Products and Product Strategy

The product and product strategy have the key role in marketing mix planning. The development of a product or service to satisfy a consumer need is the critical first step. The other elements are based on product planning.

What Is a Product?

A product is more than meets the eye. It is the total package that brings satisfaction to a consumer. "A product consists of the basic physical offering and an accompanying set of image and service features that seek to satisfy needs."[4] It is the tangible features that can be seen and the intangible image and service features that we cannot see but which make the product what it is.

As an example, an Intellevision home computer game by Mattel:

— Is a rectangular box with wires connecting it to a television set (physical characteristics)
— Has a warranty and service facilities (service characteristics)
— Has prestige associated with ownership of a relatively new product innovation (image)

These characteristics, whether tangible or intangible, are designed to produce consumer satisfaction.

Categories of Products

Product strategy involves a decision on the category of good to offer. There are two categories of goods — consumer products and industrial products.

Products are designed for the unique needs of the consumer.

Consumer Products. Consumer products are *goods intended for the personal use of the consumer.* The products in this category can be identified according to the differences in buying behavior that occur from one group of goods to another. There are three categories of consumer goods: convenience goods, shopping goods, and specialty goods.

consumer products

    Convenience goods are *products purchased with a minimum of effort.* These products are usually inexpensive and are purchased frequently. Milk, newspapers, and pencils are examples of convenience goods.

convenience goods

    Shopping goods are *items purchased after comparative shopping based on quality, design, cost, and performance.* Potential purchasers undergo an extensive shopping campaign, investigating and comparing products at competing stores. Televisions, clothes, shoes, and appliances generally fall in this category.

shopping goods

    Specialty goods are those *products that buyers prefer strongly because of their unique characteristics or image.* Consumers are willing to expend considerable energy and time to acquire these goods. Some people, for example, have specific, nonnegotiable demands for Carver stereo amplifiers, Martin guitars, or Castrol GTX motor oil. Generally, if the specific product is not available, many customers will not accept a substitute for the desired product. It is important to realize that the boundaries are personal. One person's specialty item may be another's convenience good, a difference in perception that sometimes depends on spendable income (as with jewelry) and sometimes on the effect that peer opinions and promotional efforts have on the buyer's attitude (as with motor oils, razor blades, and sporting goods). General classifications merely help producers construct broad promotion and distribution strategies that will succeed with most consumers who want or need the product.

specialty goods

Stereo equipment can be considered a shopping good or a specialty good, depending on the individual consumer's perception.

industrial products

Industrial Products. Industrial products are *goods or services purchased for the production of other goods and services or to be used in the operation of the business.* The classifications of industrial goods include installations, accessory equipment, fabricated parts and materials, raw materials, and industrial supplies.

installations
accessory equipment

Installations are *the industrial goods that are the major assets of a company.* Examples are machinery and buildings. **Accessory equipment** are *capital items that are less expensive and shorter lived than installations.* Desk calendars, hand tools, and typewriters

fabricated parts and materials
raw materials

are typical examples. **Fabricated parts and materials** are *the industrial goods that become part of the final product.* Batteries and spark plugs for automobiles illustrate this type of product. **Raw materials** are *industrial products that are composed of farm and natural products.* Minerals, iron ore, and oil are examples of raw

industrial supplies

materials. **Industrial supplies** are *items necessary in the daily operation of the firm.* They do not become part of the final product. Supplies include light bulbs, repair supplies, stationery, and pens.

Product Strategy: The Use of Brands

A major concern in developing product strategy is to distinguish your product from all others. Part of a product as we defined it earlier is its image. To create an image companies adopt a strategy

brand

of branding. A **brand** is *a name, symbol, design, or a combination of these that identifies the products or services of a company.*

There are four distinct brand identifications:

brand name

1. A **brand name** is *a letter, a word, or a group of letters or words used to identify the product.* Campbell's Soup, Mrs. Smith's Pies, and Lite Beer are brand names.

2. A **brand mark** is *a symbol or design used to identify the product and to distinguish it.* Gerber Baby Foods' picture of a baby and Prudential's rock are examples of a brand mark.

3. A **trade character** is *a brand mark that has a human quality.* Ronald McDonald, Tony the Tiger, and the Pillsbury Dough Boy provide examples.

4. A **trademark** is *a brand name, brand mark, or trade character that has legal protection.* Firms obtain the exclusive legal right to trademarks by registering them with the U.S. Patent and Trademark Office. When registered the trademark is followed by an ®. Examples include Coca-Cola and Xerox.

brand mark

trade character

trademark

Ease of Recognition. "Branding" makes the product recognizable and distinguishable. Chef-Boy-R-Dee's smiling face and Fruit-of-the-Loom fruits aid customers in distinguishing these products from others.

Projecting a Message. Brands project a message of quality and consistency. This message of quality is intended to increase consumer acceptance of the product and to help move it through the following three stages of brand acceptance.

1. **Brand Recognition** A newly introduced product becomes familiar to the public. If the product is part of a branded group of products this stage is facilitated. "Oh, Kellogg's has a new cereal."

2. **Brand Preference** Consumers who rely on previous experience with a brand choose it over competitors. "I know it's good because all their products are good."

3. **Brand Insistence** Consumers will accept no alternatives. "If you don't carry Campbell's soup, I'll shop at a store that does."

Brands Are Everywhere. The use of brands is such an effective strategy that a number of approaches have evolved. Some firms such as General Electric employ a family brand: the products produced by the company are identified by one name. On the other hand multiple branding uses separate brands for each item or product marketed by the firm. Manufacturers develop their own brands called *national brands* while retailers and wholesalers put their own "private" brands on the market. Naming a product is so important that companies have developed departments to create names. A good name won't save a lousy product, but the right name can grab attention and increase sales and market share.[5]

Generic Products: Competition for All. Some organizations have chosen an opposite approach to brands, brand names, and brand marks — **generic products.** These are *products that carry no brand name.* Generics do not have expensive packages nor preconditioned support.

generic products

The difference between generic and brand name products is often minimal. Generics may be slightly inferior in color, size, or quality of ingredients, but this has little effect on nourishment or flavor. The grade difference, coupled with the fact that the producer spends no money on promotion, enables generics to sell for as much as 30 to 40 percent less than brand-name items. Manufacturers typically use excess production capacity to process generics so regular operations may be unaffected. While generics return a lower profit per unit, they can sell in large enough volume to supermarket outlet chains that the producer enjoys satisfactory profits.

Product Strategy: The Use of Packaging

Packaging is more than putting the product in a box, bottle, or wrapper. Packaging design has a significant impact on the company's image. The proper use of shape, color, and material is an element of product strategy. Kleenex comes in decorator boxes, Pangburn's Chocolate Millionaires are in a gold box, and Lowenbrau Beer has gold foil wrapped around the neck of the bottle. An accident? Hardly. When products are almost identical, physical packaging can make the difference.[6]

In addition to the use of color, multiple use and ease of handling are conscious decisions made by marketers. Would you rather buy five 1-quart oil cans or one 5-quart plastic oil container, which you can use to store the old oil? Would you prefer plastic or glass quart bottles of cold drinks for the long car trip? Skillful marketing product designers help you with those decisions — and help you buy their products.

The Product Life Cycle

product life cycle

Products, like people, pass through several stages between birth and death. These are called collectively the **product life cycle,** *the succession of phases including the introduction, growth, maturity, and decline of a product in its market.* The length of the stages and the profits received at each stage vary according to the specific product, as Figure 10.4 illustrates.

Successful marketers are concerned about a product's position in the life cycle. It not only influences the marketing strategy that will be applied at any given moment; it also indicates the need to introduce new products. The product life cycle is a useful tool to a marketer. It reminds him or her of the necessity to watch the product and adjust the elements of the marketing mix as needed in the various stages. It also shows the vulnerability of a product and the need for new product development. Let's examine each stage in the product life cycle.

Introduction

Sales and profits are typically low during a product's introductory stage. The company may spend a great deal of money to inform potential customers about the product and convince them that it

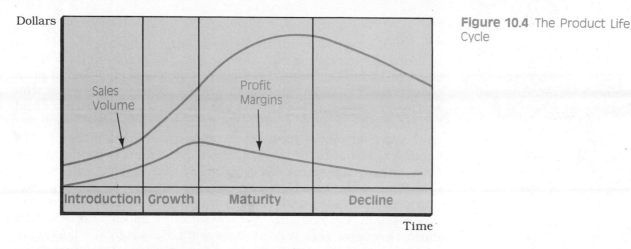

Figure 10.4 The Product Life Cycle

will satisfy their needs and wants. Because people are not familiar with the product and may doubt its usefulness, the introduction stage is a crucial get-acquainted period. In recent years computer-controlled, variable-cylinder engines (like Cadillac's V8-6-4), electric cars, and solar heating systems have entered the introduction stage of the product life cycle.

Seasoned marketing managers usually prefer to spend a relatively small amount of money marketing a new product to small geographic regions rather than offering it nationwide from the start. In a nationwide introduction, poor consumer response would cause enormous losses; so "risk a little, lose a little" usually seems a more prudent course to follow. In this small-scale introduction, called **test marketing,** *a business introduces a product in strategic geographic locations, rather than everywhere, to assess consumer response.*

test marketing

Anheuser-Busch, attracted by the size of the salted-snack market, gingerly tested its Eagle brand snack foods in various geographic locations including Tampa, Florida, and Columbus, Ohio, to determine if it wanted to enter supermarkets and convenience stores dominated by Frito-Lay's salted-snack goods.[7]

The penalty for not test marketing to determine potential consumer acceptance of a product is losses. The electric products division of 3M Corporation once invented a thin, space-saving radio speaker. It seemed ideal for use where space is at a premium, in automobiles and aircraft, for instance. Anticipating a warm market reception, the company began manufacturing the minispeaker before it discovered that existing models seemed to fill customer needs adequately. Theirs was a product that nobody wanted.[8]

Growth

If the new product sells briskly in test areas, confirming management's hopes, it enters the growth stage, during which it may be marketed nationwide with accompanying increases in sales and profits. Wide-screen home televisions and home videotape recording systems have now entered the growth stage.

Maturity

The third stage — maturity — is an important one for original manufacturers. Strong sales and profits up to this point will encourage other firms to market similar products, and cutthroat price reductions may occur. During the 1970s some entrepreneurs who started to make smoke detectors went bankrupt because they could not handle fierce price competition from well-entrenched producers who also had profits from other products to sustain them. This condition accounts for the fact that some brands of products may stay in this stage of the life cycle longer than others.

When a product is in the maturity stage, sales reach a peak and profits decline rapidly, suggesting that it is time to introduce a new product or revitalize the present one's appeal and begin the life cycle anew. This was the case with the original skateboard, which regained popularity after manufacturers invented polyurethane wheels.

When marketers at General Foods realized that customers were not eating much Jell-O gelatin because people did not have time to prepare it or want the existing calories, they quickly developed Jell-O Pudding Pops — frozen and lower in calories than ice cream.[9]

The electronic games market, which reached maturity in less than 5 years, peaked faster than many industry executives expected. One giant toymaker closed a year-old factory in the Caribbean because its production was unnecessary in a market expected to stabilize.[10]

Decline

Some products, like fountain pens, retain consumer popularity for decades before they enter the fourth stage, decline. During this stage demand virtually disappears because the product no longer suits consumer needs, life-styles, habits, or tastes. Men's oily hair cream, washboards, straight razors, and slide rules are in the decline stage now.

Products that satisfy wants instead of urgent needs sometimes appeal to a very fickle market segment, being popular today and forgotten tomorrow. Their life cycle often resembles a pyramid. Many toys and grocery items, for example, have relatively short life cycles; approximately 60 percent of the toys you see for sale today were not available 2 years ago, and over half the items now sold in supermarkets did not exist 10 years ago. Klackers, pet rocks, and mood rings are products that sped through their life cycles very quickly.

"What exactly is 'new, improved lettuce?'"

New Product Development: A Necessity

The product life cycle has a very loud message: all products eventually pass through the stages and have to be removed from the market. It is critical for the success of a company to have new products

Pause and Ponder

Think about television commercials you have seen. Have any of the products been referred to as *new* or *new, improved?* Are they new products or is the company modifying an element of the product? How do new or new, improved products relate to the product life cycle? What stage are the products in?

planned as replacements for existing ones or to find new uses for old products.

An excellent example of a company that constantly monitors the product life cycle and puts new products in the marketplace is the Gillette Company. The firm has made it a practice over decades to innovate in the face of competition and present other product alternatives to the consumer. The change from the Gillette "Blue Blade" and the Wilkinson Stainless Steel Blade to Gillette's Trac-Two and the swivel razor is a magnificent analysis and use of the product life cycle.

Another example of an industry seeking product development and innovation is provided in the fast-foods arena. What once started as selling hamburgers has now grown to barbecued ribs, chicken, biscuits and eggs for breakfast, and taco-burgers. Innovate or disappear might be the message.[11]

Summary

Marketing is a group of interrelated activities designed to identify consumer needs and develop, distribute, promote, and price goods and services to satisfy those needs at a profit. A company's long-range future is tied to the successful application of marketing.

The practice of marketing has evolved from organizations that initially were production oriented, then sales oriented, and finally marketing oriented. An organization that is marketing oriented has adopted a philosophy for the firm known as the marketing concept — a belief that the company should adopt a companywide consumer orientation directed at long-range profitability.

Marketing includes both activities and a process. Marketing activities are grouped in three major headings: exchange (buying, selling), physical distribution (transporting, storing), and facilitating (financing, risk bearing, obtaining market information, and standardizing and grading). The activities are undertaken while completing the marketing process.

The marketing process entails:

— Identifying a potential target market
— Analyzing the needs of the identified target market

The Straight Line

Columbia Pictures
Coca-Cola Goes to the Movies

The executives of Coca-Cola were ambitious for the future of their firm. Not content to rest on the success of Coke's achievements, they decided to expand their operations by acquiring a new business. Roberto C. Goizueta, chief executive, was convinced Coke's profits could not exceed 10 percent a year, and he felt that the challenge of a new business would add zest to the life of Coca-Cola. In June 1982 Coke bought Columbia Pictures for $695 million with definite plans for expansion.

Columbia's chairman, Francis T. Vincent, Jr., and president, Richard C. Gallop, were very much in favor of Coke's expansion plans and of increasing Columbia's profit growth by 20 percent a year. They contributed ideas that increased the studio's production from twelve to eighteen movies a year, and they cut the cost of the films by obtaining money from outside partners. Two of Coke's movies, *Gandhi* and *Tootsie*, received a total of twenty-one Academy Award nominations.

Victor A. Kaufman, then executive vice-president of Columbia, and Vincent believed it would not be profitable to produce more than the eighteen pictures a year as it would defeat their company's growth. With their expertise in handling bookings, they reasoned that theater owners would be more receptive to booking movies from a new studio than more movies from Columbia, because it was their experience that theater owners want good relations with all studios. As a result Tri-Star Pictures was formed in November 1982 with Victor Kaufman at the helm. This new studio is a joint venture of Columbia, CBS, and Home Box Office. Company production risks are shared by the partners, and Tri-Star pays Co-

- Researching the potential of the target market for demand, sales, and potential profit
- Creating a product or service intended to satisfy the needs of the target market
- Distributing, pricing, and promoting the product or service to the target market
- Ensuring satisfaction through after-sales service

The efforts of marketing are directed at a market. A market is a group of potential customers with the authority and ability to purchase a particular product or service that satisfies their collective demand. There are two major markets: consumer and industrial. The consumer market is composed of individuals who buy products for their personal use. The industrial market consists of businesses, government agencies, and other institutions that buy products to use either in operations or in making other products.

The large industrial and consumer markets need to be subdivided into smaller markets. This process of dividing a total market

lumbia a huge fee to handle bookings and office work.

A studio makes a profit of approximately $35 million on a movie that grosses $60 million in theatrical rentals. The fee received for the rights to show the movie on television (whether pay, network, or independent stations) can double that amount. Profits from videodisk and videocassette rentals or purchases may even surpass television rental profits in the future.

Columbia entered the field of cassettes and pay television when it formed a joint venture with Bell & Howell to manufacture videocassettes and entered a joint venture with Home Box Office, CBS, 20th Century Fox, and Goldcrest, a British filmmaker, for a pay television service.

One of Coca-Cola's greatest contributions toward the growth of Columbia has been in marketing. Peter S. Sealey, an experienced marketing man from Coke, is now the marketing executive for Columbia. Under his leadership Columbia participates in Coke's volume discounts on television advertising time and has been given Coke's unwanted air time to promote movies. Questionnaires have been used to evaluate filmed entertainment that could have far-reaching results as the economics of filmed entertainment continues to change.

Another of Coke's contributions to Columbia's growth is chief executive officer Goizueta's leadership style. He is a firm believer in listening to the consumer, surrounding himself with talented, creative people who can produce and manage the desired product, and developing an open, trusting environment where people can do their jobs.

For more about Coca-Cola's acquisition of Columbia Pictures, see Henry Eason, "The CEO Who Refreshed Coca-Cola," *Nation's Business*, March, 1984, pp. 47–49; and Myron Magnet, "Coke Tries Selling Movies Like Soda Pop," *Fortune*, December 26, 1983, pp. 119–126.

---

into subgroups with similar characteristics is called market segmentation. By using demographic, geographic, psychographic, and benefit segmentation, large markets can be divided to identify the characteristics and needs of the market. In turn the market is analyzed for sales potential, demand potential, buying power, and profit potential.

For each segment or grouping of segments, a marketing mix needs to be developed. The marketing mix is the effective meshing of product, promotion, price, and distribution strategy to achieve success.

Product strategy is the key in marketing mix planning. A product consists of the basic physical offering and accompanying set of image and service features that seek to satisfy needs. There are two categories of products: consumer products and industrial products. Consumer products include convenience goods, shopping goods, and specialty goods. Industrial goods include installations, accessory equipment, fabricated parts and materials, raw materials, and industrial supplies.

An element of product strategy includes the decision to use branding. A brand is a name, symbol, design, or a combination of these that identifies the products or services of a company. Companies choose branding to aid in recognition and to project a message. Companies choose to use brand names, brand marks, trade characters, and trademarks. Recent developments have the addition of generic products competing with family, manufacturers', and private brands.

A second element of product strategy is the choice of packaging. The proper use of shape, color, and material is important to the image, multiple use, and ease of handling of products.

Marketers need to be concerned about a product's life cycle. This refers to the succession of phases that includes introduction, growth, maturity, and decline of a product in its market. The cycle affects promotion, pricing, and distribution strategies. In addition, it points up the importance of new product development.

Key Terms

accessory equipment
brand
brand mark
brand name
consumer market
consumer products
convenience goods
exchange functions
fabricated parts and materials
facilitating functions
generic products
industrial market

industrial products
industrial supplies
installations
market
marketing
marketing concept
marketing mix
marketing orientation
marketing research
market segmentation
physical distribution functions
production orientation

product life cycle
raw materials
retailers
sales orientation
shopping goods
specialty goods
test marketing
trade character
trademark
wholesalers

For Review and Discussion

1. What is the marketing concept? What stages might a company go through before it is ready to adopt the marketing concept?

2. What are the three major marketing functions? What activities are included in each?

3. Marketers refer to marketing as "the application of the marketing process." What is included in the marketing process? What is it attempting to accomplish?

4. What is a market? What elements are necessary for a group of people to be called a market?

5. What are the two major markets? How do they differ?

6. How is a market segmented? What do demographic, geographic, psychographic, and benefit segmentation accomplish?

7. Once a market segment has been identified, what four areas are analyzed for potential?

8. What is the purpose of the marketing mix? What are its four elements?

9. What is a product? Take one product that you are familiar with and describe its physical, image, and service features.

10. What is the purpose of adopting branding as a product strategy?

11. Distinguish among brand names, brand marks, trademarks, trade characters; among family brands, manufacturers' brands, and private brands; between brands and generic products.

12. Explain the importance of the product life cycle to a marketer. What are its four stages?

13. Why is it important for a marketer always to be developing new products?

Gallery 2
Advertising: The Communication Link Between Marketers and Consumers

Advertisers sell more than products. This dramatic public service ad is a reminder to everyone about ensuring safety on the road. The simple, direct headline and the picture need no further explanation. The black background reinforces the potential risks of driving while under the influence of alcohol.

This 3M ad has a multiple message for the prospective consumer. Not only is the 3M diskette reliable (it "never forgets"), but it is compatible with a recognizable product: the Apple computer. The compatibility is reinforced with the color red — red for "apple" and thus "Apple" computers.

The clever play on words in the headline (Earth's First Soft Drink) and the unique visual image emphasize Perrier's all-natural ingredients. The ad makes an appeal to consumers who seek all that is natural and not artificial. There is an implication that consumers can rely on this product because it's been around since the beginning — much longer even than its bottlers!

Chanel is a famous name in women's perfume — so famous that nothing more needs to be said! The product (and thus its name) is even upside down. The lack of ad copy and the position of the perfume bottle show how confident the marketers were about their product speaking for itself. Note that this particular cologne is "for men."

While the Perrier ad appeals to a specific audience, the Lee jeans ad is attempting just the opposite. Blue jeans are usually popular with teenagers and young adults, but this ad is trying to reach a wider audience — consumers who are confident and who have acquired a taste for simplicity, no matter what their age. Lee jeans is "the brand that fits" . . . everyone?

THE TRIVIAL PURSUIT. SURVIVAL KIT.

While the Trivial Pursuit® game shortage lasts, please accept our apologies (and a few samples to tide you over).

G — What U.S. city has been called Little Havana?

E — What movie theater has sold the most tickets?

H — What British peerage gave its name to an overcoat, a sofa and a cigarette?

AL — What actor's autobiography is titled *All My Yesterdays*?

SN — What is xenophobia?

SL — Who retired with 755 home runs to his credit?

G — What country is home to Heineken beer?

E — How many seconds usually elapsed before the tape self-destructed on *Mission: Impossible*?

H — What date in 44 B.C. was Julius Caesar assassinated?

AL — What heroic group did D'Artagnan lead?

SN — What's the term for opposition to an electrical current in a conductor?

SL — What's the main vegetable in vichyssoise?

G — What are the only two landlocked countries in South America?

E — Who was the first host of the original *Tonight* show?

H — What British prime minister's mother was born in Brooklyn, New York?

AL — What philosopher-author lived on the shores of Walden Pond?

SN — What's the hardest bone in the human body?

SL — Who's the youngest golfer to have won the Masters?

G — What country is the resort city of St. Moritz in?

E — What film featured the line: "Open the pod bay door, Hal"?

H — What song is traditionally heard when the president of the U.S. arrives on the scene?

AL — Who wrote *The Secret Life of Walter Mitty*?

SN — What substance must mix with food to give it taste?

SL — What team did Abraham M. Saperstein establish and send on the road in 1927?

G — What city is served by Dulles International Airport?

E — Who won the 1961 best actor Oscar for his role in *Judgment at Nuremberg*?

H — What army was founded by William Booth and his wife Catherine?

AL — Whose biography is titled *Hitch*?

SN — What's the largest satellite orbiting Earth?

SL — What drink was invented by oilmen, who used their tools to stir it?

G — What's the world's smallest independent state?

E — Where did Betty meet the leader of the pack?

H — What was described as: "Two all-beef patties, special sauce, lettuce, cheese, pickles, onions and a sesame seed bun"?

AL — Who wrote the poem *The Road Not Taken*?

SN — What food got its name from the way it hung in bunches like grapes?

SL — What playing card was once known as *the devil's bedposts*?

Turn page for answers.

Supplies are short, but the makers of Trivial Pursuit are so confident that they "play" on this disadvantage. They are sure that consumers will accept no substitutes. The clever layout forces the reader to participate in the ad (play along, if you will) by turning the page for the answers.

THE TRIVIAL PURSUIT
SURVIVAL KIT
(CONT.)

If you like these, remember: there are 5,964 more questions in the Trivial Pursuit® game worth waiting for.

Genus
- **G** The Netherlands
- **E** Five
- **H** March 15, or the Ides of March
- **AL** The Three Musketeers
- **SN** Resistance
- **SL** Potato

Genus
- **G** Miami
- **E** Radio City Music Hall
- **H** Chesterfield
- **AL** Edward G. Robinson's
- **SN** Fear of strangers or foreigners
- **SL** Hank Aaron

Genus
- **G** Switzerland
- **E** *2001: A Space Odyssey*
- **H** *Hail to the Chief*
- **AL** James Thurber
- **SN** Saliva
- **SL** The Harlem Globetrotters

Genus
- **G** Bolivia and Paraguay
- **E** Steve Allen
- **H** Winston Churchill's
- **AL** Henry David Thoreau
- **SN** The jawbone
- **SL** Severiano Ballesteros

Genus
- **G** Vatican City
- **E** At the candy store
- **H** A Big Mac
- **AL** Robert Frost
- **SN** Grapefruit
- **SL** The four of clubs

Genus
- **G** Washington, D.C.
- **E** Maximilian Schell
- **H** The Salvation Army
- **AL** Alfred Hitchcock's
- **SN** The moon
- **SL** The screwdriver

Applications

Case 10.1 A Hard Lesson

Andy Hyam was in the process of achieving his goal in life. At the age of 32 Andy was about to embark on his new career as president and sole employee of Andy's Sub Shop. After scrimping and saving for 5 years he was finally taking the plunge.

Andy had grown up in New York City. When he moved to Houston, Texas, he missed the wonderful tastes and smells of the neighborhood delicatessens and submarine sandwich shops. "These people just don't know what they are missing. I'll bring the Big Apple right here to Houston."

Carrying out his plan to perfection Andy located a "perfect" little store in a quiet neighborhood. It was the only store there with the exception of a doctor's office. Andy's decision was based on the belief that "they'll flock to this place once they learn about it. It's quiet, the neighborhood is full of older people, very little traffic to contend with . . . it's perfect."

Andy next put this ad in the local newspaper:

Andy's Sub Shop
New York Style Submarine Sandwiches
Grand Opening — June 10

Andy had checked on the circulation of the paper and was convinced it was well read by the community. Andy also had some advertising flyers printed with the same message. He spent the day before the grand opening in the parking lots of two big companies, located 5 miles away, putting the flyers on car windshields.

The day of the grand opening came and went. A few customers came but not the volume Andy had expected. He received questions about home delivery, but replied that it was impossible because he was the sole employee. This same cycle continued for 3 months. Andy was getting desperate: "Where did I go wrong? I thought everyone liked submarine sandwiches."

Questions

1. What specific marketing errors did Andy commit? Cite specific examples.

2. If you had been Andy, what would you have done differently? Why?

3. What does this case indicate about the importance of target marketing and the development of a marketing mix?

Case 10.2 What's in a Name?

When a company is attempting to identify a new brand name for its product it has several potential sources and general guidelines to aid it.

General guidelines to be considered include a name that is:

1. Easy to remember
2. Easy to pronounce
3. Easy to recognize
4. Associated with a favorable mental image
5. Easy to be seen totally in one instant
6. Related to positive emotional or physical experiences

Potential sources to be investigated are:

1. Initials
2. A created name
3. Use of numbers or numbers and words
4. A person's name
5. An animal or mythological character
6. A geographic location

Questions

1. Review the potential source list for brand names. For each listed source identify three brand names you are familiar with for each category.

2. Using the names you have identified, answer the following questions.

   a. Have the creators of these brand names applied each guideline? How?

   b. Are there any brand names you consider inappropriate for the products they represent? Why?

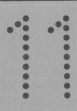

Marketing Promotional Strategy

Chapter Outline

Chapter Objectives

After studying this chapter, you should be able to:

1. Identify the principal buying motives of final consumers and those of industrial purchasers.
2. Describe the role and importance of promotional strategy.
3. Identify the four elements of promotion and explain how they are combined to form an effective mix.
4. Identify the eight elements of the communication process.
5. Define personal selling and present the seven steps in the selling process.
6. Define advertising and identify the two types of advertising.
7. List at least four advertising media and describe the advantages and disadvantages of each.
8. Define publicity and discuss its importance.
9. Define sales promotion and describe some of the sales promotion devices that can be used to appeal to middlemen and final consumers.

Nothing except the mint can make money without advertising.
— Thomas B. Macaulay, English statesman

Up Front   Daniel Fylstra

A Highly Visible Company

Daniel Fylstra is an example of today's "knowledge worker." Heavy on intelligence and experience, Fylstra had the daring to attempt things others might avoid. He currently is chairman of the board of VisiCorp, a firm that has grown from virtually nothing in January 1978 to more than 300 employees today. VisiCorp, a leader in the computer software industry, has enjoyed an average growth rate of 220 percent per year since its founding.

Fylstra's attempts to do the unconventional began as a teenager, when he tried to build a wooden submarine in his backyard. That project never made it to completion because he found another kind of engineering that offered more — electronics and computers. Pursuing that interest, Fylstra eventually obtained an electrical engineering degree from M.I.T. His abilities landed him a job at Intermetrics, where he designed computer software for NASA's space shuttle. But with little patience for the conventional way of doing things, Fylstra decided to strike out on his own. He first obtained a solid business background at the Harvard Business School, where he received an M.B.A. in 1978.

One of his projects at Harvard was to begin a small company called Personal Software, which he started with only $500, hardly a petty cash fund for many corporations. His mission was to produce and market applications programs for small computers. Within a year the company's spectacular sales curve reached $1 million, with its big seller being a computer chess game. Fylstra decided to move to California to be near the high-tech action of

"You can't sell what people don't know about" is a statement that focuses on the importance of marketing promotional strategy, the second element of the marketing mix. Regardless of how outstanding, useful, superior, or needs satisfying a product might be, marketers must inform potential customers of its existence and its merits before those customers are likely to purchase it. Through a well-developed marketing promotional strategy, consumers can learn about and gain access to the goods and services they need and want.

In this chapter we will explore the buying motives of potential consumers, the role and objectives of promotional strategy, and the role of the four elements of promotional strategy: personal selling, advertising, publicity, and sales promotion.

Silicon Valley. But before he left Massachusetts, he made an investment in Personal Software's future. Fylstra's company provided financial backing for another bright and restless Harvard student, Dan Bricklin, who had developed a program that became the highly successful VisiCalc. Within a few years, VisiCalc helped Personal Software take off. Fylstra changed his company's name to VisiCorp to capitalize on the success of VisiCalc.

The company now markets a VisiSeries of stand-alone applications programs for a variety of management and office automation tasks. With the development of the new VisiOn system, a major breakthrough in ease of use and speed has resulted in a new generation of productivity. The VisiOn system of dividing the computer screen into multiple screens allows the user (using the well known "mouse") to work on several tasks simultaneously. This system has turned the computer screen into the new generation's "desktop."

In February 1984 VisiCorp announced an agreement with Random House, which granted the publishing company exclusive distribution rights in the United States and Canada for VisiPress books. VisiPress, the publishing branch of VisiCorp, publishes how-to and problem-solving books on personal computers and software (one of the fastest growing market segments in the book trade). In addition to VisiPress, VisiCorp has extended its customer education and training services to include VisiTutor, a series of computerized training courses and VisiTraining professional seminars.

For more about Daniel Fylstra and VisiCorp, see "The Windows Battle," *Fortune*, March 19, 1984, p. 195; "Sagas of Five Who Made It — Sizzling Software," *Time*, February 15, 1982, pp. 42, 44; and "To Each His Own Computer," *Newsweek*, February 22, 1982, p. 55.

Identifying Buying Motives

Those who are involved in marketing promotional strategy must understand why consumers buy the things they do. Have you, for example, ever thought about why you bought a particular product or service? What motivated you to pick one brand or model over the other? Did you make a rational buying decision, or did emotions influence your purchase? If you are like most consumers, your buying motives vary substantially depending on the particular product you buy and the mood you are in at the time you buy it.

Marketers want to know what makes their customers buy a given product, because buying motives form the basis of effective promotional strategies. Industrial buyers and final consumers have different buying motives.

Consumer Buying Motives

consumer buying motives

Consumer buying motives are *factors that cause someone to purchase a product for personal use.* They reflect the person's needs and wants, attitudes, and self-image. They also reflect a person's experiences and the influences of social groups, culture, and family. People buy things for emotional, rational, or patronage reasons — sometimes for a blend of all three.

emotional motives

Emotional Motives. Consumers are often unaware of the emotional motives that influence their buying decisions, but they are important motives for marketers to appeal to nonetheless. **Emotional motives** are *buying reasons that arise from impulse and psychological needs rather than careful thought and analysis.* Table 11.1 summarizes the most common emotional buying motives for various products and services. They do overlap, and several of them may act simultaneously on a prospective buyer.

Many products become successful by appealing to one or more emotional buying motives. Many people purchase designer jeans out of a desire to express themselves and seek social approval by being fashionable. Guitar manufacturers anticipate heavy sales when rock stars appear in concert playing their brand. Amateur guitarists, combining emulation and self-expression motives, generate considerable demand.

Marketers work very hard to appeal to a buyer's self-image — a composite of the emotional motives listed in Table 11.1. Virginia Slims cigarettes, Adidas running shoes, and Stanley do-it-yourself kits are promoted through considerable and often subtle appeals to self-image. In short, we sometimes buy products because they

Table 11.1 Emotional Buying Motives and Products or Services That Appeal to Them

Emotional Buying Motive	Products or Services
Fear and safety	Smoke and burglar alarms Fire extinguishers Insurance
Love and social approval	Grooming aids Flowers Singing telegrams
Fun and excitement	Vacation tours Rock concerts Sporting goods Sports cars
Pride and prestige	Luxury cars Jewelry Maid service
Self-expression	Custom-painted murals on vans or trucks Personalized T-shirts Do-it-yourself books

are promoted to the kind of person we believe or wish ourselves to be. Although this behavior is not logical, it is extremely important for marketers to take into account.

Rational Motives. Although the distinction between emotional and rational buying motives is not always clear, rational motives are easier for buyers to justify: they make good sense. **Rational motives** are *buying reasons that arise from careful planning and analysis of information.* Home owners who install automatic lawn sprinkler systems want the assurance that their lawns will be watered regularly whether they are at home or away. Companies that pressure clean houses appeal to the customer's rational motives by stating that regular cleaning prolongs the life of a shingled roof and takes away the need to repaint by renewing the appearance of the exterior paint. Few consumers purchase goods for purely rational reasons. Examples of rational buying motives are summarized in Table 11.2.

rational motives

Patronage Motives. Another classification of motives, **patronage motives,** are *buying reasons based on the characteristics of a specific retail outlet or brand of product.* Some of us are loyal to a particular brand or a specific store because of past satisfactions. Patronage motives make a given brand a specialty good to some buyers. Table 11.3 lists several reasons that have been given for regularly patronizing a firm. Do some of these factors cause you to buy repeatedly from the same retailer?

patronage motives

Industrial Buying Motives

Industrial buying motives are *factors that cause an industrial buyer to recognize a logical need or want and to make a purchase that satisfies it.* They reflect the particular needs of the business and industry of the buyer. They are also a product of the development of a specific set of criteria for purchasing the product. Even though the industrial buyer makes the decision, the criteria already have been established by the purchasing system. Business purchasers

industrial buying motives

Rational Buying Motive	Products or Services
Economy and cost	Home freezers
	Auto repainting
	Freight-damaged items
Quality and dependability	Top quality watches
	Lifetime automobile batteries
	Service agreements on home appliances
Convenience	Fast-food restaurants
	Dry cleaning
	Dishwashers
	Remote control television sets

Table 11.2 Rational Buying Motives and Products or Services That Appeal to Them

Table 11.3 Patronage Motives That Cause Customers to Shop Regularly at a Particular Store

Patronage Motives

Convenient location

Pleasant salespeople

Positive public image or reputation

Cleanliness

Customer services (delivery, gift wrapping, advice on product installation and use)

Prices (high for status appeal, competitive or low to appeal to economy motives)

Variety of merchandise

An atmosphere of good will

usually buy for rational reasons and the most prevalent ones are shown in Figure 11.1.

Profit. Businesses cannot function for long without profit. Profit is therefore the governing motive for buying industrial goods. As a result most marketing promotion efforts for industrial goods ultimately appeal to this motive.

Price. Although price is important to budget-conscious industrial buyers, they may look beyond dollars to consider how the item can improve the finished product or help operations run more smoothly or efficiently. A firm may pay more to put steel-belted radial tires on its company cars, for example, because their longer wear and better gas mileage offset the higher cost. Although Sealed Air Corporation's protective air-bubble packaging wrap costs more than excelsior or Styrofoam, firms that use it as a padding in shipping cartons may save more than its cost in lower postage expenses.

Quality. Quality is a significant industrial buying motive, but it must be reconciled with price. Firms do not want to buy more quality than they need. If you bought toilet tissue for employee rest rooms and for guest rooms at a chain of luxury hotels, for example, would you buy the same quality for both? Probably not. An industrial buyer's quality standards must consider the final consumer's ex-

Pause and Ponder

Think of a major purchase you made recently — clothes, car, or appliances. What was your motive for the purchase? Was it purely rational, emotional, or a combination? What reason did you give yourself?

Figure 11.1 Industrial Buying Motives

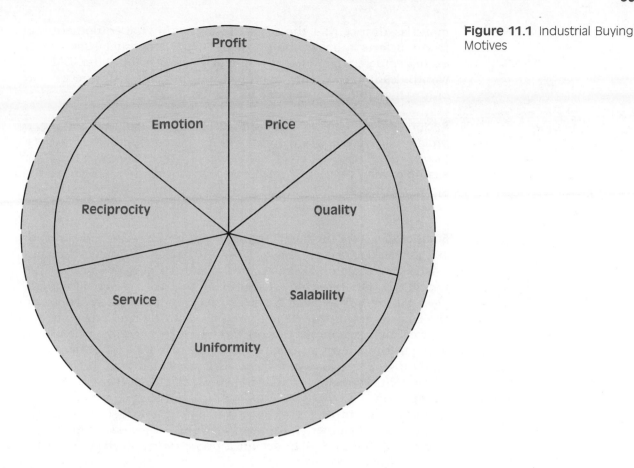

pectations, the company's image and reputation, and the budget for the product being produced.

Salability. Components and ingredients that make an end product more impressive to customers should be emphasized in marketing promotion. The paint used on a new Chevrolet Corvette, the silicone in Gillette Dry Idea deodorant, and the leather used in Nunn-Bush shoes all make those products more salable. If an industrial product will make the finished consumer product look more attractive, perform better, or take on a unique characteristic or function, that can influence an industrial customer's buying decision.

Uniformity. An industrial product that makes finished items appear identical will appeal to many company buyers. An automatic bottling machine that is guaranteed to fill each container to within 1/64 of an inch of the same level, or an automatic spray painting booth that applies paint of uniform thickness and finish to each unit, appeals to this uniformity motive.

Service. Industrial buyers are concerned about service, because the failure of one key machine can stop an entire production line or damage dozens of units. For this reason, industrial customers demand assurance that the seller will maintain vital equipment and repair defects quickly and correctly. This is a crucial factor, for example, in selling photocopying machines or computers. IBM, the world's leading computer manufacturer, attributes its success not only to high quality but also to its reputation for exceptional service.

reciprocal buying

Reciprocity. In some instances firms observe **reciprocal buying,** *a practice wherein two or more companies become mutual customers, buying each other's goods and services.* An auto repair shop, for example, may buy all of its parts from one auto parts store; the store, in turn, has its delivery fleet tuned up and repaired at the repair shop. Mutual sales mean mutual profits.

Emotion. Despite the fact that industrial buyers purchase for their companies (instead of themselves) and spend their firms' money (instead of their own), marketers of industrial goods should not ignore emotion as an industrial buying motive. A purchasing manager, for example, may like a salesperson enough to buy strictly on the basis of friendship. The owner of a copying-machine company enjoyed such exceptional rapport with one salesperson that he turned all competitors away automatically. Or there may be other emotional motives — sometimes arbitrary ones. One materials buyer for a men's hat company would not buy anything from a hatless salesperson.

Once the buying motives of the potential target markets, industrial or consumer, have been identified, the next step for the marketing manager is to design a promotional strategy to appeal to these buying motives.

Promotional Strategy: Role and Objectives

Promotional strategy is the second element of the marketing mix. It involves *the correct blending of personal selling, advertising, publicity, and sales promotion* to create the **promotional mix.**

promotional mix

Promotional strategy is the communication ingredient in the marketing mix for reaching specific target markets. Its role is to inform, persuade, and remind people about the firm's products, services, and image. By utilizing the special strengths of each element of the promotion mix, a marketing manager can focus the communication messages from four different angles to influence a prospective buyer's decision. Table 11.4 illustrates the role of promotional strategy in the marketing mix.

The Communication Process

To develop the proper blending of the promotional mix for effective communication, a starting point for the marketing manager is an understanding of the **communication process** — *the channel pro-*

communication process

— Develop a company or product image
— Explain the features and benefits of products and services
— Communicate to channel members in order to develop loyalty and enthusiasm
— Provide information to answer consumer questions
— Distinguish a company and its products from competitors
— Call for action to close the sale
— Notify consumers of sales, specials, price increases, and product developments
— Announce new product releases to the marketplace

Table 11.4 The Role of Promotional Strategy

motional messages travel to reach the purchaser. Figure 11.2 provides an illustration of the communication process. Let's examine each element.

— The **sender** is *the company, or person representing the company, who presents a message to the target market.* The sender may be a company employee, celebrity, paid actor, or customer.

sender

— **Encoding** is *the process of translating an idea into a message.* During this time a decision is made on what the message will be: price, quality, pride, love.

encoding

Figure 11.2 The Communication Process

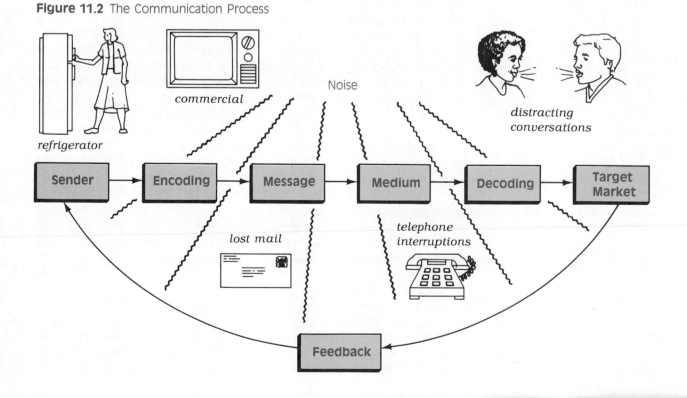

message
— The **message** is developing *the actual combination of words and symbols to be directed at the target market.*

medium
— The **medium** is *either the personal or nonpersonal means of sending the message.* One personal medium is a salesperson. Nonpersonal media include television, radio, billboards, and coupons.

decoding
— **Decoding** is *the process of interpreting the message by the target market.* The sender's message is influenced by a person's experience, culture, and family.

target market
— The **target market** is *the focus point for the sender's message.* It is either the industrial or the individual consumer.

feedback
— **Feedback** is *the target market's actions as a result of the message.* It may be a decision to purchase or not purchase or simply a new way of looking at the product or service.

noise
— **Noise** is *any possible interference with the communication process.* It can occur at any time in the process. Examples include conversations during broadcasts, lost mail, and telephone calls during sales presentations.

The Promotional Mix: Personal Selling

personal selling
The first element of the promotional mix that can be used to communicate to a target market is personal selling. **Personal selling** is *a face-to-face attempt to persuade prospective customers to buy a given product.* This technique is essential when marketing many kinds of shopping goods, and it plays an especially significant role in the marketing of industrial goods. Personal selling provides the company with the opportunity (1) to give customers individual attention, (2) to adapt a message to the customer, (3) to focus on a specific target market, (4) to receive immediate feedback, and (5) to provide the opportunity to close the sale.

selling process
Although they have varied responsibilities and earnings, salespeople share one thing in common: the **selling process.** This is *a series of seven steps that salespeople follow when persuading prospective customers to make purchases.* Figure 11.3 shows the sequence of these steps.

prospecting
Prospecting is *the step in the selling process that identifies potential customers for a product.* Although it rarely is done by retail salespeople (customers usually come to them), prospecting is essential when selling most industrial products or when selling to middlemen. Companies like Xerox and Canon, for example, seldom wait for potential photocopying-machine customers to make the first move. Instead their sales representatives seek out likely buyers.

Salespeople may get prospects from several sources: referrals by existing customers, replies to direct mail and other promotional messages, impromptu cold-canvassing calls, or the salesperson's own ingenuity. When prospecting, salespeople also must confirm that a potential buyer is qualified (i.e., can afford the product, has

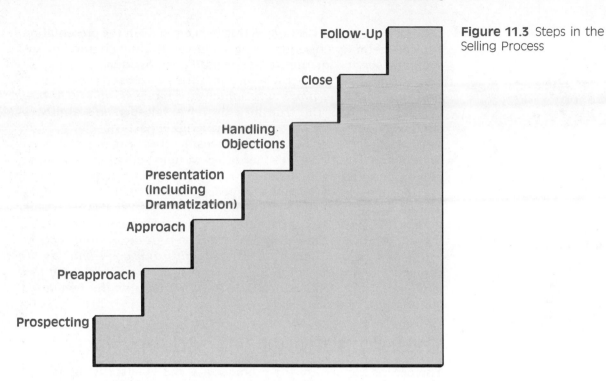

Figure 11.3 Steps in the Selling Process

the authority to buy it, and genuinely wants or needs it). This increases the likelihood that a sale will be made.

Preapproach is *the second step in the selling process where the salesperson researches the qualified prospect's background.* By reviewing census data, contacts in the industry, and company records, the salesperson attempts to put together a personal profile about the prospect. The more useful information that is gathered, the more focused will be the presentation.

preapproach

The **approach** is *the third step in the selling process; the salesperson makes actual contact with the prospect and prepares to deliver a sales presentation.* A creative, planned approach, using information gathered in the preapproach, helps the salesperson achieve rapport with and gain a more positive reception from the prospect. Each approach is tailored to the individual and the circumstances; no two are identical.

approach

Next comes the **presentation,** *the fourth step in the selling process in which the salesperson shows how the prospect can benefit by owning the product.* The salesperson must explain how the product will satisfy the prospect's wants or needs.

presentation

Some creative dramatization, including a demonstration and audiovisual appeals (charts, filmstrips, or comparative tables), can turn a mediocre presentation into a lively, exciting experience for both parties.

Objections, a basic part of the selling process, are *verbal or silent forms of resistance on the part of the potential customer to the salesperson's message.* They must be overcome before the prospect will buy. Effective salespeople anticipate most objections and

objections

address them, stating counteracting benefits early in the presentation. Typical customer objections concern price, product characteristics, company service, or the salesperson as an individual.

close

A sale does not actually occur until the **close,** which is *the step in the selling process at which the prospect agrees to buy.* Closing, which is the true measure of a salesperson's ability, is often considered one of the most challenging parts of selling. Some salespeople have difficulty closing because they fear rejection, misunderstand the prospect's needs or wants, appeal to the wrong buying motives, or mishandle one of the previous steps.

follow-up

For most professional salespeople, repeat business is the key to long-term profits, and repeat business comes from satisfied customers who feel strong patronage motives. Consequently, we see the importance of **follow-up,** *the final step in the selling process. It builds and maintains customer loyalty and good will, as the salesperson confirms that the buyer has received everything that was originally promised and clearly understands the benefits of owning the product.*

The Promotional Mix: Advertising

advertising

The second element of the promotional mix is advertising. **Advertising** is *any nonpersonal message paid for by an identifiable sponsor for the purpose of promoting products, services, or ideas.* It is an important part of any company's promotional mix. That many companies see advertising as valuable is clear from the money spent on it. Procter & Gamble, the United States number one advertiser, spent $671.8 million in a recent year to tell consumers about its products.

Why Advertise?

Effective advertising, placed where it reaches members of the right market segment, is intended to increase the likelihood that consumers will buy the product or service. Specifically advertising is used to

Personal selling provides the opportunity to answer the consumer's questions and close the sale.

inform, persuade, and remind the target market about the products or services. Advertisements can build customer awareness of products and provide information on use, quality, and performance. In addition, advertisements help create demand for products by answering prospects' questions and objections to buying. It also can remind customers about a company and its products between salespersons' visits.

Types of Advertising

Companies use two types of advertising: product and institutional. Each has its own unique characteristics and objectives.

Product advertising is *advertising intended to promote demand for a product or service* such as ads for Kodak film or Crest toothpaste. Product advertising can be directed at informing, persuading, or reminding the target market. If marketing research determines, for example, that the market segment is not aware of the new services a bank is providing, advertisements will be created to provide the information (to inform). Figure 11.4 illustrates product advertising. What is its message?

product advertising

Institutional advertising is *advertising done to enhance a company's public image rather than to sell a product.* It has long-term objectives of good will and image creation. Stressing such themes as equal employment opportunity for women, environmental protection, energy conservation, and innovation, institutional advertising highlights a company's efforts toward becoming a responsible, concerned citizen. Figure 11.5 is an example of an institutional ad.

institutional advertising

Another example is provided by Johnson and Johnson, which mounted an institutional advertising campaign to rebuild its image after seven Chicago-area consumers died from swallowing Extra Strength Tylenol capsules laced with cyanide. The advertising involved 60-second commercials directed at the public and a massive literature program distributed to doctors, dentists, nurses, and pharmacists. Both strategies were intended to "tap the reservoir of good will and trust among the public."[1]

Once the type of advertising is decided on, the best method or medium to convey the message needs to be selected.

Where to Place an Ad: Advertising Media

Advertising media are *the personal or nonpersonal means of sending a message to a target market.* Table 11.5 on page 314 compares the potential applications of advertising media. Marketers must consider such factors as cost, lead time, target audience behavior, and the company's overall promotional budget when deciding what media to use.

advertising media

Lead time, a consideration in choosing advertising media, is minimal with newspapers and radio. They are excellent for getting an advertisement aired quickly. National magazines require considerable lead time, however; advertisers may have to submit copy and pictures several months in advance. The same holds true for

Figure 11.4 Product
Advertising
Source: Courtesy Inglenook Vineyards.

INGLENOOK VINEYARDS, NAPA VALLEY, CALIFORNIA

DO YOU EAT THE RIGHT FOOD WITH THE WRONG WINE?

Everybody in the wine business seems to be avoiding giving specific advice about which wine to drink with which food.

Mainly because they want you to feel free to buy any of their wines and enjoy them with whatever you eat.

This is one way to look at it.

Looking at it this way sells more wine and there are no rules to follow.

But the trouble with leaving it all to chance is you may never experience some pretty fabulous taste combinations.

Some wines go better with some foods than others, and we at Inglenook Vineyards think you should know which is which.

We spend a lot of time and money in the making of our wines. And we want you to be able to enjoy them under the best possible conditions.

FISH?

Everybody knows white wine goes with fish, but not everybody knows why. White wine is acidic, and its acidity helps break down the oil in fish, which most people find disagreeable. Lemon is served with fish for the same reason.

Just remember that shell fish go best with the drier white wines, fish without shells taste best with a dry or semi-dry white wine.

The chart below explains which wine is which.

WHITE WINES		
Dry	Semi-Dry	Semi-Sweet
Chablis	Johannisberg Riesling	Chenin Blanc
Grey Riesling	Semillon	Sauterne
Pinot Chardonnay	Sylvaner	
White Pinot	Traminer	
	Rhine	

FOWL?

With white meated fowl, such as chicken, turkey, and cornish hen, any white wine goes well. But with red meated fowl, such as goose, pheasant, duck and quail, any red or white wine can be drunk.

CHINESE FOOD?

If you want wine with your Flaming Filet of Yak instead of tea, order any dry or semi-dry white wine. Semi-sweet whites seem to clash with the spiciness of many Chinese dishes, particularly Mandarin, and red wines are inappropriate for the same reason.

CANDIED BAKED HAM?

This is one American dish neither red nor white wines seem to go with. The dry red wines compete with the natural dryness of the meat. And the dry white wines are overpowered by it. A Rosé solves the problem and is the perfect compromise.

STEAKS, ROASTS, CHOPS, PASTA?

Red wine is the right wine for meat, but not just any red wine. It should be a dry red. The sweeter reds, combined with the richness of meat tend to fill you up and make you wish you hadn't eaten at all. Here's our chart for red wines:

RED WINES		
Dry	Semi-Dry	Sweet
Cabernet Sauvignon	Burgundy	Ruby Port
Charbono	Gamay Beaujolais	Tawny Port
Pinot Noir	Zinfandel	
Red Pinot		

CHEESE AND NUTS?

You can drink just about any red wine as you eat just about any cheese, and each does a little magic for the other. With nuts, there is really only one wine: Port. And with Port, there is really only one kind of nut: the walnut. Try them together, for one of the nicest experiences of your life.

A WORD TO THE WISE.

Now that you know the right wine to drink with your food, it's still possible to drink the wrong wine. Because if the wine you drink isn't up to the food on your table, it won't make much difference if it's red when it's supposed to be white, or vice versa.

A better argument for buying Inglenook could not be devised. Estate Bottled Inglenook is the filet mignon of wine, and unfortunately, it's just as expensive.

But for the extra money you pay, you get a wine that has been properly vintaged, aged, and bottled on our estate.

Estate bottling gives us the control necessary in order to produce a wine fine enough to be served at state dinners in Washington, and at various events in high places where money is no object.

Try Inglenook with your next feast. It's a luxury, but then, isn't every fine meal?

Inglenook

NAPA VALLEY
PINOT NOIR

INGLENOOK
We make the most expensive wine in America.

This ad is one of a series. If you'd like copies of the other ads, send your name and address to The Cellarmaster, Box F, Inglenook Vineyards, Rutherford, CA 94573.

prime outdoor billboard locations, which are sold by contract for certain periods of time. Television also requires much preparation time before an ad is aired.

Target audience behavior, another concern, causes firms to choose specific media that members of the market segment usually encounter. Firms that sell golf equipment, for example, may advertise during televised golf tournaments and buy space in such magazines as *Golf Digest.* Firms that sell to youthful market segments may advertise in such magazines as *National Lampoon*, in college newspapers, and on rock radio stations. Industrial goods marketers,

Why, why "Y"?

The problem in the Bronx neighborhood was bad and rapidly getting worse. The generation gap between youths and the elderly, always wide, had become a gulf. Stereotypes hardened into distrust, then into open hostility that was poisoning the neighborhood.

Happily, something unusual happened on the way to real trouble. The Bronx YMCA of Greater New York came forward with a unique proposal: Instead of allowing the two groups to drift still further apart, why not use the schools to bring them together? "Let the neighborhood's senior citizens go into the classrooms and tutor youngsters in reading, writing and arithmetic."

The experiment worked wonders, right from the start. For seniors, "teaching" kids provided an escape from boredom and an opportunity to grow. For kids, the program meant one-on-one instruction not usually available in big-city school systems.

To children from broken homes, the senior volunteers often became proxy parents or grandparents. In their new "teachers" they found experience and authority tempered with gentleness and, above all, caring. The youngsters responded in kind. As one child wrote to his "teacher," a 77-year-old Italian-American who had himself been unable to read when he came to this country 63 years ago: "Thank you because you helped me to read. I feel you in my heart for the rest of my life."

Fortunately, the work of the YMCA is felt all over America. While the local "Y" is as familiar as basketball—which it supports along with soccer, swimming, tennis and summer camps—it is far more than the Young Men's Christian Association.

In fact, its name has become a misnomer. Today the YMCA serves people of all ages: more and more of them with special needs and problems; 44 percent of them females. "Christian"? Yes, in that the "Y" is founded on Christian principles of love, hope and caring. But its doors are open to all.

Keeping them open is a big, expensive job, especially with YMCAs managing hundreds of essential programs in thousands of communities. Like job-finding programs for unemployed Chicagoans; employee fitness programs in California; a shelter for runaway teenagers in Louisville; home-finding for Indochinese refugees in Seattle; and minibike programs across the nation to help troubled kids get on the right track by building their self-esteem and teaching them mechanics.

The first "Y" opened in rented Boston quarters in 1852. While that was an otherwise unremarkable year—the last in Millard Fillmore's presidency—you have the opportunity to make 1984 one of the YMCA's best ever. Help support an organization that reaches out warmly and effectively to more than 12 million Americans through 2,170 units in all 50 states.

For more information on how you can reach out and help someone, contact your local YMCA.

Mobil

Figure 11.5 Institutional Advertising
Source: © 1984 Mobil Corporation. Reprinted with permission of Mobil Corporation.

logically enough, use professional and trade journals to reach their intended audience, rather than general-interest magazines or television and radio.

Often decisions about which medium or media to use boil down to the amount of money a firm can spend on advertising and the number of contacts made per dollar spent. Some media cost considerably more than others, but a relatively expensive medium may be justified by the specific market segment it reaches. *Sports Illustrated* charges $49,465 to print a full-page four-color ad in one issue of its magazine. But that large expense may be worthwhile: with a circulation of almost 2.3 million people, the magazine will help the ad reach 46 subscribers per dollar spent.[2]

Table 11.5 Advertising Media

Source: Reprinted with permission of Macmillan Publishing Company from *Essentials of Marketing* by Joel R. Evans and Barry Berman. Copyright © 1984 by Macmillan Publishing Company.

Medium	Market Coverage	Best Uses	Advantages	Disadvantages
Daily newspaper	Entire metropolitan area, local editions sometimes used	Large retailers	Short lead time, concentrated market, flexible, pass alongs, surrounded by content	General audience, heavy ad competition, limited color, limited creativity
Television	Regional or national	Regional manufacturers and large retailers, national manufacturers and largest retailers	Reach, low cost per viewer, persuasive impact, creative options, flexible, surrounded by programs	High minimum total costs, general audience, lead time, short message, limited availability
Direct mail	Advertiser selects market	New products, book clubs, financial services, catalog sales	Precise audience, flexible, personal approach, no clutter from other messages	High throwaway rate, receipt by wrong person, low credibility
Magazines	National (most with regional editions) or local	National manufacturers, mail order firms, local service retailers	Color, creative options, affluent audience, permanence of message, pass alongs, flexible, surrounded by content	Long lead time, poor frequency, ad clutter, geographically dispersed audience
Radio	Entire metropolitan area	Local or regional retailers	Low costs, selective market, high frequency, immediacy of messages, surrounded by content	No visual impact, commercial clutter, station switching, consumer distractions
Outdoor	Entire metropolitan area or one location	Brand-name products, nearby retailers, reminder ads	Large size, color, creative options, frequency, no clutter of competing messages, permanence of message	Legal restrictions, consumer distractions, general audience, inflexible
Transit	Urban community with a transit system	Firms located along transit routes	Concentrated market, permanence of messages, frequency, action orientation, color, creative options	Clutter of ads, consumer distractions, limited audience

Truth in Advertising

Through the years, many marketers have abused advertising's power and consumers' gullibility to sell products that were not all they claimed to be. Consider, for example, the outrageous claims in the early advertisement shown in Figure 11.6. As newspaper and magazine circulation increased and television coverage spanned the nation, deceptive advertising naturally flourished.

Public clamor against deceptive advertising and other misleading marketing practices became so loud that Congress responded in 1938 with the **Wheeler-Lea Act,** *the law that gives the Federal Trade Commission* (FTC; discussed in Chapter 3) *the power to issue cease-and-desist orders against firms that make false or misleading advertising claims.* The FTC can also require the company to run corrective advertising if the original message gave consumers a lasting and grossly incorrect impression of the product's capabilities.

Recently the FTC adopted a new standard requiring proof that a "reasonable" consumer had suffered actual injury before an advertiser could be charged with deceptive practices. The consumer will now have to prove that the ad "misleads" the consumer "acting reasonably in the circumstances to the consumer's detriment."[3]

In addition to the FTC, the U.S. Postal Service enjoys considerable power to protect consumers when a company uses the mails to misrepresent a product or defraud buyers. The Federal Communications Commission, which regulates interstate radio and television transmissions, can issue edicts about advertising practices in those media. The National Association of Broadcasters (NAB), a trade association representing the broadcasting industry, created its own guidelines, the Television Code, in 1952. This private set of rules governs subscribing television stations' choice of advertisements from potential customers. One of the NAB guidelines discourages television ads for hard liquor (whiskey, gin, etc.); another advises broadcasters against permitting models in beer and wine commercials to be shown actually drinking those beverages. Individual

Wheeler-Lea Act

Figure 11.6 Early Advertisement: Deceptive Advertising at Its Best

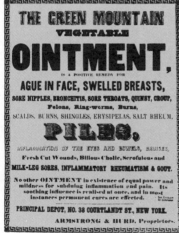

television networks also have censorship rules that apply to ads on their respective programs.

The Promotional Mix: Publicity

publicity

The third element of the promotional mix is publicity. **Publicity** is *nonpaid, nonpersonal communication to promote the products, services, or image of the company.* It is an important element of the promotion mix that can be overlooked because of its nature.

The Nature of Publicity

Publicity for the products, services, or image of the company is an ongoing goal for marketing managers; but it is often hard to gauge its success. For example, how can you measure the impact of a popular radio talk show host who declares that "Henri's has the best, I mean the best, combination of food, service, and environment I have ever experienced" or of a well-known newspaper columnist who reveals that "Hair E Natural is *the* place to have your styling done"? Publicity has greater credibility and receives more attention than advertisements. Wouldn't you believe a movie reviewer rather than the claims of a movie advertisement?

Publicity is given to a company by independent media. The media — television, radio, newspapers, or magazines — are independent because publicity is nonpaid. To take advantage of the opportunity for publicity companies have to prepare newsworthy items and send them to the media, provide the opportunity for members of the media to observe the event, hold news conferences, and have personal contacts or telephone contacts.

The Two Faces of Publicity

Publicity has two faces: positive and negative. Firms provide an ongoing stream of positive publicity: information about new products, major accomplishments, or other, similar information. On the other hand, the negative side of publicity deals with product defects, emergencies, strikes, or any other unfavorable event. A company must be able to respond in the face of adverse publicity. Some have done so successfully, others have disappeared from the marketplace.

- Tylenol rebounded after suffering through the horrors of seven deaths caused by cyanide-laced capsules of Extra Strength Tylenol.
- Procter & Gamble was forced to stop manufacturing Rely Tampons at a loss of $75 million after the item was linked to toxic-shock syndrome.
- Bon Vivant Soups filed for bankruptcy after a botulism death was traced to its vichyssoise and the Food and Drug Administration recalled all Bon Vivant products.[4]

Types of Publicity

Several types of publicity are available to a company, such as

— News publicity dealing with events of local, regional, or national importance
— Business feature articles — stories about the company or its products — that are given to the business media
— Finance releases directed toward business magazines and financial writers for newspapers
— Emergency releases related to serious problems or disasters[5]

The Promotional Mix: Sales Promotion

The fourth element of the promotional mix is sales promotion. The American Marketing Association defines **sales promotion** as *"those marketing activities, other than personal selling and advertising . . . that stimulate consumer purchasing and dealer effectiveness, such as displays, shows and expositions, demonstrations, and various nonrecurrent selling efforts not in the ordinary routine."*[6] This definition includes a host of devices, some geared toward middlemen, others toward final consumers.

sales promotion

Sales promotion supports the other three elements in the marketing mix. When directed at middlemen it aids in encouraging distribution, obtaining shelf space in stores, developing middlemen cooperation, and increasing sales. When focused on the final consumer, it assists in (1) increasing brand awareness, (2) developing impulse sales, (3) initiating a trend of a new product or service, and (4) encouraging repurchase of goods.

Promoting to Middlemen

Manufacturers use several sales promotion devices to influence the sales activities of firms that help to move products from producers to users.

Point-of-Purchase Displays. Many manufacturers promote their products with **point-of-purchase displays,** *promotional devices that are placed where sales transactions occur.* These include posters, life-size cardboard mannequins, display racks, and dummy packages. Although these attractions ultimately appeal to final consumers, they can be considered promotional appeals to middlemen because retail stores sometimes agree to carry a product only if the manufacturer provides an effective display. L'eggs hosiery, Hartz Mountain pet supplies, and Spice Islands spices are sold with the help of these visual enticements.

point-of-purchase displays

cooperative advertising programs

Cooperative Advertising Programs. Some manufacturers engage in **cooperative advertising programs,** *programs in which the manufacturer agrees to pay part of the advertising costs for the product.* Teledyne, for example, extends such a program to retailers that regularly sell its Water Pik oral hygiene appliance. The fact that producers will share the dealer's advertising costs makes dealers more willing to promote the products. Cooperative advertising is especially useful for smaller, independent retailers, who otherwise might be unable to afford advertising and thus be unable to compete effectively with chains.

Companies are aggressively pursuing the co-op industry dollar. The most innovative and flexible co-op plans are offered by high-tech computer-related companies where the co-op arrangement usually covers up to 75 percent of media costs for the retailer.[7]

specialty advertising

Specialty Advertising. Another appeal to middlemen, and also to final consumers, is **specialty advertising.** This consists of *providing "frequent reminder" items that build good will and keep a firm's or a product's name within the prospect's view.* They range from such relatively cheap items as ball-point pens, calendars, and matchbooks to staplers, coffee cups, and even skywriting. The choices have one thing in common: they all identify the product or the company.

The list of specialty advertising objects is confined only to the marketer's imagination. The Travelers Insurance Company's umbrellas protect people from the elements while its insurance policies protect them from risk; Crusty's Pizza bumper stickers slyly suggest, "Smile if you've had some lately!"; logo hats bearing corporate emblems promote Copenhagen snuff, Caterpillar heavy equipment, and Mack trucks. Many specialty advertising items are given to final consumers as well as to middlemen.

Trade Shows. Both producers and retailers find trade shows popular. At these shows, a great array of products from one or several competing firms is exhibited, attracting thousands of prospects within a region. Typical trade shows feature boats, automobiles, or mobile homes. Because these events attract such a high volume of traffic, participating companies make many sales on the spot. They also gather the names of prospects for future sales, often by having attendees register for a drawing that awards an attractive prize. The names and addresses of those who registered become a valuable mailing list after the show.

push money ("PMs" *or* "spiffs")

Push Money. As an added incentive for salespeople to devote extra personal selling effort to their brands, some producers offer **push money ("PMs"** or **"spiffs"),** which is *a manufacturer's commission paid to salespeople for selling one particular brand over all others.*

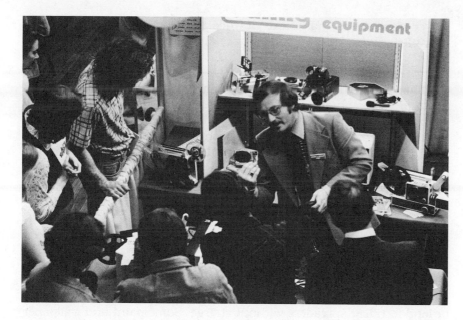

Trade shows can attract thousands of prospects within a geographic market.

Such incentives are not considered part of the salesperson's basic compensation. Push money and trade discounts have created quite a controversy in the industry. Salespeople receive money for services that they do not always perform.[8]

Promoting to Final Consumers

The other side of sales promotion involves devices that both manufacturers and retailers use to appeal to final consumers' buying motives.

Coupons. One common way to bring potential consumers and products together is by placing money-saving coupons outside or inside a product's package. Cents-off coupons also are printed in magazines and newspapers, mailed directly to consumers' homes, and distributed at retail store counters. Processed foods, consumer cleaning products, and patent medicines are examples of consumer products that have been promoted this way. Producers hope that coupon offers will generate enough new sales volume to offset the lower coupon price.

Samples. Some firms place products in consumers' hands by giving away samples. This form of promotion, which was used for Irish Spring soap and Era laundry detergent, acquaints consumers with the product in the hope of making them more likely to buy the regular size when they use up the free amount. Manufacturers of products that are used in or with certain appliances or other durable goods may arrange to distribute their product free with each of the larger items sold — a box of Bounce fabric softener comes free in every Frigidaire clothes dryer, for example.

premium

Premiums. Another appeal to final consumers, a **premium,** is *something of value given free or at a nominal charge as an incentive to buy a product.* These have special appeal to children, who in turn influence adults to buy the product. Morris the Cat T-shirts have been sold for $2.75 with ten labels from 9-Lives cat food or for $5.00 without the labels. A box of 5-ounce children's-size Dixie cups offered junior entrepreneurs a fully equipped lemonade stand for $9.95 and a proof of purchase. The classic example of a premium is the prize that comes in every Cracker Jack box.

Special Services. Some merchants appeal to patronage motives by offering consumers special services. A hardware and garden supply store, for example, may hold free classes in ornamental horticulture or lend fertilizer spreaders without charge. Some paint and wallpaper stores hold free classes in paperhanging. Banks offer such services as free travelers checks and money orders to depositors, and department stores sometimes hold such events as electric razor tune-up clinics and children's corrective shoe clinics.

Contests and Sweepstakes. Contests, another popular method of promoting products, require entrants to compete for prizes by doing things like naming a new product, writing a slogan containing the firm's or the product's name, completing a poem or limerick, or even baking a cake. Johnny Walker Scotch, Coca-Cola, and many chain supermarkets have run contests to increase product use and buyer loyalty.

Sweepstakes entrants submit their names on forms that are

Goods can be introduced to final consumers by providing in-store samples.

entered in a drawing to determine the winners. Prizes vary from exotic vacations to transistor radios. Levi Strauss staged an Olympic Opportunity Sweepstakes and offered its eighteen winners $5,000 each to spend to improve their proficiency at a skill, sport, or career; or the winners could just take the cash if they chose.

Trading Stamps. Once a popular promotional device that built patronage for gas stations, supermarkets, and other retail outlets, trading stamps have been eliminated by most stores in an effort to control escalating prices. There are, however, a few holdouts — primarily supermarkets — that continue to use them as promotional attractions. Retailers give trading stamps to customers according to how much merchandise the customer has purchased. The stamps are collected in books and can be redeemed for merchandise exhibited through a catalog or in a showroom.

Refund Offers. Money refund offers have been used to encourage sales of General Electric food processors, Minute Rice, and even (through factory rebates) new automobiles. With this device, the producer returns part of the purchase price to customers who submit a proof of purchase.

Developing Promotional Strategies

The four elements of the promotional mix need to be blended to communicate effectively to a target market. Each type of promotion serves a different function and therefore should support the other elements. (Table 11.6 on page 324 summarizes the function and value of each promotional alternative.) The blending of the elements results in a promotional strategy. There are two potential promotional strategies: push strategy and pull strategy.

A **push strategy** is *a strategy directed at the members of the marketing channel rather than the consumer.* This strategy depends heavily on personal selling with support provided by sales promotion techniques of cooperative advertising programs and push money.

push strategy

A **pull strategy** is *a strategy aimed at the consumer. The intention is for the consumer to demand that a product be available*

pull strategy

Pause and Ponder

Think of the last time you were in a supermarket. Were there any food products — soft drinks, sausage, cheese and crackers — being sampled? Did you use any coupons? Was the store having a contest? How effective do you believe these promotional techniques are?

The Straight Line

Product Placement
Using the Movies to Market Products

Do you remember which beer Dustin Hoffman drank in *Tootsie*? Or what candy lured the little alien out of hiding in *E.T.*? The use of brand-name items in movies, a practice known as product placement, has been around since the early days of motion pictures. In the early days, however, products were used by the movie studios at no charge. In return manufacturers' products were displayed on the screen, and all products eventually were returned to the manufacturers (except food and drinks, which generally were donated to the studio crew).

It was not until the mid-1970s that product placement emerged as big business and "product agents" were born. These entrepreneurs will place a company's products in a movie in return for handsome fees ranging from $5,000 to $10,000 for each product, and they have been very successful.

This innovative idea of low-key commercials has placed more and more products on the movie screen. Although the viewers aren't aware of a hard sell, subliminally they may want to drink, eat, wear, or use whatever the movie star does, and they may go out and buy that product. And product placement ads on the screen can be very lucrative: sales of Hershey's Reese's Pieces rose 65 percent after E.T. found them irresistible.

As the product placement

in the distribution channel. To accomplish this strategy marketers rely on the advertising, sales promotion, and publicity elements of the promotional mix.

Summary

Managers who are responsible for developing promotional strategy need to understand why consumers and industrial buyers buy the things they do. Consumers buy goods under the combined influence of emotional, rational, and patronage motives. Industrial buyers buy for rational reasons including price, profit, quality, salability, uniformity, service, and reciprocity.

Once the buying motives have been identified, the next step is to create a promotional strategy — the communication ingredient in the marketing mix. A promotional strategy is composed of the four elements of the promotional mix: personal selling, advertising, publicity, and sales promotion. The promotional strategy is developed with an understanding of the communication process, which includes sender, encoding, message, medium, decoding, target market, feedback, and noise.

The first element of the promotional mix is personal selling. It is a face-to-face attempt to persuade the prospective customer to buy a product. Salespersons use a seven-step sales approach that includes prospecting, preapproach, approach, presentation, objections, closing, and follow-up.

business has boomed, some movie studios — among them 20th Century Fox and MGM — have decided that they no longer need agents. These studios now try to deal directly with the manufacturers and charge fees between $10,000 and $40,000 for placing products in their movies.

Of course, not all movie studios are impressed or influenced by film commercials and their lucrative returns; they feel that brand-name products are not important to films and may even detract from the film's message. Naturally product agents disagree; they argue that film commercials are extremely important because they add realism to films. Burt Reynolds drinks a certain beer in *Hooper*. In *Rocky III* Sylvester Stallone tells his son he wants him to grow up to be big and strong as they eat a certain breakfast food. This is realism; real people eating or drinking real food in real, believable situations.

There has been some criticism that too many brand names appear in a single movie. Many movie reviewers have criticized recent movies for seeming like long commercials. This point is valid and merits attention, and corrective measures have been taken to see that the realistic display of products won't be destroyed by overexposure to too many products in a single movie.

For more about product placement "at the movies," see Aljean Harmetz, "It's No Accident When Name Brands Show Up in Movies," *The Orlando* (Florida) *Sentinel*, December 27, 1983, p. D-2; David T. Friendly, "Selling It at the Movies," *Newsweek*, July 4, 1983, p. 46; and Stephen J. Sansweet, "Why Marlon Brando Passed the Milk Duds to George C. Scott," *The Wall Street Journal*, May 24, 1982, p. 1.

The second element of the promotional mix is advertising. Advertising is any nonpersonal message paid for by an identifiable sponsor for the purpose of promoting products, services, or ideas. There are two types of advertising: product (intended to promote demand for a product or service) and institutional (done to enhance a company's public image). Once the type of advertising is determined, marketers have to select the medium for presenting the message. They may select from among direct mail, newspaper, radio, outdoor advertising, television, and magazines. Regardless of the media used, all advertising must be done within legal guidelines that prohibit false or misleading advertising claims.

The third element of the promotional mix is publicity. It is nonpaid, nonpersonal communication to promote the products, services, or image of the company. The development of a publicity element of the promotional mix requires the firm to take advantage of all opportunities to present material to independent media. Types of publicity include news publicity, business feature articles, finance releases, and emergency releases.

Sales promotion is the fourth element of the promotional mix. It involves marketing activities, other than personal selling and advertising, that stimulate consumer purchasing and dealer effectiveness. Specific types of sales promotion devices are directed at the middlemen: point-of-purchase displays, cooperative advertising programs, specialty advertising, trade shows, and push money. Other

Table 11.6 Function and Value of the Promotional Mix

Rating Criteria	Personal Selling	Advertising	Publicity	Sales Promotion
Goal	To present an individual message, to problem solve, to close the sale	To reach a mass audience; to inform, persuade, and remind	To provide a mass audience with unbiased information	To complement other promotional elements, to increase impulse sales
Type of message	Individual, specific, focused	Same message to all individuals	Same message to all individuals	Will vary depending on the specific sales promotional device
Flexibility	High flexibility	Medium flexibility	Low flexibility	Medium flexibility
Cost	High per sales call	Low per person contacted	No cost	Medium per customer
Control of message material	High control	High control	No control	High control

types are intended for the consumer: coupons, samples, premiums, special services, contests and sweepstakes, trading stamps, and refund offers.

The four ingredients of the promotional mix are blended to communicate effectively to a target market. In blending these the manager has a choice of two types of promotional strategy: push strategy or pull strategy. Push strategy is directed toward the marketing channel; pull strategy is aimed at the consumer.

Key Terms

advertising
advertising media
approach
close
communication process
consumer buying motives
cooperative advertising
    programs
decoding
emotional motives
encoding
feedback
follow-up
industrial buying motives

institutional advertising
medium
message
noise
objections
patronage motives
personal selling
point-of-purchase displays
preapproach
premium
presentation
product advertising
promotional mix
prospecting

publicity
pull strategy
push money ("PMs" *or* "spiffs")
push strategy
rational motives
reciprocal buying
sales promotion
selling process
sender
specialty advertising
target market
Wheeler-Lea Act

For Review and Discussion

1. What is the relationship between buying motives and promotional strategy?
2. Evaluate this statement: "Consumer buying motives are more emotionally oriented than industrial buying motives."
3. Explain the role of promotional strategy in the marketing mix.
4. Identify each of the elements of the communication process and explain what occurs during each part of the process.
5. Summarize the seven steps in the selling process. Should one of the steps be considered more important than the others? Why or why not?
6. What do companies advertise?
7. Distinguish between the two types of advertising.
8. Identify four advertising media and discuss the advantages and disadvantages of each.
9. What role does publicity play in the promotional mix? How can a company guarantee that it will receive publicity?
10. What is meant by the "two faces of publicity"? Provide a recent example of negative publicity.
11. What function does sales promotion perform in the promotional mix? Whom can it be targeted to?
12. Explain the purposes of four promotional devices used to appeal to middlemen and four used to appeal to final consumers.
13. Explain how the four elements of promotion are blended to create the promotional mix.
14. Discuss the purposes of a promotional push strategy and a promotional pull strategy.

Applications

Case 11.1 Marketing Madness for the Consumer

In the last few years you, the consumer, have been bombarded by personal computer ads. If you are like most people you have found yourself mystified.

- IBM, in its bakery and hat company commercials featuring Charlie Chaplin, promises that the computer will improve small-business productivity.
- Apple Computer directs its message to the independent, free-spirited person. Showing a basketball-playing female architect is one approach to attracting a different market than IBM.
- Atari, with Alan Alda as its spokesperson, assures potential buyers that its product is "user friendly."
- Commodore focuses its energy on marketing an affordable product —then adds the message to buy the supporting peripherals.
- Texas Instruments directs its energy at parents to give their children a head start in this digital world — even before they can read.
- Coleco's Adam computer promises a complete package at an attractive price. It promises benefits and takes the mystery out of buying.

All these products are intended for the mass market. The mass marketing of any product requires that the consumer receive a simple, strong message about its benefits. But the multiple messages that are coming through are extremely confusing to the consumer.

Even though IBM, Atari, Apple, Commodore, Coleco, and Texas Instruments believe that they have focused on their target markets, have identified specific needs, and have built their promotional strategies to satisfy these needs, the intended benefits are lost amid the mixed messages of all the competitors.

Questions

1. For each of the computers, identify the specific target market the companies have chosen.
2. Are the target markets or segments identical or is there a difference? If so, what is the difference?
3. What specific promotional message is being directed at each target market?
4. Why are the different promotional messages causing confusion for the consumer? Are the promotional messages able to satisfy the needs of the target markets?

Case 11.1 Adapted from Peter D. Petre, "The Computer," *Fortune*, October 31, 1983, pp. 61–67.

Case 11.2 Changing Times — And Messages

Boots Pharmaceuticals is taking a bold new direction in its promotional strategy. Boots has chosen to direct its promotional messages to the consumer for its anti-arthritis drug, marketed under the brand name of Rufen.

As part of a trial for its new strategy Boots:

- Aired a series of 30- and 60-second commercials that appeared about fifty times a day on four television channels in the Tampa Bay, Florida, area
- Sent mailgrams to doctors and pharmacists alerting them to the promotion
- Offered pharmacists entry into a drawing for a free trip to England each time they sold a bottle of a new, large-dose Rufen pill, which competes directly against the same size Motrin pill sold by Upjohn

What is so revolutionary? Prescription drugs traditionally have been promoted to doctors. In turn the doctors write the prescription for specific brands for the patients. The actual brands prescribed by doctors have the same medicinal results — but not the same price tags. Boots promotional strategy is directed at a price appeal. The only message to the consumer is that Rufen costs less than Upjohn's Motrin.

Questions

1. What risk is Boots taking in promoting its product directly to the consumer?

2. As a consumer, do you feel brand-name prescription drugs should have their promotional messages directed at you or to doctors and pharmacists?

3. This promotional strategy is based on the consumer's understanding that one brand-name prescription drug has the identical medicinal abilities as another brand. Does this need to be part of the message? How would you communicate this?

4. Do you feel that this promotional strategy is the wave of the future in the medical field?

Case 11.2 Adapted from "TV Ads for Prescription Drug to Start Today Causing a Stir," *The Wall Street Journal*, May 19, 1983, p. 37.

Distribution and Pricing Strategy

Chapter Outline

Chapter Objectives

After studying this chapter, you should be able to:

1. Describe the importance of distribution strategy.
2. List and explain the primary distribution channels for industrial goods and consumer goods.
3. Discuss the various types of middlemen and their roles as channel members.
4. Explain the components of a physical distribution system.
5. Describe the importance of pricing strategy.
6. Explain how prices are determined by supply and demand, the cost-oriented approaches of markup and break-even analysis, and the market approach.
7. Describe ten potential pricing strategies marketers can adopt.
8. Explain the importance of nonprice competition through product differentiation.

The price of a product or service is a major determinant of the market demand for the item. Price will affect the firm's competitive position and its share of the market.
— William J. Stanton, American educator

Up Front   Mo Siegel

A Millionaire on His Own Terms

Mo Siegel, a college drop-out, became a millionaire at the age of twenty-six. Now in his mid-thirties, Siegel is a very persuasive, highly intelligent individual with instinctive management ability — clearly a man with a purpose.

Mo, as he is known at work, left college after one quarter to celebrate life. He traveled about the country and finally wound up in Boulder, Colorado, where he managed a health food store. There he married and settled in a cabin out of town.

One summer Mo and some friends decided to collect herbs from the mountains and blend them into herbal tea. They distributed their tea through a local health food store, and before long this casual sideline took on the character of a company. John Hay, brother of Mo's friend Wyck Hay,

became a co-founder. Although he left the company a few years later, he is still a director and stockholder.

The firm's name echoes its unassuming origins. The nickname of a girl whom Wyck Hay had dated was Celestial Seasonings. Siegel was sure the name fit the firm to a tee. Some have termed Celestial Seasonings' operating philosophy *cosmic capitalism* because Mo's approachable management style is a reflection of his strong religious beliefs. Although he is not a churchgoer, he operates his business by the Golden Rule and describes himself as very Christian.

With a business sense as sharp as his taste buds, Mo has answered market demand in recent years by expanding Celestial Seasonings' offerings to more than

Distribution strategy and pricing strategy are the third and fourth ingredients in the firm's marketing mix. When these are "blended" with product and promotional strategy (discussed in Chapters 10 and 11 respectively), the organization has created its marketing strategy to reach the selected target market.

In this chapter we will examine the importance, objectives, and components of distribution strategy. We will also investigate pricing: its objectives, methods of determination, and potential strategies.

The Importance of Distribution Strategy

Distribution strategy involves physical distribution systems and channels used to place the product in the customer's hands. It is responsible for getting the product to the right place at the right time. A firm can have the best products in the world (product strategy),

thirty-five blends. He now imports herbs from over thirty-five foreign countries. The phenomenal growth and development of the firm can be attributed to Siegel's management techniques, which emphasize hard work, employee incentive rewards, and comprehensive employee and management training. Mo hired seasoned executives from Coca-Cola, Pepsi-Co, and Quaker Oats to generate new products, oversee marketing promotion efforts, and design a distribution strategy that has placed the tea in 70 to 75 percent of all supermarkets.

Celestial's cash position is very strong, and the company has little debt. This has been an incentive to increase advertising spending to approximately $2 million this year as opposed to $1.3 million last year; television ads are being tested in six cities. Expected sales this year are $28.5 million with an expected $100 million by 1990. But Siegel is not satisfied. His goal is to build Celestial Seasonings into a major packaged goods company. Among the more than forty products in development in his headquarters are new lines of food and beauty aids.

Mo Siegel is indeed a man who is planning for the future; and with further expansion in mind, he has purchased an additional 90 acres in Boulder. His achievements are impressive, but millionaire Mo still rides his bicycle to work, perhaps savoring his success as fully as consumers do his teas.

For more about Morris Siegel, see Thomas C. Hayes, "Health-Food Millionaire: Morris J. Siegel," *The New York Times*, April 3, 1983, p. 6-F; Eric Morgenthaler, "Herb Tea's Pioneer: From Hippie Origins to $16 Million a Year," *The Wall Street Journal*, May 6, 1981, p. 1; "What's Brewing at Celestial?" *Business Week*, March 16, 1981, p. 138.

people can know about them and want them (promotional strategy), but all this will be useless if people cannot get the products when and where they want them.

Distribution involves (1) the routes goods take and the people involved in that process and (2) the activities entailed in getting the goods to the consumer — a physical distribution system. Element one deals with the channels, choices of channels, and channel members. Element two deals with the actual components of a physical distribution system (transportation, warehousing, order processing, materials handling, and inventory control).

Channels of Distribution

A **channel of distribution** is *a route that goods follow on their journey from producers to consumers.* The channels and the organizations that compose them serve as a pipeline by which the manufacturer moves goods to the ultimate consumer.

channel of distribution

A manufacturer's choice of distribution channels varies. Some manufacturers choose to distribute the product directly to the consumer. Others choose to use a channel with a number of wholesalers and retailers. Still others who want to reach a number of market segments use several different channels. Why?

The decision to use a channel is based on a number of variables, such as:

— The industry practice
— The type of product (convenience, shopping, or specialty good)
— The degree of market coverage desired (intensive, selective, exclusive)
— The market segment (industrial, consumer)
— The ability of the firm to perform the marketing functions or the need for others to do so (buying, selling, transporting, storing, financing, risk bearing)
— The competitor's distribution strategy
— The geographic locations of the market segment

intensive distribution

selective distribution

exclusive distribution

An example of two variables is the influence of the degree of market coverage desired and the type of products offered. A firm that markets convenience products will want widespread market coverage, **intensive distribution,** that *utilizes a large number of wholesalers and retailers.* Another manufacturer that markets shopping goods may wish to emphasize image and a good sales volume through **selective distribution** that *utilizes a moderate number of retailers and wholesalers.* Finally, for a specialty good, a manufacturer may use **exclusive distribution** by *limiting distribution to one retailer or wholesaler in a geographic area.*

With these factors in mind, let's examine the two major distribution channel categories by market: the industrial goods market and the consumer goods market.

Channels for Industrial Goods

Figure 12.1 illustrates the various distribution channels that producers can use to reach the industrial goods market.

Manufacturer to Industrial Buyer. The shortest and sometimes the most practical way for a manufacturer to distribute industrial goods is to sell them directly to industrial customers. Direct distribution is used if goods are awkward to handle, the market segment is small, or the seller must train the buyer's employees to operate the product. Computers, textile manufacturing equipment, and iron ore often are distributed in this way.

Manufacturer to Industrial Wholesaler to Industrial Buyer. Industrial goods with a broad market, like welding rods, printing paper, and construction materials, need wider distribution. They utilize a distribution channel featuring wholesalers known as *industrial distributors.* These distributors resell to the industrial buyer.

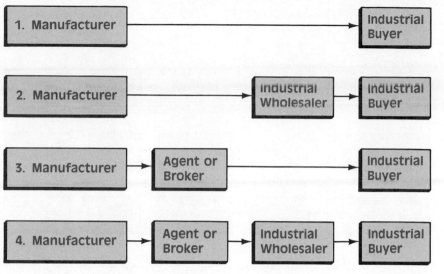

Figure 12.1 Distribution Channels for Industrial Goods

Manufacturer to Agent or Broker to Industrial Buyer. In some instances the product being sold does not require the intermediate warehousing service provided by a wholesaler. An agent or broker can serve as the contact point for the manufacturer without taking possession of or title to the goods.

Manufacturer to Agent or Broker to Industrial Wholesaler to Industrial Buyer. Small manufacturers often need to contract with an agent or broker to represent products to wholesalers. The agent serves the purpose of bringing the wholesaler and manufacturer together but does not take title to the goods.

Channels for Consumer Goods

Final consumers are reached by a variety of channels. Figure 12.2 shows distribution channels that manufacturers of consumer goods can use.

Manufacturer to Consumer. Although the direct channel is favored for reaching industrial users, only approximately 5 percent of consumer goods are moved in this way. Such products as encyclopedias and Good Humor ice cream often are sold directly to consumers. Milk used to be sold in this way but rarely is now. Firms such as L. L. Bean and various Wisconsin sausage and cheese producers also sell direct through their mail-order catalogs.

Manufacturer to Retailer to Consumer. Some manufacturers that use exclusive distribution choose to select their own retail outlets to represent them. Shoes and large household appliances are products that traditionally are distributed directly to retailers without the need for wholesalers.

Figure 12.2 Distribution Channels for Consumer Goods

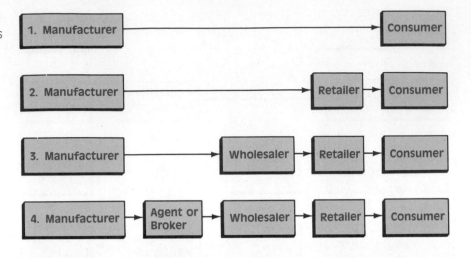

Manufacturer to Wholesaler to Retailer to Consumer. Products that require intensive distribution need a broader channel of distribution. This is provided by incorporating a wholesale and retail link in the channel. The wholesaler aids in allocating the product to the retailers in order to have the product available when and where needed by the consumer. Anheuser-Busch's impressive marketing success is a direct result of its distribution system. With the help of almost a thousand beer wholesalers (an average of more than nineteen per state), this brewer places its products in supermarkets, taverns, restaurants, and liquor stores across the country.[1]

Manufacturer to Agent to Wholesaler to Retailer to Consumer. An agent or broker does not take title to goods but performs the function of bringing buyers and sellers together. In the meat packing industry agents are used to contact wholesalers who in turn buy from manufacturers. The remainder of the channel system is as previously discussed.

Channel Members

The various channels of distribution we have examined are composed of organizations or people known as *channel members, middlemen,* or *intermediaries.* As mentioned earlier in the chapter these intermediaries provide performance of the marketing functions of buying, selling, storing, transporting, risk taking, and collecting marketing information.

There are two types of middlemen that operate between the manufacturer and consumer or industrial user: wholesalers and retailers. In the next sections we will discuss each.

Wholesaling Middlemen

Wholesalers are those middlemen who sell goods to retailers, to other wholesalers, and to industrial users, but who do not sell in significant amounts to the final consumer.[2] If wholesalers did not exist retailers would have to spend a great amount of time dealing with many different manufacturers, attempting to coordinate numerous product orders and shipments, and acquiring and maintaining huge stock inventories.

All wholesalers are not the same. Some take title to the goods (merchant wholesalers); others do not (agents and brokers). Some provide a full range of services. (As shown in Table 12.1, full-service merchant wholesalers provide credit, store and deliver, and provide sales and promotional assistance.) On the other hand, limited service merchant wholesalers simply resell goods and provide little or no service. Table 12.2 provides a sampling of the different types of wholesalers and their characteristics.

Retailing Middlemen

Retailers are the last stage in the channel of distribution; they perform the business activities involved in the sale of goods and services to the ultimate consumer for personal use. The activities may include buying and selling of products, transportation or delivery, storage of inventory, financing, and risk bearing. The activities of retailers involve both in-store and out-of-store operations.

In-Store Retailers. In-store retailers use conventional store facilities to provide products and services to the ultimate consumer. They can be classified by type of ownership and by type of store. These classifications can be broken down even further, as the following list shows.

Type of Ownership
- Independent store
- Chain store

Services to Manufacturers	Services to Retailers
Relay market information from the retailers	Advise store on layout, promotional activities, bookkeeping practices, inventory planning, and sources of credit
Employ a sales force to sell products	Tell of new products that manufacturers are bringing to market
Save manufacturers work by extending credit to retailers	Deliver merchandise faster and in smaller quantities than producers are willing to do
Store products before resale and deliver them when sold	Simplify retailers' recordkeeping and inventory handling activities by gathering many manufacturers' products into a single delivery and billing
Bear risk of market changes that may reduce demand for the product	

Table 12.1 Typical Services Provided by Full-Service Wholesalers

Table 12.2 Types of
Wholesalers and Their
Characteristics

Wholesaler	Characteristics	Takes Title
Manufacturers' agent[a]	An agent who sells products made by several manufacturers. Has little authority to approve customer requests for price concessions, expedited delivery, or credit.	No
Selling agent[a]	An agent who sells a producer's entire output. Usually has broad authority to approve customer requests for price concessions, expedited delivery, or credit.	No
Auction house[a]	Brings buyers and sellers together in one location. Allows buyers to inspect products before purchase.	No
Commission merchant[a]	An agent who represents producers. Sells products for the best price possible, takes possession of goods. Sells agricultural products.	No
Broker	Represents either buyer or seller for a commission on sales or purchases made. Products purchased through brokers usually are shipped directly to purchaser. Distributes such products as coal, grain, and produce.	No

[a]Manufacturers' agent, selling agent, auction house, and commission merchant are all categorized as agent channels of distribution.

Type of Store
- Convenience store   — Discount store
- Supermarket   — Hypermarket
- Specialty store   — Factory outlet
- Department store

independent store

Retailers can be classified according to the number of outlets. One type is the **independent store,** *an individual retail store, usually a small family-owned business.* Most independents sell a relatively narrow line of products, such as auto parts or records and tapes. Few need the sophisticated management training programs that J. C. Penney or other large retailers run. Most obtain merchandise through the wholesaler, not having the capital, sales volume, or storage space to justify buying large quantities directly from manufacturers.

Wholesaler	Characteristics	Takes Title
Rack jobber	A type of consumer-goods wholesaler. Sets up manufacturers' point-of-purchase displays in stores and restocks them as needed. Distributes such products as magazines, panty hose, and candy.	Yes
Drop shipper	Does not take physical possession of goods. Provides selling and credit. Does not provide advertising or merchandising support. Distributes primarily raw materials.	Yes
Truck wholesaler	Sells and delivers goods at the same time on a regular sales route. Provides merchandising and promotion support. Distributes potato chips, bakery, and dairy products.	Yes

A second type of store is a **chain store,** *one of two or more similar stores owned by the same company, usually a corporation.* To support relatively large-scale operations, the parent company normally buys products directly from manufacturers and distributes them to the individual stores for sale to final consumers. There are regional chains such as Winn-Dixie Stores, national chains such as Sears, and manufacturer-owned chains such as International Business Machines (IBM) Product Centers.

chain store

As we've already mentioned on page 335, in-store retailing also can be categorized by the type of store: the type of products carried or by the marketing strategy that an outlet displays. One type of retail outlet spelled the demise of the small mom-and-pop grocery stores: the **convenience store,** *usually part of a chain, which carries a wide selection of popular consumer items from groceries to motor oil.* The main attraction is convenience: many operate 24 hours a day, 7 days a week, in areas of high population or heavy highway traffic. Speedy Mart, 7-Eleven, Mini-Market, and Jiffy Stores are well-known convenience stores. Despite charging high prices for most items, their long hours, popular merchandise, and strategic locations combine to attract an ever-increasing number of customers.

convenience store

One familiar retail outlet, the **supermarket,** is *a store that sells a wide variety of food items.* Although initially intended to be a high-volume, self-service, one-stop food-shopping outlet for consumers, it has become much more. The original supermarket has evolved into the **superstore,** *a food-based retailer that carries a variety of other products.* Superstores have a minimum of 30,000

supermarket

superstore

Long hours, popular merchandise, and strategic locations offset the higher prices usually charged by convenience stores.

square feet of selling space, and carry household appliances, clothing, automobile oil and filters, and boutique items in addition to a full line of supermarket items. Safeway, Grand Union, and Giant Foods are venturing into superstores. The idea of including fresh-cut flowers, discounted cosmetics, fresh pasta, and automatic teller machines is to be everything to everybody and to make food shopping fun.[3]

specialty store

The retail outlet known as the **specialty store** is *a store that offers many models or styles of a specific product*, such as stereo equipment, cameras, or musical instruments. These make up the majority of stores located in the regional shopping centers that are anchored by one or more full-service department stores. Although many occupy their own buildings (called *free-standing stores*), others own or lease space in city business districts or in small strip shopping centers along main highways.

department store

A **department store** is *a retail outlet, usually a member of a chain, that is organized by departments and provides an extremely wide variety of merchandise including home furnishings, clothing, appliances, cosmetics, furniture, and dry goods.* Department stores provide a full line of services including gift wrapping, home delivery, and credit. In addition, a number of department stores have developed gourmet cooking classes, fashion shows, seminars, investment and career counseling programs to attract women, and evening college courses.[4]

discount store

A **discount store** is *a store that has low prices, a broad line of merchandise, self-service, a low rent location, and limited store environment.* These stores rarely offer their own credit cards, although most accept such bank credit cards as Visa and MasterCard, and they avoid home delivery, gift wrapping, and other services that would force them to raise their prices. Discount stores base their operations on their willingness to buy regular-priced merchandise and take a lower percentage of profit on the goods. Another approach is the newer, off-price discount stores, such as Mervyn's, Marshall's, Loehmann's, and Syms, that buy goods at less than regular price and sell them at less than retail.[5]

Department stores provide a wide variety of merchandise and a full line of services.

The discount approach also has moved into department stores and drugstores. Discount department stores like Zayre and K Mart offer few services but do provide a wide range of products in a department format. Discount drugstores are becoming a volume seller at low profits through buying only discounted items themselves.[6]

Popular in France, Japan, and Germany, a **hypermarket** is *a gigantic discount retail complex that combines the features of supermarkets, department stores, and specialty stores under one roof.* These stores offer few services and spartan facilities, but they provide an avalanche of merchandise, displayed in manufacturers' cartons or stacked in bins. Some stores of this type have been opened in Illinois and New Jersey and more may appear in densely populated areas.

hypermarket

Sometimes known as a seconds outlet or a manufacturer's courtesy outlet, a **factory outlet** is *a retail store that sells products directly from the plant to the final consumer at greatly discounted prices.* These outlets help producers to create good will, to sell off production overruns and out-of-season items, and to dispose of

factory outlet

Pause and Ponder

Think about a department store you have been in recently. Would you describe it as a full-service department store, a discount department store, or an off-price department store? What specific factors in this store place it in this category? Why did you choose to shop here?

products with cosmetic flaws or imperfections. Fostoria glassware, Danskin apparel, and West Bend appliances are some of the products sold in this way. Real estate developers in Reading, Pennsylvania; Orlando, Florida; and other locations have built shopping malls specifically to house factory outlets.

Out-of-Store Retailing. Out-of-store retailing includes those retailers who do not use conventional retail facilities. This category includes the following:

— House-to-house retailing
— Vending machine retailing
— Telephone retailing
— Mail-order retailing

house-to-house retailing

House-to-house retailing is *out-of-store retailing whereby salespeople call on prospective customers in their homes.* Brushes, cosmetics, encyclopedias, kitchen utensils, and vacuum cleaners are sometimes sold in this way. Fuller Brush, Amway, and Avon have built thriving businesses with this approach.

vending-machine retailing

A popular method of marketing such convenience items as soft drinks, snack foods, newspapers, candy, and gum is **vending-machine retailing,** *out-of-store retailing that distributes products to consumers by coin-operated machines.* Even though individual sales are less than a dollar, there are so many vending machines and they are so conveniently placed, total sales are high. In one recent year Americans poured an estimated 3,100 coins per second into vending machines to buy a total of $13.8 billion worth of merchandise.[7]

telephone retailing

Sales by **telephone retailing** are *out-of-store sales initiated by a salesperson who calls prospects or follows up on the customer's response to promotional campaigns.* Increases in printing and mailing costs, combined with the savings and flexibility provided by American Telephone and Telegraph's (AT&T) wide area telephone service (WATS) lines have increased the use of this technique. According to AT&T, all out-of-store retailing sales are growing at approximately 38 percent a year. In one 12-month period the number of retailers who installed toll-free numbers for telephone orders increased by 26 percent.[8]

mail-order retailing

In the form of marketing known as **mail-order retailing,** *out-of-store retailers ask buyers to order products from catalogs or brochures sent directly to their homes, or through order blanks placed in newspapers and magazines.* Some companies, like Clifty Farm (gourmet meats, poultry, and cheese) and Arlene's ("Specializing in fine cutlery by mail since 1955"), distribute most or all of their products through the mail. Others, like Hammacher Schlemmer and I. Magnin & Company, use catalogs to supplement in-store retailing efforts.

The Physical Distribution System

For goods, whether they are intended for the industrial or the consumer market, to reach their target market organizations have to create a physical distribution system. The **physical distribution system** is *the activities that take place as the goods move through the channels.* These activities include warehousing, order processing, transportation, inventory control, and materials handling. Let's discuss each briefly.

physical distribution system

- **Warehousing** is *receiving, identifying, and sorting goods.* The warehouse function can be provided by company-owned (private) or public warehouses. Public warehouses rent the space to other organizations.

  warehousing

- **Order processing** includes *the grouping of the products specified by the customer, and the accompanying paperwork.* The activities include development of the shipping orders, requisitions from inventory, and collection of the physical goods.

  order processing

- **Materials handling** includes *the activities involved in moving materials in-house.* The classification of in-house includes the manufacturer's own plants and warehouses.

  materials handling

- **Transportation** includes *the modes or means of shipping the goods.* There are five major modes: railroads, trucks, waterways, pipelines, and airways. Each has its strengths and weaknesses. Table 12.3 summarizes their operating characteristics.

  transportation

- **Inventory control** includes *the monitoring of the physical inventory of goods, monitoring inventory levels, and minimizing reorder costs.* Inventory control attempts to maximize usable inventory and minimize the costs to the organizations of that inventory.

  inventory control

The Importance of Pricing Strategy

The fourth element of the marketing mix is pricing strategy. Pricing strategy is involved with establishing prices for a product that will return a profit. The pricing decisions made by the organization are critical for the long-range survival of the company. The prices and the volume of goods sold at those prices determine the revenue received by the firm and eventually its profits. If the incorrect price is charged, products can be priced right out of the market.

Pricing decisions are important from the consumer's viewpoint. To a consumer **price** is *the exchange value of a product expressed in monetary terms.* What is a fair or unfair price to a consumer? That question can only be answered if and when the consumer buys the product. Price paid by the consumer is not just for the tangible product features, but also for the intangibles, such as being the first to own a product or having the newest product.

price

Table 12.3 Operating Characteristics of Basic Transportation Modes
Source: Adapted with permission of Macmillan Publishing Company from *Logistical Management*, Second Edition, by Donald J. Bowersox. Copyright © 1978 by Donald J. Bowersox.

Factor	Rank[a]				
	1	2	3	4	5
Speed	Airways	Truck	Railroads	Waterways	Pipeline
Dependability in meeting schedules	Pipeline	Truck	Railroads	Waterways	Airways
Availability in various locations	Truck	Railroads	Airways	Waterways	Pipeline
Cost	Pipeline	Truck	Airways	Railroads	Waterways
Frequency of shipments	Pipeline	Truck	Airways	Railroads	Waterways
Flexibility to handle different products	Waterways	Railroads	Truck	Airways	Pipeline

 Airways

 Pipeline

 Truck

 Waterways

Railroads

[a]1 = high rank, 5 = low rank.

Pricing Objectives

A company develops a pricing strategy to accomplish organizational objectives. A firm can select three general pricing objectives: sales volume objectives, profitability objectives, and other broad objectives.

- Sales volume objectives emphasize growth in sales or growth in market share.
- Profit objectives emphasize the maximizing of profit or earning a specific return on investment.
- Other broad objectives include image objectives developed by prestige pricing, status quo objectives aimed at maintaining good relationships with government agencies and channel members, and objectives focused on developing a perception of fair and ethical pricing.

Determining Prices

How does a marketer determine the price of a product or service? There are three distinct approaches to determining price: the supply and demand approach, the cost-oriented approach, and the market approach. Even though each one is a distinct alternative, in essence they complement each other. Through their use the company is assured that it will cover its costs, make a profit, respond to competition, and adjust for what the consumer thinks the product is worth. In the following pages we will examine each approach.

Supply and Demand Approach

Supply and demand describe the marketplace. Their interaction is an informal, invisible bargaining table where producers and consumers constantly negotiate the amount of a product they are willing to make or consume at a given price. Producers who are able and willing to satisfy consumer demand at a price that both find acceptable will prevail over competitors who are either unable or unwilling to adjust their prices to align with consumers' actions. Let's discuss the elements of supply and demand.

Supply refers to *the quantity of a product that producers are willing to make available at a given price.* When prices are high, producers are willing to supply more. Low prices encourage them to supply less. Part A of Figure 12.3 presents a hypothetical supply curve for hand-held electronic calculators. Notice that at a price of $5 companies are not willing to supply as many calculators as when the price is $25.

supply

Demand is *the quantity of a product that customers are willing to buy at a particular price.* High prices discourage demand, as consumers seek substitutes or simply live without a product rather than pay what producers are asking. In the case of hand-held calculators, customers may elect instead to make mathematical computations mentally or with slide rules or old-fashioned rotary calculators. Low prices, on the other hand, may attract more new customers to the product and may encourage present users to buy more than one. Part B of Figure 12.3 presents a hypothetical demand curve for hand-held electronic calculators. Notice that if a company chose to lower its price from $25 to $5 for a product consumers would demand 20,000 more units.

demand

Figure 12.3 Supply and Demand Curves and Equilibrium Price for Hand-Held Electronic Calculators

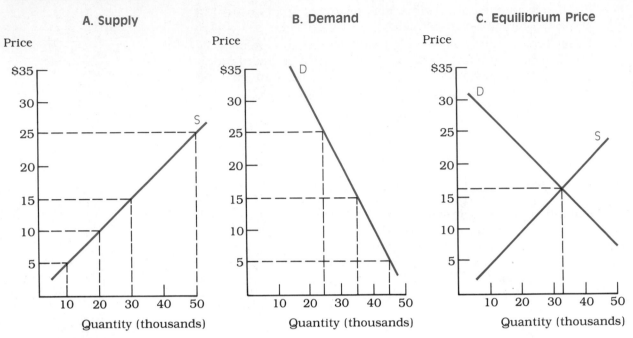

equilibrium price	**Equilibrium price** is *the point where what the consumers are willing to pay is equal to what the producers are willing to accept for a product.* At this point the buyers and sellers have agreed on the equilibrium price. The quantity supplied equals the quantity demanded. Part C of Figure 12.3 shows how the supply curve and the demand curve meet to determine the equilibrium price.

Determining the equilibrium point and price requires adjustment. The initial high prices above equilibrium that encourage producers to make and sell the product drive some consumers away. A surplus of goods results. Manufacturers may respond by lowering the price to get rid of the excess inventory. In doing so they will eventually reach an equilibrium price — an amount that both buyers and sellers find acceptable. The situation also works in reverse. An originally low price below equilibrium attracts many consumers. The resulting scarcity prompts manufacturers to supply more and charge higher prices. The price climbs until an equilibrium is reached.

The interaction of supply and demand in pricing has been very evident in the oil drilling business. With the oil glut, the number of drilling rigs in operation fell substantially. Floating oil rigs could be rented for $30,000 a day, down from $55,000 a day. In addition, the oil drilling products, pipe and tubing, have had price declines of 15 to 20 percent based on the lower drilling demands and higher inventories.[9]

Supply and demand analysis is correct in regard to the overall market for a product, but companies face the problem of setting the price for an individual product. It is difficult to determine in

The farmers market illustrates the influence of supply and demand on pricing.

advance the amount of a product that will be bought at a certain price. Business has tended to adopt cost-oriented approaches.

Cost-Oriented Approach

Some companies adopt the **cost-oriented approach** — *prices are determined by focusing on costs of merchandise, accompanying services, and overhead costs, and then adding an amount for desired profit.* There are two basic approaches: markup pricing and break-even analysis.

    Companies can use **markup pricing** by *calculating all the costs associated with the product and then determining a markup percentage to cover the costs and expected profit.*

$$\text{Markup percentage} = \frac{\text{Selling price} - \text{merchandise cost}}{\text{Selling price}}$$

If all the costs of a product (shipping, overhead, merchandise) are $6 and the selling price is $8, the markup percentage is:

$$\text{Markup percentage} = \frac{8 - 6}{8} = 25\%$$

    Companies also may choose to use **break-even analysis,** *a method of determining the number of units that must be sold at a given price to recover costs and make a profit.* In this approach a firm can compare the results on profits of using different prices.

    In doing break-even analysis the company is comparing total costs with total revenue. **Total costs** are *the total of fixed costs and variable costs.* **Fixed costs** are *costs that remain constant regardless of the number of units produced.* Rent, fire insurance premiums, payments on production equipment, and managers' sal-

cost-oriented approach

markup pricing

break-even analysis

total costs
fixed costs

variable costs

total revenue

break-even point

aries are examples of fixed costs. **Variable costs** are *costs that arise when the first unit is produced and increase with production.* Salespeople's salaries, production workers' wages, raw materials, and energy used to operate production equipment are examples of variable costs. **Total revenue** is *determined by multiplying price times the number of units sold.*

Figure 12.4 shows how fixed costs, variable costs, and total sales revenue combine to fix the **break-even point** — *the point at which sales revenue equals total costs.* Above that point, additional sales result in increasingly larger profits; below it, the firm operates at a loss. In the example, the firm must sell 20,000 calculators at the $16 equilibrium price to break even.

A break-even point (BEP) also can be determined through using the formula:

$$\text{BEP (units)} = \frac{\text{Total fixed costs}}{\text{Price} - \text{variable costs per unit}}$$

A product selling for $15 has total fixed costs of $30,000 and variable costs of $5 per unit. For the company to break even it must sell 3,000 units:

$$\text{BEP} = \frac{30,000}{15 - 5}$$

$$\text{BEP} = \frac{30,000}{10} = 3,000$$

Both cost-oriented approaches must be compared with the market demand for product. In markup pricing the markups desired

Figure 12.4 Determining the Break-Even Point

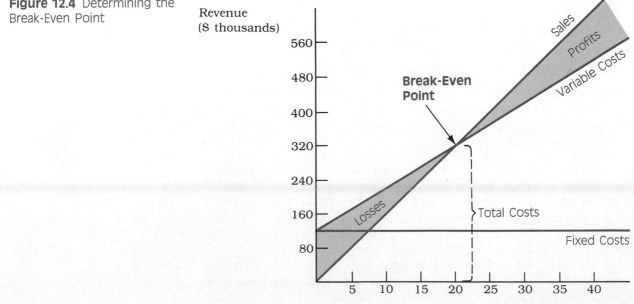

may have to be adjusted based on the consumer's reaction. Companies have to be willing to take less profit. In break-even analysis the company can evaluate different prices and their profit potential. In turn the company will have to use market research to determine what the potential sales volume is at each price.

Market Approach

Another variable to be considered is the impact of the current market prices based on the **market approach,** *a method of price determination that recognizes that variables in the marketplace influence price.* These variables include political factors, the social and cultural environment, individual perceptions, competition, and timing. The market approach has been quite evident in the price cutting in the home computer industry. With a combination of oversupply, imports, and few product differences, the computer manufacturers began to cut prices. In turn all had to live with drastic effects on profits.[10]

market approach

    All these approaches — supply and demand, markup pricing, break-even analysis, and the market approach — need to be combined to determine prices effectively. Each has strengths. If one is used without the other, gaps in information will result. Figure 12.5 illustrates the elements of price determination.

Potential Pricing Strategies

Companies have a number of potential pricing strategies to implement. The choice depends on company objectives, stage of the product life cycle, and competition.

Skimming Price Strategy. A popular pricing strategy for products during the introductory stage of the product life cycle is **skimming** (as in "skimming the cream off milk"), *charging a relatively high*

skimming

Price is influenced by the actions of competitors.

Figure 12.5 Elements of Price Determination

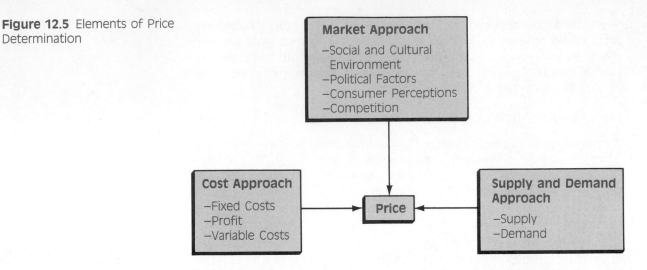

price when the product first appears on the market. Makers of new high-technology products that cost a great deal to invent, perfect, and manufacture want to recover those product development costs as soon as possible, and skimming is a logical policy to follow. Polaroid cameras, Litton microwave ovens, and Atari electronic games are all examples of products whose manufacturers followed a skimming price policy in the past.

penetration pricing

Penetration Pricing Strategy. Another pricing strategy is **penetration pricing,** which is *introducing the product at a low price intended to capture the mass market for the product or service.* The objective is to penetrate as much of the market as quickly as possible and to build brand loyalty. This strategy was followed by Pringle's potato chips (without success) and by Mr. Pibb, a soft drink.

prestige pricing

Prestige Pricing Strategy. Prestige pricing is *setting the price high to relate the image of quality.* Although price and quality are not always related (we do not always get what we pay for), many consumers believe that they are, and producers react accordingly. In fact, some marketers who have experimented with prestige pricing for shopping and specialty goods have found that their unit sales actually increased after raising prices. Rolex uses prestige pricing strategy for its watches. Rolex not only produces a quality product, but also has developed the price-quality image in the consumer's eye. This approach has taken Rolex "out of competition."

follow-the-leader pricing

Follow-the-Leader Price Strategy. Under the philosophy of **follow-the-leader pricing** *companies do not set prices but react to others' prices.* With this approach smaller companies or conservative companies choose to let others determine prices. The plumbing and steel industries, for example, have mature companies with the economic strength and market control to set the pace in product pricing.

This condition generally is referred to as *price leadership* or *administered prices*. Smaller firms, which are content to avoid rocking the boat, will raise their prices along with the industry leaders rather than keep their prices low and risk triggering a price war.

Price Lining Strategy. When a company develops more than one model of product, a price lining strategy can be used. **Price lining** *sets distinct prices for the different models in a product line.* Each model in the line is of different quality and sold at a different price. Sears sells its paints under a price lining strategy; there are distinct qualities of paint with the accompanying prices.

price lining

Relative Pricing Strategy. A **relative pricing** strategy is *a decision to set prices above the competition, below the competition, or to meet the competition.* The company makes a conscious strategy decision to base its pricing decisions on what its direct competitors are doing.

relative pricing

Psychological Pricing Strategy. With **psychological *or* odd pricing** *the seller selects as prices amounts that fall just below a major psychological threshold,* like $29.99, $19.98, or $9.95. Although we realize that those amounts are only pennies short of $30, $20, or $10, they still cushion the blow of round figures. Everything from men's cologne to used cars is priced in this manner.

psychological *or* odd pricing

Multiple-Unit Pricing Strategy. *A practice where a company offers consumers a lower than unit price if a specified number of units are purchased* is **multiple-unit pricing.** For example, products that are six for $1.50 or two for $0.99 are known to be more attractive than items that are $0.30 or $0.50 each.

multiple-unit pricing

Leader Pricing Strategy. Firms involved in retailing may employ **leader pricing,** *selling attractive items at lower than normal prices.* The objective is to increase customer traffic in the store. Low prices on soft drinks, sugar, and coffee may be offered to the consumer as attractive invitations.

leader pricing

Pause and Ponder

Think of a supermarket or superstore you have been in recently. What type of goods were priced using multiple-unit pricing strategy? What specific products were priced as leaders? What examples of psychological, or odd, pricing were evident? Were there examples of prestige pricing in the ice cream section? If so, which brands?

"For heaven's sake, Wilkins."
Source: *The Wall Street Journal.* Reproduced with permission.

The Straight Line

Off-Price Retailing

Welcome to Filene's Basement

Off-pricing has become big business. It probably had its beginning in 1909 when retailer Edward Filene, son of the founder of Filene's of Boston, decided to use the basement as an outlet for leftover goods from manufacturers or other retailers. Today this type of merchandising covers the nation, and sales for 1982 were estimated at approximately $7 billion and are growing at a 35 percent annual rate.

No longer is this segment of the retail industry relegated to the basement. Now there are well-financed chains owned by big department stores that handle designer clothes at significantly reduced retail prices. Off-price merchandisers take advantage of canceled orders, overruns, irregulars, and end-of-season goods. They make their way through the apparel industry intent on buying brand-name and designer-label merchandise at lower than wholesale prices; they also keep their selling expenses down to the discounters' level. Sometimes they can buy their merchandise for one-fourth to one-fifth of the wholesale price.

There are six big off-price chains. The largest is Mervyn's, a division of Dayton Hudson. Then there are Marshall's, owned by Melville Corp.; T. J. Maxx and Hit or Miss, owned by Zayre Corp.; Loehmann's, owned by Associated Dry Goods; and Syms, owned by Sy Syms, which is one of the fastest growing in the business.

Off-price stores are no threat to the discount stores, which are primarily merchants of hard-line goods, such as hardware, appliances, and automobile supplies;

price discounts

Price Discount Strategy. A strategy employed by nearly all organizations in one form or another is **price discounts** to encourage purchases. Price discounts are *deductions allowed from the established price.* Discounts include: cash discounts (prompt payment), trade discounts (given to a channel member by another channel member for performing marketing services), and quantity discounts (buy fifty cases and get a 10 percent discount). A recent innovation in the retail gasoline industry has been the use of cash discounts for consumers paying cash at the pumps rather than using credit cards.

Nonprice Strategy

product differentiation

The potential pricing strategy options that we have just examined place products in head-to-head competition. Rather than engage in a price battle, some companies place an emphasis on nonprice competition through **product differentiation.** *Marketers attempt to have their product perceived by the consumer as different from other, similar products.* Making the product unique in the eyes of the consumer can be accomplished through packaging, creative

however, some of the discount stores like Target and K Mart are using a part of their floor space for off-price clothing. K Mart also has launched its own Designer Depot outlets and has five in business with one hundred scheduled to open in 1984. The thirty-two-store chain of J. Brannan (Just Brand Names) is owned by F. W. Woolworth. Sears and J. C. Penney sell name-brand jeans and sportswear in their stores for less than they bring in department stores.

Manufacturers are in a dilemma. They can make sales and realize huge profits for the short term from off pricers; or at the cost of profit and growth, they can sell exclusively to department stores, continuing their long-term association as well as protecting the integrity of their brands. Even so, the manufacturers realize absolute control of distribution is impossible: there are middlemen who buy up quantities of overruns or irregulars with the stated purpose of sending them out of the country. Instead they sell to off pricers.

It has been predicted that by the end of the decade — maybe sooner — department stores will put more pressure on productivity to cut expenses, which will lead to lower prices. On the other hand, the off pricers are more and more competitive with one another, which means each one will have to spend more on services and surroundings. Eventually the department stores and off pricers may be more or less alike in decor — and price.

For more about off-price retailing, see Donna Steph Hansard, "Off-Price Retailing Reaching Maturity," and "K-Mart Hunting Sites for Off-Price Stores," *Dallas Morning News,* March 21 and 23, 1984; Ann M. Morrison, "The Upshot of Off-Price," *Fortune,* June 13, 1983, pp. 122–130; and Walter McQuade, "The Man Who Makes Millions on Mistakes," *Fortune,* September 6, 1982, pp. 106–116.

promotional strategy, specialized customer service, and other intangibles.

Summary

Distribution strategy is the third element of the marketing mix. Distribution involves (1) the routes goods take and (2) the activities entailed in getting the goods to the consumer — a physical distribution system. The actual routes, or channels, of distribution selected by a manufacturer are determined by a number of variables including the industry practice, type of product, degree of market coverage desired, market segment, ability of a firm to perform the marketing functions, competition, and geographic location of markets.

The two major channels of distribution are for industrial goods and consumer goods. Each type of good has four potential channels to use for distribution. Each one potentially can distribute directly from manufacturer to actual user. In addition, each has potential channels using wholesalers and agents. Only the consumer goods channel utilizes retailers.

The channels of distribution are composed of wholesalers and retailers. Wholesalers sell goods to retailers, to other wholesalers, and to industrial users, but do not sell in significant amounts to the final consumer. Retailers perform the business activities involved in the sale of goods and services to the ultimate consumer or user.

Goods move through the channels by means of a physical distribution system. A physical distribution system includes the activities of warehousing, transportation, order processing, inventory control, and materials handling.

Pricing strategy is the fourth element of the marketing mix. It is involved with establishing prices (exchange value of a product expressed in monetary terms) for a product that will return a profit. These prices are developed to accomplish organization objectives: sales volume, profitability, or other broad objectives.

There are three approaches for determining price: supply and demand, cost-oriented (markup and break-even analysis), and the market approach. While each is a distinct alternative, in essence they all need to be used to determine a price. They complement each other and provide information for the company to cover its costs, make a profit, respond to competition, and adjust for what the consumer thinks the product is worth.

Companies may select different pricing strategies depending on company objectives, the product life cycle, and competition. These potential strategies include skimming, penetration pricing, prestige pricing, follow-the-leader pricing, price lining, relative pricing, psychological, or odd, pricing, leader pricing, and price discounting.

Some companies choose to use a nonprice strategy to avoid price competition. They attempt to differentiate their products in order for consumers to see them as different from other, similar products. This is accomplished by packaging, creative promotional strategy, and specialized customer service.

Key Terms

break-even analysis
break-even point
chain store
channel of distribution
convenience store
cost-oriented approach
demand
department store
discount store
equilibrium price
exclusive distribution
factory outlet
fixed costs
follow-the-leader pricing
house-to-house retailing
hypermarket
independent store

intensive distribution
inventory control
leader pricing
mail-order retailing
market approach
markup pricing
materials handling
multiple-unit pricing
order processing
penetration pricing
physical distribution system
prestige pricing
price
price discounts
price lining
product differentiation
psychological or odd pricing

relative pricing
retailers
selective distribution
skimming
specialty store
supermarket
superstore
supply
telephone retailing
total costs
total revenue
transportation
variable costs
vending-machine retailing
warehousing
wholesalers

For Review and Discussion

1. Evaluate the statement "A firm can have the best products in the world, people can know about them and want them, but all this will be useless if they cannot get the products when and where they want them."

2. What variables influence the choice of distribution channels?

3. What is meant by intensive, selective, and exclusive distribution?

4. What four channels are available for industrial goods? When would each be selected?

5. Why would a manufacturer choose to use direct distribution to the ultimate consumer?

6. Why would maufacturers choose to use a channel that includes both an agent and a wholesaler?

7. Distinguish between a wholesaler and a retailer.

8. List six types of in-store retailers. For each type identify a store in your community that fits the category.

9. What type of goods normally are sold by mail-order retailing?

10. What is the difference between volume and profitability price objectives? Why would a company set volume objectives rather than profitability objectives?

11. Explain how supply and demand interact to arrive at an equilibrium point and price.

12. When markup and break-even analysis are used to determine price, what important factor(s) is not included? How can a company correct this problem?

13. What type of information does the market approach to pricing provide management? How does this complement the cost-oriented and supply and demand approaches?

14. Is there any difference between skimming price strategy and prestige price strategy? If so, what is it?

15. What is the advantage of adopting a price lining strategy?

Applications

Case 12.1 Distribution Dilemma

Ira Tevlekian had begun a second career 8 months ago. He had retired from his job as a high school history teacher to turn his hobby into a money-making business.

Ira had a green thumb. Out of a natural curiosity he had studied plants and gardening over the years. His roses, gardenias, azaleas, and even vegetables had been the biggest and healthiest in the neighborhood.

On one of his trips to California Ira had seen one of the "California fads," as he called it — topiary — wire frames in the shape of stars and animals filled with peat moss and covered with green leaves. A living decoration at its best.

Ira had gone through the growing pains. He had perfected the wirebending process to create pigs, bears, dolphins, giraffes, and rabbits. He had:

- Subcontracted with a local church group to stuff and plant the animals
- Spent hours with the local agricultural agent identifying a spray to prevent fungus
- Acquired stocks of ribbons and plastic eyes to make the animals more lifelike
- Created a promotional theme titled "Adopt Your Own Friendly Pet"

- Designed a tag that carried directions for the care and feeding of the animals
- Built a shed in his backyard to store the animals until they were sold

Despite all these accomplishments, Ira was facing a major crisis in the growth of his business: distribution strategy. He had spent long hours loading his car with his creations and making calls on florists, hotel gift shops, and hospital gift shops. This channel did not produce the anticipated volume of sales and was time consuming.

In an attempt to solve his problem Ira talked with friends, business acquaintances, and his banker. They gave him four suggestions:

- Sell directly to the consumer through major magazine ads and catalog sales
- Contract with wholesalers in the cities across the country
- Contact large grocery and nursery chains to sell through retail outlets
- Contact discount retailers directly

Questions

1. What type of products are Ira's animals?
2. What channel or channels of distribution would you recommend? Why?

Case 12.2 The Pizza Barons

"I just don't know how much longer this can go on. I'm just barely covering my costs . . . another week of no profits. I don't see how she can keep it up."

The "she" referred to by Lenny Benjamin was Mara Whitney, the owner of Mara's Pizza Palace. Lenny, the owner of Len's Pizzeria, was the elder statesman in town. He had been in business in Northcut for 25 years serving quality eastern style pizza.

Mara had arrived in the town of 2,000 just 6 months ago and had launched her pizza venture with ads featuring:

- "Thick crust pizza."
- "Pizza by the slice."
- "Buy a pizza, get the next smaller size free."

Lenny responded with:

- "Free soft drink refills."
- "Double cheese, double sauce for the same price."
- "Balloons and prizes for the kids."

The two "pizza barons" were the talk of the town. The residents could not wait to see what strategy would be used next to attract them. Soon Mara added a salad bar and an all-you-can-eat pizza lunch for only $2.95. Len countered with "homemade" lasagna and ravioli and designated Monday (a notoriously slow night) half-price pizza night. Mara began to offer specials on certain pizzas. The super deluxe with everything was *always* half-price as were several others.

Regardless of the action taken, the results were the same: the pizza baron with the lowest prices, specials, or bonus drew the crowd. The parking lot of the other was empty — except for loyal customers. On another "empty night" Lenny remarked, "I guess this town's not big enough for both of us."

Questions

1. Identify specific examples of how price setting was influenced by supply and demand, break-even analysis, and the market approach.
2. Cite specific examples of:
   a. leader pricing strategy
   b. multiple-unit pricing strategy
   c. follow-the-leader strategy
3. What specific examples are there of nonprice competition?

Sales and Product Management

Career Capsule

Sales with Atlantic Richfield

Personal selling at Atlantic Richfield Company offers challenging, rewarding opportunities. This company, which has eleven firms under its corporate umbrella, produces various petroleum, mineral, and chemical products and pursues ventures in synthetic fuels and solar energy.

The company seeks graduates with a general background in business studies or liberal arts. Once they are hired, the company's program of on-the-job training paves the way for success by providing information on products, personal selling techniques, customers' needs, and how to prepare and execute a marketing plan.

Atlantic Richfield usually sells its broad line of products to industrial users and wholesalers. Consequently, the company requires applicants for sales positions to have an assertive nature, sound communication skills, and a liking for working closely with others.

Management, by surveying its present sales staff, developed a list of how a sales representative's time is spent:

1. Selling takes up 63 percent of the work.
2. Administering is 10 percent of the work.
3. Analyzing is 8 percent of the work.
4. Consulting is 7 percent of the work.
5. Supervising and managing entails 5 percent.
6. Developing requires 5 percent of the time.

Because selling consumes more than 60 percent of a sales representative's time and is considered of paramount importance, the company further clarifies what this task entails in a fourteen-point list:

1. Calling on existing customers
2. Maintaining customer goodwill through regular contact
3. Reacting to customer complaints and questions
4. Negotiating with customers
5. Calling on prospective customers
6. Presenting proposals to customers
7. Solving service problems for customers
8. Monitoring delivery of products to customers
9. Expediting the delivery of products to customers
10. Soliciting business by phone
11. Keeping current with technical or production knowledge necessary to support sales activities
12. Suggesting new or improved ways to meet customers' needs
13. Communicating customer needs to research and development or production people
14. Projecting future levels of customer demand

Whether you begin in retail sales, commercial and distributor sales, or industrial sales, promotions would place you on the marketing staff or in various sales or marketing management positions, including sales supervision, regional or district sales management, or marketing management.

Product Management with General Foods

"General Foods is known for marketing skills and leadership, for

355

the high value it places on the marketing function, for looking on marketing as a source of future general managers. It's a company that places a premium on individual initiative and results achieved. It intends to be the best at what it does and seeks to hire people with the same commitment to excellence." That is what General Foods says in a recruiting brochure.

Interested so far? If so, you, like many other marketing-oriented college students, may build a satisfying career with this major food marketer. The firm's $8.4 billion in annual sales earned it a 41st place in *Fortune*'s 1984 list of the top 500 companies. It has almost 70,000 employees, 40 percent of whom work outside the United States in production facilities in seventeen countries. Its products are sold worldwide in more than one hundred nations.

College graduates who pursue a career in product management with this firm can expect to grow considerably through on-the-job training. You may become involved with marketing plans for a new product being test marketed, or you may work with a mature one that has become a household word — Jell-O gelatin dessert, Bird's Eye frozen foods, or Shake 'n Bake seasoned coating mix, among others.

Soon after employment, new graduates are made assistant product managers at the firm's headquarters in White Plains, New York. In that position they are responsible for market forecasting, budgeting, coordinating marketing with production planning, carrying out promotional campaigns, and performing various other activities essential to the success of their assigned product. Being highly market oriented, General Foods requires most assistant product managers to work briefly in one of the company's sales districts. There they receive firsthand experience in dealing with the retailers that buy from General Foods and learning how the company's sales force operates.

Continued personal development will be an integral part of your career at General Foods. The company's programs and activities expand and amplify the skills and talents you acquired in college. Although on-the-job training is a major ingredient in the firm's employee development program, General Foods also provides in-house workshops that cover such topics as communications, business analysis, making sales presentations, and improving supervisory skills. There are also training seminars on topics such as consumer promotions and the role of creativity in advertising. Like leaders in other industries, General Foods will reimburse your tuition for job-related college courses you take.

The firm's promotional climate is highly flexible; employees who emerge as sound decision makers and succeed as assistant product managers can expect to be recognized and rewarded with advancement into such positions as product manager, product group manager, or marketing manager.

At General Foods, marketing is a route to top management. The general managers of various foreign subsidiaries as well as an associate director of corporate planning are all alumni of the firm's product management program. The same is true of most general managers of its many divisions. If you are seeking a marketing career that includes recognition, advancement, personal growth, and challenge, you will find that General Foods' product management training programs serves these up in generous portions.

Part

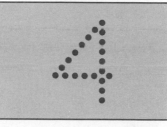

Finance and Information Systems

Money and Financial Institutions

Chapter Outline

Chapter Objectives

After studying this chapter, you should be able to:

1. Describe the functions of money in a society and list the items that make up the money supply of the United States.
2. Contrast the two causes of inflation and discuss how the Consumer Price Index monitors it.
3. Summarize the operations of a commercial bank.
4. Evaluate the role of the Federal Reserve System and discuss its organization and operation.
5. List and evaluate the devices that the Federal Reserve employs to regulate the money supply.
6. Comment on the need for the FDIC and describe its role in building public confidence in the banking system.
7. Summarize the status of interstate banking.
8. Define the three kinds of thrift institutions and compare their operations.

The marvel of banks in relation to money — the wonder of creating deposits or issuing notes — is suspended on one silken thread. The requirement is that depositors or noteholders come in decently small numbers for the hard currency that the bank is under its obligation to pay. If all come at once, the bank cannot pay. When the thought spreads that the bank cannot pay, then, often in much haste, all come. When that occurs, the deposits or notes serving previously as money cease to be available.
— *John Kenneth Galbraith, economist*

Up Front

Paul A. Volcker

Public Service Is Noble Work for the Head of the Fed

Pragmatic, competent, and intelligent. An expert's expert on monetary policy. Outstanding scholar. Brilliant economist. These words accurately describe Paul A. Volcker, chairman of the Board of Governors of the Federal Reserve System. As the most powerful central banker in history, Volcker has earned an outstanding reputation by steering the United States through one of its most distressing economic periods since the Great Depression.

The son of a Teaneck, New Jersey, city manager, Volcker distinguished himself scholastically throughout high school and college. After graduating summa cum laude from Princeton University in 1949, he accepted a scholarship to Harvard University's Graduate School of Public Administration to study government and economics. After earning his Master of Arts degree, Volcker worked briefly for the Treasury Department in Washington and then did postgraduate study as a Rotary Foundation fellow at the London School of Economics.

Volcker had worked as a summer intern at the Federal Reserve Bank of New York in 1949 and 1950. The experience so impressed him that in 1952 he returned to become a research as-

sistant on the bank's economic staff. His exceptional competency and astute judgment attracted the attention of top officers at Chase Manhattan Bank, who offered him a job as financial economist in 1957. He worked for Chase for 5 years, leaving in 1962 to accept President Kennedy's appointment as deputy under secretary for monetary affairs in the Treasury Department.

Volcker's distinguished performance in a series of appointive positions earned him the Arthur S. Flemming Award as one of the ten most outstanding young men in government service and the Treasury Department's own Exceptional Service Award. In 1975 he was appointed president of the New York Federal Reserve Bank, and four years later took a $58,500 reduction in pay to become chairman of the Fed for $57,500 at the request of President Carter.

When Volcker took over the Fed inflation seemed almost beyond control. Prices were rising at an annual rate of 13 percent, and bringing them in check demanded all the wisdom and experience he could summon. Action was not long in coming. Under Volcker's sure-handed guidance, the Fed began reducing the na-

barter system

Most nations can point to a time in their history when they operated on the **barter system,** *an economic system in which two parties trade certain goods and services that each needs to survive.* The farmer would exchange a cow for seed, the cobbler would swap shoes

tion's supply of money and credit. This economic emergency brake worked, as Volcker knew it would; by midsummer of 1982 inflation declined to less than 5 percent. Volcker's action could hardly be called an unqualified success, however, because it triggered a predictable and severe recession characterized by double digit unemployment, soaring interest rates, and a record-setting epidemic of business bankruptcies. Then in July of 1982, Volcker demonstrated one of various qualities that have earned him admiration, the quality of flexibility. The Fed began loosening the reins, pouring additional money into a floundering economy to bring it back from the precipice of a full-scale depression. By 1984 unemployment had declined, businesses were spending more to expand facilities and renew equipment, and sales of expensive consumer goods such as automobiles showed a healthy increase. Public confidence in government leadership and economic recovery seemed generally high.

The Fed's actions to avert a full-scale national economic crisis and to restore and maintain economic stability were essentially the actions of Paul Volcker himself. And Volcker undoubtedly re-alizes, perhaps more than anyone else, that his battle to ensure economic stability never will be finished. His first-term decisions provoked extensive controversy and extensive debate, as economic decisions inevitably do, and the ultimate effects of several actions may not materialize in the general economy until 1985. Nevertheless, supporters and critics seem to agree that Volcker is the most eminently qualified person to guide the Fed through these highly volatile and unprecedented economic times. A poll of top managers in large corporations revealed that 97 percent believed Volcker would exercise the necessary leadership to steer the nation to better economic health, and 90 percent of higher managers in medium-sized businesses echoed the same sentiments. The opportunity is clearly his, as Ronald Reagan reappointed him to a second term in June 1983. For Paul Volcker the man, this means continued commuting to his home in New York to see his wife. But for Paul Volcker the public servant, it means assurance that he can continue his unselfish work as the nation's foremost banker and attempt to leave his country a unique legacy indeed: economic stability.

For more about Paul A. Volcker, see Tim Carrington, "Volcker Apparently Blocks Effort To Cut Fed Authority Over Banks," *The Wall Street Journal*, January 26, 1984, p. 35; "Volcker Fan Club," *The Wall Street Journal*, January 10, 1984, p. 35; Peter W. Bernstein, "The Perils of Paul: Volcker's Scary Choices," *Fortune*, July 25, 1983, p. 36; Harry Anderson, "Volcker: Man for the Moment," *Newsweek*, June 27, 1983, p. 66; John Brecher, "Why He Wanted the Job — Again," *Newsweek*, June 27, 1983, p. 67; "Why the White House Likes Volcker Better Now," *Business Week*, June 27, 1983, p. 24; and "Washington Debate: Paul Volcker's Report Card," *Business Week*, May 2, 1983, p. 114.

for flour, and the country doctor, with a service in great demand, could trade medical care for practically everything.

This system, which flourished while we were living in agrarian societies, grew awkward and obsolete as households became less self-sufficient and specialization arrived with the Industrial Revolution. Given enough time and economic growth, every society eventually requires some form of money.

money

Money is *any object that a group of people uses to pay its debts and buy the goods and services that it needs.* In addition to money, however, an advanced economic system needs financial institutions that regulate demand for that money and make it possible for organizations and individuals to save, borrow, and transfer money as they carry out daily transactions. In this chapter we will examine money and the various institutions, such as commercial banks, the Federal Reserve System, the Federal Deposit Insurance Corporation, and the major thrift institutions, that affect its flow within our economy.

Putting Money in Perspective

What Money Does

A society's money functions as a medium of exchange, a measure of value, and a store of value, as is shown in Figure 13.1. To do so it must be relatively scarce and widely accepted. Objects that are used as money also must be durable, portable, and divisible if they are to serve people conveniently over a long period of time.

A Medium of Exchange. Money makes it easier for us to accomplish the exchange functions of marketing that you learned about in Chapter 10 — buying and selling. Although we sometimes think of money only as the bills and coins we carry in our wallets and pockets, certain societies and cultures have used some of the following unusual objects as money:

- Bison robes
- Bird-of-paradise feathers
- Bricks of tea
- Woodpecker scalps
- Manga bird feathers
- Elephant-tail hair

A Measure of Value. A society's money is a universal measure of worth. The value of everything from livestock to common stock can be expressed in a common denominator: money. This makes communication infinitely easier, because the parties to a transaction can express worth in the same units.

A Store of Value. We can convert our labor and any products we own into money of a certain value and store it in that form indefinitely. People regularly store their value in such other objects as real estate,

Figure 13.1 Functions of Money

precious metals, gems, and rare coins, but these are not as *liquid* (easily disposed of) as money. If you have stored your value in nonmonetary objects and want to purchase something like a stereo, you will have to convert those valued objects into money. This process can be costly and time consuming; you may need to have the items appraised to establish their value, and then find a buyer. Money is the most liquid asset of all — easily transferred from hand to hand.

It should be obvious, of course, that money must have a relatively stable value before people will be willing to store very much of their wealth in it. When the value of money declines, people rush to convert it to something whose value will hold steady or increase as time passes.

Money in the United States

The money supply of the United States consists of three items: coins and paper (collectively called *currency*) and checking accounts. Federal law has declared coins and paper money to be *legal tender*, which means they must be accepted when tendered as payment for debts.

Paper money takes three days to print — one day for the front, one day for the back, and one for the overprinting of such data as the serial number and the seal of the Federal Reserve Bank that will issue it. The Bureau of Engraving and Printing produces approximately 1.6 billion $1 bills each year.

The mechanics of printing and replacing paper money poses problems. Constant passing from hand to hand wears out $1 bills in 18 months. Larger denominations last slightly longer. Commercial banks return worn, damaged, and dirty bills to the Federal Reserve Bank in their district, where the Treasury Department exchanges the bills for new ones and destroys them. Damaged coins are melted down and recycled by the U.S. Assay Office.

check *or* demand deposit

A **check *or* demand deposit,** the third component of the United States money supply, is *a bank depositor's written order instructing the bank to pay a certain sum to a third party.* The bank, which owes the deposited money to the customer, provides this third-party payment, usually for a fee or service charge. Although they are not legal tender, 90 percent of all money spent is in the form of checks. Three of every four persons in America has a checking account.

Coins, which are one form of currency, must be counted, wrapped, and bagged many times throughout their lives.

A **savings account *or* time deposit** is *a sum of money, deposited with a bank, that cannot be withdrawn by writing a check.* Because the bank may require advance notice before withdrawal, time deposits are not considered part of the money supply.

savings account *or* time deposit

Inflation

Inflation, which is *a decrease in the value of a society's money,* affects both individual and business purchasing power. If it becomes acute, the public opinion of money's value erodes and economic chaos may result. Inflation has two general causes.

inflation

Demand-pull inflation *occurs when producers raise prices in response to strong consumer demand.* Items subject to demand-pull inflation have relatively inelastic demand. When market segment members appear willing to pay a higher price or view the product as a specialty item, entrepreneurs are tempted to charge more and reap a higher return for their risk. In essence, consumer tolerance encourages producers to raise prices, almost as at an auction.

demand-pull inflation

Cost-push inflation, the second type, *occurs when producers pass rising labor, materials, and other costs on to consumers by increasing prices.* Sometimes called *market power inflation,* this is a reaction to escalating costs. American Telephone and Telegraph management estimated that consumers would pay at least $1.9 billion between 1983 and 1987 in costs associated with its breakup into seven independent regional telephone companies. Much of this money will be spent on equipment changes that will allow competing long-distance service firms like MCI Corporation and GTE-Sprint equal access to local telephone customers who do not have push-button phones.[1] In the past 2 decades inflation has affected every country in the world. One of the major causes of this inflation has been escalating energy costs, a cost-push cause of inflation.

cost-push inflation

Inflation leads to witch-hunting: management, labor, and consumers look for someone to blame. Management may accuse labor of a thirst for higher wages and more costly benefits, while labor criticizes management's lust for steadily increasing profits, and consumers complain even louder as they pay even more. In essence, everyone is responsible for inflation to some degree. This does not ease the intense pressure it places on corporate and household budgets, however. Figure 13.2 shows how inflation has affected purchasing power in the last 10 years.

The Consumer Price Index

The **Consumer Price Index (CPI),** computed by the U.S. Department of Labor's Bureau of Labor Statistics, is *a figure that measures changes in purchasing power and the rate of inflation by expressing today's prices in 1967 dollars.* Prices for that base year represent 100 percent, and current prices are references to them. A CPI of 290, for example, means that consumers pay an average of $29 today for items that cost $10 in 1967.

Consumer Price Index (CPI)

Look at what inflation has done to the purchasing power of paychecks in the last decade and you'll know why many Americans feel that they've been working on a treadmill. What most would call necessities of life — a car, gasoline, electricity, and shelter, to name a few — required far more working time to acquire in 1982 than they did ten years earlier. The typical manufacturing worker, for instance, needed to work almost thirteen hours a month just to pay ordinary electric and natural gas bills, compared with about seven hours in 1972. Against these setbacks, most foods took slightly less working time to buy, as did a movie ticket and a six-pack of beer. On the whole, however, the buying power of the average factory worker's paycheck has fallen every year since 1978.

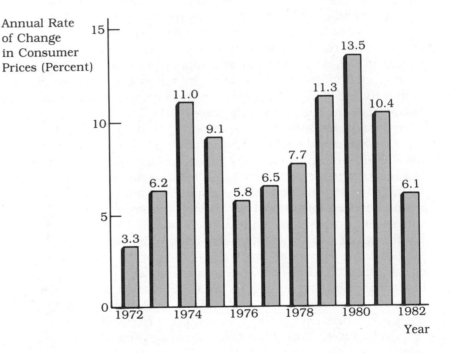

There are actually two Consumer Price Indices. The broadest one, CPI-U, tracks the impact of inflation on all urban consumers — approximately 80 percent of all citizens. The other index, CPI-W, assembles data on the purchasing power of wage earners and clerical employees and disregards self-employed and professional persons.

Early in 1983 the U.S. Department of Labor altered its method of calculating the CPI-U. One change involved adjusting the home ownership component so figures would more accurately reflect the true cost of shelter. The present CPI-U now disregards interest charges, real estate taxes, and other satellite costs of home ownership. The weights assigned to the 382 items involved in calculating this gauge of purchasing power also were adjusted. Gasoline, food, and clothing, for example, now receive greater emphasis.

The CPI is the most popular measure of how inflation dilutes buying power. The CPI-W is also a standard for computing increased

Impact on Paychecks Varies Widely

Figure 13.2, continued

Estimated Worktime Required to Purchase:	1972*	1982*
New home (median price)	42 months	47 months
New car (average price)	25 weeks	28 weeks
Washing machine	66 hr., 16 min.	55 hr., 18 min.
Hospital room, semiprivate, per day	16 hr., 37 min.	23 hr., 54 min.
Week's groceries (family of 4)	12 hr., 3 min.	11 hr., 46 min.
Motor tuneup	8 hr., 9 min.	8 hr., 34 min.
Month's electric bill (750 kwh)	4 hr., 20 min.	6 hr., 34 min.
Month's gas bill (100 therms)	2 hr., 42 min.	6 hr., 23 min.
Permanent wave	4 hr., 3 min.	3 hr., 48 min.
Tank of gasoline (18 gallons)	1 hr., 40 min.	2 hr., 43 min.
Physician's office visit	2 hr., 7 min.	2 hr., 37 min.
Man's haircut	43 min.	38 min.
Coffee (2 pounds)	29 min.	36 min.
Dry cleaning, man's two-piece suit	28 min.	31 min.
Movie admission, adult	32 min.	25 min.
Round steak (1 pound)	23 min.	21 min.
Six-pack of beer	22 min.	18 min.
Pork chops (1 pound)	20 min.	17 min.
Bacon (1 pound)	15 min.	15 min.
Toothpaste (8 ounces)	16 min.	15 min.
Sugar (5 pounds)	11 min.	12 min.
Milk (1 gallon)	11 min.	8 min.
Potatoes (5 pounds)	7 min.	7 min.
Tuna (6.5-ounce can)	7 min.	7 min.
Eggs, dozen	9 min.	6 min.
Cigarettes, pack	7 min.	6 min.
Chicken (1 pound)	6 min.	5 min.
White bread (1 pound)	4 min.	4 min.

* Figures are based on average hourly wage in manufacturing — $3.82 in 1972 and $8.50 in 1982, and assume a forty-hour workweek.

benefits to military and civil-service retirees and persons receiving social security payments. In addition, labor-management contracts covering more than 8.5 million workers tie wage increases to this measure of inflation. Each 1 percent increase in the CPI triggers approximately $1 billion in increased payments to these groups.

Pause and Ponder

How have you adjusted your personal budget and living habits to defend against the declining purchasing power of your dollars? What offensive tactics can you use to increase your money-earning ability and put you ahead of the game?

Commercial Banks

What Do Banks Do?

commercial bank

A **commercial bank** is *a profit-making corporation that accepts customers' deposits and lends them out to businesses and individual borrowers.* These banks accept both demand deposits (checking accounts) and time deposits (savings accounts), paying interest on the latter. Since December 31, 1980, both banks and savings and loan associations (which we will discuss later in this chapter) have been permitted to offer customers interest-bearing checking accounts called *NOW* accounts (for "negotiable order of withdrawal").

"And if your loan payment is in the mail, please disregard these insults."
Source: From *The Wall Street Journal*, permission Cartoon Features Syndicate.

Commercial banks earn most of their income from interest on loans, but they also invest large amounts in interest-bearing U.S. government securities. The balances in depositors' accounts are actually debts that the bank must pay at some future date, and, as John Kenneth Galbraith pointed out in the epigraph to this chapter, a bank could have difficulty paying depositors if many of them demanded their money at the same time.

Given their role as moneylenders, commercial banks occupy an influential position in our economic system. Their widespread lending operations can act as an accelerator or a brake on inflation and profoundly affect growth trends and public attitudes nationwide.

prime rate of interest

Commercial banks give their largest, most secure corporate borrowers a **prime rate of interest,** traditionally defined as *a lower rate of interest than that charged to most borrowers.* Although this definition has some validity, the concept of a prime rate has lost credibility within the last several years. A House Banking Committee survey of the nation's ten largest banks disclosed that each regularly

Commercial banks provide essential savings, checking, and lending services for individuals and businesses alike.

lent money at less than its publicized prime rate. That figure often was merely a point at which potential big borrowers could begin interest-rate negotiations. A Federal Reserve Board study found that more than half the large business loans made by several New York banks in 1 month were at less than the prime rate — by an average of 4.26 percent.

This discrepancy implies that the prime rate is a benchmark, or general guideline, and not the lowest rate available. In the survey, Chase Manhattan Corporation told the Federal Reserve Board, "We do not believe . . . that it is appropriate to consider our 'prime commercial lending rate' to be either the 'lowest' rate or a 'preferential' rate."[2]

Certificates of Deposit

Commercial banks also issue **certificates of deposit (CDs),** *bank obligations that pay higher interest than regular savings accounts because the depositor agrees to leave the money on deposit for a certain length of time.* Depositors who need the funds before the certificates mature may cash them in, but the bank will pay a lower rate of interest than if they had been held until maturity. Certificates of deposit are sold in denominations from $100 to $100,000 and up, generally for terms of 6 months to 5 years.

certificates of deposit (CDs)

The Federal Reserve System

Commercial banks keep only a small percentage of deposits on reserve, lending the rest to borrowers. Unusually heavy withdrawals, therefore, can exhaust a bank's cash, no matter how sound its loans might be. When this happens and word spreads among the bank's depositors, there can be a run on the bank with most or all depositors demanding their money at once, causing the bank to fail.

One such panic, in 1907, led Congress to pass the **Federal Reserve Act of 1913,** *a law that created the Federal Reserve System, commonly called the Fed, and made it responsible for managing the nation's supply of money and credit.* The Fed, which has been called "the nation's banker," monitors the demand for money and credit nationwide and regulates their availability so that managed, responsible economic growth can occur.

Federal Reserve Act of 1913

Organization and Membership

The Federal Reserve System consists of a seven-member Board of Governors, appointed by the president and confirmed by the Senate. Each member serves a 14-year term, but terms are staggered so that one seat is vacant every 2 years. As Figure 13.3 shows, the Fed has established a dozen Federal Reserve Banks in strategic parts of the country. These serve as "bankers' banks" for commercial banks that belong to the Federal Reserve System.

Growth in the home construction industry, like all other industries, is affected by changes in the Fed's monetary policy.

Commercial banks may be chartered by the federal government or by the states in which they are founded. Those with federal charters are called *national banks* and must belong to the Federal Reserve System. You can identify one by the word *national* in its name or the letters *N.A.* (meaning nationally associated) appearing after it. State-chartered commercial banks, called *state banks*, may

Figure 13.3 Federal Reserve Banks and Districts

— Boundaries of Federal Reserve Districts
• Federal Reserve Bank cities
✳ Board of Governors of the Federal Reserve System

* The San Francisco District includes Alaska and Hawaii.

join the Federal Reserve System if they wish, and most of the large ones have done so.

Approximately one-third of the nation's 15,000 commercial banks belong to the Fed and they hold nearly 71 percent of all commercial bank deposits. Nearly 1,000 of these Fed members are state chartered; more than 9,000 state-chartered banks are not members. Commercial banks operate under a dual banking system: they must comply with both federal and state banking laws and regulatory agencies. The Fed sets the maximum interest rates that member banks can pay on time deposits, approves mergers, and establishes specific bank management rules that its members must observe.

Why Join the Federal Reserve System?

Commercial banks join the Federal Reserve System for several reasons, chiefly for the privilege of borrowing from the Fed to meet temporary cash shortages, and to have access to the Fed's system of collecting checks written by depositors. Federal Reserve membership allows a bank to borrow from its district bank when depositors make heavy withdrawals — for Christmas spending, to pay income taxes, or to finance summer vacations, for example — thus depleting the bank's cash supply. In addition, the Federal Reserve "banker's banks" have a nationwide check-collection network that speeds a check's trip through the banking system. The Federal Reserve Bank of Minneapolis estimates that more than half of all checks are mailed to other cities and must be returned to the bank on which they are drawn through the banking system. The Fed's check-clearing service saves member banks the time, cost, and effort of sorting and mailing checks to their home banks. Instead, the Federal Reserve Banks perform this service, processing some 35 billion checks per year.[3]

The Bank Examiner

To confirm that state-chartered member banks are following regulations, bank examiners from the Federal Reserve System may arrive unannounced and audit (inspect) their records and management practices. National banks, which receive their charters from the federal government, are examined in the same manner by the Comptroller of the Currency. Examiners visit at least once a

Pause and Ponder

The Fed often employs recent college graduates to become members of its examining teams. Why would a bank examiner's job provide good preparation for a high-level position in commercial bank management?

year, and may stay from 1 week to several months, depending on the bank's size.

Regulating the Money Supply

As the legally mandated regulator of the nation's money supply, the Fed governs the availability of money — and therefore the rate of inflation — with three complementary devices:

1. Its own open market operations (buying and selling United States government securities on the open market)
2. The reserve requirements it mandates for member banks
3. The discount rate it sets for loans to member banks

These tools are employed simultaneously to increase or decrease the amount of money available for borrowing and, therefore, spending.

open market operations

Open Market Operations. Using **open market operations,** the most flexible money supply adjuster, *the Fed buys or sells billions of dollars of United States government securities daily through securities dealers in New York City.* It works in the following manner.

When the Fed wants to decrease the money supply, it sells government securities. The money that the purchasing dealers pay is kept out of circulation by the Fed, and eventually borrowing declines and interest rates rise as lenders find that there is less money to meet potential borrowers' requests.

When the Fed wants to increase the money supply, it buys government securities. Money is created the moment the Fed pays the dealers, and it filters down into the general economy as the dealers pay it to the businesses and individuals whose government securities they sold.* Figure 13.4 summarizes the effect of open market operations.

There are three types of United States government securities: Treasury bills, Treasury notes, and Treasury bonds. Examples of each, along with descriptions of their major characteristics, appear in Figure 13.5 on pages 374–375.

The securities in Figure 13.5 represent the debt of the United States government, money it has borrowed to pay its bills and purchase goods and services. These securities are considered the safest of all investments because they are backed by the government's authority to levy taxes. This ensures that they will be paid when they mature and that interest payments will be made in the meantime.

reserve requirement

Reserve Requirements. The Fed stipulates a **reserve requirement,** *a percentage of deposits that member banks must retain on deposit within their own walls or at the Federal Reserve Bank in their*

---

*Critics point out that the Fed's ability to incur debts and pay them back with interest by printing money fuels inflation. As new money enters circulation in this way, the money issued earlier immediately decreases in value.

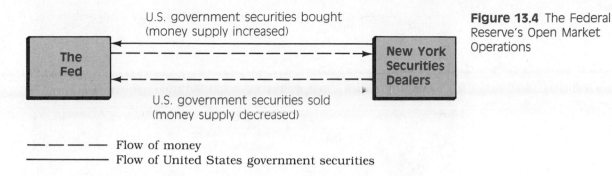

Figure 13.4 The Federal Reserve's Open Market Operations

district. When the Fed raises the reserve requirement it tightens the money supply, making loans more costly because member banks must hold a greater percentage of deposits on reserve than before. Lowering the reserve requirement instantly frees some existing reserves for lending. The Fed rarely uses this device to regulate the money supply, however. It is an extreme measure — like driving a tack with a sledgehammer. Changing the reserve requirement just a fraction of a percent liberates or restricts millions of dollars within the commercial banking system, because as was noted earlier, members of the Fed hold approximately 71 percent of the nation's total money supply.

Member banks earn no interest on required reserves, and the Fed may charge a penalty to members whose reserves fall below the required level. Reserve requirements, which vary according to a member bank's deposits, range from 7 to 16 1/4 percent on demand deposits and 3 percent for time deposits.

This reserve requirement, when coupled with open market operations, has a considerable multiplier effect on the money supply. Let's assume, for example, that the Fed wishes to increase the money supply and buys just $1 million in government securities on the open market while the reserve requirement is 10 percent. The effect at each stage as this money is deposited and lent by a succession of banks is illustrated in Table 13.1 on page 376.

The Discount Rate. As was mentioned earlier, Fed members may borrow from their district banks when depositors' heavy withdrawals endanger a bank's required reserves. The **discount rate** is *the interest rate that the Fed charges member banks for loans.* Usually this loan privilege is used only in emergencies, so the discount rate plays a relatively minor role in regulating the money supply.

discount rate

The Federal Deposit Insurance Corporation

Between 1921 and 1933, more than half the commercial banks in the United States failed; 9,000 of them after 1929 alone. This prompted Congress to pass the Banking Act of 1933 and create the

Figure 13.5 Treasury Bills, Notes, and Bonds

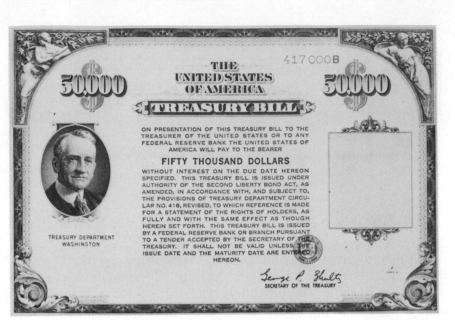

Treasury Bills

3-, 6-, 9-, or 12-month maturity. Often bought by banks and large corporations as a short-term investment.

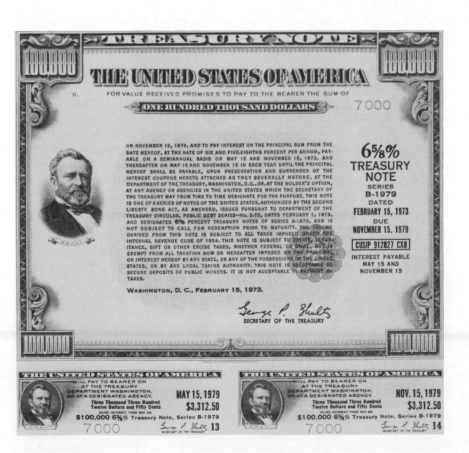

Treasury Notes

1- to 7-year maturity. Coupons must be detached and mailed in every 6 months for owner to collect an interest payment.

Figure 13.5, continued

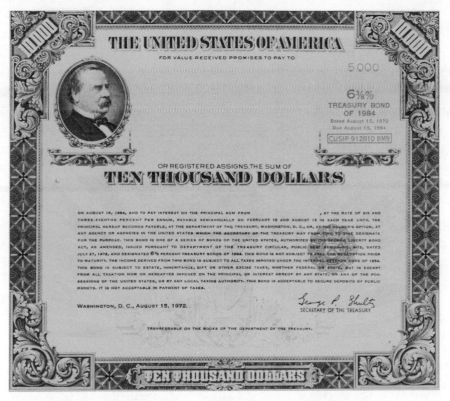

Treasury Bonds
Mature in 7 years or more. Interest is paid through coupons, as with Treasury notes.

Federal Deposit Insurance Corporation (FDIC), *a public corporation with a threefold purpose: to build confidence in the nation's banking system, insure depositors' account balances, and promote sound bank management.*

All banks that belong to the Federal Reserve System must also belong to the FDIC. Others may join if they meet its standards and conditions. As Figure 13.6 shows, almost 100 percent of all commercial banks are members of the FDIC.

Federal Deposit Insurance Corporation (FDIC)

Insurance Provisions and Examinations

The FDIC insures individual and joint accounts up to $100,000. If a bank fails, the FDIC usually begins paying depositors' claims within 10 days of its closing. The Corporation is funded by premiums assessed on its member banks.

The FDIC, like the Federal Reserve System and the Comptroller of the Currency, has a staff of examiners. Member banks are subject to their scrutiny and management guidelines. When examiners find that a bank has not followed sound practices, the FDIC may issue a cease-and-desist order. It is even empowered to remove officers of state-chartered banks that do not belong to the Fed if their personal dishonesty damages the bank financially. The FDIC's problem list carries the names of banks that may have made risky loans, suffered

Table 13.1 How Open Market Operations and the Reserve Requirement Affect the Money Supply

Level 1	
The Fed pays securities dealers $1 million for U.S. government securities that it buys.	<u>$1,000,000</u>
Level 2	
Banks that accept the securities dealers' $1 million lend out 90%.	$ 900,000
Level 3	
Receiving banks for Level 2's loans lend out 90%.	810,000
Level 4	
Receiving banks for Level 3's loans lend out 90%.	729,000
Level 5	
Receiving banks for Level 4's loans lend out 90%.	656,100
Level 6	
Receiving banks for Level 5's loans lend out 90%.	590,490
Level 7	
Receiving banks for Level 6's loans lend out 90%.	531,441
Level 8	
Receiving banks for Level 7's loans lend out 90%.	<u>478,297</u>
Total Created by All Transfers	<u>$4,695,328</u>

Figure 13.6 Percentage of Banks and Bank Assets Insured by FDIC
Source: Federal Deposit Insurance Corporation.

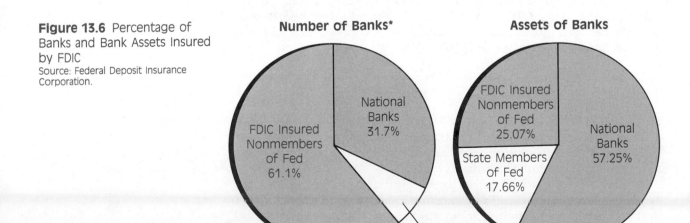

Number of Banks*

Assets of Banks

* Less than 4% of commercial banks are not FDIC insured.

employee embezzlement, or violated prescribed management practices. Problem banks are monitored closely until they regain their financial health.

If a Bank Fails

If the value of a bank's loans and other assets ever falls below its depositors' claims against it, a disaster that frequent bank examinations are designed to prevent, the FDIC may lend the bank money and accept its assets as collateral. If the possibility of recovery seems remote, the FDIC may simply pay off the bank's depositors. In this case the FDIC becomes the receiver (caretaker) of the bank's loans and collects them as they come due. It *liquidates* (converts to cash) such assets as land and equipment. FDIC liquidators have sold off such unusual items as a Houston brothel, a burning Pennsylvania coal mine, an X-rated movie theater, and a dog kennel.[4] The largest commercial bank failure in history was that of the Franklin National Bank in New York City, which owed $3.6 billion to depositors when it failed in 1974. Trailing that was the 1983 failure of the First National Bank of Midland, Texas, which owed $1.4 billion to depositors on its collapse. It later was merged with RepublicBank of Dallas.[5]

The largest FDIC payoff to insured depositors occurred when the Penn Square Bank of Oklahoma City failed in 1982. Some $250 million of accounts, most of which belonged to large institutional depositors, exceeded the FDIC's insured ceiling of $100,000 per depositor. The bank failed because it had made an unusually high number of inadequately secured loans to wildcatters who used the money to purchase drilling rigs and to prospect for gas and oil.[6]

Membership in the FDIC is the norm for commercial banks. In fact, fewer than 400 banks (holding less than 0.1 percent of all commercial bank deposits) have chosen not to join.

Interstate Banking: A Matter of Time

A pronounced trend toward interstate banking developed in the early 1980s as several huge "money center" banks in New York City found ways to expand operations beyond the borders of their home state. Although federal law still prohibits banks from accepting deposits in other states, recent federal deregulation of the banking industry has enabled megabanks such as Citicorp to offer a smorgasbord of services in several states by purchasing a controlling interest in banks or savings and loan associations already established there. Citicorp and other large New York banks also belong to computerized teller systems like CIRRUS and PULSE that form nationwide networks of some 16,000 automated teller machines. Equipped with a computer-coded plastic card and a secret identification number, customers can withdraw money, make payments, transfer funds between accounts, and conduct various other transactions (except for making deposits) in their accounts with out-of-state banks. The CIRRUS system alone claims 619 member banks.

State law permitting, banks may now acquire competitors in other states. A reciprocal agreement allowing regional mergers now exists between Massachusetts, Connecticut, and Rhode Island, and similar agreements are pending in several southern states and some states on the mid-Atlantic seaboard. Although such regional mergers may thwart the growth of true interstate banking, observers believe they may be done to prevent gigantic banks like Citicorp and Manufacturers Hanover Trust from swallowing up smaller banks when all legal barriers to interstate banking are eventually removed. Some of the largest banks in the southeast, for example, may hold no more than $11 billion worth of assets. Citicorp, by comparison, owns $130 billion.[7]

Major Thrift Institutions

The term *thrift institution* refers to three kinds of organizations: savings and loan associations, credit unions, and mutual savings banks. These institutions encourage people to save for a rainy day, and they lend their deposits to other people who want to buy or build homes or purchase certain consumer goods.

Savings and Loan Associations

savings and loan associations (S&Ls)

Originated in Philadelphia in 1831, **savings and loan associations (S&Ls)** are *thrift institutions that accept time deposits and lend them primarily to buyers of single-family homes.* In New England S&Ls usually are called *cooperative banks;* in Louisiana, *homestead associations;* and in some other locations, *building and loan associations.* Approximately 80 percent of S&L loans are made to buy or build single-family dwellings, although federal deregulation now permits them to lend money for a wide range of uses. These institutions can be organized in one of two ways.

Mutual S&Ls. Mutual S&Ls constitute approximately 78 percent of the total. They record deposits as shares of ownership, unlike deposits in commercial banks, which are considered debts or liabilities of those organizations. Payments on such shares are termed *dividends* — not interest — but the term *savings account* more recently has replaced the label *shares* in referring to deposits.

Stock S&Ls. Stock-issuing S&Ls are owned by stockholders, like any other profit-making corporation. Mutual S&Ls may be chartered by the federal government or by an individual state (more than half are state chartered), but there is no federal provision for chartering stock S&Ls. There are approximately 3,000 mutual S&LS and 800 stock S&Ls in operation. Of the total, approximately 1,700 are federally chartered, founded under the provisions of the Home Owners' Loan Act of 1933 and supervised by the Federal Home Loan Bank Board as well as by state regulators. They hold deposits from more than 80 million citizens. The state-chartered S&Ls are supervised by individual state agencies. In 1980 the Federal Home Loan Bank Board passed regulations that allow up to 20 percent of a federally chartered S&L's deposits to be lent for "personal, family, or household purposes."

Most state S&Ls and all federally chartered ones belong to the Federal Home Loan Bank System, which will lend them money against the home loans they have made. The Federal Savings and Loan Insurance Corporation (FSLIC), which is managed by the Federal Home Loan Bank Board, insures deposits in member S&Ls in the same fashion (and to the same limit) that the FDIC does in commercial banks. Federally chartered S&Ls must be insured by the FSLIC, and most state-chartered ones have elected to join. FSLIC members hold over 98 percent of all S&L deposits.[8] Table 13.2 lists the number of S&Ls that belong to the system in each district.

Credit Unions

A **credit union** is *a mutual savings and lending society for people with a common bond,* such as the same employer or union. It accepts their savings at rates comparable to those of savings and

credit union

Table 13.2 Membership of the Federal Home Loan Bank System at Year-End 1982
Source: *1983 Savings and Loan Sourcebook* (Chicago: United States League of Savings Institutions), 1983, p. 44.

Bank District	Savings and Loan Associations			Other State Chartered	Mutual Savings Banks	Life Insurance Companies	Total Membership
	Insured by FSLIC						
	Total Number	Federally Chartered	State Chartered				
Boston	141	62	41	38	77	—	218
New York	241	104	136	1	35	—	276
Pittsburgh	260	109	134	17	3	—	263
Atlanta	533	380	152	1	—	—	533
Cincinnati	430	236	172	22	—	1	431
Indianapolis	181	119	62	—	—	1	182
Chicago	388	160	228	—	3	—	391
Des Moines	217	123	93	1	—	—	217
Little Rock	541	187	354	—	—	—	541
Topeka	193	105	88	—	—	—	193
San Francisco	186	68	118	—	—	—	186
Seattle	127	77	50	—	13	—	140
Total	3,438	1,730	1,628	80	131	2	3,571

loan associations and lends them money at reasonable rates. The concept was originated in 1849 by Friedrich Wilhelm Raiffeisen, mayor of Flammersfeld, Germany, to enable drought-stricken farmers to avoid borrowing from unethical moneylenders who charged exorbitant interest rates. Technically speaking, members' savings represent shares in the organization. The group elects a board of directors, and members may volunteer their time to handle clerical and administrative duties. Larger, more sophisticated credit unions employ a salaried general manager and a full-time paid staff.

Most credit union loans are secured by such consumer products as major appliances and automobiles, but members can obtain unsecured "signature" loans up to a certain amount. Larger credit unions make both consumer goods loans and real estate loans.

Credit unions, like commercial banks and S&Ls, may be chartered by federal or state governments. Approximately 11,400 have federal charters and some 8,300 are chartered by states. The National Credit Union Administration (NCUA), a federal agency established in 1970, examines and supervises the federally chartered groups and insures their deposits (shares) in the same way that the FDIC insures deposits in certain commercial banks. Over 5,100 state-chartered credit unions have qualified for share insurance through the NCUA. All federally chartered credit unions must have this insurance.

Mutual Savings Banks

mutual savings bank

A **mutual savings bank** is *a thrift institution that accepts time deposits and lends them for home purchase and construction. Its lending policies are usually more liberal than those of a savings and loan association,* and in several states mutual savings banks accept demand as well as time deposits. If qualified, they may become members of the FDIC.

Although federal law now allows mutual savings banks to be federally chartered, most are chartered in approximately fifteen states, primarily in New England, New York, and New Jersey. There are fewer than 450 nationwide. Some of the largest are located in New York City.

Summary

Money enables citizens in a modern society to purchase goods and services conveniently, thus eliminating the need for barter. It serves as a medium of exchange, a measure of value, and a store of value. Money in the United States takes the form of coins and paper (collectively called *currency*) and checking accounts (also called *demand deposits*) in commercial banks.

Inflation, which decreases the value of a society's money, has a serious effect on purchasing power when it rises unchecked. This

Credit unions provide financial services for the employees of thousands of companies and nonprofit organizations nationwide.

occurs when producers raise prices in response to strong consumer demand or when they pass rising labor, materials, and service costs on to consumers through increased prices. The Consumer Price Index (CPI), calculated by the U.S. Department of Labor, is the federal government's inflation barometer. It expresses today's prices in 1967 dollars so concerned government agencies can monitor the rate of inflation from one period to the next and take action to bring it under control.

Commercial banks play a unique role in controlling inflation through their lending operations. Most of the larger ones, holding approximately 71 percent of all commercial bank deposits, belong to the Federal Reserve System.

The Federal Reserve System (the Fed) coordinates the nation's banking policy. The Fed's board of governors monitors inflation's growth and responds by regulating the availability of money and credit through open market operations and by adjusting reserve requirements and the discount rate for member banks.

While many commercial banks choose not to belong to the Fed, nearly all of them belong to the Federal Deposit Insurance Corporation (FDIC), a federal government corporation that will pay depositors up to $100,000 on their individual and joint accounts should a

ABA Experiment

Check Retention Gains Support

Suppose that your commercial bank stopped returning canceled checks with your monthly statement. Instead, you would receive a list of the check numbers and amounts with which to reconcile your balance. Copies of your actual checks would be preserved on microfilm and sent to you if needed.

Such a change would reduce the massive and growing burden of check handling, sorting, and transferring that has plagued the commercial banking system for generations. How big is the burden? The Fed now processes an estimated 35 billion checks per year, but that amount may be easier to relate to in this way: if you wrote one check per second, 24 hours per day, for 35 years you would write just 19 million checks — but approximately *673* million checks are cleared through the nation's commercial banking system every *week!* This figure may escalate to a staggering 1.15 billion checks per week by the late 1980s.

The American Bankers Association (ABA), whose members represent 91 percent of all United States commercial banks, proposes to deal with this avalanche of check handling through a practice called *truncation*. Its most sophisticated application requires the bank where a check is first deposited (the collecting bank) to microfilm and store it after trans-mitting the amount, account number, and other significant data by computer to the bank on which the check is drawn. A less sophisticated variation has the bank on which a check is drawn microfilm and retain the original on its return through the check-clearing system.

The ABA first conceived a pilot program to test truncation at the bank of first deposit in 1979, and in mid-1981 eight banks agreed to participate. This group, which later increased to twelve banks, was responsible for determining potential cost savings and confirming if truncation was feasible on a nationwide scale. At first, the only checks involved in the program were corporate dividend checks of $300 or less. The pilot banks later raised the face amount to $1,500 and added payroll, retirement, pension, and several other kinds of checks to the list (truncated checks were identified by a special magnetic ink computer character printed on the face).

The experiment proved so successful that the program, while still restricted to business rather than personal checks, was adopted permanently on January 1, 1983, by the group of banks involved.

This revolutionary departure from traditional banking, clearly a product of the computer age, has

---

bank fail. The FDIC, the Fed, and state banking regulators examine commercial banks' management practices and financial positions periodically to reduce the likelihood of failure.

Although federal law still prevents banks from accepting deposits across state lines, recent deregulation has encouraged larger banks, primarily those located in New York City, to offer most other services in several states by buying control of banks or savings and loan associations already established there. Banks may also operate across

caused considerable controversy. Nevertheless, it can be defended from an efficiency and economic standpoint. The Fed estimates that it costs $0.33 to process a check through the system from the collecting bank to the payor bank. This cost could be reduced to $0.18 per check (an annual savings of approximately $5.25 billion) under the truncation process. And as the volume of checks escalates, arguments for truncation are bound to grow proportionally.

The American banking system trails several foreign countries in using truncation. Banks in West Germany, Great Britain, and Japan have used the technique for a number of years. Perhaps the greatest barrier to its expansion in the United States, however, is consumer acceptance. The ABA emphasizes that truncation will be strictly voluntary, and banks that presently offer it to individual depositors report firm acceptance. Perhaps the most prominent of these, Valley National Bank of Phoenix, Arizona, reports that almost 70 percent of its 465,000 demand deposit customers elected truncation and 80 percent would recommend the practice to friends. The bank reportedly saves between $7.00 and $10.50 per account per year. Members of the ABA also emphasize that business depositors have used truncation for many years and that copies of microfilmed checks are readily available if desired.

Legal as well as consumer issues challenge the growth of truncation. For example, the Internal Revenue Service has formerly refused to accept a microfilmed copy of a check as proof of payment; however, the IRS has indicated that it may cooperate with truncation if copies of checks are accompanied by a bank's statement certifying that they are valid. There is also a possibility that some courts may refuse to accept a microfilmed copy of a check as legal evidence in lieu of the original. Accountants have their misgivings about truncation: in auditing the books of clients, for example, accountants sometimes want to compare the signatures on the companies' canceled checks with those of the executives authorized to sign them. This procedure would be more awkward and time consuming for companies whose checks are truncated. Such concerns are hardly insurmountable, however, and the ABA is moving forward to refine and implement the widespread acceptance of truncation in cooperation with major legal, accounting, data-processing, and consumer organizations. In the meantime, the volume of checks continues to multiply.

For more about the ABA's truncation concept, see: John C. Compton and W. Peter Van Son, "Check Truncation: The Auditor's Dilemma," *Journal of Accountancy*, January 1983, p. 36; "One-to-One Contact Sells Check Truncation," *Bank Marketing*, February 1983, p. 39; "Check Safekeeping to End Pilot Status by Jan. 1," *ABA Banking Journal*, August 1982, p. 86; Dolores S. Wilden, "A Model for National Interbank Truncation," *The Bankers Magazine*, May–June 1982, p. 53; and *The Wall Street Journal*, February 26, 1981, p. 1, column 3.

state lines by joining one of several nationwide automated teller machine networks. A few regions of the country have reciprocal agreements allowing banks to buy competitors in neighboring states.

In addition to commercial banks, savings and loan associations, credit unions, and mutual savings banks (collectively called *thrift institutions*) also encourage depositors to open savings accounts. Such institutions lend funds for home buying and building and for the purchase of various consumer goods.

Key Terms

barter system
certificates of deposit (CDs)
check *or* demand deposit
commercial bank
Consumer Price Index (CPI)
cost-push inflation
credit union

demand-pull inflation
discount rate
Federal Deposit Insurance Corporation (FDIC)
Federal Reserve Act of 1913
inflation
money

mutual savings bank
open market operations
prime rate of interest
reserve requirement
savings account *or* time deposit
savings and loan associations
   (S&Ls)

For Review and Discussion

1. Under what circumstances would a barter system work? Present several situations in which barter could function in our society.

2. What three functions does money perform for a society?

3. What items make up the money supply of the United States? Why are savings accounts not included?

4. Differentiate between demand-pull inflation and cost-push inflation, and give examples of each type.

5. How does the Consumer Price Index (CPI) help the federal government monitor inflation? How does this barometer affect certain citizens' incomes?

6. Discuss the functions and the purpose of commercial banks. What consideration do they give to their most secure corporate borrowers? What instrument do they offer to depositors who agree to leave money on deposit for a certain length of time?

7. Describe the organization of the Federal Reserve System. Why do banks join? How are they regulated after they become members?

8. Summarize how the Fed may use each of the following activities to regulate the money supply: open market operations, reserve requirements, and the discount rate.

9. Why was the Federal Deposit Insurance Corporation (FDIC) created? How does it affect the attitudes of commercial bank depositors?

10. How does the FDIC monitor a commercial bank's condition? What may the FDIC do if a bank gets into financial difficulty? If it fails?

11. How may out-of-state banks offer most of their services in other states despite the fact that federal law prohibits them from accepting deposits there? How have the states themselves promoted the growth of interstate banking?

12. What is the difference between a thrift institution and a commercial bank? How would you characterize the role of each in our economy?

13. Describe the ownership philosophy behind both types of savings and loan associations. What federal agency insures their depositors' accounts? What agency monitors their operations?

14. How is a credit union different from a savings and loan association and a mutual savings bank? Through what federal agency are credit union accounts insured?

15. How do the lending policies of mutual savings banks compare with those of savings and loan associations? What is their relative importance in the field of thrift institutions?

Applications

Case 13.1 Deregulation Upsets Tradition in the Banking Industry

Federal deregulation, which has made its presence felt in the trucking and airline industries, recently swept banking under its wing. One of the most significant

changes involved the removal of interest rate ceilings on time deposits. Competition flourished as banks offered successively higher interest rates on large accounts. Those customers with a minimum balance of $2,500, for example, would receive a significantly higher rate than small-balance customers. And these more affluent persons were enticed with expensive gifts such as microwave ovens or color televisions instead of yesteryear's modest travel alarm clock or cutlery set.

The higher interest paid to big depositors and the expense of competing for their business could not be passed on to borrowers because competition for their business kept lending rates down. Banks therefore were forced to increase their operating efficiency to maintain former levels of profit. This led to increasing fees for some services and changing or eliminating traditional practices that customers had taken for granted over the years.

Many banks have closed small branches, laid off personnel, and increased the use of automated teller machines. (Savings on the latter can be impressive. The cost of a teller-processed transaction may average $1.27, as compared with $0.55 at an automated teller machine.) Service charges have been increased on checking and savings accounts, and some savings accounts may receive no interest on balances under $100. Additional changes involve raising rental rates on safe deposit boxes and charging for or eliminating once-free services such as issuing traveler's checks.

Questions

1. List at least one objection that traditional bank customers may have to the regular use of an automated teller machine.

2. What incentives might banks give depositors to use the cheaper automated teller machines instead of personal tellers at drive-in windows or in the lobby?

3. Describe what you perceive to be the typical customer reaction to increased fees and decreased personal service. How do you believe a banker would reply?

Case 13.1 For more about changing traditions caused by deregulation, see John Helyar, "Banks Cut Costs, Change Strategies As Deregulation Alters the Industry," *The Wall Street Journal*, March 29, 1983, p. 37; "Banks, Consumers Debate Pros, Cons of Deregulation," *The Orlando* (Florida) *Sentinel*, August 1, 1983, p. E-3; and Orin Kramer, "Winning Strategies for Interstate Banking," *Fortune*, September 19, 1983, p. 104.

Case 13.2 Public Disclosure

Traditionally the names of banks with many risky loans outstanding have not been disclosed by examining agencies. Behind-the-scenes emergency loans or mergers arranged by FDIC officials sometimes averted a bank's failure; sometimes a bank's own managers could improve its financial health by obtaining additional collateral from risky borrowers while tightening up lending standards in general. Specific banks were identified only when they teetered on the brink of collapse.

Confidentiality was easy to justify: depositors who knew that their bank had made a large number of risky loans were apt to stage a run on the bank and virtually guarantee its failure by withdrawing all their money. Traditional secrecy and other banking safeguards are being questioned, however, as deregulation alters the character of the nation's banking system.

Despite vehement opposition by bankers, the FDIC began selling reports in 1982 that present the financial condition of every insured bank. These reports were expanded in 1983 to include data on each bank's risky loans. At present the reports have been purchased widely by financial analysts and competing banks but have received little attention from the average citizen. Nevertheless, bankers are alarmed about the potential misunderstanding or confusion these reports may cause among members of the general public.

FDIC chairman William Isaac, who favors the reports, contends that disclosure is healthy — it may force bankers to become more cautious about lending on market-sensitive collateral, such as deposits of oil and natural gas, than they have in the past. Bankers may also place greater priority on maintaining a high degree of depositor confidence as a bank's financial condition will no longer remain confidential among its examining agencies.

Variable FDIC insurance premiums could provide bankers with additional reasons to observe sound banking practices. Unlike the current FDIC rate policy, which ignores a bank's financial condition, a proposed change would charge higher premiums to banks with a larger number of risky loans outstanding. Conceivably this practice would cause lending officers to evaluate new loan applications and monitor changes in the value of existing loans' collateral more carefully. Disclosure of such variable rate premiums in the FDIC reports would further reveal a bank's potential for failure.

The FDIC's long-standing role as sole insurer of depositors' accounts also has been questioned. While proposing that the maximum balance for insured accounts be raised from $100,000 to $200,000 or more, William Isaac also has endorsed the notion that private insurance companies might offer deposit insurance (and, most likely, conduct their own bank examinations) on balances that exceed the FDIC's limit. Such action would relieve the government from being the sole guardian of banking safety. It may also prompt depositors to investigate a bank's management and operations more thoroughly before entrusting it with their money.

Questions

1. Do you agree with the bankers' contention that increased disclosure by the FDIC may alarm or confuse the general public? Why or why not?
2. What problems might the average person encounter in investigating a bank's management and operations?

3. Critics have charged that present FDIC insurance protection and examination secrecy may have insulated bankers from the consequences of bad loan decisions. Do you agree? Why or why not?

Case 13.2 For more about public disclosure, see Christopher Conte, "Regulators Say Banking Safeguards Are Faulty and Need an Overhaul," *The Wall Street Journal*, March 21, 1983, p. 23; Christopher Conte, "Government Starts Opening Banks to Public Scrutiny as Rules Ease," *The Wall Street Journal*, December 8, 1982, p. 33; and Orin S. Kramer, "Putting More Pain into Bank Failures," *Fortune*, February 20, 1984, p. 135.

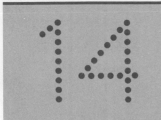

Financing for Profits

Chapter Outline

Short-Term Capital
Short-Term Financing Instruments
Institutions and Methods of Short-Term Financing

Long-Term Capital
Retained Earnings
Securities
The Law and Securities Sales
The Mechanics of a Securities Sale
Registrars and Transfer Agents

Common Stock
Dividends
The Preemptive Right
Stock Splits
Why Do People Buy Common Stock?

Preferred Stock
Preferred Stock Terminology
Why Do People Buy Preferred Stock?

Financing with Bonds
Interest and Market Price Quotations
Sinking Funds
Face Value and Format
Bond Yield
Types of Bonds
Making Decisions About Bonds
Leverage

Summary

Chapter Objectives

After studying this chapter, you should be able to:

1. Describe the various short-term financing instruments that companies may use, and compare the kinds of short-term financing institutions that companies may call on to raise working capital.

2. Discuss the contribution of retained earnings in raising long-term capital.

3. Summarize the two major laws that regulate securities sales and the mechanics of selling securities to the general public.

4. Distinguish between common and preferred stock, and prepare a summary of the features of each.

5. Describe the role and effects of a sinking fund.

6. Compute a bond's current yield and yield to maturity.

7. List and define the types of bonds that companies may issue.

8. Give reasons for investing in bonds as opposed to investing in common or preferred stock.

9. Evaluate the advantages and disadvantages of raising long-term capital by selling common stock, preferred stock, and bonds.

10. Explain the concept of leverage and the risks involved in it.

Money makes money, and the money money makes, makes more money.

— Benjamin Franklin

Up Front   Robert S. Miller

Making History Was Part of His Job

Robert S. "Steve" Miller entered Chrysler Corporation's orbit in the fall of 1979, when his Ford boss in Caracas left to join Lee Iacocca's financial brain trust there (see Up Front, Chapter 3, page 52). Six months later Miller received an offer to become Chrysler's assistant controller. For 3 days he discussed the offer and the demands of the work with his wife and three sons; then he flew to Detroit to discuss the job with Iacocca himself. Within half an hour he was hooked on the challenge, charged with enthusiasm, and ready to start work the following week. Only after leaving Iacocca's office did he realize that one detail had not been discussed: his salary. That proved to be satisfactory, but Miller's overriding reason for taking the job was the uniqueness of the company's position. He said later, "turning Chrysler around was going to be the greatest challenge in American business history."

Indeed it was. For the next 3 years, Miller worked 6 to 7 days a week. During those perilous times, he felt responsible for half a million American jobs, because the failure of Chrysler would drag down its hundreds of dealers nationwide along with thousands of parts suppliers for whom Chrysler was a major (if not the only) customer.

On January 6, 1980, Congress passed the historic Federal Loan Guarantee Act, which opened the way for Chrysler to obtain lifesaving loans, up to $1.5 billion of which would be guaranteed by the federal government. Part of the deal required the company to arrange for $2 billion in new funding on its own, and the toughest challenge was raising $650 million in new financing from Chrysler's present banks, to whom it already owed some $4 billion. With no previous banking experience, Steve Miller was made responsible for getting 400 lenders from around the world to agree to a comprehensive master plan under which the company's existing delinquent loans would be repaid.

During the next 6 grueling months Miller made more than 200 trips to confer with foreign and domestic bankers who had to approve this master plan. In the meantime, Chrysler rumbled closer toward bankruptcy. At last, a New York meeting was arranged with forty representatives of the various banks. Imagine trying to get forty people (much less forty bankers) to agree on *anything*. Miller later compared the session to trying to convert "a Saturday night saloon brawl into a Sunday morning church choir service with everybody singing from the same song sheet." Small bankers resented following the lead of executives from large banks; Canadians balked at adopting plans conceived by Washington; European bankers threatened to retaliate for lack of concern by American bankers when some of their companies faced bankruptcy. Even the delicatessen complicated things by demanding cash when it discovered the food it delivered was ordered by Chrysler Corporation.

After 2 days of bickering, Miller opened the April 1 session with this grave announcement: Chrysler Corporation had filed for bankruptcy. The group was stunned into silence as each member contemplated his bank's share of the potential loss. Then Miller reminded them of the date (April Fools' Day), and his gallows humor did the trick. Most laughed in relief and resolved to settle the problem at hand, although some Europeans, for whom the joke had no meaning, stayed worried a few moments longer than Americans. Within 2 hours an agreement in principle had been reached.

A mountain of legal paperwork still remained, as lawyers from more than fifty law firms drafted the agreement for the necessary signatures. As Chrysler's chief financial officer, Miller wrote himself into the *Guinness Book of Records* on June 6, 1980, by signing more than 4,000 documents, with a total height of 70 feet, in just 1 day. The professional fees paid to lawyers, accountants, and investment bankers who participated in writing the agreements exceeded $20 million; more than $2 million was spent on the printing bill alone. And despite some last-minute holdouts, all lenders eventually signed.

Chrysler Corporation and Steve Miller can look back with pride several years after that epic event. By the end of 1983 the company had repaid all $1.2 billion of its federally guaranteed loans 7 years ahead of schedule; the company's financial performance has earned the respect of Wall Street financial analysts and institutional investors. The implication that Chrysler was bailed out by the federal government rankles the analytical Miller, who points out that the company paid more than $800 million in interest, fees,

and other charges in connection with the federally guaranteed loans. That worked out to an annual interest rate of 24 percent — far from a bargain, and certainly not a subsidy.

In 1983 Miller achieved another financial victory by retiring a burdensome issue of Chrysler preferred stock. These securities had been given to certain creditors in payment of some $1.1 billion of loans with the understanding that no dividends would be paid until the government-backed loans were repaid. At that time, Chrysler would be obliged to pay these preferred holders some $200 million per year in dividends, an obligation the company wanted to eliminate. As repayment of the guaranteed loans seemed likely, Miller began negotiating to exchange Chrysler common stock for this preferred. His proposition began to look attractive as the price of Chrysler common climbed on the open market, buoyed by factors such as rising sales, record earnings, and a break-even point of 1.1 million vehicles, compared with 2.4 million in 1979. Seeing the wisdom of the exchange, the preferred holders agreed to the swap.

Steve Miller continues to make history at Chrysler, and his historic accomplishments during Chrysler's most dismal days have not gone unrewarded. In early 1984 he was made executive vice-president of finance and administration, and so became responsible for industrial relations, quality and productivity, Japanese operations, personnel administration, and administrative services in addition to his financial responsibilities.

For more about Steve Miller, see R. S. Miller, "The Chrysler Story," *Management Accounting*, August 1983, p. 22; "Heady Days for the Numbers Guys," *Fortune*, January 23, 1984, p. 62; Edward E. Scharff, "The Clincher for Chrysler," *Institutional Investor*, July 1983, p. 223; Richard Stolz, "Cashflow Q & A: Robert S. Miller, the Finance Man Who Kept Chrysler Afloat," *Cashflow*, May 1983, p. 35; and Matt Gryczan, "Chrysler Exec Gives Details on Comeback," *The Grand Rapids* (Michigan) *Press*, September 20, 1983, p. 3-b.

short-term *or* working capital

A company must raise two kinds of capital, which are categorized by the way in which the funds will be used. The first kind, called **short-term *or* working capital,** is *money spent on business operations covering a period of a year or less.* Working capital is used to purchase inventory and to pay daily operating expenses such as wages and salaries, insurance premiums, rent, and utilities. The demand for working capital can be enormous in large companies. Chrysler Corporation, for example, has required as much as $50 million each working day.[1]

long-term *or* fixed capital

The second kind of capital is called **long-term *or* fixed capital.** This is *money used to buy fixed assets, which are long-lived and (with the exception of land) manufactured items that will be used to produce goods and services for several years.* These fixed assets can be a microcomputer system to link all the departments in a textile plant of Burlington Industries; computer-controlled robot welding machines for a Ford Motor Company auto assembly line; or three new cargo jets for Federal Express. Unlike short-term capital, which is used to sustain a company from one day to the next, long-term or fixed capital is spent for lasting improvements that will enhance a company's ability to produce goods or services superior to those of competitors, improve or expand its existing line of products, invent new products, or even to purchase the stock of other companies in one of the business combinations that you learned about in Chapter 3.

Sources for capital are as distinct as the uses to which capital may be put. In this chapter we will examine ways to obtain both kinds of capital along with the practices and financial instruments associated with each.

Short-Term Capital

Businesses need short-term capital to amplify purchasing power and increase profit. Firms use short-term capital to buy more merchandise than they can afford to buy out of pocket. This money may be borrowed; the larger inventory that it buys should earn an increased profit when sold, even after interest payments. As a result the business is further ahead than it would have been had it bought merchandise on a cash-and-carry basis.

Short-term capital also is used to pay current debts, when cash receipts from sales and from credit customers fall below expectations. Like us, businesses have expenses that remain steady throughout the year — insurance premiums, utilities, rent, and managers' salaries, for example. Cash flowing into the business, however, is sometimes insufficient to pay such obligations, especially during slack periods. Again, management may have to find money for a short period of time.

Short-term capital also helps businesses meet unexpected expenses when sales remain steady. Even when sales and cash receipts are constant, management may have to do unanticipated maintenance or repair equipment or it may have to pay increased insurance premiums, higher-than-expected taxes, or professional fees of attorneys or accountants. When these unpleasant surprises demand more money than a firm has on hand, it must secure short-term funds.

Short-Term Financing Instruments

Table 14.1 summarizes several tools or instruments that play a part in raising short-term or working capital. We will discuss their characteristics at this point; later parts of this chapter will refer to some of them.

Promissory Note. The first and the most common, a **promissory note,** is *a short-term financing instrument, given by a debtor (called the* promisor*) to a creditor (called the* promisee*) as a legal and binding promise to pay a certain sum of money at a future date, usually with interest at a fixed rate.* A note may be *secured* (backed by specific assets that the creditor may claim if the note is not paid when due) or *unsecured* (backed only by the promisor's reputation). Figure 14.1 is an example of an unsecured promissory note.

promissory note

Although many promissory notes are payable in 1 year or less, making them short-term instruments, some extend for more than

Table 14.1 Instruments of Short-Term Financing

Instrument	Characteristics
Promissory note	A debtor's promise to pay a certain sum of money at a future date. Usually carries interest at a fixed rate. May be secured or unsecured.
Draft	Completed by a creditor ordering a debtor to pay a specific sum of money. Does not become a binding obligation until accepted by the debtor. *Sight drafts* are payable immediately; *time drafts* give the debtor a stated length of time after acceptance to produce the money.
Commercial paper	An unsecured promissory note of a large corporation (sometimes referred to as a *corporate IOU*). Used to borrow large amounts for short periods of time.
Check	A kind of draft used to make payments in financial transactions. Two kinds of checks may be used aside from a check drawn on a business's own account. A *cashier's check* is written by a commercial bank against its own money. Generally considered the safest kind of check, it may be purchased by giving the bank the amount to be paid plus a modest fee. The other kind, a *certified check*, is a depositor's own check that the bank certifies to be good. The popularity and convenience of obtaining cashier's checks have made certified checks relatively uncommon today.

Figure 14.1 Form for an Unsecured Promissory Note

No._____ $_____   _____, Florida, _____, 19____

_____ after date, for value received,

_____promise to pay to the order of_____

_____ DOLLARS,

at_____, _____, Florida

with interest thereon at the rate of_____per cent. per annum from_____until fully paid. Interest payable semi-annually. The maker and endorser of this note further agree to waive demand, notice of non-payment and protest; and in case suit shall be brought for the collection hereof, or the same has to be collected upon demand of an attorney, to pay reasonable attorney's fees for making such collection. Deferred interest payments to bear interest from maturity at_____per cent. per annum, payable semi-annually.

_____(Seal)

Due_____, 19____   _____(Seal)

a year. You may have signed a long-term note to finance the car you drive, your stereo, or your furniture.

draft

Draft. Unlike a promissory note, which is a debtor's promise to pay a debt, a **draft** is *an instrument completed by a creditor ordering a debtor to pay a specific sum of money.* A draft that orders the debtor to pay the amount immediately is called a *sight draft;* one that allows the debtor a certain time to produce the money is a *time draft.* A draft does not become a binding obligation until the debtor writes the word *accepted* on its face and signs it. Figure 14.2 shows an example of a draft.

Figure 14.2 Form for a Draft

$_____   _____ 19___

Pay to the

Order of_____

_____ Dollars

Value received and charge the same to account of

To_____

No._____   {   _____

Drafts are popular for coordinating the exchange of payment for and title to merchandise when the buyer and seller must deal at arm's length. They often are used by automobile dealers who may sell scores of cars to one another in a single transaction while never meeting personally. Figure 14.3 illustrates such a transaction and the way a draft makes it easier to accomplish.

Commercial Paper. One instrument used to borrow large amounts for short periods is **commercial paper** *(sometimes referred to as corporate IOUs), the unsecured promissory notes of large, financially sound corporations.* Usually issued in such even denominations as $50,000, $100,000, and $500,000, commercial paper can raise several million dollars of short-term capital at one time. Maturities on commercial paper range from a scant 7 days to 9 months or more.

Commercial paper houses act as go-betweens, buying these notes from borrowing firms at something less than face value and selling them to organizations with excess cash to lend. The borrowers and lenders rarely meet directly. Commercial paper lenders are often such institutional investors as large corporations, universities, and even hospitals that happen to have large amounts of cash free for short periods of time.

commercial paper

Checks. A check is a kind of draft, because the depositor is the bank's creditor (as you learned in Chapter 13). By writing a check the depositor (creditor) orders the bank (debtor) to pay a certain

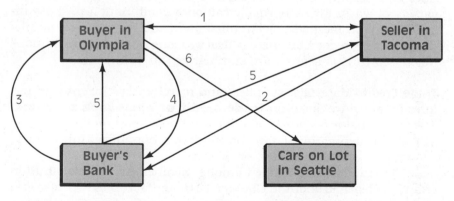

Figure 14.3 A Transaction Involving a Draft

1. Buyer and seller agree by telephone on the price of fifty cars stored in Seattle.

2. Tacoma seller sends draft to the buyer's bank ordering the Olympia buyer to pay the agreed-upon sum. (Car titles are attached to draft.)

3. Bank officer notifies buyer when draft and titles arrive.

4. The buyer accepts the draft and pays the banker.

5. The banker detaches the titles, delivers them to the buyer, and sends payment to the seller after deducting a fee.

6. The buyer, titles in hand, picks up the cars at the Seattle lot.

cashier's check

sum of money to a third party. Business transactions are conducted with two kinds of checks, in addition to those of the company itself.

The first, a **cashier's check,** is *a check written by a commercial bank against the bank's own money.* It generally is considered the safest kind of check. When a creditor doubts a debtor's ability to pay or has not dealt with that party before, the creditor may require payment by cashier's check. Getting a cashier's check is simple: you go to the proper window on the floor of your commercial bank, give them the money (plus a modest fee), and tell them to whom you want the cashier's check written. The bank deposits your money as its own, writes a cashier's check to the designated party, and gives it to you. Depositors who want to transfer funds permanently from one bank to another can do so safely by having their original bank write them a cashier's check for their balance.

certified check

The second kind of check, a **certified check,** is uncommon today. It is *a depositor's personal check that the bank certifies to be good,* usually by punching the word *certified* in the face of the check with a machine. The bank customarily sets funds aside in the customer's account so the check will be paid when it returns through the banking system. Most large commercial banks see no reason to write cashier's checks and certify personal checks, however, so when you ask for a certified check you will probably be sent to the cashier's check window.

Institutions and Methods of Short-Term Financing

Several institutions provide short-term funds to companies in a variety of ways. Firms normally call on a combination of these institutions and methods, as circumstances and business conditions dictate. It is rare for a business to deal with one alone. The institutions discussed in this section are summarized in Table 14.2.

trade credit *or* **open-book accounts**

Trade Credit. Materials, supplies, and merchandise inventories frequently are purchased on **trade credit** *or* **open-book accounts.** These are *business charge accounts that a selling firm gives buying firms.* The debtor must pay for the items bought within a given time period, usually 30, 60, or 90 days.

Trade credit is extended among members of the distribution chain you learned about in Chapter 12 (manufacturers, wholesalers, and retailers). It is not a source of actual money, but it is a way to defer payment until the buyer can resell the merchandise to the next link in the distribution chain.

cash discount

Sellers who extend trade credit or open-book accounts may give buyers a **cash discount,** which is *a discount given to encourage trade credit debtors to pay their balances before they are due.* It may be quoted, for example, as *2/10, n/30,* meaning that the buyer may deduct 2 percent if the bill is paid within 10 days after a specific date (usually the date of the billing). The buyer may, however, choose to pay the net or full amount (the total, less any returns or allowances) within 30 days of the billing date. Buyers typically manage their

Institution	Transaction
Trade credit or open-book accounts	Obtain merchandise inventory, materials, and supplies on credit.
Commercial bank	Borrow on line of credit or revolving credit agreement.
Commercial finance company	Borrow using such collateral as inventory, equipment, or trade accounts receivable.
Factoring company	Sell business customers' open-book or consumer credit accounts at a discount for cash.
Sales finance company	Sell consumers' installment sales contracts at a discount for cash.
Consumer finance company	Accept cash that consumers have borrowed from these firms as payment for merchandise.

Table 14.2 Institutions of Short-Term Financing

money so they can pay trade credit accounts within the discount period. The discounts received on an entire year's purchases can add up to impressive savings for most companies.

Borrowing from a Commercial Bank. Commercial banks, which you learned about in Chapter 13, are the most popular source of short-term business loans. Companies that obtain working capital from commercial banks usually establish a **line of credit,** which is *a maximum amount that a commercial bank agrees to lend to a business borrower if it has the funds available.* In other words the amount is assured but not guaranteed.

line of credit

A line of credit is convenient. You can borrow whatever amount you need, making payments as specified. As long as the outstanding debt does not exceed the approved maximum, you still have funds available. Interest is charged only on the amount borrowed. Large corporations may have credit lines of several hundred thousand dollars or more, and credit lines at several banks, to satisfy their short-term cash needs.

Instead of a line of credit, firms may obtain a **revolving credit agreement,** which is *a commercial bank's binding promise that the money will be available if the borrowing firm requests it.* Most banks require business borrowers to keep a compensating balance of from 10 to 20 percent of the borrowed funds on deposit, insisting that borrowers become depositors too.

revolving credit agreement

Commercial Finance Companies. An important alternative source of short-term capital is a **commercial finance company,** *a firm that makes cash loans to business borrowers, securing the loans by such assets as trade credit accounts, inventory, or equipment.* Because these companies may take greater lending risks than commercial banks, they may charge higher interest rates. But they are

commercial finance company

Business owners rely on commercial banks to supply most of the short-term capital they spend on day-to-day operations.

available should a company exhaust its bank line of credit, and they do not require compensating balances as commercial banks do.

factoring company

Factoring Companies. Some businesses raise funds from a **factoring company,** *a firm that buys a business's open-book accounts (or sometimes consumer credit accounts) and customarily absorbs all losses if the debtors do not pay.* Usually the factor performs all billing and other bookkeeping activities on the accounts. Originally used in the textile industry, factoring is now common in the container, furniture, and clothing industries as well. Even such commercial banks as Citizens & Southern National Bank in Atlanta have established factoring departments.

The factor buys the debts at a discount determined by the quality of the accounts being sold. If they are the debts of financially sound companies with good credit ratings, the discount will be lower than if they were slow-paying or otherwise shaky companies.

Debtors may be notified that their original creditor has sold their accounts to a factor, and instructed to make payments to that firm. The selling company may agree, however, to record the payments and relay the money to the factor, who thus escapes a recordkeeping burden. This arrangement is termed a *nonnotification plan.*

Factoring has undergone a face-lift in recent years as certain large retailers have sold the balances due from their credit card customers to reduce their bookeeeping load and increase their working capital. J. C. Penney Company, for example, sold more than $250 million of its credit card balances at a discount of a little under 10 percent, planning to use some of the funds to pay off some of its outstanding short-term debts.[2]

Sales Finance Companies. Another source of working capital, a **sales finance company,** is *a firm that provides short-term capital to retailers (and sometimes to wholesalers) by purchasing the installment sales contracts (promissory notes) that they have accepted from customers.* Imagine a retailer of furniture or large appliances who accepts customers' promissory notes. When the firm requires additional short-term money, it can convert the notes it holds into cash by selling them to a sales finance company. A discount is involved in these transactions, just as in the factoring of accounts receivable. The main difference between the two is that sales finance companies usually buy consumers' promissory notes for one-time purchases, while factoring companies buy the existing balances on open-book accounts owed to businesses, usually by other businesses. The concept is identical, however; the selling firm converts a future obligation into cash on the spot.

Retailers benefit from selling customers' notes to sales finance companies; they avoid keeping records on the customers' monthly payments for the remainder of the notes' lives and they convert the debts to cash, a benefit that is often worth the discount charged by the sales finance company. The sales finance company profits when it collects the full amount owed on a debt that it bought for less than face value.

Consumer Finance Companies. Indirectly involved in a firm's short-term financing activities is a **consumer finance company,** a *company that lends money to final consumers on their promissory notes.* These loans may be secured by the product the consumers intend to buy or by some other valuable item they now own. Merchants who are unwilling to accept a consumer's promissory note may make the sale if the person can borrow from one of these firms (for example, Commercial Credit Corporation or Household Finance Corporation). Consumers with good credit ratings can borrow some cash on unsecured promissory notes.

People who have exhausted their borrowing limits at commercial banks or credit unions may turn to a consumer finance company as a lender of last resort. The same holds true for people with a history of delinquent payments to more conservative lenders. The fact that these firms lend to risky borrowers justifies the relatively high rate of interest they charge on the loans that they grant.

sales finance company

consumer finance company

Long-Term Capital

Long-term or fixed capital, you will recall, is money used to buy fixed assets, which are long-lived and (with the exception of land) manufactured items that will be used to produce goods and services for several years. Huge amounts of money are required to buy or build a new plant, purchase new equipment, acquire land for a retail store, or remodel an existing facility that has become inefficient or outmoded. Companies raise money for long-term use with retained earnings and such long-term instruments as securities.

Retained Earnings

retained earnings

Retained earnings are *profits reinvested in (or plowed back into) a company for improvements and expansion.* Depending on its expected growth rate and long-term capital requirements, a firm will retain some (sometimes all) of its yearly profits for expansion. It is impractical, however — if not impossible — to pay for rapid expansion with a company's profits alone; that would be like saving enough money from your paycheck to pay cash for a home. So, while retained earnings are an important contribution, incorporated firms issue stocks and sometimes bonds to raise most of their long-term capital. Collectively, stocks and bonds are termed *securities.*

Securities

In Chapter 3 you learned that a corporation can raise large sums of money by selling shares of stock to investors who are willing to take an owner's risk. Stocks are *equity securities.* The word *equity* in this sense means ownership; stockholders are the legal owners of their corporations, and *the long-term capital raised by selling stock* is known as **equity capital.**

equity capital
bonds

Corporations also may raise money by selling **bonds,** which are *long-term, interest-bearing promissory notes.* Bonds may not mature for as long as 25 years. Bonds, as *debt securities,* represent an obligation to be paid at some future date.

The Law and Securities Sales

Before 1933 only state laws governed how corporations could sell their securities. Potential investors had no federal protection from fraudulent securities marketing schemes. After the stock market crash of 1929, however, the early years of the New Deal saw an array of federal legislation that created the present climate of regulation of corporate financing and protection of investors. Table 14.3 provides a ready reference of the most significant federal controls on the selling of corporate stocks and bonds.

prospectus

Companies usually must publish a **prospectus** before offering securities for sale. This is *a document that presents a company's financial data for several consecutive years, discusses its position in its industry, describes how it will use the funds raised by a securities sale, and summarizes other information that well-informed investors should have.* The breakup of American Telephone and Telegraph (see The Straight Line, Chapter 3, page 72) resulted in a prospectus publishing task of truly monumental proportions. All 2.9 million stockholders in the original company were required to receive a prospectus providing details about the stock of the seven

Table 14.3 Federal Laws Controlling Securities Trading

Act	Provisions
Securities Act of 1933	Requires a corporation, before it can sell a new issue of securities to the public, to supply information to the federal government in a registration statement and to potential investors in a published prospectus.
	Subjects corporations that violate this rule to criminal prosecution, and those who willfully misstate information to fine or imprisonment of responsible executives.*
Securities Exchange Act of 1934	Created the Securities and Exchange Commission (SEC), a federal government regulatory body that discharges provisions of this law and the 1933 act.
	Established specific trading rules to be followed by stock exchanges and by over-the-counter traders to prevent stock manipulation and fraud.
	Bans "wash sales" — the simultaneous buying and selling of stock to create the impression of investor interest.
	Prohibits the making of misleading statements about a security to encourage others to buy or sell it.
	Forbids organized buying or selling of a security to drive its price up or down.
	Prohibits trading of securities by corporate employees or other insiders based on information not available to the general public.
	Gives the Federal Reserve Board the power to set a *margin requirement*, a minimum payment an investor must make when buying securities (the remainder may be borrowed).†

*Registration under these provisions does not imply that the federal government supports or endorses the issue, merely that the issuing corporation has disclosed the information that will allow potential investors to make an informed decision.

†Margin buying is discussed further in Appendix B.

Note: We have used, of necessity, certain terms in this table that will be defined later in this chapter.

new corporations that were created. The company that printed this 267-page document reported that the job required 1,950 tons of paper, and that all the sheets placed end to end would circle the globe 3.4 times.[3]

Although a prospectus makes the official, or legal, offer, a company typically runs an advertisement called a "tombstone" prospectus in certain magazines or in *The Wall Street Journal* to inform potential investors that the securities are available. Figure 14.4 is an example of a tombstone announcing a new issue of Chrysler Corporation stock. Note the carefully worded message referring readers to the actual prospectus.

"*Oh, that's just our financial report and prospectus.*"
Source: From *The Wall Street Journal*, permission Cartoon Features Syndicate.

Figure 14.4 A Tombstone
Prospectus
Source: Courtesy Chrysler Corporation.

This announcement is neither an offer to sell nor a solicitation of an offer to buy these securities.
The offer is made only by the Prospectus.

March 30, 1983

26,000,000 Shares

CHRYSLER CORPORATION

Common Stock
(without par value)

Price $16.625 Per Share

Copies of the Prospectus may be obtained in any State in which this announcement is circulated
only from such of the undersigned as may legally offer these securities in such State.

Salomon Brothers Inc   The First Boston Corporation

Lehman Brothers Kuhn Loeb
Incorporated

E. F. Hutton & Company Inc.   Merrill Lynch White Weld Capital Markets Group
                                               Merrill Lynch, Pierce, Fenner & Smith Incorporated

Bear, Stearns & Co.   Blyth Eastman Paine Webber   Dillon, Read & Co. Inc.   Donaldson, Lufkin & Jenrette
                       Incorporated   Securities Corporation
Drexel Burnham Lambert   Goldman, Sachs & Co.   Kidder, Peabody & Co.   Lazard Frères & Co.
Incorporated   Incorporated
Prudential-Bache   L. F. Rothschild, Unterberg, Towbin   Shearson/American Express Inc.
          Securities
Smith Barney, Harris Upham & Co.   Warburg Paribas Becker   Wertheim & Co., Inc.   Dean Witter Reynolds Inc.
Incorporated   A. G. Becker
Sanford C. Bernstein & Co., Inc.   Alex. Brown & Sons

A. G. Edwards & Sons, Inc.   Thomson McKinnon Securities Inc.

ABD Securities Corporation   Advest, Inc.   Allen & Company   Atlantic Capital
                                                            Incorporated   Corporation
Basle Securities Corporation   Daiwa Securities America Inc.   Dominion Securities Ames Inc.

F. Eberstadt & Co., Inc.   EuroPartners Securities Corporation   Robert Fleming   Hudson Securities, Inc.
                                                                   Incorporated   Société Générale Group
Kleinwort, Benson   Ladenburg, Thalmann & Co. Inc.   Moseley, Hallgarten, Estabrook & Weeden Inc.
Incorporated
The Nikko Securities Co.   Nomura Securities International, Inc.   Rothschild Inc.
International, Inc.
Tucker, Anthony & R. L. Day, Inc.   Wood Gundy Incorporated   Yamaichi International (America), Inc.

The Mechanics of a Securities Sale

Firms rarely sell securities directly to the general public; it can take
months to dispose of the entire issue. Instead they arrange with
one or more investment banking firms to purchase the entire issue
and retail it to the public. An **investment banking firm,** not to be
confused with a commercial bank, is *a firm that purchases an
entire issue of new securities from the issuing company as a
wholesaler and resells it to the general public.* If a single investment
banking firm is unable or unwilling to take the risk of buying and
reselling an entire issue, it may form a syndicate of several investment

investment banking firm

bankers to buy the issue, divide it among themselves, and resell it. After the securities are sold the group is disbanded.

Syndication, by spreading the risk, lets one firm escape the burden of buying and reselling the entire lot of securities. It is also more convenient for the issuing corporation, which receives the money in a lump sum.

Registrars and Transfer Agents

Large corporations with thousands of owners find that keeping records on securities is a staggering burden. As a result companies normally employ large banks to act as their registrars and transfer agents. A **registrar** is *a commercial bank that monitors the number of shares of stock a corporation sells to ensure that it does not sell more than its charter has authorized.* A **transfer agent** is *a commercial bank that records changes in names and addresses for a corporation each time stocks and certain types of bonds are traded.* Earlier certificates must be canceled and current ones issued bearing the new owner's name.

registrar

transfer agent

Common Stock

Common stock, which all corporations organized for profit must issue, is *a security held by the corporation's owners.* A document called a **common stock certificate** is *legal evidence of corporate ownership. It gives the owner's name, the number of shares owned, and various data on the corporation itself.* Common stock is bought and held in groups called a **round lot** — *100 shares of a stock or multiples thereof* — or an **odd lot** — *less than 100 shares of a stock.* You saw a sample stock certificate in Chapter 3 on page 55.

Common stockholders, as the true owners of the corporation, elect its board of directors. These voting rights give stockholders ultimate control over a corporation's affairs.

common stock

common stock certificate

round lot
odd lot

Dividends

Common stockholders may receive a **dividend,** which is *a portion of company profits paid to stockholders as a return for the risk that they take as owners.* Firms that retain earnings for use as fixed capital, however, may pay a very small dividend, if any. The optional nature of dividends makes common stock a favored security to offer when a firm's financial future is cloudy. It carries no fixed payments, unlike certain other securities. Corporations are not legally required to pay dividends, because they are essentially distributed profits.

Dividends, when paid, usually are paid each quarter. The company or its transfer agent mails a check for the proper amount to the shareholders of record on a specific date. The total dividend that the board of directors approves is divided by the number of

dividend

shares of common stock outstanding to determine the amount paid on each share.

stock dividend

Firms that want to conserve cash and display concern for investors' welfare may pay a **stock dividend,** which is *a distribution of shares of the company's stock or the stock that it owns in other firms.*

The Preemptive Right

preemptive right

Corporation laws in most states require that corporations give their shareholders a **preemptive right,** which is *a shareholder's right to purchase shares of a company's new stock issues in proportion with the existing shares that he or she owns, before the new shares are offered to the general public.* This law allows you to maintain your present degree of control in the company if you wish. Without this right, your control would be diluted when others bought new shares.

warrant

A **warrant** is *a document that conveys the preemptive right to existing stockholders.* It states the number of shares the holder may purchase and the required price per share. Warrants usually have an expiration date after which the company may sell the new lot of shares to anyone. When the warrant price is lower than the market price of shares already outstanding, the warrants acquire a value of their own, and stockholders may sell them.

Stock Splits

stock split

A stock's market price is the price negotiated between buyers and sellers. It reflects investor consensus about the firm itself within its industry and the national and world economic and political outlook. If optimistic investors bid a stock's market price extremely high, the company's board of directors, with the approval of existing stockholders, may declare a **stock split.** This is *a subdivision of shares already issued, done to decrease a stock's high market price to an amount that more investors can afford to pay.* Assume, for example, that eager buyers and reluctant sellers have bid the market price for a company's common stock to $350 per share. If the firm declares a five-for-one split and you hold a round lot of 100 shares, you will own 500 shares after the split. The market price per share would be reduced from $350 to $70 ($350 ÷ 5) afterward. Although the total market value of your investment is unchanged, the market price for each share has been reduced to a more affordable level for investors. By reducing the price per share a stock split enables more investors to buy in round lots instead of odd lots and may bring the price within what some businesses believe is a psychologically attractive trading range — between $20 and $40 per share.[4]

Rising stock prices in the early 1980s led a number of large firms including Procter & Gamble, Dow Jones & Company, Dun & Bradstreet Corporation, Ford Motor Company, American Express,

Pause and Ponder

Assume that a corporation sells 1,000 shares of stock to ten people buying 100 shares each. If the firm later sold another 1,000 shares to other investors without notifying the first group, what would happen? Why do you suppose most states guarantee the preemptive right of stockholders?

and McDonald's Corporation to split their stock. The main difference between a stock dividend and a stock split is that the corporation reduces the stock's *face,* or *par, value* (an arbitrary value per share that the corporation may assign to its stock and print on the front of the stock certificate) in a stock split. The par value is not reduced when a stock dividend is distributed because no new shares have been created.

Why Do People Buy Common Stock?

Investors seeking income purchase stock in firms with a record of dividend payments that has been unbroken for several years or, in some cases, several decades. Scovill boasts an unbroken dividend payment record of 125 years. R. J. Reynolds Industries reports uninterrupted dividend payments since 1900, with increases every year since 1953 (except for 1971, when a federal wage and price control program temporarily prohibited an increase). The most intriguing and appealing reason for owning common stock, however, is **capital appreciation,** *an increase in a stock's market price caused by investor optimism.*

    If traced from their beginnings the common stock prices of many well-known companies illustrate this phenomenon. During the early years of McDonald's Corporation, for example, the company's bookkeeper agreed to take some of her pay in common stock instead of cash. When she retired her shares were worth $70 million.[5] International Business Machines (IBM) has recorded one of the most phenomenal records for capital appreciation of any common stock. If you or one of your ancestors had bought 100 shares in July 1932, they would have cost $5,250. If you held these shares until March 30, 1973, they would have grown to 13,472 shares through stock splits and been worth, on that record high date, $5,813,200. You would have become a multimillionaire from a $5,250 investment. In addition, the firm would have paid you $497,300 in cash dividends on that investment during the 41-year period — an average of $12,129.27 a year.[6] Shares of Tandy Corporation, the parent firm of Radio Shack, sold for a modest $0.60 each in 1963. A round lot purchased then was worth approximately $78,000 two decades later. Likewise, 100 shares of Jack Eckerd Corporation, which sold for $0.70 each in the early 1960s, were worth approximately $87,000 20 years later.[7]

capital appreciation

Elevators and stock prices, however, have one thing in common: they go down as well as up. During the Great Depression, when investor confidence was shaken to its roots, stocks that sold for lofty amounts in 1929 plummeted to lows that were unthinkable to many investors. American Telephone & Telegraph plunged from 310 1/4 per share to 69 3/4, and the New York Central Railroad collapsed from 256 1/2 a share to 8 3/4. But the greatest fall may have been retailer Montgomery Ward, which fell from 156 7/8 a share to a mere 3 1/2. The amounts, like all stock prices, are quoted in dollars per share, in increments of an eighth of a dollar (twelve and one-half cents).*

Preferred Stock

preferred stock

Preferred stock, which some corporations sell with the approval of the common stockholders, is *a class of stock that has a prior or senior claim on assets to that of common stock.* It is still an equity security, but it ranks ahead of common stock in receiving dividend payments and in any cash distributions should a corporation be dissolved.

Preferred stock dividends are quoted as a percentage of the face, or par, value. Most pars are either $25, $50, or $100. Some companies do not assign a par value to their stocks, however. In these cases the dividend is expressed in terms of dollars per share. Figure 14.5 is a specimen of a no-par preferred stock certificate. In the case of par preferred stock, the par value, say $100, and a dividend rate, say 7 percent, are printed on the certificate. This means that holders will receive an annual dividend of $7.00 per share. In the no-par preferred certificate shown, the dividend of $3.50 per share is stated in the upper right and left corners of the certificate.

Although preferred stock dividends are assured, they are not guaranteed. The board of directors may decide to pay no dividends at all or to make a partial payment if adverse business conditions impair the company's ability to pay the full amount due. Preferred stock dividends are fixed amounts and will change only if the stock splits.

Preferred Stock Terminology

Preferred stock also may have several features not associated with common stock. These features are stated on the stock certificate itself, or you can confirm them by checking with the company. The primary features that may apply to a given preferred stock issue are listed on the next page.

---

*When market prices are generally falling, a *bear market* is said to exist; when they are generally rising, a *bull market* is said to be present.

Figure 14.5 Sample No-Par Preferred Stock Certificate
Source: Courtesy IC Industries, Inc. Reproduced with permission.

- **Participating Preferred** This stock can pay an additional dividend beyond its standard amount, as specified by the corporation. (Most preferred stock is participating.)

- **Callable Preferred** The issuing company may require the holder to surrender these shares at a call price that is usually slightly higher than the market price at the time the company exercises its call.

- **Convertible Preferred** This stock may be converted into the company's common stock if the holder wishes. The conversion ratio (number of common shares exchanged for one preferred share) is established by the firm. Because conversion ties the company's preferred stock to its common, the market price of preferred mirrors any changes in that of the common.

- **Cumulative Preferred** Preferred stock on which the company must pay all dividends that are unpaid ("in arrears") before it can pay any dividends to its common stockholders. (Most preferred stock has this feature.)

- **Noncumulative Preferred** Preferred stock on which unpaid dividends do not carry forward to the next year.

- **Adjustable or Floating Rate Preferred** An innovative form of preferred first issued in 1982. Unlike traditional preferred, which pays a fixed dividend, the dividend rates on this variation change quarterly according to the interest rates paid on U.S. Treasury securities (discussed in Chapter 13). Dividends on most floating rate preferreds range from a minimum of 7 1/2 percent to a maximum of 16 percent.

The IC Industries preferred stock shown in Figure 14.5 is cumulative and convertible.

Why Do People Buy Preferred Stock?

Investors who buy preferred stock want less risk than those who buy common stock. The fixed but assured dividend, combined with the potential for capital appreciation, makes it an appealing security for conservative individual investors, pension funds, and others with large sums to invest.

Financing with Bonds

debt capital

When a company sells, or floats, an issue of bonds, it obtains **debt capital,** another name for *the long-term capital raised by selling bonds.* (As you learned, capital raised by selling stocks is called *equity capital.*) Bondholders are actually creditors; the corporation is their borrower or debtor. Bonds are commonly issued with a face, or par, value of $1,000 or multiples thereof, although some have face values as low as $500 or even $100. The face, or par, value is paid to the holder when the bond matures. The **bond indenture** is *a blanket agreement between the corporation and its bondholders that states the bond issue's interest rate, maturity date, and other terms and conditions.*

bond indenture

Interest and Market Price Quotations

As creditors, bondholders have a legal right to collect interest from the corporation. Interest is expressed as a percentage of the bond's face value, which you should assume is $1,000 unless you are informed otherwise. A bond's market price is expressed as a percentage of face value too. The examples in Table 14.4 illustrate how to convert interest rates and market price quotations into dollars.

You need not hold a bond until maturity once you have bought it. Bonds, like stocks, are often traded between investors, who adjust the market price up or down to compensate for the bond's fixed interest rate in relation to the short-term interest rate available from other investments at the time of sale. Because a bond's interest is fixed for its lifetime but the interest rate it is compared with is constantly changing, it will sell at either a premium or a discount.

premium

A **premium** is *the amount by which a bond's market price exceeds*

Table 14.4 Interpreting Bond Interest Rate and Price Quotations

Interest Rate	Annual Interest	Current Market Price Quotation	Market Price of Bond
8 1/2	$ 85.00	91 1/8	$ 911.25
11 1/4	112.50	119 3/4	1,197.50
10 1/2	105.00	100	1,000.00
9 3/4	97.50	87 1/2	875.00

its par value; a **discount** is *the amount by which a bond's par value exceeds its market price.* Bonds rarely sell for exactly their par value.

Sinking Funds

By floating a bond issue, a corporation incurs a multimillion-dollar debt payable on a definite future date. To prepare for this day of reckoning, companies usually establish a **sinking fund,** which is *a special fund a company creates and pays money into over the life of a bond issue so dollars will be available to pay off the bonds when they mature.* A bond sinking fund is invested in stocks and bonds of other companies and in United States government securities — the more a sinking fund can earn on its own, the less the company must pay into it.

sinking fund

By ensuring that the company will be able to retire the bonds (pay them off) when they mature, a sinking fund reduces the risk bondholders take in lending money to a corporation, which tends to prop up the market price of the bonds.

Face Value and Format

A bond's face, or par, value, like that of stock, is printed on its face; it has no relationship to market value. If you examine a bond, you will find the company's name, the serial number by which the firm keeps track of the bond, the interest rate, the face, or par, value (sometimes referred to as the *principal*), and the maturity date, on which the corporation will pay the holder the face value.

Bonds generally have one of two formats. The first, a **coupon or bearer bond** is *one with dated coupons attached, which the bondholder must cut off and mail to the company to collect interest.* When all the coupons have been clipped the bond has matured; the holder sends in the bond itself (the face) to collect the principal from the issuing firm. Bearer bonds carry no owner identification; they are transferred on delivery, meaning the present holder is presumed to be the rightful owner. These bonds, like all securities, should be kept under lock and key — preferably in a safe deposit box at a commercial bank.

coupon *or* bearer bond

The second bond format is a **registered bond,** *one whose owner's name is on record with the company and appears on the bond itself.* If the bond is registered as to principal, it carries a sheet of dated coupons that must be clipped for each interest payment, but its face amount will be paid automatically on maturity to the person whose name appears on the bond and on the company's books. A **fully registered bond** is *one without coupons. The company pays interest automatically to the owner whose name is on record with the firm, and the principal is paid to that person when the bond matures.*

registered bond

fully registered bond

Bearer or coupon bonds are a convenience to the company, which thus avoids the burden of recording ownership changes each time the bond is sold. As a rule, bond interest is payable semiannually, so coupon bonds have two coupons per year. Today most corporate bonds are registered, however, and the continued use of this format is ensured by the 1982 Tax Equity and Fiscal Responsibility Act. This federal law requires new corporate bonds sold in the United States that mature in 1 year or more to have a registered format. Corporations will thus report the interest paid to those bondholders to the federal government and so reduce the likelihood that the bondholders will fail to declare the interest income on their federal income tax returns.[8] Figure 14.6 shows an example of a coupon bond — one for the less common denomination of $500 — issued by Bethlehem Steel Corporation.

Bond Yield

bond yield

Bond yield is *the percentage return that the investor will receive.* A bond bought at 100 (face value) yields its exact interest rate, but because most are bought at a premium or a discount, the return is greater or less than the interest rate stated on the face. The current yield can be calculated, as can the yield until maturity, if the investor plans to keep the bond until then. Yield formulas and calculations are shown in Figure 14.7.

Figure 14.6 Sample Coupon or Bearer Bond
Source: Courtesy of Bethlehem Steel Corporation. Reproduced with permission.

Figure 14.7 Calculating Current Yield and Yield to Maturity

Current yield is *a bond's annual interest expressed as a percentage of the market or purchase price:*

current yield

$$\text{Current yield} = \frac{\text{Annual interest}}{\text{Purchase price}}$$

Assume a 9 1/2% bond with a $1,000 face value was bought at 105:

$$\frac{95}{1050} = 0.0905$$
$$= 9.05\% \text{ current yield}$$

Assume a 9 1/2% bond with a $1,000 face value was bought at 90:

$$\frac{95}{900} = 0.1056 = 10.56\% \text{ current yield}$$

Yield to maturity is *the percentage return an owner receives if a bond is held until it matures:*

yield to maturity

$$\text{Yield to maturity} = \frac{\text{Annual interest} \left\{ \begin{array}{l} - \text{ annual premium amortization*} \\ or + \text{ annual discount accumulation} \end{array} \right\}}{\text{Average principal (purchase price + face} \div 2)}$$

Assume an 8% bond with a $1,000 face value was bought 10 years before maturity at 90:

$$\frac{80 + \dfrac{100}{10}}{1900 \div 2} = \frac{80 + 10}{950} = \frac{90}{950} = 0.0947 = 9.47\% \text{ yield to maturity}$$

Assume an 8% bond with a $1,000 face value was bought 10 years before maturity at 110:

$$\frac{80 - \dfrac{100}{10}}{2100 \div 2} = \frac{80 - 10}{1050} = \frac{70}{1050} = 0.0666 = 6.67\% \text{ yield to maturity}$$

*Annual premium amortization and annual discount accumulation are obtained by dividing the premium or discount by the number of years to maturity.

Types of Bonds

You can categorize bonds several different ways, based on the assets that secure them and other criteria. The bond certificate itself (as shown in Figure 14.6 and Figure 14.8) states which of these categories the bond fits. The categories are summarized in Table 14.5.

Figure 14.8 Sample Equipment Trust Bond
Source: Courtesy Tiger International, Inc.

Making Decisions About Bonds

Bonds generally are considered safer investments than either class of stock because a bondholder is a creditor rather than an owner of the firm. The company pays interest on the bonds at regular intervals, and they will have a specified value when they mature. As a result conservative investors may prefer bonds to either kind of stock. Although it is impossible to prescribe a security that is appropriate for everyone's needs, the three major types are compared according to safety, growth, and income in Table 14.6.

As for the issuing company, the decision on whether to issue stocks or bonds is complex. A corporation's long-term financing mix may consist of stocks, bonds, or both. When deciding which security to issue, management compares the fixed costs and other obligations associated with each type against the company's objectives and projected earnings.

A firm that sells common stock typically sacrifices control (through voting rights) in order to raise capital on which there is no fixed cost. A firm is not obliged to pay dividends to common stockholders if profits are low or nonexistent or if the directors choose to reinvest earnings, so common stock is popular with new corporations facing an uncertain future or planning on rapid growth.

Selling preferred stock, however, creates an obligation to pay dividends if at all possible. A firm's financial reputation suffers if it does not pay dividends on preferred stock. On the bright side, preferred stock usually carries no voting rights, so common stockholders may vote to sell it to raise long-term capital without losing control of their firm.

Bonds carry a formidable set of obligations, namely, regular interest payments and a maturity date when the face value, or principal, must be paid. For these reasons, management must be confident that income will be adequate to meet the fixed interest

Table 14.5 Types of Bonds

Type	Characteristics
Mortgage bond	A bond secured by a claim against a specific company asset, such as buildings or land. The most secure of all corporate bonds.
Equipment trust bond	Often referred to as an *equipment trust certificate*. A bond issued to finance new equipment, the title to which is held by a trustee for the security of the bondholders. Popular long-term instrument for railroads and airlines (see Figure 14.8).
Income bond	A bond that pays interest only when the company's earnings permit. Unpaid interest may or may not have to be paid in the future, depending on the terms of the bond. A relatively rare type.
Debenture bond	An unsecured bond, backed only by the firm's general reputation. Considered the riskiest bonds of all; usually called, simply, *debentures*. (The coupon bond in Figure 14.6 is a debenture.)
Callable bond	A bond that the issuing firm may call in and pay off, usually at a premium, permitting the company to remove the debt early if the sinking fund earns greater income than anticipated. Interest payments end on the call date.
Convertible bond	May be exchanged for the issuing company's common stock. The market price of these bonds rises and falls with that of the company's common stock. Most are debentures. They usually pay a lower interest rate than nonconvertibles.
Serial bond	One from a bond issue that matures in lots or increments, either annually or semiannually, over several years. Essentially the issuing firm pays off a serial bond issue in installments. The bonds with later maturity dates carry a slightly higher interest rate than those with earlier dates.
Zero coupon bond	A noninterest bearing bond first marketed in the early 1980s. The bond is sold at a deep discount (perhaps 70 percent of par value or more) and redeemed for face value at maturity. The issuing firm benefits from paying nothing until the bonds mature. Although bondholders bear a greater risk (no money is received until maturity), such bonds have been bought by institutions with a specific need for future cash, such as companies that invest employee pension funds.

Table 14.6 Comparison of Three Major Types of Security

	Safety	Growth Potential	Income
Bonds	Greatest	None	Relatively certain
Preferred stock	Good	High	Assured
Common stock	Poor	Highest	Relatively uncertain

The Straight Line

Dow Jones and Company

Reporter to the World of Business

Reading *The Wall Street Journal* is as much a daily ritual as brushing one's teeth for many business-people, investors, students, and academicians. The *Journal* is the largest daily newspaper in the world and the only one uniquely devoted to reporting the news, trends, and issues affecting our business climate. Publisher Dow Jones and Company, like its renowned product, has been an integral part of the American business scene for more than a century.

It all started in late 1882 when reporters Charles H. Dow and Edward D. Jones left their native New England to create a financial news reporting company in the hub of the nation's financial district. Their original quarters consisted of a basement room beneath a soda fountain in a building near the New York Stock Exchange. Early on they hired a third reporter, Charles M. Bergstresser, and the trio worked diligently reporting the financial news of the day. Bergstresser and Dow (who reportedly took notes on his shirt cuffs) gathered and wrote the stories, submitting them to Jones for editing. Lacking printing equipment, Dow in turn dictated the final versions to secretaries who handwrote them on sheets of paper. This first product, the "Customers' Afternoon Letter," was hand carried by messengers to subscribers throughout New York's financial district.

Seven years later the staff had grown to fifty people and a Boston correspondent, Clarence W. Barron, joined the firm. In 1889 the letter, which by now ran four pages, was converted to a newspaper and named *The Wall Street Journal.* This revised publication, which carried advertisements at $0.20 per line, appeared in both morning and afternoon editions beginning in 1898.

In 1902 Charles Dow passed away and Clarence Barron purchased a controlling interest in the company. Within 2 decades the dynamic Barron had modernized Dow Jones and Company's printing facilities and expanded its reporting staff, while building daily circulation of *The Wall Street Journal* to more than 50,000 copies by 1929. Barron also conceived and introduced a new Dow Jones publication, *Barron's National Business and Financial Weekly,* in 1921.

With the onset of the Great Depression in 1929, circulation of *The Wall Street Journal* plummeted as fast as many personal fortunes. As readership declined to less than 30,000 copies per day, Dow Jones management decided to give the *Journal* a broader appeal by reporting a wider range of subjects. Several talented young writers were added to the staff to accommodate this shift in editorial philosophy, including Vermont Royster, Bernard Kilgore, and William F. Kerby. The afternoon edition was discontinued and the front page format was changed.

In the 1940s the scope of the *Journal*'s reporting was expanded even more until it was transformed into a chronicle that reported vir-

charges on its debt capital and to accumulate enough funds (usually in a sinking fund) to retire the debt at maturity. On the positive side, bond interest payments are business expenses — rent on

tually all facets of business-related news. By 1950 circulation was a healthy 100,000 copies per day as the paper reported developing trends and issues in a crisp, incisive, and engaging writing style.

During the 1960s a host of significant changes and accomplishments occurred at Dow Jones and Company including the addition of several regional editions, acquisition of a book-publishing company, and — in 1966 — a record circulation of 1 million copies per day. *Journal* reporters won six Pulitzer Prizes during this decade, and the company's researchers perfected a way to convey images among printing plants with the use of microwave transmission. The company's ownership group changed too when 110,000 shares of common stock were sold to the general public (although controlling interest — 56 percent — remains with members of the Bancroft family, who are the descendants of Clarence Barron).

The momentum of change in the 1960s carried through to the next decade and beyond to the 1980s as technology transformed almost every aspect of data recording and transmission. With more than 2 million subscribers and newsstand buyers, the *Journal* is now printed a full page at a time at seventeen plants throughout the country from images originating at a composing plant in Chicopee, Massachusetts. Dow Jones has expanded its range of publications to include a demographic magazine reporting information on population characteristics; three business and financial newswires serving subscribers in 850 North American cities; and a computerized business, financial, and consumer news and information data base that personal computer users may tap into using telephone and two-way cable lines. The company also broadcasts news reports eighteen times a day over a nationwide network of radio and television stations and a 30-minute television show produced in conjunction with the Independent Network News.

The Wall Street Journal, still at the center of this business news and information empire, exists today in a scope and formats likely to thrill its two creators. An Asian version was introduced in 1976, published in Hong Kong and printed in Hong Kong and Singapore — the only English-language daily business publication covering all of Asia. *The Asian Wall Street Journal Weekly*, published in New York, provides North American and European readers with business news from Asia. And *The Wall Street Journal/Europe*, first published in 1983, addresses the needs of European business executives and is circulated throughout Europe and parts of the Middle East. These and the American *Journal* are produced with a staff of more than 450 reporters, editors, and copyreaders working in 27 news bureaus in 8 countries, which truly makes Dow Jones and Company the world's business reporter.

For more about the global business reporting of Dow Jones and Company, see "A Brief Profile of *The Wall Street Journal*," a Dow Jones and Company news release dated February 1983; "A Brief Profile of Dow Jones," a Dow Jones and Company news release dated February 1983; *Celebrating Our First Century* (New York: Dow Jones and Company); Nancy J. Perry, "America's Most Admired Corporations," *Fortune*, January 9, 1984, p. 50; and "Dow Jones Votes New Class of Common As Stock Dividend, Raises Payout 20%," *The Wall Street Journal*, January 19, 1984, p. 5.

money borrowed — so they decrease a corporation's taxable income. In addition, financing with bonds, as with preferred stock, allows common stockholders to retain their control.

Pause and Ponder

Which do you believe is most important to the typical investor, a bond's current yield or its yield to maturity? Why?

Leverage

leverage *or* **trading on the equity**

In using **leverage** *or* **trading on the equity,** *a firm takes advantage of the sound market reputation of its common stock to sell bonds. The fixed capital thus obtained is used to improve company operations and earn back a greater return than the interest rate the company pays.* If the bond issue carries a 10 percent interest rate, for example, but the money is spent for new plants, improvements on existing plants, and more efficient new equipment, the firm may earn back, say, 20 percent on the borrowed funds. Leverage is a double-edged sword, however. The annual interest rate is fixed for the life of the bond issue, while the annual return on that borrowed capital varies from one year to the next according to business conditions. Should sales decline or expenses rise, the firm may find that the return earned on borrowed funds is less than their interest rate.

Summary

Companies must raise money for both the short and the long term to compete successfully in today's business environment. Short-term capital, the money used in day-to-day business operations, is raised to increase a firm's purchasing power, pay debts when cash receipts fall below expectations, and pay unanticipated expenses. In raising short-term capital, a company may use such instruments as promissory notes, drafts, commercial paper, and checks. It may establish trade credit or open-book accounts with several companies, or deal with such institutions as commercial banks, commercial finance companies, factoring companies, sales finance companies, and consumer finance companies.

A company raises long-term or fixed capital to buy assets that produce goods and services for several years. Retained earnings are one source of long-term capital, but few firms can finance major expansion strictly out of profits. Most will sell equity securities, which are called stocks, and perhaps debt securities, which are called bonds.

The Securities Act of 1933 and Securities Exchange Act of 1934 govern sales of securities to the general public. A corporation usually sells a new issue of securities to one or more investment banking firms, which in turn retail them to the general public.

A corporation's common stockholders may receive a cash or stock dividend as a return for their ownership risk if the corporation makes enough profit to pay it. In addition, common stockholders usually receive a preemptive right to purchase shares from new issues of their company's stock in proportion to their present holdings. Corporations sometimes also sell preferred stock, which enjoys a prior claim on the company's dividend payments and assets to that of common stock.

A corporation that finances with bonds borrows money on its long-term promissory notes. As creditors of the corporation, bondholders have a claim on assets ahead of either class of stockholders. Bondholders may trade their bonds at a premium or a discount to compensate for a bond interest rate that is higher or lower than the interest rate currently available from other investments. Corporations normally create a sinking fund so money will be available to retire a bond issue when it matures.

Companies use leverage when they borrow money through a bond issue hoping to earn a greater rate of return than the interest paid on the bonds. This practice can work against a company, however, if business conditions worsen and the return earned on borrowed funds falls below the interest that must be paid on them.

Key Terms

bond indenture
bonds
bond yield
capital appreciation
cash discount
cashier's check
certified check
commercial finance company
commercial paper
common stock
common stock certificate
consumer finance company
coupon *or* bearer bond
current yield
debt capital
discount

dividend
draft
equity capital
factoring company
fully registered bond
investment banking firm
leverage *or* trading on the equity
line of credit
long-term *or* fixed capital
odd lot
preemptive right
preferred stock
premium
promissory note
prospectus

registered bond
registrar
retained earnings
revolving credit agreement
round lot
sales finance company
short-term *or* working capital
sinking fund
stock dividend
stock split
trade credit *or* open-book accounts
transfer agent
warrant
yield to maturity

For Review and Discussion

1. How do companies use short-term or working capital? What reasons do firms have for raising such capital regularly?

2. Distinguish among the following instruments used in short-term financing transactions, and describe at least one situation in which each would be used: promissory notes, drafts, commercial paper, and checks.

3. List and discuss six sources of short-term financing and the type of transaction that characterizes each.

4. Why do companies raise long-term or fixed cap-

ital? What two sources of long-term capital are most popular?

5. Evaluate the following statement: "A well-managed company should be able to pay for expansion strictly from its earnings."

6. Name two laws that govern securities sales. What effect have they had on corporations? How have investors and potential investors benefited?

7. What is the difference between a registrar and a transfer agent? Why do large corporations use both?

8. What benefits and advantages do common stockholders enjoy? What legal right enables them to maintain their proportional control of the company?

9. Why do companies split their stock? Should stockholders view a split as a short-term or a long-term benefit? Why?

10. Contrast preferred stock with common stock. In what ways do the owners of preferred receive preferential treatment?

11. Define the following features of some preferred stock: participating, callable, convertible, cumulative, and noncumulative.

12. Compare bonds with promissory notes. What is the major difference? What do they share in common?

13. Express the following bond interest rates and market price quotations in dollars and cents. Then compute the premium or discount on each bond.

Interest	Market Price
8 1/4	87
11 1/8	113
5 1/2	71
9	101

14. Would you advise a corporation that is going to issue bonds to establish a sinking fund? Why or why not?

15. How do registered bonds and coupon bonds differ? How would you distinguish a bond that is registered as to principal from a fully registered bond?

16. Compute the current yield and yield to maturity on a 10%/$1,000 bond purchased at 115 with 10 years left until maturity. Compute both yields for the same bond purchased at 90 with 10 years to maturity.

17. Summarize the key features of each of the following: mortgage bond, equipment trust bond, income bond, debenture bond, callable bond, convertible bond, serial bond, and zero coupon bond.

18. Compare the three major kinds of securities on the bases of safety, growth potential, and income. Which are best suited for you at this time? Why?

19. What does a firm attempt to do when it uses leverage? Describe the risks and benefits of doing so.

Applications

Case 14.1 Financing with Receivables

Borrowing from commercial finance companies traditionally has been considered a last-ditch effort used only by firms that could not obtain short-term funds elsewhere. That view has changed somewhat in recent years, however.

Consider the experience of United American Food Processors, for example. This company, a supplier of top-grade beef to major hotels and restaurants, was unable to increase its inventories — and therefore attract additional customers — because banks were reluctant to lend money on beef. (It was perishable and subject to weekly price fluctuations.) Management solved this dilemma by finding a commercial finance company that would loan up to 90 percent of the value of United American's trade credit accounts. With some $2 million

made available to spend on more inventory, the company rapidly expanded its list of regular customers and within a decade sales multiplied almost three times: from $15 million to $43 million per year. Such growth would have been impossible without additional short-term financing for more inventory. The commercial finance company, then, proved to be an ideal source.

This kind of lender may loan as much as 100 percent of the value of top-quality trade credit accounts. Credit customers may be unaware that their balances are being used as loan collateral, although the commercial finance company may contact them to verify that they indeed owe the amount shown on the borrowing company's books.

A commercial finance company also may be expected to monitor the borrower's trade credit books carefully and request revised lists of credit customers and balances weekly or even daily. Interest rates on such loans may range from 2 percent to as much as 8 percent above the commercial banks' stated prime rate. That disadvantage may be offset by the fact that there are no hidden costs such as keeping a compensating balance on hand (standard practice with a commercial bank loan) that the borrower pays interest on but cannot use. Such conditions may make a commercial bank loan at the prime rate cost more than a loan from a commercial finance company.

Questions

1. Why might a commercial banker want to help a company arrange a loan from a commercial finance company?

2. Some commercial banks may also lend on the balances of trade accounts receivable. Why do you think banks have entered this more risky lending field? Do you believe bank officers in such departments fit the traditional conservative image? Why or why not?

3. Evaluate the following statement: "Granting trade credit to customers that are financially weak may be a mistake if the seller later tries to use their balances as collateral for a loan."

4. Why might it be wise to negotiate with several commercial finance companies when attempting to arrange a loan against receivables?

Case 14.1 For more about the new face of commercial finance companies, see Donna Sammons, "Receivables Financing Goes Respectable," *Inc.*, July 1983, p. 103.

Case 14.2 What's Involved in a Forced Conversion?

Corporations may issue bonds or preferred stock with both callable and convertible features. If the price of the company's common stock rises to an attractive level on the open market several years later, the firm may "force" the bondholders or preferred stockholders to convert their securities to common stock. This is done by calling them for an amount less than the market value of the common stock the holders would receive on conversion.

For example, in 1983 Grumman Corporation called an issue of 4 1/4 percent convertible debentures due in 1992 for $1,020.65 for each $1,000 of face value. The company also called its 11 percent convertible debentures due in the year 2000 for $1,093.81 per $1,000 par value. Holders of the 4 1/4 percent bonds had the choice of converting into 29.95 shares for each $1,000 face value; the 11 percent bondholders could receive 40.86 shares per $1,000 face value. Grumman common stock was trading for approximately $60.50 per share on the date the bonds were called.

In 1984 LTV Corporation called its participating convertible preferred stock, which was being traded for approximately $18.875, at $6 per share; however, stockholders could convert each share of preferred into 1.03 shares of common. The company's common stock was trading at approximately $18.625 per share on the call date. (Because companies do not issue fractional shares, the value of a partial share would be paid in cash.)

Questions

1. Calculate the dollar difference between surrendering each of the above securities for the call price and converting them to common stock.

2. What benefits would you receive by converting your bonds or preferred stock to common stock? Why would your risk increase after the conversion? What might you do?

3. Discuss the benefit to the company of staging a so-called forced conversion.

Case 14.2 For more about forced conversions, see "LTV Calls for Redemption Series 1 Preference Stock," *The Wall Street Journal*, January 10, 1984, p. 38; and "Grumman to Redeem Convertible Debentures," *The Wall Street Journal*, April 26, 1983, p. 45.

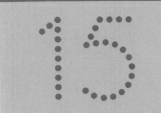

Risk and Insurance

Chapter Outline

Chapter Objectives

After studying this chapter, you should be able to:

1. Contrast the two kinds of risk that businesses encounter.
2. Outline the risk manager's role in company operations and summarize the methods that he or she can use in dealing with pure risk.
3. Explain how insurable interest, insurable risks, and the law of large numbers affect an insurance company's decision to accept a pure risk.
4. State the difference between a mutual insurance company and a stock insurance company.
5. Explain the work of actuaries and loss prevention engineers.
6. Summarize the criteria needed for an insurable risk.
7. Describe the various kinds of insurance that companies may purchase and explain the role of each one in protecting firms against pure risk.
8. Discuss the organization and operation of Lloyd's of London and explain its role in providing surplus lines of insurance coverage.

Business more than any other occupation is a continual dealing with the future; it is a continual calculation, an instinctive exercise in foresight.

— Henry Luce, founder, Time, Inc.

Maurice R. Greenberg

Pure Risk Has Its Rewards

Maurice R. Greenberg, the son of a New York dairy farmer, sits at the helm of a gigantic international insurance conglomerate, one of the biggest on the planet.

After graduating from the University of Miami and New York Law School, Greenberg had tentative plans for a career in the army or the FBI. His plans changed after a chance interview with an insurance firm, Continental Casualty Company. Irritated by the personnel director's manner during the interview, Greenberg complained directly to a company vice-president — and the fledgling lawyer was offered a job.

Through drive and outstanding ability, Greenberg rose to become east coast counsel for Continental and eventually became the youngest vice-president in the company's history. His im-pressive achievements led to an offer from another insurance firm, C. V. Starr & Company, which he accepted. Within 2 years he was president of a Starr subsidiary, American Home Assurance Company.

Greenberg moved American Home from personal lines into business insurance, which requires greater underwriting expertise but is more profitable and subject to fewer regulations. In 1968 Greenberg was named chief executive officer of the parent American International organization. Under his firm hand, American International Group (AIG) has become a global organization of more than 200 insurance companies and agencies that not only write conventional coverages, but also take on unpredictable risks, such as kidnapping,

Risk, which is the chance of loss, exists in most business decisions and transactions; indeed, it is the hallmark of a capitalistic society. Few business ventures are entirely risk free. In fact, many swashbuckling entrepreneurs embrace some profitable risks with verve. Excessive risk, however, can destroy people and companies alike, so managers must be risk conscious as well as profit conscious.

In this chapter we will discuss the kinds of risk that businesspeople face and the measures they can employ to deal with them.

Getting Acquainted with Risk

Two kinds of risk are inherent in business activities, and each has its own characteristics and its own implications for business organizations.

earthquakes, and liability lawsuits against corporate officers and directors. This kind of risk taking has paid off handsomely. Since AIG went public in 1969, it has achieved Greenberg's ambitious goal of 20 percent earnings growth every year.

More than half of AIG's employees work overseas, comprising a unique worldwide network that would be virtually impossible to reproduce even with unlimited time and money.

AIG's worldwide operations attract business from multinational companies, whose risks range from North Sea oil drilling rigs to globe-circling communications satellites. In recent years AIG has spun off specialty companies that serve the particular insurance needs of industries such as energy and entertainment.

In running AIG, Greenberg demands dedication to work and excellence in results. In turn, his exacting demands are matched with handsome rewards for those who share his commitment.

With all this success, why are other insurers not following the trail blazed by AIG? Greenberg is convinced that the reason is AIG's uniqueness: "You can't imitate our global operation. It's just incapable of being reproduced. Domestically, we have some imitators of pieces of our business, but not the entire business. And in any event, you can only imitate what we've done. You can't imitate what we're thinking. You can't copy what we're going to do tomorrow."

For more about M. R. Greenberg, see Cary Reich, "The Toughest Man in Insuranceland," *Institutional Investor*, September 1979, p. 91; Hugh D. Menzies, "The Ten Toughest Bosses," *Fortune*, April 21, 1980, p. 62; Robert J. Cole, "A High-risk Insurer," *The New York Times*, July 27, 1980, p. 7; and "Tough Guy in the Insurance Game," *Financial World*, March 15, 1982, p. 28.

Speculative Risk

A **speculative risk** is *a situation that may cause loss or gain.* Going into business for yourself is a speculative risk, but you may decide to take that risk, hoping for the reward called profit. Other examples of speculative risk, all of them ultimately taken in the hope of some gain, are:

speculative risk

— Investing time, equipment, money, and human resources to produce a new product
— Investing in the stock market or real estate
— Spending 2 or 4 years of your life, labor, and money to earn a college degree

As the examples suggest, people usually take speculative risks voluntarily — they choose to start a business, purchase stocks, or earn a college degree. The decision is up to them.

423

Pure Risk

pure risk

Pure risk is *a situation that can only become a loss.* Some examples of pure risk and the losses that result are:

— Destruction of physical property by natural disaster, riot, fire, or vandalism
— Injuries suffered in an automobile accident
— Court awards of damages to customers injured while shopping at a store or to consumers harmed by a product a company makes
— Death of a key business executive
— Medical bills arising from a serious illness

We do not expose ourselves to pure risk voluntarily, but if we lead normal lives we must get out of bed in the morning and go out into the world. Although we may not consider ourselves daredevils, we encounter pure risk constantly in the adventure called living. We share many pure risks in common with businesses, although many others are unique to their situation. In this chapter, we will focus on what businesses can do to remove, reduce, or insure against pure risk.

How Businesses Deal with Pure Risk

risk manager

Many firms now employ a full-time **risk manager,** *a person hired to identify significant pure risks that a company faces and prescribe effective techniques to deal with them.* The risk manager's responsibility is to recommend one or more of the antirisk actions: avoidance, reduction, transfer, or assumption. The first, avoidance, occurs when a firm does not undertake the venture and thus avoids the risk. Let's examine the other three antirisk actions.

Reduction

Under ideal conditions, management can reduce a pure risk so drastically that the likelihood of loss is remote, or — every risk manager's dream — nonexistent. Effective risk reduction programs can save companies thousands of dollars in employee injuries, lost production, and insurance costs. Some examples of risk-reducing activities and efforts are:

— Using flame retardant or fireproof building materials
— Storing inventory in several warehouses at different locations to minimize potential loss from fire or natural disasters
— Conducting safety programs that teach workers to use machinery properly

Funds invested in safety training are often returned many times over through lower insurance premiums and fewer lost time accidents.

— Installing drop safes in retail stores and service stations
— Monitoring customer traffic with closed circuit cameras to discourage shoplifting
— Providing cranes, hoists, dollies, hand trucks, and conveyors to reduce the likelihood of lower back injury on materials handling jobs

Companies frequently suffer severe losses from risks that could have been anticipated. One tragic example is Texasgulf, which lost seven managers and a pilot — each with an average of 17 years of service — in a single company plane crash. The managers included the firm's chairman and chief executive officer and three vice-presidents.[1] Although such group travel is commonplace, if the executives had traveled on more than one aircraft the loss would have been less serious to the firm.

Du Pont Corporation, one of several companies with exemplary safety programs, has received impressive benefits from the effort. In one year, this firm had just 129 lost-time worker accidents companywide, which was 1/23 the average lost-time accident rate for manufacturing companies according to the National Safety Council. This exceptional record enabled du Pont to avoid paying an estimated $26 million in accident-related costs.[2]

Transfer of Risk to a Noninsurer

It is often possible to let another party (not an insurance company) assume certain risks. A firm that leases vehicles, for example, can require the leasing company to insure them. Companies may dispense with risks associated with delivery vehicles altogether by employing a delivery service. A business owner who leases a building can require the landlord to insure it; and sellers may require buyers to pay for insurance on products to be shipped to them.

A business usually pays for transferring risk in this way, of course, because the other party often will charge more to enable it to pay for insurance. The business may still benefit, however, because transferring risk to a noninsuror reduces recordkeeping, reporting, and other paperwork expenses that come with insurance agreements and the filing of insurance claims.

Assumption by Self-Insurance

self-insurance fund

Large firms sometimes guard against certain kinds of pure risk by creating a **self-insurance fund,** *a special fund of cash and marketable securities that will be used to pay for losses caused by natural disasters such as fire, flood, and earthquake.* This approach is safe and practical only if the risks are very similar (buildings of the same construction housing the same kind and amount of inventory, fixtures, furniture, or equipment) and if the similar risks are scattered over a broad area. With a self-insurance fund, the firm assumes the risk.

The second condition means that self-insurance is only appropriate for firms not susceptible to massive localized losses resulting from a single natural disaster. Self-insurance is not recommended for firms with just a handful of plants or stores or for firms whose facilities are confined to one relatively small geographic area. In August 1983 hurricane Alicia caused approximately $675 million in insured losses when it struck the Texas Gulf Coast. Claims against one insurance company alone (Aetna Life & Casualty Company) were approximately $35 million.[3] At the end of that year the American Insurance Association reported that a record $1.89 billion in claims had been filed as the result of thirty-three catastrophes (a catastrophe to the insurance industry is an insured property loss exceeding $5 million).

In addition to hurricane Alicia (the second largest catastrophe on record), a massive winter storm system that blanketed thirty-eight states between December 17 and 30, 1983, caused $510 million in insured losses and ranks third in property and casualty claims records. The leader remains hurricane Frederick, whose 1979 rampage caused some $753 million in insured damage.[4] If a company with only local operations had decided to self-insure against those hazards, it would have been in serious financial trouble.

Some firms that might find self-insurance practical in certain cases are listed here.

— A retailer with many similar stores (such as Sears)
— A manufacturer or wholesaler with many similar warehouses
— A service firm with many similar offices spread over several states (such as a consumer finance company)

Of course, self-insurance should not be confined to just physical damage risks. Many firms self-insure for at least part of employees' health care and for workers' compensation claims (which will be discussed later in this chapter).

Self-insurance can be cheaper than going to an insurance company. Consider a chain of 1,000 retail stores that suffered average fire losses of $20,000 a year for the past 10 years. Management could assess each store a mere $20 annually, thus accumulating the amount of its average annual loss in a special fund that could be invested in stocks and bonds. Some of these securities could then be sold to pay for fire damage as it occurs. Besides being cheaper than purchasing fire insurance, this system also could stimulate more stringent safety programs and loss-reduction measures than if the firm had transferred the risk to an insurance company.

One problem with self-insurance is the possibility that a loss may occur before the fund is large enough to cover it. This possibility may be dealt with by making a very large initial contribution to the fund or by purchasing insurance to supplement the fund balance until it can be increased by regular contributions to a higher level.

It is somewhat rare for a company to self-insure completely against any risk. More often firms purchase insurance to cover losses that exceed the balance in their self-insurance fund. Generally a company should avoid self-insuring if it is (1) financially unsound, (2) frequently short of cash, or (3) just starting out in business.[5]

The Insurance Company

After exploring alternate ways of dealing with risk and employing one or more, management may still wish to transfer remaining risks to an insurance company. If that firm agrees to accept the risk, it will issue an **insurance policy,** which is *a legal contract that transfers risk from one party (the* insured*) to another (the* insuror*) for a fee called a* premium. Insurance is a major defense against pure risk. The insurance company will reimburse the insured up to the maximum amount specified in the policy if the risk occurs and causes a financial loss.

insurance policy

The premium that an insurance company charges for bearing a risk of loss is based on the **law of large numbers,** sometimes called the **law of averages.** This is *a mathematical law stating that if a large number of similar objects or persons are exposed to the same risk, a predictable number of losses will occur during a given period of time*. It is the concept that makes insurance work. Once an insurance company accumulates enough data on losses attributable to a certain risk to apply the law of averages, it can forecast the likelihood of loss and the average dollar amount of each loss. Then the company computes the premium it will charge. The premium will be high enough to cover expected claims, expand and improve its operations, and (for one type of insurance company) pay dividends to stockholders.

law of large numbers *or* **law of averages**

The law of averages reveals, for example, that both of the following are true:

— Those who smoke more than a pack of cigarettes a day double their chances of having heart attacks.

— Approximately half of those suffering second heart attacks will die as a result.[6]

Knowing the statistics, insurors can set life and health insurance rates for smokers that reflect the increased risk involved in insuring them. Figure 15.1 illustrates the effect of the law of averages on auto insurance rates: because younger men are involved in more accidents, rates for them are higher. As they grow older and the risk of their being in an accident decreases, the rate goes down.

insurable interest

Two other principles are essential to an understanding of insurance. The first is **insurable interest,** *the idea that the policyholder (the person who pays the premiums) must stand to suffer a financial loss before he or she will be allowed to purchase insurance on a given risk.* This prevents inappropriate persons from betting that a given risk will become a loss by paying premiums on an insurance policy and winning (by collecting the insurance money) if it does. If insurors did not require an insurable interest, you could buy insurance on anyone's life or property purely for personal gain; some unscrupulous people would be tempted to cause losses when the law of large numbers did not do the trick.

Generally speaking, married couples have an insurable interest in each other's lives, corporations in the lives of key executives, and partnerships in the owners' lives. You cannot buy life insurance on distant relatives, however, or on persons unrelated to you, and you cannot insure buildings, autos, or other property in which you have no financial investment or risk.

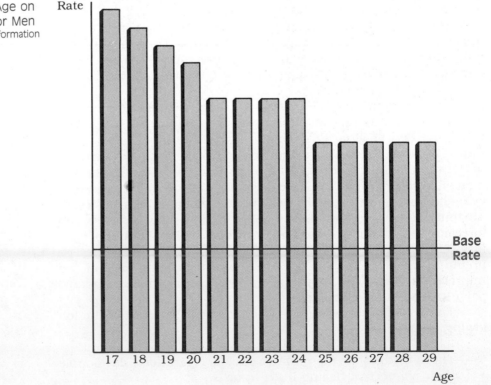

Figure 15.1 Effect of Age on Auto Insurance Rates for Men
Source: Courtesy Insurance Information Institute.

The other important insurance principle is the **principle of indemnity:** *the policyholder cannot profit by insurance.* You can buy physical damage insurance on a building to pay the replacement value of the building or the face value of the policy, whichever is less, but you cannot buy insurance for more than the building is worth. If you wanted to insure a building appraised at $300,000 for $600,000, the insurance company would reject your application; you cannot collect twice the value of property that is destroyed. And having that much insurance might encourage you to cause some accident, as the destroyed building would be so much more valuable than the building in operation.

Because the amounts of losses vary, insurance companies find it practical to offer a **deductible,** which is *an amount of a loss that the insured agrees to pay.* The deductible is actually a form of self-insurance that benefits both the insured and the insuror. The insured benefits because a deductible lowers the premium that the insurance company charges. Personal auto insurance policies with a deductible of $500 may cost several hundred dollars less a year than those with a deductible of $100. A deductible, especially a large one, also prompts management to work harder to prevent losses, because the company would have to pay a significant amount before insurance takes over. Insurors benefit because deductibles eliminate costly and irritating investigations, paperwork, and record-keeping for small nuisance claims and reduce the payout required when losses do occur.

An insurance company will pay an insured loss (less the deductible) only up to the face value of the policy. If you are under-insured, therefore, a financial loss may force you to make up the difference out of your own resources. The seventy-eight-year-old Larraburu Brothers sourdough bakery in San Francisco lost a $2 million lawsuit after one of its delivery trucks injured a child. Because the firm's insurance policy had a face value of only $1.25 million, insufficient to cover the damage award, the company had to make up the difference. The only solution was a drastic one: selling the company.

Insurance Companies and Their Personnel

There are two kinds of insurance companies, classified according to ownership. Both kinds employ two types of specially trained experts who help to make their operations efficient, accurate, and sound.

Mutual Companies and Stock Companies

A **mutual insurance company** is *one owned by its policyholders,* who elect a board of directors to oversee the company's operations. Policyholders act like stockholders in this regard, except that they are also being insured. Several examples of mutual companies are

principle of indemnity

deductible

mutual insurance company

Equitable Life Assurance Society of the United States, Massachusetts Mutual Life Insurance Company, Connecticut Mutual Life Insurance Company, The Mutual Life Insurance Company of New York (MONY), and Prudential Insurance Company of America. As the foregoing company names imply, mutual insurance companies are especially strong in the field of life insurance. Although there are only approximately 135 mutual life insurance companies in operation, they have written almost half the life insurance policies in existence and own 60 percent of the assets held by all United States life insurance companies.[7]

stock insurance company
    A **stock insurance company** is *one owned by stockholders*, like the traditional corporations you learned about in Chapter 3. Despite their different philosophies, however, the cost of identical coverage from a mutual company and a stock company of similar size is approximately equal.

Reserves

Insurance companies are required by law to keep reserves available to meet loss claims by policyholders, just as commercial banks must keep reserves available to meet depositors' demands. These reserves, like commercial bank deposits, appear as liabilities on the companies' financial statements. The funds not held in reserve are invested, making insurance companies among the largest institutional investors in the nation. They invest millions in such income-producing assets as stocks and bonds, office buildings, apartment complexes, and shopping centers. Aetna Life & Casualty Company, for example, owns two hotels in the French Quarter of New Orleans. Prudential Insurance Company of America has $66.7 billion in assets, which makes it the largest in the nation by that measurement. Its holdings include $19.8 billion in bonds, $14.7 billion in real estate mortgages, and $4.8 billion in common and preferred stocks.[8] Table 15.1 presents the total assets and the face value of the policies in force of the top seven insurance companies. Figure 15.2 shows how life insurance

Table 15.1 Top Seven Insurance Companies According to Total Assets and Coverage in Force
Source: Data provided by A. M. Best Company.

Company	Assets (Billions)	Coverage in Force (Billions)
Prudential Insurance Company of America	$66.7	$482.3
Metropolitan Life Insurance Company	55.7	426.6
Equitable Life Assurance Society of the United States	40.3	228.3
Aetna Life Insurance Company	28.6	180.1
New York Life Insurance Company	22.5	151.0
John Hancock Mutual Life Insurance Company	21.7	147.0
Travelers Insurance Company	17.4	137.9

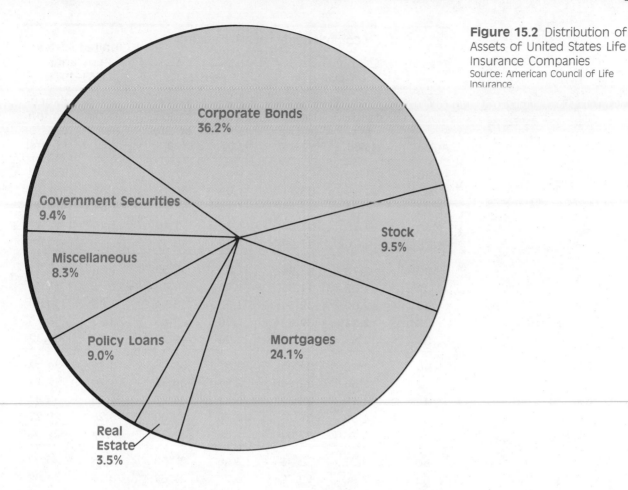

Figure 15.2 Distribution of Assets of United States Life Insurance Companies
Source: American Council of Life Insurance

companies invested money not required for reserves in one recent year.

Actuaries and Loss Prevention Engineers

An **actuary** is *a person who analyzes the likelihood of loss and the average amount of damage involved in pure risks and, applying the law of averages, computes the premium that the insurance company should charge to assume the risk.* Actuaries usually have a college education including extensive course work in mathematics and statistics. Actuaries work with tables like the one in Table 15.2. It is based on statistics about the lives and deaths of policyholders of several large life insurance companies.

A **loss prevention engineer (LPE)** is *an engineer who specializes in removing or reducing risk.* These engineers, who usually have a degree from a 4-year college, may be employed by an insurance company or by any firm that faces a wide variety of risks, such as a conglomerate with interests in chemicals, explosives, manufacturing, and mining. Because they know how to use machinery, equipment, materials, and devices to remove or reduce risks, LPEs

actuary

loss prevention engineer (LPE)

Table 15.2 Actuary's Mortality Table: Number of Deaths per 1,000 Persons at Various Ages
Source: *1983 Life Insurance Fact Book* (Washington: American Council of Life Insurance), 1983, pp. 108–109.

| Age | Commissioners' 1980 Standard Ordinary (1970–1975) | | | | United States Population (1969–1971) | |
| | Male | | Female | | | |
	Deaths per 1,000	Expectation of Life (Years)	Deaths per 1,000	Expectation of Life (Years)	Deaths per 1,000	Expectation of Life (Years)
20	1.90	52.37	1.05	57.04	1.40	53.00
22	1.89	50.57	1.09	55.16	1.52	51.15
24	1.82	48.75	1.14	53.28	1.51	49.30
26	1.73	46.93	1.19	51.40	1.43	47.44
28	1.70	45.09	1.26	49.52	1.44	45.58
30	1.73	43.24	1.35	47.65	1.55	43.71
32	1.83	41.38	1.45	45.78	1.72	41.84
34	2.00	39.54	1.58	43.91	1.95	39.99
36	2.24	37.69	1.76	42.05	2.25	38.15
38	2.58	35.87	2.04	40.20	2.66	36.32
40	3.02	34.05	2.42	38.36	3.14	34.52
42	3.56	32.26	2.87	36.55	3.70	32.74
44	4.19	30.50	3.32	34.77	4.43	30.99
46	4.92	28.76	3.80	33.00	5.28	29.27
48	5.74	27.04	4.33	31.25	6.24	27.58
50	6.71	25.36	4.96	29.53	7.38	25.93
52	7.96	23.70	5.70	27.82	8.76	24.32
54	9.56	22.08	6.61	26.14	10.43	22.75
56	11.46	20.51	7.57	24.49	12.36	21.23
58	13.59	18.99	8.47	22.86	14.52	19.76
60	16.08	17.51	9.47	21.25	16.95	18.34
62	19.19	16.08	10.96	19.65	19.74	16.97
64	23.14	14.70	13.25	18.08	23.06	15.65
66	27.85	13.39	16.00	16.57	26.99	14.38
68	33.19	12.14	18.84	15.10	31.52	13.16
70	39.51	10.96	22.11	13.67	36.61	12.00
72	47.65	9.84	26.87	12.28	42.66	10.88
74	58.19	8.79	33.93	10.95	50.75	9.82
76	70.53	7.84	42.97	9.71	60.60	8.84
78	83.90	6.97	53.45	8.55	71.53	7.93
80	98.84	6.18	65.99	7.48	83.94	7.10

Note: Mortality rates contained in the 1980 Commissioners' Standard Ordinary Table were obtained from experience of 1970–1975, but contain an added element designed to generate life insurance reserves of a conservative nature in keeping with the long-term guarantees inherent in life insurance contracts. Premiums for life insurance policies, on the other hand, are based on assumptions that include expected mortality experience.

can reduce significantly the amount of insurance an organization requires in many hazardous operations. They also can construct loss prevention programs that will reduce the premiums on the insurance purchased.

When a company first applies for insurance, an LPE may be called in to examine its operations and recommend accident prevention measures. This procedure is advantageous to the insured, the insuror, and society at large. When Marineland of Florida applied to the Hartford Insurance Group for coverage, Hartford's loss control experts surveyed Marineland's operations for hazards that could be reduced or eliminated. Responding to their recommendations, Marineland redesigned its parking area so pedestrians were better protected from moving automobiles, improved pedestrian traffic flow, and installed warning signals on the highway separating the attraction from the visitors' parking lot so drivers would watch for pedestrians crossing the road. Loss prevention engineers from Arkwright-Boston Insurance Company collaborated with the engineers of one client, textile producer WestPoint-Pepperell, to design sprinkler systems that reduced the risk of fire beneath the floors of several mills. The insurance company's LPEs also provided advice in designing a ventilation system that reduced the fire potential from synthetic dust generated during weaving operations.[9] Aetna Life & Casualty Company claims a staff of more than 600 LPEs who work out of one hundred locations nationwide.

Criteria for an Insurable Risk

Insurors are cautious about selecting the risks they insure. Their caution is justified, because an insurance company that neglects to evaluate risks carefully or issues policies indiscriminately may find itself unable to pay the claims that eventually result. Generally several conditions must be met before an insurance company assumes a risk. (Companies that do not meet these conditions may still be insured, however, through firms that issue surplus lines coverage or through Lloyd's of London, which will be discussed later in this chapter.) These conditions are:

1. A law of averages must exist.
2. The loss must be expressed in dollars.
3. The risk must be spread over a wide geographic area.
4. The insurance company reserves the right to increase the premium, to cancel the policy, or not to renew it if adverse circumstances arise.
5. The insurance company reserves the right to refuse payment under certain circumstances.

A law of averages must exist because the insurance company must possess enough data on the risk to predict how often losses will occur, the average payout associated with each claim, and other factors necessary to calculate a satisfactory premium. If no law of averages exists on a given type of risk (such as interplanetary space travel) the insurance company would be "flying blind" — it would have to guess at the likelihood of loss. Insurance against the failure of satellites has been available since 1964; however, when two satellites were lost during the Challenger space shuttle mission in February 1984 conditions changed abruptly. The satellites, owned by Western Union and the Indonesian government, were insured for $105 million and $75 million respectively. Their loss caused the insurance industry to rethink its law of averages on such hazards, and observers speculated that premiums could rise so high that future space probes by private companies and by governments would be severely handicapped. In the 6 years preceding these losses, insurance companies collected $240 million in premiums against satellite failures — but paid claims of $238 million.[10]

A second condition for an insurable risk is that the loss must be expressed in dollars. As we learned in Chapter 13, money gives us a way to measure the value of countless goods and services. If a loss cannot be expressed in dollars, the insurance company and the would-be policy owner lack a common denominator for expressing the worth of the insured item. Consider, for example, a painting that your great-great-grandmother did in high school. Even though it may have been handed down from one generation to the next and is treasured by members of your family, it has value only to them, not to the person on the street. Therefore insurance against the destruction, loss, or theft of the painting or other property that has only sentimental value may not be available.

A third condition for an insurable risk is that the risk must be spread over a wide geographic area. This concept, which was referred to in the earlier discussion of self-insurance, is equally important to insurance companies. For example, losses caused by certain natural disasters occur regularly in some parts of the country: freezing temperatures in northern states may burst pipes, and buildings may be damaged by the resulting water leakage as well as by the weight of snow and ice on their roofs. Parts of California often experience destructive brush fires and mud slides, property in the midwest may be destroyed by tornadoes, and states on the Gulf and Atlantic Coasts may suffer hurricane damage. If the insurance company spreads the risks it insures across the nation, however, a high number of loss claims in some states may be offset by a lower number in others — and this makes the law of averages work.

A fourth condition, that the insurance company must reserve the right to increase the premium, cancel the policy, or not to renew it if adverse circumstances arise, is reasonable from the insurance company's view. As the character of a risk changes, the company should be able to change its standards for accepting that risk. Consider, for example, someone with a "clean" driving record (no moving violations). If that person commits one or more major offenses (driving while intoxicated, speeding, or careless driving, for example) most insurance companies would raise the premiums significantly, cancel the policy, or refuse to renew it on its anniversary date, depending on the firm's operating policies and the severity of the offense.

A final condition for an insurable risk is that the insurance company must reserve the right to refuse payment under certain circumstances. Situations may arise that can make insurance companies the victims of their own policies or that may require them to pay claims for catastrophes that no insurance company should reasonably be expected to cover. The typical life insurance policy, for example, will not pay benefits if the insured is killed in an act of war. This stipulation is logical because wartime conditions cause more claims than the law of averages for life expectancy (which is based on peacetime conditions) predicts. Similarly, many life insurance policies will not pay if the insured is killed while piloting an aircraft, hang-gliding, driving in an automobile race, or engaging in other high-risk activities as defined in the policy itself. Such policies may not pay in the event of suicide, because self-destruction is considered intentional rather than a fateful occurrence. Health insurance policies customarily exclude preexisting conditions (illnesses that were present before the policy was issued) because such illnesses are no longer risks, they are certainties for that specific person.

What Insurance Does a Company Need?

Many of the pure risks that companies face may be protected against through insurance. The number and scope of pure risks that a large company must deal with are massive. A manufacturer, for example, may have millions of dollars of machinery, equipment, fixtures, materials, and products destroyed in a single plant fire. Businesses also are exposed to a variety of risks whenever they own and operate motor vehicles. Customers, visiting salespeople, and other nonemployees may file lawsuits to recover damages for injuries incurred on the premises, and legal action also may be brought by consumers who were injured by products the company manufactured, installed, or distributed. These examples are just a few of many potential hazards that companies encounter in the course of doing business, and they help to build a strong argument for carrying a sound and complete program of insurance. This section will provide you with a working knowledge of the types of insurance companies can purchase against various risks.

Fire insurance

A fire insurance policy covers damage caused to buildings by fire; its language may exclude the building's contents. Although a basic fire insurance policy covers only damage by fire, you may expand

allied lines *or* extended coverage

it by purchasing **allied lines *or* extended coverage,** *a feature that can be added to a fire insurance policy to encompass financial loss caused by such hazards as riot and civil commotion, hail, wind, falling objects, land vehicles, water, smoke, and possibly vandalism and malicious mischief.*

all-risk physical damage *or* multiple line coverage

One very broad category of physical damage coverage is **all-risk physical damage *or* multiple line coverage,** which fire insurance companies have offered for more than 30 years. This is *added fire insurance coverage that embraces all risks except those that the policy specifically excludes.* It may be added to a basic fire policy, and it is usually more reassuring than so-called named peril policies that cover only specifically stated risks. Damage to the building itself is not usually part of all-risk physical damage coverage (because the building is covered by the basic policy), but this extension reimburses financial loss caused by damage to inventory, materials, supplies, furniture, or fixtures. It is not unusual for chain retailers to supply merchandise to stores in several states from one gigantic regional warehouse. This practice naturally makes these large companies quite vulnerable to massive fire losses, as Kmart Corporation discovered. A major fire in that firm's 1.1 million square foot warehouse in Morrisville, Pennsylvania, choked off the supply of goods to 383 Kmart and S. S. Kresge stores in thirteen northeastern states and in Washington, D.C. Fortunately the building was insured for $38 million, its merchandise for $70 million, and equipment for $5 million. Officials estimated the structure would take at least a year to rebuild.[11]

History has recorded some massive fire losses in the United States, the largest being the San Francisco fire of 1906 that destroyed 28,000 buildings worth an estimated $350 million. This amount exceeded only the damage caused by the Chicago fire of 1871 (17,340 buildings worth $175 million) and by a 1982 fire in a retail distribution center in Pennsylvania that caused an estimated loss of $100 million.[12]

An insurance policy's language and different interpretations of that language sometimes can cause confusion. A businessperson must fully understand what assets and losses are protected in a fire insurance policy and its accompanying clauses. Fire policies usually do not cover damage caused by an exploding boiler, for example; a company usually needs a separate boiler and machinery policy.

coinsurance clause

As a rule most fire policies contain a **coinsurance clause,** *a stipulation that a company must insure a minimum (usually 80 percent or more) of a property's total value before the business will be fully reimbursed for a partial loss.* Insureds who do not purchase the stipulated amount must bear part of a loss themselves, above and beyond the deductible.

Insurance companies have no difficulty justifying coinsurance clauses. Most fire losses are partial ones; total destruction is rare. Without a coinsurance requirement, business owners would buy only enough insurance to cover the dollar amount of assets most likely to be destroyed according to the law of averages. Insurance

Fire damage can halt a company's operations temporarily or permanently. The difference may depend on adequate insurance coverage. Every business with physical assets should carry fire insurance.

companies would have trouble surviving if each policy they sold covered only the typical loss claim.

With coinsurance a firm that bought the required coverage would receive the total amount of the loss (less the deductible) up to the face value of the policy. An underinsured company (one that buys less insurance than the coinsurance clause requires) is reimbursed for a loss in the proportion of the actual amount of insurance to the coinsurance minimum. Figure 15.3 illustrates how this works.

Business interruption insurance, like allied lines and multiple line coverage, is *coverage that can be added to a basic fire insurance policy. It covers consequential losses, those that result from fire*

business interruption insurance

Figure 15.3 How a
Coinsurance Clause Works

A building is valued at $130,000. The insurance company has an 80 percent coinsurance clause.

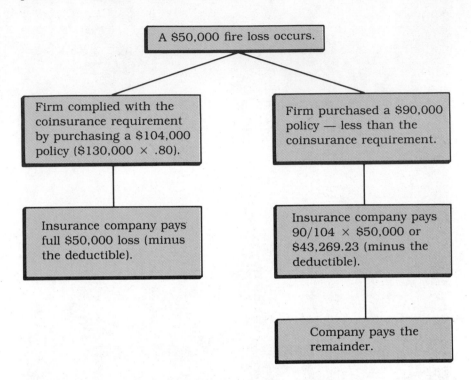

or other perils covered in the fire policy. Consequential loss coverage may, for example, pay employees' salaries or wages, business taxes, loan installments, and other fixed expenses that must be paid even if the business is closed temporarily by fire or other disasters. It also may pay the owner's normal profit while the business is being reconstructed, and pay to lease equipment and rent temporary quarters while the original facilities are being rebuilt. A drive-in theater whose screen was destroyed by a storm closed down for 26 days in midsummer. Data from the firm's accounting records showed revenues and expenses before the disaster, allowing the insuror to project them for the future. The company's insuror paid $2,990 in business interruption coverage, the projected net income lost during the shutdown.

**contingent business
interruption insurance**

A variant called **contingent business interruption insurance** is *insurance that covers a firm's losses when a key supplier's or customer's business is damaged,* something that could financially injure a company even though it suffers no physical damage itself. This coverage is not included in standard business interruption coverage.

Motor Vehicle Insurance

Many states require certain types of motor vehicle insurance (most notably bodily injury liability coverage) and leave other types optional. Businesses and individuals should avoid buying only the minimum required coverage, however, considering the losses that result from a motor vehicle accident. In this section we will explore the most common types of motor vehicle insurance and describe how they function. A deductible is applied in most of these coverages.

Collision and upset is *motor vehicle insurance that pays to repair damages to the insured vehicle up to its actual cash value (ACV) less the deductible if it collides with an object (including another vehicle) or overturns.* Property damage or personal injury done by your car is covered by property damage and bodily injury liability insurance (which will be discussed later in this section). Creditors on an auto loan protect their claim against the value of the car by requiring the borrower to supply proof of collision and upset insurance. This proof ensures that the car will be repaired or its cash value paid to the lender if it is damaged or destroyed in an accident. Because many new cars now contain highly complex miniature computers under the hood or on the dashboard that monitor or control the lights, brakes, fuel metering, and other systems, some insurance companies declare a car a total loss if the dashboard gets wet.

collision and upset

Property damage liability is *motor vehicle insurance that pays for damage the insured vehicle does to the property of others,* up to the face value of the policy. An insured vehicle easily can cause more property damage than the policy covers; when that happens, the insured must pay the difference. One hapless driver lost control of a car, jumped the curb, and sideswiped the front ends of a row of new Cadillacs parked on a dealer's lot. Another ran into and demolished an antique Packard — appraised at $100,000 — that was being driven to a classic auto rally. Neither unfortunate driver had enough property damage liability insurance to cover the damage fully.

property damage liability

Bodily injury liability, *sometimes called PIP (personal injury protection) insurance,* is *motor vehicle insurance that pays court-awarded damages for bodily injury, up to the face value of the policy, if the insured person is judged liable for a motor vehicle accident.* If you are held responsible for an accident that permanently handicaps another, that person is sure to sue you. If you lose, and the court judgment against you exceeds the face value of your insurance policy, you may have to pay the injured person a regular sum of money for the rest of your life. Because bodily injury liability suits often result in multimillion-dollar settlements today, businesses and individuals alike should be well insured against this risk.

bodily injury liability

Until recently, persons involved in an automobile accident had to engage in a lawsuit to determine which one was legally liable before insurance benefits for bodily injury liability could be collected. This process was expensive and typically delayed the payment of insurance benefits for several years. In the early 1970s, however, several states passed laws providing for **no-fault auto insurance,** which is *auto insurance that enables the parties to an accident to collect for bodily injury from their respective insurance companies, regardless of who was at fault.* Such laws were intended to streamline the settlement of bodily injury claims and reduce the backlog of auto accident lawsuits jamming the court system.

no-fault auto insurance

The provisions of no-fault insurance laws vary from one state to another. Differences exist primarily in:

— The maximum amount a person may collect for medical or funeral expenses
— The maximum a disabled person is allowed to collect to compensate for lost income
— Rights to bring suit (The parties may be legally barred from suing each other except in accidents involving death, permanent disability, disfigurement, or medical bills in excess of a stated amount.)

Prohibiting or severely limiting each party's right to sue the other would make no-fault insurance cheaper, proponents argued, because insurance companies wouldn't be paying attorneys' fees to defend their insureds in cases to establish fault. Insurance companies also would operate more cheaply assuming that state no-fault laws would limit or prohibit so-called pain and suffering claims by persons injured in accidents. Insurance analysts believed that the cost of insurance would decline under such circumstances despite the fact that both parties would collect for bodily injury from their insurors without a fault-finding suit.

In actual practice no-fault insurance has not been an outstanding success, because some states have not taken away each party's right to sue for pain and suffering. Other states prohibit these suits unless medical bills reach a certain "threshold for suit," but in several states (Colorado, Kansas, and Georgia, for example) one party can sue the other for pain and suffering after medical bills exceed just $500. This law provides an incentive for some injured persons to run up medical expenses unnecessarily just to qualify to file a pain-and-suffering suit against the other party.[13]

medical payments

Medical payments is *a form of motor vehicle insurance that pays the medical bills of the insured and of others the insured has injured while driving a vehicle,* up to the amount stated in the policy. Injured parties also may sue for bodily injury liability, but given escalating health care costs it is wise to be well protected against this particular risk.

comprehensive physical damage

Comprehensive physical damage is *motor vehicle insurance that protects the insured vehicle against most damage except that caused by collision and upset.* Some examples of hazards normally covered by comprehensive physical damage insurance are fire, flood, hail and dust storms, theft of the vehicle itself, theft of its contents (with such possible exclusions as tape decks and CB radios), vandalism, and interior damage not caused by normal wear and tear. This coverage excludes such normal deterioration as paint faded by the sun and rusted body panels, however, and it will not cover mechanical damage caused by operator negligence (as when the engine is damaged after being run without adequate oil).

uninsured motorist protection

Uninsured motorist protection is *coverage that pays the insured for bodily injuries caused by at-fault but uninsured or underinsured drivers and by hit-and-run drivers.* Damage to the

Pause and Ponder

Construct a profile of a high-risk driver. Consider such factors as age range, sex, make and model of car, special equipment, and kinds of moving violations. Which of your friends, if any, fit this profile? What might they do to improve their classification as far as the insurance company is concerned?

vehicle itself would be covered by collision and upset insurance. If you or others in your car are injured by another driver with no insurance and few or no assets, a court judgment against that person for medical payments may be of little comfort. There are no payments to be had. The "underinsured" feature provides payment in the event that you or other occupants of your car suffer injuries that exceed the dollar limits of the other driver's policy. A summary of motor vehicle coverage appears in Table 15.3.

Workers' Compensation Insurance

Workers' compensation insurance is required of most employers in all fifty states. *It pays part of an employee's wage or salary plus medical expenses, and any necessary rehabilitation, retraining, job placement, or counseling, if a worker is accidentally injured on the job or contracts a job-related disease.* It also pays a lump sum to a spouse or child of a worker killed on the job. This coverage favors both the employer and employees. The employer benefits because workers' compensation laws prohibit employees from suing employers for job-related injuries or illnesses (their relief comes through the filing of an insurance claim). Employees benefit because they receive prompt payment for medical treatment, lost wages, and other claims connected with on-the-job injuries or illnesses without having to prove the employer negligent in a costly lawsuit.

workers' compensation insurance

Table 15.3 Summary of Motor Vehicle Insurance Coverage

Bodily Injury Coverage	Policyholder Covered	Others Covered	Property Damage Coverage	Policyholder's Car Covered	Property of Others Covered
Bodily injury liability		√	Property damage liability		√
Medical payments	√	√	Comprehensive physical damage	√	
Uninsured motorist protection	√	√	Collision and upset	√	

Insured businesses can save themselves a lot of money by adopting stringent risk-reduction measures, especially employee safety programs. Workers' compensation insurance premiums are based on the following statistics:

1. Employer's accident claim rate
2. Degree of hazard or risk inherent in the job
3. Size of employer's payroll

An employer in a hazardous business, such as explosives manufacturing, will pay higher premiums than the operator of, say, a retail clothing store. Rates may vary from one-tenth of 1 percent of a company's payroll to more than 20 percent.

In some states workers' compensation laws allow employers to self-insure or join a self-insurance fund maintained by a trade association. Most companies, however, choose to cover this risk by purchasing insurance.

Public Liability Insurance

public liability insurance

Public liability insurance is *insurance that covers financial loss caused by an injury to a nonemployee that results from the business's negligence and that occurs on its premises.* (It is also available to homeowners.) Being found guilty of negligence does not mean that you deliberately caused an injury, only that you did not exercise due care to prevent it. Lawyers representing hotel guests filed public liability suits seeking more than $270 million in damages in the aftermath of the 1980 MGM Grand Hotel fire in Las Vegas. The collapse of sky bridges inside the Crown Center Hyatt Regency Hotel in Kansas City, Missouri, in 1981 resulted in the filing of $3 billion in public liability lawsuits.

Entertainment companies also find public liability insurance desirable, considering the potential injury claims that may arise after a large rock concert. Century II Promotions, which arranges concerts for Alabama, Juice Newton, the Thrasher Brothers, and various other groups, has public liability insurance provided by the St. Paul Companies. According to a St. Paul representative factors such as crowd control, barriers between the crowd and the entertainers, protection provided for the entertainers themselves, and the general nature of the crowds the group attracts must all be considered in writing such specialized public liability insurance.[14]

Businesspeople assume the responsibility of keeping their premises reasonably safe, but if an injured person sues for public liability, a jury decides what "reasonably safe" means. If it finds the company negligent, the jury also sets the amount of damages to be paid to the injured party. Because juries are holding companies strictly accountable for maintaining safe premises, a judgment easily may exceed the face value of a company's policy, and the firm may be financially strapped or even forced to liquidate its assets to pay the difference.

Product Liability Insurance

Product liability insurance is *coverage that protects a firm against financial loss when persons file suit claiming they were injured by its product.* As in public liability suits, juries decide whether the firm is at fault for the product related injury and what damages, if any, the injured party will be paid. Juries have held manufacturers liable because products did not perform as advertised, because customers were not warned about the dangers of using them, or because the warnings, though present, were not conspicuous enough. In one recent year over 80,000 such suits were filed. California juries in one year awarded damages for such suits at an average of nearly $4 million a month.

Given the present trend of court judgments in favor of the plaintiff in product liability suits, premiums have risen astronomically. Manufacturers of such products as aircraft parts, power lawn mowers, football helmets, and grinding wheels have had difficulty finding an insuror who will assume the risk of product liability.

Consumers and juries are rightly outraged at the performance failure of some products that result in unnecessary and avoidable injury. Businesses, on the other hand, are growing alarmed at the apparently punitive attitude juries are taking, sometimes blaming a manufacturer for a consumer's poor judgment. A homeowner sued a power lawn mower manufacturer because he cut off his fingers while holding the mower and using it to trim his hedge; he won the case. One result of the rise in product liability cases and awards is increased prices, for manufacturers pass their costs along to consumers. General Motors reportedly adds more than $18 to the price of each new car to cover product liability claims.

product liability insurance

"Tell the court what happened, when you drank the tonic that was supposed to restore normal growth of hair."
Source: From *The Wall Street Journal*, permission Cartoon Features Syndicate.

Fidelity Bond

Not a financing instrument, a **fidelity bond** is *an insurance policy that reimburses an employer for financial loss resulting from employee dishonesty.* The insurance company (called the *surety*) bonds or insures the acts of a second party (the employee, or *principal*), who works for the employer (the *obligee*). If the employee has been proved to have committed theft, the insurance company reimburses the employer up to a specified maximum and attempts to recover the value of the stolen property from the employee. There are three kinds of fidelity bonds:

fidelity bond

1. A blanket bond covers all present and future employees.
2. An individual bond covers a specific employee.
3. A schedule bond covers a specific group of people or jobs.

Employers commonly purchase fidelity bonds to cover retail store salespeople, bank tellers, warehouse workers, traveling salespeople who carry expensive samples, and any other workers who have custody of or access to cash or valuable inventory. One purchasing agent who bought light bulbs received a kickback from the industrial distributor. After approving each payment, the agent secretly returned the bulbs. The employer filed a $261,000 fidelity bond claim after the fraud was discovered.[15]

Surety Bond

surety bond

A **surety bond,** *sometimes called a* performance bond, is *insurance that guarantees that a contract will be completed.* It is often used in the construction industry for projects such as buildings, highways, bridges, and even ships. Miscellaneous forms are also available to guarantee the solvency of a bank or guarantee that a self-insured company can in fact pay a certain dollar amount of loss out of its self-insurance fund. A surety bond insures the principal's character, skill, and ability to complete a contract according to its terms. If the contract is not fulfilled satisfactorily, the customer may petition the insurance company that bonded the contractor to set things right. This may be done in at least three ways; the insurance company can (1) provide a loan if the contractor ran out of money, (2) hire another contractor to finish the job, or (3) pay the customer the face amount of the surety bond.

Assume that you hired a bonded construction company to build your home. Later you discover that the company used standard-grade materials instead of the premium ones that you contracted for and paid for and that they also failed to follow the blueprints correctly. If the builder does not remedy these defects, you could sue for breach of contract, requesting the firm that posted the surety bond to find another company to do the work properly.

Errors can be disastrous on large-scale construction projects. A surety bond insures that work will be done correctly.

A company that wants to obtain a surety bond must supply extensive information to the bonding company, which then conducts an investigation and decides whether to stand behind that firm's work. A contractor with a history of shoddy work and frequent customer disputes may find it difficult if not impossible to obtain a surety bond.

Life Insurance

Life insurance protects against economic loss resulting from death. It is a unique form of insurance because it covers a risk that is certain to become a loss. When the insured person dies, the face value of the policy is paid to the **beneficiary,** *one or more persons or organizations that the policyholder designates to receive the cash payment on a life insurance policy.* Most policies provide for **double indemnity,** *a feature that guarantees that twice the face value of a life insurance policy will be paid if the insured dies accidentally.* Life insurance is a flexible instrument that should be part of everyone's plan for financial security. The belief that "the insurance company is betting you'll die and you're betting that you won't" is distorted and inaccurate. There are many variations of life insurance that can be tailored to suit the insured's financial goals and circumstances. In general, life insurance can:

beneficiary

double indemnity

— Provide money to pay the deceased's debts and funeral costs
— Pay an income to survivors after the insured's death
— Guarantee that a certain amount of money will be paid to the insured person some time in the future or to a beneficiary after the insured person dies
— Provide a retirement income to supplement money received from social security, an employer's pension program, or any other sources
— Create a fund that may be borrowed against or converted to cash in an emergency

Table 15.4 summarizes the types of insurance you can buy to accomplish these goals and introduces related terminology.

Sometimes endowments (see Table 15.4) are included in higher managers' compensation packages. The firm pays premiums, which are a valid business expense for federal income tax purposes. The policy pays a generous sum to the executive at retirement or to the beneficiary if the executive dies beforehand. Because such endowments are a form of insurance, the amount the company pays as premiums is invested to earn money. Thus the employer avoids paying the full amount that the executive collects. The return, or interest, on endowments and annuities may fall short of the inflation rate, meaning they are less desirable as investments. Nevertheless, the discipline of making regular payments and the guarantee of a set rate of return makes them appealing to some people. See Figure 15.4 for a look at the growth of group life insurance in the United States.

Table 15.4 Types of Life Insurance

	Policy	Characteristics
term insurance	Term insurance	*Pays only if the insured dies during a specified period of time.* Cheapest form of coverage. Policies are often renewable (for a higher premium, as the insured is older) and also may be convertible into whole life or an endowment.
credit life	Credit life	A type of *term insurance that pays the remainder of a debt if a debtor dies.*
whole life	Whole life*	*Remains in effect for the insured's entire life; pays on death.*
straight life	Straight life	A *type of whole life. Premiums are paid until the insured's death.* Payments may be difficult for retirees on fixed income.
limited-payment	Limited-payment	A *type of whole life. Distributes over a fixed number of years the total premium the insured would pay until death according to the law of large numbers,* meaning policy is paid up after a specified period of time though coverage continues until insured's death.
universal life	Universal life	A *highly modified form of whole life insurance. Part of the premium buys insurance coverage that will be paid if the insured dies. The rest of the premium is invested in high-yield securities that are intended to increase the policy's cash value more rapidly than that of a traditional whole life policy.*
group life	Group life	*Available to employees through their employer on a master policy, usually without a medical examination required.* A popular fringe benefit (see Fig. 15.4).
adjustable life	Adjustable life	*Insured may raise or lower the face value, lengthen or shorten the protection period, or change the kind of protection as personal circumstances require.*
annuity	Annuity	A *contract that pays the policyholder (annuitant) a fixed sum at regular intervals for a specified period of time. If the annuitant dies before collecting the face value, a beneficiary receives the remainder.* Insuror may guarantee a certain percentage return on payments, and may pay more than that if investments earn more than anticipated.
endowment	Endowment	*Combines the characteristics of savings and insurance; the policyholder collects a stated sum if he or she is living when the policy matures. The beneficiary receives the amount the endowment was intended to accumulate (the face value) if the policyholder dies before the policy is fully paid up.*

*Both types of whole life accumulate a *cash surrender value,* an amount the policyholder may collect in cash if the policy is canceled before death or maturity. Policyholders also may borrow against this amount. Cash surrender values increase over time as more premiums are paid in.

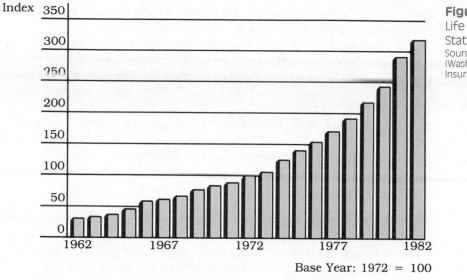

Figure 15.4 Growth of Group Life Insurance in the United States

Source: *1983 Life Insurance Fact Book* (Washington: American Council of Life Insurance), 1983, p. 29.

Base Year: 1972 = 100

Health Insurance

Health insurance is *insurance that covers medical expenses incurred by the insured and perhaps the insured's family.* It is available to individuals, but it is often provided by employers as a fringe benefit. The insuror issues a master policy establishing the terms and conditions of the insurance and describing the employees eligible for coverage. The law of large numbers makes the cost of a group health insurance plan lower than similar coverage purchased by employees as individuals.

The Department of Health and Human Services reports that consumers spend approximately $1 of every $10 for health care, and the annual total spent for health care nationwide exceeds $321 billion.[16] All of this means, of course, that health insurance now costs employers more than virtually any other employee benefit. For example, group health insurance premiums for Growth Enterprises, a New Jersey restaurant development company with 190 employees, increased by $36,000 to $121,000 in 1 year. The insurance company also indicated it would exercise considerable discretion over which claims to pay and which to deny. Although the company managed to reduce the cost of this benefit by $29,000 by creating a self-

health insurance

Pause and Ponder

Recommend the insurance coverage that the following organizations should purchase, and discuss what would affect the premiums that each would pay for different kinds of coverage: a fireworks manufacturer, a plant nursery, a children's day care center, a church, a welding shop, an auto repair service, and a traveling carnival.

insurance program that was supplemented with an insurance policy, the first-year cost of the new plan was still $92,000.[17]

Group health insurance usually contains a major medical provision that pays the cost of catastrophic illnesses involving lengthy and expensive treatment and recovery. Some policies set a maximum on this coverage — say, $250,000 — but others have no upper limit. The employee usually pays a deductible, after which coverage is provided according to the terms of the master policy. Physician, nurse, hospital, and other fees are paid according to a schedule, and the insured is responsible for the difference.

Disability Income Insurance

disability income insurance

Disability income insurance *pays a sum of money to be spent as the insured chooses if he or she is unable to work because of illness or injury.* This coverage may supplement workers' compensation payments for a job-related illness or injury, and it helps replace income the insured otherwise would have earned. In some cases the definition of *disability* has been expanded to include pregnancy.

Transportation Insurance

transportation insurance

Transportation insurance *covers loss of cargo from hazards such as contamination, spoilage, theft, fire, breakage, or collision while in transit.* Such protection is very important to firms such as R. T. French Company, which reportedly ships over $10 million worth of mustard and other products to ninety-eight countries each year. Under the terms of these policies carriers are liable for losses caused by their own negligence, but not for losses caused by floods, earthquakes, or other "acts of God," as the language of most policies has it. Of course, even a carrier who is insured against such risks may lose out if the value of a damaged shipment exceeds the face value of the policy.

ocean marine insurance

There are two kinds of transportation insurance. The first, **ocean marine insurance,** is *insurance that protects a cargo against loss on the high seas.* This insurance is the oldest in existence. Marine insurors have been called on to cover such unusual risks as the sixteen-story floating pulp mill that was moved by water the 15,000 miles from Japan to Brazil. The second, **inland transit insurance,** is *insurance that covers losses caused by catastrophes and acts of God for overland transportation.* It is often issued against such specific risks as collision, wind, lightning, derailment, or hijacking.

inland transit insurance

Power Plant Insurance

power plant insurance

Power plant insurance, *also called* boiler and machinery insurance, *covers losses caused by an exploding steam boiler, furnace, heating plant, or other equipment.* Fire insurance policies usually exclude such hazards, making separate coverage necessary. The insurance company inspects the insured equipment periodically to verify that it is properly maintained and in safe working order.

Credit Insurance

Credit insurance is *insurance that protects a firm against bad debt losses above a maximum amount on trade credit accounts.* A business can buy coverage on specific debtors, but it is more typical to insure all trade credit accounts on the books. Premiums may range from one-tenth to one-fourth of 1 percent of covered sales, and the average deductible is approximately one-fifth of 1 percent of sales.[18] The insuror will of course review the quality of the receivables on the books before quoting a premium.

credit insurance

Risk reduction is very practical with credit insurance and can save a lot in premium costs. With perpetual open-book accounts that have high average balances, it is more practical to monitor the debtor's financial health closely. The risk of truly devastating bad debt losses also may be minimized by selling to customers in a wide variety of industries, thereby reducing the risk of loss caused by an abrupt economic decline in a single industry.

Because geographic catastrophes like hurricanes or droughts may also impair the collection of trade credit accounts, selling to customers over a wide geographic area may be advisable too. Other ways to reduce the risk of bad debts are to sell on a COD (cash on delivery) basis or to sell to government agencies, which are perhaps the safest class of trade credit customer.[19]

Hazardous Waste Insurance

Hazardous waste insurance is *liability insurance required by the Environmental Protection Agency (EPA) that will provide payment to persons who are awarded compensation for bodily injury and property damage caused by accidents arising from the operation of hazardous waste facilities.* In effect since mid-1982, this regulation applies to owners or operators of some 7,000 facilities that store or dispose of such contaminants. Companies must be insured for at least $1 million per occurrence and $2 million total per year for sudden accidents such as spills, fire, or explosion and $3 million per occurrence and $6 million total per year for nonsudden accidents such as the gradual leakage of carcinogenic or toxic pollutants into the earth or atmosphere. These amounts must be earmarked exclusively for paying claims; they cannot include costs of legal defense.

hazardous waste insurance

Because few insurors offered protection against gradual accidents in the past, the EPA requirement to carry that coverage was phased in during a 3-year period starting with companies that had the greatest potential for a catastrophe. Firms with annual sales over $10 million had to be covered by January 15, 1983; those with sales between $5 and $10 million by January 15, 1984; and firms with less than $5 million by January 15, 1985.

Surplus Lines

surplus lines coverage

Surplus lines coverage is *insurance for risks on which no law of large numbers exists.* There is little or no history on the risk, the likelihood of loss, or the amount of financial damage that the risk-taker may incur if it becomes a loss. Some examples are:

— Political risk insurance, which pays if a company's assets in foreign countries are seized by the government. This type of insurance became quite popular after the revolution in Iran.

— Satellite insurance, which covers damage or loss of a satellite (see page 434). Satellites launched from the space shuttle also must carry $500 million of liability insurance in case they fail to disintegrate on a plunge to earth and cause damage on landing.

— Sexual harassment and sexual discrimination insurance, which pays up to the face of the policy if a company is judged guilty of either offense.[20]

Only a few American insurance companies — Prudential Insurance Company of America, Allstate Insurance Company, INA Corporation, and American International Group — issue this coverage.

Lloyd's of London, a legendary risk-taking institution for nearly 300 years, was born in 1687 in a London coffeehouse owned by Edward Lloyd. The coffeehouse was a gathering place for sailors

The EPA requires owners or operators of hazardous waste facilities to carry insurance against accidents that would contaminate the environment.

and sea captains who, thanks to their experience, were able to evaluate shipping risks accurately enough to insure cargoes as a profitable sideline. The organization branched out from its original marine insurance lines to become the most likely insuror in the world for surplus lines.

Technically speaking, a risk is not insured *by* Lloyd's of London; it is insured *through* Lloyd's. The organization currently has over 18,000 members (called *underwriters* or *Names*) organized into syndicates, who back the risks they insure with their personal wealth. A business wishing to obtain insurance through Lloyd's must contact an authorized agent (there are over 1,200 worldwide) and describe the risk for which insurance is sought. The agent then approaches a broker at Lloyd's headquarters, who in turn approaches underwriters who may be willing to insure part of the risk. These underwriters spread the risk among themselves, agreeing to insure a portion of the total amount desired. Should the risk become a loss, the Names who collectively insured it will pay the proportional amount for which each was committed.

Anticipating the wedding of Prince Charles and Lady Diana Spencer, British companies produced commemorative medallions and glassware, and American firms ran contests awarding free trips to London. Canadian and Australian businesses also speculated in ventures that depended on the wedding taking place. Lloyd's was asked to underwrite approximately $22 million in insurance to pay the losses suffered by such companies if the wedding were delayed or canceled.[21]

In 1981, American and National League baseball club owners purchased insurance against a players' strike through Lloyd's of London; it proved to be a sound decision. Although a major league official declined to state exactly how much insurance money was paid to the individual clubs, he acknowledged that it did help them offset losses from the lengthy strike that occurred the following summer.

Summary

Businesses deal with two kinds of risks. Speculative risk, such as the risk of doing business, may result in either a gain or a loss. Pure risk can only become a loss. To help them deal with pure risk, larger firms usually employ a risk manager, who finds ways to avoid it, transfer it to a noninsuror, or self-insure against it. Risk managers often seek insurance against a given risk if these measures do not neutralize it.

As professional risk takers, insurance companies assume a risk for a fee called a premium. Insurance depends on the law of large numbers to predict the likelihood of loss. Insurance companies are organized as mutual companies, owned entirely by their policyholders, or as stock companies, owned by stockholders. Both types employ actuaries to analyze the law of large numbers and compute premiums on various pure risks, and both hire loss prevention

The Straight Line

Kidnap and Ransom Insurance

Prominence Has Its Price

It's the kind of insurance that few companies will talk about and none will admit they carry. It's a sign of the times for many high-profile firms with worldwide operations. It's insurance against the kidnapping and ransom of prominent executives. While the very thought of such an act is repulsive and alien to most of us, kidnap and ransom, or K & R, coverage is available should that risk become a reality, as it did for brewery magnate Peter Heineken in Holland not long ago.

With international terrorism increasing and domestic social order fraying at the edges, more companies are buying these policies. Secrecy surrounds the topic, however, because potential abductors would be more likely to kidnap a key executive if they knew the company had insurance. Similarly, ransom demands would escalate with knowledge that the loss was insured.

If a key manager is abducted, the insuror may pay the expense of a ransom demand (including the fees of negotiators hired to bargain terms of the manager's release) and interest on a bank loan to obtain the cash. The ransom money itself will be reimbursed, of course, if it is not recovered. A company also may be paid for money that is lost, stolen, or destroyed before it is delivered. Because ransom demands are not always for cash, the value of property, securities, or services also will be reimbursed. One policy pays an abducted manager's family up to $5,000 per week for up to 5 weeks to cover living expenses and medical, security, or legal fees. Coverage is commonplace for extortion demands as well.

Although the maximum face value varies from one insurance policy to the next, coverage of up to $5 million per incident and $10 million per policy period (which may be 1 year or more) are available. The deductible, which is negotiable, may be expressed as a percent of each loss. At least one insurance company cites a minimum deductible of $25,000.

Several conditions must be met before coverage takes effect; for example, the company may not reveal the existence of the insurance to anyone except a select group of top managers. Management also must agree to inform the FBI or other appropriate law enforcement agencies before paying any money to the abductors.

engineers to advise clients on how to reduce or remove risk. Insurance companies only write a policy if the policyholder has an insurable interest in the person or object being insured. And insurors only allow coverage up to the replacement value of an object — the policyholder cannot profit from the loss.

The risks that insurance companies accept must meet several conditions. A law of averages must exist on the risk, the loss must be expressible in dollars, and the risk must be spread over a wide geographic area. In addition, the insurance company reserves the

The serial numbers of all currency must be recorded before payment, and management must have a written procedure to follow for notifying law enforcement officials. The procedure must not disclose that insurance has been bought, however.

Avoiding such an atrocity is better than confronting it, and there are several ways to reduce the chance that a manager will become a target for terrorism. Because outward signs of wealth are often read as price tags by potential abductors, it helps to disguise a highly paid key manager to look like just another businessperson. Executives who are not required to lead a high-profile public lifestyle may escape unwanted attention by restricting photographs of themselves and family members; removing vanity license tags from their cars and corporate logos from all company vehicles; using a modest automobile instead of a flashy limousine (and riding in front with a nonuniformed chauffeur, if the car is chauffeur driven). Still other recommendations include revealing travel plans and daily agendas only to persons who must know them and avoiding predictable patterns of behavior such as taking the same route to work each day, leaving a home or office at the same time each day, or eating in the same restaurants on certain days of the week. Some companies employ chauffeurs who also serve as bodyguards and train them in evasive driving tactics.

Foreign travel has become a concern for security-conscious managers. High-risk countries (such as some in South America and the Middle East) should be avoided if possible. Whether traveling at home or abroad, a few key people prefer to make hotel reservations under an assumed name and refuse to answer lobby pages (perhaps arranged by someone who wants to be able to recognize them on sight).

Such inconvenient and elaborate measures irritate many managers by introducing additional complications into an already complex and hectic schedule. Nevertheless, some corporations and top executives view them — and the K & R insurance they hope never to use — as necessary concessions to an increasingly uncertain world.

For more about kidnap and ransom insurance, see "Dressing for Success May Not Be Safe," *The Orlando* (Florida) *Sentinel*, February 16, 1984, p. E-12; "Insurance Decisions — Executive Security." (Philadelphia, Penn.: Insurance Company of North America); and Lisa Berger, "The Insurance Policy No One Will Talk About," *Parade*, January 8, 1978, p. 12.

right to increase the premium, to cancel the policy, or not to renew it if adverse circumstances arise, and payment may be refused under certain conditions.

Companies require several kinds of insurance, depending on the risks they encounter. Fire insurance covers losses to a building caused by fire, but it can be expanded to include coverage for the building's contents and losses owing to other calamities. Various risks of operating a motor vehicle can be insured against. Laws in all fifty states require employers to purchase workers' compensation insurance, and most firms consider carrying public liability protection. Many businesses — certainly most manufacturers — obtain product liability protection. Many firms whose employees handle money or valuable goods get fidelity bonds, and contractors get surety bonds. Firms in all lines of business offer life and health insurance to employees. Disability income insurance, transportation insurance, and credit insurance are also available. The Environmental Protection Agency now requires owners or operators of hazardous waste facilities to carry insurance that will compensate claimants for bodily injury and property damage caused by both sudden and nonsudden accidents. Companies that face risks for which no law of large numbers exists can purchase surplus lines coverage through such specialized insurance brokers as Lloyd's of London.

Key Terms

actuary
adjustable life insurance
allied lines or extended coverage
all-risk physical damage or multiple line coverage
annuity
beneficiary
bodily injury liability
business interruption insurance
coinsurance clause
collision and upset
comprehensive physical damage
contingent business interruption insurance
credit insurance
credit life insurance
deductible
disability income insurance

double indemnity
endowment
fidelity bond
group life insurance
hazardous waste insurance
health insurance
inland transit insurance
insurable interest
insurance policy
law of large numbers or law of averages
limited-payment life insurance
loss prevention engineer (LPE)
medical payments
mutual insurance company
no-fault auto insurance
ocean marine insurance
power plant insurance
principle of indemnity

product liability insurance
property damage liability
public liability insurance
pure risk
risk manager
self-insurance fund
speculative risk
stock insurance company
straight life insurance
surety bond
surplus lines coverage
term insurance
transportation insurance
uninsured motorist protection
universal life insurance
whole life insurance
workers' compensation insurance

For Review and Discussion

1. Why is risk an inherent part of any business venture? What risks do business people accept willingly? What kind must they accept whether they like it or not? Offer examples of each.
2. Describe the risk manager's job and list examples of local companies that have an especially strong need for such a position.
3. Recommend some actions that a firm could take to avoid the risk of loss by the following: fire, employee theft, robbery, explosion, motor vehicle

accident, shoplifting, and lawsuits brought by customers injured on the premises.
4. How can you transfer risk to a noninsuror? Who pays the cost in the long run? Why may this still be beneficial?
5. Describe the circumstances under which self-insurance is a reasonable way to deal with risk. List at least two risks that may be dealt with in this way.

6. Explain the following statement: "Most insurance companies will not sell insurance against a risk unless they have enough data to apply the law of large numbers."

7. What is an insurable interest? How does it protect insurance companies and insured persons and property alike?

8. Define the principle of indemnity.

9. How does a deductible benefit both the insuror and the insured?

10. What is the difference between a mutual insurance company and a stock insurance company?

11. Comment on the following statement: "Insurance companies wield considerable economic power in our society."

12. Why are actuaries and loss prevention engineers important to an insurance company? How is the insured affected by their work?

13. State the conditions that a risk must meet before a typical insurance company will accept it. What may the insurance company do if adverse circumstances arise? Why is it reasonable for an insurance company to refuse payment under certain conditions?

14. List and discuss the additional coverage that can be added to a fire insurance policy to extend it far beyond its original scope.

15. Why do insurance companies put coinsurance clauses in their policies? What do these clauses do?

16. Construct a table summarizing the various kinds of motor vehicle insurance that are available.

17. Why have several states passed no fault auto insurance laws? What has impaired the effectiveness of this insurance in some states?

18. Summarize the major features of each of the following kinds of insurance and evaluate the need for each: workers' compensation, public liability, product liability, fidelity bond, surety bond, life insurance (each type), health insurance, disability income insurance, transportation insurance, power plant insurance, credit insurance, and hazardous waste insurance.

19. What kind of life insurance accumulates a cash surrender value? What does that mean for the policyholder?

20. What sets surplus lines coverage apart from the other insurance discussed in this chapter? Give examples of risks that may have to be covered in this way.

21. How does Lloyd's of London spread the risk on insurance that it places? Describe the procedure you would follow if you wanted to insure a risk through Lloyd's.

Applications

Case 15.1 Unisex Insurance

It's an actuarial fact that women outlive men. When applied to pension plans and annuities, this statistic suggests one of the following:

1. Women should make higher contributions than men because on the average they live to collect more.

2. Women should receive lower periodic payments than men, for the same reason.

3. Members of both sexes should be paid the same, based on the average amount collected after retirement.

4. Every person should be paid a lump sum on retirement or when the annuity is paid up, regardless of which sex lives the longest.

A simple issue? Read on. It's a controversy that has caused considerable debate and concern among feminists, civil rights advocates, legislators, and insurance companies.

Insurance companies presently charge women lower premiums than men for life and auto insurance and higher premiums for annuities and health insurance based on the law of large numbers. This discrimination is mathematical rather than moral, actuaries contend, justified by data rather than bigotry.

In recent years, however, this long-standing practice has been challenged under the Civil Rights Act, which prohibits discrimination in employment, lending, and other areas based on race, sex, religion, color, or national origin. Certain legislators and special interest groups would like to extend the law's scope to include insurance. If legislation ultimately prohibits sex discrimination in insurance premiums, however, insurance company analysts predict that insurance companies would be forced to charge women some $1 billion more per year for life and auto insurance, while public and private pension plans would have to pay $1.7 billion more annually to eliminate the difference in payments to men and women.

Several states have proposed laws prohibiting the use of sex as a factor in insurance pricing and at least four have actually passed such legislation. Lobbyists for the insurance industry have urged legislators to defeat such laws in states where they are pending, while opposing factions from organizations such as the American Association of University Women, the National Organization for Women, and the National Women's Political Caucus urge that unisex pricing be adopted. Intense lobbying also is directed at federal lawmakers because bills have been introduced in the House and the Senate that would mandate the practice nationwide.

In mid-1983 a U.S. Supreme Court ruling banned sex discrimination in monthly benefit payments from an employer's retirement plan. Annuities and other insurance purchased from independent insurors by individuals weren't affected. Observers feel that it's only a matter of time, however, before any form of insurance that bases premiums on sex becomes a major issue in the political and social arena.

Questions

1. What concerns might some members of the insurance industry have in taking a stand against unisex insurance?

2. Would you consider this controversy more an ideological one than a logical one? Why or why not?

3. Which of the four possible solutions cited at the beginning of this case would you favor? Justify your choice.

Case 15.1 For more about unisex insurance, see ''A Bow to Unisex Pensions,'' *Newsweek*, July 18, 1983, p. 66; Joann S. Lublin, ''Feminists Push for Bill Requiring Unisex Insurance,'' *The Wall Street Journal*, June 3, 1983, p. 6; Daniel Hertzberg, ''Insurers Fight Bills Requiring Unisex Pricing,'' *The Wall Street Journal*, June 1, 1983, p. 33; Al Goldsmith, ''Battle Over Unisex Ratings Reaching Climax: Legislators Decry Industry Stance,'' *Best's Insurance Management Reports*, Release No. 11, May 23, 1983; and Daniel Seligman, ''Insurance and the Price of Sex,'' *Fortune*, February 21, 1983, p. 84.

Case 15.2 Insurance Information

Insurors must have a clear picture of the risks they insure if the law of averages is going to work. Dishonesty ranks high on the list of factors that can cloud that picture, distorting the degree of risk that the insurance company has actually assumed.

For life, health, and credit insurors particularly, deception by applicants may be detected through a background investigation. At least two organizations may be involved. The first is Equifax, a company that has been called the insurance industry's CIA. Founded in 1899, this firm specializes in reports on individual insurance and credit applicants. Its staff of some 3,500 field agents (private investigators) may interview friends, neighbors, or former employers in compiling a report on an insurance applicant's work habits, life-style, hobbies, and physical condition. The company's major foothold in the credit reporting industry comes through operation of the Credit Bureau.

A second large information-gathering organization, the Medical Information Bureau (MIB), is a highly computerized clearinghouse specializing in life insurance applicants. It is owned by 750 life insurance companies that write some 98 percent of all life insurance in the United States and Canada. The MIB's owner firms can identify applicants who may falsify information about their health or other facts that are significant to a life insuror. Although MIB operates on a $12 million annual budget, it reportedly saves its owners at least forty times that amount by weeding out fraudulent applicants. The names of some 12 million Americans and Canadians reside in its computer memory banks.

Questions

1. Discuss the potential such organizations have for abusing the information gathered on applicants and policyholders.

2. Defend the need for such information from the insurance companies' standpoint.

3. What safeguards (including certain forms of insurance discussed in this chapter) might these organizations employ to ensure that their information is accurate and will be used for ethical purposes?

Case 15.2 For more about the reporting of insurance information, see Daniel Hertzberg, ''Medical Files Insurers Keep Disturb Some,'' *The Wall Street Journal*, May 9, 1983, p. 33; and Aaron Bernstein, ''The Man From Equifax,'' *Forbes*, March 28, 1983, p. 115.

Gallery 3
The Computer: Its Evolution and Present-Day Uses

ENIAC, the first digital computer, was a thirty-ton monster that contained 18,000 vacuum tubes and 70,000 resistors. It could perform 300,000 calculations per minute. Today, an Apple IIe can do almost twice that many calculations in one second.

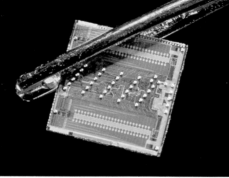

ENIAC's success encouraged advances in technology that led to the development of tiny LSI chips, or microprocessors, that can perform six million calculations per minute.

The state of the art in computers: this Cray X-MP's 240,000 LSI chips enable it to perform 400 million operations per second. Without a freon gas cooling system, the Cray would melt from the heat generated by its own circuits!

Today's microcomputers can be utilized by everyone. In some schools, pencils and paper have yielded to floppy disks. Many of today's young students consider a microcomputer to be a standard piece of classroom equipment.

Computer literacy is required of many college students. In fact, some universities require graduate students to purchase a personal computer for use in various course assignments.

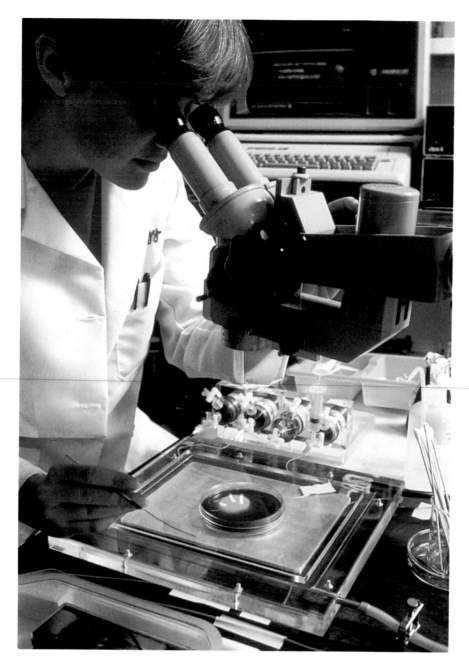

Computers facilitate the recording and analysis of large amounts of scientific data, such as that provided by this lab experiment.

A silent partner: many small-business owners have discovered how useful microcomputers can be for maintaining and summarizing data in areas such as sales, accounts receivable, and inventory. Low cost and an enormous selection of business programs have brought these machines within the reach of nearly every business owner.

A world of information at the fingertips: by accessing a commercial data base, like CompuServe, or by linking the terminal to his company's main-frame computer, this manager can obtain important information in seconds. Microcomputers give all levels of management the potential to make better-informed decisions, and the potential to reach those decisions faster than ever before.

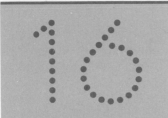

Gathering and Processing Data

Chapter Outline

Chapter Objectives

After studying this chapter, you should be able to:

1. Explain the purpose, development, and use of a formal management information system.
2. Identify each kind of data that managers use and describe situations in which both may be necessary.
3. Give examples of data that can be gathered by observation and data that may require a survey.
4. Describe three types of surveys that data collectors may use.
5. Discuss how averages, correlations, and index numbers can be used in summarizing data.
6. Differentiate between analog computers and digital computers.
7. Give examples of computer hardware and software.
8. Summarize the potential of microprocessors and give examples of how they are used today.
9. Propose at least three ways that personal computers may be used by small businesses and individuals and list at least two factors that have caused them to become so popular in recent years.
10. List several popular uses for computers.
11. Compare the advantages and disadvantages of service bureaus, time-sharing, and leasing as methods of getting access to a computer.

We provide [machines] with the data and the intelligence to do the repetitive chores while liberating the operator to define a wider variety of services for the machine to perform. What we are doing is enabling people to become more creative.
— Barney Hunts, The Singer Company

Up Front   Janet Norwood

The Nation's Statistician

The Bureau of Labor Statistics (BLS) carries out one of the most important and influential functions in the federal government. It provides accurate information on the nation's economic health for both the government and the private sector. Overseeing this massive statistical effort is Janet Norwood, a 22-year veteran of the bureau with a doctorate in international economics from Tufts University.

Dr. Norwood, praised by colleagues as "a people person as well as a numbers person," is committed to gathering and reporting dependable and timely information. This conscientious commitment to her work and, ultimately, to the nation, sometimes requires that she and her staff burn lots of midnight oil to meet an especially important deadline. On occasion she has carried one of the bureau's portable computers home to do some after-hours work there too.

She wants the bureau's reports and data-gathering procedures to reflect current social conditions. In pursuing this goal, she undertook in 1981 to change the way the Consumer Price Index (CPI) portrayed the impact of housing costs so that housing's contribution to today's CPI more accurately reflects the cost of shelter. Dr. Norwood is also adamant that the bureau's data collection and reporting practices acknowledge dynamic trends in American life-styles. This stand has led to the inclusion of two-income families and single-parent households in various statistical analyses, avoiding the stereotype that a family receives a single income and is composed of four persons, with a male breadwinner and female homemaker.

Beyond her commitment to her job and to clearly presenting statistics on contemporary social conditions, Janet Norwood is special in at least two other ways. She is the first woman to serve as commissioner of labor statistics, and she is the first bureau em-

Gathering and processing data are the foundations of the decision-making process you learned about in Chapter 4. Timely, accurate, understandable data must reach decision makers at all levels if an organization and its people hope to advance and prosper. In this chapter we will learn about the systems and methods that companies use to gather data and convert them into useful information. We will also explore the computer's role in processing large amounts of data swiftly for individuals as well as companies.

ployee to earn the commissioner's job by working her way up the ladder (she started out as an international labor law specialist in 1963).

The government, industry, and individuals alike react quickly to reports that Norwood's bureau issues, especially during uncertain economic times. Press releases that disclose increases in the cost of living or declines in national productivity have an immediate effect on investor attitudes; if the BLS sneezes, Wall Street may come down with pneumonia. As a result statistics are kept confidential until an official release date, and only one person — the president's economic adviser — is allowed to see them in advance.

The BLS systematically gathers and processes data, from government and private businesses, on employment, employee compensation, prices, and a host of other subjects that federal and state governments want to know about. The bureau's professional

journal, the Monthly Labor Review, features analytical articles and current labor statistics. Five other periodicals — CPI Detailed Report, Producer Prices and Price Indexes, Employment and Earnings, Current Wage Developments, and Occupational Outlook Quarterly — provide comprehensive reports on current data. The Bureau annually issues hundreds of news releases summarizing national, regional, and local statistics. Altogether, Norwood's organization reportedly receives 4,000 requests for information per day and disseminates some five million documents each year.

Managing the nationwide gathering and reporting of data costs money, and the bureau's annual budget exceeds $150 million. But its information is essential for governmental planning because, as Janet Norwood says, "If you are going to have effective, intelligent national policy, you need accurate data."

For more about Janet Norwood, see "Janet Norwood Is Slated to Continue at BLS Helm," *The Wall Street Journal*, May 13, 1983, p. 20; Joseph Deitch, "Portrait," *Wilson Library Bulletin*, May 1982, p. 686; "Keeping Track," *Forbes*, June 11, 1979, p. 155; and Philip Shabecoff, "She Takes Her Computers Home," *The New York Times Biographical Service*, July 1979, p. 965.

The Importance of a Management Information System

Large firms answer the challenge of gathering data by constructing a **management information system (MIS).** This system is *an organized approach to gathering data from inside and outside the company and (because of the volume involved) processing it by*

management information system (MIS)

461

*computer to produce current, accurate, and informative reports for
all decision makers.*

An MIS performs two functions. First it systematically gathers
internal data — such facts about the company as sales, inventory,
expenses, prices, rate of production, and numbers of employees —
and external data — such facts about the company's environment
as competitors' actions, market trends, demographic trends, laws
affecting the business, and changes in suppliers. The MIS then
processes this data, grouping related facts, analyzing them, and
summarizing them in a standard format. The result of these two
actions is that data are transformed into information. An MIS appears
graphically in Figure 16.1.

In small businesses such as sole proprietorships and partnerships the owners usually function as their own informal MIS.
In huge corporations like General Foods or United Technologies,
however, the role and structure of the MIS are massive. The MIS
must accumulate data from every plant and office in the firm and
also from relevant external sources such as federal government
agencies, trade associations, major consumer groups, and special
interest groups. This effort is very important, because employees
at all levels must have access to both internal and external information
if they are to reach intelligent, well-informed decisions. A company's
MIS facilitates the making of these decisions on literally thousands
of matters at every level of the organization each day.

Figure 16.1 A Management
Information System

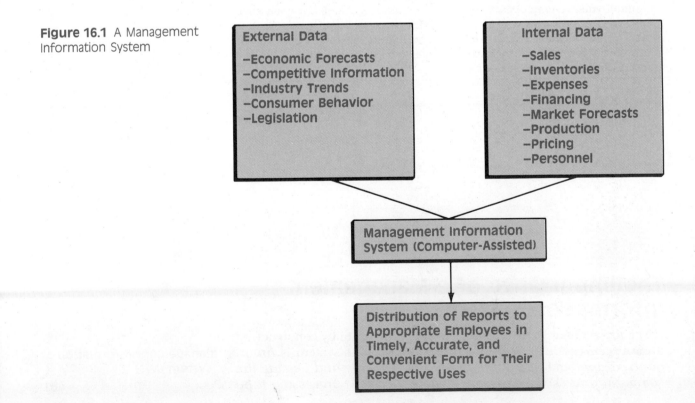

In satisfying employees' information requirements, a large MIS must arrange for essential data to be systematically gathered from all relevant sources and processed promptly and accurately for distribution to the proper persons. A management information system's design, then, must identify sources of relevant data; feed data from those sources to the central clearinghouse (a computer, in large organizations); decide on the formatting and frequency of reports to be issued; convert that data into such reports on a timely and accurate basis; and send them to appropriate recipients.

Gathering, Summarizing, and Presenting Data

Primary and Secondary Data

Businesses deal with two types of data: primary and secondary. **Primary data** are *data that a company must gather itself or employ some other firm to gather; they cannot be looked up somewhere because no one has put them together before.* Consumer buying motives, the image of a company and its products, and employee attitudes toward work are examples of primary data.

primary data

Secondary data, the other type, are *data that presently exist; they have been recorded somewhere, and management need only go to the source.* As a result secondary data are cheaper to find and to use than primary data. They are available from such public sources as federal government agencies and from such private sources as trade association publications and magazines. Your college library contains a wealth of secondary data from public and private sources. You will have noticed by this time that we have used a great deal of secondary data in writing this textbook. It has been said, after all, that much of education consists not of learning things, but of learning where to find things out.

secondary data

Businesses, like the rest of us, appreciate the savings and convenience of using secondary data, but often such data cannot answer all of management's questions; some primary data are needed. Before a company selects a location for a distribution center or a manufacturing plant it may consult data from the U.S. Bureau of the Census on population growth and income in various parts of the country, and it also may examine data provided by state agencies in several states that offer attractive locations. Typically a firm makes its own study of a potential site to supplement such published data, evaluating each location according to the criteria you learned about in Chapter 9.

Managers follow three steps in dealing with data. First they gather data, using whatever devices are appropriate; then they analyze or summarize data, following one of several methods; and finally they draw conclusions from the data and make decisions based on those conclusions. Figure 16.2 illustrates these three steps and their sequence.

Figure 16.2 The Three Steps of Dealing with Data

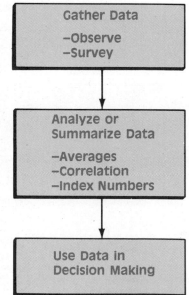

Data Collection Techniques

Management has two techniques available to gather data. The one chosen depends on the circumstances and the questions involved.

Observation. If the data you seek can be readily seen or recorded without asking questions, you can gather them by observation. Wherever possible, you should consider observing with electronic or mechanical devices. They are often cheaper to use than human researchers, and they may be more accurate because they do not suffer fatigue, boredom, and other human frailties. Also, a machine's presence does not call attention to itself and thereby potentially influence the behavior being observed. Some everyday examples of mechanical or electronic observers are:

- Jukebokes with counters that tell how many times each record has been played
- Turnstiles with counters that record the number of guests entering and leaving a tourist attraction
- Counters that gather data on traffic flow near an intersection

Surveys. Companies use surveys to gather data when they need opinions, reactions, or other information that cannot be obtained by simple observation and recording. Surveys would be used to discover the following:

- Consumer reactions to a package design or a new product flavor
- The average annual income of a family of four in a geographic region
- How employees feel about a firm's training program, promotional opportunities, and pay scale

Management must ask questions to get unobservable data. This can be done with:

- Mail surveys
- Telephone surveys
- Personal interviews

In all three methods, questions must be carefully worded, whether on a form or asked by an interviewer, so as not to influence the answer. Prejudicing the respondent invalidates the response.

Although mail surveys are ideal for reaching a farflung group of people, the response may be disappointing, especially if the survey asks for lengthy or detailed responses or for information the respondents must compute or look up. It is always easier to throw the questionnaire away.

To combat this, firms offer incentives that encourage people to answer. Respondents who do not mind identifying themselves may be offered a gift on returning the completed questionnaire. An alternative is to enclose a gift along with the questions, which makes the person feel obliged to reply. *Fortune*, *Rudder*, and *Aviation Week* have all enclosed cash incentives in their marketing surveys. According to Erdos & Morgan, a New York market research company, firms that enclose dollar bills can expect a minimum 50 percent response from mail surveys rather than a probable rate of under 10 percent.[1]

A product use card that consumers are required to return to validate a guarantee is one way to gather data from new owners of a product. Often these cards ask such questions as why you bought the product, in what store, and whether you own anything else made by the manufacturer. As you learned in Chapter 10, these data help a producer to identify consumer buying motives, popular marketing outlets, brand loyalty, and other characteristics of a market segment. An example of one such form appears in Figure 16.3.

Telephone surveys are more expensive than mail surveys because researchers must make one-to-one contact, but they can cover as wide a geographic area if a WATS (*Wide Area Telecommunications Service*) line is used. This service is available from the telephone company for a monthly fee.

It is difficult to ask someone to smell a new after-shave lotion over the telephone or to taste a new flavor of Jell-O through the mail. Under these circumstances, companies cannot avoid personal interviews, the most expensive of survey methods. Trained interviewers must contact respondents individually, face-to-face, and ask them to look, listen, taste, feel, or smell — things that they can only do in person — and give their reaction.

Sampling

It is often impractical, if not impossible, to contact every person or subject in a particular group. Consequently it becomes necessary to glean data from a **sample,** which is *a cross-section of a total group that has the same distribution of characteristics as the larger group (or* universe) *whose characteristics are being explored.* Conclusions about the larger group can be drawn from the data collected about the smaller.

sample

You learned in Chapter 9, for example, that companies test the reliability of various products they buy and make. Depending on the volume involved and the consequences of product failure, however, management may decide to test a sample of products rather than scrutinize every one. If done accurately, this sample can be as effective as 100 percent inspection, and it is certainly faster and cheaper. It is a particularly valuable method of checking virtually identical products that are mass-produced at rates of hundreds per hour.

Samples fall into two general categories. A firm may take a

Figure 16.3 A Product Use Card

PURCHASE INFORMATION CARD

To better serve you in the future, we would appreciate your filling out and returning this information card to us. Thank you.

1. ☐ Mr. 2. ☐ Mrs. 3. ☐ Ms. 4. ☐ Miss   **39B**

Name (First/Initial/Last)

Street

City   State   Zip

Date of Purchase: ___/___/___   Model Number: ☐☐☐☐
              Mo. Day Yr.

A. Store where purchased:
1. ☐ Drug store   6. ☐ Beauty salon
2. ☐ Discount store   7. ☐ Hardware store
3. ☐ Catalog showroom   8. ☐ Received as gift
4. ☐ Department store   9. ☐ Other
5. ☐ Grocery store

B. If the appliance was a gift, did you request that it be given to you?
1. ☐ Yes   2. ☐ No

C. What brand of this appliance did you previously own?
1. ☐ This is my first one   7. ☐ Pollenex
2. ☐ Conair   8. ☐ Schick
3. ☐ Clairol   9. ☐ Sunbeam
4. ☐ Gillette   10. ☐ Water Pik
5. ☐ G.E.   11. ☐ Other:_____
6. ☐ Norelco

D. How many of this appliance (any type) do you presently have in your household?
1. ☐ This is the only one   4. ☐ 4
2. ☐ 2   5. ☐ 5
3. ☐ 3   6. ☐ More than 5

E. Where did you first learn about Conair appliances?
1. ☐ Magazine advertisements
2. ☐ Recommended by friend
3. ☐ Recommended by store clerk
4. ☐ Newspaper advertisement
5. ☐ T.V. advertisement
6. ☐ Recommended by beauty professional
7. ☐ Other

F. Check the 2 most important factors influencing your selection of this Conair product:
1. ☐ Conair's reputation
2. ☐ Price
3. ☐ Style/Appearance
4. ☐ Lightweight
5. ☐ Durability
6. ☐ Special features
7. ☐ Warranty
8. ☐ Previous experience with Conair's appliances

G. Which of the following have you done in the past 6 months? (check all that apply)
1. ☐ Redeemed a product coupon
2. ☐ Ordered an item from mail order catalog
3. ☐ Sent in product inquiry card from magazine
4. ☐ Bought item from offer received in mail
5. ☐ Entered sweepstakes/contest

H. In which age group are you?
1. ☐ Under 12   5. ☐ 35 - 44
2. ☐ 12 - 17   6. ☐ 45 - 54
3. ☐ 18 - 24   7. ☐ 55 - 64
4. ☐ 25 - 34   8. ☐ 65 & over

I. Marital status:
1. ☐ Married   2. ☐ Unmarried

J. Which group best describes your family income?
1. ☐ Under $10,000   6. ☐ $30,000-$34,999
2. ☐ $10,000-$14,999   7 ☐ $35,000-$39,999
3. ☐ $15,000-$19,999   8. ☐ $40,000-$44,999
4. ☐ $20,000-$24,999   9. ☐ $45,000-$49,999
5. ☐ $25,000-$29,999   10. ☐ $50,000 & over

K. Do you have any children in any of the following age groups who are living at home?
1. ☐ Under age 2   5. ☐ Age 11-12
2. ☐ Age 2-4   6. ☐ Age 13-15
3. ☐ Age 5-7   7. ☐ Age 16-18
4. ☐ Age 8-10

L. For your primary residence, do you:
1. ☐ Own a house?
2. ☐ Rent a house?
3. ☐ Own a townhouse/condominium?
4. ☐ Rent an apartment?

M. Which of the following types of credit cards do you use?
1. ☐ Travel/Entertainment (American Express, Diners Club, Carte Blanche)
2. ☐ Bank (Master Charge, Visa)
3. ☐ Gas, department store, etc.

(over)

random sample

random sample, *one in which every member of the universe has an equal chance of being chosen.* Say the universe chosen was all supermarkets in an area. If a researcher wrote the name of every supermarket on a piece of paper, put the slips of paper in a bowl, and drew out twenty slips of paper, the supermarkets on those twenty slips would be a random sample — the ones not chosen had an equal chance of being chosen.

Researchers generally want to focus their study more closely than that, however, so they use a **stratified random sample**

stratified random sample, *one that divides the universe into subcategories, or* strata, *according*

Figure 16.3, continued

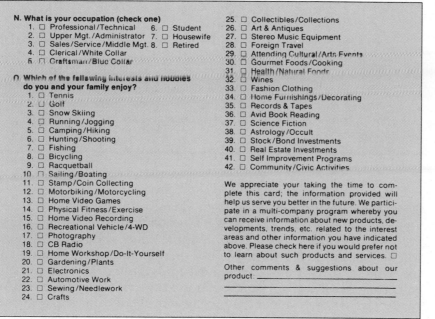

N. What is your occupation (check one)
1. ☐ Professional/Technical   6. ☐ Student
2. ☐ Upper Mgt./Administrator   7. ☐ Housewife
3. ☐ Sales/Service/Middle Mgt.   8. ☐ Retired
4. ☐ Clerical/White Collar
5. ☐ Craftsman/Blue Collar

O. Which of the following interests and hobbies do you and your family enjoy?
1. ☐ Tennis
2. ☐ Golf
3. ☐ Snow Skiing
4. ☐ Running/Jogging
5. ☐ Camping/Hiking
6. ☐ Hunting/Shooting
7. ☐ Fishing
8. ☐ Bicycling
9. ☐ Racquetball
10. ☐ Sailing/Boating
11. ☐ Stamp/Coin Collecting
12. ☐ Motorbiking/Motorcycling
13. ☐ Home Video Games
14. ☐ Physical Fitness/Exercise
15. ☐ Home Video Recording
16. ☐ Recreational Vehicle/4-WD
17. ☐ Photography
18. ☐ CB Radio
19. ☐ Home Workshop/Do-It-Yourself
20. ☐ Gardening/Plants
21. ☐ Electronics
22. ☐ Automotive Work
23. ☐ Sewing/Needlework
24. ☐ Crafts

25. ☐ Collectibles/Collections
26. ☐ Art & Antiques
27. ☐ Stereo Music Equipment
28. ☐ Foreign Travel
29. ☐ Attending Cultural/Arts Events
30. ☐ Gourmet Foods/Cooking
31. ☐ Health/Natural Foods
32. ☐ Wines
33. ☐ Fashion Clothing
34. ☐ Home Furnishings/Decorating
35. ☐ Records & Tapes
36. ☐ Avid Book Reading
37. ☐ Science Fiction
38. ☐ Astrology/Occult
39. ☐ Stock/Bond Investments
40. ☐ Real Estate Investments
41. ☐ Self Improvement Programs
42. ☐ Community/Civic Activities

We appreciate your taking the time to complete this card; the information provided will help us serve you better in the future. We participate in a multi-company program whereby you can receive information about new products, developments, trends, etc. related to the interest areas and other information you have indicated above. Please check here if you would prefer not to learn about such products and services. ☐

Other comments & suggestions about our product: _____

to one or more characteristics and chooses randomly from within the strata being examined. A stratified sample may show a market segment that a company wants to learn more about. It may be carefully defined according to such criteria as sex, age, and geographic location. A researcher who needs to understand the habits and preferences of certain drinkers of low-calorie beer, for example, might stratify, or subdivide, the universe of low-calorie beer drinkers to consider females (sex) over twenty-five (age) living in the Northeast

Telephone surveys may be used to gather data from respondents who need not be interviewed in person.

Pause and Ponder

Discuss the specific techniques you would use to gather data on the following: improvements to make on a present model of outboard motor; the eating habits of consumers of hot breakfast cereals; features that influence buying decisions about automobile tires; and future education plans of sophomores at your college or university.

(geographic region). Once defined, the stratified sample becomes its own little universe, from which a random sample is then taken.

Management's conclusions and inferences about the universe will be inaccurate if a sample is not representative. Thus design of the sample itself is one of the most important steps in any data-gathering activity. In one study of American businesses, for example, the researcher drew numerous conclusions about corporate activities and values and the characteristics and work habits of executives. The researcher's approach to gathering data was criticized, however, because he reportedly polled less than 1,100 managers using a sample of just thirteen companies. None of these firms ranked in the top one hundred industrial companies according to annual sales, and only 23 percent of surveyed businesses sold more than $1 billion annually.[2]

The A. C. Nielsen Company's many statistical reports on television viewing habits are an interesting example of sample design in action. A Nielsen electronic device called an Audimeter is attached to television sets in a sample of 2,000 homes nationwide. At 1-minute intervals the Audimeters record whether the set is off or on and (if on) which channel is selected. Nielsen's central office computer in Dunedin, Florida, can collect data from the Audimeters in less than 5 seconds, and the company converts that data into reports that summarize program preferences throughout the country.

Persons unfamiliar with Nielsen's sampling practices sometimes wonder how the habits of some 80 million television viewers can be determined accurately by using just 2,000 homes. The company, however, has prepared extensive publications that defend its sample size and the mathematical soundness with which the sample is designed (details are too lengthy to include here). Nielsen's statistics seem to enjoy high credibility with the television and advertising industries and play a prominent role in decisions made by television networks, program producers, advertisers, and advertising agencies.

Summarizing Data

Once data have been gathered, either by observation or by survey, the next move is to summarize what they mean. Three summarizing devices can put data into sharp focus — averages, correlations, and index numbers.

Averages. Three computations can produce something called an *average*. The usefulness of each computation depends largely on the nature of your data. Each computation begins by looking at an **array** of numbers, which is *a list of numbers ordered from highest to lowest or lowest to highest.*

    array

The first computation derives an **arithmetic mean,** *an average found by adding the numbers in an array and dividing by the total number of items present.* Say a sales manager is looking at the annual dollar sales that each of her salespeople was responsible for last year: $15,000, $18,000, $23,000, $27,000, $30,000, $48,000, and $56,000. Total sales were $217,000. To find the mean, she simply divides the total by the number of salespeople (seven). The mean is $31,000.

    arithmetic mean

An arithmetic mean, however, can be drawn up or down by one or a few extremely high or low numbers in the array. Assume that one salesperson in the example performed superbly and, instead of selling $56,000 worth, sold $91,000 worth. That changes the total to $252,000, making the new mean $36,000 — an increase of $5,000. Without seeing the array in question, therefore, it is difficult to judge if an arithmetic mean is reasonably close to the typical figure or not.

The second average avoids this problem: it is not affected by items in the array that are either extremely high or low. The **median** is *the number that appears midway between the highest and the lowest numbers in an array.* In the last example, the array was this:

    median

$15,000
$18,000
$23,000
$27,000
$30,000
$48,000
$91,000

The median is $27,000 because it is midway between the lowest number ($15,000) and the highest ($91,000). The median avoids the pitfall of the mean because it is determined by its position (halfway from either end), regardless of a few extremely high or low numbers. If the number of items in the array is even, add the two in the middle and divide that sum by 2 to compute the median.

The third average, the **mode,** is *the number that appears most often within an array.* Sometimes there is no mode, as in the arrays in the last examples, or there may be multiple modes when several numbers appear an equal number of times. The mode is usually the least useful of the three averages, unless your results can only fall into a few categories or numbers. Imagine, for example, that

    mode

you are standing in a gambling casino in Atlantic City or Las Vegas (for research purposes only, of course). Observing the roulette wheel for several minutes, you see these numbers come up as winners:

$$
\begin{array}{c}
5 \\
17 \\
122 \\
30 \\
11 \\
12 \\
17 \\
38 \\
17
\end{array}
$$

A mean or a median of these results would be meaningless, but the mode (17) indicates that the wheel is out of balance. Your likelihood of winning would be greatest if you bet on that number.

correlation

Correlation. You may be able to identify one or more correlations in your data. A **correlation** is *a cause-effect or if-then connection between two or more elements in a group of data.* This valuable bit of knowledge enables a researcher to forecast the likelihood that the dependent item will change when the controlling item changes. Correlation is the heart of the law of large numbers you learned about in Chapter 15. If you determine that a cause-effect relationship exists between two or more variables, you have important predicting power.

In general a correlation should be logical. It should make sense that a change in item *A* causes a change in item *B*. If you cannot explain the logic behind an apparent correlation, it may be exactly that — an *apparent* one. The elements may only seem related because they changed together and in the same manner each time you happened to record data. Many people are convinced, for example, that there is a correlation between the number of trucks parked outside a restaurant and the quality of the food inside; however, the number of trucks also could be explained by the distance from other restaurants or the fact that the business also sells diesel fuel.

The National Highway Traffic Safety Administration, which studied the repeal of motorcycle helmet laws in four states, found that deaths related to motorcycle accidents rose 23 percent in those states after the laws were taken off the books, while motorcycle registrations increased only 1 percent and total miles traveled by motorcyclists increased very little. In Colorado, where helmet use dropped to 60 percent of motorcyclists after the law was repealed, severe head injuries increased 260 percent and the death rate jumped 57 percent. A correlation seems to exist.

The surgeon general has established a correlation between smoking and lung cancer. Demand for furniture, draperies, and carpeting correlates with the rate of new home construction. Harley-Davidson Motor Company reports a correlation between the unemployment rate of young males and the sale of motorcycles, and

retailers have noted a correlation between unemployment and in-
cidents of shoplifting.

Index Numbers. A third summarizing device is an **index number**.
*This is a quantitative device that condenses or summarizes a body
of data with several characteristics into a single numerical expression.* The index number allows you to compare a complex situation
or condition in the present to an earlier time or to compare several
bodies of current data.

    Monitoring the rate of inflation, the Bureau of Labor Statistics
(BLS) issues two Consumer Price Indices (CPI-U and CPI-W), which
we discussed in Chapter 13. The BLS gathers prices on more than
400 consumer items in a monthly sampling of retail stores and
service establishments in eighty-five urban areas nationwide. Using
1967 as the 100 percent or base year, the bureau then converts
those prices into 1967 dollars. The product of this effort, the CPIs,
allows us to see how present consumer prices compare with those
of the past and to observe the rate of change. By calculating the
CPIs each month, the federal government monitors the inflation
rate and can then take appropriate action to try to keep the cost
of living under control. A chart showing the behavior of the CPI-U
over several years appears in Figure 16.4.

    In addition to the Consumer Price Index, the Bureau of Labor
Statistics prepares a Wholesale Price Index (WPI), which expresses
the prices wholesalers charge, also expressed in terms of 1967 dollars.
The data for this index are gathered by mail and telephone surveys
and a limited number of personal interviews, using a sample of
wholesaling firms across the nation. There is a correlation between

index number

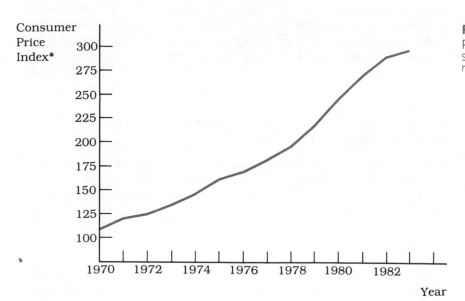

Figure 16.4 The Consumer
Price Index, 1970–1983
Source: U.S. Department of Labor, Bu-
reau of Labor Statistics.

*Consumer Price Index (CPI-U) — urban consumers only.

the behavior of wholesale and consumer prices. When the WPI rises, the CPI usually follows suit within a short time, as manufacturers and retailers pass their increased costs on to consumers.

Presenting Data

Summaries of data should be presented concisely, so users do not have to shuffle, sift, and compare mountains of paperwork to grasp the situation. There are several popular ways to condense large amounts of data into a compact form, each suitable for particular kinds of data:

- A *pie chart* shows how 100 percent of one unit, such as one dollar, is allocated among various areas. Figure 16.5 is a pie chart showing the market share of soft drinks.
- A *horizontal bar chart* (Fig. 16.6) compares different items at the same time.
- A *vertical bar chart* (Fig. 16.7) compares the same item at different times.
- A *line graph* indicates the general trend of one or more elements of data over time. Figure 16.4 is a line graph.
- A *statistical map* (Fig. 16.8) compares several geographic regions on the basis of one or more factors.
- A *pictograph* (Fig. 16.9) uses drawings to compare or present data.

Learning About Computers

computer

The most popular and efficient way to process large amounts of data in a management information system is to use a **computer,** *a device that performs large numbers of repetitive calculations automatically and at high speeds, usually with considerable accuracy.* Your electronic calculator can perform many math operations at lightning speeds, but you still have to feed data into it and tell it which operations to perform. Computers, on the other hand, can follow a set of instructions without human intervention until the data-processing job is complete. Computers are useful for such jobs as the following:

- Adding or subtracting units from inventory and calculating the current balance
- Adding purchases to and deducting payments from a company's trade accounts receivable
- Calculating payroll records, including deductions for such items as taxes, insurance, and union dues

Although computers cannot *think* in the human sense, they can *decide* by remembering, analyzing, and comparing two elements to determine if one is greater than, less than, or equal to the other.

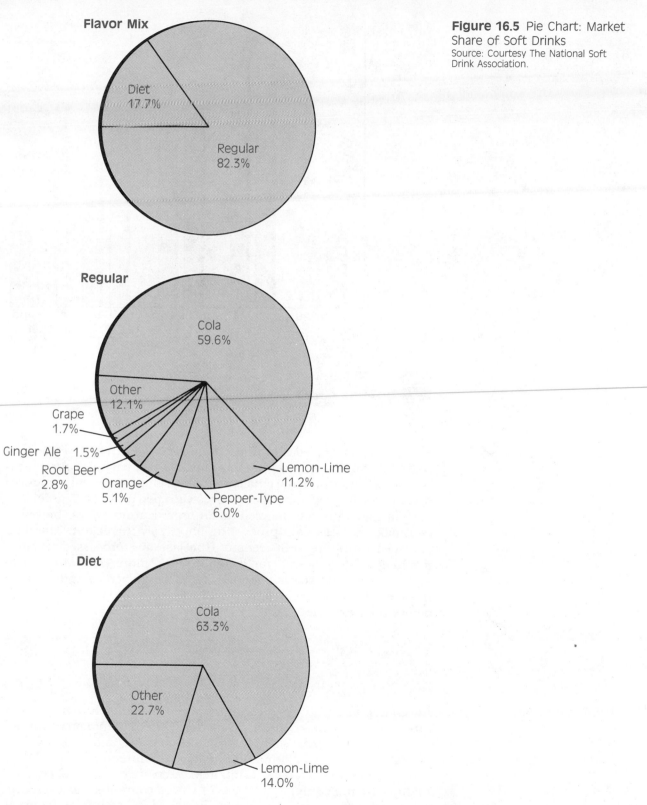

Flavor Mix

Diet
17.7%

Regular
82.3%

Regular

Cola
59.6%

Other
12.1%

Grape
1.7%

Ginger Ale 1.5%

Root Beer
2.8%

Orange
5.1%

Pepper-Type
6.0%

Lemon-Lime
11.2%

Diet

Cola
63.3%

Other
22.7%

Lemon-Lime
14.0%

Figure 16.5 Pie Chart: Market Share of Soft Drinks
Source: Courtesy The National Soft Drink Association.

Figure 16.6 Horizontal Bar Chart: Percentage of Drivers by Age
Source: Courtesy Motor Vehicle Manufacturers Association of the United States.

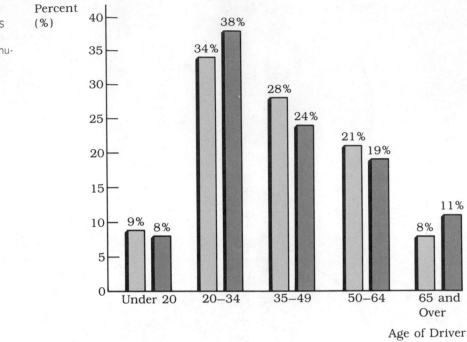

1970
1982

You do not need a machine to process data. They can be processed manually, as you probably do when you balance your checkbook every month. Some small businesses employ clerical personnel to maintain payroll and other records with pen and ink. The volume of data that must be handled as an organization grows, however, can make manual data processing hopelessly inefficient. The data obtained from the 1880 census (the last one processed without mechanical assistance), for example, took more than 7 years to summarize, underscoring the need for more efficient ways to handle the mountain of facts: that census was summarized just 2 years before the next one began.

Types of Computers

Analog Computers

analog computer

An **analog computer** is *a computer that takes measurements and processes these data against a model of the problem or situation.* A cable-driven speedometer, a spring-driven clock, and cruise control on automobiles are examples of analog computers.

Businesses use analog computers extensively to control complex manufacturing equipment. Once an analog computer has been programmed with the desired speed, pressure, temperature, or other elements of a machine's operation, it monitors and adjusts the

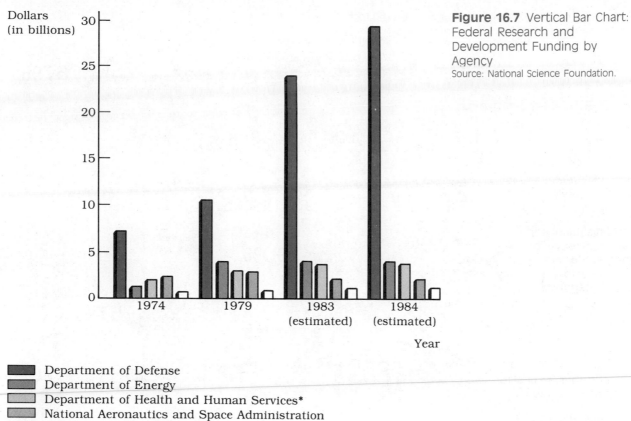

Figure 16.7 Vertical Bar Chart: Federal Research and Development Funding by Agency
Source: National Science Foundation.

Department of Defense
Department of Energy
Department of Health and Human Services*
National Aeronautics and Space Administration
National Science Foundation

*Data have been adjusted to reflect only health and human services programs (without education).

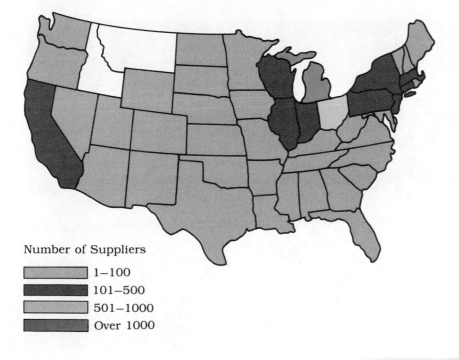

Figure 16.8 Statistical Map: Suppliers to Motor Vehicle Manufacturers in Forty-Eight States
Source: Courtesy Motor Vehicle Manufacturers Association of the United States.

Number of Suppliers

1–100
101–500
501–1000
Over 1000

Figure 16.9 Benefits That Organizations Are Most Likely to Adopt
Source: *Families: Strengths and Strains at Work.* Report published 1981 by General Mills. Used by permission of General Mills, Inc., 9200 Wayzata Boulevard, Minneapolis, MN 55440.

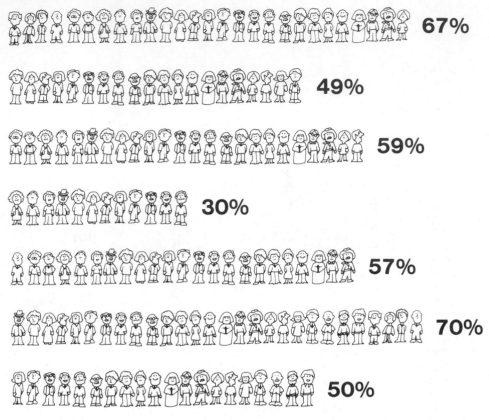

Child care at the place they work — **67%**

Paid personal days specifically for children and family responsibilities — **49%**

Job counseling and job hunting services for a spouse if relocated — **59%**

Paid disability and personal leave for mothers for more than six weeks for pregnancy and maternity — **30%**

Paid personal leave for fathers for paternity — **57%**

Freedom to pick and choose the employment benefits that are best for their family's needs — **70%**

Part-time work two or three days a week with full-time employment benefits — **50%**

Like an electronic orchestra conductor, this Chrysler Corporation employee monitors the operation of fifty-eight robots from a master computer control station. Robots make ninety-seven percent of the welds on these vans.

machine's performance automatically to ensure that the machine performs according to specifications. In a typical automated engine assembly line, the rough engine block can be bored, honed, drilled, tapped, and milled by computer control to the required engineering tolerances with little human intervention.

One of the more promising applications of analog computers in these energy-conscious times is in automated climate control for large buildings. Reading temperatures relayed by sensors at strategic points throughout a building, a computer automatically adjusts the heating, air conditioning, and ventilation systems. Even with the cheapest system costing more than $20,000, International Business Machines (IBM) and Honeywell alone have sold more than 2,500 in recent years.

Digital Computers

Unlike an analog computer, which deals with measurements, a **digital computer** is *a computer that processes exact data according to a set of instructions.* It has the potential for 100 percent accuracy, if the following conditions hold:

digital computer

1. The data are 100 percent accurate.
2. The instructions for processing the data are accurate and complete.
3. The computer's electronic components do not fail (a rare occurrence, but possible).

Digital computers are used more widely because they can do so many repetitive chores in such areas as inventory control and payroll recordkeeping. Their applications are limited only by management's ingenuity.

The first digital computer, built in 1946 at the University of Pennsylvania, was a behemoth called ENIAC (*Electronic Numerical*

DOONESBURY   **by Garry Trudeau**

Integrator *and* Calculator). Large enough to fill a two-car garage, this 30-ton monster had 70,000 resistors, 10,000 capacitors, and 6,000 switches. On the average, 1 of its 18,000 vacuum tubes failed every 7 minutes. Compared with today's computers, it was a dinosaur. Transistors developed by Bell Laboratories in the late 1950s made smaller computers possible and reduced computing time to millionths of a second, a remarkable improvement over ENIAC's ponderous speeds. Modern microprocessors (discussed later in this chapter) perform calculations in billionths of a second (*nanoseconds*) and are approaching the trillionth-of-a-second threshold. By comparison a person performing 1 calculation per second, 24 hours a day for 70 years, would do fewer than 2.25 billion. The blinding speed of today's computers is the result of miniaturization. As electronic components are reduced in size, the time they require to perform computing tasks decreases accordingly.

You probably will encounter digital computers in many places, because they are easily applied to so many business operations. The rest of this section focuses on them by describing their components.

hardware

Hardware. When we speak of computer **hardware,** we are referring to *the five tangible parts or units of a digital computer* as shown in Figure 16.10. These are as follows:

input unit

— The **input unit,** *the device used to enter data into the computer for processing.*

memory unit

— The **memory unit,** *the computer's electronic warehouse, which stores data as instructed by the program.*

arithmetic unit

— The **arithmetic unit,** *the unit of the computer that performs mathematical computations on data.*

Figure 16.10 Parts and Terminology of a Digital Computer System

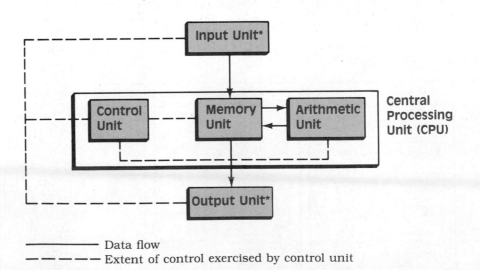

Data flow
————— Extent of control exercised by control unit

*Peripheral equipment (need not be used in the same location as the CPU).

— The **control unit,** *the coordinating part of a computer, which directs the other parts to perform their respective functions to complete the data-processing job.*

control unit

— The **output unit,** *the part of a computer that presents the processed data in a form that management can use.*

output unit

The memory, arithmetic, and control units are located in the computer's central processing unit (CPU). The input and output units, sometimes called *peripheral equipment*, need not be located with the CPU; they often are located elsewhere and connected to the CPU by telephone lines or other electronic means.

Data can be input to the computer on punched paper tape; magnetic tape, cards, or disks; punched cards; a keyboard; or an optical scanner that "reads" them directly off a source document. Processed data emerge as information through various output media. Video display terminals (VDTs) display the processed data on cathode ray tubes (CRTs), something like a television screen. Information can also be printed on paper or recorded on punched cards, punched paper tape, or magnetic (*mag*) cards, disks, or tape.

Software. Software generally can be defined as *all elements of a computerized data-processing system other than hardware.* More specifically, software includes operating manuals and other printed matter, customer training programs, maintenance services, and programming assistance. The term is most often used to refer to programs themselves and to the media (such as magnetic tape and floppy or hard disks) on which programs and output can be recorded.

software

A **program** is *a software element stored in the memory unit that feeds step-by-step instructions to the control unit, which then commands one of the other hardware units to perform whatever operation is needed.* Each data-processing job requires a separate program; without it a computer is useless.

program

Writing a program is time consuming and expensive; the programmer must anticipate every conceivable decision or computation that must be made during the job and tell the computer what to do in each case. Some computer manufacturers provide little programming support, which can make a computer seem like a car without a driver: all the hardware is there, but it lacks the key element to set it in motion. Firms that cannot use ready-made programs because their computing requires certain particular operating characteristics or information must hire software companies to write custom programs. This can be an expensive obstacle when converting from manual to computerized data-processing systems.

Computer Languages. Programs must be written in a language that is compatible with the computer itself and with the type of data it will process, whether commercial or scientific. Such a language is a set of symbols that the machine understands, a communications bridge between person and computer. Some of the most popular computer languages are listed on the next page.

— FORTRAN (short for *formula translation*). This language can be used to write programs for a great many scientific data-processing jobs. It is quite simple to learn, but its popularity also stems from the fact that it was developed in 1957 by IBM employees for IBM equipment, some of the most commonly used hardware. It can be used with numerous other brands as well.

— COBOL (*common business oriented language*). This language was developed in the late 1950s to meet the needs of the U.S. Department of Defense, the largest computer user in the nation at that time. The department wanted a language that could be used with many different computer brands and models at many locations. COBOL is designed for processing commercial rather than highly scientific data.

— PL/1 (*Programming Language One*). This language was developed as a bridge between FORTRAN and COBOL, combining the best features of both. An extremely flexible language, it accommodates scientific and commercial data.

— BASIC (*Beginner's All-purpose Symbolic Instruction Code*). This language is relatively simple to use, making it popular as a fundamental programming language. Its simplicity and technical capabilities make it particularly suitable for sophisticated business data-processing applications, including payroll, accounts receivable, and other accounting tasks. It is probably the most popular language today.

Microprocessors

microprocessor

A **microprocessor,** also called a *computer on a chip,* is *a microscopic maze of circuits etched on a layered piece of silicon a fourth of an inch square.* Invented in 1974 these snowflake-sized large-scale integration (LSI) chips contain thousands of electronic components that are almost too small to imagine. Chips used for memory storage in today's desk-top computers easily hold more than 256,000 (*256K*) bits of information, the equivalent of a large city's telephone directory, in cells a 30th of the width of a human hair. Microprocessors can perform 6 million calculations per minute, compared with ancient ENIAC's 300,000 per minute. This almost incomprehensible speed has decreased the cost of some computer calculations from a dollar to less than a penny in just 10 years.

Within the past 5 years refined production methods and better engineering have expanded the reliability and capabilities of microprocessors impressively. These developments, coupled with increased competition among manufacturers, have caused a steady decline in computer prices. One researcher summarized the extent and magnitude of these changes in efficiency and price by claiming that if the trend had occurred in the auto industry a Rolls-Royce would now get 3 million miles to the gallon and cost $2.75.[3]

Manufacturing LSI chips demands fanatical precision and

cleanliness. Circuits usually are drawn hundreds of times larger than their actual size and then photographically reduced and transferred to a silicon chip using a complex variation of photoengraving called *photolithography*. Light passing through a glass negative etches each circuit's intricate pattern onto the chip, one at a time, layer on layer, until the complex of circuits is complete. (An even more precise procedure using electron beams has been developed than can inscribe lines visible only with a microscope.) More than 2,000 of the latest chips, holding more than 100,000 transistors each, can fit on a wafer 6 inches in diameter.[4]

The production environment for these virtually invisible components must be immaculate. A particle of dust will cause a microprocessor circuit to fail and so ruin the entire chip. Assembly takes place in sterile "white rooms" where employees are prohibited from wearing makeup, hair and beards must be covered, and workers dress in sterile garments that reduce the contamination of circuits by debris from street clothing. Production costs naturally rise as chips become more complex; today's 256K versions, for example, may cost as much as twenty times more to manufacture than earlier 64K models.[5] Some extremely advanced microprocessors are capable of retaining data after power has been turned off. These chips may be used in computer-controlled machine tools, for example, automatically and constantly adjusting the tool's settings to allow for internal wear on its own gears and bearings.[6]

Silicon-chip microprocessors now are used in cash registers, microwave ovens, electronic memory typewriters, and traffic light controls. Some of the more expensive luxury cars have microprocessors that report driving miles available at a given speed on the remaining fuel supply and maintain climate control to within 1 degree. Nearly all of today's new cars contain microprocessors that regulate their ignition, carburetion, and pollution control equipment.

The Personal Computer Revolution

Three general categories of computers are in use today. The first group, mainframe computers, may cost several million dollars and form the heart of a large company's management information system. The second group, minicomputers, cost up to $100,000 and are often used by medium-sized companies. The third category, microcomputers, or personal computers (PCs), have prices ranging from

Pause and Ponder

List the products you own that contain at least one microprocessor. Name some products whose performance would be enhanced or whose applications could be expanded by the use of microprocessors.

several hundred dollars to as much as $30,000. Microcomputer owners range from computer "hackers" (or hobbyists) and curious consumers to engineers, small-business owners, and authors — including the team that wrote this textbook. According to International Data Corporation, there are roughly 60,000 mainframe computers and 600,000 minicomputers in existence, but the popularity of personal computers has made usage estimates difficult.[7] Sales at this time exceed 2 million machines per year, and one source reports that as many as 80 million will have been sold by 1990.[8]

Powered by microprocessors, which we discussed in the previous section, PCs have revolutionized the way that millions of us work, play, learn, communicate, make decisions, and otherwise process data. Personal computers are commonplace teaching tools in every course from foreign languages to physics. *Computer literacy* — the ability to use a personal computer in a nontechnical fashion — is a graduation requirement at many educational institutions. Some observers believe that a working knowledge of computers will be essential for future citizens to function effectively in a world that will embrace computers in so many ways.

Beyond educational and game applications, PC owners now put these compact, powerful, and tireless machines to work in areas such as small-business accounting, investment analysis, budgeting personal finances, performing complex engineering calculations, and

It's not a fad; it's a way of life. Personal computers have already carved their niche in millions of homes and offices throughout the country.

word processing, complete with color graphics. By the mid-1980s PC sales to companies alone reached $6 billion per year.[9] Although declining prices have spurred the growth of PC sales, another significant factor is simplicity. Most machines tend to be *user friendly*, which means that a novice can learn to run them without knowing what really goes on inside, and without knowing how to program them. Because technical jargon, baffling codes, and complicated keyboard procedures have been simplified through user-oriented instruction manuals and programs, microcomputers are less intimidating to the first-time user. Figure 16.11 presents a user-friendly breakdown of the parts of a personal computer.

Tasks within their capabilities are typically cheaper to perform on microcomputers than on their bigger brothers, mainframe computers, because microcomputers need neither highly trained operators nor special facilities (which may include under-the-floor wiring and additional air conditioning to keep components cool). All reputable microcomputer software companies provide instructional manuals so first-time users can learn to run the programs in a matter of hours with no programming knowledge. One company claimed that graphs of financial forecasts that cost $36 in mainframe computer time were produced for $0.06 on a microcomputer.[10]

As you may have guessed, this enormous growth in the PC market has triggered proportional growth in markets for support products and services. Companies that manufacture the 5 1/4-inch floppy disks that fit most models (see Figure 16.11) report industry sales of $700 million per year.[11] One firm that fixes and services printers, disk drives, and other PC system components estimates that the repair market alone will reach $5 billion nationwide by 1986. Xerox Corporation reportedly can service as many as thirty-three microcomputer-related products made by sixteen different companies.[12] Personal computer software sales may reach $4.8 billion by 1987, while satellite markets for items such as PC-related furniture, disk drive head-cleaning kits, dust covers, floppy disk file boxes, printer ribbons, paper, and stands also will grow at a rapid pace.

Uses for Computers

Computers can fill several roles within an organization. Their applications are restricted only by management's imagination and willingness to initiate change.

Simulation

Computer simulation, which has grown in step with the complexity of business operations, requires a mathematical model of a particular operation, piece of equipment, or situation. The computer can then reproduce the model electronically. For example, duplicating the conditions of an automobile crash test with computer simulation lets Chrysler Corporation escape the cost of demolishing a real $10,000 automobile.[13]

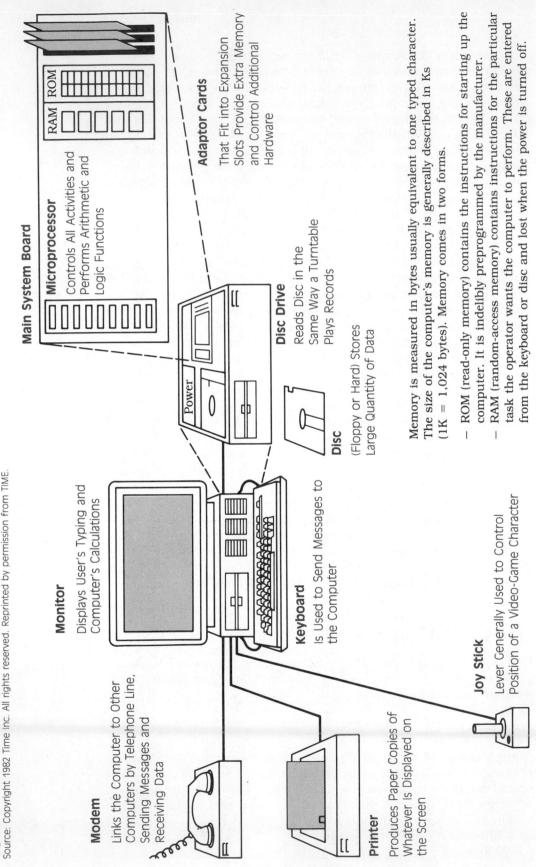

Figure 16.11 Parts of the Personal Computer and What They Do

Main System Board

Microprocessor
Controls All Activities and Performs Arithmetic and Logic Functions

RAM ROM

Adaptor Cards
That Fit into Expansion Slots Provide Extra Memory and Control Additional Hardware

Disc Drive
Reads Disc in the Same Way a Turntable Plays Records

Power

Disc
(Floppy or Hard) Stores Large Quantity of Data

Monitor
Displays User's Typing and Computer's Calculations

Keyboard
Is Used to Send Messages to the Computer

Joy Stick
Lever Generally Used to Control Position of a Video-Game Character

Modem
Links the Computer to Other Computers by Telephone Line, Sending Messages and Receiving Data

Printer
Produces Paper Copies of Whatever Is Displayed on the Screen

Memory is measured in bytes usually equivalent to one typed character. The size of the computer's memory is generally described in Ks (1K = 1,024 bytes). Memory comes in two forms.

- ROM (read-only memory) contains the instructions for starting up the computer. It is indelibly preprogrammed by the manufacturer.
- RAM (random-access memory) contains instructions for the particular task the operator wants the computer to perform. These are entered from the keyboard or disc and lost when the power is turned off.

Computers also are used to train pilots, by controlling the Link flight simulator, to simulate an actual aircraft cockpit under flight conditions. The simulation is so faithful that the Federal Aviation Administration has declared Link trainer experience to be the equivalent of actual flying time. A computer reproduces natural engine and weather sounds, projects pictures of actual airport runways under all weather, light, and speed conditions onto the pilot's windshield, and instructs hydraulic equipment to move the cockpit exactly the way an actual aircraft would respond to the pilot's touch in every situation. Microprocessors perform over 500,000 calculations per second to make the Link reproduce the feeling and reaction of a high-speed aircraft accurately.

Applied to the training of railroad engineers, the newest $8 million simulator can faithfully reproduce the feel and behavior of a train pulling various numbers of cars under all track conditions and situations. The line between simulation and reality vanished completely for one trainee who, confronted with an impending collision, leaped from the make-believe cab and fractured his ankle.[14]

Burger King's computerized site selection procedures have saved the firm more than $1 million in a single year. Programmed in advance with significant demographic data, computers compare the attractiveness of a potential location with an ideal simulated one, indicating each site's relative benefits and disadvantages. This capability reportedly allowed Burger King to reduce average decision-making time on a new location from 2 weeks to 1 day.[15]

The most complex simulations require computers that perform millions of calculations per second to create the hypothetical conditions that engineers or managers want to duplicate. When simulation demands stretch the capabilities of conventional machines, companies must employ so-called supercomputers like those built by Cray Research of Minneapolis, Minnesota. The $11 million Cray X-MP weighs several tons, houses 240,000 silicon chips, and can perform 400 million operations per second (compared with a humble Apple IIe, which has 31 chips and does only half a million operations per second). This and competing machines generate so much heat that they require internal freon gas cooling systems to keep them from self-destructing. Their abilities are as impressive as their statistics, however. Users such as General Motors can simulate solid objects so realistically that they are virtually indistinguishable from actual photographs — including highlights reflected by automobile paint and chrome strips.[16] Automotive engineers can simulate wind tunnel tests on automobiles electronically without leaving their desks, or create and observe the heat and pressures that occur inside the combustion chambers of a running engine — almost as if they were looking through a window.[17]

File Maintenance

A more humble but also more universal job that computers do well is maintaining data files on such subjects as accounts receivable and payable, sales, payroll, and inventory. One of the biggest examples of this burdensome task is the Social Security Administration's periodic update of each citizen's personal account during his or her working life. It would require an army of clerks and mountains of handwritten records to do this task manually.

Summaries

Computers can be used to summarize data for reports on such subjects as overtime hours worked by a department, actual versus budgeted sales and expenses, and income by division or product. Crompton Company, a textile manufacturer, has a computerized system that summarizes the output of weavers at its Leesburg, Alabama, plant. The system has generated lively competition among loom operators, who can check with the computer to compare their output for a given period with that of co-workers.

Automated Control

Another popular computer application, mentioned in our discussion of analog computers, is automated control of machines that perform repetitive operations. Many cities use computers to synchronize traffic lights along busy streets. Electronic sensors suspended above the streets monitor the flow of cars passing underneath at any given time and inform the computer, which automatically adjusts traffic light cycles along the route so traffic can flow freely around the clock.

Computerized control systems are essential in complex manufacturing situations too. Firms such as Honeywell, Leeds & Northrop, and Foxboro produce systems, which cost from $1 million to $17 million, that are tailored to specific customers' needs. For example, A. E. Staley Manufacturing Company controls syrup production with a Foxboro system that feeds operators constant data on liquid flows and other matters connected with making syrup.[18] Employees of Atlantic Richfield Company use Honeywell systems to regulate as many as 3,000 variables during the petroleum refining process. Exercising perpetual and precise control over operations ensures that the end products of refining (an example of which appears in Chapter 9 on page 252) conform to quality assurance standards.[19]

Sorting

Many companies use computers to sort data into certain categories. Your college may have computer-sorted lists of students by alphabetical order, zip code, major field of study, and alphabetical order within each zip code and major. Such data also can be sorted according to campus at large state universities with several campuses. Law enforcement agencies have computerized auto registration lists by license number and registered owner, which allow police officers to make a radio check for outstanding warrants and other important information before stopping a vehicle.

Service Bureaus, Time-Sharing, and Leasing

Not all companies that wish to use a computer must purchase one. Three other ways of gaining access to computers have become popular in recent years, making powerful computing capacity available to smaller firms.

A **service bureau** may be a practical way for small companies to avail themselves of automated data processing. This is *a firm that processes clients' data on its own computer (or one that it has access to) for a fee.* Once the service bureau has written a program to process the customer firm's data, the customer simply delivers its documents to the service bureau, which processes the data as agreed and returns the information or other output. Companies that keep records manually and employ large staffs of clerical personnel may find that a service bureau can do the same work faster and cheaper. A service bureau can write a company's paychecks, maintain its payroll records, update its inventory records, bill its trade credit customers and record payments received from them, write checks to the business's creditors, record and summarize sales and expense data, and produce financial statements that management can use to evaluate the company's financial health. Table 16.1 on page 490 presents a checklist that small firms can use in deciding if a service bureau would be worth hiring.

After the customer firm has paid the service bureau's programming fee, or selected a standard program to avoid this initial expense, it is charged for the time the service bureau spends on each data-processing job. Firms that hire a service bureau to process their data must comply with the service bureau's schedules, delivering complete and correct data on time. If they fail to do this, their job may be backed up in the service bureau's work flow, and important information may not reach the customer firm when it is needed.

Large companies with excess computing capacity may also act as service bureaus, a practice that has become a profitable sideline for some. With certain standard programs already written, these firms can process competitors' data for a fee rather than letting their own computer sit idle for a time.

Time-sharing is *a form of computer use in which several firms buy or rent access to a computer that is owned by another firm.* Input and output hardware units at the clients' locations are linked by telephone line or other method to the central processing unit on the time-sharing company's premises. More than 2,000 time-sharing companies operate nationwide. Time-sharing, like service bureaus, is used commonly for routine data-processing operations such as preparing payroll, updating inventory records, and running monthly statements for open-book account holders.

The time-sharing market has been affected by the growth of microcomputers in small-business data processing. Nevertheless, some small-business owners may adopt time-sharing before deciding to purchase their own microcomputer, while others have data-processing jobs that require greater memory storage than the typical

service bureau

time-sharing

The Straight Line

CAD/CAM

Computers Change Manufacturing

Imagine the savings in cost, time, and efficiency if products were designed on computers that communicated specifications to computer-controlled tools that readjusted themselves to make those items. Such a process, called *CAD/CAM*, exists today — and its possibilities are enormous. According to the National Science Foundation CAD/CAM (*C*omputer-*A*ided *D*esign and *C*omputer-*A*ided *M*anufacturing) has "greater potential to increase productivity than any invention since electricity." Perhaps you'll agree as you read on.

Computer-aided design grew from an early 1960s alliance between IBM and General Motors, who combined forces to improve engineering and drafting techniques. Complex computer programs enabled engineers to rough out the design of a machined part on a video screen and command the computer to calculate the dimensions of the finished product. Today the procedure has been so highly refined that CAD can reduce the time to produce many engineering drawings from several weeks to several days. Once an engineer has input all product dimensions into a computer, the computer can be used to modify, manipulate, and illustrate those dimensions on its screen, much the same as text is manipulated on a word processor.

Early CAD programs produced computer graphics that resembled wire mesh. These models were awkward for engineers to manipulate and did not represent the final product very well. Improvements in computers and programming techniques lent momentum to the growth of CAD, and today the state of the art permits engineers to model solid objects graphically on computers instead of making them out of clay. Applicon's Solids Modeling program, for example, allows engineers to simulate an object on a video screen complete with texture, color, and other details. Given the nature of the material (steel, aluminum, or plastic) the program also will calculate the part's final weight, center of gravity, area, and volume. Parts may be subjected to computer-simulated heat, stress, and pressure or abused in a host of other ways to determine their durability and performance. They can be enlarged, reduced, viewed from any angle, or cut into sections — all done electronically, which means tremendous savings in personnel and time.

Thanks to CAD, engineering drawings that once required a full day to do by hand can be done in just an hour. When you consider that drafting employees may receive more than $25 per hour in salary and benefits, annual savings from a CAD system can

personal computer contains. Software features are another advantage. Most time-sharing companies have programs that process and manipulate data in more ways than the word-processing or accounting programs that run on personal computers.

Time-sharing offers more flexibility than does a service bureau. Time-sharing customers have direct access to the computer virtually

be tremendous. Some analysts maintain that many manufacturers may recover the cost of a CAD system, which can range from $55,000 to $200,000, in less than 3 years.

The CAM part of CAD/CAM involves linking design computers with those controlling machine tools or even robots, which you learned about in Chapter 9. The design computer can communicate the engineer's specifications directly to the machine's computer, which adjusts its settings accordingly to produce the finished part to exact standards. CAM's savings result from the fact that machines may be reprogrammed to perform a wide range of repetitive movements and tasks consistently and accurately.

Companies such as Pratt & Whitney Aircraft, General Motors, and General Electric have produced some of the most successful CAD/CAM marriages in industry today. Pratt & Whitney, one of the more advanced CAD/CAM users, reportedly produces turbine blades directly from computerized drawings. Northrop Corporation's CAD/CAM system has compressed the lag time between the release of engineering drawings and the production of custom-bent hydraulic tubing (which snakes its way through an aircraft fuselage) from 6 weeks to 18 *minutes*. General Motors' CAD/CAM system re-

duced production time for auto body panels by 50 percent, while General Electric's use of CAD/CAM in troubleshooting potential problems with plastics molding operations promises to save the company $100 million per year. Engineers can identify design problems with molds before the molds are even produced. A programming system coupling both CAD and CAM may cost more than half a million dollars, excluding, of course, the cost of the production equipment itself.

As the price of computers and CAD/CAM systems declines, their amazing power to graft design computers with manufacturing equipment will fall within the reach of more small companies. Indeed some forty firms currently make ready-to-run CAD systems and prices are expected to fall below $40,000 for a system and a graphic plotter (which converts the computer design to an engineering drawing) by the late 1980s.

In the very near future, the time usually needed to convert an engineer's idea to a finished product may be expressed in hours rather than months for many companies. CAD/CAM will have changed forever the basic relationship between engineering and manufacturing that has existed since the Industrial Revolution.

For more about CAD/CAM, see Harry B. Thompson, "CAD/CAM and the Factory of the Future," *Management Review*, May 1983, p. 27; John Teresko, "CAD/CAM Goes to Work," *Industry Week*, February 7, 1983, p. 40; Lawrence Stevens, "Designs of the Times," *Inc.*, January 1983, p. 106; and Gene Bylinsky, "A New Industrial Revolution Is on the Way," *Fortune*, October 5, 1981, p. 106.

around the clock, and the computer's lightning speed permits it to handle the data-processing load of many time-sharing customers simultaneously. Customers usually rent the peripheral equipment and pay a fee for the amount of computer time used during a given period.

Considering the rapid technological advances that are char-

Table 16.1 Checklist to Determine If a Business Can Benefit from Using a Service Bureau
Source: John D. Caley, *Computers for Small Business*, Small Business Administration, Small Marketers Aids No. 149, p. 4.

How Many of These Do You Have Each Month?	Give Yourself These Points	Your Points
Number of checks written	10 points for each 100	_____
Number of employees (including salespeople)	1 point per employee	_____
Number of customers' accounts receivable	10 points for each 100	_____
Number of invoices you prepare	10 points for each 100	_____
Number of purchases or purchase orders	10 points for each 100	_____
Number of different items you carry in inventory	10 points for each 1,000	_____
Do you have very large items in inventory, such as trucks?	10 points if answer is yes	_____
Do you need help in keeping track of your inventory?	10 points if answer is yes	_____
Total points for your business		_____

If you fill in the blanks honestly and your total comes to 100 or more, you would probably benefit from using a service bureau. Even if your total is less than 100, you might be able to benefit. But no simple test such as this can make the decision for you. Look into it carefully. Remember that EDP should reduce costs or increase income enough to repay every dollar you put into it.

acteristic of the computer industry, many firms choose to lease machines rather than buy them. This lets them avoid being stuck with a new yet technically obsolete computer, because the leasing company often allows its customers to exchange their present computers for newer models after several years. Unlike time-sharing and service bureaus, leasing gives a company full control over its own computerized data processing.

Leasing costs vary according to the size and capabilities of the computer. Management should select a machine that can be adapted to changes in the company's data-processing requirements and business operations over several years.

Summary

Large companies gather and process internal and external data in a formalized management information system. Such data are classified as primary if they have not been assembled before and secondary if they have. Managers use both types of data when examining a problem or exploring a business opportunity.

Observation is a suitable method of data collection if it is not necessary to ask questions. Firms use mail, telephone, or personal interview surveys, however, when they require opinions, reactions, or other data that cannot be gathered by simple observation.

Averages, correlations, or index numbers may summarize data succinctly and meaningfully. The choice depends on the characteristics of the data. Such visual aids as pie charts, bar charts, statistical maps, and pictographs help to present data in a meaningful, easy-to-understand fashion.

Computers are used to process large quantities of data rapidly because they can perform many repetitive calculations quickly and accurately without human intervention. Analog computers, widely used to control manufacturing equipment, process measurements against a model of the problem or situation. Digital computers, the type that businesses use more often, accommodate such data-processing jobs as payroll calculations, inventory recording, and billings for trade accounts receivable. They require programs that feed them step-by-step instructions. Programs must be written in a computer language that is compatible with the computer and the type of data it processes.

Microprocessors, mazes of circuits photographically etched on layers of snowflake-sized silicon chips, have pushed the frontiers of data-processing speed far beyond what transistors made possible in the 1950s.

Powered by microprocessors, microcomputers (personal computers) have revolutionized the way that many of us process data. In fact some educational institutions now require computer literacy as a prerequisite to graduation. Declining prices combined with simplicity of operation have accelerated sales of personal computers to individuals and small businesses. Their popularity naturally has encouraged the growth of support companies that supply floppy disks, software, and accessories.

Businesses have put computers to work in such areas as simulation, file maintenance, summarizing information, controlling automated equipment, and sorting information. Many firms gain access to computers through service bureaus, time-sharing, and leasing. The choice depends on the company's size, the degree of flexibility it requires in its computerized data processing, and the nature of the data that the computer must process.

Key Terms

analog computer
arithmetic mean
arithmetic unit
array
computer
control unit
correlation
digital computer
hardware

index number
input unit
management information system (MIS)
median
memory unit
microprocessor
mode
output unit

primary data
program
random sample
sample
secondary data
service bureau
software
stratified random sample
time-sharing

For Review and Discussion

1. Describe the differences as you see them between the management information system in a large corporation such as General Foods and the one in a small local company that customizes vans. List three examples of internal and external data that each firm must gather and process.

2. Discuss at least one major personal decision you have made that required you to gather primary data. List one decision you have made using strictly secondary data, and one that involved both.

3. Indicate whether you would use observation or a survey to gather data on each of the following circumstances, and why you would make that choice: traffic flow past a potential retail store location; spendable income of teenage customers in a record and tape shop; the number of drivers who use city streets instead of a new crosstown expressway charging a toll of a quarter per car; peak customer traffic periods at a popular fast-food restaurant; and the most popular breeds of dog and cat purchased from a pet store.

4. Evaluate mail, telephone, and personal interview surveys on each of the following criteria: geographic coverage, cost, need for interviewer training, control over the accuracy of responses, language bias, interviewer bias, and flexibility.

5. Why is a representative sample essential to a reliable observation or survey? Cite one situation in which a random sample would be desirable and another that would call for a stratified random sample.

6. Calculate the mean, median, and mode of the following array:

    12
    15
    23
    34
    40
    40
    56
    72
    95

7. Under what circumstances can a mean be misleading? What other average may be more representative in such a case, and why? In what situation would a mode be more meaningful than either a mean or a median? Why?

8. Give at least two examples of pieces of information that show a correlation. How do you explain the correlation? Why would knowledge of it be valuable?

9. Under what circumstances would an index number be a useful way to summarize data? Is this a more complex summarizing tool than averages or correlations? Why or why not?

10. List at least one example of data that could be displayed on each of the following visual aids: pie chart, horizontal bar chart, vertical bar chart, line graph, statistical map, and pictograph.

11. What makes a computer different from a hand-held electronic calculator? Why is this difference significant?

12. What is the difference between an analog computer and a digital computer? Which has the greater potential for business use? Why?

13. List and briefly describe the function of each of the five units of a digital computer's hardware.

14. Name some tangible examples of computer software. What is the most important piece of software in actual computer operation? Why?

15. List some potential uses of microprocessors. What products that you own or work with, if any, contain them?

16. What is the difference between mainframe computers, minicomputers, and microcomputers or personal computers?

17. What factors have caused personal computers to become so popular? List at least three ways that personal computers may be used by individuals and by small-business owners.

18. List at least one example of how computers are used in the following: simulation, file maintenance, summaries, automated control, and sorting.

19. What data-processing features can service bureaus offer small companies? What restrictions and conditions must customer firms accept in using a service bureau?

20. Contrast time-sharing with the use of a service bureau and a microcomputer. Should a company's size be a factor in choosing one over the other? Why or why not?

21. What characteristic of the computer industry can make leasing more attractive than purchasing for a company that needs its own in-house computer? What should management consider when selecting a machine to lease or buy?

Applications

Case 16.1 Terminal Irritation

Compared with many work environments it sounds ideal: modern desks, comfortable chairs, soft lighting, pastel colors, carpeted floors, and background music. Practically the only noise is the rhythmic clicking of co-workers' fingers on their computer keyboards. Despite such creature comforts some data-processing clerks find their jobs almost intolerable.

To understand something about the work of these employees, you must appreciate the extent of automation in many businesses. Organizations such as insurance companies, banks, and credit card firms have tens of thousands of customers, and their records all reside on computer files. This means that huge volumes of data must be input each day to update and correct existing policies or accounts and to create new ones. So every day in highly computerized organizations nationwide data-processing clerks toil away at rows or clusters of terminals in environments that are not as pleasant as they may appear.

Some data-processing clerks maintain that their jobs are today's variation of the factory sweatshops that existed around the turn of the century. Compensation programs may be blamed for part of this attitude, because many firms pay these workers according to the number of forms they input during a work period. Under these conditions, workers complain, a trip to the restroom comes out of your paycheck. They also complain of monotony caused by keying in the same data from the same standardized forms time and time again.

Then there's the computer itself, which may seem like an electronic galleymaster to these toilers, many of whom contend they are rowing as fast as they can. While digesting the data its attendants input, the computer also keeps exact records on their performance. Clerks who consistently fail to input the standard number of coded insurance claims or credit card account applications per hour, for example, will be identified, counseled, and eventually released if their productivity does not improve.

The relationship between the workers' machines and their bodies (referred to as *ergonomics*) may pose problems too. Some clerks complain of stress, headaches, eyestrain, and blurred vision caused by long hours of staring at a video screen. Others suffer from back and neck aches attributed to holding their bodies in a rigid pose in front of the machine or stiff, sore wrists caused by hours spent at a keyboard. Complaints have become so pronounced, in fact, that some unions view these workers as prime targets for an organizing campaign.

Questions

1. What recommendations would you have to a manager whose subordinates made several of the above complaints?

2. Many companies today manufacture ergonomic furniture that can be adjusted to alleviate several physical problems mentioned in this case. Considering the nature of the work as outlined here, what kinds of adjustments would be needed to help alleviate complaints?

3. In what ways might management redesign these jobs or the company's data input procedures to make the work more varied and challenging?

Case 16.1 For more about the problems of data processing clerks, see Sharon Begley, "Making Machines Fit People," *Newsweek*, August 29, 1983, p. 68; Wim J. H. Selders, "Ergonomic Work Stations: Are They Really Needed?" *The Office*, June 1983, p. 154; and John Andrew, "As Computers Change the Nature of Work, Some Jobs Lose Savor," *The Wall Street Journal*, May 6, 1983, p. 1.

Case 16.2 Taking the Byte out of Crime

Computers have enjoyed a secure niche in processing banking transaction data for several decades; however, as bank services have expanded in step with increased computer capabilities, the potential for electronic larceny has grown proportionally. Today one truly adept computer hacker might be able to steal more from a bank than all the traditional robbers in history have taken — and with considerably greater finesse.

Banks transfer $400 billion per day on networks of automated teller machines that are linked by telephone lines to their central computers. Transactions of this sort are not usually sent in code, which means they can be intercepted. Conceivably a computer expert could tap into lines that link remote teller machines to a bank's main computer, record withdrawal transactions made by legitimate depositors, and play the recorded data over the same lines later. The computer would recognize this as a new round of withdrawals and dispense money from the machine. Although such a theft would require someone who was an expert on computers, telecommunications, and electronic equipment, it is entirely feasible. A similar scheme in Japan cost three banks almost $6,000 before the thief was caught.

One obvious solution to this potential problem would be to automatically encrypt (encode) messages exchanged by remote tellers and the bank's central computers. The expense of encrypting equipment — $5,000 per automated teller machine — makes it very impractical at this time. And even if the price were cheaper, security could be breached with those systems that require one or more persons to set or change the code.

Computerized theft isn't restricted to teller machines, of course. On an even larger scale, the Fed and its member banks swap more than $64 trillion by computer every year. Electronic hijackers who were truly ambitious could channel millions of dollars' worth of funds in transit into one or more personal accounts. At the present time some of these computerized transfer commands are coded, and the Fed plans more stringent safeguards in the near future. Nevertheless, some observers estimate that it will be at least 5 years before most banks have truly made their automated teller machine networks safe from the threat of computerized larceny.

Questions

1. In addition to encryption, what measures might banks use to minimize the likelihood of this new form of robbery?

2. Relate the following comment to the attitude of some computer hackers: "The satisfaction is in the chase."

Case 16.2 For more about computerized bank robbery, see Susan Dentzer, "Tapping the Bank's Wires," *Newsweek*, April 25, 1983, p. 58.

Accounting for Profits

Chapter Outline

Chapter Objectives

After studying this chapter, you should be able to:

1. Discuss the history of accounting.
2. Discuss the functions of accounting that an accounting system is organized to perform.
3. Describe the six groups that need accounting data for decision making.
4. Contrast the work of a bookkeeper with that of an accountant.
5. Summarize the credentials and qualifications that set a CPA apart from other accountants.
6. Explain the purpose and significance of the audit function of CPAs.
7. Give reasons for choosing a fiscal year that is different from the calendar year.
8. Describe an income statement and the information this statement contains.
9. Describe a balance sheet and the information this statement contains.
10. Explain the purpose of a statement of changes in financial position.
11. Perform certain financial analyses based on the income statement and the balance sheet, and one that requires data from both statements.
12. List several sources of information for comparative financial analysis.

I guess business is never going to get back to normal. . . . We have learned the hard way over the last four years that it's a competitive world, and we have to do a more effective job of managing our assets.

— *E. Mandell de Windt, Chief Executive Officer, Eaton Corporation*

Up Front   Wayne G. English

Success Began with an Accounting Degree

What's the key to a successful career? If you asked Wayne English that question, he might point to his degree in accounting, which set the stage for extraordinary success throughout his career. He seems to have reached the pinnacle of his profession, however, as chief financial officer at MCI Communications Corporation. English's skill at creative financing has helped that company become the undisputed leader in the telecommunications market.

After earning his Bachelor of Science degree at Ohio State University and serving in the U.S. Air Force, English began his career as a junior accountant with the national accounting firm of Coopers & Lybrand. A scant 3 years later he had earned his CPA certificate and risen to the post of senior accountant. The auditing responsibilities that came with the work provided little spice and fire for English, though: he began leaning more toward financial than accounting responsibilities. A series of significant jobs followed: financial analyst for Ford Motor Company; controller of a Ford truck plant; vice-president of finance and director at Aeroquip Corporation, vice-president of finance at Pullman, senior vice-president of finance and director of Trans World Airlines (TWA), and executive vice-president and director of Hallmark Cards.

What could surpass such an exceptional history of responsibilities with so many prestigious firms? For Wayne English, it has been his achievements at MCI.

In 1975 English and Hallmark Cards parted company and English was shopping for a position worthy of his background and reputation. People of English's caliber don't have to look very long for new challenges, and soon an executive recruiter told him about MCI, which badly needed an astute chief financial officer. The company's finances were a shambles. It owed $100 million, its banks had refused to lend additional capital, and to make matters worse, the struggling telecommunications company was competing in the marketplace — like David against Goliath — with huge American Telephone and Telegraph (AT&T).

The more English learned about the company, the more interested he became. Unlike his former employers, which had been in business for generations, MCI was new, it had a relatively informal way of doing business, and its management atmosphere was charged with promise and prog-

Italy, the hub of world trade during the fifteenth century, honed the skills of business to a sharper edge than any other nation at that time. Such business practices as accounting originated and flourished there as a natural result.

A Venetian monk named Luca Paciolo wrote the first book

ress. If the company survived, it would be special in its field — and English could be the designer of its survival plan. What MCI needed most was a financial officer with English's proved expertise at raising capital (after all, he'd raised almost $1 billion at TWA and Hallmark Cards). Put simply, the company's growth had outpaced its present ability to raise money, although its potential to compete in the telecommunications market was outstanding.

English knew the company would be doomed if its bankers demanded payment of their loans, so he interviewed them before taking the job. The company's major bankers agreed to restructure the pay-back agreements on its loans and also agreed to let MCI pay only the interest (suspending principal payments) for 2 years. English took the job, and in doing so he made some solemn promises: he would raise capital using methods that would place MCI on solid financial ground; he would obtain enough capital to enable the company to exceed $1 billion in sales by 1987; and he would ensure the company's continued survival by employing additional financial personnel with similar talent who would carry the company forward after he retired.

By all accounts Wayne English is a man who keeps his promises. His initial strategy was to issue convertible preferred stock, followed by convertible debenture bonds (see Chapter 14). This capital was invested in the business, and similar securities offerings followed. As the company thrived on its new diet of badly needed capital, holders of both securities converted them to common stock. The plan worked so well, in fact, that MCI paid off its bank loans within 2 years after the moratorium on principal payments expired.

Wayne English's success as MCI's financial wizard has been the capstone of a distinguished career. With the company's balance sheet restored to good health and his promises kept, English now looks forward to playing golf with his wife and savoring gourmet foods. And while his achievements reach far beyond the scope of the accountant's work, his education and subsequent CPA certificate equipped him, in retrospect, to build the kind of reputation that is the envy of many financial officers — and to build a financially sound future for MCI.

For more about Wayne G. English, see "Heady Days for the Numbers Guys," *Fortune*, January 23, 1984, p. 63; Gregory Miller, "MCI's Struggle for Survival," *Institutional Investor*, September 1983, p. 89; and Ann Monroe, "Financing Profile," *Corporate Financing Week*, October 26, 1981, p. 5.

about bookkeeping in 1494, basing it on his work as a tutor to a merchant's son. It clearly reflected the author's background as a mathematician, but this work also outlined most of the bookkeeping practices and procedures that are part of the broader field of accounting today. Paciolo introduced the principles of double-entry bookkeeping, in which each transaction is recorded in at least two accounts. This system, fundamental in today's bookkeeping, provides checks and balances through which bookkeepers may detect and correct errors and verify accuracy. It is sometimes referred to as "the method of Venice." Paciolo's clear, precise, and accurate work became the standard bookkeeping reference of its day, and his ideas have been used throughout the centuries with few changes.[1]

Management has always considered accounting data to be guide-posts to profit, but they took on additional importance when the securities laws that you learned about in Chapter 14 placed larger corporations under federal scrutiny. Today publicly held companies must report their financial standing to federal and state regulatory agencies. This government regulation, combined with the growing sophistication of management techniques and the increasing complexity of corporate operations, has increased the demand for accountants and accelerated accounting's popularity as a career.

Accounting in Perspective

accounting system

A firm's **accounting system** is *an organized approach to gathering, recording, analyzing, summarizing, and interpreting financial data to determine a firm's financial condition.* Accounting is a highly specialized part of a company's management information system, which you learned about in Chapter 16. As the preceding definition implies, a company often must employ many people to ensure that its accounting system performs its required functions efficiently and effectively. For a large corporation with many facilities, this usually means making one or more persons responsible for accounting functions at each plant or office. These individuals will gather, record, analyze, summarize, and interpret accounting data for their respective locations and send it to divisional or regional offices, where it may be combined with data from other plants or offices and relayed to headquarters for use by top management.

The tasks performed in an accounting department are summarized in Figure 17.1, which shows the accounting cycle. For small companies, these operations may be performed by hand. As you learned in Chapter 16, for many large corporations, the volume of data to be processed is so great that many of these operations must be performed by computer. Either way, the result of the work carried on during the accounting cycle is to produce reports that help management perform the controlling function you learned about in Chapter 4. These reports enable decision makers to compare what is happening to a company financially with what they expected to happen, and to evaluate the causes and effects of the difference.

Who Needs Accounting Data?

Accounting data must acknowledge the concerns and needs of many different groups and individuals both inside and outside a company. Many decisions that these parties make will be based largely, if not

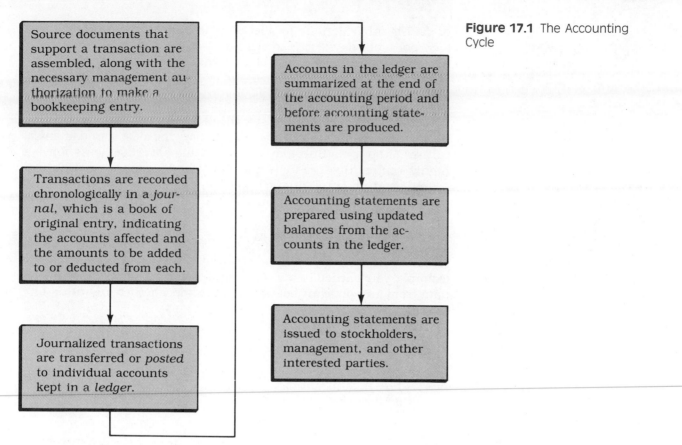

Figure 17.1 The Accounting Cycle

entirely, on information contained in financial reports and other accounting documents.

Management. Management at all levels uses accounting data to monitor the success of plans and progress toward objectives. Accounting data reveal, for example, the number of units sold during a given period, revenue received from sales, expenses associated with selling and those connected with the general operation of the business, production costs, inventory levels, and a host of other significant facts. Managers simply could not function without periodic feedback of this sort.

Owners. Owners use accounting data to evaluate their decision to become owners. By reporting the health of their company, accounting data enable owners (whether sole proprietors, partners, or stockholders) to determine if the risk they have taken is providing a sufficient return on their investment. If they are satisfied with their company's financial performance, they may decide to increase their risk (by investing more capital or purchasing additional shares of stock). If accounting data disclose financial difficulties, owners may react, for example, by reducing costs, attempting to increase sales, or taking other actions to alleviate the problems. Stockholders of a corporation may decide to sell their shares if the company seems destined to operate at a loss or to earn disappointing profits in the foreseeable future.

Potential Investors. Would-be stockholders also scrutinize accounting data to decide which companies seem to have the most sound financial future. Although a firm may run appealing advertisements, have a highly competitive product, and enjoy high employee morale, its present and potential financial future, as indicated by accounting data, are the ultimate factors on which to base an investment decision.

Creditors. Potential creditors use a company's accounting data as justification for approving or denying a loan. In Chapter 14, for example, you learned that a commercial bank must have accounting data from an applicant before it can decide whether to grant a line of credit.

Unions. Unions examine a company's accounting data closely before negotiating a new labor-management agreement. The company's past, present, and anticipated financial condition form the basis for union proposals on wages and fringe benefits.

Government. All levels of government require companies to submit accounting data to comply with the law. This is true from the Internal Revenue Service on a federal level to county and city governments, which base certain taxes on the value of assets reported on a company's books.

Bookkeeping and Accounting

bookkeeper

accountant

Many persons use the terms *bookkeeping* and *accounting* as synonyms, but business students should realize that they differ significantly. Bookkeeping is a routine clerical function within the field of accounting, and a **bookkeeper** is *a clerical worker who maintains the financial records that an accountant shapes into usable information.* Accounting, on the other hand, has a much broader scope. An **accountant** is *a person who has the education and experience to evaluate the significance of information derived from a company's financial records, interpret its impact on operations, and participate in higher management decisions that are made as a result.*

The CPA

The definition of an accountant states that accountants usually have extensive training. Some people may adopt the label *accountant* with few formal credentials, but a certified public accountant (CPA)

Leaving the bookkeeping to bookkeepers, this accountant examines, analyzes, and interprets the effect of financial information contained in a company's records.

is a recognized professional who must receive specific training and meet certain requirements, just like a lawyer or a physician. A CPA achieves this stature by completing required academic study (usually a 4-year college degree in accounting) and passing a rigorous 3-day examination prepared and administered by the American Institute of Certified Public Accountants (AICPA). After successfully completing this test, which encompasses accounting theory, accounting practice, auditing, and law, the candidate receives a CPA certificate.

Many states require a minimum of 2 years' work experience in a CPA office, in addition to the certificate, before a person may begin private practice as a CPA. Beyond this states have continuing education provisions that require CPAs to attend courses or seminars regularly so they will keep abreast of changes in their profession. State regulations on work experience and continuing education are not uniform, but the state board of accountancy can supply details on becoming a CPA in your state.

The Audit Function

State and federal laws require corporations to have their books audited or examined at least once a year by an independent certified public accounting firm. Before the 1930s audits mostly verified mathematical correctness using a sample of a client's accounts. Then McKesson & Robbins, a major drug company, was found to have reported fictitious inventories in nonexistent warehouses on its financial statements, and auditing took on new significance. A certified public accounting firm's regular audit is not done specifically to detect fraud, however, nor does it vouch for the accuracy of a company's financial reports. It does enable the firm to evaluate the extent to which the client's accountants followed generally accepted accounting practices and to express a professional opinion on how

The CPA's audit function: corporations employ certified public accounting firms to audit their books each year.

fairly the client's financial statements reflect its financial position. This opinion, which only CPAs are legally qualified to provide, is given considerable weight by lenders, current and potential stockholders, such government regulatory agencies as the Securities and Exchange Commission, labor unions preparing for contract renegotiations, major suppliers, customers, and firms that may wish to acquire the company.

The CPA's responsibility in auditing a client firm acquired greater significance as bankruptcies rose in the late 1970s. Escalating bankruptcies prompted lawsuits by disgruntled creditors and stockholders who claimed that reckless or indifferent auditing by the certified public accounting firm prevented it from uncovering evidence that bankruptcy was imminent. Thus, argued the plaintiffs, the accounting firm should be held liable for their losses. At least two major accounting firms lost such cases and were liable for a total of $8.4 million in damages. The AICPA's auditing standards now declare that an auditor should be alert to the possibility of fraud and must examine a client's accounting records with "professional skepticism." Although fraud detection remains a lesser audit objective, accountants in the future must be more sensitive to evidence of fraud than ever before.[2]

The Accountant's Discretion

"Everyone to the tax shelter."

From *The Wall Street Journal*, permission Cartoon Features Syndicate.

Although accounting deals with quantifiable data (usually dollars and cents), accountants enjoy some discretion in applying generally accepted accounting principles. Within the limitations of the Internal Revenue Code and the accounting profession's own guidelines, a firm may legitimately apply one set of accounting rules for financial reporting purposes and another set when computing federal and state income taxes. A company may select one of several methods of computing the value of its year-end merchandise inventory and cost of goods sold, for example, or of calculating annual depreciation on assets that it owns. Each approach produces a different net profit figure and alters the other amounts that appear on the business's financial statements.

The generally accepted accounting principles are established, clarified, and modified by the **Financial Accounting Standards Board (FASB),** *a group created in 1973 through the joint efforts of the American Institute of Certified Public Accountants and several other accounting organizations to be the overall rule-making body for the accounting profession.* The FASB's periodic pronouncements significantly affect the decisions of accountants in designing accounting systems, interpreting financial statements, and advising companies on financial matters.

Financial Accounting Standards Board (FASB)

The Fiscal Year

A **fiscal year** (also termed *budget year* or *management year*) is *the 12-month period that a company adopts for financial accounting purposes.* Although the fiscal year is frequently the same as the calendar year, other beginning and ending months may be chosen to correspond with the business's natural 12-month cycle if customer behavior (as with tourist attractions) or model or style changes (as with clothes, cars, or lawn and garden equipment) create such a cycle.

fiscal year

By declaring a fiscal year that begins and ends when business activity is slowest, management can summarize financial results when the number of daily accounting transactions to be recorded is lowest. The data-processing burden on personnel and equipment thus becomes as light as possible. Automobile dealers may choose a fiscal year of September 1 through August 31, closing the books for financial reporting purposes during the changeover to new models, when sales activity and inventories are minimal. Toy manufacturers and retailers often operate from July 1 to June 30, placing Christmas, their busiest time, at midyear.

Accounting Statements

The document in which businesses summarize their financial condition each year is called an **annual report.** Management needs financial information more often that that, however, to control op-

annual report

Pause and Ponder

How would you use the information provided by a firm's accounting system in making the pricing decisions discussed in Chapter 12? How could accounting information help in selecting a new plant site, discussed in Chapter 9? In expanding a plant? In expanding marketing efforts into new regions?

erations effectively, so certain documents are produced quarterly too. Stockholders usually receive quarterly or interim financial reports as well as the annual report.

This was not always so, however. In the nineteenth century many companies did not issue annual reports. One reason, of course, was that they were not required to do so. The chief reason, though, was that most corporations before the turn of the century were owned by small groups of local stockholders, many of whom were related to or friends of the top managers. Thus it was relatively easy for stockholders of that time to stay abreast of how their company was performing. Only since the early 1900s, when corporate ownership extended to large numbers of widely scattered stockholders, has this formal summary of financial condition become an annual publication, expected by stockholders and required by law.[3]

The terminology and format of the accounting statements found in companies' annual reports vary from one company to another and from industry to industry, so we will depart from our habit of using examples from actual companies and discuss major accounting statements with fictitious firms as examples.

17

A complete financial report contains three major accounting statements, each with its particular purpose. They are the income statement, the balance sheet, and the statement of changes in financial position.

The Income Statement

income statement *18*

The **income statement**, popularly called the *profit and loss*, or *P & L*, statement, is *an accounting statement that summarizes a company's revenues, cost of goods sold (if it sells merchandise), expenses, and net profit or loss over a period of time.* Although an income statement may reflect such time spans as a month or a quarter, the example shown in Table 17.1 covers one year.

19 **revenue**

The **revenue** section presents *cash or other items received in exchange for merchandise or services.* In a merchandising firm, customers may return certain items or receive sales allowances for such reasons as buying shopworn goods. As a result the dollar value of these returns and allowances is subtracted from the gross sales figure to produce net sales for the period.

cost of goods sold

Under **cost of goods sold,** the statement shows *the cost of obtaining the merchandise that was sold to produce the net sales.* This cost is computed very logically. The merchandise inventory at the beginning of the accounting period is added to net purchases during the period to determine the total value of goods available for sale. The ending inventory is then subtracted from this figure to get the cost of merchandise actually sold during this period.

19 **gross profit on sales**

Gross profit on sales is *the profit that a company made after deducting cost of goods sold from net sales but before subtracting operating expenses.*

operating expenses

The section on **operating expenses** presents *the value of items or services used or consumed in normal company operations during an accounting period.* In our example, expenses are classified

Table 17.1 Sample Income Statement

PROFIT-MAKING ENTERPRISES, INC.
Income Statement
Year Ended December 31, 198X

Revenue		
Sales		$778,918
Less returns and allowances		14,872
Net sales		764,046
Cost of goods sold		
Beginning inventory, January 1, 198X	$ 37,258	
Plus net purchases	593,674	
Goods available for sale	630,932	
Less ending inventory, December 31, 198X	41,540	
Cost of goods sold		589,392
Gross profit on sales		174,654
Operating expenses		
Selling expenses		
Sales salaries	$56,718	
Advertising expense	7,418	
Sales promotion expense	5,780	
Total selling expenses	69,916	
General and administrative expenses		
Office salaries	14,378	
Administrative salaries	26,612	
Telephone expense	700	
Insurance expense	2,100	
Depreciation expense, building	3,250	
Depreciation expense, furniture and fixtures	1,780	
Utilities expense	6,250	
Total general and administrative expenses	55,070	
Total operating expenses		124,986
Net income before taxes		49,668
Less federal and state income taxes		18,315
Net income		$ 31,353

into two main categories, *selling* and *general and administrative*, with individual accounts for each. This separation allows management to monitor and control spending in each area and decide if it should be curtailed or increased. **Net income before taxes** is *the amount a firm earned from operations before state and federal income taxes are deducted.* **Net income** is *the amount of profit*

net income before taxes

net income

that a company earned during an accounting period. The accountant's discretion that you learned about on page 504 may suggest that companies decrease net income for anticipated as well as documented expenses. This decrease may be justified if a company must make a significant, one-time expenditure in the near future and wants its financial statements to show the effects of that decision. For example, Johnson & Johnson, the makers of Tylenol, charged $50 million against profits in one 3-month period to offset the cost of recalling and destroying 22 million bottles of capsules after receiving evidence that some had been tampered with in the stores. This action reduced the company's net income 26 percent in that quarter and depressed its earnings per share on common stock from $0.78 per share to $0.51 per share.[4]

The Balance Sheet

balance sheet

A **balance sheet** is *an accounting statement that shows a firm's status on the last day of an accounting period.* If you compare a company's accounting period to a reel of movie film, with each frame representing a day's operations, the balance sheet is the last frame on the reel. The firm is frozen on that day for reporting purposes.

The balance sheet shows subtotals and totals in three general areas: assets, liabilities, and owners' equity. These relate to one another in the basic accounting equation:

Assets = liabilities + owners' equity*

The balance sheet presents a detailed view of this equation. Like the income statement, it has various categories of accounts. Table 17.2 shows an example of a balance sheet for our hypothetical corporation. Familiarize yourself with the important terms that it shows.

assets 14

Assets may be defined as *things of value that businesses, government, or individuals own.* Here we focus specifically on things of value that a company owns. They can be classified in several ways. The sample statement presents two common categories of assets. **Current assets** consist of *cash, items that will become cash within 1 year* (such as inventory and trade accounts receivable), *and prepaid expenses* (such as insurance premiums, rent, and office supplies). **Plant and equipment,** *sometimes called* fixed assets, is *an asset category that includes land and expensive manufactured items that a company will use in its operations for several years.* The sample balance sheet in Table 17.2 shows a building and some furniture and fixtures included in this classification.

current assets

plant and equipment

All plant and equipment assets except land are depreciated. **Depreciation** is *an accounting technique by which management gradually recovers the cost of expensive fixed assets over the course*

depreciation

*Depending on the firm's form of organization, this third element also may be called *capital, net worth, proprietorship, partners' equity,* or *stockholders' equity.* However it is referred to, it reports the owners' claims against the business on the day the balance sheet was prepared.

PROFIT-MAKING ENTERPRISES, INC.
Balance Sheet
December 31, 198X

Table 17.2 Sample Balance Sheet

Assets

Current assets

Cash	$ 17,280	
Accounts receivable	84,280	
Inventory	41,540	
Prepaid expenses	12,368	
Total current assets		$155,468

Plant and equipment

Building	$43,980		
Less accumulated depreciation	10,550	$ 33,430	
Furniture and fixtures	19,200		
Less accumulated depreciation	5,250	13,950	
Land		14,000	
Total plant and equipment assets			61,380
Total assets			$216,848

Liabilities

Current liabilities

Notes payable	$ 10,000	
Trade accounts payable	41,288	
Salaries payable	400	
Taxes payable	14,000	
Total current liabilities		$ 65,688

Long-term liabilities

Mortgage payable	$ 8,000	
Bonds payable	3,280	
Total long-term liabilities		11,280
Total liabilities		$ 76,968

Stockholders' Equity

Common stock, 1,000 shares at $100 par value	$100,000	
Retained earnings	39,880	
Total stockholders' equity		139,880
Total liabilities and stockholders' equity		$216,848

of their expected lives. In doing so, it acknowledges their decline in value as a result of obsolescence, use, and age. Part of the cost is recorded as an expense on the income statement each year, and that amount is added to a running total in an account called *accumulated depreciation*, which is deducted from the asset's original cost on the balance sheet (as you can see in Table 17.2). The difference

This view of a Boeing aircraft plant in Seattle, Washington, shows a host of plant and equipment assets, including the machinery and the building. The airplanes, which are inventory to Boeing, will be recorded as plant and equipment assets by the airlines that ordered them.

between the original cost and accumulated depreciation is the asset's *book value*, its value to the firm on the day the balance sheet is prepared. A fixed asset's annual depreciation does not necessarily reflect changes in its market value, so book value may not represent what the company would receive if it sold the asset on the balance sheet date.

liabilities

Liabilities are *debts or creditors' claims that a firm owes on the day the balance sheet is prepared.* Table 17.2 shows two categories of liabilities. **Current liabilities** are *debts that must be paid within 1 year.* **Long-term liabilities** are *debts that are due in more than 1 year.* In the sample, the company has an outstanding mortgage balance of $8,000 and corporate bonds of $3,280, both of which are payable in some future year. These are long-term liabilities.

current liabilities
long-term liabilities

stockholders' equity

The balance sheet section that shows owners' claims against a corporation is called **stockholders' equity.** Listed in that section will be the total capital that the firm obtained when it sold shares of common stock — in the sample in Table 17.2, $100,000 from 1,000 shares at $100 par value. In addition, the retained earnings balance is the cumulative total profit reinvested in the firm as of the balance sheet date. This amount also is considered part of the owners' equity, giving the stockholders in the sample a claim of $139,880 against their company.

Note that the accounting equation balances in Table 17.2: assets of $216,848 equal combined liabilities and stockholders' equity of $216,848. The accounting equation must always balance. Assets are things of value the business owns, but those things must come from somewhere; they must be supplied either by someone in the company or someone outside it. The proportion of assets that comes from inside or outside the company is shown in the other two parts of the accounting equation (and of the balance sheet): owners' equity

Pause and Ponder

Would a businessperson not having formal accounting training be well equipped to interpret the information on a company's financial statements and make decisions based on that interpretation? Why or why not? Some observers say all accounting functions soon will be performed by computers. Do you think a computer could replace an accountant?

and liabilities. The equation must balance, that is, assets must always equal the total of liabilities and equity, because it must be clear where the total value of assets came from.

The Statement of Changes in Financial Position

The **statement of changes in financial position,** *also referred to as a* source and use of funds statement *or simply a* funds statement, *accounts for increases and decreases in a company's net working capital throughout an accounting period.* More specifically, it discloses where funds came from, in what amounts, and how they were applied in operations. *Working capital is determined by subtracting the firm's current liabilities from its current assets.*

statement of changes in financial position

Fluctuations in a company's net working capital and its annual change as a result of operations are important things to know in planning day-to-day operations. Working capital must be adequate to purchase inventory and other needed current assets and to pay debts as they come due. Insufficient working capital can seriously handicap a firm, which may find itself unable to pay its debts as they mature, to take advantage of cash discounts from suppliers, or to purchase enough inventory to receive quantity discounts. Management should monitor changes in working capital from one accounting period to the next to ascertain that it remains high enough to permit sound, economical operations. A sample statement of changes in financial position appears in Table 17.3.

Financial Analysis

The income statement and balance sheet present summarized totals and account balances, but many valuable facts are obscured by the format of the statements themselves. It is difficult to draw conclusions about certain financial relationships from a cursory reading of these statements. Financial analysis becomes necessary.

Financial analysis is *the use of mathematics to bring important facts and relationships on accounting statements into sharp focus,* enabling management and other interested parties to determine the firm's financial health with greater precision and clarity. Most

financial analysis

Table 17.3 Sample Statement of Changes in Financial Position

PROFIT-MAKING ENTERPRISES, INC.
Statement of Changes in Financial Position
Year Ended December 31, 198X

Sources of working capital		
Current operations		
Net income for the year	$31,353	
Plus:		
Depreciation expense, furniture and fixtures*	1,780	
Depreciation expense, building*	3,250	
Total new working capital		$36,383
Uses of working capital		
Purchase of store fixtures	5,110	
Addition to building	18,710	
Payment on mortgage	6,000	
Total uses of working capital		29,820
Net increase in working capital		$ 6.563

*Depreciation does not cause a physical flow of funds into the firm, but it is an unusual expense in that it does not require an outflow of funds. Proper accounting procedures require that depreciation be added to net income.

ratio

such computations are designed to produce a **ratio,** which is *a mathematical statement of the relationship or proportion between two elements, derived by dividing one into the other.* Such ratios and other results are used in making decisions that ultimately affect every segment of the company.

Income Statement Analysis

The following calculations will improve your understanding of the income statement in Table 17.1. Ratios derived from the income statement frequently use sales as a 100 percent, or base, figure and compare all other elements on the statement to that item.

Ratio of Net Income to Net Sales

$$\frac{\text{Net income}}{\text{Net sales}} = \frac{31,353}{764,046} = 0.04 : 1 \text{ or } \$0.04 : \$1$$

ratio of net income to net sales

The **ratio of net income to net sales** is *a statement of the net income a company earned from each dollar of sales during an accounting period.* Like the results of most financial analysis calculations, it becomes meaningful when compared with the industry standard for a firm of this size. It is a measure of a company's efficiency, answering the question, "How much of each sales dollar ended up as profit?"

A low ratio like the one in the previous calculation is not always a negative sign. Companies that sell a high volume of merchandise at a low profit per unit can survive handsomely, given the proper location, purchasing decisions, and management and marketing techniques.

Ratio of Net Sales to Net Income

$$\frac{\text{Net sales}}{\text{Net income}} = \frac{764{,}046}{31{,}353} = 24.37{:}1 \text{ or } \$24.37{:}\$1$$

The **ratio of net sales to net income,** the inverse of the previous ratio, is *a statement of the amount of sales a firm had to make to earn a dollar of net income.* If competitors are selling less to earn a dollar of net income (or earning more on each dollar of sales), management should reevaluate the firm's purchasing habits, sales efforts, marketing techniques, and expense controls to discover the reasons.

ratio of net sales to net income

Inventory Turnover

$$\frac{\text{Cost of goods}}{\text{Average inventory [(beginning inventory + ending inventory)} \div 2]}$$

$$= \frac{589{,}392}{(37{,}258 + 41{,}540) \div 2}$$

$$= \frac{589{,}392}{39{,}399} = 14.96 \text{ times}$$

Inventory turnover is *a calculation of the number of times a firm sold and replaced (or turned over) its average stock of goods during an accounting period.* If the firm's rate of turnover is higher or lower than that of competitors, there may be cause for celebration or criticism — it depends on the reason for the difference. Higher turnover may be traced to superior location or marketing efforts; it also could be caused by purchasing inventory hand-to-mouth, which makes the firm lose quantity discounts, process more paperwork than is necessary, and pay progressively higher prices during inflationary times. Inventory turnover is affected by the nature of the merchandise itself as well as by management's purchasing and marketing decisions. Stores that sell jewelry, clocks, or pianos, for example, almost always have lower turnover than stores that sell health food, shoes, or tires and mufflers.

inventory turnover

Balance Sheet Analysis

The following calculations are used to analyze balance sheets such as the sample you studied in Table 17.2.

Current Ratio

$$\frac{\text{Current assets}}{\text{Current liabilities}} = \frac{155{,}468}{65{,}688} = 2.37{:}1 = \$2.37{:}\$1$$

current ratio

The **current ratio** is a measure of safety, *an expression of a firm's ability to pay its current debts from its current assets.* A relatively low current ratio can signal trouble: the company could have difficulty paying current liabilities as they mature. On the other hand, a high current ratio may indicate that a company is keeping unnecessarily large balances of cash, inventory, or other current asset items on hand. If so, management will be criticized for not allocating funds to such long-term uses as buying more efficient equipment or renovating outdated manufacturing facilities. If a large inventory is mainly responsible for a high current ratio, the goods may fall out of style before they are sold. An overstock of seasonal items may have to be marked down drastically to attract buyers before the season ends, or the products will have to be stored until the season starts next year. Many authorities believe that 2:1 is a reasonably safe current ratio.

Acid Test Ratio

20

$$\frac{\overset{\text{(Quick assets)}}{\text{Cash + accounts receivable + marketable securities}}}{\text{Current liabilities}}$$

$$\frac{17,280 + 84,280}{65,688} = \frac{101,560}{65,688} = 1.55{:}1 = \$1.55{:}\$1$$

acid test ratio

The **acid test ratio,** more realistically than the currrent ratio, is *a measure of a firm's ability to pay current debts from its most liquid, or quick, assets — cash and near-cash items.* Such nonliquid items as inventory and prepaid expenses are ignored. Profit-Making Enterprises has $1.55 in quick assets standing behind each $1.00 of current debts on the balance sheet date. It is not unusual for this ratio to approach 1:1, but if it is 1:1 or less management must quickly determine when the current liabilities mature and confirm that enough cash will be received from sales and accounts receivable collections to pay the debts as they fall due. An extremely low acid test ratio may prompt a firm to borrow against its line of credit at a commercial bank or find some other way to raise short-term cash so it can pay its current debts on time.

Ratio of Debt to Stockholders' Equity

$$\frac{\text{Liabilities}}{\text{Stockholders' equity}} = \frac{76,968}{139,880} = 0.55{:}1 = \$0.55{:}\$1$$

ratio of debt to stockholders' equity

The **ratio of debt to stockholders' equity** is *the value of claims that creditors have against a firm's assets for each dollar of owners' claims.* This ratio expresses the relative control or claim that different parties have against the business. Highly leveraged companies have a high ratio of debt to stockholders' equity because they have raised so much long-term capital through the sale of bonds. An extremely high ratio of debt to stockholders' equity suggests that the company may have difficulty paying short-term debts, paying interest on bonds, and making contributions to its bond sinking fund, which you learned about in Chapter 14. In our example, however, stockholders' equity is roughly twice creditors' claims.

Book Value of Common Stock

$$\frac{\text{Stockholders' equity}}{\text{Common stock shares outstanding}} = \frac{139,880}{1,000}$$

$$= \$139.88 \text{ per share}$$

The **book value of common stock** is *the amount per share that stockholders would theoretically receive if a company's assets were sold on the balance sheet date.* During a bear market, when uncertain investors drive a stock's market price down, the book value of some stocks has exceeded the market value. In other words, investors were not willing to pay for shares on the open market the amount that present stockholders would have received (according to balance sheet figures) had the firm's assets been sold. Many investors consider a company's stock a good buy if its book value is greater than its current market value.

book value of common stock

Combined Statement Analysis

Certain analytical computations relate an item on the income statement to another on the balance sheet. One is usually considered most significant.

Rate of Return on Stockholders' Equity

$$\frac{\text{Net income}}{\text{Stockholders' equity}} = \frac{31,353}{139,880} = 0.224 = 22.4\%$$

The **rate of return on stockholders' equity** is *the percentage return that the company earned on the owners' investment during the previous accounting period.* It is a measure of management's ability to use stockholders' investment effectively. A return that is consistently low suggests that it might be wise for the company's owners to invest their capital in some other venture or to replace certain top managers in the company with ones who would improve leadership and performance. In the sample, the firm earned $0.224 cents on each $1 of owners' investment — a return of 22.4 percent.

rate of return on stockholders' equity

It would be convenient if just one calculation revealed a firm's financial condition, but in this case, what would be convenient is not possible. Financial analysis provides ways of looking at a firm from many angles, and the typical company will look strong by some measures and weak by others. If financial analysis indicates a current or potential problem, management must act rather than simply react to the situation. This means meeting with various departments, analyzing the problem, and taking action to restore the company to firmer financial ground as soon as possible.

Sources of Comparative Data

Virtually all of the calculations just discussed are most meaningful when compared with a standard in the company's industry or general line of business. In fact some calculations are practically useless unless the analyst has a yardstick, a typical figure that expresses the condition of competing firms. Knowing how a company stands in relation to competitors can be at least as important as knowing how it stands alone.

Business owners can get comparative data from several sources. Perhaps the best source is a trade association. These organizations act as clearinghouses of financial information for the businesses they represent. They produce statistics on typical ratios, turnover figures, and other data by sampling member firms of various sizes throughout the country. Table 17.4 shows a trade association's summary of operating ratios for over 350 profitable hardware stores, using net sales as a base.

Dun & Bradstreet, another popular source, publishes an annual report of key business ratios for 125 lines of business in retailing, wholesaling, manufacturing, and construction. Robert Morris Associates, a national association of bank loan and credit officers, reports ratios for more than 350 different kinds of companies. The Accounting Corporation of America and NCR Corporation also publish some industry ratios. Finally, a CPA can recommend additional sources of comparative data to supplement those mentioned here.

Summary

Management has a fundamental interest in accounting data because they provide guideposts to profit, but federal securities laws have made accounting even more important as corporations have become legally obligated to report their financial status. Six key groups need accounting data: management, owners, potential investors, creditors, unions, and government.

A firm gathers, records, analyzes, summarizes, and interprets financial data in an organized way through its accounting system. Accounting has a much broader scope than the routine clerical function of bookkeeping: the accountant evaluates financial information, interprets its impact on operations, and participates in higher management decisions that are made based on that information.

Certified public accountants (CPAs) are recognized professionals in accounting, having passed a national certifying examination and met state requirements. Only CPAs are legally qualified to evaluate a company's adherence to generally accepted accounting principles and to state how fairly the firm's financial statements reflect its actual financial position. Although accounting deals primarily with quantifiable data, accountants enjoy some discretion in applying

Net sales	100.00*
Cost of goods sold	64.92
Margin (gross profit on sales)	05.00
Expenses	
Payroll and other employee expenses	16.23
Occupancy expense	3.23
Office supplies and postage	0.40
Advertising	1.49
Donations	0.08
Telephone	0.24
Bad debts	0.30
Delivery	0.47
Insurance	0.66
Taxes (other than real estate and payroll)	0.46
Interest	0.61
Depreciation (other than real estate)	0.57
Supplies	0.37
Legal and accounting expenses	0.31
Dues and subscriptions	0.08
Travel, buying, and entertainment	0.19
Unclassified expenses	0.64
Total operating expense	26.33
Net operating profit	8.75
Other income	1.65
Net profit before income taxes	10.40

*Numbers expressed as a percentage of sales.

Table 17.4 Sample Operating Ratios for Hardware Stores
Source: Courtesy National Retail Hardware Association.

generally accepted accounting principles. The Financial Accounting Standards Board (FASB) is the professional rule-making body that approves the application of certain accounting principles, and its pronouncements have a considerable effect on the way some transactions will be recorded and referred to in a firm's accounting system.

Companies summarize their financial condition each year in a document called an annual report. This report contains an income statement, a balance sheet, and a statement of changes in financial position. By summarizing the firm's revenues, cost of goods sold, and expenses during the accounting period, the income statement reveals its net income or loss for that time. The balance sheet shows

The Straight Line

Procter & Gamble

Accounting Is a Cornerstone of Its Success

Accounting data are essential to effective decision making in every company. Gathering that data in a timely, accurate, and efficient manner can be a formidable challenge, but one that the Procter & Gamble Company meets surpassingly well.

Each of the company's various divisions has its own accounting or comptroller's department. Employees in this area are responsible for gathering data that will be used to develop the division's — and eventually the entire company's — financial plans. The comptroller's employees work closely with marketing, manufacturing, research and development, purchasing, and all other areas as part of their everyday jobs.

The financial plans that arise from these collective efforts are complex and extremely important. They include forecasts of sales, costs, expenses, and profits and help management reach decisions on how and where to spend the more than half a billion dollars of long-term capital that management uses to improve the business each year. Financial plans prepared by the comptroller's department help to ensure that the company and its shareholders eventually will receive their money's worth from each dollar spent. Financial plans

from each division are condensed into periodic reports that top managers use in constructing company-wide financial plans.

Most employees in the comptroller's organization work in cost accounting. Many are assigned to manufacturing plants in their divisions, where they report to the plant accounting manager. Cost accounting can be especially important in divisions like Procter & Gamble's Paper Products, where raw materials, packaging, and manufacturing expenses amount to roughly 75 percent of the product's cost. The gathering, reporting, analysis, and control of such costs are essential to keep prices competitive and achieve profitability goals. Each division's financial employees must coordinate their work not only among other areas in the division but also with counterparts in other divisions and in the home office in Cincinnati, Ohio.

June and July are especially hectic months for the comptroller's department because the company's fiscal year ends on June 30. Employees must take inventory at every office and plant around the world, bring all the accounts up to date, and relay this information to the home office for preparing the annual report.

the firm's status on the last day of the accounting period by presenting the balances of assets, liabilities, and owners' equity. The statement of changes in financial position accounts for increases and decreases in the company's net working capital throughout the accounting period.

It is difficult to evaluate a company's financial condition simply by reading its accounting statements. To get a true picture one

Computers are a vital ingredient in accounting at Procter & Gamble. In marketing promotion, for example, programs run simultaneously for dozens of products, which means that advertising cost by brand and consumer response to sales promotion efforts such as premiums, samples, and coupons must be accounted for separately by brand. Advertising production costs, another area that demands attention, have been the focus of cost-control programs that saved the company $3.3 million in one year alone without impairing the effectiveness or creativity of the ad campaigns themselves.

Employees of the comptroller's department also play an active role in setting pricing strategy for each brand in their division. Using data from financial plans, computerized financial models are prepared and used to calculate anticipated costs and profits by geographic sales district for each brand. Obviously accuracy demanded that every department in the division report its data correctly and on time to the comptroller's office.

Procter & Gamble's internal auditors, also part of the comptroller's department, follow up to verify that cost-reduction measures are actually implemented and followed at every level in the company. Furthermore, internal auditors examine every plant, department, and office in the company at least once every 2 years to ensure that such functions as purchasing, receiving, and check writing are not performed by the same persons, a practice that could allow collusion and dishonesty. A newer but extremely important responsibility is that of monitoring controls that prevent unauthorized access and unethical use of proprietary accounting data that reside in the company's computerized data banks.

What is the result of these far-flung, interrelated, and highly coordinated accounting activities? To Procter & Gamble's stockholders, it is an annual report. But to groups such as management, employees, suppliers, government agencies, and others mentioned in this chapter, the comptroller's organization exists to provide reports that influence literally thousands of internal and external decisions that can only be as sound as the accounting data on which they are based. At Procter & Gamble, the comptroller's organization aims to make these data extremely sound indeed.

For more about the accounting function at Procter & Gamble, see "More Than Keeping Score," *Procter & Gamble Moonbeams*, July 1983, p. 3.

must learn the mathematics of financial analysis. Financial analysis calculations clarify the relationships (usually ratios) between important items in a firm's accounting statements and thus bring a firm's financial health into sharper focus. Current industrywide data, available from a trade association or other reliable source, can enable a company to determine its relative financial standing in its line of business.

Key Terms

accountant
accounting system
acid test ratio
annual report
assets
balance sheet
bookkeeper
book value of common stock
cost of goods sold
current assets
current liabilities
current ratio

depreciation
Financial Accounting Standards
   Board (FASB)
financial analysis
fiscal year
gross profit on sales
income statement
inventory turnover
liabilities
long-term liabilities
net income
net income before taxes

operating expenses
plant and equipment
rate of return on stockholders'
   equity
ratio
ratio of debt to stockholders'
   equity
ratio of net income to net sales
ratio of net sales to net income
revenue
statement of changes in financial position
stockholders' equity

For Review and Discussion

1. How does a firm's accounting system relate to its management information system? How does it relate to management's controlling function?

2. Relate each of the following steps to the function of an accounting system after placing them in the correct sequence: summarizing, interpreting, recording, gathering, analyzing.

3. State at least one way in which each of the following groups uses accounting data: management, owners, potential investors, creditors, unions, and government.

4. Distinguish between a bookkeeper and an accountant. Which occupation requires greater preparation? Why?

5. What must one do to become a certified public accountant? How do individual states regulate the practice of CPAs?

6. State the purposes of a certified public accounting firm's regular audit. Why would it be unrealistic to require a CPA to vouch for the accuracy of a firm's financial reports after this audit?

7. What individuals and groups are interested in a CPA's opinion of a firm's financial statements? Give a reason for the interest of each.

8. Explain the following statement: "Accountants are allowed some discretion in applying many generally accepted accounting principles."

9. How does the Financial Accounting Standards Board influence the practice of accounting?

10. State at least one situation or condition that might induce a firm to use a fiscal year that does not coincide with the calendar. Give an example of a business that could justify this choice.

11. What time is usually covered in an income statement? List and discuss the types of information that this statement provides.

12. What time does the balance sheet cover? How does it serve as a detailed expression of the accounting equation (assets = liabilities + owners' equity)?

13. What kinds of assets are depreciated? Why does this treatment make sense?

14. Describe the role of a statement of changes in financial position. What two general categories of information appear on it?

15. Evaluate the following statement: "If you can't perform financial analysis and interpret your results, you won't know much about a company's financial condition."

16. The following calculations are used to analyze an income statement. Explain what information must be assembled to calculate them, and what they reveal: ratio of net income to net sales, ratio of net sales to net income, and inventory turnover.

17. The following calculations are used to analyze a balance sheet. Explain what information must be assembled to calculate them, and what they reveal: current ratio, acid test ratio, ratio of debt to stockholders' equity, and book value of common stock.

18. What does the rate of return on stockholders' equity reveal? How is it computed?

19. Why is accurate comparative information essential for accurate and complete financial analysis?

20. Where can a business owner find information for comparative financial analysis? Which source is the most valuable? Why?

Applications

Case 17.1 Controlling Costs

In the mid-1970s United States automakers earned some $5.1 billion by selling 7.9 million cars. In the early 1980s profits rose to $6.5 billion. Every business manager hopes that profits will climb from one period to the next, but what makes the auto industry's story exceptional is that it made record profits by selling one-third *fewer* cars than it sold a decade earlier.

Although automobile prices — as any casual window-sticker watcher will confirm — have risen in step with inflation, the cost of making a car has declined to a point where profits are earned at significantly lower sales volume than in the late 1970s.

Since 1977 General Motors Corporation, Ford Motor Company, and Chrysler Corporation have engaged in an orgy of cost cutting the like of which the auto industry has never experienced before. By the mid-1980s the "big three" auto producers had slashed production costs by $10 billion.

Personnel reductions figured prominently in the automakers' plans: staff cuts reduced fixed costs by $2.5 billion. Ford Motor Company, for example, eliminated 21,000 salaried employees — 29 percent of its North American salaried work force. Other efficiencies were implemented, such as stopping production lines during employee work breaks (which eliminated the need for 500 relief workers and saved one producer $23 million per year in pay and benefits for those employees). Closing antiquated plants saved companies $70 million annually in insurance, maintenance expenses, and taxes on assets. The use of robots (see page 245) is a connecting theme throughout this economy wave.

Some observers believe that the past decade has brought truly revolutionary cost controls to an industry that seemed to be the victim of its own momentum before the Japanese influx. Benefits are now beginning to materialize, and they're impressive. In a recent year all three producers made 25 percent more cars than the previous year and required only 8 percent more production workers to do so. Ford reports producing approximately twenty-seven cars per worker today, versus eighteen per worker in 1979.

Despite these victories in efficiency and productivity, Japanese producers still build cars for an estimated $1,500 less than their American competitors. This fact means that more than ever before cost controls must become a way of life for one of America's senior industries.

Questions

1. Discuss the morale problems associated with cost-cutting measures.

2. Assume the role of an accountant and justify continued cost reduction efforts as a means to keep American producers competitive with Japanese firms.

3. What problems should management expect to have with employee cooperation and recruitment, given that intense cost orientation is a way of life for United States automakers? How would you propose that these problems be solved?

Case 17.1 For more about cost reductions in the United States auto industry, see Robert L. Simison and John Koten, "Auto Makers' Earnings Are Increasing Sharply Despite Mediocre Sales," *The Wall Street Journal*, December 19, 1983, p. 1; Ralph E. Winter, "Expecting Lean Times, Many Firms Try Hard to Increase Efficiency," *The Wall Street Journal*, November 28, 1983, p. 1; and John Koten, "U.S. Auto Makers Face Severe Challenge of Holding Down Costs As Profits Grow," *The Wall Street Journal*, August 5, 1983, p. 42.

Case 17.2 Constructing Accounting Statements

Income Statement

Use these year-end account balances and other figures to answer questions 1 and 2.

Operating expenses	$ 45,800
Net purchases	73,000
Sales returns and allowances	5,000
Net income	24,200
Merchandise inventory, January 1, 198X	23,500
Merchandise inventory, December 31, 198X	26,500
Sales	115,000

Balance Sheet

Use these year-end account balances and other figures to answer questions 3, 4, and 5.

Delivery equipment	$ 10,065
Building	52,321
Cash	755
Salaries payable	1,721
Accumulated depreciation, building	8,286
Mortgage payable	14,200
Accounts receivable	1,200
Accumulated depreciation, delivery equipment	2,365
Taxes payable	198
Interest payable	160
Total current liabilities	2,300

Prepaid insurance premiums	2,310
Inventory	26,500
Stockholders' equity	66,000
Total assets	82,500
Accounts payable	221
Total plant and equipment	51,735

Questions

1. Construct an income statement. (Use Table 17.1 as a model.)

2. After completing the income statement, use financial analysis to compute the ratio of net income to net sales, the ratio of net sales to net income, and the inventory turnover.

3. Construct a balance sheet. (Use Table 17.2 as a model.)

4. After completing the balance sheet, use financial analysis to compute the current ratio, the acid test ratio, the ratio of debt to stockholders' equity, and the book value of common stock, assuming 2,000 shares are outstanding on the balance sheet date.

5. Using the income statement you constructed in questions 1 and 2 and your balance sheet, compute the rate of return on stockholders' equity.

Information and Finance

Information Systems with Standard Oil

With assets worth in excess of $20 billion, Standard Oil Company (Indiana) stands in the top twelve firms in the United States and ranks fifth within the petroleum industry. It does business in more than forty nations around the world.

A company this large and successful must employ a large information services department. The company has two computing centers, one at its Chicago headquarters (housed in the eighty-story Standard Oil Building, the fourth tallest building in the world) and another in its complex in Tulsa, Oklahoma. It also has satellite computing centers in Houston, Denver, New Orleans, and London, England.

In applications development, one area where entry-level positions exist, new graduates join teams headed by seasoned project leaders. They work closely with experienced peers to improve the company's existing systems for handling information and to create new ones in response to the company's dynamic business environment. Increased responsibility accompanies increased experience, and after a period of time new employees will work with various areas and departments of Standard Oil, creating and maintaining information systems to suit their needs.

In software support services, another information systems area that offers entry-level work, new graduates maintain existing software, distribute it to in-house users, and evaluate its performance and suitability in light of current company requirements and changing conditions. They may propose modifications in the existing information system to enhance its value to the company and to its individual operating units. Advancement from this position, as from applications development, moves employees into a variety of higher-level positions within the department, including jobs as group leader, project manager, and perhaps a management position at one of the computing centers. The company promotes from within whenever possible.

At Standard Oil, as with all large employers, the education employees bring to the job is only part of what is required for long-term success. Additional education and training comes through a professional development program that combines on-the-job training and classroom training. The latter is provided by the company's instructors, who introduce information systems employees to techniques of information processing used by the company. Programmer trainees receive extensive in-house training in computer languages, hardware, and software as well as introductory course work in computers. Advanced courses on programming, systems analysis, and principles of supervision bring information services employees up to date on the most recent technology and enhance their promotability.

In a field like information systems where technology, applications, and an organization's needs are never static, Standard Oil encourages employees to take classes and attend seminars provided by outside organizations. The company also has an educational assistance plan that pays most of the cost of additional education.

Finance with International Business Machines

International Business Machines Corporation (IBM) has become synonymous with computers.

Being a business enterprise first, however, IBM must recruit and train college graduates in many fields to do the multitude of jobs required to ensure its leadership in manufacturing, marketing, and servicing a broad line of products — not only computers, but also electronic and magnetic memory typewriters and copying and dictation equipment. This career capsule focuses on IBM's opportunities in finance.

IBM is a demanding and competitive place to work; but then, it did not rise to prominence by employing people who would settle for less. Successful, competent, and loyal IBMers, however, receive abundant personal and professional recognition and rewards from an employer that places a high value on each worker's individual dignity and worth.

Graduates who accept a job offer from IBM's financial area receive prompt and meaningful responsibility by working at various locations such as a plant, laboratory, regional office, or division headquarters. Most postemployment training is on-the-job training, but it is supplemented by in-house and external classroom training.

Entry-level jobs exist in financial analysis, financial planning, accounting, and other finance-related areas. The employee beginning in financial analysis may study financial trends, justify the development and marketing of a new product from a financial point of view, and attempt to forecast the financial climate throughout a product's life cycle by considering reactions by competitors, customer needs, product pricing, and the return on investment the company will receive from the product.

Employees who begin work in financial planning will help devise short-term financial operating plans (which project sales, expenses, and profits for a relatively short period of time) and conceive financial strategies to cope with the expected business environment several years from now. In doing so, financial planners, like their counterparts in financial analysis, work closely with personnel in such areas as marketing, service, product planning, research and development, and manufacturing. They become familiar with all facets of the company and receive ample opportunities to exercise professional judgment and make significant decisions very early in their careers.

Employees who take entry-level positions in accounting find that their decisions influence every aspect of the company's operations. The accounting organization creates and administers financial controls that affect all company activities, from pricing to general management. Furthermore, IBM's accountants are called on to make changes in the company's accounting system in response to changes in governmental regulatory policies and rulings by the Financial Accounting Standards Board.

Regardless of an employee's starting assignment within the finance area, he or she can look forward to promotion solely on merit. Performance, not seniority, is the criterion for advancement at IBM.

IBM has achieved success by seeking uncommon people and recognizing and rewarding their performance uncommonly well. When you join IBM you enter an employer-employee relationship many consider unmatched in American business. Exceptional students who thrive on challenge, enjoy competition, and welcome responsibility can build highly successful and rewarding careers in this exceptional company.

Part

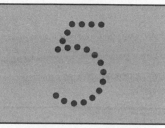

Special Challenges and Issues

The Small Business and Franchising

Chapter Outline

A Board of Advisers

Lawyer
Accountant
Insurance Counselor

Starting a Small Business

Legal Requirements
Start It Right the First Time

Sources of Financing

Personal Savings
Credit from Suppliers
Manufacturer Financing of Equipment
Commercial Banks
The Small Business Administration
Selling Stock
Venture Capital Firms

Sources of Continuing Help

The SBA
SCORE
ACE
The National Family Business Council
Students Make Good Teachers
Local Educators and Consultants
Trade Associations
Wholesalers

Franchising

What Is a Franchise?
What Does Franchising Offer You?
What Do You Have to Sacrifice?
Investigate Before You Sign

Summary

Chapter Objectives

After studying this chapter, you should be able to:

1. List three key people whose advice a new business owner should seek, and explain the need for each.
2. Describe the licenses and permits that must be obtained, and other general details that must be observed, in starting a new company.
3. List the things a small-business owner must know about to be successful.
4. Suggest several potential sources of capital for a small business.
5. Name several sources that provide continuing management advice after a small business begins to operate.
6. State the potential advantages and disadvantages of entering into a franchise agreement.

A new enterprise is like a canoe — a slight mistake and over it goes.

— Thomas P. Murphy, head of venture capital firm

Up Front   Sandra Kurtzig

ASK Computer Systems, Inc.

Many businesspeople dream of becoming millionaires before they reach forty, but few achieve that goal. Sandra Kurtzig, founder and president of ASK Computer Systems, did so 7 years early.

After earning a master's degree in aeronautical engineering from Stanford University, Kurtzig worked in marketing and technical jobs at TRW and General Electric for several years before resigning to raise a family. Chafing at her housebound condition, she soon turned her energy toward writing computer programs that newspapers could use to maintain records on delivery personnel. With no management background and just $2,000 in capital, she worked in a spare room in her home and kept her money in a shoe box. If the shoe box had more money in it on the last day of the month than it had on the first, Kurtzig knew she'd made a profit.

Soon Kurtzig's cottage industry picked up momentum. Her newspaper software programs sold well, and new, more challenging programming applications came to mind. If she could write software tailored to the newspaper industry, why not write it for other kinds of businesses too? Drawing on her background at General Electric, where she worked with manufacturing companies, Kurtzig decided that manufacturing software applications were needed. She quickly hired several recent graduates with degrees in computer science and

The more than 10 million small businesses in the United States account for more than 40 percent of our gross national product.* These companies provide livelihoods for their owners and employees while creating goods and services for millions of citizens. The definition of small business varies, but Table 18.1 shows some guidelines established by the **Small Business Administration (SBA),** *a federal government agency started in 1953 to give financial and managerial assistance to owners of small businesses.*

Small Business Administration (SBA)

Small-business owners assemble some very special ingredients in their quest for success. Seeking economic independence outside the boundaries of traditional jobs and large, formalized employers, these individuals combine courage, determination, resourcefulness, ambition, self-confidence, and optimism into a business enterprise as unique as themselves. The pioneer spirit is alive and well in dens, garages, small stores, and utility sheds nationwide.

A study released by the Massachusetts Institute of Technology revealed that within a 5-year period small businesses employing

*These totals do not include farms or farm production.

engineering, and they set to work with verve. Within a matter of months her new staff churned out 10 business-oriented programs for small and medium-sized manufacturing companies. ASK was on the move.

Lacking the computers to develop and refine more sophisticated programs, Kurtzig and her small but ambitious staff received a generous gift from a neighbor, gigantic Hewlett-Packard Company. They were allowed to use an H-P 3000 minicomputer after hours. Working at night, sometimes napping on the floor, they toiled for months to perfect an inventory control program for the H-P 3000, and in 1978 the job was done. Its completion meant instant success for Kurtzig's company, because any customer who bought an H-P 3000 computer could also buy ASK's inventory control software, which was written especially for that machine.

The company's reputation and product offerings grew as steadily as its sales. By 1980 Kurtzig's firm was selling $12 million worth of business software per year. Within 5 years sales reached $65 million, employees numbered 350, and profits were $6.1 million. Kurtzig, who had by then formed a corporation, held shares valued at $66.9 million — much more money than she could fit into her humble old shoe box, even with the aid of a shoehorn.

For more about Sandra Kurtzig, see Earl C. Gottschalk, Jr., "More Women Start Up Their Own Businesses, With Major Successes," *The Wall Street Journal*, May 17, 1983, p. 1.

twenty or fewer people created two-thirds of all new jobs in the country; companies with one hundred or fewer workers created 80 percent of all new jobs during the same time period.[1] The SBA reports that small businesses with fewer than 500 employees added some 1.7 million jobs to the economy within just 2 recent years. Small businesses, then, form a very special and significant pattern in today's economic tapestry.

In this chapter we will discuss starting and maintaining a small business and investigate franchising as a way to establish a firm's identity and draw on other management talents. The discussion will be of special value to those who are planning to start their own companies or who have already done so.

A Board of Advisers

The opinions of an experienced lawyer, a certified public accountant, and an insurance counselor are vital to an infant business, and pave the way to later prosperity. Few small-business owners are qualified to provide their own legal, accounting, or insurance advice.

529

Table 18.1 Guidelines Defining a Small Business
Source: The Small Business Administration.

Industry	Definition
Manufacturing	A company with up to 1,500 employees
Wholesaling	A company with annual sales from $9.5 million to $22 million
Services	A company with annual sales from $2 million to $8 million
Retailing	A company with annual sales from $2 million to $7.5 million
Agriculture	A company with annual sales not exceeding $1 million

Finding a competent professional in each of these fields is a challenge. One way is to ask friends and business acquaintances for recommendations. Local newspapers often interview outstanding local professionals who have earned special awards or recognition. Such service clubs as Rotary or Lions International usually have members who are active in these areas. The business owner must make an organized and thoughtful search; the people selected will be the firm's navigators, advising its owner, the pilot, on the direction he or she should take.

Lawyer

A lawyer provides in-depth legal advice on choosing forms of business organization (discussed in Chapter 2 and Chapter 3). If an owner decides to incorporate, a lawyer can prepare the required forms using the legal language needed to give the company maximum operating flexibility under its charter. The lawyer also can help by drawing up a partnership agreement for a business choosing that form.

In addition, a competent lawyer can help the small-business owner avoid legal confusion in such areas as the following:

— Contracts with outside parties (suppliers, landlords, creditors, customers, and service and repair firms)
— Liability for customer and employee injuries and for injuries caused by a product, service, or operating method
— Compliance with government regulatory agencies (Federal Trade Commission, Department of Justice, Occupational Safety and Health Administration, and others)

Accountant

An accountant helps ensure the financial success of a business venture. Certified public accountants, whom you learned about in Chapter 17, provide advice on the tax aspects of operating as a sole proprietorship, a partnership, or a corporation and custom-build accounting systems to suit the legal and operating characteristics of companies. More specifically, an accountant helps a business owner do the following:

Good things sometimes come in small packages. The collective sales and employment provided by small businesses make them a driving force in the nation's economy.

— Determine how much beginning capital the firm requires
— Make decisions to lease or purchase major fixed assets
— Project cash collections and payouts to ensure that the firm has an adequate supply of cash on hand at all times
— Choose methods for raising short-term and long-term capital
— Manage finances so the owner receives the most favorable federal and state income tax treatment possible

Insurance Counselor

A business's **insurance counselor** is *an advisor who recommends a comprehensive program to protect a firm against insurable risks and to meet legal or quasi-legal insurance requirements*, including workers' compensation insurance, mortgage insurance, or insurance required by your lease. This risk expert should have the same professional concern for a firm's success as its lawyer and accountant. A conscientious insurance counselor should maintain close ties with the owner, recommending changes in coverage when changes occur in the company's size, the kind of risks it faces, or the owner's personal circumstances.

insurance counselor

Starting a Small Business

Legal Requirements

Small-business owners must follow several steps before offering a product or service to the public. They generally must obtain documents and approvals before starting operations.

First of all, the business must meet applicable **zoning ordinances.** These are *city and county regulations defining the type*

zoning ordinances

One ingredient for a small business's success is complete insurance coverage, backed by sound advice and continuing service from a qualified insurance counselor.

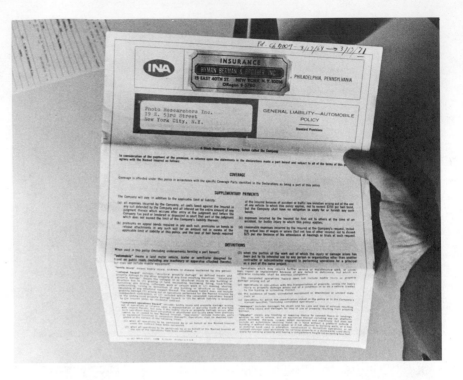

of business activity that can be conducted at certain locations. The firm also must obtain city and county business permits, and perhaps a state occupational license, if setting up shop as a cosmetologist, realtor, barber, or electrician, or in some other state-regulated business. Local government officials also will inspect a company's building to verify that it conforms to local fire and safety codes. Retailers, who act as sales tax collection agents for the state, must contact the state revenue department for registration forms and instructions on how to collect and pay sales tax.

The Internal Revenue Service (IRS) has various tax forms and reporting requirements that affect every type of business. This agency provides a Business Tax Kit that describes the many taxes, deductions, and payment schedules companies must be aware of.

Most firms have to conform to a state's fictitious-name act. This means that if the name of the business is not simply the name or names of its owners, the owners' names must be registered at the county courthouse and published along with the company's name in the Legal Notices section of the newspaper.

This is a very general introduction to the formalities involved in starting a business. The board of advisors discussed earlier will provide detailed information on additional steps that are required in your city, county, and state.

Start It Right the First Time

Infant companies have a fairly high mortality rate. Dun & Bradstreet reports that approximately half of all business failures occur within the first 5 years.[2] The early years, then, are usually the most critical in a firm's life. There are many things to do, and the owner's success in doing them will determine the success he or she will enjoy in the business. Figure 18.1 shows some of the factors that people who start their own businesses must consider.

Experience. Get experience in the line of business. A business presents many challenges to management, so a would-be owner needs as much experience as possible before striking out alone. Knowledge of finance, customer relations, marketing, inventory purchasing, personnel requirements and management, and technologic developments is necessary. Ira H. Latimer, executive vice-president of the American Federation of Small Business, suggests that you first become an employee in the kind of business that you plan to start. Avoid dead-end jobs that will isolate you from the rest of the organization and strive to become involved in every area of the company's business, however unfamiliar at first.

Dun & Bradstreet Corporation's causes of business failure are shown graphically in Figure 18.2. They build a strong argument for receiving sound experience before starting out on your own. According to these statistics, 65 percent of businesses failed because their owners were deficient in some key management area or lacked balanced experience. This figure also points out the need for management experience — intimate, first-hand knowledge of the planning, organizing, staffing, directing, and controlling functions that we

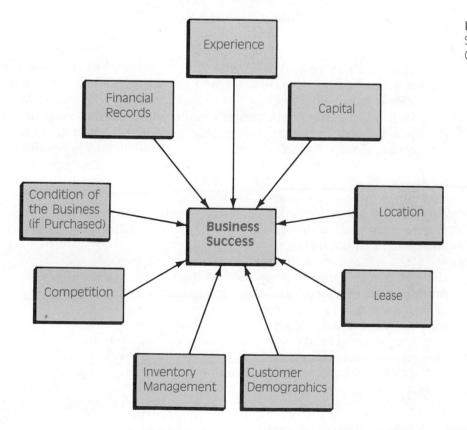

Figure 18.1 Factors for a New Small-Business Owner to Consider

Figure 18.2 Causes of
Business Failure
Source: *The Business Failure Record*
(New York: Dun & Bradstreet), 1983,
p. 12. Courtesy Dun & Bradstreet
Corporation.

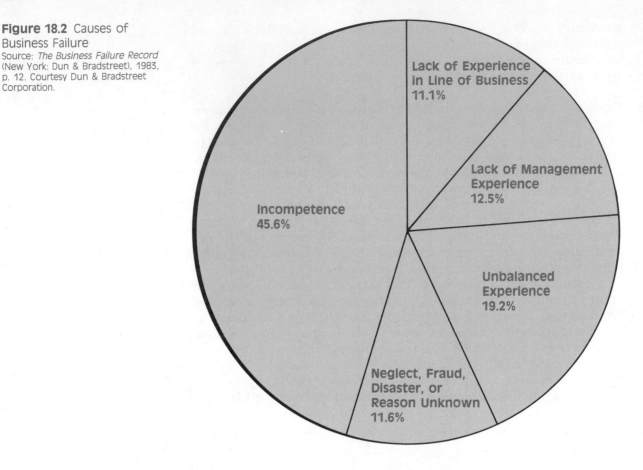

discussed in Chapter 4. Approximately 11 percent of all these entrepreneurs failed because they did not know enough about the line
of business they went into.

Dun & Bradstreet, the nation's major source of statistics on
business failures, reported that 31,334 businesses failed in one
recent year alone.[3] The effects of these failures extend far beyond
the owners themselves, however, because companies never operate
in a vacuum. Shock waves from a failed company have an impact
on many groups — employees, creditors, suppliers, customers, and
governmental bodies (through lost tax revenue), to name a few. The
failed companies totaled in Figure 18.2 owed creditors more than
$1.5 billion in liabilities.

It is not necessary to start small to get the needed experience,
though. Many small-business owners learned the basics of sound
management in a large firm, then applied them to a small company
of their own. Basic management practices remain the same regardless
of a company's size. Some business owners have worked for low
pay or even as volunteers to learn the basics of an industry, with
an eye to the day when they would become their own boss. Keeping
a diary of this work experience reinforces the memory and makes
the most of the time spent. Courses and self-education supplement
the lessons of experience. Business owners also can exchange ideas

with one another by participating in service clubs and trade associations.

Capital. It is essential to start with sufficient capital. A company with inadequate financing is like a rowboat with a hole in the bottom: given enough time, it is bound to sink. Some small-business owners dream and save for so long that they reach the end of their patience and open the business come hell or high water. Rather than start a company on a shoestring, it is best either to wait until there is enough capital to ensure success or to begin on a smaller scale than originally planned. Both accountants and trade associations can help potential business owners decide if they have enough capital to make a sound beginning.

How much capital does a business need? There is no easy answer. It depends on such variables as location, credit terms given by suppliers, distance from markets, and the nature of the product or service. It may take a construction company several months to complete its first projects, for example, but the owner must meet weekly payrolls, buy materials, make payments on leased or purchased equipment, maintain office facilities, and pay insurance premiums, taxes, utilities, and other business expenses in the meantime. These payments demand a large fund of operating capital. The Small Business Administration offers the form shown in Figure 18.3 to help business owners estimate their starting cash needs.

Location. Pick a sound site for operations, a spot that favors the type of customer you seek and the product or service that your firm will provide. A wag once declared that the three keys to business success were "location, location, and location." Neighboring businesses should be complementary. Undesirable neighbors can repel traffic, while several businesses with supporting lines or comparable target markets attract more customers together than any one of them could alone. Many business people also realize today that there is strength in numbers. This factor accounts for automobile alleys — rows of competing car dealers lined up next to each other — and shopping centers with two or more major department stores.

Site selection decisions often require a traffic study, an analysis of the traffic pattern around a location to confirm what type of person drives by, when, and why. Ideally, many people in the target area will need what the business sells and will find easy access to the premises. Traffic lights, pedestrian safety islands, and other traffic modifications should make it possible for customers to stop with a minimum of inconvenience. It also helps to consider plans for future street and highway improvements or business and housing developments. Such changes can make the area the hub or rim of traffic.

Lease. If a business owner decides to rent a facility, a lawyer should review the lease and explain what the tenant and the landlord are responsible for. Some business owners like to negotiate a short-

Figure 18.3 Form for Estimating Small-Business Start-Up Costs
Source: The Small Business Administration.

WORKSHEET NO. 2			
ESTIMATED MONTHLY EXPENSES			
Item	**Your estimate of monthly expenses based on sales of $ _____ per year**	**Your estimate of how much cash you need to start your business** (See column 3.)	**What to put in column 2** (These figures are typical for one kind of business. you will have to decide how many months to allow for in your business.)
	Column 1	Column 2	Column 3
Salary of owner-manager	$	$	2 times column 1
All other salaries and wages			3 times column 1
Rent			3 times column 1
Advertising			3 times column 1
Delivery expense			3 times column 1
Supplies			3 times column 1
Telephone and telegraph			3 times column 1
Other utilities			3 times column 1
Insurance			Payment required by insurance company
Taxes, including Social Security			4 times column 1
Interest			3 times column 1
Maintenance			3 times column 1
Legal and other professional fees			3 times column 1
Miscellaneous			3 times column 1
STARTING COSTS YOU ONLY HAVE TO PAY ONCE			Leave column 2 blank
Fixtures and equipment			Fill in worksheet 3 on page 12 and put the total here
Decorating and remodeling			Talk it over with a contractor
Installation of fixtures and equipment			Talk to suppliers from who you buy these
Starting inventory			Suppliers will probably help you estimate this
Deposits with public utilities			Find out from utilities companies
Legal and other professional fees			Lawyer, accountant, and so on
Licenses and permits			Find out from city offices what you have to have
Advertising and promotion for opening			Estimate what you'll use
Accounts receivable			What you need to buy more stock until credit customers pay
Cash			For unexpected expenses or losses, special purchases, etc.
Other			Make a separate list and enter total
TOTAL ESTIMATED CASH YOU NEED TO START WITH		$	Add up all the numbers in column 2

Pause and Ponder

Identify at least four specific business locations you pass by frequently. Which two seem to be well-suited to the firms that operate there? Which two appear to be undesirable or mismatched? What factors account for your assessment?

term lease with an option to renew for a longer period, so they can see how the location actually works out before making a long-term commitment.

Customer Demographics. Before business owners can create effective advertising, sales promotion, or personal selling appeals, they must know customers' **demographics.** These are *statistics on such subjects as age, income, marital status, recreational habits, and ethnic customs for people who live within a given geographic area.* U.S. Bureau of the Census tracts help here, providing data on income, social characteristics, and occupations for as broad or as narrow an area as necessary. By combining census data with demographic reports from the chamber of commerce and the city and county government, business owners can define the population features of their trading areas clearly and accurately.

demographics

Inventory Management. Demographic knowledge enables business owners to identify the most popular items to carry in inventory. Businesspeople who stock excessive inventory use too much storage space and pay too much for recordkeeping and insurance. Furthermore, the dollars invested in unneeded merchandise could be better spent on improved marketing efforts or more modern facilities and equipment. An understocked inventory is just as serious. The business can lose sales, good will, and customer loyalty if it cannot satisfy the needs of its clientele.

Major suppliers and trade associations provide information on seasonal trends and buying practices to help retailers stock the correct inventory at the desired levels throughout the year.

Competition. Still another aspect of running a successful small business is analyzing the practices of competitors. What do they do exceptionally well? Where could they improve? An alert newcomer, after observing the ways established competitors do business, can use their most effective practices and procedures from the beginning and avoid measures that they have found too costly, inefficient, or unproductive. Examine competitors' approaches to such subjects as price, inventory selection, service, customer conveniences, and employee relations before committing yourself to any policy.

Condition of the Business. An entrepreneur who buys an existing business rather than starting from scratch must investigate the business thoroughly. The prospective buyer's lawyer and accountant should obtain records that fairly present the business's legal and financial condition. A sole proprietor who claims that a business has earned $35,000 a year should be able to document that claim by showing copies of his or her personal income tax returns, for example. Equipment and merchandise should be physically inspected to verify its age and condition. Responsibility for any repairs should be clearly stated in the sales agreement between the present owner and the prospective owner.

One novice restaurant owner who closed a deal without verifying the equipment inventory thought he was buying twenty more chairs than the building actually contained. On top of that, the seller had stopped servicing the equipment, which required expensive overhauling just after the sale was closed. The buyer also should obtain a clear statement of which items will stay with the business and which will be taken by the seller, covering such things as drapes, special fixtures, paintings, decorative wall hangings, and display equipment.

Financial Records. Doing it right the first time means keeping accurate and timely financial records. Knowing the current balances of accounts receivable and payable, levels of inventory, sales, expenses, and payment due dates gives an owner a view of the company's financial picture and of marketing trends and overall profitability. A certified public accountant (CPA) can develop an orderly accounting system that a bookkeeper can maintain with minimal effort. Sound and accurate accounting records let you monitor your financial condition from one period to the next and chart a course for success.

Sources of Financing

In Chapter 2 and Chapter 3 we introduced some fundamental points on the financing of sole proprietorships, partnerships, and corporations, and in Chapter 14 we discussed the topic of finance at length. Beyond what you learned there, however, it is necessary to explore specific sources of financing for small businesses.

Personal Savings

Personal savings is the source of financing used most often. Many observers advise small-business owners to avoid excessive borrowing. Firms that start off under the heavy weight of creditors' claims may take years to struggle out of debt, while their owners have to put up with the nervous questions and suggestions of the creditors. Still, under the right circumstances, a firm can profit impressively using the leverage of borrowed money. Thus the question of how much debt a firm should carry in relation to the owner's investment has no simple answer.

Credit from Suppliers

Businesspeople, especially retailers, buy inventory on trade credit or open-book accounts with suppliers. Under this arrangement, which was discussed in Chapter 14, payment is not due for a credit period such as 30, 60, or 90 days, giving the buyer time to sell the goods before the bill is due.

A credit pyramid of sorts may arise within at least one distribution chain discussed in Chapter 12. Assume that a manufacturer gives a wholesaler 90 days' credit and the wholesaler in turn decides to give its retail customers a 60-day credit period. Under that relationship, the retailer could conceivably sell the goods to final consumers and pay the wholesaler, and that party could in turn pay the manufacturer so each bill is paid within its respective credit period.

Manufacturer Financing of Equipment

Manufacturers (and sometimes distributors) of equipment and fixtures may be willing to finance purchases made by financially sound customers or help them to arrange financing through a commercial bank. Even if they do not get involved directly, the supportive phone call from a well-established manufacturer to a bank lending officer might make it considerably easier for a customer firm to get a loan. An equipment manufacturer could also cosign for a loan along with the buyer or be a reference for that buyer at a bank where the manufacturer obtains financing.

Commercial Banks

A commercial bank may make a term loan that the small business can pay off within several years. In addition (recalling Chapter 14), commercial banks give qualified small businesses a line of credit or a revolving credit agreement. Naturally the business owner will have to provide financial statements listing personal and company assets and debts. Unfortunately banks are often reluctant to lend money to companies that have only been operating for a few years unless the loan also is secured by the Small Business Administration.

The Small Business Administration

The federal government defines a small business as a profit-making concern with less than $9 million in assets, a net worth under $4.5 million, and profits below $450,000 for the last 2 years of operation. The SBA, however, uses different yardsticks to determine smallness among firms in different industries (see Table 18.1, page 530). A nearby SBA field office can provide you with specific standards for a business in a particular industry.

Under its guaranteed loan program, the SBA can secure up to 90 percent or $350,000 of a bank loan, whichever is less. If the bank declines to be involved in that arrangement, the SBA can lend up to $150,000 directly to the business.

The Reagan administration has endorsed the work of the SBA by budgeting $3.3 billion for loans in fiscal 1985. Marine Midland Bank of Buffalo, New York, was the recent leader in making SBA-guaranteed loans, with a total of $32.8 million in one fiscal year and an average of $111,200 per loan.[4] Guaranteed loans averaging $118,000 apiece were granted to a total of 15,359 companies in 1983; 74 percent of those loans matured in 6 years or more.[5]

Entrepreneurs who start a new firm instead of buying a functioning business are expected to contribute approximately half of the required funds before qualifying for SBA assistance. They must **pro forma financial statements** also present **pro forma financial statements,** which are *financial statements that forecast expected sales, expenses, profits, and other financial data for a future accounting period.* These statements are evidence that the owner can make payments on SBA loans and any other long-term debts incurred to finance the business. The SBA is prohibited from lending to a company that can borrow money from another source, so applicants must first attempt to borrow from such private lenders as commercial banks.

The steps in the SBA lending process are:

1. Describe the kind of business to be started.
2. List the owner's experience and management capabilities.
3. Estimate the amount the owner is prepared to invest and the amount he or she will need to borrow.
4. Prepare a personal financial statement listing the owner's assets and debts.
5. Develop pro forma statements of the business's sales, expenses, and profits for the first 2 years.
6. List the owner's collateral (security) for the loan, at current market value.
7. Ask a commercial bank for a letter stating the amount of the loan the owner requested, the interest rate, the payment terms, and the reason for rejecting the application.
8. If the bank agrees to be involved in the SBA's guarantee or participation plans (in which the bank joins with the SBA to make the loan), the banker will contact the SBA to negotiate the terms.
9. If the bank declines to be involved, contact the SBA for a direct loan.

Selling Stock

Some small businesses raise money by issuing and selling stock. Only corporations can sell stock, and open corporations, those whose stock is traded publicly, must comply with extensive state and federal regulations on stock sales. The founder of a company also must be concerned about surrendering control if a majority of the shares are sold to other persons. The firm could remain a close corporation if the owner raises capital from a select and restricted group of investors. In Chapter 14 we discussed the kinds of stock a corporation can sell and the characteristics of each kind.

Venture Capital Firms

A **venture capital firm** is *a company that buys stock in new firms that make products or offer services with strong profit potential.* It takes greater risks than such lenders as the SBA or commercial banks. Venture capital firms often are owned by successful entrepreneurs who have come up the hard way themselves. The certified public accounting firm of Deloitte Haskins & Sells reports that there are approximately 2,000 venture capital firms in the United States.[6] These companies shop for soundly managed firms with unique products or services in growing markets. Many specialize in specific industries (such as high technology, consumer products, or manufacturing companies). Recently companies with ideas for new minicomputers, electronic medical instruments, or communications equipment have been looked on favorably by venture capital firms.

Although venture capital firms are willing to take large risks, they also want large rewards. Typically these companies may want 50 percent or more of the fledgling corporation's stock in exchange for an infusion of cash and will require that their own people be seated on the small company's board of directors. Venture capital firms customarily expect the value of their investment to increase fivefold within 5 or so years.[7]

A really sound venture capitalist should provide far more than just capital, however. The small-business owner should deal with a firm that can help arrange short-term financing through a network of sympathetic commercial banking contacts. A venture capital firm also should be able to place the company in touch with potential customers for its products and help negotiate favorable contracts with suppliers. Companies such as Atari, Apple Computer, Compaq Computer, and Lotus Development Corporation (a producer of popular microcomputer software) all got assistance from venture capital firms during their infancy.[8]

venture capital firm

Sources of Continuing Help

Most small-business owners find they need advice after their business opens it doors. Several sources can provide this ongoing assistance after the firm is on its feet.

The SBA

The Small Business Administration has more than 300 free or inexpensive booklets with information on everything from procedures for incorporation to personnel selection. Approximately eighty field offices provide management advice and offer management training for owners with the assistance of nearby colleges and business schools. In addition, SBA assistance loans help companies that have been damaged by natural disaster or by the economic changes brought on by urban renewal or other government-funded construction programs. There are even loans to help small companies meet federal air and water pollution standards.

SCORE

Service Corps of Retired Executives (SCORE)

The **Service Corps of Retired Executives (SCORE)** is *a volunteer organization of over 3,000 retired higher managers who advise small-business owners in conjunction with the Small Business Administration.* Business owners can request the assistance of a SCORE advisor whether or not they have received an SBA loan. They need only apply at an SBA field office. An advisor whose expertise fits the nature of the problem (finance, personnel, marketing) will meet with the owner to analyze the problem and develop a solution. A team of volunteers may be called on to attack problems with a broad scope. The advice is free, but the company will be expected to pay the SCORE volunteer's out-of-pocket expenses.

ACE

Active Corps of Executives (ACE)

The **Active Corps of Executives (ACE)** is *a volunteer organization of active managers who supplement SCORE's services with the most current expertise and techniques for small-business owners.* Like SCORE, ACE works through the Small Business Administration, and its services can be requested at the nearest SBA field office. ACE volunteers are business executives, officers of trade associations, management educators, lawyers, and accountants. They are an excellent source of advice to those who cannot afford the fees of professional consultants.

The National Family Business Council

The National Family Business Council (NFBC) consists of employees of family-owned companies who work in managerial or trainee positions and are related to the owners by birth or marriage. Any company that hires relatives of the owners — a common situation in closely held corporations — may benefit from joining this organization, which focuses attention on the unique interpersonal management problems found in family-operated businesses. In addition to its various chapters and management education programs, the NFBC publishes a newsletter and stages cooperative educational programs with leading universities and private management development firms.

Students Make Good Teachers

Many business professors include a small-business assistance project among the requirements for their graduate courses. Students may be called on to answer a business owner's request for help, analyze problems (possibly as part of a team or task force), and design and implement plans that will help a small firm back onto its feet. This type of program, which may be available through the business school at a nearby university, offers an inexpensive and reliable introduction to many of the latest concepts in the study of business operations. Priority 1 Electronics, a California mail-order house that sells computer parts, saved $100,000 per year after a team of graduate students from Brigham Young University dissected and recommended changes in the company's management information system, inventory control techniques, and order-processing capabilities. The only cost was travel expenses for the students and one professor.[9]

Local Educators and Consultants

In his famous lecture, "Acres of Diamonds," noted nineteenth-century clergyman and educator Russell Conwell dramatized how easy it is to overlook riches in one's own backyard. Business owners who live in a moderately or heavily populated area with colleges and universities nearby will find abundant management advice available from local business professors, authors of books on management, and consultants. Some recommendations of specific people to contact may be obtained from the local chamber of commerce.

Trade Associations

There is at least one trade association for practically every line of business, from funeral parlors to massage parlors. Some confine themselves to highly specialized fields, such as the Power Crane and Shovel Manufacturers Association and the Fir and Hemlock Door Association. Others, such as the National Association of Manufacturers and the National Retail Merchants Association, cover more ground. Trade associations can give advice on financing, inventory management, personnel management, accounting procedures, physical layout, marketing research, supplier relations, site selection, and advertising for their specific lines of business. They exist to help member firms prosper by communicating proved management practices and information.

Wholesalers

Well-equipped wholesalers can boost a small retailer's success in merchandise promotion by doing the following:

- Pooling orders from many customers, buying in large quantities, and receiving lower prices, thus allowing independent firms to offer prices that compete with those of chains and larger independents
- Selling certain items at cost, thus encouraging retailers to buy others later at regular prices
- Providing an inventory rotation plan to ensure fresh merchandise and ideal stock levels

— Distributing manufacturers' point-of-purchase displays to help retailers sell merchandise more effectively

They can make market information available by:

— Assessing market trends by monitoring trends in sales to competing retail firms
— Distributing market information in newsletters and bulletins
— Forewarning customers of trends and changes in demand
— Providing information on competitors' prices and marketing practices
— Staying abreast of changing conditions that influence the supply of staple items
— Notifying customers of new products, improved store fixtures, and innovative equipment
— Advising on efficient store layouts, effective marketing practices, and productive floor displays.

Wholesalers can give small retailers financial help too by selling merchandise on open-book accounts and by delaying billings for seasonal merchandise until the selling season arrives and sales improve. They also can provide accounting forms and booklets that help customer firms establish and maintain good recordkeeping habits, and offer accounting services through an umbrella contract with a local accounting firm.

Franchising

What Is a Franchise?

franchise

A **franchise** is *a license sold by one firm (the* franchisor*) to another (the* franchisee*), allowing it to produce and sell a product or service under specific terms and conditions.* Although franchisees sacrifice considerable independence, they gain the right to use operating procedures that the franchisor has created and refined through experience. A franchise is like a series of chain stores: the outlets look alike, each one makes and sells the product or service the same way, and each dealer adopts the same set of management techniques. Franchises differ from chain stores in that the owner of a franchise is not an employee, but owns his or her own business. Franchisees are trained in effective production, marketing, and employee selection and training practices by the franchisor.

Franchise opportunities exist for an array of companies ranging from day care centers to funeral homes. McDonald's Corporation, which began in 1955, is the largest, with 7,259 outlets nationwide and in 31 foreign countries.[10]

Since the 1960s franchising has grown to have a significant impact on the nation's sales and employment levels. Approximately 70,000 franchised outlets now sell some $38 billion worth of fast

McDonald's, a household word in many countries, is one of the largest franchise companies in the world.

food each year. The Department of Commerce estimates that $436 billion worth of franchised goods and services were sold in 1983 through a total of 465,000 outlets that provided jobs for 5.2 million citizens. Approximately one-third of all retail sales are made by franchised outlets. Franchising is expected to grow especially fast in services such as insurance, law, accounting, home repair, dental work, smoking control, weight control, and physical fitness.[11]

What Does Franchising Offer You?

The franchisor sells proved techniques for success in a specific business. The International Franchise Association's franchisor members reported that only 175 outlets of a total of 26,581 failed in one recent year, for a low 0.7 percent failure rate.[12]

Unlike independent business owners, who build a company and reputation from scratch, franchisees receive a combination of the following benefits:

— National reputation
— National advertising and sales promotion programs
— Proved work layout refined for maximum efficiency in minimum space
— Advice about site selection
— Assistance in negotiating leases and purchase agreements for equipment and other items
— Blueprints and bill of materials for constructing the building
— Training in how to manage the business for maximum profitability
— An accounting system developed to meet the needs of this business and the reporting requirements of the parent company

— An employee training program
— Grand opening materials and the assistance of parent company employees
— Group business insurance program through the parent company (at a lower cost than if the franchisee bought insurance alone)
— Ability to purchase furniture and equipment from the parent at a lower cost
— Advertising and sales promotion allowances
— Advertising materials geared to various national promotions
— Purchase of inventory items and supplies through the parent company at lower cost
— Well-defined and protected territory
— Financing assistance

What Do You Have to Sacrifice?

It is unusual to benefit without sacrifice, and franchising does involve some sacrifices. Franchise contracts include several of the following restrictions and conditions:

— Investment of a minimum amount of capital
— Payment of a percentage of gross profits (and possibly a fixed fee) to the parent company at specified times
— Payment of several additional items as required
— Approval from parent company for choice of location; installation of any furniture and fixtures; deviation from prescribed menu or inventory; purchase of disposables or inventory from anyone other than the parent company; pricing changes; involvement in any other business of a similar nature; and even changes in prescribed hours of operation
— Full involvement in management and daily operations
— Personnel required to present a specified appearance
— No members of owner's family working in the franchise
— Detailed accounting reports furnished to the parent company
— Management techniques and methods of operation kept confidential
— Minimum amount of insurance purchased as dictated by the parent company
— Shelf-life standards dictated by the parent company for perishable inventory
— Minimum amount of money spent each year for advertising and sales promotion
— Periodic training as required by the parent company at a specified location

Being a franchisee is like driving a car with dual controls. The franchisor, like an experienced driving instructor, can intervene if

Pause and Ponder

Examine the lists of benefits and restrictions of owning a franchise. Which three benefits most appeal to you? Which three restrictions would you find most difficult to accept? Why?

the driver seems headed for trouble. The franchisee, the driver, finds a reassuring presence nearby. The cost of starting a franchise for several well-known firms is broken down in Table 18.2.

Investigate Before You Sign

Have a lawyer review any franchise contract, examining the contract thoroughly, and clarify what the franchisee and the franchisor are responsible for. In addition, a prospective franchisee should talk with present franchisees, asking if they receive the services and advice promised in the contract, discovering if the franchisor's demands are reasonable, soliciting opinions on the worth and timeliness of the management advice they received, and asking if the franchisor's forecasts of sales, expenses, and profits are reliable.

Table 18.2 Cash Investment Needed to Start Business for Selected Franchises
Source: *International Franchise Association Directory of Membership 1983–1984* (Washington, D.C.: International Franchise Association, 1984).

Franchise	Cash Investment Needed	Number of Outlets*
Auto products and services		
AAMCO Transmissions	$ 35,000	950
Midas	141,000	1,250 (34)
Personal computers		
Entre' Computer Centers	85,000–100,000	60+ (1)
Campgrounds		
Kampgrounds of America	60,000	706 (12)
Employment Services		
Snelling and Snelling	20,000–80,000	450+
Equipment rentals		
Taylor Rental	60,000	600 (approximate)
Foods		
Carvel	100,000	700 (2)
Arby's	100,000	1,067 (149)
Dunkin' Donuts	50,000–100,000	1,100 (70)
Motels		
Holiday Inns	1,125,000	1,512 (229)
Printing		
Postal Instant Press	15,000 minimum	850+ (10)

*Number in parentheses is the number of franchisor-owned outlets.

The Straight Line

ComputerLand Franchises

Wiring the Gap Between Retailing Success
and the PC Boom

In Chapter 16 we discussed the phenomenal growth of personal computers (PCs) for both home and small-business applications. Aspiring entrepreneurs who wish to sell PCs, printers, and accessories can improve their chance for success by becoming a franchisee of ComputerLand Corporation, the world's largest franchisor of retail computer stores. Started in 1976, this California-based company had more than 590 outlets operating in 1984. Its franchisees sell more kinds of computers under one roof than any other retailer in the world.

ComputerLand franchises are the brainchild of William Millard, a Californian who has worked on both the manufacturing and the retailing sides of the PC explosion. Millard theorized that consumers deserved to shop at one store that carried many competing brands of PCs, printers, software, and accessories. None existed in 1976. Tandy Corporation marketed its products through Radio Shack stores and several retailers had exclusive contracts to sell other brands, but no retailers sold a wide range of brands and models from several manufacturers. Millard's franchises give consumers a choice.

The growth of these one-stop shopping centers for PCs has been amazing. Beginning with its first franchised store in Morristown, New Jersey, in February 1977, the chain grew to twenty-four stores in thirteen states by the end of that year. In November 1979 there were 100 outlets, which expanded to 241 in fourteen countries by January 1982. By late 1983 franchised stores were opening at the rate of one per day.

While the franchisees may change their store's inventory to suit the product preferences of their clientele, they have access through ComputerLand's central purchasing department to approximately 5,000 products made by more than 400 manufacturers including Atari, Digital, Hewlett-Packard, International Business Machines, Texas Instruments, and Zenith. Most products are sold to small-business owners who use them for keeping payroll and inventory records and for word processing. At the present time there are more than forty ComputerLand stores in Europe, thirty-eight in Canada, eighteen in Australia, and fifteen in Japan. Such globe-circling distribution suggests that this company may well become the McDonald's of PC franchises. In fiscal 1984 franchisees sold an estimated $1.5 billion worth of PCs and related products.

A ComputerLand franchise, like most others, begins with ComputerLand's top management reviewing an applicant's financial condition. Also reviewed are qualities such as energy, persistence, initiative, motivation, and sales and merchandising ability. A background in data processing is desirable but not essential. A business plan provided by ComputerLand's top management provides guidance about obtaining loans from banks or other sources, store budgeting, and identifying the market potential. Management must approve the location, lease, and interior specifications of each store; a company architect approves the interior design and layout.

A successful ComputerLand franchisee must raise at least

$237,000 in starting capital. This amount will ensure the store's survival, because the following must be paid or available for payment as required by the franchise agreement and normal business operations:

Franchise fee	$75,000
Fixtures	15,000–25,000
Furniture and equipment	15,000–25,000
Opening inventory	80,000–120,000
Purchase and installation of sign	2,000–3,500
Leasehold improvements on building	20,000–40,000
Working capital	20,000–40,000
Training and other start-up costs	10,000–20,000

Rental costs vary with the size, location, and condition of the building. Franchises are not limited to locations in free-standing buildings or shopping centers, however. In late 1983 the company also began experimenting with franchises inside several major department stores, including Bullock's, Meir & Frank, and Sanger-Harris. These outlets operate on leased floor space of between 400 and 600 square feet.

After all financial and legal details have been resolved, franchisees and ComputerLand management sign an agreement granting the franchise owner the exclusive 10-year right to operate a store within a half-mile radius of the location. Agreements may be renewed for another 10 years on expiration. Franchisees, who must organize their companies as corporations, pay a monthly royalty of 8 percent of gross sales and an advertising contribution of 1 percent of gross sales to the parent company. The latter amount goes to pay for national and international advertising programs in print, direct mail, and broadcast media.

Unlike many franchisors, ComputerLand allows its store owners to buy inventory from any source, although the monthly royalty applies to all items sold in the store, regardless of where they were purchased. One of the most powerful benefits of dealing through the parent company, however, is that franchisees receive their merchandise at cost. And the cost can be relatively low, considering that ComputerLand's central buying organization purchases in huge quantities from the nation's leading producers of PCs, printers, software, and accessories.

Before their store opens, ComputerLand franchisees receive 2 weeks of formal training at the company's home office, with follow-up training available through regional and international conferences. A 2 1/2-day course in personal selling and time management is also available.

A ComputerLand franchise can be a financial life raft for an independent computer retailer, many of whom are struggling for survival. ComputerLand's concept has attracted some 14 percent of all independents, and the arrangement can be financially rewarding to say the least. The typical ComputerLand store sells more than $2 million worth of merchandise per year, and net profit before taxes reaches or exceeds $200,000 annually. Multiply that amount by the six or more stores that some franchisees own and you'll find, as they have, that joining forces with ComputerLand has made them millionaires.

For more about ComputerLand's retail franchising concept, see Kathleen E. Wiegner, "The Instant Billionaire," *Forbes*, December 5, 1983, p. 39; Karen Blumenthal, "ComputerLand's Satellite Stores Test New Approach to Retailing," *The Dallas* (Texas) *Morning News*, October 10, 1983; and "Store a Day," *Fortune*, September 19, 1983, p. 12.

The Council of Better Business Bureaus in Washington, D.C., has summaries of data on many franchise firms, and the International Franchise Association (IFA) is another reputable source of data. This highly selective organization, whose membership consists of over 200 sound franchisors, has a code of ethics that all members are expected to observe. Franchisors who wish to join the IFA must have been operating for at least 2 years, be in sound financial condition, meet minimum requirements for number and age of outlets, comply with applicable state and federal laws, and supply satisfactory business and personal references.

The Federal Trade Commission (FTC) has come to the aid of prospective buyers of franchises with a Trade Regulation Rule adopted in 1979. The rule requires franchisors to provide information on business experience, backgrounds of key managers, present or past bankruptcy or lawsuits, and financial condition for the past year. Franchisees must be told of recurring fees required by the contract and the conditions under which the contract may be terminated, sold, or renewed by the franchisor. The rule also requires the parent firm to supply a list of the ten franchisees closest to a buyer's proposed location, the names of all franchisees in the United States, or all those in a buyer's state. Individual state laws may require that considerably more information be disclosed than is demanded by this FTC rule.

Summary

Prospective small-business owners need a board of advisors (lawyer, accountant, and insurance counselor) to assist on technical matters of law, finance, and risk management. These individuals help ensure the company's success from the outset. It is also necessary to obtain certain licenses and permits, some of which vary with the firm's location and the nature of the business.

A small-business owner should have sound experience, adequate capital, a good location, and favorable lease terms if the building is rented. Entrepreneurs should know the demographics of their market, identify the most popular inventory to stock, and find out about competitors' operating techniques. Someone who buys an existing company must obtain accurate information on its condition from the seller before closing the purchase. Finally, the small-business owner must keep accurate, up-to-date accounting records to monitor the company's financial condition and profitability.

Prospective small-business owners have several avenues of financing available. Personal savings is the most obvious and popular one, but they also can buy merchandise on credit from suppliers, finance equipment through distributors or manufacturers, get a commercial bank loan, or borrow through the Small Business Administration. Corporations can sell stock to the general public or to a venture capital firm.

After a company starts operating, the SBA can provide continuing management advice, as can the National Family Business

Council. SCORE and ACE, which work through the SBA, make the management expertise of retired and active executives available to small-business owners. Business students from nearby universities, local management authorities, trade associations, and wholesalers also can provide assistance.

Some entrepreneurs elect to buy a franchise, which is a license to sell a widely recognized product or service. There are many advantages to becoming a franchisee, but the franchisor's contract also sets forth various conditions and restrictions on operating freedom. The decision to buy a franchise should be made with the advice of a lawyer and accountant as well as some awareness of the experience of existing franchisees.

Key Terms

Active Corps of Executives
(ACE)
demographics
franchise

insurance counselor
pro forma financial statements
Service Corps of Retired Executives (SCORE)

Small Business Administration
(SBA)
venture capital firm
zoning ordinances

For Review and Discussion

1. Name the three advisors you need before starting a business. Why do you need them? How would you choose them?

2. Describe the procedure a business owner must follow before a company opens its doors. Why would this procedure vary somewhat from area to area and type of business to type of business?

3. Give at least one reason why a small-business manager must consider each of the following: experience in the type of business started, capitalization, location, lease terms, customer demographics, inventory management, competitors' practices, condition of a purchased business, and financial recordkeeping.

4. Why might it be a good idea to finance a business as much as possible with your personal savings? How does this method of financing affect your chances of success?

5. What kind of financing do merchandise suppliers offer? How does this complement a retailer's sales activities?

6. Should distributors or manufacturers of equipment be concerned about helping you finance purchases from them? Why or why not?

7. Describe the types of loans available through the Small Business Administration. What prerequisite must you meet before becoming eligible for SBA loans?

8. How does the attitude of venture capital firms differ from that of such conventional capital sources as the SBA or commerical banks? What do you sacrifice when dealing with a venture capital firm?

9. Describe the type of management assistance offered by the SBA. How does it differ from that offered by the National Family Business Council?

10. Contrast the contributions of SCORE and ACE advisors to small-business managers. In what ways might they complement each other?

11. Discuss the value and the limitations of graduate business students' advice to small-business managers as compared with that of SCORE and ACE volunteers.

12. How might local management authorities' advice be preferable to that of experts located several hundred miles away? In what ways could the distant advisors' views be preferable to those of local people?

13. Should you consider a trade association a source of highly specialized management assistance? Why or why not?

14. Discuss at least two areas in which wholesalers can help their retailer-customers. Why is it to their advantage to do so?

15. List at least four benefits of entering into a franchise agreement. What must you be prepared to sacrifice? What suggestions would you offer to potential franchisees?

Applications

Case 18.1 Mobile Moneymakers

Consider the advantages of owning a small business that pays no rent, utilities, real estate taxes, building insurance, or maintenance costs for painting, janitorial services, lawn care, and so forth. A large number of entrepreneurs enjoy these advantages today, because they've put their companies on wheels.

More than ever before, consumers seem to value service, convenience, and the saving of time. Ambitious and creative small-business owners are cashing in on this trend by delivering services right to the customer's door, and it can be a very profitable trip. Consider the following examples:

- Lawn Doctor, a franchised lawn care service, boasts 290 franchisees operating 700 vans in 23 states. Franchise owners' annual revenue reportedly totals $100,000 per truck.

- Decorating Den Systems, also a franchise, is a mobile interior decorating service that brings samples of everything from upholstery to floor coverings to the customer's home by a fleet of 175 vans owned by 140 franchises.

- A mobile pet clinic in Wheaton, Maryland, makes house calls for $20 each. Its major asset is a $24,000 motor home outfitted with the equipment necessary to perform vaccinations, minor surgery, and other procedures not requiring general anesthesia.

- A former florist, secretarial service owner, and real estate agent conceived Pac Van, a secondhand schoolbus that she converted into a rolling video game arcade. It rents for $70 to $130 per hour to private parties, carnivals, or other gatherings. Electricity for the eleven video games, heating, and air conditioning is supplied by a portable, gasoline-powered generator.

- The owner of a mobile dog-grooming service brings all his equipment to the owner's home in the bed of a Datsun pickup truck. He can wash, dry, comb, trim, and pedicure his shaggy customers by appointment — right in the driveway.

These small-business owners have eliminated the problems associated with permanent facilities. Some, like the husband-and-wife veterinary team in Maryland, had to rework the interiors of their vans or motor homes to fit the special needs of their clientele.

Promotional costs may be minimal, depending on the entrepreneur's boldness and luck. Several convinced local newspaper reporters to write human interest articles on them, and business started rolling in immediately. A combination of direct mail, radio, television, and newspaper advertising often is needed, however, to start a fledgling enterprise moving. Referrals from satisfied customers usually add new prospects, while the vehicles themselves serve as their own advertisements.

Questions

1. List at least two types of businesses in addition to those mentioned in this case that might succeed by "going on the road."

2. What risks do such mobile entrepreneurs face that they could avoid by setting up shop in a permanent facility?

3. Name at least one specific company in your area that does business from a vehicle instead of a traditional permanent location.

Case 18.1 For more about mobile entrepreneurs, see Carol Dilks, "Business on the Move," *Nation's Business*, March 1984, p. 66.

Case 18.2 Who Needs a Paycheck?

Many small-business owners sever themselves from a paycheck because they want independence — no rigid schedules, no bosses, and no standards but their own. Perhaps the most liberated businesspeople, though, are the worksteaders. These entrepreneurs operate out of dens, living rooms, bedrooms, and garages nationwide and make everything from hats to stuffed toys. And while cottage industries have thrived for generations, some observers view today's scattered army of worksteaders as a new breed of small-business owner.

An estimated 5 million people support themselves in this way. Working at home is especially well suited to computer-oriented small businesses. Many free-spirited entrepreneurs have invested in an expensive personal computer, for example, and set up shop at home writing software or doing freelance word-processing or accounting services. Others simply found themselves so adept at a hobby or a second job that consumer demand propelled them into a full-fledged and highly profitable business.

Such was the case, for example, with Jackson Hole Hat Company. Its owners, Paul and Marilyn Hartman, decided to supplement their income as waiters in Jackson Hole, Wyoming, by blocking Western hats in their home. Before long they started repairing hats and manufacturing hats and marketing hats and, well, you can imagine the rest. The sideline business became a thriving company. Peggy Glenn, an underpaid and overly skilled secretary, quit to start a home typing service. Working on a rented typewriter on a typing table in the corner of her living room, she made enough money in her first 3 months to buy the $1,100 typewriter. Before long she was making $250 per month by working just 18 hours a week. Her business prospered so quickly that she eventually wrote a book (*How to Start and Run a Successful Home Typing Business*), started a 1,100 member association of home typists like herself, and finally quit typing altogether to start a publishing company.

At least one group of worksteaders, the National Alliance of Homebased Businesswomen, has founded its own 1,400-member trade association. Their products and services include quilting, landscape painting, calligraphy, baking custom-ordered cakes, reweaving damaged sweaters, and making leather sandals. A trip to work is usually just a journey from the bedroom to the den.

Worksteaders are often pleased when they add up the savings they realize on transportation, clothing, child care, and other costs associated with being someone else's employee. If they feel like it, they can work in pajamas, sleep late, or simply take the day off.

Questions

1. Weigh the advantages and disadvantages of being a worksteader. What aspects of this life-style appeal to you most? List at least three negative aspects about being a worksteader.

2. Name at least one acquaintance who would be a successful worksteader. In your opinion, why hasn't this person done so?

3. Visualize yourself as a worksteader. What kind of product or service would you attempt to sell? How would you attempt to sell it? Describe how you would arrange your workweek.

Case 18.2 For more about worksteaders, see Lynn Langway, " 'Worksteaders' Clean Up," *Newsweek*, January 9, 1984, p. 86; and Carol Krucoff, "Former Secretary Leads Revolution in Growth of Home Typing Business," *The Orlando* (Florida) *Sentinel*, July 27, 1982, p. E-2.

Multinational Business

Chapter Outline

Chapter Objectives

After studying this chapter, you should be able to:

1. Describe the scope and importance of international trade.
2. Explain the major concepts involved in international trade: balance of trade, balance of payments, exchange rate, and absolute and comparative advantage.
3. Explain why a business chooses to participate in international business.
4. Summarize the alternative approaches a business firm may use to operate in international business.
5. Describe the development of multinational corporations and the strategies they use.
6. Identify and explain the barriers to international trade.
7. Describe the aids to international trade.
8. Identify and describe the conflicts that occur between an international business and the host and home countries.

Interdependence is no longer something one is for or against, but rather a fact that all nations must learn to live with.
— *J. Paul Sticht, R.J. Reynolds Industries*

Willard C. Butcher

Chase Manhattan's Premier Strategist

Willard C. Butcher, The Chase Manhattan Bank's chief executive officer since 1980 and its chairman since 1981, has a formidable task facing him. After a few highly publicized missteps, the world's flagship international bank of the 1970s is back on its feet, fighting to become the premier corporate bank in the world. Currently, Chase is America's third largest bank (out of 14,000 banks in the country) and the 14th largest multinational corporation.

Butcher has what he considers to be a clear, multifaceted rebuilding strategy. He intends to emphasize corporate banking on an international level, and technology for consumer and corporate banking at home and abroad. In his 37 years with Chase, Butcher has been in charge of the New York City branch system and has overseen the bank's business and operations in Europe and Africa. The bank's international network, which he put together, is still one of Chase's proudest accomplishments. Butcher clearly has the experience and expertise to make his strategy work.

Part of Butcher's plan leans heavily on the bank's consumer banking sector. Chase has invested $20 million in a home banking system and has put together a "universal account" — a comprehensive package of personal banking services. These —

"No man is an island" is a saying that could apply to the business community. As we have learned, businesses are all interrelated; they do business with one another and affect one another's operations. One area we have not explored is business on an international scale — the whys, hows, and difficulties entailed in involvement on the international scene.

Why do we need to examine the international scene? The world is like an international department store. Many products whose brand names are household words are produced in other countries. Norelco razors, Volvo automobiles, and Heineken beer are produced abroad and marketed in the United States.

On the other hand, products produced in the United States are found in the marketing channels of other countries. Gillette razor blades, Jeep four-wheel-drive vehicles, International Business Machines (IBM) computers, and Chris Craft yachts are produced in America and are sold worldwide.

Multinational business is not an element of the future. It is here now. American automobile, petroleum, farm machinery, and chemical companies have become multinational operations. In this

and the burgeoning of ATMs (automatic teller machines) — will allow Chase to continue cutting costs while offering service enhancements to its customers. Fewer branches will be needed to handle customer transactions: since 1978, Chase has closed 51 branches.

In the corporate banking area, Butcher's strategy is to move toward "globalization" — an approach to the market that defines customers according to the industry they're in and the worldwide geographic dimensions of their businesses. He has also called for ever-increasing emphasis on and growth in electronic technology and investment bank-

ing services. All this is being done at a time when management is more concerned than ever about internal controls, which have been reviewed, revised, and tested in the wake of Drysdale and Penn Square.

Spirits are high at Chase with Butcher at the helm. He is gregarious, at ease with himself and others. He is respectful of subordinates and their talents. He is, however, a man of action who does what has to be done. (In 1982, 8 executives responsible for Chase's involvement in Penn Square and Drysdale were sent packing.) Financial analysts have seen the changes Butcher is making — and have pronounced Chase well and making progress.

For more about Willard C. Butcher, see "Chase's Battle to Catch Up," *Business Week*, April 9, 1984, pp. 74–80.

chapter we will examine the importance of international business and the concepts involved in conducting it.

Scope and Importance of International Trade

Imagine that all world trade ceased at 11:00 A.M.

- How would you get your morning coffee or the sliced bananas for your corn flakes?
- How would your car get you to work on time without imported oil refined to gasoline?
- What would you wear without your imported clothes from Taiwan, Korea, or Singapore?
- What would you do after dinner with no French or German wine to sip and no Sony television to watch?

The International Picture

The scope of international trade is enormous. It has become an increasingly important part of world economic activity. For some countries their very economic health is significantly affected by their ability to sell to global markets. Examples of this situation are Japan and Germany, which export 16 and 27 percent of their gross national product (GNP) respectively.

Beyond the economic reasons, trade between nations benefits those involved by:

— Increasing the variety of goods and services available to people of all nations and thus improving their standards of living.

— Encouraging interactions that facilitate understanding. Countries that communicate with one another and depend on each other economically are less likely to go to war with each other.

Closer to Home

**importing
exporting**

How important is international trade to the United States? Although we export less than 8 percent of our GNP, international trade is important both to us as a nation and to our individual domestic companies.[1] As a nation we are involved in international trade through **importing,** *buying goods and services abroad,* and **exporting,** *selling goods and services abroad.* In a recent year the U.S. Department of Commerce reported that exports of goods and services totaled $332,304 billion and imports totaled $363,743 billion.[2] International trade is big business! Table 19.1 presents a summary of the nations the United States marketed to (exports) and was supplied by (imports). In addition, Table 19.2 supplies a geographic view of United States trade with selected countries.

Exports are now a significant percentage of total sales and revenue for many companies. Opening up new markets is a major element of many firms' marketing strategies. Table 19.3 shows the leading exporters among United States corporations. Note the significance of the export sales as a percentage of total sales.

Major Concepts in International Trade

Business on an international scale has a language all its own. The critical terms include balance of trade, balance of payments, exchange rate, and the concepts of absolute advantage and comparative advantage.

Balance of Trade

balance of trade

A nation's **balance of trade** is *the difference between the dollar value of a nation's exports and the dollar value of its imports for a stated period of time.* If exports exceed imports, a *trade surplus*

Top Twenty-Five U.S. Markets (Exports)		Leading U.S. Suppliers (Imports)	
World Total	**$200.5**	**World Total**	**$258.0**
1. Canada	38.2	1. Canada	52.1
2. Japan	21.9	2. Japan	41.2
3. United Kingdom	10.6	3. Mexico	16.8
4. Mexico	9.1	4. West Germany	12.7
5. West Germany	8.7	5. United Kingdom	12.5
6. Saudi Arabia	7.9	6. Taiwan	11.2
7. Netherlands	7.8	7. South Korea	7.1
8. France	6.0	8. Hong Kong	6.4
9. South Korea	5.9	9. France	6.0
10. Belgium and Luxembourg	5.0	10. Italy	5.5
11. Australia	4.8	11. Indonesia	5.3
12. Taiwan	4.7	12. Brazil	4.9
13. Italy	3.9	13. Venezuela	4.9
14. Singapore	3.8	14. Nigeria	3.7
15. Switzerland	3.0	15. Saudi Arabia	3.6
16. Egypt	2.8	16. Algeria	3.6
17. Venezuela	2.8	17. Netherlands	3.0
18. Spain	2.8	18. Singapore	2.9
19. Hong Kong	2.6	19. Switzerland	2.5
20. Brazil	2.6	20. Sweden	2.4
21. China	2.2	21. Belgium and Luxembourg	2.4
22. South Africa	2.1	22. Netherlands Antilles	2.3
23. Israel	2.0	23. China	2.2
24. U.S.S.R.	2.0	24. Australia	2.2
25. India	1.8	25. India	2.2

Table 19.1 The Leading United States Export and Import Partners (Figures in Billions of Dollars)
Source: "U.S. Trade Outlook," *Business America* (prepared by the Office of Trade and Investment Analysis, International Trade Administration), February 20, 1984, pp. 2–6.

exists and the country has a favorable balance of trade. If the imports exceed exports, a *trade deficit* exists and the country has an unfavorable balance of trade. In 1983 the United States had an unfavorable balance of trade of $31 billion.[3]

Balance of Payments

A nation's balance of trade determines its **balance of payments,** *the amount of money that flows into or out of the country.* When a country experiences a trade deficit there is an outflow, or unfavorable balance, of payments to pay for the goods. When the opposite situation occurs, there is a favorable balance of payments, or inflow of payments.

Other activities affect the balance of payments; these include banking, transportation, military transactions, and profits from companies operating in foreign countries.

balance of payments

Table 19.2 United States Trade with Selected Countries (in Millions of Dollars)
Source: *Business America* (prepared by the Office of Trade and Investment Analysis, International Trade Administration), February 20, 1984, p. 55.

Area and Country	U.S. Exports				U.S. Imports			
	1980	1981	1982	1983	1980	1981	1982	1983
Western Hemisphere								
Barbados	136	149	155	195	96	81	106	202
Belize	58	69	64	36	60	43	36	27
Bermuda	136	150	172	185	13	18	12	11
Bolivia	172	189	99	102	182	177	109	166
Cayman Islands	56	59	73	67	3	4	15	9
French Guiana	14	17	10	70	17	27	29	25
French West Indies	67	69	51	38	7	20	8	22
Guyana	96	106	56	36	120	104	71	69
Leeward, Windward Islands	152	282	174	166	36	32	27	39
Surinam	137	138	128	117	109	179	60	63
Western Europe								
Gibraltar	4	53	47	28	2	1	1	2
Iceland	79	71	77	53	200	198	184	219
Ireland	836	1,025	983	1,115	417	498	556	560
Malta	26	33	48	65	9	10	14	10
Near East—North Africa								
Bahrain	197	296	220	136	16	35	30	23
Cyprus	70	86	86	54	6	4	3	15
Iran	23	300	122	190	456	64	585	1,130
Lebanon	303	296	294	484	33	18	19	17
Libya	509	813	301	191	8,595	5,301	512	1
Oman	95	100	173	175	344	348	334	360
Qatar	129	157	153	108	235	115	106	11
Syria	239	143	138	112	26	83	10	8
Tunisia	174	222	213	216	60	10	59	33
Yemen (Sana)	77	44	38	108	1	(*)	1	(*)
Far East—South Asia								
Bangladesh	292	158	227	190	85	85	70	88
Brunei	70	45	79	58	280	329	211	19
Burma	29	34	34	16	9	15	17	11
Macao	2	1	14	1	114	154	201	226
Pacific Islands, Trust Terr.	49	58	62	69	7	16	6	12
Papua New Guinea	38	55	66	84	53	50	18	18
Sri Lanka	62	90	198	75	125	154	175	185
Sub-Sahara Africa								
Benin	15	19	24	12	(*)	1	1	27
Botswana	6	6	5	4	87	132	18	42
Burundi	3	4	4	4	40	28	41	3
Chad	2	1	2	13	(*)	(*)	(*)	68
Congo	22	25	69	16	143	286	652	821
Ethiopia	72	62	43	42	87	83	102	87
Gabon	48	128	110	63	343	432	610	657
Ghana	127	154	116	119	207	246	362	120

*Less than $500,000.

Table 19.2, continued

Area and Country	U.S. Exports				U.S. Imports			
	1980	1981	1982	1983	1980	1981	1982	1983
Sub-Sahara Africa (continued)								
Guinea	34	53	28	22	94	96	121	104
Ivory Coast	185	130	96	61	288	344	303	343
Kenya	141	150	98	69	54	52	71	65
Malagasy Republic	7	16	24	22	91	70	63	71
Malawi	4	5	3	3	25	62	31	14
Mauritania	20	27	26	28	(*)	(*)	1	1
Mauritius	22	18	15	8	50	20	30	32
Mozambique	69	35	26	20	105	83	51	28
Rwanda	5	6	6	6	68	40	33	28
Senegal	41	42	30	38	9	1	1	2
Sierra Leone	21	26	15	11	77	45	35	22
Somalia	56	59	47	46	(*)	(*)	1	(*)
Swaziland	6	7	2	4	58	66	28	13
Tanzania	62	48	41	32	32	19	29	14
Zaire	155	141	90	83	418	423	407	366

*Less than $500,000.

Exchange Rate

Each country has its own currency. When a contract for the sale of goods between countries is made it requires the price to be converted from one country's currency to another's. *The rate at which money of one country is converted or exchanged for another* is known as the **exchange rate.**

    The rate of exchange can be established through a floating exchange rate where the rate varies with market conditions. It can also be established by the government — a controlled exchange rate.

    The government of a country can affect the exchange rate and in turn the attractiveness of goods. The government can practice **devaluation,** or *increasing the rate of exchange at which foreign currency will be traded for domestic currency.* As an example, if the United States raised the exchange rate for British pounds from $3.50 for £1 to $5.00 for £1, it would encourage the British to buy more United States exports (£1 buys $1.50 more of goods after the devaluation) and would increase the cost of British goods to American importers by $1.50 for each £1. As exports to Britain rose and imports from that country declined, the trade deficit with Britain might be eliminated.

    The government can practice **revaluation,** or *decreasing the rate of exchange at which foreign currency will be traded for domestic currency.* In the previous example if the United States lowered the exchange rate for British pounds from $3.50 to £1 to $1.00 to £1, the result would be to discourage the British from buying American exports.

exchange rate

devaluation

revaluation

Table 19.3 Leading Exporters Among United States Corporations

Source: Andrew Kupfer, "The 50 Leading Exporters," Fortune, August 8, 1983, pp. 88–89. © 1983 Time Inc. All rights reserved.

Rank 1982	Rank 1981	Company	Products	Exports ($000)	Fortune 500 ($000) Sales	Fortune 500 Rank	Exports as Percent of Sales Percent	Exports as Percent of Sales Rank
1	2	General Motors (Detroit)	Motor vehicles and parts, locomotives, diesel engines	4,673,800	60,025,600	2	7.79	39
2	3	General Electric (Fairfield, Conn.)	Aircraft engines, generating equipment, locomotives	3,921,000	26,500,000	11	14.80	22
3	1	Boeing (Seattle)	Aircraft	3,879,000	9,035,000	34	42.93	1
4	4	Ford Motor (Dearborn, Mich.)	Motor vehicles and parts	3,733,000	37,067,200	5	10.07	38
5	5	Caterpillar Tractor (Peoria, Ill.)	Construction equipment, engines	2,619,000	6,469,000	45	40.49	2
6	7	E.I. du Pont de Nemours (Wilmington, Del.)	Chemicals, fibers, polymer products, petroleum, coal	2,559,000	33,331,000	8	7.68	41
7	8	United Technologies (Hartford)	Aircraft engines, helicopters	2,271,721	13,577,129	20	16.73	17
8	6	McDonnell Douglas (St. Louis)	Aircraft, missiles, space systems	2,076,500	7,331,300	43	28.32	4
9	9	International Business Machines (Armonk, N.Y.)	Information-handling systems, equipment, and parts	1,875,000	34,364,000	6	5.46	45
10	10	Eastman Kodak (Rochester, N.Y.)	Photographic equipment and supplies	1,853,000	10,815,000	26	17.13	16
11	*	Chrysler (Highland Park, Mich.)	Motor vehicles and parts	1,795,900	10,044,900	29	17.88	14
12	11	Westinghouse Electric (Pittsburgh)	Generating equipment, defense systems	1,356,700	9,745,400	31	13.92	24
13	23	Occidental Petroleum (Los Angeles)	Agricultural chemical products, coal	1,205,000	18,212,226	15	6.62	44
14	22	Phillip Morris (New York)	Tobacco products	1,142,000	9,101,600	32	12.55	29
15	17	Hewlett-Packard (Palo Alto, Calif.)	Computers, electronic equipment	1,083,000	4,254,000	81	25.46	5
16	12	Signal Companies (La Jolla, Calif.)	Trucks, engines, chemicals, audio-video systems	1,075,400	4,935,600	69	21.79	10
17	14	Union Carbide (Danbury, Conn.)	Chemicals, plastics	979,000	9,061,500	33	10.80	34
18	18	Weyerhaeuser (Tacoma, Wash.)	Pulp, logs, lumber, wood products, newsprint	924,000	4,186,224	82	22.07	9
19	13	Raytheon (Lexington, Mass.)	Defense electronic systems, aircraft	917,000	5,513,370	58	16.63	18
20	20	Archer Daniels Midland (Decatur, Ill.)	Soybean meal and oil, wheat, corn	876,000	3,712,977	102	23.59	7

*Not on last year's list

With only one motorcycle producer in the United States, we are a prime target for Japanese exports.

Absolute and Comparative Advantage

Trade is an important element in minimizing economic hardships among nations that need one another's goods and services. Companies sell to people and firms in other nations for the same reason that they sell in their own countries — to earn a profit. How do countries determine what to export to earn the most profit? The decision is made by evaluating the potential profit of products by the concepts of absolute and comparative advantage.

    A nation has an **absolute advantage** when it *has a monopoly on a product or can produce it at the lowest cost.* The country can export the product because the country either controls it or can do it more efficiently. This situation occurs infrequently, however; most often the country has a comparative advantage.

absolute advantage

    A nation has a **comparative advantage** when it *is better equipped to produce one product or service than other nations.* Essentially a nation produces for export whatever it is in the best

comparative advantage

position to make relative to other nations. This specialization may arise from such characteristics as climate, soil, technological development, labor supply and skills, indigenous agricultural products (mahogany or teak, for example), or mineral and petroleum deposits. Table 19.4 shows several nations and the products in which they enjoy a comparative advantage. As an example, in relationship to the goods it could produce, Australia has the terrain and environment to produce sheep, which leads Australia to export sheep and wool.

Now that we have looked at the scope and language of international business, let's examine why an individual company engages in international business.

Why Do Businesses "Go International"?

Why should a company take the giant step into the unknown and venture into international business operations? The most obvious reason is the profit potential available to an organization. Just as companies working within the borders of the United States target profitable market segments, internationally oriented companies visualize the world market as their overall target market for profitable operations.

Three other reasons can motivate a business to participate in the international arena:

1. The potential of obtaining a higher percentage of earnings than can be received from domestic operations.

Table 19.4 Nations That Enjoy a Comparative Advantage in Producing Certain Goods

Nation	Product
Argentina	Sheep, wool, beef, hides
Australia	Sheep, wool, rutile ore for titanium
Bolivia	Zinc, tin
Brazil	Industrial diamonds, coffee, manganese
Canada	Grain
Colombia	Coffee
France	Wine, cheese
Indonesia, Venezuela	Petroleum
Italy	Glass
Japan	Motorcycles, automobiles, electronics
Norway	Forest products
South Africa	Manganese, platinum, chromium
South Korea	Labor, steel
Surinam, Jamaica	Bauxite
Sweden	Seafood
Switzerland	Chocolate
United States	Aircraft, coal, grain, chemicals
Zambia, Zaire	Cobalt

California oranges for sale in a Hong Kong street market are an example of comparative advantage.

2. The potential to take advantage of an established demand for American goods. In effect a company may not have to pioneer new markets where a demand exists, but simply piggyback on the efforts of other American firms.

3. The long-range opportunity to provide capital, technology, and expertise to improve the overall economic development of the country and in turn the standard of living. This has a circular effect: the higher standard of living can then lead to an increase in the demand for American goods and a higher profit potential.

Now we know why companies choose to enter international operations, but what approaches can a firm use to participate in international business?

Alternative Approaches in International Business

A company can select from a number of alternative strategies when it decides to become involved in international trade. Each alternative increases the level of commitment of the organization's resources. As a result companies normally evolve from one strategy to another as their success increases.

The potential alternatives include export department or foreign intermediary, foreign licensing, joint venture, foreign-operated sales branches, and wholly owned subsidiaries. Let's examine each.

Export Department or Foreign Intermediary

foreign trade intermediary

The initial commitment to international operations can be approached in one of two ways: an export department can be created or the company can employ the services of a **foreign trade intermediary,** *a wholesaler or an agent who performs marketing functions for firms that wish to do business in other countries.*

Of the two alternatives, the creation of an export department requires more internal capital and management talent. The use of an intermediary is one of the least risky ways for a novice company to venture into foreign markets. It requires little investment of capital, time, or effort. Intermediaries often serve a large number of firms, however, so they might not market products as aggressively or as effectively as some of their clients would wish.

Foreign Licensing

licensing

As foreign markets expand, some firms take the step of **licensing.** This is *an agreement between one company (the* licensor*) and another (the* licensee*) that permits the licensee to manufacture and market a product owned by the licensor.* The licensee pays a royalty to the licensor for each unit sold.

Licensing agreements enable a producer to reach markets that for various reasons might otherwise be impossible to penetrate. Levi Strauss, for example, entered into a licensing agreement with Hungary in the late 1970s allowing genuine Levi's jeans to be made and sold in that country. Anheuser-Busch considers licensing the key to expanding its operations in foreign markets. The firm has licensed such leading brewers as Labatt Brewing Company in Canada, the Oetker group in Germany, and Société Européene de Brasseries in France to make and market its brands in those nations.[4]

Joint Venture

Another step for involvement in international trade is to create a joint venture. By entering a joint venture, a company shares ownership of the foreign operations with foreign nationals — individuals, a company, or the nation's government itself.

An example is provided by the American Motors Corporation (AMC) who negotiated a joint venture with the People's Republic of China. The deal is the largest joint industrial venture in China. It calls for AMC to invest $8 million in cash and $8 million worth of technological expertise to modernize the Peking Auto Works. The result: a plan to produce a new line of four-wheel-drive vehicles like the American-made AMC Jeep and market them in Southeast Asia.[5]

Both licensing and joint ventures are active commitments to international business. In licensing the firm permits someone else to produce and market the products. In a joint venture the company becomes a partner. A next step in commitment is to become a "resident" in a foreign country. This can be done through a foreign-operated sales branch.

Foreign-Operated Sales Branch

A **foreign-operated sales branch** is *a firm's wholly owned sales organization in a foreign country.* Branch employees (either foreign nationals or citizens of the home country) are hired to sell the products made in the company's domestic plants. This approach gives the producer control over the marketing effort abroad.

foreign-operated sales branch

Wholly Owned Subsidiaries

The final alternative strategy for involvement is to control both the foreign production and the marketing facilities. This is achieved through the formation of a **wholly owned foreign subsidiary** — *a set of manufacturing and distribution facilities located in a foreign country but owned by a parent company located elsewhere.* An example is J. I. Case Company, owned by Tenneco, which makes and sells its own heavy earthmoving equipment overseas. Companies that have made this major commitment to international business are referred to as *multinationals.* Just what are multinationals?

wholly owned foreign subsidiary

Multinational Corporations: The Ultimate Involvement

A business organization resulting from the growth of and importance of international business is the multinational corporation. The **multinational corporation** is *a corporation that operates on an international level, is based in one country but has operations in other countries also, and does a substantial amount of its total business in other countries.* Multinationals may work in partnership with host country firms, form joint ventures with host country firms or governments, or simply establish operations on their own. Whatever the arrangement, they can be found producing sewing machines in England, mining bauxite in Australia, and selling insurance in Thailand. Table 19.5 lists the largest United States multinationals. Notice the dominance of the oil-related industries.

multinational corporation

Table 19.5 The Twenty Largest United States Multinationals
Source: Carol E. Curtis, "Better Late Than Never," *Forbes*, July 2, 1984, pp. 129–130.

Rank	Company	Foreign Revenue (Millions)	Total Revenue (Millions)	Foreign Revenue As Percent of Total	Foreign Operating Profit (Millions)	Total Operating Profit (Millions)	Foreign Operating Profit As Percent of Total	Foreign Assets (Millions)	Total Assets (Millions)	Foreign Assets As Percent of Total
1	Exxon	$61,815	$88,651	69.7	$2,913	$5,390	54.0	$28,297	$62,963[5]	44.9
2	Mobil	32,629[1]	55,609[1]	58.7	1,010[2]	1,503[2]	67.2	16,529	35,072	47.1
3	Texaco	25,157	40,068	62.8	900[2]	1,233[2]	73.0	10,376	27,199	38.1
4	Phibro-Salomon	20,100	29,757	67.5	235[2]	470[2]	50.0	5,000	42,017	11.9
5	IBM	17,058	40,180	42.5	2,142[2]	5,485[2]	39.1	15,121	37,243	40.6
6	Ford Motor	16,080	44,455	36.2	351[2]	1,867[2]	18.8	13,723	23,869	57.5
7	General Motors	14,913	74,582	20.0	258[2]	3,730[2]	6.9	11,422	45,694	25.0
8	Gulf	11,535	26,581	43.4	604[2]	978[2]	61.8	7,240	20,964	34.5
9	Standard Oil Calif.	10,952	27,342	40.1	755[2]	1,590[2]	47.5	8,678	24,010	36.1
10	El du Pont de Nemours	10,816	35,173	30.8	436[3]	1,638[3]	26.6	6,778	24,432	27.7
11	Citicorp	9,650[4]	17,037	56.6	468[2]	860[2]	54.4	75,553[5]	127,923[5]	59.1
12	ITT[6]	7,808	20,249	38.6	692	1,201	57.6	9,619	30,612	31.4
13	BankAmerica	5,943	13,299	44.7	185[2]	390[2]	47.4	49,381[5]	123,045[5]	40.1
14	Dow Chemical	5,726	10,951	52.3	382	516	74.0	5,333	11,981	44.5
15	Standard Oil Indiana	5,363[1]	27,937[1]	19.2	663[2]	1,868[2]	35.5	6,498	25,805	25.2
16	Chase Manhattan	4,943	8,523	58.0	181[2]	430[2]	42.1	46,350	81,920	56.6
17	General Electric	4,758[1]	27,681[1]	17.2	358[2]	2,024[2]	17.7	5,322	23,288	22.9
18	Occidental Petroleum	4,544[1]	19,709[1]	23.1	310[3]	844[3]	36.7	2,300	11,775	19.5
19	Safeway Stores	4,528	18,585	24.4	84[2]	183[2]	45.9	1,099	4,174	26.3
20	Sun Co.	4,282[1]	14,928[1]	28.7	70[7]	558[7]	12.5	2,542	12,466	20.4

[1] Includes other income.
[2] Net income.
[3] Operating income after taxes.
[4] Estimate.
[5] Average assets.
[6] Includes proportionate interest in unconsolidated subsidiaries or investments.
[7] Profit before interest and after taxes.
D/P: Deficit over profit.
P/D: Profit over deficit.
NA: Not available.
General notes: 1984 data were used for those February and March reporting companies that reported before press time. United Brands, ranked 110 last year, was excluded as information by geographic area is not available because of a change in fiscal year-end.

Origins of Multinationals

The impetus for the eventual development of United States multinational corporations occurred after World War II when European nations badly needed recovery assistance. The United States Government could not solve European recovery problems merely by exporting domestic production. The best approach seemed to be for American firms to produce needed products overseas. As a result corporations were encouraged to invest abroad.

In the majority of instances foreign nations welcomed the involvement of American companies in their industrial recovery. Encouraged by this response, United States corporations have steadily increased their foreign investment from approximately $7 billion in 1946 to better than $200 billion today.

The growth of multinationals is a two-way street. Foreign multinationals also are opening operations in the United States or buying existing businesses. Foreign investment in the United States almost tripled between 1971 and 1983. Table 19.6 lists the largest foreign multinationals.

Operational Strategies

Multinational corporations are specialists in international business. They attempt to minimize costs and maximize marketing opportunities. In doing this they focus on producing the product where it can be done the most economically and target their marketing to focus on growth areas.

One production strategy available to multinationals to minimize costs is known as **production sharing,** *a manufacturing process that integrates production operations along international lines. A company may assemble part of an item in one nation, ship it to another for further processing, and market the finished product in yet another country.* Such products as hand-held calculators, for example, may be classified as imports, but that does not tell the whole story. The microcomputer chips that are the heart of a calculator may be made in America, shipped to a developing nation like Mexico or South Korea for assembly into an end product, and then marketed in such developed countries as the United States, Canada, and England.

production sharing

Another element of the operating strategy of some multinationals is the tactic of **dumping.** It is *selling the same product in different markets at different prices for the purpose of disposing of excess production and maximizing total profits.* The term should become clear with an illustration.

dumping

Assume a multinational company controls most of the output and sales of television sets in its home country. As a result of its dominant domestic market position, it is relatively free to charge a higher price in its home country than it could in other countries where greater competition exists. Also assume that it has excessive productive capacity that enables it to produce more televisions than it can sell domestically. Consequently the managers decide to dump

Table 19.6 The Twenty Largest Foreign Multinationals
Source: Carol E. Curtis, "The Ever-Rising Sun," *Forbes*, July 2, 1984, pp. 134 and 136.

Rank	Company	Fiscal Year-End	Revenue[1] (Millions)	Net Income (Millions)	Assets (Millions)	Market Value of Common[2] (Millions)	Corporate Headquarters	Industry	Employees (Thousands)
1	Royal Dutch/Shell Group	Dec	$80,610	$4,178	$70,766	$21,138[3]	Neth/UK	energy	156.0
2	Mitsui & Co. Ltd.	Mar	63,149	27	21,017	1,558	Japan	wholesaler	12.9
3	Mitsubishi Corp.	Mar	62,831	102	21,340	2,981	Japan	wholesaler	14.3
4	British Petroleum Co. Plc	Dec	49,231	1,564	39,419	10,739	UK	energy	131.6
5	C Itoh & Co. Ltd.	Mar	48,436	1	15,612	1,149	Japan	wholesaler	10.0
6	Marubeni Corp.	Mar	46,816	2	16,543	1,093	Japan	wholesaler	10.6
7	Sumitomo Corp.	Mar	45,806	92	10,914	1,327	Japan	wholesaler	11.5
8	Nissho Iwai Corp.	Mar	34,039	20	9,835	604	Japan	wholesaler	7.7
9	ENI-Ente Nazionale Idrocarburi	Dec	25,166	−915	26,713	none[4]	Italy	energy	140.0
10	IRI-Istituto Ricostruzione Industriale	Dec	24,532	−2,141	41,384[5]	none[4]	Italy	multicompany	515.9
11	Toyota Motor Corp.	June	21,470	920	13,431	17,416	Japan	automotive	57.8[6]
12	Pemex-Petroleos Mexicanos	Dec	20,756	6,685	38,804	none[4]	Mexico	energy	160.0
13	Unilever	Dec	20,306	579	11,211	5,014[3]	Neth/UK	consumer goods	267.0
14	National Iranian Oil Co.	Dec	19,000E	NA	NA	none[4]	Iran	energy	NA
15	VEBA Group	Dec	18,859	146	11,969[5]	2,072	Germany	energy	77.3
16	Deutsche Bundespost	Dec	18,650E	NA	46,906[5]	none[4]	Germany	communications	505.0E
17	Hitachi Ltd.	Mar	18,479	707	20,521	9,968	Japan	elec equipment	161.5
18	TOTAL Group-Française des Pétroles	Dec	18,314	102	10,992	561	France	energy	43.6
19	Elf Aquitaine Group	Dec	17,587	488	17,994	1,870	France	energy	75.5
20	Nippon Tel & Tel Public Corp.	Mar	17,189	1,481	42,810	none[4]	Japan	communications	323.0

[1]Revenue figures are for group or consolidated operations and exclude excise taxes and duties.
[2]As of Dec. 31, 1983.
[3]Combined market value.
[4]Not publicly traded.
[5]Figures from latest available balance sheet.
[6]Not fully consolidated.
[7]Based on current cost accounting.
NA: Not available.
E: Estimated.
P: Preliminary.
General note: revenue and net income are converted at an average rate of exchange for the fiscal year; assets are converted at fiscal year-end rate. For companies with February and March fiscal year-ends, 1983 figures are used when more current data are not available.

570

its excess capacity in other countries, charging a lower price than in its own country. The American steel industry has criticized Japanese steelmakers for dumping their products in the United States, thus dramatically underselling domestic producers.

Barriers to International Trade

Companies that decide to enter international business operations are confronted with barriers that can hamper their operations. These barriers include language, customs and cultural differences, currency conversion, and protectionist practices.

Language

A potential problem on the international business scene includes the language and customs of the host nation. Language can prove to be a large stumbling block even with the use of interpreters. In the American Motors negotiations to create a joint venture with the Republic of China no problems were encountered on the big issue: the millions each party would contribute. The big problem? The meaning of the word *etc.*, as in "acts of God such as flood, etc.," took hours of negotiation to resolve.[6]

Another illustration of this potential barrier is found in Japan. Japanese communication is 70 percent nonverbal. With Americans it is just the opposite — 70 percent verbal. Body language, facial expressions, and hand gestures are extremely important in the Japanese method of expression. Managers unaware of that can miss vital communication or potentially can give nonverbal communication that contradicts verbal communication.[7]

Customs and Cultural Differences

Limitations in cultural knowledge may create problems. Did you know that:

— In Bangkok offices speaking softly is the rule.
— In Sydney, Australia, managers treat workers almost as equals and in taxis riders sit up front with the driver.
— In Madrid, at business meals, executives don't do business until after eating.[8]

Knowledge of cultural values can assist in making the correct decisions. The efforts of Beatrice Foods to develop a joint venture in China were aided by the decision to use one of their chief executive officers in the negotiations. This was seen by the Republic of China as a sign of commitment. The choice of an agent rather than a corporate officer would have been greeted with mistrust because agents are seen as exploiters of Chinese workers.[9]

When companies take their operations to a foreign country, they need to adopt the customs and language of the host country.

On the other hand, lack of cultural understanding forced both Gerber Products and Campbell Soup to abandon their Brazilian markets. Campbell's canned soup was a marketing failure because a Brazilian housewife felt she was not fulfilling her role as a homemaker if she served her family a soup she could not call her own. Gerber's dilemma was almost identical: Brazilian mothers were not willing to accept prepared baby food as a good substitute for fresh food made by themselves.[10]

Currency Conversion

A third potential barrier to international trade is the problem of currency conversion. A firm transacting business with a company in another country faces the ongoing problem of converting its currency to that of the trade partner's currency. Earlier in the chapter we introduced the concept of the exchange rate and the fact that this exchange rate "floats" based on market forces. What problems does this create? Pricing negotiations for the sale of a product are made with the realization that the worth of the money can change from day to day.

Pause and Ponder

Based on the experience of Campbell Soup and Gerber Products, how can a company protect itself against cultural marketing problems? Can a company ever really be *sure* that its product will be a success in an international market? Why or why not?

"Have Jensen find out what effect, if any, the collapse of the economies of the Western industrial nations would have on sales."
Source: *Changing Times*, August 1981, page 24. Used with permission.

Protectionism

Even though countries ideally support unrestricted free trade between one another, the realities of economics, inflation, and recessions have helped to create legal barriers — quotas, tariffs, and embargoes — to implement a philosophy of **protectionism.** This is *an international trade philosophy that favors the creation of barriers against the importing of goods to shelter domestic industries from foreign competition.* Protectionist arguments run the gamut, but all are centered on limiting foreign imports of products of home industries.

protectionism

Home Industries Protection Argument. The **home industries protection argument** is *the argument that trade with other nations will cause domestic industries to lose their customers to foreign competitors, forcing firms out of business and throwing workers out of jobs.* This argument has considerable emotional appeal, but a nation that takes an extreme protectionist stance may expect retaliation from other countries. Protective legislation also tends to reward less efficient domestic producers, allowing them to avoid competing with foreign firms that may be doing a better job.

home industries protection argument

Infant Industries Protection Argument. The **infant industries protection argument** is *the argument that endorses placing protective tariffs and quotas on certain imports so that fledgling domestic industries can become well established.* Theoretically, as these infant industries gain strength, the nation would eventually achieve a comparative advantage in providing the products or services in question and the trade barriers would be abandoned.

infant industries protection argument

Diversification for Stability Argument. The **diversification for stability argument** is *the argument that trade with other nations will reduce or inhibit the development of a variety of domestic*

diversification for stability argument

industries and thus reduce economic stability. This reasoning is behind the protectionist measures of governments in such one-industry economies as Cuba (reliant on sugar), Honduras (bananas), Brazil (coffee), and countries in the Middle East (oil). Diversification develops a stable economy. The stability argument might be valid for countries with a few industries, but it does not apply to an already diversified economy such as that of the United States.

wage protection argument

Wage Protection Argument. The **wage protection argument** is *the argument that trade with other nations depresses domestic wages because domestic producers cannot compete with cheap foreign labor.* Although this argument has strong patriotic and humanitarian overtones, applicability to the United States has lessened in recent years. American wages, although higher than those in many nations, are no longer the highest among developed countries. Many northern European workers enjoy higher average pay than their American counterparts.

national security argument

National Security Argument. The **national security argument** is *the argument that a nation must strengthen and protect its domestic industries that produce strategic defense materials to be able to maintain its defenses.* If this is not done, a country will become dependent on other nations for strategic materials needed during wartime, thus jeopardizing its own military capabilities.

This argument is logical, but difficult to implement. For a nation such as the United States, with many resources and a large production capacity, it is relatively easy to maintain independence in production of military hardware. Problems are still encountered, however, in connection with maintaining steady supplies of scarce but crucial raw materials. For this reason, the U.S. Department of Defense has established stockpiles of important raw materials essential to the production and maintenance of military equipment.

For a smaller nation that does not have the plants or sophisticated technology to produce its own war material, the national security argument is impossible to follow. For a smaller nation to compete militarily in this age, it must have a highly advanced army, navy, and air force. To obtain the material, it often is forced to buy those weapons and replacement parts for them abroad. A certain reliance on other nations for its own defense thus becomes unavoidable.

Pause and Ponder

After reviewing the arguments for protectionism, how valid do you think they are? How much protection do American industries need? What dangers are there of retaliation in the international business community if America adopts a protectionist mentality?

Now that we have discussed the reasons for protectionism, let's examine the tools of protectionism — tariffs, quotas, and embargoes.

Tariff. A **tariff *or* import duty** is *a tax imposed on imported goods to raise their market prices, making the cost of competing domestic products attractive by comparison.* The demand for domestic products may then increase, benefiting domestic producers and wage earners. Trade associations, labor organizations, and government agencies have encouraged tariffs against such items as leather jackets from Italy and Spain, steel from Japan, wooden and plastic clothespins from Taiwan and China, and fishing tackle from Japan, France, Mexico, Taiwan, and South Korea.

In an effort to protect Harley-Davidson Motor Company from the competition of Japanese motorbikes, a tariff raising import duties more than tenfold has been enacted. Harley-Davidson is the last remaining United States motorcycle maker. The 5-year tariff program (which applies to motorcycles with engines of 700 cubic centimeters or larger) raised the duties from 4.4 percent to 49.4 percent of the machine's cost in the first year. Over the remaining years the additional duty will drop to 35, 20, 15, 10, and 4.4 percent.[11]

tariff *or* import duty

Quota. A **quota** is *a trade barrier that restricts the quantity of a foreign product that can be brought into a country for resale.* Quotas are more restrictive and absolute than tariffs. They reduce or eliminate the possibility of purchase by placing a ceiling on the number of units imported.

In the past quotas have been imposed on foreign steel, televisions, textiles, and petroleum products. More recently, spurred by the continued pressure of Japanese imported cars, General Motors, Ford, Chrysler, and the United Auto Workers all worked successfully for more stringent import quotas. With large numbers of American autoworkers on indefinite suspension and the domestic auto industry just coming out of its worst depression, even more relief will be requested.[12]

quota

Embargo. An **embargo** is *legislation that prohibits firms from importing some or all of the products made in a given country.* For example, the United States has in the past imposed embargoes on goods from China, and it maintains them against Cuba, North Korea, and Vietnam. An operator of an art gallery in Salt Lake City learned about embargoes the hard way. After importing $24,000 worth of art objects from an embargoed nation, he was convicted of trading with the enemy and faced a maximum sentence of 10 years in prison or a $1,000 fine.

After Fidel Castro won control of Cuba, Americans who wanted Havana cigars had to buy them in Canada or Europe and smoke them before returning to the United States. Most embargoes, like

embargo

the one against Cuba, are politically motivated; domestic economic concerns are secondary.

Aids to International Trade

A number of aids facilitate international trade. These, as the list below shows, include international agreements, means for financial support, attempts at exchange rate stabilization, and the development of economic alliances.

- General Agreement on Tariffs and Trade
- Export-Import Bank
- International Monetary Fund
- Economic alliances

General Agreement on Tariffs and Trade (GATT)

The **General Agreement on Tariffs and Trade (GATT)** is *an international accord setting trade rules.* It is an attempt to have all nations work together to lower trade barriers. The agreement was created with the idea of limiting the possibility of a country's making a unilateral trade policy and having other nations retaliate. All signers of the agreement have agreed to work together to reduce import tariffs.

Export-Import Bank

The **Export-Import Bank** *attempts to promote international trade by lending money to importers and exporters who have not been able to obtain funds from other sources, and by lending money to foreign governments to help the development of international trade.* The **International Monetary Fund** *provides a vehicle for foreign exchange by assisting in stabilizing exchange rates in the world economic community.*

International Monetary Fund

economic alliances

Economic alliances *are agreements among independent nations to promote trade.* These nations create agreements to allow trading among themselves without tariffs, or to develop one set of trade rules. The most famous of these economic alliances is the European Economic Community (EEC), also called the Common Market. Table 19.7 lists the member nations in the EEC as well as those in other economic alliances.

International Business: The Problem of Conflict

Businesses operating in the international arena, especially multi-nationals, face ongoing conflicts with both the home country (where they originated and are headquartered) and the host country (where they have affiliates). These conflicts arise from questions of economics and power.

Table 19.7 Economic Alliances

Economic Alliance	Membership
Association of Southcentral Asian Nations	Indonesia, Malaysia, Philippines, Singapore, Thailand
Central American Common Market	Costa Rica, El Salvador, Guatemala, Honduras, Nicaragua
European Economic Community	Belgium, Denmark, England, France, Greece, Ireland, Italy, Luxembourg, Netherlands, West Germany
European Free Trade Association	Austria, Norway, Portugal, Sweden, Switzerland, Iceland, Finland (an associate member)
Latin American Free Trade Association	Argentina, Bolivia, Brazil, Chile, Colombia, Ecuador, Mexico, Paraguay, Peru, Uruguay, Venezuela
Organisation Commune Africane et Mauricienne	Benin, Central African Republic, Ivory Coast, Mauritius, Niger, Rwanda, Senegal, Togo, Upper Volta
The Nordic Council	Denmark, Finland, Iceland, Norway, Sweden

Home Country Conflicts

Conflicts between international businesses and the home country are usually economic in nature. They result in the following criticisms:

— Rather than building a plant in another country, a United States company, for example, should build another plant in the United States to provide jobs and keep dollars in the country.

— Moving operations to foreign countries to take advantage of lower wages there tends to depress domestic industry and eliminate jobs for domestic workers.

— The profits of foreign-based operations, by staying in foreign countries, are not taxed by the home nation, which reduces government revenues and allows multinationals to escape their duty to support their countries financially.

The responses to these criticisms are:

— Although production may move to another country, income is still entering the home country because company headquarters are based there — a net gain in productive income for the home country.

— Jobs are not lost by these operations except in declining industries. In the long run those jobs will be replaced by the creation of new positions generated by the income the businesses receive.

The Straight Line

American Companies Go International

Innocents Abroad

Companies that deal in international markets encounter unlimited opportunities to embarrass themselves. Many blunders are caused by language differences and inaccurate translation; others arise from ignorance of the social customs or business practices of the host nation.

Charles D. Tandy, founder of Tandy Corporation and its Radio Shack stores, discovered that he had to have a government tax stamp on windows in Belgium, and that he broke laws in Germany by giving away flashlights. Cultural and technical conflicts arose more than once during American Motors Corporation's licensing and sales negotiations with the French automaker Renault. Japanese managers may be offended if you attempt to arrange a meeting over the phone; hand-delivered notes are the traditional method. Italian customers limit the first meeting to socializing, reserving business decisions for future conferences.

Translation difficulties also have proved embarrassing. Parker Pen Company's Latin American ads claimed its Super Quink ink would prevent unwanted pregnancies; Otis Engineering's Russian language promotion materials promised that its oil well equipment would improve one's sex life; Germans interpreted Pepsi-Cola's German translation of "Come Alive with Pepsi" as a claim that the drink could resurrect the dead.

Some firms have recognized the need for preparing their employees to live and work in foreign countries. They hold cultural orientation seminars to acquaint workers with the customs, language, history, work habits, and religion of the host country. As a result employees are more able to adjust to living in a foreign country and are better equipped to handle the inevitable culture shock. Having a basic knowledge of the language of a country enables employees to establish rapport more

---

— The difficulties of double taxation: profits of the affiliate are taxed by the host country and then, when some profits are returned to the company's headquarters, they are taxed again by the home country. For the investor, profit is the measure and companies should try to minimize double taxation.

Host Country Conflicts

Possibly more fierce are the arguments between host countries and multinationals, particularly between host countries of the developing Third World (Asia, Africa, and Latin America) and American companies. Conflict centers on the fact that multinationals have different goals than does the government of the society in which they begin operations. The conflicts include:

quickly, thereby breaking down social and business barriers, which will benefit both the employee and the firm.

From 1980 to December 1981, Procter & Gamble conducted a unique exchange manager-training program between Akashi, Japan, and Modesto, California, that brought the two cultures together in the common goal of establishing an elasticized Pampers diaper production facility in Akashi. Extensive training in one another's language and culture was given to the American and Japanese managers and their families. They were taught by instructors from the International Relations Institute at Stanford University. This comprehensive program is credited with the success of the plant in Akashi.

Coca-Cola's international relations are good because the firm believes in becoming integrated in the countries in which it operates; and if possible, it sup-

ports community projects. Coke's personnel policies adhere to the country's local practices and to government requirements that follow the firm's philosophy of fairness in handling salaries, representation rights of labor unions, compensation, and benefits. In addition, Coke recognizes how important it is for employees and their families to be able to adapt to an overseas assignment. Among other things, the firm provides language courses to help employees and their families adjust to a foreign environment.

Cultural reorientation is now being considered by companies whose employees have experienced reentry trauma when moving back home after several years of living abroad. A period of transition would include help in adjusting to changes in America and in reestablishing the employees and their families in the company and the community.

For more about international trade, see Susan Nelson, "Learning to Work Overseas," *Nation's Business*, March 1984, pp. 59–60; "Exchanging and Training for Akashi," *Procter & Gamble's Moonbeams*, August 1983, pp. 3–5; and "The Coca-Cola Company: Personnel Topics — International Personnel," a one-page information sheet provided by the Consumer Information Center of The Coca-Cola Company, November 1979.

— Who controls the nation's business. The government of the host country wants to ensure control over the way its economy develops and resources are used, while the business wants the freedom to pursue its own operations.

— The direction of industrial growth. Governments that see multinationals under the control of their foreign-owned parent company fear that their own plans for economic development can be undercut by decisions made elsewhere.

— The question of possible nationalization of key industries to avoid their control by foreign countries.

— The fact that the government cannot control the companies' ability to take profits made in its country and move them elsewhere rather than reinvest them. The goal of the business is overall profit, which may even be paid to stockholders living in another country, whereas the goal of the government is further economic growth. Obviously the two conflict. The ability of the business to move money from one operation to another can endanger a host country's balance of payments and undermine the value of its currency.

The problem of who is running the company. Many multinationals send experienced personnel from headquarters to run foreign operations. The result, host countries feel, is a lack of responsiveness to host country needs and no gain in the business skills of its population. Many host countries are interested in multinationals setting up training programs to prepare host country nationals to run the affiliate themselves. These governments do not just want the businesses to provide jobs for many individuals, they want the companies to prepare members of its population for greater responsibility.

Summary

International trade has become an increasingly important part of world economic activity. In addition to economic growth it aids in increasing the standard of living and assisting in worldwide communication and understanding. International business has its own unique language. Among the major concepts are balance of trade, balance of payments, exchange rate, and absolute and comparative advantage.

Businesses choose to go international because of the profit potential (an opportunity for obtaining a higher percentage of earnings than can be done on a domestic scale), to take advantage of established demands for goods, and to improve the overall standard of living in foreign countries.

When a business chooses to operate on an international level it has a number of options. Each option requires the use of more resources and a greater commitment to international operations. The options include an export department or foreign intermediary, foreign licensing, joint venture, foreign-operated sales branches, and wholly owned subsidiaries.

The ultimate involvement by a corporation is becoming a multinational. Multinationals are corporations that operate on an international level, are based in one country but have operations in others as well, and do a substantial amount of business in other countries.

When a business tries to conduct international operations it must overcome potential barriers. The barriers include language, customs and cultural differences, currency conversion, and protectionism.

In the face of these barriers there are a number of aids to assist a business. These include the General Agreement on Tariffs and Trades, the Export-Import Bank, the International Monetary Fund, and economic alliances such as the European Economic Community.

Businesses operating on an international level also face conflicts between themselves and the home and host countries. The conflicts are involved with economics and power.

Key Terms

absolute advantage
balance of payments
balance of trade
comparative advantage
devaluation
diversification for stability argument
dumping
economic alliances
embargo
exchange rate
Export-Import Bank

exporting
foreign-operated sales branch
foreign trade intermediary
General Agreement on Tariffs and Trade (GATT)
home industries protection argument
importing
infant industries protection argument
International Monetary Fund
licensing

multinational corporation
national security argument
production sharing
protectionism
quota
revaluation
tariff *or* import duty
wage protection argument
wholly owned foreign subsidiary

For Review and Discussion

1. "Some countries rely on international trade for their basic survival." Respond to this statement.
2. Relate the concepts of balance of trade and balance of payments.
3. Distinguish between absolute advantage and comparative advantage.
4. What is the importance of the exchange rate in international business?
5. What are three reasons a business might choose to go international?
6. "A firm can select how deep it wants to wade into international waters by the approach it takes in international business." Explain this statement and provide examples of the different degrees of commitment a company can make to its involvement in international business.
7. What is a multinational corporation? What operational tactics does it focus on? What is meant by production sharing and dumping?
8. Why is protectionism considered a barrier to international trade? What are three arguments for protectionism? How is protectionism implemented through tariffs, quotas, and embargoes?
9. Identify and explain four aids that facilitate international business. Which one is most important to an individual business?
10. What types of conflicts can arise between a host country and an international business? How can some of these concerns be resolved?

Applications

Case 19.1 How Free Is Free Trade?

Representative Bill Frenzel, Minnesota The protectionist pressures are waxing hot.

Representative Bill Frenzel, Minnesota We'll see if the administration, which seems committed to free trade, can hold off Congress, which seems committed to protectionism.

Representative Barbara Kennelly, Connecticut The individual citizen is asking us to do something.

In recent years the protectionism movement and free trade supporters have been in a constant tug of war. In Congress the protectionist sentiments can be seen through:

- "Buy America" amendments cropping up on all kinds of bills
- Concerns that nations openly flaunt rules against unfair competition because the General Agree-

ment on Tariffs and Trade does not have any enforcement mechanisms

- An attempt to develop "reciprocity" legislation that would write into law the principle of United States retaliation against countries that restrict American goods and services

- Proposals to require foreign automakers to use specific percentages of American parts and labor for autos sold in the United States

On the other hand, the free trade forces do not want to take actions that could worsen the situation. The goal in this camp is to keep negotiating. Protectionist actions are seen as a way to ensure mediocrity on the home front and to minimize the ability of the United States to compete on the international scene.

Questions

1. From the standpoint of an American businessperson how do you feel about each of the potential protectionist actions? Why?

2. From the standpoint of an American consumer how do you feel about each of the potential protectionist actions? Why?

3. What actions if any would you take to ensure free trade as well as to protect American businesses? Is it possible to do both?

Case 19.2 Politics of Free Trade

Embargoes are political tools. In the recent past the United States has chosen to place embargoes on trade with the Soviet Union on two separate occasions.

1. An embargo on United States grain sales to the Soviet Union was imposed by the Carter administration after Russia invaded Afghanistan. It resulted in a $2.5 billion decrease in total trade between the two nations from the previous year.

2. An embargo by the Reagan administration barred United States subsidiaries and licensees abroad from aiding construction of a Soviet gas pipeline after Moscow's support of a military crackdown in Poland. It resulted in friction between the United States and its allies in addition to loss of business by American companies.

Eventually these embargoes were removed. But, based on the state of international relations, there is always the possibility that an embargo can and will be used again.

Questions

1. What was the intended purpose of the embargo in each instance?

2. How effective do you feel it was in achieving its goal? Why?

3. What effect did the embargoes have on the American farmer (situation #1) and on high technology companies (situation #2)?

4. Do you think the price of the embargoes was worth the cost?

Business Law and the Legal Environment of Business

Chapter Outline

The Legal System of the United States

Torts and Crimes
The Federal Court System

Business Law

The Law of Contracts
The Law of Agency
The Law of Sales
The Law of Property
Negotiable Instruments Law
The Law of Bankruptcy

The Legal Environment of Business

Business Regulation Today
What Price Regulation?
Responses to Regulation
Deregulation

Summary

Chapter Objectives

After studying this chapter, you should be able to:

1. Differentiate between common law and statutory law.
2. Distinguish between torts and crimes, and name the two general categories of each.
3. Discuss the organization and operation of the United States court system.
4. Describe the major subdivisions of the Uniform Commercial Code, including laws having to do with contracts, agency, sales, property, negotiable instruments, and bankruptcy. Also discuss the specific characteristics of patents, secrecy, trademarks, and copyrights.
5. Summarize the legal and regulatory environment in which today's business operates.

America is like a ship sailing on an ocean swept by crosscurrents. Government is one force behind those currents, a force that can be either constructive or destructive.

— Robert F. Dee, Smithkline Corporation

Up Front   Frank McCormack

General Counsel Helps ARCO Remain a Leader in Its Field

As Atlantic Richfield Company's (ARCO) chief attorney, Frank McCormack holds an awesome responsibility: safeguarding the legal health of one of the nation's largest corporations. With a staff of 160 lawyers, billions of dollars in pending lawsuits, and a perpetual burden of government regulations to oversee, McCormack's role is essential to ARCO's continued leadership in the petroleum and chemical industries.

McCormack's job requires him to play multiple roles: adviser, legal strategist, legal problem solver, and administrator. He meets regularly with the lawyers on his staff to remain abreast of legal problems in their areas and consider their recommendations on legal strategy. McCormack ultimately may be the one to decide whether to settle a major lawsuit or how to respond to a new government regulation that threatens the way ARCO operates.

"Corporation general counsels are becoming more important," McCormack says. "As a nation, we're over-legislated and over-regulated, burying ourselves in laws and litigation. Things have gotten so complex that management can't move without talking to the lawyers." To cope with the explosion of legal activity, McCormack expanded the company's staff to its present size, which ranks approximately tenth in the nation. Such growth naturally required some delegation; McCormack now has two deputy general counsels and three associate general counsels reporting to him on the status of operating companies owned by ARCO as well as the company's finance and corporate services, major litigation, and staff support.

Although the company's staff and operations have grown impressively in the past decade, its basic areas of legal concern have remained the same: litigation against the company, the legal aspects of corporate finance, and coping with government regulations. McCormack pays close attention to litigation, which he considers the "corporate jugular vein." Under McCormack's direction, ARCO has successfully defended itself against approximately twenty major antitrust suits within the past decade. Like other companies in its industry, ARCO is named occasionally as defendant in the growing number of toxic tort lawsuits. A large and prominent employer, ARCO is often the target of employee and labor relations

Many legal concerns influence business conduct. In fact, certain points of law were integral parts of material you studied earlier involving forms of business organization, labor relations, marketing,

lawsuits that demand the expertise of Frank McCormack and his staff.

McCormack is not your taciturn, one-dimensional, corporate legal eagle. He's very much a people person and a very special individual to work for. Shunning status symbols and protocol he says, "Everyone can swear at the boss. I encourage people to disagree. I hate turf fighting and will not allow it because it's counterproductive. . . . I try to make [my staff of 160 attorneys] a group of equal colleagues." One of the attorneys on his staff commented, "Frank's down-to-earth and candid, and also sensitive to people's feelings. He has good interpersonal relations. Because people feel at ease, they open up with him."

It would be easy for someone at McCormack's management level to relinquish the operating portion of his department to subordinates and avoid the nuts-and-bolts aspects of corporate law. That's hardly appealing to McCormack, however, who loves being a "shirtsleeve lawyer." "Many general counsels are pure administrators," he says, "but if I just do administration, I lose confidence in my legal ability. So I keep my hand in."

Often, he says, an ARCO executive will ask him to become personally involved in a special legal problem such as a merger, acquisition, or divestiture deal. And he loves the special legal cases, complex and critical ones that demand concentrated effort and long hours. Such cases, which typically have tight deadlines and may involve millions of dollars in their outcomes, tap the very core of Frank McCormack as a lawyer. He attacks them with special enthusiasm.

A dedicated family person, McCormack has encouraged other executives to place their families first in their lives. He follows his own advice by rarely bringing work home and by planning activities that he, his wife, Peggy, and their six children (ranging in age from twenty to twenty-nine) can still enjoy as a group. One of their favorite forms of recreation involves the family boat, Community Property, which they sail from a marina on the California coast. Reflecting on his life and his career, Frank McCormack says, "I'm fulfilled. I have six lovely kids, a good marriage, a nice house and a good job. I got what I always wanted and never thought I'd have. I've exceeded all my expectations."

Condensed with permission from Bill Stephens, " 'Shirtsleeve Lawyer,' " *Arco-Spark*, May 27, 1983, p. 3.

and finance. In this chapter we will not try to give you a comprehensive view of the laws relating to business; rather, we will introduce you to certain basic aspects of the legal system in the United States, summarizing major areas of business law and exploring the legal environment in which business has gained its ever-increasing influence on our society.

The Legal System of the United States

common law

In the democratic form of government found in the United States, regulation of business and personal conduct falls into two general categories: common law and statutory law. **Common law** is *a body of law based on records of early English court decisions settling disputes that involve people and property.* A historical legacy that stands apart from written rules of law, common law has evolved in and influenced court decisions in America since before the Revolutionary War. Common-law cases follow the doctrine of *stare decisis* (Latin for "to stand by the decisions"), which holds that prior court decisions set a precedent for future decisions on cases that have the same elements of controversy or similar relationships among the parties.

statutory law

Statutory law is *a written body of rules created and approved by a group of persons (generally referred to as a* legislature*), which presumably expresses the will of the citizens it represents.* Statutory law is enforced in the appropriate courts and administered by law enforcement agencies and their duly authorized representatives, including police officers, game wardens, the marine patrol, and sheriff's deputies. Statutory laws require that certain penalties be levied against violators.

Torts and Crimes

tort

A **tort** is *a private or civil wrong or injury committed against a person or property for which a court will award damages if the wronged party (called the* plaintiff*) can submit adequate proof that the accused wrongdoer (called the* defendant*) was guilty, through either negligence or intent, of committing the act in question.* A personal damage tort is wrongful harm to an individual, including damage to the person's reputation or feelings. This can occur, for example, if someone intentionally spreads lies about another person's private life. A property tort is wrongful damage to someone's property, as when a crop duster accidentally sprays a defoliant on a farmer's field of wheat. Most torts involve acts of negligence.

crime

A **crime,** on the other hand, is *a violation of a law passed by a legislative body.* The appropriate government (federal or state) will bring charges in its own name against the offender. (A tort requires a private individual to charge that a wrongful act has been committed.) Criminal laws most often cover crimes against person or property such as robbery or murder. Sometimes, however, businesspersons commit actions that violate criminal statutes, such as arson, fraud, embezzlement, or bribery.

Cases involving crimes are heard in criminal courts. Tort cases are aired in civil courts. Statute law may give certain courts special jurisdiction over such cases as juvenile offenses, probation, and domestic matters between husband and wife. In criminal cases, the plaintiff (which is always a government) must prove the defendant guilty beyond a reasonable doubt. In cases involving torts it is not necessary to prove the injury or damage beyond a reasonable doubt; the plaintiff need only prove by a preponderance of the evidence that a wrong was done. Criminal cases are decided by juries, with judges presiding over the proceedings and ruling on technical legal questions. Civil cases can be handled similarly, but if both parties to a civil case agree to do so, the question may be decided by a judge rather than by a jury.

The Federal Court System

Criminal cases that violate federal statutes are heard in the federal court system. (Each state has a similar court system for hearing cases involving violations of state law.) The lowest federal courts, district courts, are those in which juries decide questions or disputes of fact involving violations of federal law. The court, represented by a judge, rules on legal questions and ensures that attorneys for the plaintiff and defendant observe proper legal procedure. Each state has between one and four federal district courts, depending on its size.

Acting as buffers between the district courts and the Supreme Court, the courts of appeals (also called circuit courts) hear appeals based on alleged procedural errors that occurred in district court trials. Cases appealed to the circuit courts and the Supreme Court are heard only by judges. Circuit court decisions are final unless the United States Supreme Court agrees to review a case appealed beyond that level. Decisions of the Supreme Court are final; they can only be overturned by a later Supreme Court decision or a constitutional amendment. The circuit courts also review and enforce orders and rulings of such quasi-legal bodies as the Federal Trade Commission and the National Labor Relations Board. Figure 20.1 illustrates the hierarchy of the federal court system. The Supreme Court also may agree to hear appeals from state courts.

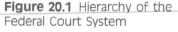

Figure 20.1 Hierarchy of the Federal Court System

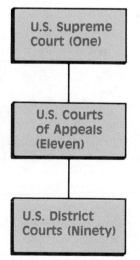

Business Law

The **Uniform Commercial Code (UCC)** is *a comprehensive body of business law that encompasses various kinds of transactions.* Drafted by the National Conference of Commissioners on Uniform State Laws, it has been adopted by all states except Louisiana, thus ensuring that business transactions will be handled consistently

Uniform Commercial Code (UCC)

from state to state. In this section, we will examine several areas of business law covered by the UCC.

The Law of Contracts

contract

A **contract** is *a legally binding agreement between two or more parties obliging them to do or refrain from doing certain acts.* When you sign a contract you voluntarily give up certain legal rights that you would otherwise enjoy. Although some contracts may be wholly or partly oral, the law requires that a contract be written if it involves any of the following:

— A purchase or sale of real estate
— A sale of goods for a price that exceeds $500
— An agreement to pay another's debt
— An obligation that cannot be performed within 1 year of the date of the agreement

A valid contract must have each of the elements illustrated in Figure 20.2 and described in the following paragraphs.

Offer. Extreme precision is not necessary, but the offer must be clear enough for a reasonable person to understand what the offeror meant. In addition, the offeror must have intended to make the offer and to communicate it to the offeree. Such frivolous offers as

Figure 20.2 The Elements of a Valid Contract

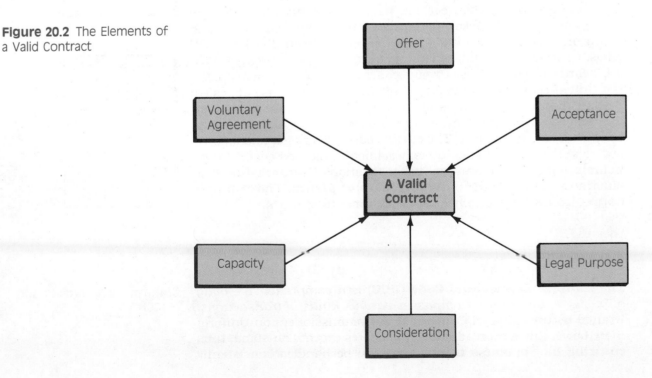

Pause and Ponder

A student standing in the cafeteria line at your college nudges his friend and comments, "I'd give a week's pay if that girl behind me would go out with me Saturday night." She taps him on the shoulder and says, "Here's my address. Pick me up at eight." He fails to appear, and she sues him for breach of contract. What defenses are available to him?

jokes or casual remarks or offers that were not intentionally communicated may be declared invalid by a court.

Acceptance. A valid acceptance of the offer requires the same general conditions as a valid offer. Intent to accept, clarity of acceptance, and intentional communication to the offeror must all be present.

Legal Purpose. A contract's purpose or object must comply with the law. One party to a contract cannot bring suit against the other for breach of contract if the act required by the agreement is illegal.

Consideration. A valid contract requires that both parties exchange something of value, which is called consideration, or *quid pro quo* (Latin for "something for something"), as an inducement to enter the agreement. Each party thus establishes an obligation to the other. Consideration may be an act performed or withheld, money, goods, or services rendered, or any combination of such things that lends weight to each party's obligation. In general, it need not be tangible or possess economic value. The law usually does not attempt to weigh the relative worth of each party's consideration.

Capacity. Capacity is a requirement that the contracting parties be of sound mind, understand what they are agreeing to, and be of legal age to enter into a contract. Persons who can prove that they made a contract while under the influence of alcohol or drugs, or while senile, insane, or not of legal age to make a contract may successfully avoid their obligations under it.

Although minors may not be required to fulfill most contracts they make before they reach the age of majority (either 18 or 21 in most states), they may be held liable for contracts they made to acquire items essential to their maintenance (rent, food, clothing, medical care) if they are self-supporting.

Voluntary Agreement. A final requirement of a legally valid contract is that both parties make the agreement voluntarily, without restraint or influence, acting of their own free will. A person who signed a contract because he or she was threatened or otherwise placed under duress cannot be compelled by a court to perform the agreement.

If all of these requirements are met in a contract that you signed, you are bound to carry out your share of the bargain, whether or not you understood its terms. The law assumes that you understood the contract if you signed it.

The Law of Agency

agent
principal

An **agent** is *one who is authorized to transact business and exercise authority on behalf of another party.* The **principal,** *the person whom an agent represents*, grants the agent authority to act on his or her behalf.

The law of agency exists because it is sometimes necessary or desirable to employ someone who has a special knowledge or skill to act on your behalf. Because you cannot be in two places at the same time, you may also employ an agent to close a deal in a distant location. Agents are used to buy or sell real estate, purchase securities, make travel arrangements, find work for actors and musicians, sell various products, and accomplish many other business transactions.

The Law of Sales

warranty

The law of sales, also covered by the Uniform Commercial Code, deals only with the sale of new, tangible personal property. Companies that sell such property often issue a written **warranty,** *a document that states certain facts and conditions about a product's operation and correct use and clarifies the limits of its performance under various circumstances.* A warranty's terms include conditions under which the product or its parts will be repaired or replaced and the kinds of use or abuse that would void the company's obligation to fix or replace the product. The manufacturer's express warranty usually is printed on a piece of paper packed with the product.

The law of sales also holds sellers to certain implied warranties regardless of the terms of their express warranty. Implied warranty under the law of sales falls into four general categories that are discussed in Table 20.1.

The Law of Property

Another subdivision of the Uniform Commercial Code encompasses the ownership and transfer of *real property*, which is the earth and things firmly attached to it, including crops, buildings, trees, and minerals. Property law also covers certain rights having to do with *personal property*, which is simply defined as objects other than real property and any intangible rights or interests held in such objects. Real property is generally immovable, and personal property

Category	Terms
Implied warranty of title	The seller implies that he or she is the lawful owner and can convey that ownership to the buyer.
Warranty of sale by sample or description	The seller warrants that the merchandise that is delivered will match the sample merchandise or the description used to make the sale. (This term can be important when buying merchandise from a catalog or from such samples as the swatches of material used to sell rugs.)
Warranty of fitness for a particular purpose	The seller is responsible for a product's failure if he or she assumed the role of expert advisor to the buyer.
Warranty of merchantability	Goods must be suitable for ordinary usage. (This is a central issue in many product liability cases.)

Table 20.1 Categories and Terms of Implied Warranties

consists of transportable objects or rights to them: bonds, furniture, or a sailboat, for example.

One area of property law that has particular importance for businesspeople is intellectual property: patents, trademarks, and copyrights. Because these properties have a significant bearing on a firm's identity in the marketplace and its survival in the world of business, we will explore them in some detail.

Patents. The Patent and Trademark Office of the U.S. Department of Commerce grants a **patent,** *a legal right allowing an inventor to exclude others from making, using, or selling an invention, a design, or a plant for a stated length of time.* An invention becomes public property after its patent expires, and anyone may then produce and sell it. Patents are only renewable by act of Congress.

patent

The abbreviation *Reg. U.S. Pat. Off.* followed by a patent number confirms that the product is patented and duly registered in the Patent Office. Labels saying *Patent pending* or *Patent applied for* afford no legal rights; they simply mean that the inventor applied for a patent and expects to receive it.

Three kinds of patents can be obtained. The choice depends on the nature of the item. A *utility patent* is a patent with a life span of seventeen years awarded to those who invent a new, useful, and unobvious industrial or technical process, machine, or chemical composition or a new, useful, or novel improvement on existing machines, processes, or materials. "Useful" simply means that the invention must perform its intended function.

A *design patent* is a patent awarded on an ornamental device for a period of 3 1/2, 7, or 14 years, whichever the applicant chooses. Such patents may protect designs on floor coverings or styles of automobile bodies.

A *plant patent* provides seventeen years of protection for a new species of plant that is asexually reproduced (grown from cuttings, grafting, or other nonseed methods). A horticulturalist who produces a new variety of rose or apple may obtain the exclusive right to produce and market it by obtaining a plant patent.

How to Obtain a Patent. Patenting is a horse race. The first inventor who files an application stands the best chance of receiving the patent. If two people apply for patents on identical devices almost simultaneously, each may have to establish the date on which the idea was conceived.

The first step is the preliminary search, an examination of existing patents filed in the search room of the Patent Office, to determine if a similar or identical device already has been patented. Patent records are open to the public, enabling you to make your own search, but it is usually faster and cheaper to employ a patent attorney, who can have a search made within several days.

If a search reveals that no invention like yours has been patented, your attorney probably will advise you to apply for a patent. A patent application includes an oath, a description of your device, a drawing (where possible), and a statement of claims about the unique character of your invention. You must also pay a filing fee.

Because applications are examined in the order in which they are received, several months will pass before your application is reviewed by a patent examiner, who is familiar with the category into which the invention falls. If the examiner finds the device is similar to an already patented one, you will be informed of this and advised to alter the invention in a manner that would make it patentable before reapplying. If the invention is unique, the Patent Office will award you a patent. You must then pay an issue fee. An applicant who is denied a patent may appeal the decision to the board of appeals of the Patent Office.

It takes the Patent Office approximately 26 months to award a patent because of its backlog of 200,000 applications. Presently there are 24 million documents on record, and they must be filed manually. The Reagan administration has taken steps to streamline this archaic information system by adding several hundred staff members and computerizing its records at a cost that may exceed $300 million. If these efforts succeed, the waiting time for a patent may decrease to 18 months by 1987.[1]

One alternative to obtaining a patent, of course, may be to keep certain product information secret. Secrecy may be practical if products are made from formulas with several ingredients that must be measured in exact proportions and blended in a precise sequence. Secrecy also may be applied to a manufacturing process that gives an end product a unique appearance, finish, durability,

or other characteristic. Bailey's Original Irish Cream, a liqueur, is made with a secret formula that competitors have been unable to duplicate to date, giving Bailey's sales of 1 million cases per year. The formula somehow prevents the cream from curdling in the bottle for up to 2 years.[2]

Although secrecy prevents a company's exclusive right to a product from expiring in seventeen years (as it would if it were patented), secrecy requires management to take considerable precautions to safeguard its formulas or processes from accidental or intentional disclosure by employees.

Many companies veil their developmental laboratories in secrecy until new products have been perfected and are ready for marketing. Such is the case at Wendy's International, for example, where doors to test kitchens have coded locks and information on new products is distributed on a "need-to-know" basis only.[3]

Trademarks. In addition to awarding patents, the Patent and Trademark Office also registers trademarks. A **trademark** is *a brand name, brand mark, or trade character that has legal protection.* A company uses trademarks to identify its products and to distinguish them from competitors. A company's name (also referred to as a *trade name*) may be registered with the Patent and Trademark Office if it appears in or forms part of the trademark that identifies its products.

trademark

Once a firm's trademark is approved and registered, it receives legal protection for 20 years. Registration may be renewed for 20-year periods thereafter unless the firm cancels it or surrenders the trademark. If over time the public comes to use a trademark generically to identify a product rather than one company's specific version of it, the courts may strip the firm of its trademark protection. Some former trademarks that have been held to be generic are linoleum, shredded wheat, aspirin, yo-yo, brassiere, kerosene, aerosol, cellophane, harmonica, escalator, and zipper.

Registered trademarks usually are followed by the symbol ® or ™. A firm may also register its **service mark,** which is *a mark or words used in sales or advertising literature to distinguish a firm's services from those of its competitors.*

service mark

Companies treasure the financial value and consumer recognition of their trademarks and service marks, and they defend them vigorously to discourage generic use. The word *brand* is stated or printed after the product's name in television and print advertising and on package labels for such products as Sanka decaffeinated coffee, Scotch cellophane tape, and ReaLemon reconstituted lemon juice in the hope that this will reinforce the idea that these are registered trademarks and not generic words. Table 20.2 presents some trademarks that have been registered for many years, along with the products they refer to.

One of the most widely publicized legal battles over trademark protection began in the early 1970s when Parker Brothers threatened to sue an economics professor at San Francisco State University

Table 20.2 Well-Known Trademarks and the Products They Refer To

Registered Trademark	Generic Product
Kleenex®	Paper tissues
Jeep®	Four-wheel drive vehicles
Coke® and Coca-Cola®	Cola-flavored drinks
Xerox®	Photocopying machines
Levi's®	Jeans
Band-aid®	Adhesive bandages
Formica®	Plastic laminate
Q-Tips®	Cotton swabs
Teflon®	Nonstick coating
Vaseline®	Petroleum jelly
Styrofoam®	Foam insulating material
Magic Marker®	Felt-tip marking pen

for naming his new board game "*Anti-Monopoly.*" The company contended that his name infringed on its right to use the word "*Monopoly*" as the registered trademark for its board game ("Monopoly" had been protected by trademark since 1935). After Parker Brothers reportedly declined offers by the professor's lawyers to alter the name of his game, he sued in California district court to have the trademark "Monopoly" declared invalid. Nine years of decisions and appeals followed as Parker Brothers pursued the matter all the way to the U.S. Supreme Court. In early 1983 that court let stand a circuit court of appeals ruling that stripped "Monopoly" of trademark protection, thus making it generic.[4]

copyright

Copyrights. Registered by the Copyright Office of the Library of Congress, a **copyright** is *a set of legal rights granted to the creator of an original work of authorship, such as an artistic, dramatic, literary, or musical production.* The creator of a copyrighted work may be called an author, artist, or composer, depending on the nature of the work. A copyright owner may do the following with a copyrighted work:

— Reproduce it
— Create works derived from or based on it
— Sell duplicates of it
— Perform it or display it publicly
— Authorize others to do any of the above

Examples of works that are copyrighted rather than patented are as follows:

— Books
— Musical scores and lyrics to songs
— Dramatic works (including accompanying music)
— Choreography

- Photographs, sculpture, or works of graphic art
- Motion pictures, slides, filmstrips, videodisks, videotapes, televised productions, and other audiovisual works
- Phonograph records and tapes

Under the provisions of the Copyright Act of 1976, works created after January 1, 1978, are protected until 50 years after the creator's death. Works originated by more than one person and copyrighted jointly receive protection for 50 years after the last surviving creator's death. The creator receives automatic copyright protection the moment the work is placed in a visual or audible form — written, filmed, or otherwise recorded.

Notice of copyright on nonsound works usually appears as the symbol © or the abbreviation *Copr.* followed by the owner's name and the year the work was first published or produced.

The issue of copyright protection became especially important to the film industry after videocassette recorders (VCRs) were introduced in the early 1970s. Walt Disney Productions, Universal City Studios, and other filmmakers claimed that home taping of movies violated copyrights and caused them financial losses. After a 7-year battle between moviemakers and VCR manufacturers, the U.S. Supreme Court ruled in 1984 that taping televised movies does not violate copyright laws as long as copies are strictly limited to home viewing and not used for personal gain.[5]

Negotiable Instruments Law

The Uniform Commercial Code addresses various transactions involving **negotiable instruments,** which are *written promises or requests that certain sums of money be paid to the bearer or to order.* Negotiable instruments include promissory notes, checks, and drafts, all of which you learned about in Chapter 14. To be negotiable, an instrument must be:

negotiable instruments

1. In writing
2. Signed by the maker

Pause and Ponder

The U.S. Supreme Court ruled 5 to 4 that recording programs on a VCR for personal viewing does not violate copyright. Hollywood film producers, obviously displeased by the decision, have resolved to lobby for a federal law that would levy a minimum $0.50 surcharge on the sale of each blank video tape and $100.00 on each video recorder. Proceeds would be paid to film producers and artists to offset income allegedly lost because of home taping. Defend or criticize their position.

3. An unconditional promise to pay
4. For a specific sum of money
5. Payable on demand or at a definite time
6. Payable *to order* or *to bearer*

The UCC also specifies several types of indorsement, each of which has special meaning when used on a negotiable instrument. A *blank indorsement* is a simple signature: "Paul J. Owens." Blank indorsement creates a bearer instrument, one that can be transferred from one subsequent party to the next without further indorsement. Whoever possesses a bearer instrument is presumed to own it and can cash it.

A *special indorsement* is generally the safest kind. An example would be: "Pay to the order of Ellen Johnson (signed), Paul J. Owens." Johnson must now indorse the instrument before it can be transferred to another party, because Owens's indorsement dictated that it be paid only to Johnson.

A *restrictive indorsement* dictates a specific purpose or use and so restricts future handling: "Pay to the order of National Bank for deposit only, account number 93476-007-8 (signed), Paul J. Owens." In this case, the instrument's future is restricted. It can only be deposited in Owens's bank account. If Owens should lose it, the restrictive indorsement would prevent the finder from forging Owens's name as a blank indorsement and receiving cash for the instrument.

A *qualified indorsement* allows the holder to avoid responsibility for paying the instrument if the maker refuses or fails to pay and causes the instrument to bounce: "Paul J. Owens, without recourse." If you indorse a check this way, however, you may have trouble finding another party who will give you cash for it, because that party cannot bring legal action against you if the maker refuses to pay. On the other hand, a qualified indorsement may be the safest in situations where you doubt that the maker will pay and you want to avoid liability for payment as a subsequent holder of the instrument. Agents sometimes receive instruments payable to them that were written to pay debts owed to their principals. In this case, a principal would not expect the agent to stand behind the instrument merely because it was payable to the agent, but should be willing to accept it from the agent with the agent's qualified indorsement.

The Law of Bankruptcy

bankruptcy *or* insolvency

Bankruptcy or insolvency is *the state of being unable to pay one's creditors' claims as they come due.* As you learned in the discussion of accounting in Chapter 17, a firm's assets must equal the sum of its liabilities and its capital. When the firm operates at a loss over several years, capital and assets decline and liabilities may increase to a point where debts outweigh assets, thus destroying the accounting equation, and also the business.

A firm that is besieged by creditors may petition the federal district court to declare it bankrupt, a procedure called *voluntary bankruptcy*. When a group of creditors petitions the court to declare a debtor bankrupt so they may collect at least part of their claims, that is called *involuntary bankruptcy*.

The new federal bankruptcy law that became effective October 1, 1979, streamlined and simplified bankruptcy procedures. In the absence of fraud or gross mismanagement, a company's present management team is allowed to stay in place and negotiate a reorganization plan that will permit the firm to pay off its creditors over an extended period of time. Further legal actions may be taken if repayment proves to be impossible.

The Legal Environment of Business

Various state and federal government agencies possess legal or quasi-legal power to regulate business operations. Table 20.3 introduces the most influential federal regulatory agencies. (You will recall that some agencies were discussed earlier, particularly the Occupational Safety and Health Administration in Chapter 6 and the Securities and Exchange Commission in Chapter 14.)

The creation of these agencies began with the Interstate Commerce Commission in 1887. Today at least 116 government agencies and programs control some facet of business activity. Figure 20.3 shows a sample of the 310 federal regulations that affect pizza.

Business Regulation Today

Companies sometimes engaged in questionable business practices that harmed consumers, smaller competitors, or the environment. As some of the more serious abuses came to light, federal and state governments began to mandate social consciousness through intensified regulation. Some observers today, however, feel that overzealous regulators unnecessarily inhibit business efforts to pursue their goals. When Eli Lilly & Company petitioned the Food and Drug Administration for clearance to market a drug for arthritis, the required paperwork reportedly exceeded 100,000 pages. Exxon Corporation, a firm whose complex operations are subject to scores of external controls, averages ten reports apiece to forty government agencies each year.[6]

Under the Food and Drug Administration's system of testing, it takes 7 to 10 years for a drug company to develop, test, and clear for sale new drugs to combat various diseases and illnesses. Consequently, among nations in the world, the United States ranked

- 32nd in approving the anticancer drug doxorubicin
- 51st in approving the antituberculous drug rifampin
- 64th in approving the antiallergenic drug cromolyn
- 106th in approving the antibacterial drug co-trimoxazole

Table 20.3 Principal Federal Regulatory Agencies

Agency, Year Established	Major Activities
Interstate Commerce Commission (ICC), 1887	Approves rates, routes, and methods of operation for truck, bus, and rail carriers operating in interstate commerce. (Its scope was reduced somewhat by the Motor Carrier Act of 1980.)
Federal Reserve Board, 1913	Regulates the operations of commercial banks belonging to the Federal Reserve System. Governs national policy on money and credit.
Federal Trade Commission (FTC), 1914	Administers the terms of several laws passed to protect consumers. Investigates incidents of alleged monopoly, restraint of trade, or unfair or deceptive trade practices: its goal is to maintain fair and free competition.
Food and Drug Administration (FDA), 1931	Sets standards of quality for food and drug products. Grants operating licenses to drug manufacturers and distributors.
Federal Communications Commission (FCC), 1934	Awards operating licenses to radio and television stations. Regulates interstate and international telephone and telegraph operations.
Securities and Exchange Commission (SEC), 1934	Regulates the issue of stocks and bonds and the operation of the various stock exchanges.
Civil Aeronautics Board (CAB), 1938	Regulated domestic air routes until 1982. Approved domestic air fares until 1983. Slated for dismemberment by January 1, 1985, by Airline Deregulation Act of 1978.
Federal Aviation Administration (FAA), 1948	Sets airport safety standards. Monitors aircraft fitness and maintenance. Licenses pilots.
Equal Employment Opportunity Commission (EEOC), 1964	Monitors and attempts to eliminate discrimination based on race, color, religion, sex, national origin, or age in all places of employment and in labor unions.
Environmental Protection Agency (EPA), 1970	Protects and enhances the environment through the control and abatement of air, water, solid waste, noise, radiation, and toxic substance pollution.
Consumer Product Safety Commission, 1972	Sets standards for product safety to protect the public against unreasonable risk of injury. Has the power to recall defective or hazardous products through their manufacturers.

Table 20.3, continued

Agency, Year Established	Major Activities
Nuclear Regulatory Commission, 1975	Licenses persons and companies to build and operate nuclear reactors and to own and use nuclear materials.
	Inspects sites to ensure that rules and standards are being observed.
Federal Energy Regulatory Commission, 1977	Sets rates and charges for the transportation and sale of natural gas and the transmission and sale of electricity and licensing of hydroelectric projects.
	Sets rates for the transportation of oil by pipeline, as well as the valuation of such pipelines.

This is *not* to argue that drugs should be allowed on the market without adequate safeguards to confirm their performance and effects. Thalidomide, a tranquilizer whose use by pregnant women caused many birth defects in Europe in the 1950s and early 1960s, was never approved for use in the United States. Nevertheless, the lengthy test procedure can keep helpful drugs off the market for years.

What Price Regulation?

The total cost businesses pay to comply with federal regulations alone is estimated at more than $100 billion per year. A survey by the National Federation of Independent Business (NFIB) disclosed that small-business owners ranked government regulations and red tape their fourth most important problem after taxes, interest rates and financing, and poor sales.[7] General Motors Corporation reported that compliance with all levels of government regulations in one recent year cost approximately $1.8 billion and consumed the efforts of roughly 22,000 full-time employees. The company claims it has spent more than $14 billion to comply with federal, state, and local governmental regulations in the past decade.[8]

Compliance procedures usually apply as stringently to small firms as to large ones. Government report formats are generally identical for both large and small firms; the same data may be required from a 500-employee company as from one with 50,000 workers. The smaller firm, lacking the full-time regulatory compliance staff that many large firms have created, will find the report more costly to complete. As a result the small-business owner's time and attention is drawn away from management to matters of less value to the business itself. An NFIB poll concerning government surveys disclosed that small-business owners averaged almost 9 hours and spent $238 preparing just one large report — the federal government's Annual Survey of Manufacturers. Federal agencies most subject to criticism for burdensome paperwork are the Internal Revenue Service and the Departments of Health and Human Services, Transportation, and Agriculture.[9]

Figure 20.3 Selected Regulations Affecting Pizza
Source: Adapted from a chart by Ron Taylor and Carl Vansag, and from basic data provided by the United States Department of Agriculture, Food and Drug Administration, appearing in "A Pizza with the Works — Including 310 Regulations," *U.S. News & World Report,* May 31, 1982, p. 55.

When it comes to snacks, few foods can rival pizza in popularity. Since New York City restaurants first offered the tangy pies in 1936, pizza has grown into a booming, six-billion-dollar-a-year business.

Last year, Americans gobbled up more than 1.5 billion pizzas at home, in schools and sporting arenas, and in the more than 20,000 restaurants that serve it. That breaks down to about seven pizzas for every man, woman, and child in the U.S.

But with the popularity have come scores of regulations from the Food and Drug Administration and the Department of Agriculture on the ingredients in what the government describes as "a bread-base meat food product with tomato sauce, cheese, and meat topping." In all, the rules governing what goes on a pizza and how those toppings can be described on labels and menus take up more than forty pages of federal documents, including some 310 separate regulations. Here's a sampling of just a few of those standards for a pizza — with everything.

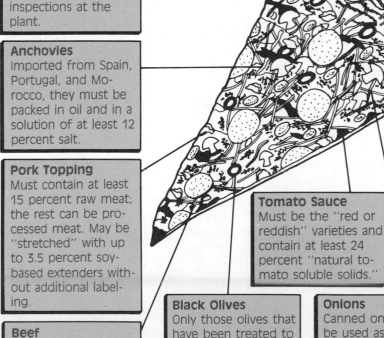

Mushrooms
Only ascorbic acid (vitamin C) — up to 37.5 milligrams per ounce — and water are allowed in canned mushrooms. No vinegar is permitted.

Crust
Each pound of flour must contain 2.9 milligrams of thiamine, 24 milligrams of niacin, and at least 13 — but not more than 16 — milligrams of iron.

Green Peppers
Calcium chloride or other salt preservatives in canned green peppers must not be more than .026 percent of the food's weight.

Italian Sausage
Uncured, unsmoked sausage containing at least 85 percent meat. Sausage consisting of more than 13 percent extenders must carry the notice "texturized soy flour added."

Mozzarella Cheese
This low-moisture, part-skim cheese must contain at least 30 percent but no more than 45 percent fat and come from pasteurized cow's milk.

Pepperoni
To meet nutrition requirements, 18 to 21 percent of its content must be protein. If used in school lunches, the meat must pass daily USDA inspections at the plant.

Anchovies
Imported from Spain, Portugal, and Morocco, they must be packed in oil and in a solution of at least 12 percent salt.

Pork Topping
Must contain at least 15 percent raw meat; the rest can be processed meat. May be "stretched" with up to 3.5 percent soy-based extenders without additional labeling.

Beef
Ground beef must be no more than 30 percent fat.

Tomato Sauce
Must be the "red or reddish" varieties and contain at least 24 percent "natural tomato soluble solids."

Black Olives
Only those olives that have been treated to remove bitterness, packed in a salt solution, and oxidized can be called black olives.

Onions
Canned onions may be used as long as the onions come from the bulb of the plant and not the stalk.

Responses to Regulation

Responses to regulation have ranged from combative to cooperative. Between these two extremes can be found various measures that companies, managers, and regulators alike may adopt in achieving their respective goals constructively. Several of them are explored here.

Improved Self-Policing. Greater self-policing and voluntary attention to the matters scrutinized by government regulators may minimize the need for future regulations. By keeping their own houses in order and publicizing their voluntary controls, industry leaders can discourage government interference. This has long been the practice within the legal, accounting, and medical professions, and it certainly could be transplanted to business in general. The result might be the demise of various regulatory agencies as legislators agree to let the private sector be its own watchdog. Self-policing might begin with a voluntary code of conduct, stringently enforced industrywide by committees or examining boards composed of executives from the companies involved.

The Power of Lobbying. Individual firms and trade associations can lobby to have lawmakers consolidate overlapping government authority and eliminate agencies' duplication of regulatory activities, so that, for example, one report or inspection would satisfy the needs of several agencies at once. In addition, regulators could be required to justify each form and inspection and to stop gathering unnecessary or irrelevant information.

Some opponents of excessive regulation hope that regulators will someday be required to produce economic impact statements disclosing the effect of new reports and external controls on a business's costs, employee productivity, and other vital matters. This would require a comprehensive law, however, because many large agencies, such as the Consumer Product Safety Commission and the Federal Trade Commission, operate with considerable autonomy. Nevertheless, a law requiring bureaucrats to balance the costs of controls against the expected benefits would help to ensure that future regulations place no greater burden on society than do the conditions they seek to alleviate.

Nearly 400 firms, including Union Carbide, Texaco, Ford, International Paper, and Dow Chemical, have their own lobbyists or other employees in Washington to keep their fingers on the pulse of government and to maintain positive relations with influential lawmakers whose decisions will ultimately affect company operations. Anheuser-Busch has a vice-president of national affairs, Allied Corporation has created a senior vice-presidency in charge of government affairs, and INA Corporation has established a similar position within its corporate structure.

Focusing on Results. Regulators (and legislators who make regulatory proposals) might also concentrate on the results they want business to achieve — reduced accidents, healthier working environments

— rather than on the way the business community must reach them. Goal-oriented government, like goal-oriented business managers, would establish the results to be achieved, leaving the mechanics of getting there up to the companies involved. At present, a host of specific, prescriptive regulations are in place, at a greater cost than if management were allowed to use its own judgment about ways to reach the ultimate objectives that regulations address.

Financial Penalties and Rewards. One government report that examines the cost of federal paperwork to American industry suggests that fines be levied on companies that fail to reach mandated results. Financial penalties would decrease as firms aligned their operations with legal guidelines. The government might also consider providing tax incentives to firms that met legislated goals and levying greater taxes on those that did not. Ultimately firms that operate within legally acceptable bounds in such areas as workplace and product safety and pollution abatement would pay lower taxes, charge lower prices for their products, and enjoy a competitive advantage over companies that complied with the law less fully or enthusiastically.

Positive Response by Government. In 1982 President Reagan formed a blue-ribbon panel of 150 business leaders to perform an 18-month review of all federal government operations, searching for wasteful and inefficient management practices. Formally called the Private Sector Survey on Cost Control, the group came to be known as the Grace Commission after its leader, J. Peter Grace, chairman of W. R. Grace & Company. The committee was assisted by more than 2,000 volunteer managers whose contributed time was valued at $75 million; 850 corporations, private persons, and foundations paid the cost. Participating firms included such companies as Goodyear Tire & Rubber Company, Aetna Life & Casualty Company, PPG Industries, and Borden.

Although joint efforts of this sort are not new between government and private industry, this survey has received more publicity and did a more extensive examination of government's management practices than any in recent memory. After completing its review, the Grace Commission submitted 2,478 recommendations involving 750 separate issues.[10]

The Commission projected savings of $424 billion by 1987 as a result of improved management of federal programs, reduction or elimination of wasteful management practices, and the reorganization or streamlining of various governmental activities.

Although all the Commission's recommendations won't be examined until 1986, approximately one-third had been considered by the White House by mid-1984. Eighty-five percent of those were adopted, and their impact on government efficiency will save a projected $6 billion in the 1985 federal budget alone.

Another government cost-control review group, the President's Council on Integrity and Efficiency, saved approximately $31 billion by reducing incidents of waste and fraud in internal management practices within federal agencies. This panel's work resulted in a 143 percent increase in prosecutions for defrauding the federal government and a 137 percent rise in reports of alleged wrongdoing by federal government contractors and suppliers. Government publications, a point of constant criticism, were reduced by 3,800 pamphlets (150 million copies) per year. This action, coupled with the elimination of unneeded printing facilities, is expected to save $85 million per year in government printing expense.[11]

Deregulation

Deregulation emerged in Washington on a limited scale in the late 1970s and early 1980s, as Congress and the administrations of President Carter and President Reagan, spurred by public opinion and aggressive lobbying, began limiting the investigatory powers of many agencies and repealing outdated and ineffective rules. Deregulation currently has expanded to include banks, savings and loan associations, and the telecommunications industry as well as all modes of shipping and public transportation. The intent is to encourage the growth of productivity as marketplace incentives fill the gaps left by decreased government regulations.

Following passage of the Airline Deregulation Act of 1978, twenty-two new national and regional airlines started business, compared with none from 1973 through 1978. Several of these new carriers devised interesting market segment appeals by catering to budget-conscious travelers, wealthy "carriage trade" customers, or (in the case of Muse Air) nonsmokers. Long-distance customers also benefited from the epidemic of fare wars that accompanied increased competition. For a short while at least one airline sold one-way tickets between New York and Los Angeles for $99, but such bargains were offset by higher fares and reduced service to smaller cities. Following the shakeout in route changes, a total of seventy-three small towns had regular air service terminated.[12]

Such dramatic changes in operations affected airline workers too. More than 50,000 were laid off, while others approved pay freezes or wage decreases, fewer fringe benefits, and longer work hours. Some airlines gave workers shares of stock in exchange for these concessions to a new, competitive environment.

The deregulation that eliminated the Interstate Commerce Commission's financial requirements to start a trucking company caused the birth of 11,000 of these new firms. Unfortunately such increased competition, aided by a recession in the late 1970s (which decreased shipping volume), triggered a price war that cut truckers' income by as much as 30 percent. Consequently the number of independent truckers declined from almost 300,000 in the late 1970s to 100,000 by the early 1980s.[13] Shippers have realized material gains from trucking deregulation, however, as more companies were forced to compete on price alone. The traffic manager at one large manufacturing plant estimated that his facility saved $1 million in

The Straight Line

Product Piracy

Manufacturers Wage War Against Illegal Reproductions

What do Pineapple computers, Everlight flashlight batteries, and Vansayline hair tonic have in common? They're all pirated products that are deceivingly similar in name and appearance to their trademarked counterparts — Apple computers, Everready batteries, and Vaseline hair tonic. Such fakes, manufactured abroad and marketed in many countries, are causing significant problems for some manufacturers.

Companies that make internationally known products are being victimized by fly-by-night firms that make knockoffs or counterfeits of their brands. The difference, although subtle, is definite. A *knockoff* is a product that's extremely similar: the shape of the container, the name, and the colors on the label are nearly identical to the real thing. A *counterfeit*, on the other hand, is an exact duplicate of a company's product in virtually every detail. Both knockoffs and counterfeits cost bona fide producers a great deal in lost profits, reputation, and legal action to defend their trademarks, while confusing less observant consumers.

Although Korea and Brazil have their share of illicit manufacturing companies, Taiwanese firms are the undisputed leaders in product piracy. The practice has long been ignored or treated leniently there because many Taiwanese government officials and business owners felt U.S. trademark protection on brand names, package colors, and other unique aspects of a company's products unreasonably limited their rights to compete.

No product is immune from being copied. In addition to Apple computers, pirates have duplicated E.T. (the ExtraTerrestrial) dolls, Cartier and Rolex watches, Charlie cologne, and Prince tennis racquets. Although many of these products are sold eventually in Europe or Asia, some find their way into the United States and virtually all of them cost the companies whose products they resemble millions of dollars in lost

shipping costs as deregulation caused cheaper rates. Deregulation has brought intensified price cutting among rail carriers too.

In the financial area, deregulation of banks and savings and loan associations led to a rise in interest rates that benefited thrifty consumers; however, this development had a negative impact on real estate borrowers and the users of bank-sponsored credit cards such as Visa and MasterCard. The breakup of massive American Telephone and Telegraph (see The Straight Line, pages 72–73) is ultimately intended to introduce more competition within the communications industry.

All these deregulatory moves, and many more, indicate that the federal bureaucracy is responding to public and business protest against excessive control. There is also congressional support for a dual system of reporting and inspection based on the size of a business.

profits. Schaper Manufacturing Company, manufacturer of the popular Stomper 4 × 4 four-wheel drive toy truck, claimed that illegal manufacturers of that item cost the firm $30 million in annual sales. Union Carbide reportedly lost half a million dollars in sales owing to knockoffs of its Everready brand batteries, while Kamar International, which owns the rights to manufacture E.T. dolls, believes $3 million worth of illegal dolls have been made and sold worldwide. Illegal reproduction of the many Disney characters reportedly has cost Walt Disney Productions $4 million in royalties from sales by licensed producers each year. The International Anti-Counterfeiting Coalition, a trade group formed to combat product fakery, has estimated that worldwide losses traceable to counterfeit and knockoff products reached $20 billion in 1983.

Damage from product piracy is not confined to dollars, of course. Fraudulent products are rarely as good as their genuine counterparts, so their performance may disappoint consumers who believed they bought a legitimate item. Therefore the reputation of the authentic manufacturer may be criticized unjustly for shoddy performance by fakes.

Large manufacturers wage perpetual war against ersatz products, and the cost of the battle (which may include private investigator's fees) runs high. Union Carbide spent more than $50,000 to track down and prosecute one Taiwanese company; Ideal Toy Corporation's cost to defend trademark rights to Rubik's Cube totaled $5 million; Schaper and the inventor of the Stomper miniature 4 × 4 truck spent a total of $1 million in 1 year to prevent illegal copies from being produced. And, while Taiwan has passed laws that provide much stricter penalties for cheap imitators than previously existed, the underground industry still flourishes in back rooms, sheds, and full-scale production plants throughout the island.

For more about product piracy, see "CPI Fights Counterfeiters of Company Products," *Chesebrough-Pond's World*, Fall 1983, p. 6; Louis Kraar, "Fighting the Fakes From Taiwan," *Fortune*, May 30, 1983, p. 114; and Dennis Kneale, "Toy Companies Starting to Combat the Big Trade in Illegal Imitations," *The Wall Street Journal*, November 15, 1982, p. 31.

Summary

The law in the United States consists of common law, based on the evolution of court decisions from the earliest English courts to the present, and statutory law, a written body of legislated rules. Torts, private or civil wrongs, are tried in civil courts, and crimes, public wrongs, are tried in criminal courts. The three-tiered federal court system allows for appeals of court decisions; most states have a similar court system.

Much of business law is covered by the Uniform Commercial Code, which virtually every state has adopted. The UCC law of contracts specifies what contracts must be written and presents the six elements required for a contract to be valid. The law of agency governs the legal relationship of an agent to the principal he or she represents. The law of sales, which pertains only to new, tangible

1.   JOAN: Have you noticed how friendly AT&T is lately?

2.   Oh sure, now that you have a choice of long distance phone companies it's "Hello. Thank you for calling. Have a nice day."

3.   And why? Grow up. It's not because they love you.

4.   It's because they're afraid you'll do what I did, which is switch to MCI.

5.   Because MCI saves me up to 30, 40, even 50% on long distance calls

6.   to any phone in any other state from coast to coast.

7.   Now that's what I call a friend. Who needs Hello...Hello...

MCI
The nation's long distance phone company.
Toll free
1-800-624-2222

8.   ANNCR: (VO) Call MCI, Joan Rivers and nearly two million others saving up to 30, 40, even 50% on their out-of-state calls.

Can we talk long distance? As deregulation changed the communications industry, companies like MCI jumped at the opportunity to provide telecommunications services that were immune to competition beforehand.

personal property, enumerates several implied warranties that sellers make to buyers.

The UCC's law of property covers both real and personal property. Federal laws govern the ownership and use of intellectual property: patents, trademarks, and copyrights. Inventors apply to the Patent and Trademark Office for a utility patent, a design patent, or a plant patent. Once a patent is awarded, the holder has the right to exclude others from making, selling, or using the item for a fixed length of time. The Patent and Trademark Office also registers trademarks and service marks, which are words, names, symbols, or devices that firms use to identify their products or services and to distinguish them from those of competitors. A copyright, recorded by the Copyright Office of the Library of Congress, guarantees certain rights to persons who create an original work of authorship. The Uniform Commercial Code also deals with the law of negotiable instruments, which affects the transfer of promissory notes, checks, and drafts, and the law of bankruptcy.

Businesses operate within an intricate network of state and federal regulations issued by a variety of regulatory agencies. Regulations are administered by at least 116 different federal agencies and programs. The cost of meeting the reporting requirements of these agencies is eventually paid by the consumer in the form of higher prices. Because living in today's legal environment can be costly, companies are concerned about reducing and streamlining regulatory demands. Companies and individual managers have found that they can respond to excessive regulation by improving self-policing, staying abreast of legislative trends, and lobbying for legislative change. Sympathetic regulators have been able to reduce the burden on businesses by setting regulatory objectives and leaving the choice of methods to business and by creating a system of financial penalties and rewards for affected firms. The federal government itself has demonstrated concern about efficient operations by examining its own management practices with the aid of the Private Sector Survey on Cost Control and the President's Council on Integrity and Efficiency. In response to public opinion and aggressive lobbying, some regulatory agencies have had their powers limited and some regulations have been rescinded. There also has been support for the idea of reducing the burden of regulations on small companies, which are hit especially hard by the cost of compliance.

Key Terms

agent	crime	statutory law
bankruptcy *or* insolvency	negotiable instruments	tort
common law	patent	trademark
contract	principal	Uniform Commercial Code (UCC)
copyright	service mark	warranty

For Review and Discussion

1. Where did our body of common law originate? What is the doctrine on which it is based? How does statutory law differ from common law?

2. What is the difference between a tort and a crime? What is the difference between a personal damage tort and a property tort?

3. Diagram the hierarchy of the federal court system. Which courts conduct jury trials? Which act as buffers? Which concern themselves with procedural errors? Which serves as a last resort for appeals?

4. What advantage does a state receive when it adopts the Uniform Commercial Code?

5. List and define the six elements of a legally binding contract.

6. What four types of contracts must be made in writing? Give the reasons for that requirement in each case.

7. Cite several business transactions that might require the involvement of an agent.

8. Evaluate the following remark about written warranties: "The big print giveth and the small print taketh away." What does it mean? Is it true? If so, what implications does it have for consumers?

9. Discuss the four implied warranties covered in the law of sales. Give examples of business transactions in which each would play an important role.

10. Define the two kinds of property that are covered by the UCC law of property.

11. Discuss the importance of patents, trademarks, and copyrights in a business firm's marketing.

12. What are the principal features of the three kinds of patents? What procedure would an inventor follow to apply for a patent?

13. Do you think the commercial lives of most patents are equal to, less than, or greater than their legal lives? Give reasons for your answer, and cite examples.

14. Under what conditions may secrecy be preferred to patenting? What measures should management take to protect the security of trade secrets?

15. What things can be registered as trademarks? What action can a firm take to prevent its trademark from being used generically?

16. What rights would you enjoy if you copyrighted a commercially valuable work?

17. What three instruments of payment fall under the UCC negotiable instruments law? List the six conditions each such instrument must meet to be negotiable.

18. Describe the conditions under which each of the following indorsements might be used: blank indorsement, special indorsement, restrictive indorsement, and qualified indorsement.

19. Under what circumstances might someone be declared bankrupt?

20. What problems does the federal bureaucracy present for small and large businesses alike?

How does regulation inhibit new product development?

21. Recommend several measures that companies and individual managers can take to reduce the regulatory burden. How might sympathetic regulators fulfill their mandate without placing undue demands on businesses?

Applications

Case 20.1 Licensing: Profitable Characters Earn Millions

A company or person who owns a trademarked character may license others to reproduce that character. Although this practice is nothing new in business law, it has become enormously popular — and extremely profitable — since the early 1980s. In 1 year the creators of trademarked characters made $20.6 billion from royalties paid to them by licensees, while the licensees themselves enjoyed excellent profits selling merchandise with the likenesses of popular characters.

Consider for example Coleco Industries, owner of a license to make products using the Smurfs, conceived by Belgian artist Pierre Culliford. These pleasant little blue characters, who look like a cross between an elf and one of Snow White's seven dwarfs, adorn products ranging from picnic tables to wading pools. They even star in a Coleco video game. Smurf-related products accounted for $650 million in retail sales in one year alone.

Not one to rely on a solitary license, Coleco recently bought a license from creator Xavier Roberts to produce his Cabbage Patch Kids soft sculpture dolls and related products. In almost no time the Cabbage Patch Kids trademarked characters appeared on umbrellas, doll carriers, and various items of children's clothing. Coleco also has the right to license other companies to make Cabbage Patch Kids products, soon to include children's books and lunch kits. Video games and traditional toys and games are in the works as a result of Coleco's license from Dr. Theodor Seuss Geisel to use his famed Dr. Seuss characters.

Then there's E.T. (the ExtraTerrestrial), a charming little space character popularized by the movie of the same name. After appearing at your local theater, he showed up on items made by more than forty firms — dolls, riding vehicles, notebooks, stickers, and so forth. At least one expert predicts that $1 billion worth of E.T.-related products will be sold by the mid-1980s.

Kamar International, the licensee for E.T. dolls, tripled its sales after purchasing the license to make those products.

Some of the best planning on trademarked characters, however, went into development of the Care Bears. Joint products of American Greetings Corporation and General Mills, the Care Bears emerged from hibernation with a $6 million promotional budget. More than twenty-five businesses promptly signed up for licenses to make stuffed bears, drinking mugs, notebooks, bed sheets, lamps, and children's clothing all featuring one or more of these cuddly commercial characters. American Greetings and General Mills have scored previously with the extremely profitable Strawberry Shortcake characters, whose licensees are expected to sell more than half a billion dollars' worth of products by the mid-1980s.

Generally trademark owners receive a royalty rate of between 5 and 15 percent of the retail sales of their licensed characters. The licensing agreement customarily includes a large initial payment to the licensor, but if the characters become a hit with consumers — especially children — both parties may reap handsome rewards from the arrangement.

Questions

1. Defend a licensor's decision to require a multimillion-dollar initial payment before allowing a licensee to reproduce popular cartoon characters or other trademarked items.

2. Respond to the comment: "Licensing is a no-risk deal for the licensor."

3. How can a manufacturer justify spending millions of dollars to obtain a license to use characters such as those referred to in this case?

Case 20.1 For more about licensing, see *Coleco Industries 1982 Annual Report*; "E.T. and Friends Are Flying High," *Business Week*, January 10, 1983, p. 77; Betsy Morris, "More Businesses Licensing Trademarks," *The Wall Street Journal*, October 14, 1982, p. 33; Margaret Yao, "The Marketing of Licensed Characters for Kids, Or How the Lovable Care Bears Were Conceived," *The Wall Street Journal*, September 24, 1982, p. 56; and "MCA Sues to Stop 7 Firms Selling 'E.T.' Products," *The Wall Street Journal*, September 16, 1982, p. 6.

Case 20.2 Manville Corporation: Taking the Heat for Asbestos

Why would a healthy corporation with $1.1 billion in net worth want to file for bankruptcy? In virtually every case, it wouldn't — and under the law it would not be allowed to — but consider the plight of beleaguered Manville Corporation, which makes it somewhat special under bankruptcy law.

Until a decade ago Manville was the free world's largest producer of the insulating material called asbestos. Then the product was proved to cause lung cancer, asbestosis (similar to emphysema), and other respiratory diseases. This news was the catalyst for a monumental epidemic of lawsuits revolving around the product: employees, manufacturers, distributors, and installation companies filed lawsuits against each other that will not be settled for years. Manville, of course, was the target of many because of the company's prominence as a manufacturer. The company was hit with 16,500 product liability lawsuits from persons who had worked with asbestos as far back as World War II. Because asbestos-related diseases may take between 20 and 40 years to materialize, management expected as many as 52,000 lawsuits to be filed as more of the 8 to 11 million workers exposed to asbestos became ill. Nearly all of Manville's insurance companies went to court to avoid paying these massive product liability claims, and the final decision on their responsibility has yet to be made by the courts.

In 1982 Manville reacted to the catastrophe by filing for protection under Chapter 11 of the federal Bankruptcy Code. This tactic was permissible because bankruptcy law will consider the projected cost of future as well as current lawsuits. Manville's lawyers and accountants predicted that legal claims from persons harmed by asbestos would reach $2 billion — more than twice the company's net worth.

Chapter 11 temporarily suspends the settlement of existing and future lawsuits so that management may reorganize the company and work out a way to pay creditors and court-awarded damages. As an added benefit, Chapter 11 protection enables a firm to lump similar claims together and settle them collectively. Manville may therefore avoid defending itself against individual asbestos suits. Following a reorganization plan approved by the court, each plaintiff would receive his or her proportional share of the money allocated to pay all asbestos-related claims.

Although asbestos plaintiffs and their lawyers were incensed at this legal maneuver, it was not intended purely to frustrate their proceedings. With $1.1 billion in net worth and $2 billion in claims anticipated, Manville couldn't pay all asbestos claims even if the company were liquidated, there simply wouldn't be enough money to go around. Furthermore, not having to defend itself against thousands of individual claims saves Manville millions in legal fees, therefore providing more money that may eventually be set aside under bankruptcy proceedings to pay all legitimate asbestos claims. Chapter 11 filing, followed by a negotiated reorganization and claims payment program, means that future asbestos plaintiffs will receive *something* for their injuries. Had the company continued to do business as usual, future claimants would have received nothing as the company's assets were gradually drained away through payment of prior judgments.

The bankruptcy filing has frustrated Manville's creditors too. Their claims for amounts due on open-book accounts and short-term loans are in limbo until a reorganization plan can be worked out and approved by creditors' committees and by the bankruptcy court. Patience is wearing thin. And, while the bankruptcy court's ruling on creditors' claims and asbestos-related payments will be final, it will tend to sympathize with the wishes of a large number of militant creditors who, fed up with delays caused by the bankruptcy maneuver, could vote to liquidate the company for whatever it will bring instead of prolonging work on a reorganization plan.

Questions

1. Do you agree that this company has operated within the spirit as well as the letter of the Bankruptcy Code? Why or why not?

2. Defend the insurance companies' reluctance to pay on product liability policies in this case. Refer to Chapter 15 (Risk and Insurance) if necessary.

3. How would Manville stockholders be affected by a reorganization under bankruptcy proceedings, as compared with liquidation?

Case 20.2 For more about the Manville Corporation bankruptcy, see Dean Rotbart, "Manville Corp. Faces Increasing Opposition to Bankruptcy Filing," *The Wall Street Journal*, January 31, 1984, p. 1; Anna Cifelli, "Management by Bankruptcy," *Fortune*, October 31, 1983, p. 69; Jeremy Bulow, Thomas Jackson, and Robert Mnookin, "Winners and Losers in the Manville Bankruptcy," *The Wall Street Journal*, November 4, 1982, p. 30; Neil Maxwell, G. Christian Hill, and Raymond A. Joseph, "Manville's Big Concern As It Files in Chapter 11 Is Litigation, Not Debt," *The Wall Street Journal*, August 27, 1982, p. 1; "Despite Strong Business, Litigation Forces Manville to File for Reorganization," *The Wall Street Journal*, August 27, 1982, p. 29 (a commentary by Manville Corporation on conditions that led to its bankruptcy filing.); and Craig R. Waters, "The Private War of James Sullivan," *Inc.*, July 1982, p. 41.

The Social and Ethical Environment of Business

Chapter Outline

The Concept of Social Responsibility

The Evolution of Social Responsibility

Enlightened Self-Interest Phase
Social Awareness Phase
Social Responsiveness Phase

Areas for Social Responsibility

Small-Business Investment
Education and Training
Employment Opportunities for Minorities and Women
The Handicapped in Business
Urban Renewal
Community Involvement
Environmental Concerns
Energy Concerns
Employee Health
Consumer Protection

Implementing Social Responsibility: The Commitment

The Ethical Environment of Business

The Ethical Dilemma: What Is Unethical?
Causes of Unethical Practices
What Can Be Done?

Summary

Chapter Objectives

After studying this chapter, you should be able to:

1. Define social responsibility.
2. Explain the evolution of social responsibility.
3. Describe the reasons for, and the socially responsible actions taken by, business in the following areas: small-business investment, education and training, employment opportunities for minorities and women, the handicapped in business, urban renewal, community involvement, environmental concerns, energy concerns, employee health, and consumer protection.
4. Describe the importance of the social audit.
5. Discuss the importance of a personal code of conduct and a company's code of conduct in developing ethical behavior in business.

Business, in partnership with government and other institutions, must be intimately involved in addressing the major unmet needs of society, not as something over and above its normal operations but as an integral part of the business itself.
— William C. Norris, founder, chairman, and chief
executive officer, Control Data Corporation

Zoltan Merszei

Working for Today and Tomorrow

Among the many executives leading major industrial corporations in new directions of social responsibility is Zoltan Merszei, vice-chairman of the board of Occidental Petroleum Company, a California-based multinational conglomerate. While maintaining "Oxy's" successful position in oil, coal, and chemicals, Merszei has expanded its role in pursuing alternative energy sources, contributing to the communities in which Oxy operates and participating actively in the education of tomorrow's citizens.

Oxy spent more than $150 million on environmental programs in 1982. An additional $50 million was spent on environmental control equipment that included a state-of-the-art disposal vault for chemical waste.

Community contributions include agribusiness donations for libraries and ambulance services, particularly in rural communities, and continued support of a child abuse prevention project in Texas. In the area of medical research an annual cash award for cancer research is provided by the Hammer Prize Foundation. A standing award of $1 million has been set aside for the person(s) who discovers a cancer cure similar to Salk's polio vaccine.

In support of education Occidental has an employee matching-funds program for contributions to educational institutions and provides funding for several

Business does not operate in a vacuum, nor are business decisions made without evaluating the total effect of those decisions on the business, on society, and on employees. Today's business firms operate in an environment of interdependence. Society, government, and private enterprise must interact to ensure their mutual survival and success.

Business managers cannot divorce their decisions, objectives, and resources from social and governmental influence. They must pursue their overriding goal of profit within a social and political framework. In this respect, American business is in a pioneering era. It is dealing with relationships and challenges that were either nonexistent or of no concern to managers just a few decades ago.

Modern business is one part of a vast complex of social, governmental, and private enterprise activities. No company, and certainly no industry, can realistically declare itself independent of this interrelatedness or fail to let it influence the decisions of its leaders. The basic dilemma faced by managers is to balance the conflicting demands of these factors as they attempt to allocate and manage their organization's resources.

National Merit scholarships. Oxy's Armand Hammer Foundation financed the sixth United World College with the goal of improving world relations. The first of its kind in the United States, the college began classes in its New Mexico facilities in September 1982 with students from forty-six countries. With the same goal of world peace and understanding in mind, the company supports the Annual Armand Hammer Conference on Peace and Rights.

Merszei takes a personal interest in the education of future business leaders, which he shows by participating in the executive forum of the Krannert School of Management at Purdue University. The school arranges lectures by well-known executives who speak to and socialize with students and faculty. Students are then asked to write critiques of the participants; the most lucid of these reactions are sent on to the speakers. Merszei demonstrates his commitment to this program by responding in writing to each student whose critique he receives. He also views the program as an opportunity for Oxy because he directs the personnel department to contact the most impressive students about possible future employment. Observes Merszei, "I think those of us in the real world should participate in the education of the next generation."

For more about Zoltan Merszei, see *Occidental Petroleum Company 1982 Annual Report*, pp. 32–34; and Paul B. Carroll, "At Purdue Students Rate Executives," *The Wall Street Journal*, April 26, 1982, p. 29.

Just what responsibilities do managers and their organizations have to society? What is the definition of good corporate citizenship? Unfortunately there is no rule book to provide the answers. Companies and their managers must develop their own approaches.

In this chapter we will examine social responsibility, its nature, evolution, and areas of involvement. In addition, we will discuss the ethical climate of business operations.

The Concept of Social Responsibility

The concept of social responsibility is a relatively new business challenge that has evolved over the last few decades. Concerned individuals, special interest groups, and society in general have recognized that business organizations exert considerable influence on the general well-being of society. Regardless of whether the business is confined to a city, spans the nation, or has worldwide operations, there is a recognition that its actions, products, and services

social responsibility

directly affect the environment, the welfare of suppliers, and its customers' standard of living.

As a result of these observations the need has developed for organizations to practice **social responsibility** — *a belief that, as organizations and managers function, their decisions should be made within the confines of both social and economic considerations.* Social responsibility is based on a sincere belief that as a business achieves its ultimate goal of profit it should turn its attention to matters of the public need that it can pursue simultaneously as profitable business opportunities.

An integral element of this concept is the belief that:

— What is good for society is good for the business firm.
— Social objectives actually enhance a firm's profitability over the long term.
— Companies should contribute to healthy social conditions to ensure that the society in which they earn their profits will remain so in the future.
— Business must not only enjoy its social environment but also work to sustain the social home in which it lives. In doing so it builds a hospitable environment for tomorrow's business success.
— Companies with a high social consciousness further their own goals when they help to strengthen the social structure.

Social responsibility as presented here did not happen overnight. It has evolved over a number of years.

The Evolution of Social Responsibility

The concept of social responsibility has three observable stages: enlightened self-interest, social awareness, and social responsiveness. These stages represent degrees of acceptance of social responsibility and levels of involvement by companies.

Enlightened Self-Interest Phase

In this stage professional managers are responsible to the owners and the owners' interests are primary. The only social responsibilities a manager has are to make profits and to obey the law.[1] As recently stated by Nobel Prize winning professor of economics Milton Friedman, managers:[2]

— Are employed by owners to make as much money as possible while conforming to the law and to ethical custom
— Are exclusive agents for their employers and owe primary responsibility to them

– Are agents for stockholders and should not make decisions about social responsibilities and social investments because they represent tax decisions (These matters are government functions.)

In short, social responsibility is not the business of business.

Social Awareness Phase

This stage is referred to as the *hand of government* or the *activist* phase. It is characterized by business firms that follow the letter of the law but not its true intent or spirit. Business does only what it is mandated to do and does that with little enthusiasm. Little League teams are sponsored, managers attend business affairs, and quotas for minorities are set and once reached, minorities are ignored.

Social Responsiveness Phase

In this phase management has recognized that the long-range future of business is dependent on the health and well-being of the society of which it is a part. This view requires that business anticipate possible problems and changes and adopt an active approach to deal with them. Business must understand it is a part of society and that anything that threatens society threatens the future of business.

This phase calls for business to partner with society — with labor, government, and religious and civic groups — in addressing society's needs. It also calls for business to assume the leadership role because it has the majority of the country's technical, financial, managerial, and professional resources. In short, business needs to be proactive, not reactive.

Figure 21.1 presents an overview of the social responsibility continuum. Firms that evolve to the social responsiveness phase focus their energies on specific areas of social responsibility, including small business, education and training, employment opportunities, the handicapped in business, urban renewal, community involvement, environmental concerns, energy concerns, employee health, and consumer protection. Firms that pursue these areas do so with the purpose of investing their energies and resources toward the

Figure 21.1 The Social Responsibility Continuum
Source: Adapted from Grover Starling, *The Changing Environment of Business,* 2nd edition (Boston, Mass.: Kent Publishing Company), 1984, p. 313. © 1984 by Wadsworth, Inc. Reprinted by permission of Kent Publishing Company, a division of Wadsworth, Inc.

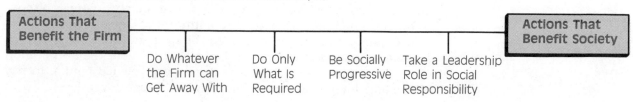

long-range goal of profitability — not as a philanthropic activity. The next section will examine areas for social responsibility.

Areas for Social Responsibility

Small-Business Investment

Businesses have taken a socially active role in providing substantial resources to assist the development of small-business opportunities. Recognizing that a healthy business economy is built on the spirit of free enterprise found in small businesses, major corporations have committed financial, human, and technical resources to aid the formation and profitable growth potential of the small-business sector. Control Data Corporation has developed a wide range of services to assist small business including financial assistance, data-processing services, education and training, management and professional consulting, and technology transfer. In addition, Control Data has established business and technology centers to provide combinations of consulting services. It has shared laboratory, manufacturing, and office facilities, as well as other services to facilitate the start-up and growth of small businesses.[3]

A number of companies, including Control Data, have either partnered with major corporations or formed their own small-business investment corporations (SBICs). These SBICs provide funds to finance the start-up of small business enterprises. Through their investments in SBICs the large corporations in essence take an equity position in the small business of tomorrow.

In addition to the previous programs, businesses have made major commitments to promote the development of minority businesses. Shell Oil Company, General Motors, and other large firms have formed **minority enterprise small-business investment companies (MESBICs),** which are *venture capital firms designed specifically to provide funds to minority-owned small businesses.* Shell has contributed $100,000 to Gulf South Venture Company, a New Orleans MESBIC licensed by the Small Business Administration to provide capital as well as management and technical advice to minority-owned businesses.

minority enterprise small-business investment companies (MESBICs)

The MESBIC Financial Corporation of Dallas has ninety-eight corporate shareholders, including LTV, Texas Instruments, Zale Corporation, International Business Machines (IBM), Xerox, Mobil, Frito-Lay, and Dr. Pepper, plus all the major Dallas banks. In the past 14 years it has been responsible for providing $3.5 million in capital for minority-owned companies; it invested $700,000 in 1983.

Anheuser-Busch, Shell Oil Company, du Pont, and General Motors demonstrate their commitment to minority business by consciously doing business with and maintaining deposits in minority-owned banks. In a program entitled the "National Hispanic Business Agenda," Coca-Cola USA pledged to maintain more than $3 million of deposits and lines of credit with Hispanic-owned banks, to pay $5 million for goods and services from Hispanic vendors, and to set aside $5 million to create Coca-Cola ads in Spanish using Hispanic-owned advertising agencies and broadcast facilities.[4]

Numerous organizations are committed to a minority vendors program. Through this vehicle a major corporation commits to and aids in developing minority suppliers with which to do business. Western Electric, du Pont, and General Motors have actively engaged in and supported this practice.

Education and Training

Another area for social responsiveness of business leaders is in education and job training. Recognizing that the future of their corporations, their communities, and America are directly linked to the opportunities for and quality of education and job training, corporations have committed funds, personnel, and equipment. Wang Laboratories provided the equipment and trained the operators on computer systems it donated to twenty-eight colleges and universities in Massachusetts.[5] Texas Instruments has made significant donations of microcomputers to the Dallas County Community College System for classroom and laboratory use. Companies in all industries, man-

Du Pont participates in twenty trade fairs each year to help develop minority vendors.

ufacturing, retailing, and service continue to support creative co-operative educational programs. The companies provide support, facilities, time, and management expertise in assisting high school and college students to gain both practical experience and an education.

A number of major companies provide ongoing tuition and grant support for higher education. The Exxon Education Foundation recently announced a $15 million program to relieve serious faculty shortages in the engineering field. These funds go to sixty-six colleges and universities to create one hundred teaching fellowships that provide salary support grants for junior faculty. The foundation also gave $1.8 million to the engineering schools of six traditionally black colleges to support faculty development.[6]

Xerox has developed programs to provide for industry and college faculty exchange. The benefit from such a program: current industry practices are brought into the classroom and the college instructors move into the "real life" laboratory for skills updating. In Dallas more than eighty Frito-Lay employees have given their time to two elementary schools.[7] Anheuser-Busch has developed an urban league community college scholarship program for adults who seek a second chance to embark on a new career. Begun in St. Louis, the program has been expanded to Newark and Chicago.[8]

Control Data devised a job training program known as Fair Break that prepares disadvantaged persons to find and keep jobs. Operating in more than 200 locations throughout the country, each center delivers training in basic skills, job readiness, life management, and job seeking skills. Since its inception more than 10,000 students have enrolled with an 83 percent completion rate and an 80 percent job placement rate.[9] Chevron USA made a $325,000 donation to fund a job training program in Oakland, California, for 300 unemployed persons.[10]

Employment Opportunities for Minorities and Women

Business has long had the incentive of affirmative action programs to stimulate the development of employment opportunities for minority groups and women. Spurred on by the concerns of society and the commitment to social responsibility, organizations have been complying beyond the letter of the law. With an eye to the future, companies like Atlantic Richfield, Xerox, and Exxon now recruit minority and women job applicants and provide the opportunity for them to advance into higher-paying positions — especially management ranks — as fast as their ambition, their ability, and job vacancies allow.

For example, minorities currently compose 18 percent of the total work force of Anheuser-Busch. In addition, minorities are heavily involved in management decision-making roles and hold positions on the board of directors of Anheuser-Busch, and of the parent corporation, Anheuser-Busch Companies. At Exxon 17 percent of the work force are minorities and 27 percent are women. The number of minority and women employees who hold managerial and professional jobs has continued to increase.[11]

The St. Paul Companies has developed a number of programs to implement its corporate philosophy — to give each person an opportunity to develop skills and grow professionally. These include:

— A series of informational sessions for supervisors conducted by the Employee Relations and Communication Departments titled Management Briefing Live. The purpose: to provide goals and directions for hiring and developing qualified minorities and women.

— A 3-day program called "Men and Women Moving Up" designed to build supervisory and communication skills by focusing on the issues of men and women communicating and interacting in the work setting.

— A 4-day program entitled "Seminar for Minority Professionals" targeted at minority employees who hold technical and professional positions. The seminar is intended to increase participants' awareness of their skills, values, and the overall corporate environment.[12]

The Handicapped in Business

Another area of social concern for business is the employment of handicapped workers. Businesses that contract with the government are required by federal law to hire handicapped workers and to make their facilities accessible to handicapped employees. But, even without legislative encouragement, many large companies are committed to both hiring handicapped workers and modifying the physical work environment to accommodate handicapped workers.

The Joseph Bulova School, which teaches watch repair to handicapped workers, reports that they have seen "an incredible change" in employer attitudes toward hiring the handicapped. Employers not only have actively recruited workers; Control Data Corporation, IBM, Walgreen Company, and several Chicago banks have taught handicapped employees to write computer programs at home. Other companies have employed handicapped persons as typists or in other jobs that can be performed more conveniently at home.[13]

Employers have voluntarily accommodated the special needs of handicapped employees by installing wheelchair ramps and electric doors; lowering elevator button panels, pay telephones, and water fountains; widening doorways; and providing wider than usual handicapped parking spaces close to buildings. IBM employees have designed new cafeteria trays made to fit on wheelchairs, and Sears has installed a dog walk for its blind workers' seeing eye dogs.[14]

Urban Renewal

Another area for business commitment has been as a community citizen. Rather than deserting troubled cities at the first signs of urban decay, many firms now channel their resources toward **urban revitalization programs,** *intensive efforts by large businesses to*

urban revitalization programs

Companies continue to provide expanded job horizons for the handicapped.

build new offices or plants or refurbish old ones in cities, thus providing new jobs and improving the city's economic health.

Corporate involvement in urban renewal is at least 2 decades old. Hallmark built the $400 million Crown Center in Kansas City, Missouri, in 1968, and 4 years before that Alcoa constructed a shopping complex and housing development in Pittsburgh. Responding to the inner-city riots that broke out in several large cities in 1967 and 1968, Control Data Corporation built five manufacturing plants in the heart of such cities as Minneapolis, St. Paul, and Washington, D.C., which provide employment for more than 1,400 persons, many of whom were once considered hard-core unemployed.

In an ambitious undertaking, Control Data, several other corporations, and two church organizations created City Venture Corporation. City Venture plans and manages comprehensive programs for the revitalization of urban centers. Its approach stipulates that plans for restoring a community must be based primarily on meeting the needs of residents for high quality, accessible, and affordable education and training, and more importantly their needs for decent jobs. During its existence City Venture has promoted numerous projects. Government-funded contracts have been obtained for programs in Minneapolis, Toledo, Philadelphia, Baltimore, St. Paul, Charleston, South Carolina, San Antonio, Benton Harbor, Michigan, Miami, and the South Bronx.[15]

Community Involvement

Business organizations have come to identify more closely with the communities in which they do business. They recognize that the health and well-being of the community are major factors in recruiting and retaining talented employees. As a result community involvement

Control Data and other large corporations have made commitments to large programs of urban revitalization.

works to the advantage of corporate citizens, local residents, and the city itself. Community involvement is exhibited both through providing leadership and through multiple means of support.

- The organizing campaigns for initiating mass transportation programs in southern cities of the United States have been strategically guided and publicly led by major community business leaders.
- The last three mayors of Dallas, Texas, have been presidents of major businesses in that city. In essence, each has taken a leave of absence from corporate commitments to provide management expertise to the public sector.
- Business leaders have undertaken leadership roles in local charitable programs. By being able to network (interact) with other business leaders a number of programs have received valuable support. Figure 21.2 provides an example of this commitment.

Business has recognized that making investments in the community is good business.

Environmental Concerns

A major area of concern for business has been the environment. Environmental preservation, maintenance, and restoration must rank high on any corporation's list of social concerns. The advent of synthetic chemical compounds and materials and of exotic manufacturing processes means that our environment is no longer self-cleansing. Firms that produce damaging waste must be held re-

Figure 21.2 Example of Commitment to Community Involvement
Source: Courtesy Willow Distributors, Inc.

Help The Hungry In Dallas Survive

WILLOW DISTRIBUTORS, INC.

Coors BEER DISTRIBUTORS
2601 COCKRELL, P.O. BOX 15491
DALLAS, TEXAS 75215
214/426-5636

March 11, 1984

Dear Caring Dallas:

The North Texas Food Bank is supported by many caring businesses and organizations in the Dallas area. It supplies food to the underprivileged through many charitable groups such as Meals on Wheels, the Red Cross, the Salvation Army, area churches and many other charitable organizations.

Many people would go hungry, and in some cases - starve, without the help of contributors. These contributors supply the food bank with canned goods and staple foods. But with the beginning of a new year, the shelves have been emptied due to extra holiday giving, and the supply is now at an all time low.

On behalf of Willow Distributors, Inc., I ask you to assist us in replenishing the North Texas Food Bank canned goods supply.

Over 2400 retailers in this area have allowed us to place a box and poster requesting your support in prominent positions within their stores. We hope as you visit these stores that you will donate one or more canned goods to this worthy cause. Route salesman will pick up the contributed canned goods during the first week of April.

We thank you for helping the needy people in Dallas. A recent article in the Dallas Morning News indicated 30,000 children are hungry in our city.

Yours faithfully,

Bill Barrett

Bill Barrett
Executive Vice President
WILLOW DISTRIBUTORS, INC.

P.S. If you are interested in helping the North Texas Food Bank sponsor a canned goods drive, contact Dub Nelson at 330-1396.

sponsible for its safe disposal. Experience and mistakes with waste disposal over the last 3 decades have shown that waste cannot be thrown away. Unless it is converted into usable material or neutralized, all a company can do is shift the disposal burden to someone else. Perhaps the most bizarre evidence of this pass-the-buck pollution occurred on June 22, 1969, when in a now legendary display of pollutant power, the Cuyahoga River, which flows through Cleveland, Ohio, caught fire. The flames were fueled by oil and other combustible matter that ran into the river from various industrial plants lining its banks.

Industrial Wastes. According to recent estimates, industrial operations produce 41 million tons of hazardous waste each year, an average of 13.8 tons for each square mile of land mass in the forty-eight contiguous states. While generating products that benefit consumers in various ways, many manufacturing processes produce toxic chemical waste faster than it can be disposed of. Farsighted business leaders see this and give more than lip service to environmental concerns.

Environmental Maintenance. In addition to the disposal of solid waste problems, industry has another major social concern: overall environmental maintenance and protection. Our rivers have become polluted, our air contaminated, and our land resources have suffered. What has business done in answer to these problems?

"Now they say we can't dump our industrial wastes in the river anymore! My God! What's a river for?!?"
Source: From *The Wall Street Journal*, permission Cartoon Features Syndicate.

The once polluted Naugatuck River in Connecticut has been cleaned up by a combination of environmentalists and the industries that function along the river.[16] Companies like Phillips Petroleum and Shell Oil Company have made major commitments to replenish the earth by carefully planning drilling sites with an eye to maintaining the ecological environment. Major concerns still need to be addressed, such as pollution through acid rain and dioxin contamination.

Another attempt at environmental maintenance has been **recycling,** *the practice of reclaiming or producing materials from previously manufactured products and using them to make other items.* It is common in the aluminum, glass, steel, and paper industries. Armco has produced shredders that can reduce a junked car into chunks of recyclable steel fragments that fit nicely into the furnaces at the firm's steel mills. Armco claims to have recycled more than 800,000 automobiles in 1 year.

recycling

Kimberly-Clark has six of these bobbing aerators installed on the Miami River. They are part of the company's water treatment system at its paper plant in Moraine, Ohio.

Recycling opportunities exist in all areas of a business. Instead of discarding its cocoa-bean hulls, Hershey Foods Corporation reportedly grinds them up and sells them as garden mulch. Fiberboard and pressboard made from sawdust and wood chips enable economy-minded forest products firms to convert virtually every splinter of a tree into a salable product. In some manufacturing plants, heat from production processes is cycled through the heating system to heat the building. The Adolph Coors brewery once generated most of its needed electricity from recycled waste materials. The cumulative effects of recycling are impressive:

- Mississippi River water is used at least eight times on its journey to the Gulf of Mexico.
- Forty percent of all new copper is made from recycled copper.
- Twenty percent of the glass we use comes from recycled scraps and shards that are melted down and mixed with new material.

Energy Concerns

Social responsibility extends to the area of energy conservation. The rising cost of energy hits hard those large companies whose monthly utility bills run into the tens of thousands of dollars. Such companies attempt, if possible, to secure adequate supplies of energy in advance, perhaps through captive sources. United States Steel, for example, which derives 70 percent of its energy from coal, obtains two-thirds of its coal from company-owned mines, making it almost 50 percent self-sufficient on energy supplies. du Pont and various other firms have created top executive positions to deal with creating and obtaining adequate energy supplies to ensure smooth, uninterrupted operations.

Companies have addressed the energy situation with a variety of alternatives. A promising but expensive windmill experiment is being run by Pacific Gas & Electric Company (PG&E) 40 miles northeast of San Francisco. The firm has contracted with Boeing Company to manufacture and install a 200-foot tubular steel tower capped with a turbine generator that will produce 2,500 kilowatts of electricity in winds above 27 1/2 miles per hour. If this $10 million pilot project succeeds, PG&E plans to add 80,000 more kilowatts of wind-generated electricity by 1990. The experiment could lead to colonies, or farms, of windmills erected where prevailing winds are high enough.[17]

For more than 75 years, Great Northern Nekoosa Corporation burned fuel oil to fire its boilers in two Maine pulp and paper mills. During that time, each plant accumulated a 15-acre pile of scrap bark 60 feet deep that smoldered and stank year round. When fuel costs rose, management decided to build a $36 million boiler at one plant to burn the bark as fuel. The solution not only removes a smelly eyesore, it saves 800,000 barrels of oil per year. Because the stockpile of fuel is expected to last 15 years, the company will reap the advantages for a long time.[18]

To conserve energy some firms encourage **van pooling,** *an*   van pooling
energy conservation measure whereby employees are asked to
commute to work in groups using their own vans or those supplied
by the company. This practice also reduces traffic congestion. The
Baltimore plant of Control Data has provided a dozen vans to ferry
managerial employees to work from various pickup points on the
outskirts of the city, which saves an estimated 2 million miles of
passenger car driving and 34,000 gallons of gasoline a year. Conoco,
which has used van pooling for a decade, owns a fleet of more than
a hundred vans. By substituting them for the more than 800 private
autos that employees would otherwise drive to work, the program
saves nearly a million gallons of gasoline every year.

Employee Health

For humanitarian reasons, and not just to protect an investment
or save on insurance bills, many companies promote healthful living
habits and even pay employees for observing them. Antismoking
campaigns head the list of corporate health activities. A Dartnell
Institute of Business Research survey disclosed that nearly a third
of the companies in the United States have developed antismoking
policies that either flatly prohibit smoking on company premises
or confine it to designated areas. This survey also indicated that 3
percent of all firms actually pay workers not to smoke. Obviously,
larger companies may have trouble identifying those who break
their pledge, but in firms where all the employees know one another
management can implement a quit-smoking campaign with some
degree of success. The president of Cybertek Computer Products,
estimating that time lost because of smoking amounted to 3 percent
of an employee's yearly salary, offered workers $500 apiece to quit
smoking. Houston-based Neon Electric Corporation battled smoking
by banning ashtrays and smoking on its premises and giving all
who quit a raise of $0.50 an hour. Westminster Business Systems
in Illinois added *nonsmoker* to all its job specifications several years
ago, while allowing smokers who were employed before that to smoke
only in designated areas.

Some employers pay membership fees in health clubs and the
YMCA as yet another incentive to remain physically fit. Integral Data
Systems offers its employees a discount of at least 20 percent on
membership fees at a local health club by making the initial payment.
Integral's discount program cost about $10,000 in 1982. "That's a
relatively small price to pay for what we get in return," according
to Sara Joyce, Integral's personnel director.[19]

Consumer Protection

In recent years another major area of concentration for businesses
has been consumer protection. To genuinely partner with society
businesses can no longer simply produce a product and place it on
the market. Consumer protection involves both product safety and
providing consumer information.

Product Safety. Businesses have spent time and money to improve the safety of products. Spurred on by the fear of lawsuits and consumer action, business has initiated a number of innovative ideas to ensure product safety.

Companies spend millions of dollars researching the safety of products. The auto industry has developed padded dashboards, shock-absorbing steering columns, and stronger gasoline tanks to improve consumer safety. Companies also have delayed the release of products until conclusive results of testing have been obtained, initiated product recalls when their testing has discovered problems, and attempted to identify product purchasers to make these recalls less difficult.

Consumer Information. Companies have become more sensitive to the needs of consumers for product information. A number of organizations have established toll-free numbers for consumers to use to solve operating problems or receive product advice. In addition, companies have co-sponsored with retailers workshops or clinics where consumers can see demonstrations of products and receive answers to their questions. Finally, companies have packaged extensive operating instructions, safety procedures, and practical uses of products to be provided to consumers at the time of purchase.

Implementing Social Responsibility: The Commitment

The organization that accepts the view that it has obligations to persons other than its insiders and makes managerial decisions on every level from this point of view is an organization that is socially responsible. Its leadership at the top demonstrates this by taking the lead in meeting social challenges. Implementing social responsibility entails three events:

- Fixing the area of social responsibility in the organization
- Developing policies for implementing socially responsible programs
- Auditing the results of its efforts

Pause and Ponder

Identify a company in your community that is considered socially responsive. What areas of social responsibility is the company involved in? How do these efforts affect the community? How is this company viewed by the community for its actions?

When an organization is truly committed to meeting its social responsibilities, it reflects that commitment in its routine approaches to management decision making and its ongoing planning operation. Figure 21.3 presents an illustration of an organization's policy for social responsibility.

For social responsibility to be truly effective in an organization it needs the backing of all managers. It needs to be part of daily operations, not subordinate to them. The manager needs to know what is being done in terms of social responsibility, what can be expected in the future, and what results have been for past actions and plans. The means of achieving this is the **social audit,** *a report on the social performance of a business.* It is becoming standard procedure for many of our nation's largest businesses. Although no standard format exists, the social audit usually includes a summary of corporate activities under these headings: charitable contributions, support of local community groups and activities, employment of women, minorities, and the handicapped, pollution control, support for minority enterprises, and efforts to improve the health and quality of work life for employees.

social audit

Progress may be stated in terms of goals set and met as well as in monetary terms. Those who benefit are clearly labeled, and the extent to which they benefit is quantified when possible. The results of the social audit should be shared with all employees so that awareness of the commitment to and success of programs can be reinforced.

The Ethical Environment
of Business

Whenever two parties interact in business the quality of their relationship — the honest exchange of information, the openness, the "on the table" discussions — are the result of two forces: the

In developing policies governing social actions, companies are reexamining their profit concepts. The following profit objective statement is suggested for companies reevaluating their responsibilities:

> It is the policy of the company to take action in the name of social responsibilities but not at the expense of the rising profit level required to maintain the economic strength and dynamism desired by top management. Actions taken in the name of social responsibility should enhance the economic strength of the company and/or the business community. The overall mission of the company is two pronged: to set forth and achieve corporate objectives both internally and externally, that meet specified social challenges in areas ranging from product quality to quality of life; and to increase the company's earnings per share at a rate that meets shareowner/profit expectations *and* these new social requirements.

A number of companies have adopted similar profit policy statements.

Figure 21.3 A Recommended Policy to Govern Business Social Actions
Source: George A. Steiner, "Institutionalizing Corporate Social Decisions," *Business Horizons,* December 1975. Copyright, 1975, by the Foundation for the School of Business at Indiana University. Reprinted by permission.

ethics

laws that govern the transaction and their ethics. **Ethics** are *the standards that govern moral conduct.* They have been narrowly referred to by people as "individual codes of conduct," "being honest," "fair play," and a "person's value system."

Regardless of how ethics are defined, they play a significant role in the business environment. Laws cannot and should not be developed to govern all business interactions. If this is the case, then people must rely on the ethical practices of others to ensure the open conduct of business.

The Ethical Dilemma: What Is Unethical?

Ethics in the business world creates a dilemma for people. What makes a practice unethical? An action that is simply shrewd to one manager may be unethical to another. Practices in an organization that managers might condemn in profitable times might not seem so offensive when a firm is battling for its financial survival, with thousands of jobs and the welfare of supplier firms hanging in the balance. The following are some situations governed by ethics. What are your reactions to each situation?

— The company allows 20-minute coffee breaks. All the members of department *A* take 30 minutes or more. What would you do?
— The head buyer for the company has been receiving gifts from vendors, a practice frowned on by the company. What would you do?
— As a potential major supplier to an electronics corporation you have been assured that shipments can be made if the "right arrangements are made" (kickbacks). What would you do?
— A business acquaintance who has personally guaranteed business loans states that he will "file personal bankruptcy before he will pay off the loans." What do you think?
— A person in a land development company who sees company plans to purchase large undeveloped farm lands immediately purchases some. What do you think?
— A loan officer in a bank grants a friend a loan at 0.5 percent less than other loans are made. What do you think?

Causes of Unethical Practices

What causes unethical conduct in business? Although the cause of every unethical action cannot be identified, one of the major causes appears to be pressure on middle managers to execute top management's expectations. In a survey that guaranteed their anonymity, a group of Pitney-Bowes managers disclosed that they felt pressured to sacrifice their personal ethical standards to reach certain corporate objectives. Two specific, supporting illustrations show managers who altered company records to reach company goals.

Believing that his job and those of 300 employees were at stake, the manager of a glass plant altered records to show a 33 percent

---

Pause and Ponder

Think of a newspaper story or news event reported on television that involved the ethical practices of a business. Was the action of the company illegal or unethical? What factors were reported that led to this activity? What would you do if you were in the same situation?

---

increase in production. But instead of destroying the true records, a janitor hid them behind a chicken coop and gave them to the company's internal auditors. The manager was fired, and the company had to recalculate its financial statements for the preceding 2 years to adjust for the effects of his deception.[20]

Glenmore Distilleries Company decreased its earnings in one fiscal year by $0.51 per share because a manager in the barrel-making division, under pressure to achieve production goals, had falsified inventory data to inflate actual production. Investigating a rumor, company officials found that inventory tags had been altered. The manager resigned after admitting what he had done.[21]

Competition also can be a cause of unethical business practices. Some firms slip into questionable business practices as a way to keep pace with competitors, who may in turn have established their dominant market position by using under-the-table practices to attract and retain large numbers of important customers. Companies on the edge of bankruptcy may employ dubious means to get or keep customers whose business can make the difference between survival and financial failure.

What Can Be Done?

From a business standpoint it is undesirable to legislate ethics. Ethics and ethical practices can be influenced from two major sources: personal and company codes of conduct.

Personal Codes of Conduct. An individual's personal value system is the greatest influence on the businessperson as he or she conducts business transactions. These personal codes of conduct, developed through home environment and personal experience, are the best barometers of "business right and wrong." Companies hire employees as well as their value systems and with these comes a code of ethical behavior.

Company Codes of Conduct. The actions of subordinate managers and company actions reflect the standards, attitudes, and values of top management. Its willingness to condone or to ignore ethically questionable activities becomes an unwritten code in itself. In a recent survey of middle managers the respondents believed that top management is primarily responsible for setting the ethical tone of the company and that enforcement should be directed primarily at top executives. Why? The same survey also revealed that it was the perception of lower-level managers that those at the top knew about violations at the time they occurred or soon after.[22]

code of ethics

Many companies have addressed the problem by developing a written **code of ethics,** *formal guidelines for the ethical behavior of individuals in an organization, job, or profession.* An Opinion Research Corporation survey of 241 companies disclosed that 73 percent had written codes of ethics, half of which had been developed since the mid-1970s. These codes are only effective if companies live by them. The fact that a company has developed a code but ignores its presence in the conduct of business creates a question of credibility. Figure 21.4 presents an illustration of a company's policy on business ethics.

Aids to Ethical Conduct. In addition to personal codes and business codes of conduct, the support of other organizations is necessary to focus attention on ethical practices. These include the efforts of fraternal and professional organizations to promote ethical practice. For example, Delta Nu Alpha, a fraternity of transportation industry executives, and the Instutute of Internal Auditors, a professional organization of auditors, are actively involved in promoting ethical practice. The ethics code of the Institute of Internal Auditors appears in Figure 21.5.

Industry's continued support for the teaching of ethics courses and seminars in business schools is necessary. Both managers and college professors feel that discussing ethical problems in an academic setting lays the foundation for building and maintaining workable standards when students enter the real world of business.

Industry needs to develop guidelines for everyday relations with customers, suppliers, and government regulators. Kaiser Aluminum and Chemical Corporation has attempted to clarify and minimize such conflicts by having employees fill out the questionnaire shown in Figure 21.6.

Firms also must involve middle-level managers in corporate planning. The Mead Corporation, a manufacturer of folding boxes, attempts to reduce pressure on middle managers by involving more of them in top-level goal-setting and planning sessions. These sessions are intended to set goals that are attainable with effort but without violating ethical standards and criminal laws. Mead's top management also studies the ways in which the company's earlier goals were met, something that firms have ignored in the past.[24] This enlightened philosophy could be a model for companies to follow in setting realistic goals that reduce the pressures that often lead to wrongdoing.

Summary

Today's business firms operate in an environment of interdependence with society and government. Out of this interdependence has come the realization that they must pursue their overriding goal of profit

Policy on Business Ethics

The policy of this Corporation, as stated by the Board of Directors years ago and reaffirmed by the Board at its September 1975 meeting, is one of strict observance of all laws applicable to its business.

Our policy does not stop there. Even where the law is permissive, Exxon chooses the course of the highest integrity. Local customs, traditions, and mores differ from place to place, and this must be recognized. But honesty is not subject to criticism in any culture. Shades of dishonesty simply invite demoralizing and reprehensible judgments. A well-founded reputation for scrupulous dealing is itself a priceless company asset.

An overly ambitious employee might have the mistaken idea that we do not care how results are obtained, as long as he gets results. He might think it best not to tell higher management all that he is doing, not to record all transactions accurately in his books and records, and to deceive the Corporation's internal and external auditors. He would be wrong on all counts.

We do care how we get results. We expect compliance with our standard of integrity throughout the organization. We will not tolerate an employee who achieves results at the cost of violation of laws or unscrupulous dealing. By the same token, we will support, and we expect you to support, an employee who passes up an opportunity or advantage which can only be secured at the sacrifice of principle.

Equally important, we expect candor from managers at all levels, and compliance with accounting rules and controls. We don't want liars for managers, whether they are lying in a mistaken effort to protect us or to make themselves look good. One of the kinds of harm which results when a manager conceals information from higher management and the auditors is that his subordinates think they are being given a signal that company policies and rules, including accounting and control rules, can be ignored whenever inconvenient. This can result in corruption and demoralization of an organization. Our system of management will not work without honesty, including honest bookkeeping, honest budget proposals, and honest economic evaluation of projects.

It has been and continues to be Exxon's policy that all transactions shall be accurately reflected in its books and records. This, of course, means that falsification of its books and records and any off-the-record bank accounts are strictly prohibited.

Figure 21.4 Business Ethics
Source: Reprinted from *Ethics and Responsible Behavior*, Exxon Corporation employee booklet, January 1979, pp. 4–5. Courtesy Exxon Corporation.

within a social and political framework. This in turn has led to an emphasis on social responsibility — the belief that as organizations and managers function their decisions should be made within the confines of both social and economic considerations.

The concept of social responsibility has evolved over a number of years. There are three stages of social responsibility: the enlightened self-interest phase, the social awareness phase, and the social responsiveness phase. In the last phase business focuses its energies on a number of socially important concerns.

Business has taken a socially active role in providing substantial

The Certified Internal Auditor has an obligation to the profession, management, and stockholders and to the general public to maintain high standards of professional conduct. In recognition of this obligation, The Institute of Internal Auditors, Inc., adopted this Code of Ethics for Certified Internal Auditors.

Adherence to this Code, which is based on the Code of Ethics for members of The Institute, is a prerequisite to maintaining the designation Certified Internal Auditor. A Certified Internal Auditor who is judged by the Board of Directors of The Institute to be in violation of the provisions of the Code shall forfeit the Certified Internal Auditor designation.

Preamble

The provisions of this Code of Ethics cover basic principles in the various disciplines of internal auditing practice. Certified Internal Auditors shall realize that their individual judgment is required in the application of these principles. They have a responsibility to conduct themselves in a manner so that their good faith and integrity should not be open to question. Furthermore, they shall use the "Certified Internal Auditor" designation with discretion and in a dignified manner, fully aware of what the designation denotes and in a manner consistent with all statutory requirements. While having due regard for the limit of their technical skills, they will promote the highest possible internal auditing standards to the end of advancing the interest of their company or organization.

Articles

I. Certified Internal Auditors shall have an obligation to exercise honesty, objectivity and diligence in the performance of their duties and responsibilities.

II. Certified Internal Auditors, in holding the trust of their employer, shall exhibit loyalty in all matters pertaining to the affairs of the employer or to whomever they may be rendering a service. However, a Certified Internal Auditor shall not knowingly be a party to any illegal or improper activity.

III. Certified Internal Auditors shall refrain from entering into any activity which may be in conflict with the interest of their employer or which would prejudice their ability to carry out objectively their duties and responsibilities.

IV. Certified Internal Auditors shall not accept a fee or a gift from an employee, a client, a customer or a business associate of their employer without the knowledge and consent of senior management.

V. Certified Internal Auditors shall be prudent in their use of information acquired in the course of their duties. They shall not use confidential information for any personal gain or in a manner which would be detrimental to the welfare of their employer.

VI. Certified Internal Auditors, in expressing an opinion, shall use all reasonable care to obtain sufficient factual evidence to warrant such expression. In reporting, Certified Internal Auditors shall reveal such material facts known to them which, if not revealed, could either distort the report of the results of operations under review or conceal unlawful practice.

VII. Certified Internal Auditors shall continually strive for improvements in the proficiency and effectiveness of their service.

Figure 21.6 Kaiser Aluminum's Employee Questionnaire on Conflicts of Interest
Source: Courtesy Kaiser Aluminum & Chemical Corporation.

DEFINITIONS

1. **"Kaiser Aluminum or its Affiliates"** means Kaiser Aluminum & Chemical Corporation and all corporations and other entities in which Kaiser Aluminum & Chemical Corporation owns beneficially 20 percent or more of the total equity interest.

2. **"Supplier"** means anyone (other than Kaiser Aluminum or its Affiliates) who, during the period covered, has sold, rented, or furnished materials, equipment, or services or any other thing of value to Kaiser Aluminum or its Affiliates either directly or indirectly, such as in the capacity of a subcontractor or subvendor.

3. **"Customer"** means anyone (other than Kaiser Aluminum or its Affiliates) who, during the period covered, has purchased, rented, or otherwise acquired products, equipment, services, or any other thing of value from Kaiser Aluminum or its Affiliates.

4. **"Family Group"** means you, your spouse, and any children or other relative of yours or your spouse living in your household. The term also includes any other relative of yours by blood or marriage of whom you have any knowledge, information, or belief with respect to the subject matter of this questionnaire.

5. **"Material"** means any investment or interest which in the case of the Family Group as a whole equals or exceeds the lesser of (a) one percent of the estimated value of the outstanding securities or net worth of the Supplier or Customer or (b) a value of $25,000.

QUESTION 1: Does your Family Group now have or has it had at any time, during the period covered, any material investment or interest in any Supplier or Customer? Yes ☐ No ☐

QUESTION 2: Is there now, or has there been during the period covered, any creditor-debtor relationship existing between your Family Group and any Supplier or Customer (other than for the purchase by your Family Group of goods or services at prices and upon terms and conditions applicable to the public generally)? Yes ☐ No ☐

QUESTION 3: At any time, during the period covered, has any member of your Family Group received from any Supplier or Customer or from any employee, agent, or representative of a Supplier or Customer, or from any person acting for a Yes ☐ No ☐

Supplier or Customer, any commission, fee, compensation or remuneration of any kind (other than salary or wages received by another member of the Family Group for services performed at rates customary for such services)?

QUESTION 4: At any time, during the period covered, has any member of your Family Group received from any Supplier or Customer or from any employee, agent, or representative of a Supplier or Customer, or from any person acting for a Supplier or Customer, any vacation trips, gifts or benefits of any kind (other than meals or entertainment which did not continue beyond one day, or gifts or gratuities with a value not in excess of $100)? Yes ☐ No ☐

QUESTION 5: At any time, during the period covered, has any member of your Family Group engaged directly or indirectly in any business venture or dealings of any nature whatsoever with any Supplier or Customer or any employee, agent, or representative of a Supplier or Customer, or with a person acting on behalf of a Supplier or Customer (except transactions in which you were acting solely on behalf of Kaiser Aluminum or its Affiliates, and except transactions involving the purchase by your Family Group of goods or services at prices and upon terms and conditions applicable to the public generally)? Yes ☐ No ☐

QUESTION 6: At any time, during the period covered, has any member of your Family Group been a director, officer, consultant, agent, employee, or representative of, or acted in any capacity for, any Supplier or Customer? Yes ☐ No ☐

QUESTION 7: At any time, during the period covered, has any member of your Family Group had any direct or indirect financial or business relationship with any Supplier, Customer, or other party which has not been disclosed in the answers to any of the preceding questions and which might reasonably be considered to be or to occasion a conflict of interest with Kaiser Aluminum or its Affiliates? Yes ☐ No ☐

(If your answer to any of the foregoing questions is yes, furnish as a separate attachment full and complete details on each investment or interest, transaction, or circumstance involved.)

_____
Date

_____
Signature

The Straight Line

Control Data Corporation

Addressing Social Needs

In September 1982 Control Data Corporation, in cooperation with the American Academy of Arts and Sciences, hosted a conference entitled "Social Needs and Business Opportunities." More than 200 business, government, and academic leaders from around the world discussed the ramifications of addressing the major unmet needs of society as profitable business opportunities.

Peter Drucker, who served as a consultant to the conference, drew some comparisons to make his point in one of the keynote speeches: Andrew Carnegie and Julius Rosenwald represent the two classic corporate approaches to social need. Carnegie made his fortune, then spent the rest of his life endowing libraries: he did well in order to do good. Rosenwald, who purchased Sears at a low ebb in the company's history, realized something had to be done to raise the earning (and buying) power of rural Americans — so he invented the county agent system and the 4-H Club. Sears ran the county system for 3 years before the government recognized its worth and took it over. Rosenwald succeeded in his goal and Sears benefited: he did good in order to do well.

According to Drucker, William C. Norris, founder and chairman of the board of Control Data, represents a third and absolutely necessary alternative. Rosenwald applied the resources of a corporation to the marketplace, but he did it indirectly. Norris applies those resources directly: the business strategy of Control Data is to address the major unmet needs of society as profitable business opportunities.

This strategy means something more than corporate philanthropy or voluntarism — it means investment. The concepts are quite

resources to assist the development of small-business opportunities. Major corporations have committed financial, human, and technical resources to aid the formation and profitable growth of the small-business sector.

Business leaders have made commitments to education and training. Recognizing that the future of their corporations, their communities, and America are directly linked to the opportunities for and quality of education and job training, corporations have provided funds, personnel, and equipment.

Beyond the letter of the law, business organizations are committed to the development of employment opportunities for minorities and women. These opportunities include not only active recruitment but also special employment seminars, internships, and programs to facilitate retention and promotional opportunities.

Business has committed to both hiring handicapped workers and modifying the physical environment to accommodate them. Companies have initiated programs to employ handicapped workers who work at home.

simple (their enactment is not). First, business must play a load ership role in addressing social needs, because business has the vast majority of the country's financial, technical, managerial, and professional resources. Second, none of the needs can be adequately addressed by any one business or any one sector of society alone — they must be cooperatively addressed by business, government, educational institutions, religious organizations, labor unions, community groups, and so on. Third, business involvement must be profit driven — there must be a reason for business to apply the full breadth of its resources to an area of need.

Of course, the profits will not be short term, and that is one of the reasons Norris has had such difficulty getting other corporations to follow Control Data's lead, although some are now doing so.

The investments Control Data, City Venture, and others are making today often will not bear fruit for a decade or more, but in Norris's view, they will be the foundation of corporate survival well into the twenty-first century. In his mind, addressing complex social needs such as job creation, education, and training for the disadvantaged and people with physical handicaps, health care, assistance to small business, and urban and rural revitalization is no different than addressing the need for food by putting soup in a can and selling it for a profit — it's just that the process is more difficult.

The important thing to understand is that the emerging businesses in which Control Data has become involved are part of an overall information services strategy that capitalizes on all the resources the corporation has assembled during the past 25 years.

Information supplied by Control Data Corporation, March 1984.

Recognizing that the lifeblood of their companies is founded in the communities in which they function, companies have become involved in community programs and urban renewal projects. Major accomplishments have been made in urban revitalization, the arts, and local charity programs.

Although a long way from perfection, businesses have become more concerned with environmental concerns. They have focused attention on disposal of industrial wastes and environmental maintenance of air, land, and water resources.

Business has initiated programs to support energy conservation. Not only has business attempted alternative sources of energy, but also it has initiated programs to reduce energy consumption through improved operations and van pooling.

Many companies have established programs designed to maintain and improve their employees' health. These programs include attempts to discourage smoking and encourage physical exercise.

Consumer protection has been a major concern for business. Companies have concentrated on product safety improvement and

637

programs providing consumer information to accomplish this objective.

Ethics are the standards that govern moral conduct. They have been referred to as individual codes of conduct, being honest, fair play, and a person's value system. Ethics are important because they affect all business transactions. The problem in the business environment is that ethics have been modified by changing situations. Pressure to perform and the actions of competitors have resulted in business managers displaying unethical behavior. For a positive code of ethics to be practiced, there is a dependence on the person's code of ethics and the development and reinforcement of a company's code of ethics.

Key Terms

code of ethics

ethics

minority enterprise small-
    business investment
    companies (MESBICs)

recycling

social audit

social responsibility

urban revitalization programs

van pooling

For Review and Discussion

1. Explain in your own words what is meant by social responsibility.

2. Why do you think companies have become socially responsive? Do you believe it is voluntary or involuntary? Why?

3. Distinguish among the three phases of social responsibility. For each phase write one sentence that describes management's operating philosophy on social responsibility.

4. Why do major business corporations invest in small-business opportunities?

5. Why would a company choose to participate as a shareholder in an SBIC or a MESBIC?

6. Evaluate this statement: "Companies that initiate programs for hiring and promotion of minorities and women are simply doing what the government demands."

7. Explain why businesses have been reluctant to hire handicapped workers. Why has this reluctance been changing?

8. Why has business taken a leadership role in urban revitalization and overall community involvement?

9. "Community involvement is the thing to do. It is expected." Evaluate this statement from the standpoint of social commitment.

10. In the area of environmental concerns provide an illustration of a company's action that would illustrate the three phases of social responsibility.

11. "Energy conservation is just another phase. If it wasn't for the cost factor we would not worry about it." Evaluate this statement from the standpoint of social responsibility.

12. What specific benefit do employers and employees receive when employers invest in a company health program?

13. Why are product safety programs and consumer information programs considered a function of social responsibility?

14. "Social responsibility is the job of every manager." Explain this statement as it relates to the social audit.

15. What effect does ethics have on business transactions? How can a company bring pressure on an individual that could create unethical practices? Can this be avoided?

Applications

Case 21.1 Crime and Punishment

Despite the general acceptance by corporations of the necessity to practice social responsibility, some corporations have initiated socially irresponsible behavior. These behaviors include:

- The development and implementation of policies resulting in the manufacture and sale of life-threatening products
- The continued pollution of the environment
- Collusion in the establishment of prices

When discovered, the actions are not traceable to a single person. The corporation is the one responsible — its values, its support of the actions, and its inability or unwillingness to respond are the causes.

The actions taken by society to punish the offending corporations are either to levy fines or to require civic contributions. The primary penalty in both cases is the loss of funds to the corporation. But these funds can quickly be recovered in the marketplace.

An indirect punishment as a result of the publicity that often accompanies the attention this type of situation attracts is public embarrassment. The amount of negative publicity a corporation receives is based on the public's awareness of the events, the importance of the corporation, and the seriousness of the offense.

A concept that has been discussed is to increase the negative public image a company receives as the punishment for the actions. The court would require the company to develop appropriate publicity by advertising in designated media. In essence, the company would publicly proclaim its guilt. This would be done in addition to any fines or civic contributions.

Questions

1. Do you believe a company is deterred from social wrongdoings by monetary punishment? Why or why not?

2. Which do you believe is more effective in correcting behavior, monetary punishment or negative publicity? Why?

3. What is your reaction to the proposal requiring business to advertise its wrongdoings publicly?

4. What should companies be allowed to do to state their cases publicly?

Case 21.1 Adapted from Peter French, "Crime and Tarnishment," *Dallas Morning News*, March 4, 1984, p. 1-H.

Case 21.2 Unethical or Good Business?

"It's not a matter of ethics, it's a matter of survival!" After making this pronouncement, Sukie James terminated the conversation and stalked from the room. For the last 2 hours Sukie and Jack Stedman, two general partners of Creation I, had been embroiled in a heated discussion.

The company desperately needed to find someone who could come in and take over the research responsibilities for Creation I. Charley Wesnouski, the original creative genius, had left the company to begin his own operation. Since that day the technological advances so necessary in the computer industry were just not happening at Creation I.

Quite by accident Sukie had found the solution to the problem. While attending a computer conference in Chicago she had literally bumped into Tighe McGauliffe, a former college classmate and the resident wizard for a large computer manufacturer.

After returning from the conference, Sukie had begun a campaign of recruiting Tighe for Creation I. Although Tighe insisted she was perfectly happy and had been for years, gradually Sukie's offer of three times the present salary, a full partnership, and unlimited potential began to interest the potential recruit.

"Just think of what she can do for us, Jack. She's got access to all that technical information. We'll cut our research time in half. She's also told me she would like to bring along some of her top researchers."

Jack had protested vehemently to the action. "Pirating is just not the way we operate. Besides, when Tighe tries to leave they'll make her read the fine print in her contract — she will be prohibited from working for us."

Questions

1. Discuss the ethics of the situation from the standpoint of Creation I.

2. Discuss the ethics of the situation from the standpoint of Tighe McGauliffe's employer.

3. What, if any, are the ethics involved in this situation?

Appendix: The Business of Getting a Job

Most of you reading this book will eventually earn a degree and enter the job market. This appendix is designed to give you some basic information on ways to identify a potentially satisfying career, find job openings in that field, clear an employer's selection hurdles, and understand how large corporations — the primary employers of college graduates — recruit on college campuses.

Choosing a Career

You probably have several friends or acquaintances who enjoy their work. They feel challenged by it, enthusiastic about doing it, and rewarded by the experience of going to work each morning. These fortunate people probably selected their career with care. The close mesh between their personal preferences and the work they have come to do is probably no accident. You, too, can identify a satisfying career if you will invest some time and effort.

Explore Your Interests

Perhaps the fundamental step in choosing a career is to get to know yourself well — to define and describe clearly the aspects of jobs that suit you well and the specific work activities you would prefer to avoid.

One way to do this is to complete a personality inventory questionnaire and checklist like the ones in Figure A.1. Your self-knowledge and suitability for a particular career can be further confirmed by taking one or more tests in your college's counseling department or career guidance office. Two of the more popular ones are:

- The Hall Occupational Orientation Inventory, which requires you to rate the strength of your interest in various activities.

Figure A.1 A Personality
Inventory Questionnaire and
Checklist
Source: From the book *The Job Hunt:
How to Compete and Win* by Joseph T.
Straub, pp. 3–6. © 1981 by Prentice-
Hall, Inc. Published by Prentice-Hall,
Inc., Englewood Cliffs, New Jersey
07632.

1. What kinds of hobbies do you like to work with in your spare time? What is it that makes them appealing to you?
2. Which sports, clubs, and other extracurricular activities do you like best? Why do you like them?
3. What jobs have you had that you liked best? Why did you like them?
4. Do you like to work with abstract ideas or tangible objects? Why?
5. Do you keep calm and cool when being rushed? Do you meet deadlines regularly?
6. Would you prefer to work with a large group, in a small group, or by yourself?
7. Do you like to have well-organized and predictable work assignments or would you rather have a dynamic job that changes every day? Why?
8. Are you comfortable supervising others or would you rather let someone else be the boss? List several reasons for your answer.
9. Which high school and college courses did you enjoy the most? What was it about each that appealed to you?
10. What offices or special honors have you held or received? What personal qualities were responsible for this?
11. Without mentioning a type of work, describe yourself ten years from now. What physical living arrangements do you want? What recreational interests and hobbies do you intend to follow? What kind of people do you want to socialize with and work with? How much income would you like to have?

Yes	No	Personal Characteristic
_____	_____	Work successfully under pressure.
_____	_____	Prefer to work with ideas and concepts.
_____	_____	Prefer to work with tangible objects.
_____	_____	Like routine, methodical work.
_____	_____	Like to supervise others.
_____	_____	Meet deadlines promptly.
_____	_____	Enjoy traveling.
_____	_____	Prefer challenging work assignments.
_____	_____	Am comfortable in the company of strangers.
_____	_____	Would rather work alone or with a small group.
_____	_____	Like to be thought of as a "take-charge" person.
_____	_____	Appreciate a regular paycheck.
_____	_____	Like to associate with people who are members of the "upper class."
_____	_____	Enjoy assignments that require persuading others.
_____	_____	Like to speak in front of groups.
_____	_____	Have little trouble communicating with others.
_____	_____	Prefer to make decisions rather than have others make them.
_____	_____	Ask lots of questions.
_____	_____	Willing to try out new ideas.
_____	_____	Like to help others with their problems.
_____	_____	Make friends easily.

In doing so, you indicate characteristics a job must have to attract and satisfy you, and you reveal certain job characteristics that you would find unappealing.

— The Strong Vocational Interest Blank, which measures your preference for various kinds of work, school subjects, recreation, and personal characteristics in other people. The interest profile that emerges can be compared with the preferences, interests, and attitudes required in occupations from accountant to zoologist to determine how compatible you would be with each occupation.

Although brief personality inventories and exercises cannot provide a formula for finding an agreeable job, they should enable you to be reasonably certain of the job characteristics you find attractive and the ones you do not want to encounter.

Build a Career Profile

After you have completed the personality inventory and the tests offered by your college counseling department, you will be ready to build a profile of potential careers that seem appealing. Some methods of obtaining career information are illustrated in Figure A.2.

One of the most interesting ways to obtain information about a career is to interview someone who already does that kind of work. The procedure is simple — merely identify several companies or organizations that employ persons in that field, telephone their local offices (consult the Yellow Pages), and ask for the head of the appropriate department. Tell that person your name, request a meeting, and give the reason for your request, and you probably will be able to make an appointment at a mutually convenient time. You also may be able to get names of people to talk to from your college placement office; many colleges and universities maintain lists of alumni who are willing and happy to talk to students about their careers.

Figure A.2 How to Build a Career Profile

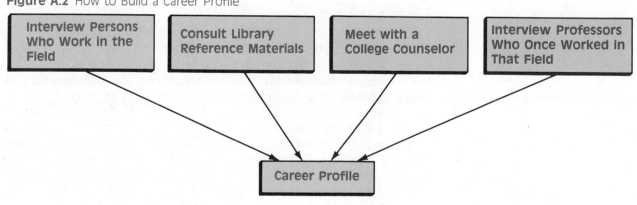

Interviewing people who work in the field serves two purposes. First, it gives you an opportunity to ask questions of someone with firsthand, intimate experience in the career. Second, it gives you the opportunity to contact a potential sponsor, someone who might recommend you for a job should you eventually decide to pursue that career. Your initiative in seeking these people out and your candor in approaching them also portrays you as a bright, ambitious, and thoughtful self-starter. Be sure to arrange meetings with several people in each field to obtain a balanced impression of what the work is like.

In addition to meeting with those who are employed in the field, read current reference materials about careers that interest you. One good source of information is the latest edition of the *Occupational Outlook Handbook*, published annually by the United States Department of Labor, which provides data on required training and other qualifications, expected demand, nature of the work, typical job environment, approximate salary ranges, and various other topics for hundreds of jobs. This information can be supplemented from such other sources as the *Handbook of Job Facts* and the *Encyclopedia of Careers and Vocational Guidance* to build an even more thorough profile of your particular field. Collectively these sources should provide you with considerable information on a career, including average starting pay, promotional opportunities, and ways to prepare yourself.

Supplement the information you gain from interviewing practitioners and reading reference materials with a visit to your college counseling department or career guidance office, which should have specific information from prospective employers, as well as information about the careers other graduates have pursued.

If you are a student at a large university you probably will find one or more faculty members who formerly worked in the field you are researching. You can identify them by calling the office of the appropriate department or division or by consulting a faculty directory that presents a brief biography of each professor. Arrange an interview to talk about their experiences and opinions of your potential career.

Choose a Major

The next move is to choose a major field of study that will prepare you for a career that interests you. Colleges offer quite an academic menu; if you have not discovered this by now, you soon will. You have so many choices that you may decide to change majors several times between your freshman year and your senior year. You may be able to pursue a certain career by following one of several academic routes. Large companies employ marketing trainees with majors in psychology, business administration, and various other areas. Many firms fill their needs for college-educated employees from a host of majors, and certain majors may qualify you to work in several areas. The career capsules that follow parts 2, 3, and 4 of this book indicate the variety of majors that lead to some jobs.

Fortunately for most of us, the choice of major is not an all-or-nothing commitment. Should you find, after completing several preliminary courses, that the course work is not intellectually gratifying or stimulating, you can change to another field.

Work closely with a college counselor in selecting a major. It is especially important to schedule your courses strategically and in the correct sequence. If possible, balance your schedule so you do not find yourself taking several courses that require large amounts of out-of-class work in the same session (English literature, chemistry, and accounting, for example). Verify the need for prerequisite courses and complete them before enrolling in the more advanced ones.

Depending on the size of your college, some courses may only be offered infrequently. Realizing this will enable you to sign up at the best time for you and to graduate on schedule.

Selling Yourself in a Resume

Many of the marketing concepts you learned about in Chapter 10 apply to your job search, because getting a job means marketing a unique product — yourself. You are selling a package of education, attitude, ambition, dedication, and potential that will be developed both on the job and through additional training. You must present yourself clearly and impressively to people who can make or influence a hiring decision. This involves developing a resume, which demands an understanding of the importance that appearance plays in making a good impression.

A good resume is the bait that hooks an employer's attention. It should be confined to *1 page* and designed so a reader can scan it quickly and easily. It should give your name, address, and telephone number, and summarize information about your education, work experience, and any extracurricular activities, hobbies, or interests that are relevant to your desired career. An example of a concise resume appears in Figure A.3.

The work experience section is especially important. You must show that your responsibilities were meaningful and that you had to exercise maturity, independent judgment, and initiative (see Figure A.3). Action words such as "developed," "processed," "designed," "supervised," "submitted," and "administered" give the impression of meaningful activity and responsibility.

Before writing your resume, you should make a rough draft listing all the information you want to present, then rewrite and polish it until it is concise and descriptive. You may want to have someone in the counseling center or guidance office or a business or English professor look over your final version.

Several mechanics of resume preparation deserve your attention.

1. A resume should always be typewritten or typeset.
2. Grammar, spelling, and punctuation must be flawless.
3. Always give a prospective employer an original or a high-quality offset copy, never a carbon copy or a mimeographed copy.

Figure A.3 A Sample Resume

Source: From the book *The Job Hunt: How to Compete and Win* by Joseph T. Straub, p. 21.
© 1981 by Prentice-Hall, Inc. Published by Prentice-Hall, Inc., Englewood Cliffs, New Jersey 07632.

RÉSUMÉ

NAME: Paul J. Owens   PHONE: (904) 672-4359

ADDRESS: 2317 Crest Street
          Tallahassee, Florida 23692

CAREER GOAL: Retail Sales Management

EDUCATION: B.S., Marketing, Florida State University, August, 198x.
              G.P.A. 3.40 out of 4.0 possible.

              A.A., Business Administration, St. Petersburg Junior College,
              June, 198x.

WORK
EXPERIENCE: June, 198x to present: Barrows Department Store, Tallahassee,
              Florida. Retail salesperson responsible for cash and credit
              sales, inventory control, merchandise marking, and producing
              various internal reports used by store and regional manage-
              ment.

              August, 198x to June, 198x: Sampson's Auto Supply, Tallahassee,
              Florida. Counter clerk and warehouse worker. Recorded cash
              and credit sales, processed telephone and catalog orders,
              gathered items for shipment, received and processed incoming
              merchandise.

EXTRA-
CURRICULAR
ACTIVITIES: President and Treasurer, Delta Chi fraternity; Secretary,
              F.S.U. Collegiate Chapter of the American Marketing Associa-
              tion; member, Campus Youth for Christ; President's list;
              intramural racquetball, baseball, and soccer.

HOBBIES,
INTERESTS: Water skiing, racquetball, tennis.

REFERENCES: Furnished upon request.

Prospective employers draw many conclusions about applicants from the condition of their resumes. A sloppy appearance (smudges, smeared corrections, or overstrikes) implies that the applicant is slipshod, messy, unkempt, and careless. Numerous spelling or grammatical errors imply carelessness or stupidity. Haphazard spacing or an inconsistent format indicates that the person has no concern for consistency or detail. A resume speaks for you when you may not be present to speak for yourself. Be sure it says what you want it to say.

Finding Out About Job Openings

The most obvious source for finding out about job openings is a newpaper's help wanted listings. But relying on that source alone — or even primarily — can severely limit a student's chances of finding a satisfying job. The fact is, many jobs are never advertised in the newspaper; those jobs, often the most interesting and rewarding, will never be found by the avid paper reader. To get a good job, you must pursue other sources of job information.

Co-ops and Internships

Cooperative employment programs (co-ops) permit students to attend college for part of the year and apply their learning to a full-time job for the remainder. Such federal agencies as the Treasury Department and the General Accounting Office have established co-op programs, as have such leading corporations as Deere & Company, General Electric, and General Motors.

The popularity of cooperative education has grown impressively over the last several years. In 1981 the Cooperative Education Research Center of Northeastern University reported that the number of colleges and universities that have developed cooperative education programs in conjunction with employers had increased from 120 to 1,050 in less than 15 years, and that student enrollment in these programs had increased by 34 percent in just 6 years.[1] A sound academic record usually ranks very high in an employer's decision to admit a student to a co-op program.

One appealing aspect of cooperative education is that the organization you work for during part of your academic year has an opportunity to get to know you as a person and as a potential employee. And at the same time, after working for part of 3 or 4 years for the same employer, you can come to understand that employer's operations, systems, and philosophy. If the relationship is mutually satisfying, you might be able to step into a full-time position with the employer after graduation. In many cases the step is virtually automatic. Furthermore, several years of co-op training enhances your bargaining power in the job market. Usually co-op program alumni can negotiate a more responsible position and a higher starting salary than graduates with less meaningful experience who were recruited directly out of the classroom.

The organization and operation of Dow Chemical Company's co-op program provides some interesting insights. Students are given responsibilities related to their major fields of study in areas such as research and development, manufacturing, marketing, and business administration. Dow ensures that they will be considered for full-time employment after graduation. Salaries are based on academic experience, experience in the program, and job performance; responsibility naturally increases with subsequent co-op assignments. The duration of each assignment is tailored to the student's academic year. Dow pays the cost of round-trip transportation from campus to the work location in addition to group medical insurance and perhaps a paid vacation (depending on how long a work period lasts). Students receive assistance with finding suitable living quarters at each location. Those who take job-related courses while working on a co-op assignment are reimbursed the full amount of their tuition and books. Many other large companies including du Pont, Aetna Life & Casualty Company, and Datapoint Corporation have summer intern programs.

Although a co-op program might extend your projected graduation date by a year, many co-op alumni swear that the valuable work experience they accumulated and the head start they got in their search for employment after graduation made the delay well worth it. Cooperative education also has been the only way some financially strapped students could afford a college education. By working full time for part of the academic year, they were able to save enough money to pay for the next semester.

You can gain meaningful work experience and valuable personal contacts by participating in a summer co-op program. This arrangement is common in government agencies, where students may work full time or part time. You also may be able to enter a private employer's internship program, earning college credit and perhaps a nominal salary for the time. One-semester internships can earn an average of six credit hours, if the student's work responsibilities are related to his or her major. Internship pay is sometimes meager or nonexistent, but this arrangement, like co-op training, allows you to make valuable personal contacts in an organization while experiencing work that you think might interest you. It also helps you accumulate credit toward your degree. Your counseling office or placement office will be able to supply information on cooperative education or internship programs that are available through your college.

The Placement Office

The placement office is central to every college student's job hunt. Its function is helping students get jobs before they graduate. It does this by performing the following activities and services:

1. Offers data on demand trends in various careers
2. Polls perspective employers on the relative popularity of various fields of study

3. Publishes starting salary surveys tabulated by industry and major field of study

4. Distributes recruiting literature from specific employers that discuss kinds of jobs available, majors and degrees desired, potential work locations, starting salary ranges, the nature of operations, and specific characteristics and qualities that the employer finds most desirable in a prospective employee

5. Provides facilities and procedures for employer representatives to meet and interview graduating seniors

6. Counsels students on how to interview effectively to make a favorable impression on prospective employers.

Generally you will not be permitted to interview with prospective employers through the placement office until your senior year. Nevertheless, you should find where it is located and explore the materials and services it offers as soon as possible. Most colleges also have alumni placement programs to help graduates conduct job searches later in their careers.

Professors in Your Major Field

The professors who teach courses in your major are a valuable source of job leads if they maintain regular contact with potential employers. Professors in schools of business and engineering, for example, may have worked with or are consultants to large corporations and so may know influential managers with the authority to hire several outstanding graduates each year. It is not unusual for large firms to have such back-door recruiting arrangements with professors, who recommend students to fill high-paying, top-notch entry jobs. The challenge here is to make sure that your professors know and respect you as a student and as a person. This will take a conscious, discreet effort on your part, but it may pay dividends. Active class participation, volunteering for light research assignments, and other signs of thoughtfulness and diligence should make you stand out.

Networking

Networking requires that you cultivate a system of influential persons who may help you get job interviews. In fact, some network members may be in a position to hire you themselves. Your personal network may include the following:

— Friends, other students, and members of their families
— Professors
— Family friends
— Associates, clients, suppliers, or customers of relatives who are in business
— Members of fraternities or sororities
— Faculty advisors and members of campus clubs related to your major

> — Counselors
> — Members of your church
> — Prominent executives in local companies that you often deal with (such as department stores, restaurants, clothing stores, off-campus bookstores, and supermarkets)

You should become acquainted with these contacts on a personal level and make them aware that you're actively seeking employment. Then follow up periodically and discreetly to remind them that you'd appreciate their assistance.

Other Sources

You may land a job through a private employment agency, but these firms typically deal with experienced people. If you have no meaningful work experience, an agency may not be willing to help you. An employment agency acts as your agent (see Chapter 20), and you will pay for its services according to a fee schedule and policy discussed at the time you sign a contract with that agency. The fee may be equal to at least a month's salary from the job the agency helps you find. An employer may be willing to pay all or part of the fee on your behalf, but the fee is legally your responsibility. Tax-supported state employment services have jobs available too, but most of them are nontechnical and nonsupervisory positions and relatively few require a college background. Most employers with jobs that require a college education fill them from other sources.

Corporate Recruiting

You may not graduate with a major in business, but if you are like most college graduates, you will accept your first career position with a large corporation. This is true whether you majored in anthropology, theology, or zoology, so it is important that you understand the way large companies recruit graduating seniors for entry-level jobs. Figure A.4 illustrates the steps, which are described in the following sections.

What Are Recruiters Looking For?

First, however, you need to have an idea of what the corporations are looking for. Allen Blitstein, a professor of economics at Southwest State University in Marshall, Minnesota, surveyed several kinds of

Figure A.4 Typical Corporate Recruiting Procedure

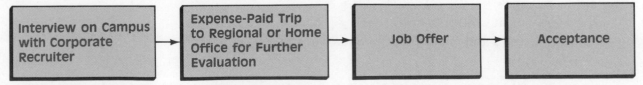

private and government employers to determine the importance they attach to various factors when evaluating business and agribusiness majors. The results, shown in Table A.1, are noteworthy for job-seeking students from any major. The table shows the percentage of those surveyed who answered that a particular factor was very important, important, or not important. Notice the emphasis on factors that you can demonstrate to them in your resume and interview: written communication skills, oral communication skills, poise, appearance, and personality.

The Campus Recruiter

When you investigated the campus placement office, you learned that large employers send representatives called *campus recruiters* to interview graduating seniors there. The placement office periodically announces the names of firms whose recruiters will visit the campus, the dates of those visits, and the specific majors they are looking for. You must then reserve an appointment with any companies you are qualified to interview with and interested in learning about. A recruiter typically spends 1 or 2 days on campus, during which time he or she interviews as many as two dozen prospective employees. Because a recruiter may recommend only two or three students for further consideration, qualifying and signing up in time for this campus interview is a major hurdle in a student's job search.

Preparing for the Interview

An interview is a personal sales presentation, and like any effective salesperson you must be prepared to present your most impressive features, make clear the ways they would benefit your prospective employer, and demonstrate your potential to excel in the work for which you have applied. Some contend that the interview is the single greatest challenge facing a jobseeker. It is an exchange of information and impressions upon which job offers and career decisions hinge.

Table A.1 Importance of Various Factors in Getting a Job

Source: Reprinted with permission of Allen Blitstein, Southwest State University, from *The Collegiate Forum* (Winter 1980–1981): 7. Published by Dow Jones and Company, Inc., Princeton, New Jersey, 08540. Copyright 1981, all rights reserved.

Factor	Very Important	Important	Not Important
Grade point average	23.7%	64.5%	11.8%
Oral communication skills	69.0	30.0	1.0
Written communication skills	38.3	52.2	9.5
Poise	42.9	57.1	0
Appearance	37.9	56.9	5.2
Social graces	6.8	64.0	29.2
Personality	44.1	51.6	4.3
School attended	1.1	51.6	47.3
Recommendations	16.9	52.8	30.3

Interviewing is like anything else — the more you practice, the better you should become. Serious jobseekers interview often, getting comfortable with the experience of being scrutinized by strangers who may hold the key to a job offer.

A successful interview starts at the library. You will need facts about such things as major products or services, sales and profit trends, and major markets that the firm sells to. Thorough preliminary research will benefit you in at least two ways. First, you will learn more about the employer's industry position, potential for future success, and scope of operations, so you can make a better-informed decision if you receive a job offer. Second, you gather a body of knowledge that you can use, tactfully, to show the interviewer that you have initiative, foresight, and curiosity (you went to the library on your own and dug it up). Because many students show up for interviews knowing nothing but the employer's name, information from personal research, conveyed during your interview, makes you look more attractive as a potential employee.

Several library sources provide all the information you will probably need. Assuming you are interviewing a company, refer to the list of sources of financial information in Appendix B, on page B-8. The two best sources for the purpose of job interviews are *Standard & Poor's Stock Reports* and *The Value Line Investment Survey*. Between them they provide a condensed history of a company's financial performance, mention some of its major products, and state any subsidiary firms that the company owns (or the parent company that owns it). These references have facts that are not common knowledge. An alert interviewer will realize that you did some respectable research if you can refer to such facts during your interview.

It also is equally important to read and make notes from recent magazine articles about the company. These may be found by looking in the *Business Periodicals Index*, which lists articles indexed by company name and gives the title, magazine, date, and page number on which the article appears.

A genuine interview is a two-way exchange. The employer wants applicants to understand the organization and its job requirements. The employer also wants to assimilate as much information as possible about the applicant's ambitions, plans, background, priorities, and potential for being a solid candidate for the job. Some questions that many employers ask college students who are applying for jobs are presented in Table A.2. Study them and prepare yourself to offer responsible, intelligible, and interesting answers. But remember: it is impossible to condense the dynamic experience of an interview into a formula. Be prepared for anything.

Prospective employers also expect (and are impressed by) inquiring minds, so you should come to an interview prepared to ask as well as answer questions. Table A.3 presents some questions that many job applicants want to ask during the interview.

In getting ready for an interview, it is helpful if you analyze what you think the employer will require from a prospective employee like yourself. You have an inventory of features — background,

Table A.2 Questions You May
Be Asked in a Job Interview

— What do you have to offer our organization?

— What have you accomplished during your years in college?

— What do you know about our organization?

— What do you expect us to do for you? Why?

— Tell me about yourself.

— What do you expect to be doing in (3, 5, 10, 15) years?

— If you had your life to live over, what would you do differently? Why?

— If you were to start college over again, what would you do differently? Would you choose the same major? Why or why not?

— How much of your education did you pay for yourself? Why so much (or so little)?

— What kind of training do you expect to receive from our organization?

— What are your plans for future education?

Table A.2 Questions You May
Be Asked in a Job Interview

education, experience, and skills — and during the interview you must translate these features into benefits you can offer the employer that will satisfy that employer's needs. By role-playing the interview beforehand and anticipating probable questions, you can develop acceptable answers that focus on those things that you alone can offer the employer. Simply put, your goal is to appear to be the most ideal applicant for the available position.

Some additional hints for interviewing effectively are as follows:

1. Be on time. Lateness shows rudeness or indifference.
2. Maintain steady eye contact with the interviewer. Shifty glances imply insecurity or deception.

Table A.3 Questions You
Might Want to Ask in a Job
Interview

— What responsibility can I expect to have in my starting position? What is the typical career path from that job?

— What kind of training can I expect to receive? Who is responsible for it? How is it provided?

— What is your tuition reimbursement policy for courses taken toward an advanced degree?

— What efforts does your organization make to ensure that new trainees are exposed to meaningful work experience? How will my progress be monitored?

— What is the typical background of a supervisor to whom I would report in my starting position?

— How easy is it to transfer among various departments or divisions within your organization?

— Have there been any recent layoffs of persons in jobs like the one I would have? If so, how did management decide who to retain and who to release?

— Describe the kind of location at which I might be employed. What facilities does it have for education, recreation, housing, and health care?

3. Speak clearly and concisely, avoiding such irritating verbal crutches as "you know," "really," "you're kidding," or other fad words or phrases.

4. Bring a copy of your resume, an updated copy of your transcript, and any letters of recommendation you have from professors, employers, or influential persons in case the interviewer asks to see them.

5. Do not smoke, even if invited to; it introduces an unnecessary distraction. (One organization admits that its interviewer may offer you a cigarette in a room without ashtrays to test your ability to handle the awkward situation that would arise if you lit up.)

6. Dress conservatively. There is no record of anyone being criticized for presenting a traditional appearance.

7. Do not take notes during the interview. Make a summary of important facts and impressions immediately after leaving.

8. Do not ask questions only about salary. Employers usually reject applicants who put dollars ahead of such job factors as training, promotional opportunity, and meaningful responsibility. Some questions about compensation are reasonable, however. Asking what criteria are used to determine the actual starting salary within a range (if there is a range), what the potential for salary growth is, and what the company's benefits include are legitimate concerns of potential employees, and interviewers should understand your desire to clarify these matters.

After Your Campus Interview

During the interview, the recruiter should be able to say how long it will be until you have some feedback from the company. If the recruiter does not volunteer this information, it is perfectly reasonable to ask. In addition, it is appropriate for you to write a letter of thanks to the interviewer for the time and information he or she shared with you on campus. This effort, like the preinterview research that was recommended earlier, sets you apart; it is something that less-motivated candidates probably will not do.

Soon after the interview, you should receive one of two letters. One will inform you that no vacancies exist for which you are qualified. This could be a polite rejection, but it could also be the truth — the firm may indeed have no present openings. If that is the case, the letter probably will mention that the company will keep your name on file for a specified period of time in the event something opens up. The other letter, however, usually offers an expense-paid trip for further evaluation. Your destination may be a regional office or the company's main headquarters, depending on the firm's size and hiring procedures. As a rule, you can expect to spend a day at the facility being interviewed by a succession of executives who constitute a hiring committee. They may plan to interview quite a number of students like yourself (on different days, of course) and extend job offers to only a select few.

The offer of a trip requires that you arrange an absence from campus with your professors and make travel plans with the company official who contacted you. You will most likely have to plan air transportation, ground transportation, meals, and at least one night's lodging at your destination. Some employers have travel departments that handle most of these details once the date is set; others leave the arrangements to you. If the latter occurs, you may want to use a travel agent. Respect the company's budget by traveling modestly. Fly coach class, eat adequate meals in respectable restaurants, and generally show as much concern for thrift as you would if you were employed by the firm or if you were spending your own money.

The Company Interview

Once you arrive at your destination and check in with the official who helped arrange your trip, you will be told whom you will be meeting during the day and at what times. You will be escorted from one executive's office to the next by a secretary or by the last person you interviewed with.

The managers you interview with may cover a broad spectrum of organizational functions, including labor relations, marketing, manufacturing, finance, and human resources management. Each will be a seasoned executive within his or her area, and their questions will be more extensive and less predictable than those asked by campus recruiters. At lunchtime you will dine with one or more members of this group, giving them an opportunity to evaluate your social skills.

When your day of interviewing is over, the executive who helped arrange your interview should tell you when to expect the final decision on a job offer. Then you will return to campus, submit a statement of travel expenses for reimbursement (supported by receipts), and wait.

Evaluating Job Offers

Job offers usually are made in a letter (perhaps preceded by a telephone call) describing such details as the formal job title and the starting location, date, and salary. The prospective employer also should provide a written description of your duties and responsibilities and be ready to answer all your questions. You will be asked to communicate your decision within a few days. The deadline can be negotiated, of course, if you are awaiting results from other trips to other companies. No reasonable employer will expect you to make a snap decision on such a critical matter.

Many people experience one of the most dramatic transitions in their lives when they leave college and begin work. Changing, for example, from a full-time student who gets money from home to an independent, self-supporting individual is a radical change. Therefore, in addition to the previously discussed factors, you should evaluate the offer of a starting salary against the budget you have determined you will need to support yourself adequately.

You will have to allow for such items as food, clothing (including, most likely, a more extensive wardrobe than you needed as a student), rent, utilities, and probably the cost of owning and operating an automobile. You also should allocate money for insurance you need that will not be paid by your employer and set aside a sum for savings and for an investment program.

Taking 25 percent off the salary figure offered to you will give the approximate net or take-home pay. If your budget exceeds that figure, you can either recalculate the budget or contact the employer and try to negotiate a higher salary. If you try to do the latter, however, realize that most employers' starting salaries are relatively fixed unless an applicant has meaningful work experience; the amounts do vary, of course, according to the cost of living in a given area of the country. Admittedly, applicants with exceptional qualifications or high-demand degrees may be able to deal for a higher starting salary without meaningful experience; however, many employers adhere to a uniform figure for the sake of fairness.

A job decision is an awesome one. The course you choose will affect you for the rest of your life. Consider the work itself. Does it seem to coincide with the personal and career objectives that you determined? Does the organization appear to be one that you could be comfortable in and satisfied working for? Are its operations stable enough to offer a reasonable degree of job security? Do its demands and those of the job you have been offered reflect the kind of life-style you want to pursue after graduation? These and many other questions must be answered as clearly as possible. Remember, however, that no one truly knows what a job or an organization is like until he or she actually goes to work there.

Discuss your job offer with several professors who are knowledgeable about the employer or the work itself. You might also ask the opinion of several of the people whom you interviewed when you were exploring your interests and comparing them with career profiles. Still, regardless of how many outside opinions you seek out, the final decision is yours and it may be the most profound one of your life. We do not mean to imply that you will be locked into this employer or career for the rest of your life. You may change employers several times during your career if competitors offer faster advancement, greater challenge, more responsibility, or (naturally) more money. Furthermore, you may decide to pursue an altogether different career some time in the future, as time and experience change your preferences, interests, and personal priorities. Those things change naturally as part of the adventure called life. Whatever your present or future goals, though, we wish you good luck and good job hunting!

Appendix: The Stock Market and Personal Investing

B

Once securities are sold to the general public, they may be traded on the secondary market, which includes various stock exchanges and the over-the-counter (OTC) market. When investors decide to sell their stocks or bonds, they need to contact other potential investors who may be willing to buy. Thus the national and regional stock exchanges and the OTC market were born. Both stocks and bonds are traded on exchanges and over the counter, so a stockbroker is a bond broker too.

Where to Trade Stocks

Stock Exchanges

Companies list their stocks on an organized stock exchange primarily for prestige and for the convenience of buyers and sellers. Prestige comes especially from a listing on one of the two national exchanges, the New York Stock Exchange (NYSE) or the American Stock Exchange (ASE or "Amex"). Listing on a national exchange implies size, profitability, and popularity — things a corporation can point to with pride. In addition, a company's investors can buy and sell their securities rapidly and conveniently when they can be traded on one of these centralized auction markets. The number of firms whose stocks are traded on these exchanges varies from year to year. Stocks of approximately 1,550 companies are listed on the New York exchange and 822 on the American exchange.[1]

There are also regional exchanges, the largest of which are the Midwest (in Chicago and Cincinnati), Pacific (in Los Angeles and San Francisco), and the Philadelphia-Baltimore-Washington Stock Exchange. In addition, there are local exchanges in such cities as Boston, Detroit, Honolulu, Pittsburgh, Salt Lake City, and Spokane. The regional and local exchanges deal primarily in local stocks, but they may also handle larger, national corporations' issues.

A stock exchange is simply a gathering place where the representatives of buyers and sellers of securities meet to make trades in those securities. All but a handful of the exchanges are regulated by the Securities and Exchange Commission, and all have their own boards of governors as well.

Before a stock can be listed on an exchange, exchange officials require the corporation to provide specific operating information and to pay a listing fee plus a few cents for each share of stock outstanding at the time of listing. Qualifications for listing, which vary among the exchanges, are based on the number of publicly held shares, their total market value, the total number of stockholders, and the company's earnings. Brokerage houses that belong to a stock exchange are permitted to make trades there through their representatives who work on the floor of the exchange. Table B.1 shows the listing requirements of the two national exchanges.

The Over-the-Counter Market

The over-the-counter market has no central location. It is an informal marketplace, made up of brokers who communicate by telephone and computer. The stocks of approximately 3,900 companies are traded on this market.[2] Price per share and other trading data for OTC stocks are reported by NASDAQ, a computerized quotation system maintained by the National Association of Securities Dealers. These stocks are said to be unlisted because the companies are either unqualified or unwilling to comply with the listing requirements

Table B.1 Listing Requirements of the Two National Stock Exchanges
Source: Courtesy American Stock Exchange, Inc., and New York Stock Exchange, Inc.

	American Stock Exchange	New York Stock Exchange
Shares publicly held	500,000, of which 150,000 must be in 100- to 1,000-share lots	1,000,000
Market value of publicly held shares	$3,000,000	$16,000,000
Number of stockholders	1,000, including 800 holders of round lots of which 500 must be holders of 100- to 1,000-share lots	2,000 holders of round lots
Net income	$400,000 last fiscal year	
Pretax income	$750,000 last fiscal year	$2,000,000 preceding two years; $2,500,000 latest year
Net tangible assets	$4,000,000	$16,000,000

of an organized exchange. This does not imply that OTC stocks are second-rate. Some nationally known corporations have their shares traded over the counter, including Apple Computer, Adolph Coors Company, Hoover Company, and Pabst Brewing Company.

Learning About Securities

Understanding the Financial Pages

As a rule, investors can learn certain facts about a company's securities by consulting the financial pages of a daily newspaper or *The Wall Street Journal*. These contain current information on stocks and bonds traded on the New York and American exchanges, at large regional exchanges, and over the counter.

Although they do not provide financial data on the company itself, the financial pages tell how a stock behaved in open trading on a given day and present several other pieces of information. Table B.2 shows you how to interpret the stock listings on the financial pages.

The Dow-Jones Industrial Average

The Dow-Jones Industrial Average, conceived by Charles Henry Dow, has been used as an indicator of stock market trends since it was first published in 1896. Although there are actually three Dow-Jones averages — for industrial, transportation, and utilities corporations — the industrial average is the one most widely quoted. It is calculated using information such as price-earnings ratios, stock splits, and dividends of thirty firms that are believed to present an accurate sample of American industry. Table B.3 shows the firms presently used in computing this average. Calculating the Dow is a major mathematical challenge because of the number of stocks listed, the daily trading volume, and the occasional stock splits that further complicate computations. Still, formulas that adjust for stock dividends and splits over the years allow us to compare today's average to those of earlier years and decades. Thus the Dow-Jones average indicates general stock market price trends. The Dow is an index number, not a dollar amount. As an index number, it allows us to contrast the condition of the present market with that of earlier years, noting differences and similarities and identifying reasons for changes.

Working with Stocks

A *stockbroker* (also called an account executive) is a person who buys or sells securities for members of the general public. Many stockbrokers majored in finance in college, and most have earned at least a bachelor's degree.

Table B.2 Interpreting Stock Listings

	1	2	3	4	5	6	7	8	9
52 Weeks					P-E	Sales			Net
High	Low	Stock	Div	Yld.%	Ratio	100s	High	Low	Close	Chg.
113¼	65¼	Digital	• •	• •	16	593	98½	96⅝	98	+⅜
67⅛	41½	Disney	1	1.6	16	354	64¼	63⅞	64	+¾
15¼	10¼	DrPepp	.76	5.7	10	303	13½	13¼	13¼	• •
43	28¾	Donnly	1.28	3.2	11	301	41	40¼	40½	+⅜
31	12¾	Dorsey	1	3.7	9	12	27½	27	27	−½
64¾	37⅜	Dover	1.04	1.8	14	66	58½	58¼	58¼	−⅛
39	30¼	DowCh	1.80	5.4	9	1962	34⅜	33½	33½	−½
56	36	duPont	2.40	4.6	12	654	53⅜	52½	52⅝	−⅜
39	30	duPnt	pf 3.50	11	• •	30	30½	30⅛	30½	−½
50½	38¼	duPnt	pf 4.50	11	• •	116	41	38⅞	40	• •

1. Highest and lowest price per share over the past 52 weeks.
2. The firm's abbreviated name. For example, *Digital* is Digital Equipment Corporation, *Disney* is Walt Disney Productions, and *DowCh* is Dow Chemical Company.
3. Annual dividend (if any) that the company is paying on each share. The abbreviation *pf* in the last two entries identifies preferred stock.
4. Yield or rate of return (as a percentage) that an investor would earn based on the closing price. Determined by dividing the dividend per share by the closing price.
5. Price-earnings ratio, based on the company's most recent earnings. This ratio indicates the level of investors' confidence in the company. It is calculated by dividing the stock's market price by its most recent earnings per share. If a stock now sells for 25 1/4 and the company reported earnings per share of $2.50, its price-earnings ratio would be 10.10 ($25.25 ÷ $2.50 = 10.10). A high price-earnings ratio indicates that investors are optimistic that the firm will perform well. They are willing to pay a relatively high price to become owners in anticipation of what the firm will earn. A low price-earnings ratio indicates that investors are pessimistic about the company's performance.
6. Number of shares sold today, in hundreds.
7. Highest and lowest price at which shares were traded today.
8. Price at which the last trade was made today.
9. Net change between today's closing price and yesterday's closing price.

To illustrate, let us use du Pont as an example. Shares of this stock have sold for as high as $56 and as low as $36 during the preceding year. The company's most recent annual dividend was $2.40 per share, which represents a 4.6 percent yield based on today's closing price of $52.625 per share. The stock presently has a price-earnings ratio of 12, which suggests that it recently earned $4.385 per share ($52.625 ÷ $4.385 = 12). Investors traded 65,400 shares (654 round lots) today. The highest trade was made at $53.375 per share, the lowest at $52.50. Today's closing price, $52.625, is $.375 lower than yesterday's closing price.

Brokers must complete an extensive training program run by their companies, and they also must pass licensing examinations administered by the Securities and Exchange Commission, the National Association of Securities Dealers, and the New York Stock Exchange. These examinations verify that they have the knowledge of corporate finance and the securities industry that is necessary to soundly advise investors on which securities to buy and sell.

Table B.3 Stocks Used to Compute the Dow-Jones Industrial Average

— Allied Corporation
— Aluminum Co. of America
— American Brands, Inc.
— American Can Company
— American Express Company
— American Telephone and Telegraph Company
— Bethlehem Steel Corporation
— E. I. du Pont de Nemours & Company
— Eastman Kodak Company
— Exxon Corporation
— General Electric Corporation
— General Foods Corporation
— General Motors Corporation
— Goodyear Tire & Rubber Company
— Inco Limited
— International Business Machines Corporation

— International Harvester Company
— International Paper Company
— Merck & Co., Inc.
— Minnesota Mining and Manufacturing Company
— Owens-Illinois, Inc.
— Procter & Gamble Company
— Sears, Roebuck & Company
— Standard Oil Company of California
— Texaco Inc.
— Union Carbide Corporation
— United States Steel Corporation
— United Technologies Corporation
— Westinghouse Electric Corporation
— F. W. Woolworth Company

After completing the necessary training and becoming licensed, brokers buy and sell stocks for clients in the over-the-counter market or on the various exchanges to which their employer, the brokerage firm, belongs. Brokers receive a commission each time they buy or sell securities for their clients, but they are prohibited from *churning,* advising clients to buy or sell without good reason merely to generate commissions for themselves.

Investing in Securities

Investment Objectives

When you contact a stockbroker and open an account, the broker will meet with you and have you select a main investment objective: growth, safety, or income. Your decision will be influenced by such factors as your age, income level, financial condition, present and desired standard of living, and the degree of risk you are willing to take.

If you set growth (or capital appreciation) as a goal, you want the value of your investment to multiply as much as possible. Your broker may recommend that you buy stocks in companies that have the potential to earn high profits if their products or services (which may be in the developmental stages or relatively new on the market) succeed.

If your investment goal is safety, you will want to see your investment dollars used conservatively. The broker may therefore recommend that you buy stock in so-called blue chip companies — soundly financed industry leaders with prospects for steady, profitable, but not spectacular performance. You also may be advised to buy bonds issued by financially sound corporations or by municipalities, states, or the federal government.

If your investment goal is income, your broker will recommend that you buy stocks of firms whose dividend payments have been uninterrupted for many years or bonds of financially sound companies that will be able to pay the interest when it is due and retire the bonds at maturity. In either case, you want money to be paid to you regularly.

As mentioned earlier, your broker must be trained and licensed to ensure that he or she is qualified to evaluate and suggest securities that conform to your investment objective.

The Specialist

Another important figure on the stock exchange is the specialist, who works independently of the brokerage firms, either alone or in association with other specialists. Each specialist is assigned exclusive responsibility for a stock or several stocks (only one specialist, for example, handles General Motors or IBM stock); every stock on the exchange has a specialist assigned to it. Specialists play two main roles.

In one, specialists preserve the integrity and stability of trading on the exchanges by adjusting the supply of and demand for listed stocks in an orderly way. That is, they must buy their companies' stocks when most investors are selling and sell their accumulated inventory of shares when most investors want to buy. In this way specialists work for the benefit of the exchange and the companies listed thereon by preserving an orderly market. Either a bear market, a bull market, or mere coincidence may cause the number of buyers and sellers of a company's stock to vary widely at a given time and temporarily imbalance supply or demand.

In the second role, specialists act as brokers' brokers. For example, they may briefly hold a sell order from a particular broker on one of their stocks until approached by another broker who wants to buy the same stock. In this role, they are agents, charging a commission to execute orders for busy brokers who do not have time to wait until another broker with a buy or sell order happens to walk up.

Persons who want to be specialists must be approved by the stock exchange. They must be extremely wealthy because they need to have capital on hand to dampen temporary inequities in supply by buying shares of their assigned stock when necessary.

How to Buy Securities

After setting your investment objectives with your broker, you instruct him or her to purchase securities accordingly; these instructions can be given over the telephone. You could tell your broker to purchase a round lot (100 shares) of, say, Dow Chemical. She would check the price on a computer on her desk and tell you that it was currently selling at $35 a share. You would then advise her to buy "at market" or make a "limit order."

If you bought *at market* you would be authorizing the stockbroker to purchase 100 shares at the lowest price she could obtain that day, which would be around the $35 she quoted you. In the end, say she was able to get the shares for $34.50 each — that would cost you $3,450 for the stock, plus the commission for the broker. If you made a *limit order*, you would be instructing the broker to buy the shares for no more than a certain price, say $33 a share. The broker could not purchase any Dow stock for you until she could obtain that price. Limit orders generally are valid only until the end of the day on which they are made, but you can give your broker an open order, which keeps the order valid until you cancel it.

Regardless of what kind of an order you place, the transaction is accomplished by the broker transmitting your order to a representative of her brokerage firm on the floor of the stock exchange. That representative goes to the trading post for Dow Chemical, a spot where all transactions in Dow stock are made, to look for a representative of someone who wishes to sell the same amount of stock at the price you desire. When the sale is concluded, the representative wires the information back to your broker, who informs you verbally. Shortly afterward, printed confirmation of the transaction is sent to you; you send your broker a check within 5 business days of the date of the transaction. A simple purchase or sale of stock handled through a broker can take less than 5 minutes from the time the order is placed.

How to Hold Securities

You can have your broker deliver your new securities to you. If so, we recommend that you rent a safe deposit box at a commercial bank or your credit union and keep them under lock and key, because it is extremely difficult to get lost or stolen securities certificates replaced.

To avoid the problems and inconvenience of keeping securities yourself (and having to deliver them yourself to your broker if and when you sell them), we suggest that you set up your brokerage account in *street name*. This means that the broker keeps your securities and sends you a statement each quarter for your records. You will also receive a confirmation slip each time you buy or sell. If you keep securities in street name, the statement you receive reports the shares of stock or number of bonds you own and the price at which each was bought. Dividends or interest may be paid to you or you can have them credited to your account to buy more securities.

Although street name securities could be lost or stolen, the brokerage firm is fully responsible for their safekeeping and must carry insurance to cover such risks. Most active investors prefer the convenience of having an account in street name.

Making Your Own Investment Decisions

Many investors prefer to rely on the advice of their brokers about which securities to buy and when to sell, and full-service brokerage firms have extensive research departments that provide brokers with detailed financial information of hundreds of companies.

You may prefer, however, to do your own company research and decide for yourself which securities to buy or sell. If so, there are several valuable financial reference publications that you can consult. They contain information about areas such as company sales, profits, dividend payments, projected growth, industry position, acquisitions and mergers, product lines, and projected financial performance. Most college and public libraries subscribe to one or more. You should, of course, add your broker's opinion to the information gathered from these. Be sure, too, to consult the most current issue or edition. Some of the most popular of these sources are:

- *Standard & Poor's Stock Reports*
- *Moody's Handbook of Common Stocks*
- *The Value Line Investment Survey*
- *Moody's Manuals* (organized by category to provide information on industrial, over-the-counter, transportation, utility, and bank and financial stocks)
- *Moody's Dividend Record*
- *Moody's Bond Record*
- *Standard & Poor's Security Owner's Stock Guide*
- *Standard & Poor's Bond Guide*
- *Moody's Handbook of Over-the-Counter Stocks*

Investment Strategies

Short Selling

A *short seller* is a person who borrows stock from a broker and sells it, hoping to replace the borrowed shares at a lower price if and when the market price declines. In other words, short sellers hope to make money during a bear market. A short sale happens like this:

Borrow and sell a round lot of XYZ Corporation stock at $32 per share	$3,200
Pay back broker by purchasing a round lot of XYZ stock at $10 per share (assuming market price declines to that point)	1,000
Profit (less broker's commissions)	$2,200

Short sales can be extremely risky. You owe your broker shares of stock, not dollars, and should the stock's market price rise instead of fall, it will cost you more to replace the borrowed shares than you collected when you originally sold them. Because of this, short sales are wise only when you have reliable information that investors will bid a stock's market price down. Such information might be news of an impending lawsuit against the firm for making a hazardous product or a government antitrust action that would break the company up into smaller independent companies or advance information that the firm is about to report heavy financial losses.

You cannot make a short sale with empty pockets. The short seller must place a deposit with the broker equal to the borrowed stock's market price, so that the broker may replace the stock if necessary. The adage, "It takes money to make money," is especially true in making a short sale.

To prevent a group of manipulators from selling a firm's stock short to give a false impression of lost investor confidence, each short sale must be identified as such. Stock exchange personnel can then monitor short selling activity on each stock and, if a rash of short sales occur, suspend trading on the target stock to protect small investors who are not privy to special information.

Margin Buying

A *margin buyer* borrows part of a stock's purchase price. The *margin* is the percentage of the total price that the investor must pay out of pocket. Margin requirements, which affect inflation rates and investor activity, are set by the Federal Reserve Board. Requirements have been set as low as 40 percent and as high as 100 percent, meaning that investors could enter the market with as much as 60 percent of their funds borrowed. In recent years margin requirements have hovered around 55 percent. Figure B.1 shows what happens when a stock is bought on margin.

Margin buyers benefit from a bull market. In the example in Figure B.1, if the market price of the stock rose to $80 per share, the margin buyer could sell 250 shares to pay off the loan (250 × $80 = $20,000) and still hold $60,000 worth of stock at market price. The original investment of $30,000 has doubled in value even though the market price only rose 60 percent because some of the purchase was borrowed as cash and paid back as cash. In addition, if the stock pays dividends, they will offset at least part of the interest on the loan.

As long as the margin stock's market value is greater than the amount of the loan, the lender — which may be a bank or the brokerage firm itself — is satisfied. Should the stock ever become worth less than the loan, however, the broker will place a margin call on the investor, demanding that he or she supply cash or other securities to bring the value of the account up to the value of the loan. If the investor cannot meet this ultimatum, the broker, who has custody of the stock, sells it and the customer must pay any difference between the cash received and the balance of the loan. Stocks, bonds, and certain United States government securities can be bought on margin.

Figure B.1 How Margin
Buying Works

A purchase of $50,000 worth of stock when margin requirements are
60 percent.

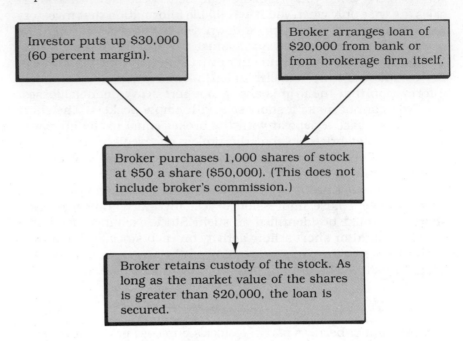

Old Stock Certificates

In Chapter 3 we discussed various business combinations that occur
today. Depending on the kind of combination, a corporation's stock
may be exchanged for that of another, or an entirely new corporation
may arise. In either case, one or more of the combining firms loses
its original identity altogether. The stock certificates of companies
that were absorbed into another firm years ago, however, may be
far from worthless.

Is an old stock certificate bearing the name of a corporation
that you cannot identify valuable? It may be. There have been many
cases in which people found yellowed stock certificates behind attic
wallpaper or in old trunks and the certificates turned out to be
valuable because the original company had become part of another,
still existing corporation. The original shares are then exchanged
for an appropriate number of shares in the present firm, figuring
subsequent stock splits and stock and cash dividends that the new
company paid to date. In one notable case a St. Petersburg, Florida,
woman paid $75 for 300 shares of stock in an oil exploration firm
in the 1930s. The company owned oil rights in northern Germany,
and it ceased business during World War II. It was revived in 1957
when oil was discovered in that region, and the fortunate stockholder,
now eighty years old, found that her certificates were worth $54,550.[3]

Old stock and bond certificates may also be worth a great deal
of money to *scripophilists*, who are collectors of unusual securities.
Certificates are valuable if signed by famous business personalities,

for example. Old American Express stock certificates signed by founders Henry Wells and William Fargo may bring $1,000 as collectibles. Scripophilists also will pay several hundred dollars for colorful Barnum & Bailey Circus stock certificates or elaborately engraved certificates issued by Marconi Wireless Telegraph Company, the forerunner of RCA Corporation.[4]

If you have stock certificates of companies that you cannot trace through your stockbroker or through directories in your public library, the following organizations can help you determine if they are valuable:

- The New York Stock Exchange
  Public Information Office
  11 Wall Street
  New York, NY 10005
- The American Stock Exchange
  Rulings and Inquiries Department
  22 Thames Street
  New York, NY 10006
- The Office of Consumer Affairs
  Securities and Exchange Commission
  500 North Capitol Street NW
  Washington, D.C. 20549
- Stock Market Information Service Inc.*
  P.O. Box 120, Station K
  Montreal, Quebec H1N 3K9
  Canada
- R. M. Smythe & Company, Inc.*
  170 Broadway
  New York, NY 10038

* These firms charge a fee for conducting a stock search.

References

Chapter 2

1. *Statistics of Income Bulletin* (Washington, D.C.: Internal Revenue Service, Summer 1981).
2. "Business Partnerships — the Joys and Pitfalls," *The Orlando* (Florida) *Sentinel*, May 1, 1983, p. E-11.
3. Laura Landro, "If You Have Always Wanted to Be in Pictures, Partnerships Offer the Chance, But with Risks," *The Wall Street Journal*, May 23, 1983, p. 60.
4. "Partnerships Help Investors Bet on the Thoroughbreds," *The Orlando* (Florida) *Sentinel*, August 15, 1983, p. E-3.
5. Dennis Kneale and Laura Landro, "IBM, CBS, and Sears Plan a Joint Venture in At-Home Marketing through Video-Tex," *The Wall Street Journal*, February 15, 1984, p. 3.

Chapter 3

1. Philip Revzin, "AT&T: It Works and It's Interesting," *The Wall Street Journal*, February 20, 1981, p. 28.
2. "Tensor's Annual Meeting Hits Snag — Nobody Came," *The Wall Street Journal*, May 17, 1979, p. 16.
3. "America's Oldest Companies," *Nation's Business*, July 1976, p. 36.
4. "Merger Activity Hits 9-Year High," *The Orlando* (Florida) *Sentinel*, January 16, 1984, p. E-9.
5. "FTC Approves Socal's Merger with Gulf Corporation," *The Wall Street Journal*, April 27, 1984, p. 3; and "Ten Largest Corporate Mergers," *The Wall Street Journal*, March 7, 1984, p. 22.
6. Aaron Bernstein, "Making Dough," *Forbes*, April 25, 1983, p. 60.
7. Office of the Federal Register, *United States Government Manual*, 1983–1984, p. 522.
8. Harry Anderson with Rich Thomas and Christopher Ma, "Rewriting Antitrust Rules," *Newsweek*, August 29, 1983, p. 50.
9. Andy Pasztor, "U.S.-Backed Synfuels Program Is Likely to End in 1984; $5 Billion Seen Returned," *The Wall Street Journal*, December 19, 1983, p. 8.
10. Meg Cox, "Speedier Chickens Fowl Up Their Jobs, Inspectors Grouse," *The Wall Street Journal*, October 12, 1979, p. 1.
11. Jeff Blyskal, "Sleepless Nights in Iowa," *Forbes*, October 25, 1982, p. 172.
12. Sue Shellenbarger, "Shakeout Begins for Cooperatives As Slump, Competition Take Toll," *The Wall Street Journal*, May 17, 1982, p. 29.

Chapter 4

1. Henry Mintzberg, "The Manager's Job: Folklore and Fact," *Harvard Business Review*, July–August 1975, pp. 49–61.
2. Robert L. Katz, "Skills of An Effective Administrator," *Harvard Business Review*, September–October 1974, pp. 90–102.

Chapter 5

1. Harold Koontz and Cyril O'Donnel, *Management* (New York: McGraw-Hill, 1976), p. 375.
2. Keith Davis, *Human Behavior at Work: Organizational Behavior*, 6th ed. (New York: McGraw-Hill, 1981), pp. 328–330.

Chapter 6

1. U.S. Congress, Senate, Subcommittee on Labor of the Committee on Labor and Public Welfare, *The Equal Employment Act of 1972*, March 1972, p. 3.
2. James Ledvinka and Robert Gatewood, "EEO Issues with Pre-Employment Inquiries," *The Personnel Administrator*, February 1977, pp. 22–26.
3. Howard Black and Robert Pennington, "Labor Market Analysis as a Test of Discrimination," *Personnel Journal*, August 1980, pp. 649–652.
4. Anthony Pell, *Recruiting and Selecting Personnel* (New York: Regents, 1969), pp. 96–98.
5. "Gestetner Feels Technical Training Begins at Home," *The Office*, March 1983, p. 40.
6. Stephen Wermeil, "Court Order that Shields Minorities from Layoffs Generates Bitterness," *The Wall Street Journal*, March 23, 1983, pp. 33, 42.

7. Craig R. Waters, "The New Malpractice," *Inc.*, June 1983, pp. 136–140.
8. "Pay for Production," *The Wall Street Journal*, June 14, 1983, p. 1.
9. Robert A. Mamis, "Golden Handcuffs," *Inc.*, August 1983, pp. 59–69.
10. *The Dallas Morning News*, July 10, 1983, p. 35.
11. Lynn Phillips, "When Corporations Play Baby-Sitter," *The Orlando* (Florida) *Sentinel*, October 17, 1983, pp. E1, E8.

Chapter 7

1. Abraham H. Maslow, *Motivation and Personality* (New York: Harper and Row, 1954).
2. Frederick Herzberg, "One More Time: How Do You Motivate Employees? Business Classics: Fifteen Key Concepts for Management Success," *Harvard Business Review*, 1975, pp. 16–17.
3. Robert Tannenbaum and Warren H. Schmidt, "How to Choose a Leadership Pattern," *Harvard Business Review*, May–June 1973, pp. 162–180.
4. *The Wall Street Journal*, March 9, 1978, p. 1.
5. "Stunning Turnaround at Tarrytown," *Time*, May 5, 1980, p. 87.
6. Charles G. Burck, "What Happens When Workers Manage Themselves," *Fortune*, July 27, 1981, pp. 62–65, 68, 69.
7. Bill Stephens, "A Fine Balance, Shared Job Frees Time, Provides New Options," *ArcoSpark*, July 22, 1983, p. 5.
8. Heywood Klein, "Interest Grows in Worksharing, Which Lets Concerns Cut Workweeks to Avoid Layoffs," *The Wall Street Journal*, April 7, 1983, p. 31.
9. David Robinson, "Du Pont's Twelve Hour Shift Improves QWL and Employee Self Esteem at Six Continuous-Process Plants," *World of Work Report*, February 1978, p. 1.

Chapter 8

1. *Collective Bargaining: Democracy on the Job* (Washington, D.C.: AFL-CIO, 1965) p. 6.
2. Ibid., p. 8.
3. Harry Anderson et al., "The Rise and Fall of Big Labor," *Newsweek*, September 5, 1983, pp. 50–54.
4. Daniel Seligman, "Who Needs Unions?," *Fortune*, July 12, 1982, pp. 54–66.
5. Leonard M. Apcar, "Unions, Forced to Retrench More, Fear Their Clout May Not Return," *The Wall Street Journal*, May 20, 1983, p. 33.

6. Harry Anderson et al., "The Rise and Fall of Big Labor," *Newsweek*, September 5, 1983, pp. 50–54.
7. Bill Saporito, "Unions Fight the Corporate Sell-Off," *Fortune*, July 11, 1983, pp. 145–152.
8. Harry Anderson et al., "The Rise and Fall of Big Labor," *Newsweek*, September 5, 1983, pp. 50–54.
9. Dale D. Buss, "Lifetime Job Guarantee in Auto Contracts Arouse Second Thoughts Among Workers," *The Wall Street Journal*, April 18, 1983, p. 29.
10. Daniel Seligman, "Who Needs Unions," *Fortune*, July 12, 1982, pp. 54–66.
11. Peter Drucker, "Where Union Flexibility's Now a Must," *The Wall Street Journal*, September 23, 1983, p. 30.
12. "Pulp and Paper Mills in British Columbia Threaten a Lockout," *The Wall Street Journal*, January 24, 1984, p. 12.
13. "Ford Threatens to Shut Edison, N.J., Plant if Union Doesn't Yield," *The Wall Street Journal*, March 15, 1983, p. 16.
14. Dale D. Buss, "Ford's Demand for Givebacks at Steel Unit Creates Painful Choices for UAW Officials," *The Wall Street Journal*, June 22, 1983, p. 58.
15. "Swift Says Rejection of Labor Pact to Cause Closing of Four Facilities," *The Wall Street Journal*, September 14, 1983, p. 4.
16. Joann S. Lublin, "NLRB Rules Firms May Move Operations to Avoid Higher Costs of Unionized Labor," *The Wall Street Journal*, January 25, 1984, p. 3.
17. Robert A. Liff, "Labor Lobbyist Says Airlines Won't Get Away with Bankruptcy Tactics," *The Orlando* (Florida) *Sentinel*, October 1, 1983, p. A-12.
18. "President Intervenes to Stop Strike Against Rail Freight Line for Third Time," *The Wall Street Journal*, February 15, 1983, p. A-8.
19. Robert S. Greenberger, "More Firms Get Tough and Keep Operating in Spite of Walkouts," *The Wall Street Journal*, October 11, 1983, p. 1.
20. Robert S. Greenberger, "AT&T's Managers Weather Strike Despite Long Hours, Tedious Work," *The Wall Street Journal*, August 17, 1983, p. 25.
21. Joann S. Lublin, "Both Sides Made Mistakes in Controllers' Strike," *The Wall Street Journal*, September 15, 1981, p. 28; Joann S. Lublin, "Firings of Air Controllers Begin as Efforts to Resume Talks Stall," *The Wall Street Journal*, August 6, 1981, p. 3; and "Why PATCO Strikers Are Out of Luck," *Business Week*, November 16, 1981, p. 51.

22. "Procter & Gamble Boycott Urged by AFL-CIO Panel," *The Wall Street Journal*, November 16, 1981, p. 17.
23. Robert S. Greenberger, "More Unions Try Slick Advertising to Educate and Influence the Public," *The Wall Street Journal*, September 30, 1980, p. 39.
24. Robert S. Greenberger, "Unions Organizing Their Retirees to Lobby and Work in Companies," *The Wall Street Journal*, July 7, 1982, p. 23.
25. Tom Nicholson with Richard Manning and Frank Gibney, Jr., "Labor Bends to Big Steel," *Newsweek*, March 14, 1983, p. 55.
26. Joann S. Lublin, "Use of Arbitration May Be Expanded by NLRB Rulings," *The Wall Street Journal*, January 24, 1984, p. 5.

Chapter 9

1. Leslie Schultz, "A Good Garage Is Hard to Find," *Inc.*, April 1983, p. 91.
2. "The Pizza Is Coming!" *Newsweek*, January 17, 1983, p. 18.
3. Michael Cieply, "East of Eden," *Forbes*, January 31, 1983, p. 34.
4. *The Wall Street Journal*, June 7, 1983, p. 1.
5. Amanda Bennett, "Small Tennessee Town Waits Restlessly for Word on Site of Datsun Truck Plant," *The Wall Street Journal*, October 30, 1980, p. 33.
6. Charles W. Stevens, "GM's Plan to Skip '83 Corvette Model Riles Some Buyers," *The Wall Street Journal*, February 4, 1983, p. 1.
7. John A. Byrne, "Whose Robots Are Winning?" *Forbes*, March 14, 1983, p. 154; Craig R. Waters, "There's a Robot in Your Future," *Inc.*, June 1982, p. 64; Carol Hymowitz, "Manufacturers Press Automating to Survive, But Results Are Mixed," *The Wall Street Journal*, April 11, 1983, p. 1; and Eugene Carlson, "Robot Report . . . State Efforts to Get Jobs . . . Inflation Race," *The Wall Street Journal*, February 1, 1983, p. 35.
8. "Robots in Phillips Future," *PhilNews*, January 1984, p. 7.
9. "GM, Citing the Lack of Parts, Closes 2 Plants for Week," *The Wall Street Journal*, December 13, 1983, p. 16; and "GM's Subcompact Recall Stalled by Lack of $1 Part," *The Wall Street Journal*, April 7, 1983, p. 37.
10. Harold C. Livesay, *American Made* (Boston: Little, Brown, 1979), pp. 20–21.
11. Shel Holtz, "Coordinators Save Money for Projects," *ArcoSpark*, June 3, 1983, p. 7.

12. Richard S. Sabo, "Effective Utilization of Personnel Through Incentives," *Journal of NAME* 4, no. 1 (Spring–Summer 1979): 24.
13. Steven Flax, "How Detroit Is Reforming the Steelmakers," *Fortune*, May 16, 1983, p. 126.
14. Robert L. Simison and John Koten, "Auto Makers' Earnings Are Increasing Sharply Despite Mediocre Sales," *The Wall Street Journal*, December 19, 1983, p. 1.
15. Anne B. Fisher, "Winners (and Losers) from IBM's PC Jr.," *Fortune*, November 28, 1983, p. 44.
16. "Where Macs Are Made," *Fortune*, February 20, 1984, p. 94.
17. "Where Robots Can't Yet Compete," *Fortune*, February 21, 1983, p. 64.

Chapter 10

1. Bill Abrams, Susan Chase, Laura Landro, and Erik Larson, "Home Computer Firms Begin to See Marketing as an Industry's Salvation," *The Wall Street Journal*, August 12, 1983, pp. 1, 21.
2. Lawrence A. Klatt, *Small Business Management* (Belmont, Calif.: Wadsworth Publishing Co., 1973), p. 157.
3. Dean Rotbart, "In Spite of Huge Losses, Procter & Gamble Tries Once Again to Revive Pringle's Chips," *The Wall Street Journal*, October 7, 1983, p. 29.
4. Joel R. Evans and Barry Berman, *Essentials of Marketing* (New York: Macmillan Company, 1984), p. 162.
5. Carrie Dolan, "Concocting Zingy New Names Starts Turning into a Business," *The Wall Street Journal*, August 5, 1982, p. 19.
6. Bill Abrams, "Packaging Often Irks Buyers, But Firms Are Slow to Change," *The Wall Street Journal*, January 28, 1982, p. 29.
7. David P. Garino, "Anheuser-Busch Tests Eagle Brand Salted-Snack Foods," *The Wall Street Journal*, February 14, 1983, p. 10.
8. Lee Smith, "The Lures and Limits of Innovation," *Fortune*, October 20, 1980, p. 84.
9. Janet Guyon, "General Foods Gets a Winner with Its Jell-O Pudding Pops," *The Wall Street Journal*, March 10, 1983, p. 33.
10. Steve Weiner, "Growth of Electronic Games Slows; Oversaturation of Market Is a Factor," *The Wall Street Journal*, December 17, 1980, p. 18.
11. Judith B. Gardner, "A Burger-Battle with Everything," *U.S. News & World Report*, November 8, 1982, p. 76.

Chapter 11

1. Michael Waldholz, "Tylenol Maker Mounting Campaign to Restore Trust of Doctors, Buyers," *The Wall Street Journal*, October 29, 1982, p. 33.
2. *SBDS Consumer Magazine and Farm Publication Rates and Data* 64, no. 2 (March 27, 1982): 185, 369.
3. "FTC Relaxes Rules on Deceptive Advertising," *The Orlando* (Florida) *Sentinel*, October 19, 1983, p. 10.
4. Judith B. Gardner, "When a Brand Name Gets Hit by Bad News," *U.S. News & World Report*, November 8, 1982, p. 71.
5. N. Frazier Moore and Bertrand R. Canfield, *Public Relations: Principles, Cases and Problems*, 7th ed. (Homewood, Ill: Richard D. Irwin, 1977), pp. 140–147.
6. Committee on Definitions, *Marketing Definitions: A Glossary of Marketing Terms* (Chicago: American Marketing Association, 1960), p. 5.
7. Sara Delano, "How to Get Tax Free Dollars," *Inc.*, July 1983, pp. 94, 96.
8. Monci Jo Williams, "The No-Win Game of Price Promotion," *Fortune*, July 11, 1983, pp. 92–102.

Chapter 12

1. David P. Garino, "If Anheuser-Busch Gets Its Way, Saying 'Bud' Won't Say It All," *The Wall Street Journal*, January 15, 1981, p. 25.
2. Adapted from Ralph S. Alexander (Chairman), *Marketing Definitions: Report of Definitions Committee* (Chicago: American Marketing Association, 1960), p. 47.
3. Janet Guyon, "Supermarkets Change to Lure More Shoppers," *The Wall Street Journal*, November 14, 1983, p. 33.
4. Barbara Toman, "Department Stores Start Adding Seminars and Services to Attract Working Women," *The Wall Street Journal*, July 19, 1982, p. 17.
5. Ann M. Morrison, "The Upshot of Off-Price," *Fortune*, June 13, 1983, pp. 122–126, 128.
6. Bill Abrams, "Discount Drugstores Thriving with Tricky Buying Strategy," *The Wall Street Journal*, March 17, 1983, p. 29.
7. "Vending Machines Hit $13.8 Billion," *The Orlando* (Florida) *Sentinel*, November 29, 1981, p. D-3.
8. "Large Retailers Upgrade Equipment to Increase Telephone Sales," *The Wall Street Journal*, April 23, 1981, p. 1.
9. "Oil Drilling Gear Declines in Price As Demand Drops Off," *The Wall Street Journal*, August 19, 1982, p. 1.
10. Bro Uttal, "Sudden Shake-Up in Home Computers," *Fortune*, July 11, 1983, pp. 105–106.

Chapter 13

1. James A. White, "AT&T Sees Cost of Shedding Bell Units at $1.9 Billion, to Be Passed to Customers," *The Wall Street Journal*, March 3, 1983, p. 52.
2. "The Term Is Called Meaningless," *The Orlando* (Florida) *Sentinel*, April 30, 1981, p. D-12.
3. Patricia M. Scherschel, "The Mighty 'Fed' — How It Really Works," *U.S. News & World Report*, July 25, 1983, p. 27.
4. Robert S. Greenberger, "A Liquidation Sale by FDIC Can Range from Bawdy to Nice," *The Wall Street Journal*, September 20, 1978, p. 1.
5. G. Christian Hill and Richard B. Schmitt, "Bank in Midland, Texas, Has Assets Sold by FDIC," *The Wall Street Journal*, October 17, 1983, p. 2.
6. "The Stain from Penn Square Keeps Spreading," *Business Week*, August 2, 1982, p. 60; Paul A. Gigot, "Banks Hurt by Penn Square Collapse Were Victims of Oil Slump, Greed," *The Wall Street Journal*, July 19, 1982, p. 17; and *Federal Deposit Insurance Corporation 1982 Annual Report*, p. 6.
7. Daniel Hertzberg, "Banks Consider Regional Mergers, But Exclude Big New York Firms," *The Wall Street Journal*, November 25, 1983, p. 15.
8. *1983 Savings & Loan Sourcebook* (Chicago: United States League of Savings Institutions, 1983), p. 48.

Chapter 14

1. From a speech by R. S. Miller, Jr., executive vice-president of finance and administration, Chrysler Corporation, to the Financial Executives Institute, Chicago, Illinois, January 19, 1984.
2. "Penney to Sell 10 Percent of Credit Accounts to Unit of CitiCorp," *The Wall Street Journal*, January 30, 1980, p. 12.
3. "AT&T's Prospectus Is Massive Printing Job," *The Wall Street Journal*, November 17, 1983, p. 26.

4. Lawrence Ingrassia, "Recent Increase in Share Prices Has Led to Flurry of Stock Splits, Stock Dividends," *The Wall Street Journal*, January 27, 1983, p. 56.
5. Associated Press, "McDonald's Founder Kroc Dies At 81," *The Orlando* (Florida) *Sentinel*, January 15, 1984, p. A-1.
6. Ross and Norris McWhirter, *The Guinness Book of World Records* (New York: Sterling Publishing, 1978), p. 350.
7. "Investing," *American Business*, January 1982, p. 1.
8. *The Wall Street Journal*, September 8, 1982, p. 1.

Money Stolen by Their Employees," *The Wall Street Journal*, January 5, 1981, p. 13.
16. *Insurance Facts*, 1983–1984 edition (New York: Insurance Information Institute, 1983), p. 54.
17. Donna Sammons, "Risky Business," *Inc.*, January 1984, p. 115.
18. "Bad Debt Insurance," *Small Business Report*, March 1983, p. 7.
19. H. Allan Legge, Jr., "Should You Insure Against Bad Debt?" *Inc.*, November 1982, p. 148.
20. "News & Trends," *Inc.*, October 1983, p. 49.
21. Daniel Hertzberg, "When It Comes to Royal Romance, Business Leaves Nothing to Chance," *The Wall Street Journal*, March 10, 1981, p. 37.

Chapter 15

1. *Texasgulf 1980 Annual Report*, p. 53.
2. Jeremy Main, "When Accidents Don't Happen," *Fortune*, September 6, 1982, p. 62.
3. "Aetna Life Estimates Hurricane-Loss Claims Will Total $35 Million," *The Wall Street Journal*, August 26, 1983, p. 4.
4. "Insurors to Pay Claims Totaling $1.89 Billion on Catastrophes in '83," *The Wall Street Journal*, January 9, 1984, p. 12.
5. Donna Sammons, "Risky Business," *Inc.*, January 1984, p. 115.
6. "Using Common Sense To Avoid Heart Attacks," *Business Week*, April 7, 1980, p. 99.
7. Daniel Hertzberg, "Top Executives at Mutual Insurers Get Large Raises, Drawing Criticism," *The Wall Street Journal*, May 14, 1982, p. 27.
8. "Assets," *Best's Review*, October 1983, p. 62.
9. From an Arkwright-Boston Insurance Company advertisement that appeared in *The Wall Street Journal*, November 16, 1983, p. 6.
10. "Double Indemnity," *Newsweek*, February 20, 1984, p. 55; and James L. Rowe, Jr., "Satellite Misfires Put Insurance Premiums on Launch Pad," *The Orlando* (Florida) *Sentinel*, February 12, 1984, p. E-1.
11. "K mart Says Fire Badly Damaged Major Warehouse," *The Wall Street Journal*, June 23, 1982, p. 18.
12. *Insurance Facts*, 1983–1984 edition (New York: Insurance Information Institute, 1983), p. 62.
13. Mary Williams, "No-Fault Auto Policies Are Widely Attacked As Costly, Ineffective," *The Wall Street Journal*, November 16, 1983, p. 1.
14. Greg Bailey, "Country Super Stars Sizzle with the St. Paul," *The St. Paul News*, January–February 1984, p. 3.
15. Paul A. Gigot, "Companies Try Harder To Recover

Chapter 16

1. *The Wall Street Journal*, July 31, 1980, p. 1.
2. Frank Allen, "A New Study of Corporations in the U.S.," *The Wall Street Journal*, December 1, 1982, p. 26.
3. Otto Friedrich, "The Computer Moves In," *Time*, January 3, 1983, p. 14.
4. Bro Uttal, "The Coming Glut of Semiconductors," *Fortune*, March 19, 1984, p. 125.
5. William D. Marbach, "Racing to Build a Bigger Chip," *Newsweek*, July 25, 1983, p. 53.
6. Richard A. Schaffer, "Computer Chips Are Getting Smarter," *The Wall Street Journal*, January 28, 1983, p. 33.
7. William M. Bulkeley, "Microcomputers Gaining Primacy, Forcing Changes in the Industry," *The Wall Street Journal*, January 13, 1983, p. 33.
8. Otto Friedrich, "The Computer Moves In," *Time*, January 3, 1983, p. 14.
9. Earl C. Gottschalk, Jr., "Companies Scramble to Grab Share of Microcomputer Repair Market," *The Wall Street Journal*, February 6, 1984, p. 27.
10. William M. Bulkeley, "Microcomputers Gaining Primacy, Forcing Changes in the Industry," *The Wall Street Journal*, January 13, 1983, p. 33.
11. Ed Leefeldt, "Major Firms' Move Into Floppy Disks Market Is Prompting Analyst Predictions of Shakeout," *The Wall Street Journal*, February 6, 1984, p. 49.
12. Earl C. Gottschalk, Jr., "Companies Scramble to Grab Share of Microcomputer Repair Market," *The Wall Street Journal*, February 6, 1984, p. 27.
13. Robert L. Simison and John Koten, "Auto Makers' Earnings Are Increasing Sharply Despite Mediocre Sales," *The Wall Street Journal*, December 19, 1983, p. 1.

14. Albert R. Karr, "Locomotive Simulator Brings Realism to Engineer Training," *The Wall Street Journal*, November 25, 1983, p. 15.
15. Edward Meadows, "How Three Companies Increased Their Productivity," *Fortune*, March 10, 1980, p. 101.
16. William D. Marbach, "The Race to Build a Supercomputer," *Newsweek*, July 4, 1983, p. 58.
17. Tom Alexander, "Reinventing the Computer," *Fortune*, March 5, 1984, p. 86.
18. Alacia Hills Moore, "The New Cockpits of Industry," *Fortune*, November 28, 1983, p. 109.
19. C. Anne Vitullo, "On-Lining Refining: Employees' Bytes Give Competitive Edge," *ArcoSpark*, October 24, 1983, p. 1.

Chapter 17

1. Richard Brown, ed. *The History of Accounting and Accountants* (New York: A. M. Kelley, 1968), p. 108.
2. John A. Byrne, "Deep Pockets," *Forbes*, November 8, 1982, p. 174.
3. *Understanding Financial Statements* (New York: The New York Stock Exchange, 1978), pp. 1–2.
4. "Drug Maker Says Recall of Tylenol Cut Profit by 26%," *The Wall Street Journal*, October 29, 1982, p. 4.

Chapter 18

1. Frederick C. Klein, "Some Firms Fight Ills of Bigness by Keeping Employee Units Small," *The Wall Street Journal*, February 5, 1982, p. 1.
2. *The Business Failure Record* (New York: Dun & Bradstreet, 1983), p. 3.
3. "Business Failures Rose 24% to 31,334 in '83, Dun & Bradstreet Says," *The Wall Street Journal*, January 9, 1984, p. 48.
4. Sanford L. Jacobs, "Employee Traits . . . Problems in SBA Computers . . . Loans," *The Wall Street Journal*, February 6, 1984, p. 27.
5. Tom Richman, "Will the Real SBA Please Stand Up?" *Inc.*, February 1984, p. 85.
6. *Raising Venture Capital: An Entrepreneur's Guidebook* (New York: Deloitte Haskins & Sells, 1982), p. 45.
7. Sanford L. Jacobs, "Firms Seeking Venture Capital Must Weigh Strings Attached," *The Wall Street Journal*, August 1, 1983, p. 17.
8. Richard A. Shaffer, "To Increase Profits, Venture-Capital Firms Are Investing Earlier in Fledgling Concerns," *The Wall Street Journal*, October 31,

1983, p. 33; and James Cook, "Happy Valentine," *Forbes*, November 22, 1982, p. 250.
9. "Matter of Degrees," *Inc.*, June 1982, p. 91.
10. International Franchise Association Directory of Membership (Washington, D.C.: International Franchise Association, 1983–1984), p. 133.
11. Bernie Ward, "Franchising as Phenomenon," *Sky*, October 1983, p. 102.
12. Sanford L. Jacobs, "Operating a Franchise Often Pays, But Demands on Buyer Are Great," *The Wall Street Journal*, November 3, 1980, p. 33.

Chapter 19

1. Andrew Kupfer, "The Fifty Leading Exporters," *Fortune*, August 8, 1983, p. 88.
2. Bureau of Economic Analysis, U.S. Department of Commerce, "Survey of Current Business," *Business America*, February 20, 1984, p. 5.
3. Ibid.
4. "Anheuser Tries Light Beer Again," *Business Week*, June 29, 1982, p. 136.
5. Tom Nicholson with Larry Rohter and James C. Jones. "AMC Joins the China Trade," *Newsweek*, May 16, 1983, p. 75.
6. Amanda Bennett, "Four Years of Tortuous Negotiations Led to AMC Jeep Venture with China," *The Wall Street Journal*, May 6, 1983, p. 34.
7. "Exchanging and Training for Akashi," *Procter & Gamble's Moonbeams*, August 1983, p. 3.
8. "Culture Shock," *The Wall Street Journal*, February 1, 1983, p. 1.
9. Sue Shellenburger, "Beatrice Foods Finds the Pace Lags in China," *The Wall Street Journal*, November 22, 1982, p. 33.
10. "Gerber Abandons a Baby Food Market," *Business Week*, February 8, 1982, p. 45.
11. "Reagan Slaps Tariff on Motorcycles," *The Orlando* (Florida) *Sentinel*, April 2, 1983, p. A-4.
12. "Striking a Reluctant Compromise on Autos," *Newsweek*, November 14, 1983, p. 94.

Chapter 20

1. Desiree French, "Mother of Invention," *Forbes*, February 28, 1983, p. 110.
2. "Baileys Creams the Competition," *Newsweek*, March 21, 1983, p. 62.
3. John Koten, "Fast-Food Firms' New Items Undergo Exhaustive Testing," *The Wall Street Journal*, January 5, 1984, p. 25.
4. Donna Sammons, "The Name of the Game," *Inc.*, September 1983, p. 28; and "Monopoly: More

Than a Game," *Newsweek*, March 7, 1983, p. 66.

5. Aric Press, "A Blank Tape for Hollywood," *Newsweek*, January 30, 1984, p. 57; and Associated Press, "Movies to Ask Surcharge on Videotaping," *The Orlando* (Florida) *Sentinel*, January 19, 1984, p. A-3.

6. *Technology and Overregulation, or, Why Our Standard of Living Might Not Get Better* (Rolling Meadows, IL: Gould).

7. *NFIB Quarterly Economic Report for Small Business*, report no. 42 (San Mateo, California: National Foundation of Independent Business Research and Education Foundation, 1984), p. 31.

8. *1983 General Motors Public Interest Report* (Detroit: General Motors Company, 1983), p. 37.

9. Clemens P. Work, "Washington's Red Tape Just Keeps Rolling Out," *U.S. News & World Report*, April 4, 1983, p. 62.

10. Peter A. Holmes, "The Saving Grace," *Nation's Business*, March 1984, p. 33.

11. United Press International, "War on Waste Saves $31 Billion," *The Orlando* (Florida) *Sentinel*, January 7, 1984, p. A-6.

12. Suzy Hagstrom, "Airline Deregulation — Survival of Fittest," *The Orlando* (Florida) *Sentinel*, January 1, 1984, p. E-1.

13. Bill Richards, "Independent Truckers Who Hailed Deregulation Reconsider As a Rate War Rages and Taxes Rise," *The Wall Street Journal*, March 31, 1983, p. 56.

Chapter 21

1. Kenneth E. Goodpaster and John B. Matthews, Jr., "Can a Corporation Have a Conscience?" *Harvard Business Review*, January–February 1982, pp. 133, 138.

2. Milton Friedman, "The Social Responsibility of Business Is to Increase Its Profits," *New York Times Magazine*, September 13, 1970, p. 142.

3. *Report from the Social Needs and Business Opportunities Conference*, Control Data Corporation, September 22, 23, 1982, p. 4.

4. Sonia L. Nazarro, "Coke Plans Program to Improve Its Links with Hispanic Firms," *The Wall Street Journal*, March 15, 1983, p. 16.

5. James M. Hildreth, "When Business Comes to Cities' Rescue," *U.S. News & World Report*, August 9, 1982, p. 43.

6. *Exxon Corporation Annual Report*, February 21, 1983, p. 20.

7. James M. Hildreth, "When Business Comes to Cities' Rescue," *U.S. News & World Report*, August 9, 1982, p. 43.

8. Anheuser-Busch Companies, *Partnership*, May 28, 1982, p. 3.

9. *Report from the Social Needs and Business Opportunities Conference*, Control Data Corporation, September 22, 23, 1982, p. 3.

10. *Exxon Corporation Annual Report 1982*, p. 20.

11. Ibid.

12. "Affirmative Action Enriches Life for All Employees," *The St. Paul News*, 26, no. 8 (October 1983): 1.

13. "Disabled Workers Programs Expand As Training and Placement Improve," *The Wall Street Journal*, September 9, 1980, p. 1.

14. "Work Accommodations for the Disabled Often Cost Little and Benefit Others," *The Wall Street Journal*, November 22, 1983, p. 1.

15. *Report from the Social Needs and Business Opportunities Conference*, Control Data Corporation, September 22, 23, 1982, p. 5.

16. Liz Roman Gallere, "Connecticut's Naugatuck River Became a Sewer; Now Even Its Polluters Are Cheering the Cleanup," *The Wall Street Journal*, July 16, 1982, p. 36.

17. "A Summary of PG&E's Wind Energy Plans," *Pacific Gas* release, October 21, 1980.

18. Steven Grover, " 'Jaws' Invades Forest Products Industry as Use of Wood Waste Replaces Fuel Oil," *The Wall Street Journal*, August 12, 1981, p. 10.

19. "Ideas You Can Use," *Inc.*, October 1983, p. 162.

20. George Getshow, "Some Middle Managers Cut Corners to Achieve High Corporate Goals," *The Wall Street Journal*, November 8, 1979, p. 1.

21. "Distiller Says Errors in Its Inventories Caused by Manager," *The Wall Street Journal*, October 23, 1980, p. 19.

22. "Retired Corporate Aids Say Regulation Needed to Prevent Misdeeds, Poll Finds," *The Wall Street Journal*, May 16, 1983, p. 12.

23. George Getshow, "Some Middle Managers Cut Corners to Achieve High Corporate Goals," *The Wall Street Journal*, November 8, 1979, p. 1.

Appendix A

1. *The Wall Street Journal*, April 30, 1981, p. 1.

Appendix B

1. Scott McMurray, "Amex, NASD Officials Exchange Salvos As Rivalry for Listing of Stocks Heats Up,"

The Wall Street Journal, February 10, 1984, p. 8.

2. Ibid.

3. Dick Marlowe, "Stock Certificate Sleuth Tracks Down Big Bucks for Shareholders," *The Orlando* (Florida) *Sentinel*, March 4, 1984, p. E-1; and Associated Press, "50 Years Later, Woman Nets $54,550 on Stock Bought to Cheer Boyfriend," *The Orlando* (Florida) *Sentinel*, July 9, 1983, p. C-7.

4. "Those Old Stocks and Bonds — Are They Worth Anything?" *The Orlando* (Florida) *Sentinel*, October 17, 1983, p. E-5; and Lisanne Renner, "Securities Sleuthing Her Specialty," *The Orlando* (Florida) *Sentinel*, March 23, 1983, p. E-1.

Glossary

absolute advantage A nation has a monopoly on a product or can produce it at the lowest cost.

accessory equipment Capital items that are less expensive and shorter lived than installations.

accountability Having to answer to someone for your actions.

accountant A person who has the education and experience to evaluate the significance of information derived from a company's financial records, interpret its impact on operations, and participate in higher management decisions that are made as a result.

accounting system An organized approach to gathering, recording, analyzing, summarizing, and interpreting financial data to determine a firm's financial condition.

acid test ratio A measure of a firm's ability to pay current debts from its most liquid, or quick, assets — cash and near-cash items. (Found by dividing the sum of cash, accounts receivable, and marketable securities by current liabilities.)

acquisition Results when one firm buys a majority interest in another, but both retain their identities.

Active Corps of Executives (ACE) A volunteer organization of active managers who supplement SCORE's services with the most current expertise and techniques for small-business owners.

actuary A person who analyzes the likelihood of loss and the average amount of damage involved in pure risks and, applying the law of averages, computes the premium that the insurance company should charge to assume the risk.

adjustable life insurance Life insurance on which the insured may raise or lower the face value, lengthen or shorten the protection period, or change the kind of protection as personal circumstances require.

advertising Any nonpersonal message paid for by an identifiable sponsor for the purpose of promoting products, services, or ideas.

advertising media The personal or nonpersonal means of sending a message to a target market.

Affirmative Action Programs to eliminate the present effects of past discrimination on women and minorities.

agency shop Nonunion members must pay union dues because the union acts as their agent when bargaining with management.

agent One who is authorized to transact business and exercise authority on behalf of another party.

alien corporation A firm incorporated in a country other than the one in which it operates.

allied lines *or* extended coverage A feature that can be added to a fire insurance policy to encompass financial loss caused by such hazards as riot and civil commotion, hail, wind, falling objects, land vehicles, water, smoke, and possibly vandalism and malicious mischief.

all-risk physical damage *or* multiple line coverage Added fire insurance coverage that embraces all risks except those that the policy specifically excludes.

amalgamation *or* consolidation Occurs when one firm combines with others to form an entirely new company; former identities are relinquished.

analog computer A computer that takes measurements and processes these data against a model of the problem or situation.

analytic process Raw materials are broken down to form new products.

annual report The document in which businesses summarize their financial condition each year.

annuity A life insurance contract that pays the policyholder (*annuitant*) a fixed sum at regular intervals for a specified period of time. If the annuitant dies before collecting the face value, a beneficiary receives the unpaid balance.

anticipatory purchasing A purchasing agent stockpiles an extremely large supply, well in advance of need, anticipating future problems.

approach The third step in the selling process; the salesperson makes actual contact with the prospect and prepares to deliver a sales presentation.

arbitration Labor and management empower an impartial third party called an *arbitrator* to act as judge and hand down a legally binding decision that both sides have agreed in advance to accept.

arithmetic mean An average found by adding the numbers in an array and dividing by the total number of items present.

arithmetic unit The unit of the computer that performs mathematical computations on data.

array A list of numbers ordered from highest to lowest or lowest to highest.

articles of partnership A contractual agreement that establishes the legal relationship between partners.

assembly process The variation of synthetic production in which materials or parts are combined without substantial changes.

assets Things of value that businesses, government, or individuals own.

authority The right to commit resources (that is, to make decisions that commit the organization's resources) or the legal right to give orders (to tell someone to do or not to do something).

autocratic leadership style Characterized by decision making solely by the manager; subordinates are excluded from the process.

balance of payments The amount of money that flows into or out of the country.

balance of trade The difference between the dollar value of a nation's exports and the dollar value of its imports for a stated period of time.

balance sheet An accounting statement that shows a firm's status on the last day of an accounting period.

bankruptcy *or* **insolvency** The state of being unable to pay one's creditors' claims as they come due.

barter system An economic system in which two parties trade certain goods or services that each needs to survive.

beneficiary One or more persons or organizations that the policyholder designates to receive the cash payment on a life insurance policy.

bid purchasing A policy of requesting bids from several vendors and selecting the most attractive one.

blacklist A list of prounion workers in a given area.

bodily injury liability Sometimes called *PIP (personal injury protection) insurance*; motor vehicle insurance that pays court-awarded damages for bodily injury, up to the face value of the policy, if the insured person is judged liable for a motor vehicle accident.

bond indenture A blanket agreement between the corporation and its bondholders that states the bond issue's interest rate, maturity date, and other terms and conditions.

bonds Long-term, interest-bearing promissory notes.

bond yield The percentage return that the investor will receive.

bonus Incentive money paid to employees in addition to their regular compensation.

bookkeeper A clerical worker who maintains the financial records that an accountant shapes into usable information.

book value of common stock The amount per share that stockholders would theoretically receive if a company's assets were sold on the balance sheet date. (Found by dividing stockholders' equity by the number of common stock shares outstanding.)

boycott A refusal to do business with a given party until certain demands are met.

brand A name, symbol, design, or a combination of these that identifies the products or services of a company.

brand mark A symbol or design used to identify the product and to distinguish it.

brand name A letter, a word, or a group of letters or words used to identify the product.

break-even analysis A method of determining the number of units that must be sold at a given price to recover costs and make a profit.

break-even point The point at which sales revenue equals total costs.

business An organization engaged in producing goods and services to make a profit.

business interruption insurance Coverage that can be added to a basic fire insurance policy; it covers consequential losses, those that result from fire or other perils covered in the fire policy.

bylaws Internal rules that govern the general operation of a corporation.

capital The total of tools, equipment, machinery, and buildings used to produce goods and services.

capital appreciation An increase in a stock's market price caused by investor optimism.

capitalism An economic system where the factors of production are in private hands.

captive supplier A vendor firm in which the customer firm owns controlling interest or from which it obtains an exclusive supply contract.

cash discount A discount given to encourage trade credit debtors to pay their balances before they are due.

cashier's check A check written by a commercial bank against the bank's own money.

centralization A philosophy of organization and management that focuses on the selective concentration of authority within an organization structure.

certificate (articles) of incorporation The application to incorporate that must be filed with the secretary of state, which becomes the corporation's charter after it is approved.

certificates of deposit (CDs) Bank obligations that pay higher interest than regular savings accounts because the depositor agrees to leave the money on deposit for a certain length of time.

certified check A depositor's personal check that the bank certifies to be good.

chain of command Hierarchy of decision-making levels in the company.

chain store One of two or more similar stores owned by the same company, usually a corporation.

channel of distribution A route that goods follow on their journey from producers to consumers.

check *or* **demand deposit** A bank depositor's written order instructing the bank to pay a certain sum to a third party.

classroom training Training conducted away from the pressures of the work environment.

close The step in the selling process at which the prospect agrees to buy.

close corporation A corporation whose stock cannot be purchased by the general public; it is usually owned by a few individuals.

closed shop Agreements stipulating that employees had to be union members at the time they were hired.

code of ethics Formal guidelines for the ethical behavior of individuals in an organization, job, or profession.

coinsurance clause A stipulation that a company must insure a minimum (usually 80 percent or more) of a property's total value before the business will be fully reimbursed for a partial loss.

collective bargaining The process whereby employer and employee representatives jointly negotiate a contract that specifies wages, hours, and other conditions of employment.

collision and upset Motor vehicle insurance that pays to repair damages to the insured vehicle up to its actual cash value (ACV) less the deductible if it collides with an object (including another vehicle) or overturns.

commercial bank A profit-making corporation that accepts customers' deposits and lends them out to businesses and individual borrowers.

commercial finance company A firm that makes cash loans to business borrowers, securing the loans by such assets as trade credit accounts, inventory, or equipment.

commercial paper (Sometimes referred to as *corporate IOUs*) the unsecured promissory notes of large, financially sound corporations.

commission A percentage paid to a salesperson of the price of each item sold.

common law A body of law based on records of early English court decisions settling disputes that involve people and property.

common stock A security held by the corporation's owners.

common stock certificate Legal evidence of corporate ownership; it gives the owner's name, the number of shares owned, and various data on the corporation itself.

communication process The channel promotional messages travel to reach the purchaser.

communism An economic system under which the government controls the factors of production.

comparative advantage A nation is better equipped to produce one product or service than other nations.

comprehensive physical damage Motor vehicle insurance that protects the insured vehicle against most damage except that caused by collision and upset.

computer A device that performs large numbers of repetitive calculations automatically and at high speeds, usually with considerable accuracy.

conceptual skill The mental ability to view the organization as a whole and to see how the parts of the organization relate to and depend on one another; the ability to imagine the integration and coordination of the parts of an organization — all its processes and systems.

conglomerate merger Occurs when one firm buys other firms that make unrelated products.

consumer buying motives Factors that cause someone to purchase a product for personal use.

consumer finance company A company that lends money to final consumers on their promissory notes.

consumer market Individuals who buy products for their personal use.

Consumer Price Index (CPI) A figure that measures changes in purchasing power and the rate of inflation by expressing today's prices in 1967 dollars.

consumer products Goods intended for the personal use of the consumer.

contingent business interruption insurance Insurance that covers a firm's losses when a key supplier's or customer's business is damaged.

continuous process A production method that uses the same machinery to perform the same operations repeatedly over relatively long periods of time.

contract A legally binding agreement between two or more parties obliging them to do or refrain from doing certain acts.

contract purchasing The company negotiates with the supplier (perhaps after soliciting bids) a contract that defines prices, delivery dates, and other conditions of sale.

controlling The management function of establishing standards, measuring actual performance to see if standards have been met, and taking corrective action if required.

control unit The coordinating part of a computer, which directs the other parts to perform their respective functions to complete the data-processing job.

convenience goods Products purchased with a minimum of effort.

convenience store Usually part of a chain, which carries a wide selection of popular consumer items from groceries to motor oil.

cooperative An enterprise created and owned jointly by its members and operated for their mutual benefit.

cooperative advertising programs Programs in which the manufacturer agrees to pay part of the advertising costs for the product.

copyright A set of legal rights granted to the creator of an original work of authorship, such as an artistic, dramatic, literary, or musical production.

corporate charter A document issued by a government that contains all information stated in the original application for a charter plus the powers, rights, and privileges of the corporation as prescribed by law.

corporation A legal form of business organization created by a government and considered an entity separate and apart from its owners.

correlation A cause-effect or if-then connection between two or more elements in a group of data.

cost of goods sold The cost of obtaining the merchandise that was sold to produce the net sales.

cost-oriented approach Prices are determined by focusing on costs of merchandise, accompanying services, and overhead costs, and then adding an amount for desired profit.

cost-push inflation Occurs when producers pass rising labor, materials, and other costs on to consumers by increasing prices.

coupon *or* **bearer bond** One with dated coupons attached, which the bondholder must cut off and mail to the company to collect interest.

craft *or* **trade unions** Associations of workers with a specific skill.

credit insurance Insurance that protects a firm against bad debt losses above a maximum amount on trade credit accounts.

credit life insurance Term insurance that pays the remainder of a debt if the debtor dies.

creditors Those to whom the company owes money.

credit union A mutual savings and lending society for people with a common bond.

crime A violation of a law passed by a legislative body.

current assets Cash, items that will become cash within 1 year, and prepaid expenses.

current liabilities Debts that must be paid within 1 year.

current ratio An expression of a firm's ability to pay its current debts from its current assets. (Found by dividing current assets by current liabilities.)

current yield A bond's annual interest expressed as a percentage of the market or purchase price.

customer departmentalization Groups activities and resources in response to the needs of specific customer groups.

debt capital The long-term capital raised by selling bonds.

decentralization A philosophy of organization and management that focuses on the dispersal of authority within an organization structure.

decision making The process of making rational choices among alternatives.

decoding The process of interpreting the message by the target market.

deductible An amount of a loss that the insured agrees to pay.

delegation The downward transfer of formal authority from one person to another.

demand The quantity of a product that consumers are willing to buy at a particular price.

demand-pull inflation Occurs when producers raise prices in response to strong consumer demand.

demographics Statistics on such subjects as age, income, marital status, recreational habits, and ethnic customs for people who live within a given geographic area.

demotion A movement from one position to another that has less pay or responsibility attached to it.

departmentalization The process of creating the basic format or departmental structure for the organization; forming groups, departments, and divisions on the basis of the objectives of the organization.

Department of Justice An arm of the federal government; works closely with the FTC to preserve competitive markets through investigations by its Antitrust Division.

department store A retail outlet, usually a member of a chain, that is organized by departments and provides an extremely wide variety of merchandise including home furnishings, clothing, appliances, cosmetics, furniture, and dry goods.

depreciation An accounting technique by which management gradually recovers the cost of expensive fixed assets over the course of their expected lives.

devaluation Increasing the rate of exchange at which foreign currency will be traded for domestic currency.

digital computer A computer that processes exact data according to a set of instructions.

directing The management function that builds a climate, provides leadership, and arranges the opportunity for motivation.

disability income insurance Pays a sum of money to be spent as the insured chooses if he or she is unable to work because of illness or injury.

discount The amount by which a bond's par value exceeds its market price.

discount rate The interest rate that the Fed charges member banks for loans.

discount store A store that has low prices, a broad line of merchandise, self-service, a low rent location, and limited store environment.

dispatching The production control step in which a production planner releases a job to the first production department on its route.

diversification for stability argument The argument that trade with other nations will reduce or inhibit the development of a variety of domestic industries and thus reduce economic stability.

dividend A portion of company profits paid to stockholders as a return for the risk that they take as owners.

domestic corporation The term applied to a corporation in the state where it is incorporated.

dormant *or* sleeping partner A partner who is both secret and silent. This person is only interested in investing funds in the company for financial profit.

double indemnity A feature that guarantees that twice the face value of a life insurance policy will be paid if the insured dies accidentally.

draft An instrument completed by a creditor ordering a debtor to pay a specific sum of money.

dumping Selling the same product in different markets at different prices for the purpose of disposing of excess production and maximizing total profits.

economic alliances Agreements among independent nations to promote trade.

economic order quantity (EOQ) Compares the cost of buying an item in various quantities with the cost of carrying those units in stock, and identifies the point at which the cost of the item and the cost to store it are equal.

economic system The method society uses to allocate its resources (land, labor, capital, and entrepreneurship) to satisfy its needs.

embargo Legislation that prohibits firms from importing some or all of the products made in a given country.

emotional motives Buying reasons that rise from impulse and psychological needs rather than careful thought and analysis.

employees' association An organization that represents an occupational group, but appeals to white-collar workers.

employers' association A group that represents several companies in bargaining with a union that has organized their workers.

encoding The process of translating an idea into a message.

endowment Life insurance that combines the characteristics of savings and insurance; the policyholder collects a stated sum if he or she is living when the policy matures. The beneficiary receives the amount the endowment was intended to accumulate (the face value) if the policyholder dies before the policy is fully paid up.

entrepreneur An individual or individuals who are willing to take risks in return for profits.

entrepreneurship The group of skills and risk taking needed to combine the other three factors of production to produce goods and services.

environmental impact study A report describing how a proposed plant will alter the quality of life in an area.

Equal Employment Opportunity Legislation designed to provide an employment environment in which both job applicants and present employees are free from discrimination in their pursuit of employment opportunities.

equilibrium price The point where what the consumers are willing to pay is equal to what the producers are willing to accept for a product.

equity capital The long-term capital raised by selling stock.

esteem need The need to feel important, admired, and worthwhile.

ethics The standards that govern moral conduct.

exception principle Routine actions and decisions should be handled by subordinates; only exceptional decisions should be referred to a higher level.

exchange functions Buying and selling activities — complementary activities that relay products to their intended users.

exchange rate The rate at which money of one country is converted or exchanged for another.

exclusive distribution Limiting distribution to one retailer or wholesaler in a geographic area.

Export-Import Bank Attempts to promote international trade by lending money to importers and exporters who have not been able to obtain funds from other sources and by lending money to foreign governments to help the development of international trade.

exporting Selling goods and services abroad.

fabricated parts and materials Industrial goods that become part of the final product.

fabrication process A variation of synthetic production in which new products are created from those already manufactured by changing their form.

facilitating functions Financing, risk bearing, obtaining market information, and standardizing and grading.

factoring company A firm that buys a business's open-book accounts (or sometimes consumer credit accounts) and customarily absorbs all losses if the debtors do not pay.

factors of production The resources used to provide goods and services: land, labor, capital, and entrepreneurship.

factory outlet A retail store that sells products directly from the plant to the final consumer at greatly discounted prices.

Fair Labor Standards Act A 1938 federal law that requires most employers to pay a minimum hourly wage and overtime pay of one-and-one-half times the base rate for any hours worked in excess of 40 per week.

Federal Anti-Injunction Act (Norris-LaGuardia Act) of 1932 A federal law that prohibits courts from issuing injunctions against labor's nonviolent protest activities; requires an open hearing before the issuance of an injunction; outlaws "yellow dog" contracts.

Federal Deposit Insurance Corporation (FDIC) A public corporation with a threefold purpose: to build confidence in the nation's banking system, insure depositors' account balances, and promote sound bank management.

Federal Reserve Act of 1913 A law that created the Federal Reserve System, commonly called *the Fed*, and made it responsible for managing the nation's supply of money and credit.

Federal Trade Commission (FTC) A government agency established by the Federal Trade Commission Act of 1914; a quasi-judicial body empowered to issue cease-and-desist orders against companies whose combinations would significantly lessen competition.

feedback The target market's actions as a result of the message.

fidelity bond An insurance policy that reimburses an employer for financial loss resulting from employee dishonesty.

Financial Accounting Standards Board (FASB) A group created in 1973 through the joint efforts of the American Institute of Certified Public Accountants and several other accounting organizations to be the overall rule-making body for the accounting profession.

financial analysis The use of mathematics to bring important facts and relationships on accounting statements into sharp focus.

first-line management The lowest level of management; their subordinates are nonmanagement workers.

fiscal year The 12-month period that a company adopts for financial accounting purposes.

fixed costs Costs that remain constant regardless of the number of units produced.

flextime *or* **flexible working hours** Allows employees to decide, within a certain range, when to begin and end each workday.

follow-the-leader pricing Companies do not set prices but react to others' prices.

follow-up The production control step in which production planners monitor each job's progress along its route, and report and attempt to deal with any delays or difficulties that occur. *Also*, this is the final step in the selling process. It builds and maintains customer loyalty and good will, as the salesperson confirms that the buyer has received everything that was originally promised and clearly understands the benefits of owning the product.

foreign corporation The term applied to a United States corporation in states other than the one in which it is incorporated.

foreign-operated sales branch A firm's wholly owned sales organization in a foreign country.

foreign trade intermediary A wholesaler or an agent who performs marketing functions for firms that wish to do business in other countries.

formal organization The official organization that top management conceives and builds.

forward purchasing A policy of purchasing relatively large quantities to fill needs over longer periods of time.

franchise A license sold by one firm (the *franchisor*) to another (the *franchisee*), allowing it to produce and sell a product or service under specific terms and conditions.

free-rein *or* **laissez-faire leadership style** Characterized by the leader permitting the subordinates to function independently.

fringe benefits Nonfinancial rewards provided for employees.

fully registered bond One without coupons; the company pays interest automatically to the owner whose name is on record with the firm, and the principal is paid to that person when the bond matures.

functional authority The authority to make decisions on specific activities that are undertaken by personnel in other departments.

functional departmentalization Groups activities under the major headings that nearly every business has in common.

functional organization An attempt by management to provide expert technical supervision to operating employees by providing separate supervisors for each task.

General Agreement on Tariffs and Trade (GATT) An international accord setting trade rules.

general partner A partner having specific authority, specific operational responsibilities, and unlimited liability.

general partnership An association of two or more people, each with unlimited liability, who are actively involved in the business.

generic products Products that carry no brand name.

geographic *or* **territorial departmentalization** Groups activities and responsibilities according to geography.

goods Commodities that have a physical presence.

government *or* **public corporation** A corporation organized by a city, county, state, or federal government to serve a specific segment of the population.

grievance procedure A series of steps to be followed by an employee whose complaint to a supervisor has not been resolved satisfactorily.

grievances Disputes caused by contract violations or different interpretations of contract language.

gross national product (GNP) The total market value of all goods and services that a country produces in one year.

gross profit on sales The profit that a company made after deducting cost of goods sold from net sales but before subtracting operating expenses.

group life insurance Life insurance available to employees through their employer on a master policy, usually without a medical examination required.

hand-to-mouth purchasing Purchasing an item in small quantities, as needed.

hardware The five tangible parts or units of a digital computer: input unit, memory unit, arithmetic unit, control unit, and output unit.

hazardous waste insurance Liability insurance required by the Environmental Protection Agency (EPA) that will provide payment to persons who are awarded compensation for bodily injury and property damage caused by accidents arising from the operation of hazardous waste facilities.

health insurance Insurance that covers medical expenses incurred by the insured and perhaps the insured's family.

home industries protection argument The argument that trade with other nations will cause domestic industries to lose their customers to foreign competitors, forcing firms out of business and throwing workers out of jobs.

horizontal merger Occurs when one firm purchases other firms that produce similar or competing products.

household Any person or group of people living under the same roof and functioning as an economic unit.

house-to-house retailing Out-of-store retailing whereby salespeople call on prospective customers in their homes.

human resources forecasting Attempts to predict the organization's future demands for people and for jobs.

human resources inventory Provides information about the organization's present personnel.

human resources management The staffing function of the organization. It includes the activities of human resources planning, recruitment, selection, orientation, training, performance appraisal, compensation, and safety.

human resources planning Includes forecasting the demand for and supply of personnel.

human skill The ability to interact with other persons successfully.

hypermarket A gigantic discount retail complex that combines the features of supermarkets, department stores, and specialty stores under one roof.

importing Buying goods and services abroad.

income statement An accounting statement that summarizes a company's revenues, cost of goods sold (if it sells merchandise), expenses, and net profit or loss over a period of time.

independent store An individual retail store, usually a small family-owned business.

index number A quantitative device that condenses or summarizes a body of data with several characteristics into a single numerical expression.

industrial buying motives Factors that cause an industrial buyer to recognize a logical need or want and to make a purchase that satisfies it.

industrial market Businesses, government agencies, and other institutions that buy products to use either in operations or in making other products.

industrial products Goods or services purchased for the production of other goods and services or to be used in the operation of the business.

industrial supplies Items necessary in the daily operations of the firm.

industrial unions Associations of workers employed within a given industry, such as coal mining or steel or automobile manufacturing, regardless of skill.

infant industries protection argument The argument that endorses placing protective tariffs and quotas on certain imports so that fledgling domestic industries can become well established.

inflation A decrease in the value of a society's money.

informal organization A network of personal and social relationships that arises spontaneously as people associate with each other in the work environment.

injunction A court order prohibiting a party from performing an unjust, inequitable, or injurious act.

inland transit insurance Insurance that covers losses caused by catastrophes and acts of God for overland transportation.

input unit The device used to enter data into the computer for processing.

installations The industrial goods that are the major assets of a company.

institutional advertising Advertising done to enhance a company's public image rather than to sell a product.

insurable interest The idea that the policyholder (the person who pays the premiums) must stand to suffer a financial loss before he or she will be allowed to purchase insurance on a given risk.

insurance counselor An advisor who recommends a comprehensive program to protect a firm against insurable risks and to meet legal or quasi-legal insurance requirements.

insurance policy A legal contract that transfers risk from one party (the *insured*) to another (the *insuror*) for a fee called a *premium*.

intensive distribution Utilizes a large number of wholesalers and retailers.

intermittent process A production process that shuts down equipment periodically and readjusts it to make a slightly different product; production does not run the same day in and day out.

International Monetary Fund Provides a vehicle for foreign exchange by assisting in stabilizing exchange rates in the world economic community.

inventory control Balances the need for adequate stock against the costs of purchasing, handling, storing, and keeping records on it.

inventory turnover A calculation of the number of times a firm sold and replaced (or turned over) its average stock of goods during an accounting period. (Found by dividing the cost of goods sold by the average inventory.)

investment banking firm A firm that purchases an entire issue of new securities from the issuing company as a wholesaler and resells it to the general public.

job analysis The gathering and analyzing of data about a specific job so that a job description and job specification can be written.

job description A written summary of the scope, function, duties, responsibilities, and relationships involved in a job.

job enlargement Increases the variety or the number of tasks a job includes.

job enrichment Directed at giving the worker more authority over the work, providing a variety of tasks, and increasing responsibility.

job evaluation A technique of placing each job within its order of importance in the organization to establish its proper compensation.

job rotation Assigns people to different jobs or different tasks to people on a temporary basis.

job sharing *or* twinning Permits two part-time workers to divide one full-time job.

job shops Companies that make products to customers' individual specifications.

job specification A document that describes the characteristics and qualifications needed in someone who could successfully perform a given job.

joint venture A partnership established by two or more persons to carry out a specific "adventure" or undertaking. It usually is dissolved after the objective has been achieved. For the duration of the agreement, each partner has unlimited liability.

labor The total human resources required to turn raw materials into goods and services.

Labor-Management Relations Act (Taft-Hartley Act) of 1947 A federal law that permits the president of the United States to seek an 80-day injunction to delay a strike or lockout if evidence suggests that the strike would "imperil the national health and safety"; declares the following union activities to be unfair labor practices: (1) closed shops and secondary boycotts, (2) featherbedding, and (3) refusal to bargain in good faith; empowers states to pass "right-to-work" laws.

Labor-Management Reporting and Disclosure Act (Landrum-Griffin Act) of 1959 Creates a bill of rights for union members; requires unions to file copies of their constitutions, bylaws, and various reports (including financial reports) with the secretary of labor where they become public record; bars persons convicted of certain felonies from serving as union officers; requires that union officers be bonded (insured).

labor union A legally sanctioned, formally organized association of workers who have united to represent their collective views for wages, hours, and working conditions.

laissez-faire *or* hands-off approach The government does not interfere in the economic system.

land The natural resources that can be used to produce goods and services.

law of large numbers *or* law of averages A mathematical law stating that if a large number of similar objects or persons are exposed to the same risk, a predictable number of losses will occur during a given period of time.

layoff A temporary separation dictated by the level of business a company is experiencing.

leader pricing Selling attractive items at lower than normal prices.

leadership The process of influencing a group or individual to set or achieve a goal.

leadership style The approach a manager uses to influence subordinates.

lead time The time a supplier requires to process and ship an order.

leverage *or* trading on the equity A firm takes advantage of the sound market reputation of its common stock to sell bonds. The fixed capital thus obtained is used to improve company operations and earn back a greater return than the interest rate the company pays.

liabilities Debts or creditors' claims that a firm owes on the day the balance sheet is prepared.

licensing An agreement between one company (the *licensor*) and another (the *licensee*) that permits the licensee to manufacture and market a product owned by the licensor.

limited liability A feature inherent in corporations; stockholders' responsibility for debts is restricted to the amount of their investment in the corporation.

limited partners Partners who are legally barred from participating in the partnership's management but enjoy limited liability for debts incurred by the firm.

limited partnership A partnership arrangement in which the liability of one or more partners is limited to the amount of assets they have invested in the firm.

limited-payment life insurance Whole life insurance that distributes over a fixed number of years the total premium the insured would pay until death according to the law of large numbers.

line-and-staff organization Blends into the line organization staff personnel that advise and serve the line managers.

line authority Direct supervisory authority from superior to subordinate.

line of credit A maximum amount that a commercial bank agrees to lend to a business borrower if it has the funds available.

line organization A straight line of authority originating from the top manager that connects each successive management level until it reaches the operating employee level.

lobbying Employing persons to influence state and federal legislators to sponsor laws that further one's own interests or inhibit those of one's opponents.

lockout Management locks the doors and prevents workers from entering the building.

long-term liabilities Debts that are due in more than 1 year.

long-term *or* fixed capital Money used to buy fixed assets, which are long-lived and (with the exception of land) manufactured items that will be used to produce goods and services for several years.

loss prevention engineer (LPE) An engineer who specializes in removing or reducing risk.

mail-order retailing Out-of-store retailers ask buyers to order products from catalogs or brochures sent directly to their homes, or through order blanks placed in newspapers and magazines.

maintenance *or* hygiene factors Those job factors that prevent dissatisfaction but do not generate satisfaction or motivate workers to greater effort.

make versus buy *or* in-house versus out-of-house An either-or question: whether to create your own supply of an essential item or rely on an outside producer to make it for you.

management The process of setting and achieving goals through the execution of five basic management functions that utilize human, financial, and material resources.

management by objectives (MBO) A technique designed to improve motivation and commitment by having the manager and employee jointly set objectives, assess progress on the objectives, and evaluate the end results.

management functions The five broad activities that managers perform to achieve organizational goals: planning, organizing, staffing, directing, and controlling.

management hierarchy The pyramid arrangement of the several levels of managers.

management information system (MIS) An organized approach to gathering data from inside and outside the company and (because of the volume involved) processing it by computer to produce current, accurate, and informative reports for all decision makers.

manufacturing company A firm that converts raw materials and component parts into consumer and industrial goods.

market A group of potential customers with the authority and the ability to purchase a particular product or service that satisfies their collective demand.

market approach A method of price determination that recognizes that variables in the marketplace influence price.

marketing A group of interrelated activities designed to identify consumer needs and to develop, distribute, promote, and price goods and services to satisfy these needs at a profit.

marketing concept A belief that the company

should adopt a companywide consumer orientation directed at long-range profitability.

marketing mix The effective meshing of product, price, promotion, and distribution strategies to achieve success.

marketing orientation An emphasis on identifying the needs and wants of specific consumer groups, then producing, promoting, pricing, and distributing products that satisfy these needs and earn the company profits.

marketing research The facilitating function of collecting and interpreting data on customer demands and characteristics so that firms can develop new products and sell existing ones profitably.

market segmentation The process of dividing up a total market into subgroups with similar characteristics.

markup pricing Calculating all the costs associated with the product and then determining a markup percentage to cover the costs and expected profits.

materials handling The activities involved in moving materials in-house.

matrix organization Temporarily groups together specialists from different departments or divisions to work on special projects.

mean See *arithmetic mean.*

median The number that appears midway between the highest and the lowest numbers in an array.

mediation A process by which an impartial person acceptable to both sides encourages them to communicate, bargain, and work toward a satisfactory compromise.

medical payments A form of motor vehicle insurance that pays the medical bills of the insured and of others the insured has injured while driving a vehicle.

medium Either the personal or nonpersonal means of sending a message.

memory unit The computer's electronic warehouse, which stores data as instructed by the program.

merger Occurs when two or more companies become a single enterprise; the controlling corporation retains its identity and absorbs the others.

message The actual combination of words and symbols to be directed at the target market.

microprocessor A microscopic maze of circuits etched on a layered piece of silicon a quarter of an inch square.

middle management Managers below the rank of vice-president but above the supervisory level; their subordinates are other managers; they are responsible for implementing top management policies.

minority enterprise small-business investment companies (MESBICs) Venture capital firms designed specifically to provide funds to minority-owned small businesses.

mixed capitalism An economic system based on a market economy with limited government involvement.

mode The number that appears most often within an array.

money Any object that a group of people uses to pay its debts and buy the goods and services that it needs.

morale The attitude workers have toward the quality of their total work life.

motion study A study that identifies the number and kind of movements required to perform a given operation.

motivation Feelings that drive someone toward a particular objective.

motivation factors Those job factors that provide satisfaction and therefore motivation, but whose absence causes no satisfaction to be achieved.

multinational corporation A corporation that operates on an international level, is based in one country but has operations in other countries also, and does a substantial amount of its total business in other countries.

multiple-unit pricing A practice where a company offers consumers a lower than unit price if a specified number of units are purchased.

mutual insurance company One owned by its policyholders.

mutual savings bank A thrift institution that accepts time deposits and lends them for home purchase and construction. Its lending policies are usually more liberal than those of a savings and loan association.

nationalization The change from private ownership of an industry to government ownership.

National Labor Relations Act (Wagner Act) of 1935 Prohibits management from interfering with, attempting to influence, or punishing employees' union organizing activities; requires management to bargain in good faith; establishes the 5-member National Labor Relations Board to supervise employee elections for union representation, and to prevent and remedy unfair labor practices by either employers or unions.

national security argument The argument that a nation must strengthen and protect its domestic industries that produce strategic defense materials to be able to maintain its defenses.

needs Deficiencies a person is feeling at a particular time or things that are missing from a person's life.

negotiable instruments Written promises or requests that certain sums of money be paid to the bearer or to order.

net income The amount of profit that a company earned during an accounting period.

net income before taxes The amount a firm earned from operations before state and federal income taxes are deducted.

no-fault auto insurance Auto insurance that enables the parties to an accident to collect for bodily injury from their respective insurance companies, regardless of who was at fault.

noise Any possible interference with the communication process.

nominal partner An individual who is neither a part-owner of the partnership nor an active participant in the firm's affairs. Often this is a well-known person who lends a famous name to the company.

nonprofit corporations Organizations formed to further the interests and objectives of educational, religious, social, charitable, and cultural groups. No stock is issued, but the members of the organization enjoy the advantage of limited liability.

objections Verbal or silent forms of resistance on the part of the potential customer to the salesperson's message.

objective performance appraisal system The specific performance areas are indentified for the employee as are the results expected.

objectives The results that plans are made to achieve.

Occupational Safety and Health Act A federal law that requires most employers to create and maintain safe, healthful working conditions.

ocean marine insurance Insurance that protects a cargo against loss on the high seas.

odd lot Less than 100 shares of a stock.

on-site inspection The buyer's inspectors examine purchased items throughout the supplier's manufacturing operations.

on-the-job training (OJT) A technique of teaching job skills while the person performs the job.

open corporation A corporation whose stock can be purchased by anyone who can afford the price.

open market operations An activity in which the Fed buys or sells billions of dollars of United States government securities daily through securities dealers in New York City.

open shop Workers have not elected a union to represent them in dealing with management.

operating expenses The value of items or services used or consumed in normal company operations during an accounting period.

order processing The grouping of the products specified by the customer, and the accompanying paperwork.

organization A group of two or more people that exists and operates to achieve clearly stated, commonly held objectives.

organization chart The visual representation of the way an entire organization and each of its parts fit together.

organizing The management function concerned with (1) assembling the resources necessary to achieve the organization's objectives and (2) establishing activity-authority relationships of the organization.

orientation program A series of activities that gives the new employees information to help them adapt to the organization and their new jobs.

output unit The part of a computer that presents the processed data in a form that management can use.

participative leadership style Characterized by the manager involving the subordinates in the decision.

partnership An association of two or more people who are co-owners of a business for profit.

patent A legal right allowing an inventor to exclude others from making, using, or selling an invention, a design, or a plant for a stated length of time.

patronage motives Buying reasons based on the characteristics of a specific retail outlet or brand of product.

pay grades Pay categories that relate dollar values to the job ladder developed through job evaluation.

penetration pricing Introducing the product at a low price intended to capture the mass market for the product or service.

pension plan A program to provide a retirement income to workers by holding a percentage of their earnings in reserve.

performance appraisal A formal measure or rating of an employee's job performance compared with established job standards.

personal selling A face-to-face attempt to persuade prospective customers to buy a given product.

philosophy of management A manager's attitude about work and the people who perform that work.

physical distribution functions Transporting and storing goods.

physical distribution system The activities that take place as the goods move through the channels.

physiological need The fundamental need for food, clothing, and shelter.

picketing Workers publicly air their complaints against an employer by staging a demonstration outside the building, with protest signs and explanatory leaflets.

piecework Pays employees according to the number of units they produce.

planning The management function that establishes organizational goals or objectives and creates the means for accomplishing them.

plant and equipment Sometimes called *fixed assets;* an asset category that includes land and expensive manufactured items that a company will use in its operations for several years.

point-of-purchase displays Promotional devices that are placed where sales transactions occur.

policy A plan that describes how a question or subject should be addressed; it helps guide management decisions.

power plant insurance Also called *boiler and machinery insurance;* covers losses caused by an exploding steam boiler, furnace, heating plant, or other equipment.

preapproach The second step in the sales process where the salesperson researches the qualified prospect's background.

preemptive right A shareholder's right to purchase shares of a company's new stock issues in proportion with the existing shares that he or she owns, before the new shares are offered to the general public.

preferred stock A class of stock that has a prior or senior claim on assets to that of common stock.

premium Something of value given free or at a nominal charge as an incentive to buy a product. *Also,* the amount by which a bond's market price exceeds its par value. *Also,* a fee paid on an insurance policy.

presentation The fourth step in the selling process in which the salesperson shows how the prospect can benefit by owning the product.

prestige pricing Setting a price high to relate the image of quality.

price The exchange value of a product expressed in monetary terms.

price discounts Deductions allowed from the established price.

price lining Sets distinct prices for the different models in a product line.

primary boycott Employees or a union agree not to purchase goods from a particular firm.

primary data Data that a company must gather itself or employ some other firm to gather; they cannot be looked up somewhere because no one has put them together before.

prime rate of interest A lower rate of interest than that charged to most borrowers. (Given by commercial banks to their largest, most secure corporate borrowers.)

principal The person whom an agent represents.

principle of indemnity The policyholder cannot profit by insurance.

private enterprise system An economic system where both the resources necessary for production and the businesses are owned by private individuals, not by public institutions like the government.

procedure A set of step-by-step, chronological instructions for carrying out a given policy.

processing company A firm that converts natural resources into raw material.

product advertising Advertising intended to promote demand for a product or service.

product departmentalization Assembles the activities of creating, producing, and marketing each product into one department.

product differentiation Marketers attempt to have their product perceived by the consumer as different from other, similar products.

production A business activity that uses people and machinery to convert materials and parts into salable products.

production control Coordinating the interaction of people, materials, and machinery so that products are made in the proper amounts at the required times to fill orders.

production management The job of coordinating and controlling all the activities required to make a product.

production orientation The number one priority is to produce a good to keep up with demand.

production plan A document that contains a list of materials and equipment needed to manufacture a finished product that also specifies which operations will be performed in-house or out-of-house.

production sharing A manufacturing process that integrates production operations along international lines; a company may assemble part of an item in one nation, ship it to another for further processing, and market the finished product in yet another country.

product liability insurance Coverage that protects a firm against financial loss when persons file suit claiming they were injured by its product.

product life cycle The succession of phases including the introduction, growth, maturity, and decline of a product in its market.

profit The difference between a business's total revenues or sales receipts and the total of its production costs, operating expenses, and taxes.

profit sharing Paying a portion of company profits to employees as a performance incentive in addition to their regular compensation.

pro forma financial statements   Financial statements that forecast expected sales, expenses, profits, and other financial data for a future accounting period.

program   A software element stored in the memory unit that feeds step-by-step instructions to the control unit, which then commands one of the other hardware units to perform whatever operation is needed.

promissory note   A short-term financing instrument given by a debtor (called the *promisor*) to a creditor (called the *promisee*) as a legal and binding promise to pay a certain sum of money at a future date, usually with interest at a fixed rate.

promotion   A movement by a person into a position with higher pay and greater responsibilities.

promotional mix   The correct blending of personal selling, advertising, publicity, and sales promotion.

property damage liability   Motor vehicle insurance that pays for damage the insured vehicle does to the property of others.

prospecting   The step in the selling process that identifies potential customers for a product.

prospectus   A document that presents a company's financial data for several consecutive years, discusses its position in its industry, describes how it will use the funds raised by a securities sale, and summarizes other information that well-informed investors should have.

protectionism   An international trade philosophy that favors the creation of barriers against the importing of goods to shelter domestic industries from foreign competition.

proxy   A document that expresses a stockholder's voting intentions on corporate matters when he or she cannot attend the annual meeting.

psychological *or* odd pricing   The seller selects as prices amounts that fall just below a major psychological threshold.

publicity   Nonpaid, nonpersonal communication to promote the products, services, or image of the company.

public liability insurance   Insurance that covers financial loss caused by an injury to a nonemployee that results from the business's negligence and that occurs on its premises.

pull strategy   A strategy aimed at the consumer. The intention is for the consumer to demand that a product be available in the distribution channel.

purchasing agent   A company's in-house expert on where to buy various products. Each will buy a broad or narrow line of products, depending on the size and complexity of the company and the characteristics of its end product.

purchasing procedure   A series of steps that a company follows when buying products.

pure capitalism *or* market economy   An economic system in which economic decisions are made freely according to the market forces of supply and demand.

pure risk   A situation that can only become a loss.

push money ("PMs" *or* "spiffs")   A manufacturer's commission paid to salespeople for selling one particular brand over all others.

push strategy   A strategy directed at the members of the marketing channel rather than the consumer.

quality assurance   The production control step in which the product is inspected at various stages along the route to ensure that it meets standards.

quality circle   A cooperative effort by workers and supervisor to find ways to improve operations and quality.

quota   A trade barrier that restricts the quantity of a foreign product that can be brought into a country for resale.

random sample   One in which every member of the universe has an equal chance of being chosen.

rate of return on stockholders' equity   The percentage return that a company earned on the owners' investment during the previous accounting period. (Found by dividing net income by stockholders' equity.)

ratio   A mathematical statement of the relationship or proportion between two elements, derived by dividing one into the other.

rational motives   Buying reasons that arise from careful planning and analysis of information.

ratio of debt to stockholders' equity   The value of claims that creditors have against a firm's assets for each dollar of owners' claims. (Found by dividing liabilities by stockholders' equity.)

ratio of net income to net sales   A statement of the net income a company earned from each dollar of sales during an accounting period. (Found by dividing net income by net sales.)

ratio of net sales to net income   A statement of the amount of sales a firm had to make to earn a dollar of net income. (Found by dividing net sales by net income.)

raw materials   Industrial products that are composed of farm and natural products.

reciprocal buying   A practice wherein two or more companies become mutual customers, buying each other's goods and services.

recruitment   An activity in which the organization attempts to identify and attract candidates to meet the requirements of anticipated or actual job openings.

recycling The practice of reclaiming or producing materials from previously manufactured products and using them to make other items.

registered bond One whose owner's name is on record with the company and appears on the bond itself.

registrar A commercial bank that monitors the number of shares of stock a corporation sells to ensure that it does not sell more than its charter has authorized.

relative pricing A decision to set prices above the competition, below the competition, or to meet the competition.

reserve requirement A percentage of deposits that member banks must retain on deposit within their own walls or at the Federal Reserve Bank in their district.

resignation A voluntary separation in which a worker leaves to accept another position.

responsibility The obligation to carry out one's assigned duties to the best of one's ability.

retained earnings Profits reinvested in (or plowed back into) a company for improvements and expansion.

retirement A person's intention to stop working for the rest of his or her life.

revaluation Decreasing the rate of exchange at which foreign currency will be traded for domestic currency.

revenue Cash or other items received in exchange for merchandise or services.

revolving credit agreement A commercial bank's binding promise that the money will be available if the borrowing firm requests it.

right-to-work laws Allow workers to obtain and keep jobs without having to join or pay money to a labor organization.

risk manager A person hired to identify significant pure risks that a company faces and prescribe effective techniques to deal with them.

robot A reprogrammable, multifunctional manipulator designed to move material, parts, tools, or specialized devices through variable programmed motions to accomplish a variety of tasks.

role Any one of several behaviors a manager displays as he or she functions in the organization.

round lot 100 shares of a stock or multiples thereof.

routing The production control step in which a logical sequence is established for the operations that the product must undergo on its way to completion.

safety and security need The need to avoid bodily harm and uncertainty about one's well-being.

salary Compensation based on weeks or months worked.

sales finance company A firm that provides short-term capital to retailers (and sometimes to wholesalers) by purchasing the installment sales contract (promissory notes) that they have accepted from customers.

sales orientation The energy of the company is focused on selling the products produced.

sales promotion Those marketing activities, other than personal selling and advertising that stimulate consumer purchasing and dealer effectiveness, such as displays, shows and expositions, demonstrations, and various nonrecurrent selling efforts not in the ordinary routine.

sample A cross-section of a total group that has the same distribution of characteristics as the larger group (or *universe*) whose characteristics are being explored.

savings account *or* **time deposit** A sum of money, deposited with a bank, that cannot be withdrawn by writing a check.

savings and loan associations (S&Ls) Thrift institutions that accept time deposits and lend them primarily to buyers of single-family homes.

scheduling The production control step that allots time for each operation along the route.

S corporation One that may elect, under Subchapter S of the Internal Revenue Code, to be taxed as a sole proprietorship, if owned by one stockholder, or as a partnership, if owned by several stockholders.

secondary boycott Third-party companies are threatened with harassment and internal labor problems if they continue to do business with the target firm.

secondary data Data that presently exist; they have been recorded somewhere, and management need only go to the source.

secret partner A partner who may be an active manager but does not want his or her identity revealed to the general public.

selection The process of deciding which candidate, out of the pool of applicants developed in recruiting, has the abilities, skills, and characteristics that most closely match job demands.

selective distribution Utilizes a moderate number of retailers and wholesalers.

self-actualization *or* **self-realization need** The need to get the maximum reward from one's life experience; to maximize one's skills, abilities, and potential.

self-insurance fund A special fund of cash and marketable securities that will be used to pay for losses caused by natural disasters such as fire, flood, and earthquake.

selling process A series of seven steps that salespeople follow when persuading prospective customers to make purchases.

sender The company, or person representing the company, who presents a message to the target market.

separation The loss of an employee to an organization through layoff, termination, retirement, or resignation.

service bureau A firm that processes clients' data on its own computer (or one that it has access to) for a fee.

Service Corps of Retired Executives (SCORE) A volunteer organization of over 3,000 retired higher managers who advise small-business owners in conjunction with the Small Business Administration.

service mark A mark or words used in sales or advertising literature to distinguish a firm's services from those of its competitors.

services Activities that benefit consumers or other businesses.

shareholders or stockholders A corporation's owners but frequently not the individuals who control and manage the firm day by day.

shopping goods Items purchased after comparative shopping based on quality, design, cost, and performance.

short-term or working capital Money spent on business operations covering a period of a year or less.

silent partner A partner who assumes no active role in managing the firm, but who may be known to the general public as a partner.

simple-recognition shop An arrangement wherein all employees, whether union members or not, receive the same pay, work assignments, and benefits.

single-source purchasing Buying a product from one company only.

sinking fund A special fund a company creates and pays money into over the life of a bond issue so dollars will be available to pay off the bonds when they mature.

skimming Charging a relatively high price when the product first appears on the market.

Small Business Administration (SBA) A federal government agency started in 1953 to give financial and managerial assistance to owners of small businesses.

social audit A report on the social performance of a business.

socialism An economic system in which much ownership is private, but the government controls the operation and direction of basic industries.

social need The need to be accepted by people whose opinions and companionship you value.

social responsibility A belief that, as organizations and managers function, their decisions should be made within the confines of both social and economic considerations.

software All elements of a computerized data-processing system other than hardware.

sole proprietorship A business owned by one individual.

span of control The number of subordinates under the direction of each manager.

specialty advertising Providing "frequent reminder" items that build good will and keep a firm's or a product's name within the prospect's view.

specialty goods Products that buyers prefer strongly because of their unique characteristics or image.

specialty store A store that offers many models or styles of a specific product.

speculative risk A situation that may cause loss or gain.

staff authority The authority to serve in an advisory capacity (the authority to advise).

staffing The management function that attempts to attract good people to an organization and to hold onto them.

statement of changes in financial position Also referred to as a *source and use of funds statement* or simply a *funds statement;* accounts for increases and decreases in a company's net working capital throughout an accounting period.

statutory law A written body of rules created and approved by a group of persons (generally referred to as a *legislature*), which presumably expresses the will of the citizens it represents.

stock certificates Documents that provide legal evidence of ownership of shares in a corporation.

stock dividend A distribution of shares of the company's stock or the stock that it owns in other firms.

stockholders' equity The balance sheet section that shows owners' claims against a corporation.

stock insurance company One owned by stockholders.

stock option A plan that permits employees to buy shares of stock in the employees' firm at or below the present market price.

stock split A subdivision of shares already issued, done to decrease a stock's high market price to an amount that more investors can afford to pay.

straight life insurance Whole life insurance in which premiums are paid until the insured's death.

stratified random sample One that divides the universe into subcategories, or *strata,* according to one or more characteristics and chooses randomly from within the strata being examined.

strikebreakers Workers who perform the jobs until

the striking workers come to terms with management.

strikes Temporary work stoppages by employees to protest certain working conditions and reinforce demands for their correction.

subjective performance appraisal system Based on the personal viewpoint of the manager.

supermarket A store that sells a wide variety of food items.

superstore A food-based retailer that carries a variety of other products.

supply The quantity of a product that producers are willing to make available at a given price.

surety bond Sometimes called a *performance bond;* insurance that guarantees that a contract will be completed.

surplus lines coverage Insurance for risks on which no law of large numbers exists.

synthetic process Materials are combined instead of separated to form a certain product.

target market The focus point for the sender's message.

tariff *or* import duty A tax imposed on imported goods to raise their market prices, making the cost of competing domestic products attractive by comparison.

technical skill The knowledge of and ability to use the processes, practices, techniques, or tools of a specialty responsibility area.

telephone retailing Out-of-store sales initiated by a salesperson who calls prospects or follows up on the customer's response to promotional campaigns.

termination A permanent separation from the company.

term insurance Life insurance that pays only if the insured dies during a specified period of time.

test marketing A business introduces a product in strategic geographic locations, rather than everywhere, to assess consumer response.

Theory X A philosophy of management with a negative perception of subordinates' potential for work and general attitudes toward work. It assumes that subordinates dislike work, are poorly motivated, and require close supervision.

Theory Y A philosophy of management with a positive perception of subordinates' potential for and general attitudes toward work. It assumes that subordinates can be self-directing, will seek responsibility, and find work as natural as play or rest.

time-sharing A form of computer use in which several firms buy or rent access to a computer that is owned by another firm.

time study A study that determines the amount of time an average worker takes to perform a given operation.

top management Managers who are responsible for the overall management of the organization, for establishing organizational or companywide objectives or goals and operating policies, and directing the company in relationships with its external environment.

tort A private or civil wrong or injury committed against a person or property for which a court will award damages if the wronged party (called the *plaintiff*) can submit adequate proof that the accused wrongdoer (called the *defendant*) was guilty, through either negligence or intent, of committing the act in question.

total costs The total of fixed costs and variable costs.

total revenue Determined by multiplying price times the number of units sold.

trade character A brand mark that has a human quality.

trade credit *or* open-book accounts Business charge accounts that a selling firm gives buying firms.

trademark A brand name, brand mark, or trade character that has legal protection.

training Supplies the skills, knowledge, and attitudes needed by subordinates to improve their abilities to perform their jobs.

transfer A lateral move from one position to another that has similar pay and responsibility levels.

transfer agent A commercial bank that records changes in names and addresses for a corporation each time stocks and certain types of bonds are traded.

transportation The modes or means of shipping the goods.

transportation insurance Covers loss of cargo from hazards such as contamination, spoilage, theft, fire, breakage, or collision while in transit.

Uniform Commercial Code (UCC) A comprehensive body of business law that encompasses various kinds of transactions.

uninsured motorist protection Coverage that pays the insured for bodily injuries caused by at-fault but uninsured or underinsured drivers and by hit-and-run drivers.

union shop Agreements stipulating that a company's new employees must join a union within a certain number of days after being hired in order to keep their jobs.

union steward A worker who is both an employee and a union representative.

unity of command Each person in an organization should take orders from and report to only one person.

universality of management The concept that all managers do the same job regardless of title, position, or management level; they all execute the five management functions and work through and with others to achieve organizational goals.

universal life insurance A highly modified form of whole life insurance. Part of the premium buys insurance coverage that will be paid if the insured dies. The rest of the premium is invested in high-yield securities that are intended to increase the policy's cash value more rapidly than that of a traditional whole life policy.

unlimited liability The owner's personal responsibility for any debts or damages incurred by the operation of a business.

urban revitalization programs Intensive efforts by large businesses to build new offices or plants or refurbish old ones in cities, thus providing new jobs and improving the city's economic health.

van pooling An energy conservation measure whereby employees are asked to commute to work in groups using their own vans or those supplied by the company.

variable costs Costs that arise when the first unit is produced and increase with production.

vending-machine retailing Out-of-store retailing that distributes products to consumers by coin-operated machines.

venture capital firm A company that buys stock in new firms that make products or offer services with strong profit potential.

vertical merger Occurs when one firm unites with others that contribute to its product's manufacture or distribution.

vestibule training Training conducted in a simu-lated work environment complete with sample equipment.

wages Compensation based on hours worked.

warehousing Receiving, identifying, and sorting goods.

warrant A document that conveys the preemptive right to existing stockholders.

warranty A document that states certain facts and conditions about a product's operation and correct use and clarifies the limits of its performance under various circumstances.

Wheeler-Lea Act The law that gives the Federal Trade Commission the power to issue cease-and-desist orders against firms that make false or misleading advertising claims.

whole life insurance Life insurance that remains in effect for the insured's entire life and pays on death.

wholesalers Middlemen who sell goods to retailers, to other wholesalers, and to industrial users, but who do not sell in significant amounts to the final consumer.

workers' compensation insurance It pays part of an employee's wage or salary plus medical expenses, and any necessary rehabilitation, retraining, job placement, or counseling, if a worker is accidentally injured on the job or contracts a job-related disease.

"yellow dog" contract An agreement by workers that they will not join a union.

yield to maturity The percentage return an owner receives if a bond is held until it matures.

zoning ordinances City and county regulations defining the type of business activity that can be conducted at certain locations.

Credits

zaschi/Stock, Boston, Inc. *Page 345:* ©Frank Siteman 1980/Jeroboam, Inc. *Page 347:* ©1980 Michael Uffer/Photo Researchers, Inc.

Chapter 13

Page 361: Paul A. Volcker/Board of Governors of the Federal Reserve System. *Page 364:* ©Christopher Morrow/Picture Group photo. *Page 368:* ©John Maher/EKM-Nepenthe. *Page 370:* Rogers/Monkmeyer Press Photo Service. *Page 381:* ©1981 Peter Morgan/Picture Group photo.

Chapter 14

Page 391: Robert S. Miller/Chrysler Corporation. *Page 398:* Rogers/Monkmeyer Press Photo Service.

Chapter 15

Page 423: Maurice R. Greenberg/American International Group, Inc. *Page 425:* Courtesy Industrial Training Systems Corporation, Mt. Laurel, New Jersey. *Page 437:* Gamma-Liason. *Page 444:* Ellis Herwig/Richard Upton Pickman/Stock, Boston, Inc. *Page 450:* ©1980 Bryce Flynn/Picture Group photo.

Chapter 16

Page 461: Janet Norwood/Bureau of Labor Statistics. *Page 467:* ©Hazel Hankin/Stock, Boston, Inc. *Page 476:* Chrysler Corporation. *Page 482:* Harris Corporation. Reproduced with permission.

Chapter 17

Page 499: Wayne G. English/MCI Communications Corporation. *Page 503:* ©John Maher/EKM-Nepenthe. *Page 504:* ©Elizabeth Hamlin/Stock, Boston, Inc. *Page 510:* ©1980 Peter Menzel/Stock, Boston, Inc.

Chapter 18

Page 529: Sandra Kurtzig/ASK Computer Systems, Inc. *Page 531:* ©David Perrotta/Picture Group photo. *Page 532:* ©Van Bucher 1978/Picture Researchers, Inc. *Page 545:* ©George W. Gardner.

Chapter 19

Page 557: Willard C. Butcher/The Chase Manhattan Bank. *Page 563:* ©1976 Josephus Daniels/Photo Researchers, Inc. *Page 565:* ©Kent Reno 1978/Jeroboam, Inc. *Page 572:* ©Mark Antman/The Image Works, Inc.

Chapter 20

Page 587: Frank McCormack/ArcoSpark. *Page 608:* Courtesy MCI Communications Corporation.

Chapter 21

Page 615: Zoltan Merszei/Atkinson Business Photography. *Page 619:* Courtesy of E. I. du Pont de Nemours & Company. *Page 622:* Freda Leinwand/Monkmeyer Press Photo Service. *Page 623:* Charles Gatewood/The Image Works, Inc. *Page 625:* Monkmeyer Press Photo Service.

Gallery 1

Page 1, top: Robert V. Eckert, Jr./EKM-Nepenthe. *Page 1, bottom:* ©Peter Menzel/Stock, Boston, Inc. *Page 2:* Tim Jewett/EKM-Nepenthe. *Page 3:* ©Barbara Alper/Stock, Boston, Inc. *Page 4, top:* Burger King Corporation. *Page 4, bottom:* Owen Franken/Stock, Boston, Inc.

Gallery 2

Page 1, top: ©The Advertising Council, Inc. *Page 1, bottom:* Courtesy 3M. *Page 2, top left:* Courtesy of The Perrier Group/Great Waters of France. *Page 2, top right:* ©1978 Chanel, Inc. *Page 2, bottom:* ©1983 Lee Company. *Pages 3 and 4:* Courtesy of Selchow & Righter Company. Trivial Pursuit® is the registered trademark of Horn Abbot, Ltd. (Canada) for the game manufactured and distributed in the United States under license to Selchow & Righter, Bay Shore, N.Y.

Gallery 3

Page 1, top: Courtesy of the University of Pennsylvania Office of Communications and Publications. *Page 1, middle:* Courtesy of the IBM Corporation. *Page 1, bottom:* Cray Research, Inc. *Pages 2 and 3, and page 4, top:* Courtesy Apple Computer, Inc. *Page 4, bottom:* Courtesy of the IBM Corporation.

Subject Index

Marginal terms and their page numbers appear in boldface.

Name and Company Index